Braman

100 Years of Farm Journal

By the Editors
of Farm Journal

Published by Countryside Press
a division of Farm Journal, Inc.
Philadelphia, Pennsylvania

Distributed to the book trade by
Doubleday & Company, Inc.
Garden City, New York

Contents

This book was compiled by the editors of FARM JOURNAL, current and retired, with the help of Marshall Ledger, who excerpted the early issues.

Book Design: Michael Durning

ISBN: 0-385-12522-4
Library of Congress Card Number 76-17449
Printed in the United States of America

Introduction

If a farmer of the American Revolutionary years of the 1770s could have returned 100 years later in the 1870s, he probably would have been mildly surprised to see draft horses in the field instead of oxen and improved harvesting tools of the day like the reaper and binder. But almost everything else in ordinary farming would have been quite familiar. Take the farmer of the 1870s, however, and wake him up today on a modern commercial farm in any good farming area of the country, and he'd surely go into instant shock.

During the second century of our Bicentennial, nearly everything in agriculture changed—from seed the farmer plants and the livestock he raises to the way he sees himself, his occupation and his role on the world scene. He was a member of the majority group in American life in the 1870s. Today, he and other farm workers represent one in 20 in the work force, and he and his family constitute only 4½% of the total U.S. population.

This kind of drastic change over the past century may be true of other occupations. But it is especially significant to us at FARM JOURNAL, because farmers have been "our people" since the first issue published by founder Wilmer Atkinson in March 1877. He called readers that, and the pages of FARM JOURNAL from the beginning have reflected the revolutionary changes in their life and productive ability that at the least made possible the totally industrialized society we have today.

In the first issue, reproduced entirely in this book, and in subsequent pages selected over the next 40 years, you'll first sample the personal journalism so characteristic of this era.

Farmers (and editors) of this time often had to be *sold* on "new-fangled" things. The age-old complacency, self-sufficiency and moral superiority of farmers gave way slowly at first, then more rapidly with the coming of tractors, automobiles, running water, electricity, farm chemicals, growth in Land-Grant colleges and Extension services, experiment stations, breeding stock from abroad—a whole flood of innovations.

There's not much question that reading the pages from the Wilmer Atkinson years will give you an insight into rural thinking of the late Nineteenth Century and into the "golden age" of agriculture from 1900 to 1914. That was a time when the frontier had passed. Seemingly, the entire country was "filled up" and farm supply and demand were in a neat balance. Atkinson had a unique ability to focus on interests common to all farmers of his day regardless of what they produced and where they lived. So without great effort in that direction, the magazine which he designed "for farmers within a day's drive of Philadelphia" rapidly acquired a nationwide audience. And he announced proudly in an early issue that only one other magazine surpassed it in circulation on the farm. It became the leading farm magazine among the nation's farmers which it is still today.

The upheaval of World War I is written in FARM JOURNAL in more ways than one, including changes in the magazine itself, between 1917 when Atkinson retired and 1920 when his nephew, Arthur H. Jenkins, assumed the editorship. Active and alert in his 90s as we assembled this book, Mr. Jenkins said he ached to make changes in FARM JOURNAL for a long time before he had a chance.

By 1927, when FARM JOURNAL was 50 years old, Jenkins had converted Atkinson's journal for farmers into a "general interest magazine with a farm angle to it," as he puts it. You can see what this new magazine for the "modern" farmer looked like in the reproduction of the 50th anniversary issue. We have included it in its entirety because it gives a good review of farming in the post-World War I years.

FARM JOURNAL itself fell on hard times in the 1930s, when hard times hit most businesses. But better days were ahead for it, too, as the Pews of Philadelphia, successful founders of the Sun Oil Co., bought and revitalized it. They wanted to maintain the institution in their city and its strong conservative editorial voice among farmers nationally during the hotly controversial New Deal days.

Gradually, a totally new editorial team assumed the helm at FARM JOURNAL. This included Wheeler McMillen, editor-in-chief, Carroll P. Streeter, managing editor and later editor, and Gertrude Dieken, editor of the *Farmer's Wife*. The *Farmer's Wife,* originally a separate magazine, merged into FARM JOURNAL as a magazine within a magazine.

Farm families they wrote for endured the strenuous years of World War II and came into the late 1940s and 1950s with an insatiable appetite for the innovations in farm and family living, the better practices and better things. These had been developed but were not available during the depression and the war because of shortages of everything including money. Focused to satisfy these wants and needs, FARM JOURNAL became "The Magazine Farm Families Depend on." The advance of mechanization both on the farm and in the farm home is reflected in FARM JOURNAL in some of the 75th anniversary pages included in this book.

While the focus was on the whole farm family in the 1950s and 1960s, FARM JOURNAL clearly emphasized the news of the exploding technological revolution in agriculture. Editor Lane Palmer points out FARM JOURNAL's leadership in farmer acceptance of (1) continuous corn cultivation, (2) narrow-row corn, (3) chemical weed killers, and (4) the adoption of the latest, even-larger and more-efficient farm power and equipment.

American agriculture assumed the status of a mature industry in the 1960s, and FARM JOURNAL changed again. The reader's increasing need for more specialized information was recognized. And the magazine was completely changed in the next few years by its editors and president, R. J. Babcock, a veteran of 35 years at FARM JOURNAL and today principal stockholder.

They converted it from a "something for everybody" magazine to a magazine in which *every* article was intended to be of importance to *every* farm family. They did this by asking readers to state their commodity interests when they renewed subscriptions, by remaking the magazine regionally and adding sections of EXTRAS to meet these specific interests. Corn stories went to Midwest readers, cotton to the Southerners, beef stories to cattlemen subscribers to BEEF EXTRA and so on.

Gradually, the interest in technical agriculture transformed FARM JOURNAL into a business magazine. As innovators became more numerous, FARM JOURNAL responded with a separate magazine devoted to the common interests of upper-income farmers who were way out in front of the rest in their need for information on taxes, business organization, marketing, financing and the like. This was called *Top Operator*.

In 1972, an explosion of world demand for American food and feed, epitomized by the "Russian grain deal," helped to end a long period of over-production. By then, farm numbers and the farm population had stabilized after the 200-year long migration of farm people to urban areas. All commercial farmers, not just a few hundred thousand, were rather suddenly faced with the whole gamut of problems faced by all businessmen and some other problems peculiarly their own. Again FARM JOURNAL was remodeled to reflect reader needs and assume the role it fills today as "The Business Magazine of American Agriculture," under its new publisher and president, Dale E. Smith. Closing pages of this book reflect the businessman-farmer of today. He feeds himself and over 50 other Americans and many more overseas, and his efficiency is still increasing.

—Roe C. Black
Executive Editor
Farm Journal

Wilmer Atkinson

Founder and editor for 40 years expressed the self-sufficiency, family orientation of his readers

The following pages, culled from FARM JOURNAL's earliest years, tell the story of Wilmer Atkinson, the founder and first editor. His personality and opinions dominated the magazine from its beginning in 1877 to his retirement in 1917—the first 40 years.

In 1877, no one seemed to know a paper was needed which specialized in the daily stresses and strains of farm life. When Atkinson produced his monthly journal for "practical, not fancy, farming," he tapped thousands upon thousands of readers who didn't know until they read it that they needed FARM JOURNAL.

Not only farmers, but their wives and children were part of Atkinson's audience. He conceived the farm as a total enclosure, perpetuated by successive generations of boys and girls taking their parents' place. FARM JOURNAL was to minister to their specific needs. By providing a medium for the exchange of information, it also served to unite the otherwise isolated family units.

Nothing expresses better than Atkinson's own columns his attitude toward his audience—paternalistic, protective and imperious. Lying behind advice on hogs, strawberries or games for children is the imperative "Look to it!" His readers loved it. He called them "Our Folks," and they returned the chumminess by sending in their know-how on farm methods, by subscribing and by voluntarily acting as agents to round up more subscribers.

The paternalistic attitude determined what ads would appear in FARM JOURNAL. Atkinson screened them to protect his readers from swindlers and from what he deemed harmful or useless products. He established the first "Fair Play" code by which he personally made good the claims of his advertisers. This policy was in keeping with his life-long hatred of cheats. It had the ancillary advantage of building rapport between editor and reader. And it guaranteed advertisers that their readers would be pre-sold on the quality of goods or services they could expect.

Atkinson was alive to agricultural change and proved himself open to new information. He thought agricultural schools were at first expensive sinecures for professors who could write but not farm. He came to appreciate their experiments and analyses (not blindly, however), and eventually enshrined a few professors in his "Portrait Gallery." At first he opposed ensilage as being slightly on this side of humbuggery and eventually yielded to the large number of farmers who were getting good results. He opposed barbed wire as too costly and over-barbed, again yielding to its success. He opposed rural free delivery, but, in a dialogue conducted right on the pages of FARM JOURNAL, was persuaded that farmers have the right to home delivery "just as town folks do." And he ended up helping make it a reality.

Sometimes his opinions changed without particular consciousness on his part. He always claimed FARM JOURNAL was going to be free from politics. Yet he discussed issues which were inherently politically loaded and took unequivocal stands. He supported minimum wage, private property, the Grange, the heavy taxing of millionaires and women's suffrage. He was vigorously against trusts and monopolies, opposed the head of the Department of Agriculture becoming a cabinet officer (because that rank would bring the position under partisan patronage) and urged rigid restrictions on immigration.

Even though he acknowledged political implications when he wrote a headline "Fair Play (Not socialism)," he persisted in thinking that FARM JOURNAL was above party. It was even above the self-interest groups which farmers began on their own behalf, the uniting factor among all the granges, alliances, and leagues.

He began FARM JOURNAL with scrupulous editorial standards. He promised no "puffery" for merchandise, no self-praise, no special subscription rates. He ridiculed the offer of premiums for goods, especially magazines. Reluctantly, we gather, he was forced to hedge on his editorial purity. He constantly recommended one item or another (not always from his own list of advertisers). By enlisting his readers as his subscription agents, he found it necessary to remind them how special they were and how essential FARM JOURNAL was to their lives. And when he did finally offer giveaways, he outdid his competitors (first prize in one subscription contest was the payment of the winner's taxes).

Yet through these pages there is a refreshing honesty. When he changed his mind on R.F.D., he told us in a tone not of pride but of human error acknowledged. He realized after publication that an ad for tobacco seed was contrary to his general policy against tobacco and dropped it with an apology. He was intrigued by gadgets, even though many such items were new and untested and the ideal ground for swindlers. He advised, "Experiment a little, but not too much."

Over forty years a man's ideas could easily go stale, be overrun by time. Luckily for Atkinson his ideas were so deeply rooted in quintessential America that they were never completely eclipsed. The more mechanized and commercial the farm became, the more perilous the qualities of self-sufficiency and family-togetherness. These qualities he never lost. If there was a measure of innocence to Atkinson's magazine, it was something farm families were happy to embrace when threatened by an ever more complex outside world.

An epigram for April 1895, goes: "Many a man with a hard hand has a tender heart." And so with Atkinson. His austere paternalism was humanized by his contradictions, reversals and changes of opinion, and always by the warmth he had for his enterprise and his readers.

—Marshall Ledger
The Pennsylvania Gazette

THE
FARM JOURNAL
DEVOTED TO THE FARM, ORCHARD, GARDEN, AND RURAL ECONOMY.

A NATION'S GREATNESS DEPENDS ON THE VIRTUE AND INTELLIGENCE OF ITS FARMERS.

Vol. 1. PHILADELPHIA, MARCH, 1877. No. 1.

PUBLISHED MONTHLY AT

NO. 726 SANSOM STREET,

SATURDAY EVENING POST BUILDING,

At 25 Cents a Year.

WILMER ATKINSON, - - - *Publisher.*

Publisher to Reader.

THE FARM JOURNAL offers no terms to clubs, and no premiums to subscribers. The price of THE FARM JOURNAL is 25 cents a year.

There will be 25,000 copies of the first number of THE FARM JOURNAL printed and mailed to farmers and other rural residents, within a day's ride of Philadelphia. Subscriptions should be mailed direct to the Publisher, or they may be handed to Postmaster to forward. The Publisher will insert advertisements of an unobjectionable character, at 40 cents a line. No lottery swindles, cheap jewelry announcements, quack medical advertisements, nor Wall Street speculator's cards, can find admittance at any price.

The postage on THE FARM JOURNAL will be paid by the Publisher.

The Publisher does not intend to occupy much space with puffs of THE FARM JOURNAL, leaving it for the intelligence of the reader to discern merit, if any exist.

Enough said; send along the 25 cents.

Go West!

Yes, go to Kansas. If the grasshoppers do not overrun your farm, the prairie soil will yield a good crop; then you can send it to market and pocket the proceeds. You can get for butter—choice, 16 to 18 cents per pound; butter, medium, 12 to 14 cents; eggs, per dozen, 18 to 20 cents; corn, per bushel, 25 cents; oats, 17 to 20 cents; wheat, $1.05 to $1.25; rye, 50 cents; sweet potatoes, 50 cents; hay, per ton, $3.50 to $4.50; chickens, per dozen, $2 to 2.25; chickens, dressed, 4 to 5 cents per pound; turkeys, per pound, 8 to 8½ cents per pound; cabbage, per head, 10 cents; cheese, per pound, 12 to 15 cents; wood, per cord, $4 50 to $5.

Go West, young man, go West!

Strawberries—Essex Beauty.

BY WILLIAM PARRY.

As the time approaches for setting out strawberries, it may be well to consider what kinds to plant. In the early stages of strawberry culture, when it was difficult to raise enough to supply the demand, the main question was What kind will yield the most bushels, and bear transportation best to market? quality not claiming much consideration, as any strawberry that looked well, was considered good enough to sell. Then the general sentiment was in favor of Wilson's Albany, which was very productive, turning red before it was ripe and palatable, could be carried a greater distance to market than other more delicious berries, which did not color up well until they were ripe enough to eat without sugar. Now we have many varieties, large and excellent, and if they are not so generally adapted to all soils and climates as the Wilson, some of them can be found to thrive well wherever the Wilson does, and are of much better quality; among which may be named: Charles Downing, Colonel Cheney, Captain Jack, Cumberland, Triumph, Great American, Jucunda, Kentucky, Monarch of the West, Seth Boyden, Triomphe d'Gand, and others—large, luscious, and sufficiently productive to supply the demand; and sometimes, when the markets are overstocked with berries, the Wilsons are left unsold for the want of purchasers.

The accompanying engraving is intended to represent a medium-sized berry of a new variety, recently introduced, called

ESSEX BEAUTY,

being four and a half inches in circumference. It might be called large, compared with the berries most commonly seen in market; yet we have measured berries of the same variety six and a half to seven inches in circumference. It was raised from seed by E. W. Durand, who also originated the Great American, and is second in size only to that wonderful strawberry, single specimens of which have measured nine inches in circumference and weighed from 2¼ to 2¾ ounces each. When exhibited at the U. S. Centennial Exhibition last summer, the International Judges of the Pomological Department were of the opinion that the flavor of the Essex Beauty was superior to that of the Great American. Ripening earlier than the Great American, and of superior flavor, it possesses in a high degree two good qualities, much sought after by producers and consumers. Both varieties are of a beautiful, bright, crimson color, excellent qualities, firm and very productive, yielding from thirty to one hundred berries to a single plant, and frequently more than a quart to a hill.

They are both desirable to cultivate, and should be grown in preference to the small, sour Wilsons, which have been grown in such quantities as to overstock our markets. A neighbor of ours last year sent to market in one day four wagon-loads of Wilson strawberries (120 crates), which sold at 12½ cents per quart. Another person sent to the same stall, on the same day, one load (30 crates) of large, sweet strawberries, which brought 50 cents per quart, yielding as much money as the four wagon-loads of Wilsons, with only one-fourth the expense for picking and hauling to market.

CINNAMINSON, N. J.

Sheep on the Farm.

BY EASTBURN REEDER.

In successful sheep husbandry at least three conditions are essential

First. Location and adaptation of the farm for the business.

Second. Adaptation of the breed to accomplish the object sought—mutton, wool, or both combined.

Third. Care and skill in their management.

There are very few farms but what are well adapted to keeping sheep. If the surface of the ground is not too wet, sheep will do well almost anywhere. There are many farms that will perhaps pay a better return for the investment if devoted to dairying or general agriculture. It is upon those farms which are unsuited to the purposes of grain raising or dairying that I would urge the claims of sheep husbandry. Steep hillsides, broken and new land, rocky and stony places, will often make excellent sheep pastures, and cannot profitably be devoted to anything else. There is much land of this kind which is now producing nothing but briars and weeds, which, if stocked with sheep, would contribute much to the owner's income. The value of sheep as aids to the farmer in subduing weeds and briars is not sufficiently understood or appreciated. But while it is true that sheep can be kept profitably upon land that cannot be well be devoted to anything else, it is still equally true that upon good land, with care and skill in their management, they will pay as well as any other kind of stock, and with less labor to secure it.

As the principal object sought to be produced, mutton or wool, so should the farmer be governed accordingly in selecting his stock of sheep. Where land is high, and hay and grain bring good prices, it will not pay to keep sheep for the purposes of wool-growing alone. On such land and in such locations the value of the carcass must be combined with that of the fleece to make the business remunerative. The average amount received for the wool of a single sheep ranges from one to two dollars at present prices. On land worth $100 an acre it will not pay to keep sheep for wool-growing when hay is $20 a ton, or corn 60 cents per bushel. The relative gross receipts per acre would stand in something like this proportion:

1 acre of land, cutting 2 tons of hay, worth $40.

1 acre of land, yielding 50 bushels of corn, worth $30.

1 acre of land, pasturing 10 sheep, yielding wool, worth $20.

But if these 10 ewes each produce a lamb worth four or five dollars, then the gross receipts per acre will be swelled above that received from either hay or corn. It is no uncommon thing for the farmer to purchase say 20 ewes for $5 apiece, making $100 for the lot, and before the expiration of a year to sell $25 worth of wool, and lambs amounting to $80 or $100, making over 100 per cent. on the investment, and have the original stock on hand, worth as much or more than at the time of starting. Of course this is not all to be set down as profit. Neither is the whole amount received for a crop of hay or grain to be considered as profit. In determining the actual profit on any crop there are many items of debit and credit to be counted before the true result is reached. In sheep husbandry the credits come in under the heads of wool, lambs, mutton, manure, improvement of the farm, etc., while the principal charges are for provender consumed and labor in their care.

Early Chickens—A Glass-Covered Run for Them.

There is nothing that a farmer can produce that pays a better profit than early chickens, to be hatched in February or March. In June and July they are ready for market, and always command a high price. But it is difficult, and has been found by many impossible, to hatch the chickens in March and keep them growing right along until the warm days of April when they can go out to range at will. It is useless to attempt to raise early chickens without proper arrangements for the business. The building in which the hen sits should front the south, and the southern side should admit the sun freely through glass. But it is not difficult to get the eggs hatched in February or March, but after the chicks are out of the shell then the trouble begins. The chicks must be kept warm and dry, and have a clean, dry, sunny place to run in. This may be provided, as shown in the accompanying

CHICKEN RUN.

engraving. Three ordinary hot-bed sash, covering a space of seventy-two square feet, are enough for four clutches. The coops should open at the back, so they can be readily cleaned out and the mothers fed. A covering should be provided for the glass in case the place gets too hot, and the sash can be raised a little at the upper end to admit fresh air. Fresh horse manure should be placed around the run, and covered with earth to provide heat, as in very cold weather it will be needed. By means of this arrangement the young chickens can be kept in a thriving condition until warmer weather comes.

Shade Trees—No. 1.

BY G. A.

The place to be selected to plant a tree should be well drained and have good rich soil; some kinds prefer a sandy loam and others a more clayey soil, and it would be well for planters to select such kind as suits their soil.

The aim in planting a tree is to put the roots as near as possible in the same position as they were before the tree was removed from its original place. For this purpose the hole should be made so large that the lateral roots do not require any bending or crowding, and so deep that, when planted, the roots are as deep in the ground as previous to their removal. In such a hole the tree must be placed, and the dirt, which must be good rich soil, thrown in little by little, placing it all around each root and treading it firm, so as to bring the soil close around each root, not leaving any hollow spaces. After filling up the hole within about two or three inches of the surface, the tree must stand *firm*, so as to withstand the pressure of the wind If the season should be dry, a bucket of water should be poured around the tree, and then the hole filled in with loose soil, which must not be trodden, as loose soil retains the moisture better. A mulching—that is, a covering of half-rotten straw—is very recommendable. Large trees must be staked so that the wind cannot move them, in order that the roots may have a chance to grow and take hold of the soil. There is a fashion of digging the holes several days before the trees are planted, which is a very wrong practice, as it allows the dirt and the hole to dry out; it should always be dug the same day—or, better, the same hour—when the tree is to be planted.

In taking up a tree in the nursery, it can hardly be avoided that some of the roots are cut shorter, and in this case it cannot be expected that the so shortened roots should obtain nourishment for the same amount of top branches as the tree had before. The branches, therefore, must be cut back accordingly, more or less, in proportion to the roots. Many persons who have planted their trees with the utmost care have failed in making the trees grow by neglecting to follow this rule.

Any tree can be transplanted in the spring, but it is far better to plant such in the fall, which are not liable to be injured by severe winters after the transplanting, as the roots may form new fibres before the winter sets in, and is ready to grow in spring at the arrival of the first warm spell.

If trees are lifted too soon in the fall, the winter will trim them very severely by killing all the unripened wood. The best time to take up a tree for transplanting is when they shed their leaves.

The list of really good *shade* trees is not a very long one for this section. The most beautiful—probably the most common—are the different kinds of maples. They rank among the first, and with right, as—beside their beauty—they answer all requirements. The *Norway Maple* (Acer plasanoides), with its dark green leaves, gives a very dense shade, and forms naturally a regular round spreading top. It is perfectly hardy; is an excellent street or lawn tree, which can be planted in the fall without risk, and it will thrive in almost any good drained soil. Its slowness in growth is the only objection, and therefore its cost, as nurserymen cannot afford to sell trees which take more time for their completion for the market for the same price as more rapidly growing kinds.

Very similar to the Norway is the *Sycamore Maple* (Acer pseudo-platanus), which is a more rapid grower in rich loam soil, forms a regular round head; is hardy, easily transplanted, and is well suited for a street tree or for the lawn. Its bearing large quantities of seed is a little objectionable.

The *Sugar Maple* (Acer saccharinum) makes also a fine tree, which is particularly admired in the fall, when its foliage changes to golden yellow with red. It will thrive in almost any good soil, and can be planted safely in the fall.

The *Red* or *Swamp Maple* (Acer rubrum) is very desirable as well for shade as for beauty. The leaves change to all different shades of red in the fall, and in the spring its red fruit and flowers give it a pleasing appearance. It is also hardy; bears transplanting in the fall well; will thrive in any soil—even if a little wet.

The most rapidly growing tree of the Maple tribe is the *Silver Maple* (Acer dasycarpum). This must have a good loamy soil, and in such it makes a beautiful shade tree, with its leaves being silvery under the surface. Wherever the soil is suitable it is a good street tree; not giving such a dense shade as the others, it allows some air and sunlight to penetrate the top, making it more healthy to inhabitants living on streets where a narrow sidewalk does not allow trees to be planted far enough from the house. This tree is often confounded with the Silver Poplar, which suckers from the roots to a terrible extent; but the former does not at all. Although the Silver Maple can be transplanted in the fall, it is preferable to do it in spring.

There are several more kinds of Maple which are not mentioned here, as they are more suitable for ornament than shade.

The Model Coffee House.

A brief sketch of the "Model Coffee House" of Philadelphia, will prove interesting to the readers of THE FARM JOURNAL

"A PINT OF COFFEE AND A ROLL, 5 CENTS."

Joshua L. Baily, dry goods merchant of the city, is the philanthropic individual to whom the credit must be given of having established this most excellent institution.

Mr. Baily conceived the idea, that if we ask men to abandon their beer and whiskey, we must furnish them a substitute every way better. Hence he determined to establish a coffee house, and supply all applicants with a cup of coffee and a roll at the mere price of a glass of beer. In October, 1874, he opened a small store at 15th and Market Streets, and placed in charge thereof a woman as cook and waitress. A full pint of the best Java coffee was served, together with a roll, for five cents. Custom flowed in with marvelous rapidity until three more stores were added to the first one rented, and, in place of one woman, a score were employed to serve the increasing number of patrons. Now there are 1,400 persons who daily lunch at this place, not simply on a roll and coffee, but a dozen other dishes are prepared and served in the best manner. This was called the "Workingmen's Coffee House."

In December of the same year another house was opened at 31 South Fourth Street, which proved to be so popular that Mr. Baily erected a new building adjoining Nos. 27 and 29, and fitted it up in an admirable manner for its intended purpose. In June of last year this building was opened to the public. It is called the "Model Coffee House."

The main hall seats 218 persons, and about 2,400 persons lunch here daily. Though it was originally intended to provide only a cup of coffee and a roll, the bill of fare now is greatly extended, and a hungry man for five or ten cents can feast to his satisfaction. In the bill of fare no article costs over five cents. One may order an Irish stew, or adish of baked beans, a bowl of oat meal or wheat mush, with milk, dumplings, corned beef, custards, pies, soups, fruit in season, each item, five cents. A pint glass of milk, with a roll, costs five cents. Nothing is handed out in meager quantities, but it must be a famishing man, indeed, if ten or fifteen cents' worth does not more than satisfy his cravings. The cooking is admirably done, and served by cleanly and obliging waitresses, and with exemplary dispatch. The "Model" is often thronged during the day with all classes of people—merchants, bankers, editors, clerks, mechanics, working men, bootblacks. The throng is always a genteel one, and rude or unbecoming behavior is unusual.

Mr. Baily has been apprised of many cases where his "Coffee Houses" have been the means of rescuing from the drinking saloons persons who had been lured thereto, and were on the rapid road to destruction, and we have no doubt he is doing a wonderful amount of good to the community through these instrumentalities. He says that he has received scores of letters from those who acknowledge themselves to have been benefited, and fathers, mothers, and sisters have called to express their gratitude for the restoration of sons and brothers. We understand that the receipts at the counters cover all running expenses—a gratifying fact. Our country friends, when in the city, may find no small amount of pleasure in calling and satisfying themselves of the merit of the bill of fare, and of the good work being done by Mr. Bailey's "Model Coffee Houses."

Agricultural Societies.

The annual meeting of the Oxford (Chester County) Agricultural Society took place in January. This Society is not in a flourishing condition. It has a floating debt of $3,000, and a mortgage debt of $6,500. Its property is valued at $20,000. In the election of officers for the ensuing year the following were chosen: President, J. Lacey Darlington; Recording Secretaries, Theodore K. Stubbs, George B. Passmore; Corresponding Secretary, Henry L. Brinton; Treasurer, D. M. Taylor.

At the annual meeting of the Chester County Agricultural Society, on January 29th, the following officers were elected to serve the ensuing year, viz.: President, Evans Rogers, West Chester; Recording Secretaries, William H. Morgan, J. F. Ingram, West Chester; Corresponding Secretary, Josiah Hoopes, West Chester; Treasurer, William H. Morgan.

The Doylestown (Bucks Co.) Agricultural and Mechanics' Institute held its annual meeting January 27th. The old board was elected except Joseph W. Cornell in place of R. W. Grier, deceased, and Isaac Ely instead of Charles Phillips, declined. The actual expenses of the current year were $5,498.42, and income, $4,245.99, showing a difference of $1,252.43. Dr. Isaiah Michener is President, and J. Watson Case, Secretary.

The annual meeting of the Burlington County (N. J.) Agricultural Society was held on Saturday, January 27th. According to the Treasurer's report the indebtedness of the Society is $10,300, and a cash balance in the treasury of $1,080.24. The following are the newly elected officers of the Society: Isaac Fenimore, of Lumberton, President; J. B. Collins, of Mount Holly, Secretary, and E. B. Jones, of Mount Holly, Treasurer. The next annual exhibition will take place on October 9th, 10th and 11th, 1877.

At the annual meeting of the Montgomery County and East Pennsylvania Agricultural Society, held on February 14th, John Kennedy was elected President, and A. S. Hallman, Recording Secretary.

The Montgomery County Agricultural Society held its annual meeting on February 12th. Dr. M. L. Newbery was elected President; David Dunnett, Treasurer; and Joseph Rex, Recording Secretary.

The Sitting Hen.

BY DR. A. M. DICKEY.

A seasonable subject just now in many far ms and households in the Middle States is the sitting hen. Most farmers know, or should know, how to manage her. But there are many readers, into whose hands THE FARM JOURNAL will fall, who perhaps do not know all they would like to about it.

In our section of country poultry-keeping is not confined to farmers. Almost every one who has any accommodations does something at it. Retired people, mechanics, laborers, etc., raise nearly as much poultry in the vicinity of Philadelphia as the farmers.

Many people like to have early-hatched chickens. These are the most profitable and desirable, but what are called early chickens nowadays are hatched in January and February. Broods got out at that time of year require a great deal of nursing and attention, more, I always thought, than they were worth to me: hence, I do not indulge in them, nor would I encourage any one to, unless he had the special accommodations necessary for the business.

March is early enough to hatch broods anywhere north of 40°. Broods brought out in this month do not require a tithe of the care January or February chicks do, and they grow to as good size, and may still be sold as broilers in May and June, if they have been raised for that purpose.

As soon after the 1st of March as a hen shows a disposition to become broody, if she is a desirable hen for the purpose, she should be indulged, and given a clutch of eggs. A wild, or nervous, or fidgety hen should not be chosen for the purpose of rearing a brood. Her nest should be clean and fresh, and *placed where other hens ca not disturb her*. The nest box should be whitewashed; if this cannot be done conveniently, the box must, at least, be thoroughly cleaned, and the corners and bottom treated to a dressing of coal-oil—this is to prevent trouble from lice.

The nest should be put on the ground for various reasons. Hens are often set in the cellar, and where this can be done, there is no better place. If convenient, a nest may be made on the ground, which will, ordinarily, be the best. A few bricks, or sticks of stove wood, may be be placed so as to prevent the nest from being displaced, or the eggs from rolling away.

The mistake of giving a hen a large number of eggs at this time of year is to be avoided. Nine are enough. More can be hatched, without doubt, but the trouble is to raise them after they are hatched. Better success in the end will follow with seven or eight chicks than with ten or twelve. A good mother hen will raise seven or eight chicks without loss, but few hens can do more than this with March chicks, unless under more than ordinarily favorable circumstances.

The sitting hen should have food and water once a day, and she should have the opportunity to take a dust bath while she is off her nest; she must not be allowed to be too long absent, or the eggs will get chilled.

With these precautions, if the eggs are fertile, and the hen is not disturbed, success may be counted on, and in our next we shall try and give some directions for managing the chicks.

What Shall We Do About It?

BY E. M. DILWORTH.

The suggestion has been frequently made, and, truly, with some appearance of reason, that farmers in the Eastern and Middle States will eventually be driven out of their business by the cheapness, the wonderful fertility, and the vast extent of Western farm lands. Let us see what, if any, difficulties may arise in our way from this source.

That the immense tracts of land brought into grain production during the last twenty years, affect the market, cannot be doubted, though we have also in that time increased our market for grain both at home and abroad, and it would be hard to persuade ourselves that we should not obtain more money for our crops if the surplus in our country were smaller; still, a little thought will convince us that we necessarily have some advantages over our Western fellow-laborers. The chief of these is our easy communication with shipping ports, as compared with the long railroad routes over which Western grain must be brought to these same ports. It is very evident that, whatever the competition, no railroad will carry freight at less than cost, and this cost is increased by every mile and by each branch road; now, however low the freight may be made on railroad lines, those who have water communication to the coast do not need to pay it at all, and by just so much have the advantage of Western producers. A vivid illustration of this may be seen in the shipping of peaches from the Delaware and Maryland peninsula; from points on the Delaware and Chesapeake Canal, and from all landings on the two bays within twelve hours of Philadelphia or Baltimore, boats are run throughout the season, and 5 or 6 cents will cover the freight, while the expense on the same fruit to those who must ship by rail is from 16 to 25 cents; the result being that when fruit is lower than 20 cents, growers on the line of railroad cannot ship without being actually brought into debt, while all having water communication can at least make a few cents toward paying other expenses. The cases are identical save that the Western grain-grower may choose his time for shipment. Nor is this all; the gradual defertilization of the older and nearer Western States, gives farmers there the alternative of going still further west to "fresh fields and pastures new," or of supplying their failing lands with artificial manures, such as we in the older States have been so long using; either course must necessarily add still more to freight expenses. Another view of this subject, however, must probably be taken very shortly. The accomplished fact of a twenty-foot channel at the mouth of the Mississippi cannot fail to affect the grain-growers of the vast country drained by it and its tributaries. Western men have built great hopes upon this project; whether they are now to be realized is a question which cannot remain long unsolved.

But, however it may be decided, a second advantage remains with the grain-grower of the Middle States in the ease with which he obtains farm labor. At our very doors the three chief ports of immigration, we can, with no trouble, obtain our pick of those who come to our shores seeking employment. Nor is this a small matter, for beside the convenience of abundant help, wages cannot, under these circumstances, be exorbitant. Still another thing greatly in our favor is the readiness with which we can avail ourselves of sudden favorable changes in the grain market, which in these days of fluctuation varies with every hour.

But suppose, with all these favoring circumstances, we find the price of grain falling, till the margin left us is hardly a living one, small comfort then to know that our Western brothers are no better off. Is there no way left to help ourselves and them also? Surely there is. *They must* raise grain, cattle, horses, hogs, etc.; they *can* do nothing else; but the same necessity is not laid upon *us*. The immense demand, not only in the cities of New York, Philadelphia, and Baltimore, but in the innumerable smaller cities, towns and villages between and around them, for fruits, vegetables, milk, poultry, eggs and hay, must be supplied from the comparatively neighboring country, and there is no reason why all our farmers should not go much more largely into this branch of their business than they now do. Granted that the cities seem sometimes overstocked; but this rarely, perhaps never, occurs in reference to all the products mentioned in one season, and diversified farming is what our Middle States farmers should look forward to in the near future; nor, as already hinted, must they overlook the smaller cities and towns in marketing their produce. In many of them the articles named will, at any time, bring a higher price than in the city, simply because the neighboring farmers send everything to "the city" forgetting that towns-people also will live—if they can.

Surplus stock of fruits and vegetables will readily be disposed of to local canneries and drying establishments, which in their turn will afford employment to many in the country who cannot take an active part in farm labor. It is needless to say that the market for *these* articles is full, for in the comparatively few years since their introduction, they have only begun to make a market, and the world is open to them. This, then, seems to me the easiest and best mode of solving the grain question between East and West.

PORT PENN, DEL.

Home-made Fertilizers.

A large number of farmers and truckers now manufacture their own chemical manures at a saving of from 25 to 50 per cent. in the cost. Others adhere to the old method of buying their manures of those who deal in or manufacture them. Thousands are using the recipe given by Harrison Brothers & Co., of this city, which is as good as any we have seen. For the benefit of those who have not met with it we present it below: Select a good wooden floor of a barn, or make a box floor of thick plank, laid tight. On this first throw the bones. If not ground very fine, it would be well to sift them, and place only the coarser part on this floor, putting the finer portion aside for mixing in afterward. By this means, the coarse bone will come in contact with the strong acid first, and be more effectually acted upon by it, while the finer parts can then be added to dry up. No metal should be used on the floor, or where the acid can reach. Water, equal to about one-fourth the weight of the bone, is first to be poured upon it, well stirred in with a spade or hoe, and left for two or three days to heat and ferment; if convenient, it would be well to use the water boiling hot. After the bones have fermented, then add the oil vitriol, mixing well with a wooden spade or board; the mass effervesces or boils; stir twice a day thoroughly for two days, so as to turn the whole mass over; let it stand for two or three days to dry; add the fine bone, and mix it in well. If not dry, use some absorbing substance, as sawdust, dry peat or muck, or dry earth, in small quantities, and mix well. Do not use, for this purpose, lime, ashes, or marl, as they would destroy the super-phosphate, and spoil the whole work.

Now, when your super-phosphate has become thoroughly dry, the addition of sulphate of magnesia, muriate of potash, nitrate of soda, land plaster, or other elements which are to compose your complete fertilizer, may be made. Stir them in thoroughly one at a time, reserving the land plaster to be worked in the last thing.*

SPECIMEN GARDEN WINDOW.

Window Gardening.

Some random suggestions in relation to the above subject, may rightfully occupy space in THE FARM JOTRNAL.

A pile of sods laid by and well rotted, containing a good deal of sand, is the basis of the best soil for window gardening.

A teaspoonful of guano in a quart of water may occasionally be used as a fertilizer to advantage.

When the soil in the pots gets dry, water it *thoroughly*.

The temperature should be such as is healthy for human beings to live in; but at nights it should be twenty degrees lower.

The plants should be aired every fine day, and thoroughly washed once a week, at least.

Every one knows that most plants *must* have plenty of sun to thrive.

Any floral guide will give you directions applicable to the destruction of insect enemies; but if the conditions named above are complied with, no insects will come to give trouble.

The wood-cut of the charming window garden, which we give herewith, was kindly furnished us by that prince of florists, Mr. James Vick, of Rochester, New York.

The Wheat Prospect.

Many farmers feared during January that the wheat would be badly damaged by the ice which was upon all low places in the fields; but it now appears that the injury from that source will not be great. There will be patches of grain killed, here and there, but the wheat generally looks green and healthy, and so far bids fair to yield a good crop.

New Agricultural Works.

Norristown has been selected as the site of the new Hubbard Agricultural Works, owned by Rochester, N. Y., parties. Plans of the buildings are now completed, and estimates are being made by contractors for their erection. The main building will be 170x48 feet; the foundry will be 115x48 feet. The Company will engage chiefly in the manufacture of the Hubbard self-raking, self-binding reaping-machine. We are pleased to learn that these works will locate in this section, and hope the owners will meet with success.

All communications intended for publication should be addressed to the editor, and should give the name of the writer.

The editor expects the practical and scientific cultivators of the soil, who are among the readers of this paper, to tell what they know in the columns of THE FARM JOURNAL, and he depends largely for success upon their encouragement and aid.

WILMER ATKINSON, - - *Editor and Proprietor.*

THE FARM JOURNAL.

PHILADELPHIA, MARCH, 1877.

Introductory.

Believing that there is a field uncultivated for the establishment of an agricultural paper in this city that shall meet the requirements of those engaged in rural pursuits in this immediate section—not seeking a circulation outside of the three States of Pennsylvania, New Jersey, and Delaware—we bring THE FARM JOURNAL into existence, and send it forth upon its mission.

While appreciating the difficulties that are sure to beset an enterprise of this kind, we enter upon our task cheerfully and with hope, but knowing well that in this field of labor, as in most others, no one can attain success without earning it.

We shall use our best endeavor to make THE FARM JOURNAL a newspaper that shall possess *real value* to the class for whom it is published—the cultivators of the soil—and an entertaining monthly visitor to rural firesides. The future will determine the measure of our success.

More than this, at present, we need not say, but we will let our paper speak for itself, month by month, as it shall appear.

Our Contributors.

THE FARM JOURNAL has cause to feel proud of the character of its contributors. No veteran agricultural journal can boast of a more respectable list. Of writers more fit to address the public on the topics they have selected to discuss, William Parry, Eastburn Reader, E. M. Dilworth, Dr. Dickey, and William Dean, are names that any journal may well feel pleased to rank among its contributors, and no person within our acquaintance can write more intelligently upon shade trees and kindred subjects than G. A., a gentleman too modest to allow his name to appear in print. It is such material as this that the editor of THE FARM JOURNAL has selected to aid him in making the paper acceptable to its readers. But these are not all; other practical writers will be heard from, of equal merit, in future numbers.

Procuring Names for Evil Purposes.

In spite of the able and tireless efforts of the *American Agriculturist* to show up that large class of scoundrels, to be found chiefly in the city of New York, who get a livelihood by preying upon ignorant and simple people throughout the country, of whom there seems to be a vast number, these gentry seem to be doing a good business yet—as good, if not better, than when the *Agriculturist* began its warfare fifteen or twenty years ago.

A circular recently came under our notice, sent out to a young person, requesting a "list of the names and post-office addresses of all the young people you are acquainted with." Of course some worthy object was to be forwarded, and these young people were to be greatly benefited! We cannot say what the actual purpose is of the one who sent out the circular, but it is doubtless a bad one, and parents should caution their children against ever replying to such circulars. To comply with such a request from an unknown person might be the cause of bringing an untold amount of misery upon a companion or acquaintance. It is not pleasant for parents to reflect that the names of their boys and girls are booked already by these birds of prey—but such is the fact—even in regard to many parents whose attention is called to this article. The Publisher of this paper, in sending to postmasters for lists of persons to mail the first number of THE FARM JOURNAL to, found that his prospectus, in some cases, was torn up without being read, those officials having become suspicious of all applications of the kind, one postmaster saying that he received a dozen circulars daily of parties who want a "list of names."

THE FARM JOURNAL intends to go to the aid of the *American Agriculturist*—we are glad to follow such noble leadership—in its fight against these scoundrels who live by their evil wits and seek a livelihood by crooked paths and vicious methods, to the injury of society and the ruin of many victims. We shall thank our readers to keep us posted in regard to the movements of any of the tribe that may come under their notice.

Real Estate Exchange.

There will be found in this number of THE FARM JOURNAL a new feature, which, it is expected, will become a prominent one, useful to many, and interesting to all of our readers—we allude to the Real Estate Department.

If, at the present time, a resident of this city, or elsewhere, wishes to buy a farm, how will he go about finding one to suit his purse and purpose? Will he hunt up all the local papers around Philadelphia? will he search out all the real estate agents and obtain their lists? will he daily ponder the advertising columns of the *Public Ledger?* Of course he will, and very likely by the time he concludes the above programme he will have relinquished the idea of purchasing!

Now, our design is to place before him, in the columns of this paper, which he can get at the nearest news stand, just the information he needs to place him upon the right track; we will give him a list of the properties for sale in Bucks, Montgomery, Chester, and Delaware Counties; or if he cares to secure his acres over the river, we will show him what can be bought in Gloucester, Camden, and Burlington.

Moreover, we will report sales that have taken place in all these counties; who sold, who bought, and the price of the land.

Our list for March is not as perfect as we should like, but it will serve to show our purpose, and perhaps arouse the attention of persons in any way interested in the buying and selling of farms and other rural property.

Sugar-Beet Culture.

Mr. Lea Pusey, one of Delaware's best citizens, has been accumulating information, for the last year or two, concerning the culture of the sugar beet, and the adaptability of the soil and climate of his section thereto. Last season he procured seed from Europe, and distributed it to farmers in various sections of Delaware, Chester County, Pa., and West Jersey, and in the fall tested the product as to its sugar-yielding capacity. By means of newspaper articles and pamphlets he has disseminated an immense array of facts and figures, and has awakened a large degree of interest in the subject among the people.

A meeting of the leading business men of the city of Wilmington was held on February 14th to consider the matter, at which it was resolved to ask the Legislature of the State to make an appropriation for the purpose of offering premiums for the years 1877 and 1878 for the best results in growing sugar beets, and an influential committee was appointed to present the petition to the Legislature.

This subject of sugar-beet culture is not a new one in this country, by any means, it having been talked about more or less for fifty years; and whether the present movement in Delaware will prove to be mere talk or not, is more than we are able, as yet, to determine. We are, however, somewhat of the opinion of the *Germantown Telegraph*, that our farmers will be able to find, for many years to come, fruits of the soil that will be more profitable to cultivate than the sugar beet. They will most likely continue to sell their corn and wheat, their pork and beef, their fruits and vegetables, and to buy their sugars with the proceeds. Still, we will watch Mr. Pusey's efforts with a good deal of interest, and hope indeed that they may be crowned with success.

Is This True?

Mr. Alexander Ramsey, Jr., of this city, in a communication to the *Ledger*, says:

"Calculi in the stomach and bladder of horses is frequently caused by feeding them adulterated feed obtained from dishonest millers who mix plaster of paris, which is very heavy, with the chop and other feed. When the animal eats this horrible mess, the moisture of the stomach causes the plaster to 'set,' and thus makes the stones."

Now, then, who is it that mixes plaster of paris with horse feed? Such villainy ought to be ferreted out and the villain punished. The Norristown *Herald* recently reported a case of a horse having died from the presence of a stone in the bladder, and Mr. Ramsey thinks the disease came from the use of food adulterated in this way.

Write for the Farm Journal.

We desire to have concise, practical articles from our readers on various agricultural, horticultural, and domestic topics, when they can speak from actual experience or observation.

Will not some successful fruit-grower tell the readers of this paper what he knows about the apple and pear, and how to grow them?

Will not some one accustomed to managing a small-fruit farm, tell us what he knows about cultivating the strawberry, the raspberry, the currant?

Will not some experienced trucker acquaint THE JOURNAL with his methods of growing and harvesting profitably his celery, tomato, asparagus, egg-plant, and ruta-baga crop?

Will not the owner of some profitable egg-farm inform the public how he manages his poultry successfully?

Will not some prosperous stock-raiser write what he knows for the benefit of THE FARM JOURNAL readers?

Will not the women tell us how to make palatable bread and gilt-edged butter?

Come, friends, disseminate the knowledge you are possessed of for the benefit of others and the advancement of the community in general. THE FARM JOURNAL will spread what you may say before the eyes of its fifty thousand readers, who, in common with the editor, will thank you for your effort in their behalf.

Tramps.

In the annual report of the Directors of the Poor of Chester County, an item of considerable interest is to be found relating to "tramps." The showing is as follows: "In the year running from October 1st, 1873, to October 1st, 1874, there were 3,152 entertained at the Almshouse, to which 8,898 meals were given. From October 1st, 1874, to 1875, the callers numbered 3,351, to whom 8,400 meals were distributed. From October 1st, 1875, to 1876, 5,258 made calls, and received 11,464 meals. In March, 1876, 915 tramps were cared for, and in August of the same year, the number was 977. These people in March claimed to be then *en route* for the Jersey vegetable farms, and in August they were wending their way to Delaware to engage in peach picking."—*Record.*

Since New Jersey has passed a law bearing heavily against the tramp nuisance, the question is, Which way will the bummers travel in March? Before August, Delaware will have her law enacted; then what route will he go in August? The likelihood is that the Sheriff of Chester County will have to prepare a few thousand additional meals for 1877 for the wretched vagabond.

TOPICS IN SEASON.

The Farm.

Give me, ye gods, the product of one field,
That so I neither may be rich nor poor,
And having just enough, not covet more.—DRYDEN.

Clover seed will be sown before the ground becomes hard. The seed should be selected with care.

Plaster should be sown early in the month to have the benefit of the spring rains.

Potatoes for early crops should go in as soon as the ground will admit.

Give particular attention to cows that have calved.

Succulent food, such as ruta-bagas, beets, etc., increase the flow of milk, and should always be given in addition to grain and hay.

Clean thoroughly and whitewash poultry houses.

If any of our readers have had experience in raising poultry on a large scale, we trust they will give the results of their efforts, whether successful or not.

Get the corn ground well covered with manure, if not already done.

If you desire to get a large yield of rich milk, give your cow, three times a day, water slightly warm, slightly salted, in which bran has been stirred, at the rate of one quart to two gallons of water. You will find, if you have not found this by daily practice, that your cow will gain twenty-five per cent. immediately under the effect of it. She will become so attached to the diet as to refuse to drink clear water, unless very thirsty, but this mess she will eat almost any time, and ask for more. The amount of this is an ordinary water-pail full each time, morning, noon, and night. Your animal will then do her best at discounting the lacteal. Four hundred pounds of butter is often obtained from good stock, and instances are mentioned where the yield was even at a higher figure. So says a writer who is worthy of attention.

An Upper Dublin, Montgomery County, farmer, who raised a fine crop of potatoes last summer when nearly every one else had an extremely light yield, informs THE FARM JOURNAL how he did it. He says: "The best potatoes to plant in this section are the Early Rose and Peerless. On a good clover sod is the best place to plant; I put them on corn stubble because it suits our rotation better; my good crop last season was raised in this way: A good, stiff blue grass sod was plowed six inches deep for corn the previous year, on which was spread, after plowing, about 800 pounds per acre of concentrated fertilizers, composed of equal parts of Peruvian guano, super-phosphate, and ground bone. This was harrowed in; brought only a medium crop of corn. For potatoes I spread on a good coat of barn-yard manure and sprinkled bone in the rows. The previous summer being dry the sod did not rot, consequently could not plow the ground as usual for potatoes four inches deep, but had to run under sod, hence plowed six inches. I worked the ground with Pheifer's corn-plow three times, as deep as team could pull, once while the plants were in blossom. On six acres I harvested 1,200 bushels of Peerless, on two acres, 250 bushels of Early Rose, and on one acre, which was not manured, but treated otherwise the same, 100 bushels of Peerless. The potatoes were nearly all large. I used for seed the second size potato, cut in four pieces, of my own growing, and also some of large size bought in Philadelphia; my own seed proved the best."—J. Q. A.

While it is true that some of our growers claim that they are able to gather a much larger yield per acre than that above recorded, who among them actually did harvest an equal crop last year. Let us hear from Edwin Satterthwaite and the "growers in his neighborhood" on this point!

The Garden.

"Well must the ground be digged, and better dress'd,
New soil to make, and meliorate the rest.—DRYDEN.

In the neighborhood of Philadelphia the soil may or may not become dry enough in March to be a fit receptacle for seed. Should the spring open early, beets, carrots, lettuce and peas may be planted. Peas cannot be got into the ground too early in the year if the ground is fit. To secure an early start for potatoes for family use, the tubers may be placed in a box of earth near the kitchen fire and kept moist. They can be planted out the moment the ground becomes mellow, and come forward very early. Those who have no hot-bed can very readily raise early tomato-plants in a box in the house. Onion sets may go in the ground as early as they can be got there. Celery should have an early start; after the young plants get a start, keep them growing; when too dry, sprinkle them as often as needed. Of peas the dwarf kinds are of little use when sticks can be had for the taller sorts.

If the hot-bed is not yet started, no time is to be lost. Fresh stable manure only, not exceeding six weeks old, is suitable for the purpose. Turn it over into a compact heap, protected from heavy rains or snow; allow it to remain a few days, when it should be put into the frame; tramp it firmly and evenly; place thereon the sash; put in the rich earth, and, in about four days, sow the seed, having previously stirred the earth freely, to destroy any seeds or weeds therein.

Be sure to have the ground where you put onions rich, and, to make it so, cover it over with manure *now*, running over it and raking off all the coarse parts before planting.

If not done before, trim currants, grapes, and gooseberries.

The end of March is a good time to set out roots you have saved for seed, such as turnips, carrots, parsnips, cabbage, celery, leeks, lettuce, etc. Draw the earth up around them to keep from frost.

Sugar Corn.—In sending for seed, if one has not tried Stowell's evergreen, put it in the list. Although not a very early sort, it really has no equal, all things considered.

It is of much importance to know when is the best time to prune grape-vines. This question has received an intelligent answer from S. Printz Rush, of Media, Delaware County, in the *American*. Mr. Rush says: "Having pruned at various times for my neighbors from the first to the fifteenth of April, and apparently with good results, I became of the opinion that the sap never ceased to flow in a healthy vine, and so I adopted the plan of clipping a vine every warm day in March until I noticed a decided increase in the flow of sap. When that occurred I pruned all the vines immediately. Within two years I found a marked increase in the quantity of fruit as well as in flavor and richness. The vines also began to throw out healthy shoots from near the ground, with which I was enabled to renew. To the novice I would say, prune between the 25th of March and the 5th of April, according as the season is favorable. To the practical gardener I would say, prune any time after the 15th of March, when, by cutting off a branch, there will be sufficient sap flow to hermetically seal over the stump in fifteen or twenty minutes."

Celery seed should be sowed very early in the spring, in rich ground, which should be kept moist. When the plants are four or five inches high, they should be transplanted into trenches three inches deep. The trenches should be about three feet apart, and the plants seven inches. The soil should be very rich, and the plants should be well watered in case of drought. Some cultivators earth up at intervals, while others permit the plants to retain their full growth, and earth up all at once, which is the best method. About the 1st of October, earthing up may proceed without injury; but let it be done firmly and evenly, and on a sloping direction, from the base to nearly the top of the leaves; in this state it will remain sound for a long time; should the weather become very severe, dry litter or straw should be spread over the plants.

Blackberry plants should be pinched back so as not to grow more than three feet high. This treatment keeps them partly in a dwarfed condition, and insures productiveness. If cultivated more the growth would become too rank on rich soil, and they would bear less, become more straggling, and be more liable to winter killing. This is now well understood by blackberry planters, and is in accordance with the remark which we have from boys who gather wild blackberries," that if they find a bush which the cows have browsed, it is always sure to be full of berries." A plant affected with yellow rust should be removed upon its first appearance.

Landscape Art.—The publisher, D. M. Dewey, of Rochester, New York, has sent us an excellent little work on landscape gardening, written by B. R. Elliott. It is a practical work by an old and experienced gardener, presenting a number of plans, marking the spot for each building, shrub and tree. It has been very much needed, and all who contemplate laying out or improving a country place ought to have a copy.

The Orchard.

Nor is it hard to beautify each month
With files of party-colored fruits.—PHILIPS.

This is a proper time to prepare a list of fruit trees for spring planting, if not attended to earlier. Too much care cannot be exercised in the selection, and, in fact, if one has not already given a good deal of study to the matter, he had better postpone planting to another season. It is a fearful waste of time, energy, and money, to set out an orchard of which one-half of the trees will never bear fruit. A majority of the orchards in the country are of this character. A few choice varieties of apple, pear, or peach, are sufficient either for small or extensive fruit growing. After the list is selected, the best plan is to write to the near-by nurserymen who are known to be honest and fair-dealing, and ascertain if they have the varieties needed; then, in the planting season, take the list to the nursery, and make your own selection of trees. Do not have the trees sent by railroad or express, but have the whole process of taking up the trees, tying up the roots so they will not become dry, conveyance home, and transplanting, done under your own supervision. Healthy trees, taken up with ample roots, which are never allowed to become dry, and transplanted in soil fit to receive them, the roots being carefully spread out, and the tops trimmed to the same extent that the roots have been by the process of transplanting, will surely take root and grow, and, under proper after-cultivation, will rapidly come into a fruit-bearing orchard. The rule is a simple one: Do not order trees until you know which kinds are worthless, and which are not; then go yourself to the nursery, and get them, and transplant in ground as thoroughly tilled as your corn ground at planting time; *then learn how to take care of them.* Where this plan is adopted, you will soon rejoice in an abundance of the finest fruit, and have no worthless trees to "cumber the ground."

The time to set out fruit trees in the spring is in April and May, and as soon as the soil can be got into a dry and mellow condition to receive them.

Throw your coal ashes around your fruit trees. Don't throw away or sell wood ashes, but use them around your peach and other fruit trees.

Cut off from the twigs on trees any nests of caterpillar eggs, and burn them.

We doubt the reasonableness of the indiscriminate abuse of tree agents indulged in by most of the agricultural newspapers of the country. Some of these agents are honest, responsible persons, and do business for nurserymen who are worthy of confidence. That there are fraudulent characters engaged in traversing the country offering to sell trees, we do not doubt; but every farmer ought himself to be able to select the worthy from the worthless.

In grape culture it seems that the finer varieties, which grow weak, and liable to disease, can begrafted on Concord and Clinton roots, and then grow as well and as strong as these robust varieties. The French are importing Concord roots for grafting their own kinds upon from this country.

One of the most prolific of early winter apples for this section is the Wine, or Hayes. Its quality is excellent, and we know of no fault it has, unless it be that some seasons it may show a disposition to rot earlier than others. It always brings a good price in market where it is known, and is a regular and immense bearer.

The Household.

A Word to our Lady Readers.—Fifteen Dollars in Premiums. We have concluded to offer to the lady readers of THE FARM JOURNAL fifteen dollars in premiums, thus: five dollars to the one who will send us the best response to the following queries and requests, viz.:

- How to make good coffee.
- How to make good bread.
- How to make good butter.
- Name ten of the most valuable household receipts.
- Give the best methods of preserving fruits and meats for family use.

And ten dollars to the one who will send us the best five essays on the following topics, viz.:

- How to manage the baby.
- How to manage children without scolding or whipping them.
- What shall a farmer's wife read, and when?
- How shall the mother of five or more healthy children maintain a sweet temper?
- Name ten of the most desirable flowers for the embellishment of the lawn or garden, and tell how to manage them.

All responses to the above offer will be submitted to a competent tribunal of ladies for judgment, who will, after thorough consideration, determine the successful competitors, and award the premiums accordingly. All papers submitted that are deemed worthy, and for which we can find room, will be printed in the columns of THE FARM JOURNAL, after the prizes shall have been awarded. How many of our lady readers shall we hear from? The more the merrier.

In scouring knives use a cork instead of a cloth. This recipe, simple as it is, is worth the price of THE JOURNAL for a year. So says the lady who gives it to us.

A Young Housekeeper wishes a recipe for yeast. Who will furnish it? Let us have one that will stand the test of trial.

Coffee roasted, ground and exposed in an open vessel, is one of the best possible deodorizers, quite equal to chloride of lime without its disagreeable smell.

Cayenne pepper will keep the pantry and store-room free from cockroaches and ants.

The kitchen should be as cheerful, clean and attractive, as any room in the house.

A grocer had a pound of sugar returned with a note stating "Too much sand for table use, and not enough for building purposes."

Some women won't be happy in heaven unless they can scrub it out once a year.

Our lady readers can preserve the smoothness and softness of their hands, by keeping a small bottle of glycerine near the place where they habitually wash them, and whenever they have finished washing, and before wiping them, put one or two drops of the glycerine on the wet palm and rub the hands thoroughly with it as if it were soap, then dry lightly with a towel.

To remove ink from linen, cotton, etc., wash the article in sweet milk, leaving it to soak over night, or as long as the stain remains, rubbing and wringing the cloth freely. No water should touch the article until after it has been soaked in the milk, and it should be taken before the ink has dried.

A good bunion remedy is to use pulverized saltpetre and sweet oil; obtain at the druggists five or six cents' worth of saltpeter, put into a bottle with sufficient olive-oil to nearly dissolve it; shake up well, and rub the inflamed parts night and morning, and more if painful. This is a well-tried remedy.

A little pure nitric acid carefully applied every other day will soon destroy warts. Touch the wart only with the acid. Should any of the acid get on the skin, apply sweet oil.

Fat people who wish to get lean should eat freely of lean meat, avoiding pastry, sugar, fat meat, and generally all kinds of farinaceous articles of food.

This is how a colored woman makes the delicious corn bread for which the South is so famous: "Why, darlin', sometime gen'ally I takes a little meal, and sometimes gen'ally I takes a little flou', an' I kine o' mixes 'em up with some hot water, an' I puts in eggs enuff an' a little salt, an' then I bakes it jist 'bout enuff. An' you do so, jess so, honey, an' you'll make it as good as I do."

Chandler Darlington, of Chester County, says we should not use sugar, and therefore should not learn how to make it. He is consequently not interested in the culture of the sugar beet.

The Queen of Puddings.—One pint of fine bread crumbs to one quart of milk, one cup of sugar, the yolks of four eggs beaten, a piece of butter the size of an egg, portion of the juice of a lemon. Bake until done, but not watery. Whip the whites of the eggs stiff, and beat in a teacupful of sugar in which has been stirred the juice of the lemon. Spread over the pudding a layer of jelly, or any sweetmeats you prefer. Pour the whites of the eggs over this, and replace in the oven and bake lightly. To be eaten cold with cream.

Another Nice Pudding.—Three tablespoonfuls melted butter mixed with one cup of sugar; 1 egg well beaten; 1 pint of flour; 2 teaspoonfuls cream of tartar; 1 of soda; 1 cup of sweet milk. Beat well, and bake 30 minutes. Serve hot with flavored cream. J.

UPPER DUBLIN, PA.

Oliver Raldsterson, of Solebury, Bucks County, thinks that a cord of hickory wood will go as far as a ton of coal. Oliver is also of the opinion that milk is a good substitute for meat as a feed for poultry, and that ground oats and corn mixed with milk is an excellent diet for fowls.

REAL ESTATE.

In times of business depression like the present, the tendency is for wealthy residents of the city, who have idle funds, to seek investments in the country, either in mortgages or in the purchase of farms; and we understand that a large number of Philadelphians are now looking for country mortgages and farms to buy. Lands are perhaps as cheap now as they ever will be in this section of the country, and buyers will likely be plentier than they have been for some years. We will report, under this head, the sales that have taken place, and will also give a list of farms and other country property that are seeking purchasers. Those who want to either buy or sell will find this department of use to them.

RECENT SALES.—BUCKS COUNTY.

IVYLAND HOTEL, on March 6, public; by Samuel A. Firman, assignee of Ivyland Hotel Company.

HARTSVILLE HOTEL, private. Apply to C. Michener, agent for Elias Krewson.

27 ACRES, in Solebury, $2,000; estate of Emily M. Sowener, to Susan Shellenberger.

54 ACRES, in Tinicum, $1,480.50; estate of Peter Gray, deceased, to Michael McEntee.

162½ ACRES, in New Britain, $75.50 per acre; T. O. Atkinson & Co., assignee of John Todel, to John Kront, of same place.

85 ACRES, in Plumstead, $74 per acre; T. O. Atkinson & Co., for William Heacock, to John M. Trainer, of Solebury.

35 ACRES, in Springfield, $2,925; T. O. Atkinson & Co., for Michael Boehel; public sale, to John Beck, of Philadelphia.

35 ACRES, in New Britain, $2,000; Z. Leidy, agent of James Rafferty, to John Zimmerman (a Russian,) of Philadelphia.

61 ACRES, at Carversville, $6,850; Jacob Booz, to George Large, of Danborough.

MONTGOMERY COUNTY.

93 ACRES, in Limerick Township, $8,000; Lydia Danehower, to Warren Fry, of Trappe.

10 ACRES, in Horsham, $4,000; sold by Yerkes, Bready & Yerkes, for Warner J. Kenderdine.

14 ACRES, near Blue Bell; R. R. Corson, agent, sold for Howard Cadwallader, to H. H. Wheatland, of Philadelphia.

57 ACRES, at Willow Grove, $19,700; George R. Berrell, assignee, to the Abington Building Association.

40 ACRES, in Lower Merion, $6,500; sheriff, for Samuel Atkinson, to N. P. Stichter, of Pottsville.

11 ACRES, oil and powder mill, in Frederick, $3,775; sheriff, for James Wood, to James Wood.

18 ACRES and store, at Hopperville, in Marlboro', $3,100; sheriff, for Benjamin H. Roth, to Jacob S. Geller.

CHESTER COUNTY.

PAPER MILL AND FARM, on Buck Run, East Fallowfield; bought by Isaac Broomall of Mrs. Truman for $6,000.

150 ACRES, in Warwick, $9,500; John Lewis, to Samuel Love, of the same township.

10¾ ACRES, in Willistown, $1,800; assignee of David Bishop, to William L. Alexander, of the same township; also, 8 acres in Easttown, to Samuel Biddle, of West Philadelphia, for $662.

55 ACRES, adjoining Experimental Farm, $5,500; Thomas M. Harvey, to Samuel C. Kent, of Richmond, Va.

73 ACRES, in New Garden, $7,000; Isaac J. Yerkes, to Elwood Wollaston, of same township.

27 ACRES, in East Nautmeal, $3,300; Jacob Hoffecker, to Clayton R. Pike, of same township.

60 ACRES, in East Nottingham, $3,000; James S. Dulin, to J. A. Lloyd, of Oxford.

125 ACRES, in Warwick, $76 per acre; John Lewis, to Samuel Lahr, of same township.

73 ACRES, in Newlin, $70.30 per acre; estate of Joseph Hoopes, to John M. Windle, of East Marlborough.

36 ACRES, in West Pikeland, $4,045; estate of Thomas Hines, deceased, to Uriah Williams, of same township.

BURLINGTON COUNTY.

HOUSE AND LOT, in Burlington, $1,000; Sheriff Lee, to Elisabeth S. Martin, for Daniel S. Purdy.

FOR SALE.—BUCKS COUNTY.

(Notices of properties for sale will appear under this head at the rate of 50 cents per line.)

101 ACRES, in New Britain Township; price reasonable; Thomas MacReynolds, Chalfont Post-office.

MONTGOMERY COUNTY.

50 ACRES, in Moreland, $165 per acre; J. J. Morrison, for Thomas W. Wright, to David Martin, of Cheltenham.

30 ACRES, at Springhouse, Gwynedd; Samuel Fleck to Zieber Marple, of Montgomery Township.

116 ACRES, in Horsham, 1 mile from Hatboro' Station; price $140 per acre; Yerkes, Bready & Yerkes.

125 ACRES, in Abington, 11 miles from Philadelphia; price $165 per acre; Yerkes, Bready & Yerkes.

54 ACRES, in Moreland, 2 miles from Hatboro' Station; terms easy; Yerkes, Bready & Yerkes.

12 ACRES, in Horsham, 1½ miles from Three Tons; price, $3,000; terms easy; Yerkes, Bready & Yerkes.

CHESTER COUNTY.

40 ACRES, grist and saw mill, near Lincoln University. Address Robert F. Hoopes, West Chester.

30 ACRES, in East Fallowfield, 1 mile from Ercildown. Apply to Pyle & Brown, West Chester.

135 ACRES, in London Grove, 2 miles from West Grove Station. Apply to William P. Harper, West Grove Post-office.

DELAWARE COUNTY.

110 ACRES, on West Chester and Philadelphia Railroad, near Baltimore Central Station. Isaac L. Miller, 705 Walnut Street.

25 ACRES, on the West Chester and Philadelphia driving road, near 5-mile stone. Isaac L. Miller, 705 Walnut Street.

56 ACRES, in Concord Township; $130 per acre. Isaac L. Miller, 705 Walnut Street.

4 ACRES, near the Rose Tree, $2,800. Isaac L. Miller, 705 Walnut street.

70 ACRES, in Newtown Township; abundance of fruit; terms easy. Edward Worth, 737 Walnut Street.

40 ACRES, in Upper Chichester, near Linwood Station, Philadelphia, Wilmington and Baltimore Railroad. David Morrow, Sr.

GLOUCESTER COUNTY.

127 ACRES, near Almshouse, now occupied by Edmund T. Wood.

53 ACRES, at junction of the Blackwoodstown road aforesaid, with the County House road, occupied by Samuel Wood.

70 ACRES, 1 mile from depot, at city of Woodbury. D. J. Freas.

38 ACRES, in Mantau Township, near Clarksboro. For particulars, apply to William P. Haines, Mickleton.

BURLINGTON COUNTY.

24 ACRES, in Shamony; public sale on March 10th; Chalkley Willetts, administrator, for estate of Amos T. Decon, deceased.

FARM, WOODLAND AND CEDAR SWAMP, 1½ miles from Pemberton; public sale on March 3d; Thomas S. Logan, acting executor, for estate of Abraham Fort, deceased.

235 ACRES, in Shamony, ½ mile from Indian Mills; terms easy. R. H. Brown.

74 ACRES, at Crosswicks; plenty of fruit. Apply to David R. Kelley, on the property.

MARKETS.

It will be the province of this paper in its reports to give the tendency of market prices—whether up or down—rather than to give the present ruling prices. A journal that is p .blished but once a month can quote prices only upon the one day preceding the issue, and we are glad to know that our American farmers are so wide awake and enterprising that they demand daily, at least weekly, reports of the markets, and are satisfied with nothing less. We shall, of course, quote figures in some cases, but it will be our endeavor, chiefly, to give *facts* upon which our readers may base an intelligent estimate of their own, of the course of prices, and the probable future condition of the markets.

For the first number, we frankly confess, we have few facts or theories to present, as we have not had time to look about us, and not being posted ourselves, we do not propose to make ourselves appear ridiculous by undertaking to inform others, and we shall not make the market column the dumping-ground for cart-loads of rubbish, as we fear some of our cotemporaries do.

We shall, however, seek to become informed, and carefully study the wants of our readers in these matters, and supply information that will be of benefit to them in marketing their products and purchasing their supplies.

PHILADELPHIA, February 21.

GRAIN.—Prime Pennsylvania red and amber Wheat is quoted at $ .52 to $1.56. Wheat is scarce in this market, and price advancing. Corn is also firmer, and selling at 56 to 56½c. Rye, 75 to 80c. Oats, 37 to 38c.

It is estimated that of the wheat crop of 1876 the farmers still hold 15 to 30 per cent.

An English paper, the *Builder*, in the course of a recent article, refers to the immense system of irrigation, railroad and river improvements now being perfected in India, which, it is thought, will have a bearing upon the future of the wheat market in this country. The *Builder* says that the public works at this time under construction in India embrace 7,000 miles of canal and 6,000 miles of railway. The former include an immense system of irrigation lines, but are also intended to a large extent for purposes of internal navigation. The cheapness of labor in India renders these vast undertakings practicable and dividend-paying. The outlay for railroads in India is not over one-third of the cost in the British Islands. This will illustrate the low price at which the English expect to obtain wheat from their India possessions, as soon as the improvements now under way are completed. The *Builder* thinks that wheat may be landed in England for about 55 cents per bushel, and felicitates itself on the prospect. Should this happen, we may yet see the novel spectacle of wheat importation into this country, as we now see that of potatoes.

The war cloud still hangs threateningly over Europe, ready to burst forth at any moment. Should a great conflict ensue, as now seems not only possible but probable, the price of grain will no doubt advance.

SUGARS, it is believed, will be higher during 1877, there being a short crop in European countries where the sugar beet is grown, and there is a large deficiency in Cuba. The amount of sugar manufactured in 1876 will fall very considerably below the average of consumption.

CLOVER SEED is firmly held at 15½ @ 17c. ℔ pound.

HAY AND STRAW.—For week ending February 17, 1877: Loads of Hay, 347; Straw, 127 loads. Average price during week: Prime Timothy, $1.05 @ 1.17; Mixed, 90c. @ $1.05; Straw, 65c. @ 75c. ℔ 100 lbs.

POTATOES have fallen slightly in price, owing to the arrival of a few thousand bushels from Ireland, and several cargoes from New England and Nova Scotia. The Irish potatoes were soon sold out, being sought after by Irishmen. The wholesale prices to-day range from $1.15 to $1.35—a decline of about five cents a bushel. The retail price is $1.25 to $1.60. Dealers generally are of the opinion that the supply from Nova Scotia is nearly exhausted, and that potatoes, as the season advances, will advance rather than decline in price. We express no opinion.

THE GRANGE.

Pomona Grange, No. 8, of Montgomery County, endorses the proposition for holding an inter-State Council in this city some time in March, and promises to attend in a body. This Grange meets March 1 for the installation of officers. The Council above alluded to is to "discuss and mature a plan for co-operation."

William Dean, the *livest* Patron in the State of Delaware, and ought to be, some day, made Master of the National Grange, is in favor of a Grange-supply house in Philadelphia. By the way, Brother Dean, have you got that law passed in Delaware concerning "Tramps"? If so, what is the purport of it?

Mortimer Whitehead, Secretary of the ex-Committee of New Jersey State Grange, lately visited Chester County, and seems to have fallen among the Philistines. Two doctors challenged him to discuss the merits of our Order, and "went for" him right and left. We think, however, that the two doctors found a tough subject, and one hard to dissect, in Brother Whitehead

There are thirty-five farmers in the Pennsylvania Legislature; thanks to the Grange.

Burlington County Pomona Grange, No. 1, is in a flourishing condition, judging from the late annual reports from the subordinate Granges. Mount Laurel made purchase to amount of $1,800; Edgewood, $1,362; Columbus, $6,245.78. John E. Darnell is Master, and Abel H. Burr, Secretary.

William R. Hancock, of Columbus, is Deputy for Burlington County; Isaac W. Nicholson, of Camden, for Camden County, and Frank B. Ridgeway, of Mullica Hill, and John C. Thompson, of Hurffville, of Gloucester County.

Pomona Grange, No. 3, of Chester and Delaware Counties, met recently, and installed Samuel R. Downing as Master. E. M. Harlan is Secretary.

Asa P. Horner is Master of Union Grange, Merchantville, N. J. Joseph M. Kaighn is Secretary.

William S. Taylor, of Burlington, is Master of the New Jersey State Grange. Wm. C. Kates, of Woodstown, is Secretary.

The post-office address of Samuel R. Downing, lecturer of the Pennsylvania State Grange, is West Chester. He is open to engagements to lecture. Brother Downing will keep the ball rolling.

John J. Rosa, of Milford, is Master of the Delaware State Grange, and has been since its organization. Brother Rosa is a good farmer, a devoted Patron, and in every sense worthy of the position he fills.

[The following letter from William Dean, the efficient Chairman of the Executive Committee of Delaware State Grange, contains statements that are well worth the consideration of Patrons everywhere.—EDITOR OF THE FARM JOURNAL.]

MR. EDITOR: Will you allow me space in your columns to say a few words to Patrons of Husbandry in regard to their slow method of doing their business. The position which I occupy in the Order has given me opportunities to see what I consider are the mistakes made by the members of our Order. In January of 1876, I could have bought clover seed at $7 per bushel, and issued a circular to the Granges of our State to that effect; yet none were ready to buy. On the last day of February I had orders for about three hundred bushels, yet had received only $1,500 of money with which to make purchases. The asking prices at this time for clover seed were $9.50 to $10 per bushel, but when I said to the dealers that I had $1,500 of cash in my pocket to spend for clover seed, that meant business, and I found a party who took my money and gave me first-class seed at $8.80. At this time seed was rapidly advancing, and the money for the remaining orders came in every week, and I continued to purchase on the best possible terms I could, yet many patrons had to pay as much as $11 per bushel for their seed. What I want to convey to Patrons is that they should make up their minds at the earliest possible time in regard to their wants for spring and fall seasons, and as soon as they have ascertained their wants get the money ready as soon as possible, and by combining their wants and their capital they will always be able to realize the greatest amount of advantage. Last fall had the Patrons of Delaware made up their minds in regard to the amount of bone they should want for the season just three weeks sooner than they did, I could have saved upon what was purchased by Patrons that came under my observation not less than $1,000. Owing to advance in freights our bone cost us all the above amount over and above what it should have done had Patrons acted on correct business principles, and made their purchase when at the lowest point of price. Farmers heretofore have been in the habit of being plucked by every person with whom they had business transactions. Their confidence in mankind is very limited. This must be changed if the Patrons expect to derive the advantages which it is in the power of the organization of Patrons to convey. They must place none but competent and honest men in positions of trust, and secure themselves against fraud by taking bonds in sufficient amount to guard against loss.

WILLIAM DEAN.

THE CITY.

The market companies of Philadelphia seem to thrive, one of them paying a dividend to stockholders of 5 per cent. for the last six months. We intend in an early number of THE FARM JOURNAL to give some facts and figures about them that may be interesting.

We intend also, to look into the doings of the milkmen of Philadelphia soon, and make a report to the readers of THE FARM JOURNAL. We shall give some facts and statistics of the milk business that will be of interest to our readers, many of whom are milk dairymen.

The New Jersey Centennial Building, which will be remembered by all our readers, has been removed to Haddonfield, New Jersey. The farmers went to the Park with their farm wagons, and in one day hauled thirty-seven loads of the structure away. The remainder, about one-half, was brought away at another time. Mr. Braddock, the purchaser of the building, treated all engaged in the work of hauling to an oyster supper.

At the Abattoir, on the Schuylkill at Arch Street, the building possesses all proper appliances whereby waste material from the slaughtered animals is done away with, and the health and comfort of the neighborhood is not interfered with in the least. The Abattoir has capacity for slaughtering 600 beeves, which is more than the city consumes. We have no doubt that private slaughter-houses will eventually be done away with, as they ought to be, for the health of the city's people.

The Philadelphia Almshouse has 4,300 occupants.

Franklin Square contains a little over seven acres.

A statue of William Penn is to crown the dome of the new Public Buildings. The entire altitude of the structure will be 4.0 feet.

The *Germantown Telegraph* does not entertain a very high opinion of the Pennsylvania State Agricultural Society.

Philadelphia lost one of its citizens recently, who was formerly widely known among rural people, in the person of Edmund Deacon, for many years one of the publishers of the *Saturday Evening Post*. He was in his sixty-seventh year.

The Philadelphia Agricultural Society has rented a new room in which to hold its meetings, at 258 South Third Street. The Society meets on the first Wednesday of each month at 11 o'clock, A. M.

The average weekly sales at the "North Philadelphia Butchers' and Drovers' Live-Stock Yard Association," since its formation in April last, have been 1,000 head of cattle, 2,000 sheep, 1,000 hogs, besides many cows.

The Kansas and Colorado Building at the Centennial goes to Ocean Beach for a boarding-house.

About March 1st the Market Street Passenger Railway will commence to run steam-cars. The fare will be five cents. A street-car horse will soon be among the animals "that were."

The new bell goes up on Independence Hall about March 1.

The important steps now being taken by Mr. John Wanamaker, in converting his great establishment, at Thirteenth and Market Streets, into a mammoth dry goods store, has awakened a large degree of interest among Philadelphians. The immense clothing trade of Wanamaker & Brown will be principally, though not entirely, confined to "Old Oak Hall," at Sixth and Market Streets, the largest clothing house in America, and perhaps more widely known than any other business concern in the city.

At the new house, which, by the way, covers more than two acres, the preparations are now going on for the change, and in a few weeks there will be opened a magnificent store, which will inevitably be to the retail dry goods trade what "Oak Hall" is to the clothing business—the central point of interest; in fact, this new establishment will be the "Stewart's" of the Quaker City, to which the ladies will come from far and near, in never-ending streams, to purchase their dry goods and wearing apparel of every description—for the house will supply all articles of a lady's wardrobe, from a paper of pins to a camel's hair shawl.

One portion of the building, as at present, will be devoted to the sale of gentlemen's goods—hats, boots and shoes, shirts and underwear, gloves, rubber clothing—in fact, it is intended that here a gentleman may procure a complete outfit, and a lady may do all her shopping under one roof and on one floor.

We presume that the same principles of conducting business that have distinguished the firm of Wanamaker & Brown, will still be maintained: that is, *one price*, with every article plainly labeled, and no solicitation on the part of the salesman, and prices fixed on the basis of small profits and big sales. If these features prevail in the new department the ladies will know hereafter where to do their shopping.

HUMOROUS.

Why is old age like a dog's tail? Because it is in-firm.

A good kind of a miser—Economizer.

Often a man drives a pair of grays, while he himself is driven by duns.

A peanut dealer says business is at a stand-still.

An old Scotch woman recommended a preacher, who arrived at the kirk wet through, to get at once into the pulpit: "Ye'll be dry enough there."

A tall man having rallied a friend on the shortness of his legs, the friend replied: "My legs reach the ground—what more can yours do?"

A man recently knocked down an elephant, a lion, and a rhinoceros. He was an auctioneer.

The man whose voice was taxed to its utmost is requested to call round and see the assessor.

Church fairs are good things. They teach a man how to preserve a look of deep humility while paying out two dollars of his hard-earned money for a ten-cent pin-cushion.

A white boy met a colored lad the other day, and asked him what he had such a short nose for. "I spect's so it won't poke itself into other people's business."

He was carving at dinner, and thought he must talk to the æsthetical-looking angel on his right. "How do you like Beethoven?" said he at a venture. "Well cooked," said she, interested in the business at hand.

A Philadelphia vagrant, who had been fined regularly every week for begging, requested the magistrate to fine him by the year at a reduced rate.

Said a clerk to a young lady who bluntly asked for stockings instead of hose: "What number do you wear, miss?" She looked at him an instant with ineffable scorn, and then replied: "I wear two, sir. Do you think I am a centipede?"

"If there's no moonlight, will you meet me by gaslight, dearest Juliana?" asked he. "No, Augustus, I won't; I am no gas-meter," replied she.

DOCTOR.—"I am pleased to say, Mrs. Fitzbrown, that I shall be able to vaccinate your baby from a very healthy child of your neighbor Mrs. Jones." MRS. FITZBROWN.—"Oh, dear doctor, I could not permit that! We do not care to be mixed up with the Joneses in any way."

Dr. Louis, of New Orleans, who is something of a wag, called on a Baptist minister, and propounded a few puzzling questions. "Why is it," said he, "that you are not able to do the miracles that the apostles did? They were protected against all poisons and all kinds of perils. How is it that you are not protected in the same way?" The colored brother responded, promptly: "Don't know about that, doctor; I s'pect I is. I've t'ken a mighty sight of strong medicine from you, doctor, and I is alive yet."

Josh Billings says that "truth kan take kare of itself, but a lie has got to be watched as kareful as a sore thum." Josh says, also, "There never waz a man yet but what thought his lame back waz a good deal lamer than anybody else's."

A grave-digger, who buried a Mr. Button, put the following item in the bill which he sent to Mrs. Button: "To making one Button-hole, $5."

Mrs. Partington remarks that few persons nowadays suffer from suggestions of the brain. She also remarks that Ike has bought a horse so spirituous that he always goes off in a decanter.

ADVERTISEMENTS.

FOR SALE—A NO. 1 PRINTING PRESS, WORTH $35; will be sold for $20; new. A real bargain for some live boy. Apply to THE FARM JOURNAL. 1t

POMONA NURSERY.

FRUIT, SHADE AND ORNAMENTAL TREES, VINES AND PLANTS, of the most certain bearing, hardy kinds. EVERGREENS for hedging or single planting. CAROLINA POPLARS, best trees for lawn or street. Best Strawberries, Raspberries and Grapes. Send for a catalogue.

WILLIAM PARRY,
March* Cinnaminson, N. J.

TREES!

FRUIT AND ORNAMENTAL,

Shrubbery, Grapevines, &c.

"MORRIS NURSERIES,"

G. ACHELIS, PROPRIETOR,
WEST CHESTER, PA.

ADVERTISEMENTS.

SEED POTATOES.

PEERLESS, EARLY VERMONTS, PEACHBLOWS, EARLY Rose, Mercers, Jackson Whites, and other varieties.
FLING, SHRIGLEY & CO.,
1t* 811 and 819 North SECOND Street, Philada.

1877, Dreer's Garden Calendar. 1877,
contains Descriptive and Price-List of Vegetable, Flower, and Grass Seeds, Plants, Bulbs, Novelties, and every GARDEN REQUISITE. Containing 192 pages. Beautifully illustrated. Mailed free.
HENRY A. DREER, 714 Chestnut St., Philadelphia.

EGGS TO HATCH!

THE PLYMOUTH ROCK IS LARGE, DOMINIQUE IN color, matures early, lays well.

THE BEST FARMERS' FOWL.

The BROWN LEGHORN is small, handsome,

GREAT LAYER.

Price of eggs, either kind, $2 per doz.

ORDER EARLY.

Dr. A. M. DICKEY,
DOYLESTOWN, Pa.

ECONOMY IN FERTILIZERS.

HOME-MADE

Chemical Manures.

THE MOST EFFECTIVE AND CHEAPEST.

Buy reliable Chemicals, and make your own Fertilizers AT HOME. Write for circular, giving full information on this subject.

We make or import all kinds of Fertilizing Chemicals, including

OIL OF VITRIOL,	DISSOLVED BONES,
GROUND BONES,	LAND PLASTER,
SULPHATE OF POTASH,	NITRATE OF SODA,
AGRICULTURAL SALT,	SULPHATE OF AMMONIA,
MURIATE OF POTASH,	BONE CHARCOAL,
SULPHATE OF SODA,	SULPHATE OF MAGNESIA.

Address, HARRISON BROS. & Co.,
105 South Front Street,
PHILADELPHIA.

Established as Manufacturers of Fertilizing Chemicals in 1793.

NO. 1 PERUVIAN GUANO.

THE SUBSCRIBERS HAVE EFFECTED AN ARRANGEment with the Peruvian Government Agents by which they have constantly on hand

PURE NO. 1 PERUVIAN GUANO,

which they will deliver from their own stores in Philadelphia, or the Government stores in New York or Baltimore.

We Sell no Guano but what we receive direct from Government Stores,

therefore, parties buying of us can rely on receiving none but a pure article.

CHRISTIAN & CO.,
No. 141 North WATER Street, Philadelphia.

PELICAN

GUANO
REGISTERED TRADE-MARK.

PELICAN GUANO!

$38.00 Per Ton.

SOLUBLE

MARINE GUANO

Reduced to $45.00 per ton—Quality Strictly Maintained.

PHILADELPHIA LAWN FERTILIZER

Promotes a rapid growth of rich green grass.

NO ODOR! NO LUMPS!

IN NEAT BAGS OF 10 LBS., 50 LBS., AND 100 LBS. EACH.

Send for Circulars.

J. J. ALLEN'S SONS,
124 SOUTH DELAWARE AVENUE, below Chestnut Street,
March. PHILADELPHIA.

ADVERTISEMENTS.

LIME!

-BUILDING LIME-

SUITABLE FOR

BRICK WORK,

PLASTERING, ETC.

Sent to any point on the line of the Philadelphia, Wilmington, and Baltimore and Delaware Railroads, and Maryland and Delaware Railroad, and over all the United Railroads of *New Jersey*, from

RAMBO'S

—CELEBRATED—

Schuylkill Lime Quarries.

The undersigned is now prepared to ship in quantities of

FROM 100 TO 10,000 BUSHELS

EITHER FOR

BUILDING OR LAND, Etc.

This Lime is considered by competent judges to be beyond all question

THE BEST

NOW OFFERED IN THIS MARKET.

Analysis of Schuylkill Lime.

ST. JOHNS COLLEGE, *Annapolis*, January 11, 1860.

P. T. Tyson, Maryland State Geologist:

Dear Sir: During our interview at Annapolis, some months since, you expressed the opinion that the analysis of lime for publication in your reports, should be of samples taken *as the cargo is delivered on the farm*. You will remember that I told you that I had such a sample taken last April, while on a visit to my farm. I annex the analysis, and think that it represents one of the best varieties of the "Schuylkill lime of Pennsylvania." The sample was taken before it was slaked, and represents a grea many lumps from different parts of a cargo of 2,000 o 3,000 bushels. These were powdered and fairly sampled, the balance of the sample being preserved in glass in our cabinet.

I paid 12½ cents per bushel unslaked, and have since obtained 1,000 bushels from the same source. The sample taken from the second load was taken beneath the surface of the heap, and from several parts of the heap after it had been slaked for several weeks on my farm.

I am thus particular in giving you the circumstances under which this sample was taken, as you told me that it was your intention to procure samples representing the lime that the manufacturer sells to the farmer, "and not such as is sent for analysis."

The cargo was "accidentally" presented at the landing during my visit to my farm, and the captain assured me that it was from the quarries of W. B. Rambo, near Norristown, Montgomery County, Pennsylvania.

Moisture, &c., expelled by a full red heat, continued for about 15 minutes	05 64
Sand or insoluble matter	00 85
Phosphoric acid, iron and alumina	03 65
Lime, oxide of calcium, or quicklime	56 24
Magnesia	32 79
Soluble silica	00 83
	100 00

The slaked lime referred to above, was soluble in *dilute* acetic acid except about six per cent. (6.22) and yielded 107. of pure carbonate of lime, obtained by precipitating the acid solution with oxalic acid, and then heating the oxalate by the usual process.

Yours respectfully,
DAVID STEWART, M. D.

This lime is also delivered by boat, in cargoes of from thirty-five hundred to four thousand bushels, to all points on the Delaware Bay and its tributaries.

Address,
WM. B. RAMBO,
NORRISTOWN, Montgomery Co., Pa.

THE
FARM JOURNAL
DEVOTED TO THE FARM, ORCHARD, GARDEN, POULTRY AND HOUSEHOLD ECONOMY.

VOL. V.—NO. 1. PUBLISHED BY WILMER ATKINSON, PHILADELPHIA. PRICE FIVE CENTS.
October, 1880. *Practical not Fancy Farming.* 50 Cents a Year.

Editor Atkinson moved Farm Journal into a new "home" in October 1880

OUR NEW HEAD.

How do you like it? By hunting up the September number you will see that we have moved out of a somewhat characterless farm house into the substantial, dignified old homestead pictured above. This old house may have stood a hundred years—in fact it is a correct representation of a mansion that was built more than a hundred years ago—and to all appearances it will stand a hundred years more. It has an air of comfort, of refinement and of stability that to us is very pleasing, and we think it must impress our readers in like manner. We have "moved in"—as it were—have got "fixed," and are now ready to entertain our friends. We have anchored at the old homestead and hope to abide there for many a day.

The main features of the FARM JOURNAL—Real Farming, Fruit Growing, Stock Breeding, Poultry Keeping and Practical Housekeeping—are outlined or suggested in other portions of the engraving, clearly, and we think with a fair degree of taste and artistic beauty.

While the art critic may possibly point out faults in the design and blemishes in its elaboration, and our readers may miss the old, familiar head, yet we think all will come to acknowledge that it has some merit visible to the naked eye, and that the FARM JOURNAL has taken another step in the right direction.

But our readers may take this improvement—with the complete dress of new type in which we clothe our journal, the beautiful, tinted paper and elegant typography, the best attainable—as a simple manifestation of a fixed purpose to excel in our vocation, and to print not only the most practical, most useful, and the cheapest, but the handsomest Agricultural and Household paper in this or any other country. They will observe that we take high aim, and that our arm is steady, that our finger is on the trigger, and that we expect to hit the mark.

OUR EDITORIAL PLAN.

It is our constant endeavor to treat all subjects in season; to be concise and to the point; to be practical rather than theoretical; to exclude long-winded discussions and fine-spun theories of fancy farmers; in short, to give our readers CREAM, not skim-milk.

The Editor was born on a farm and reared at the plow handles, and our contributors are mostly practical men and women, who write with their sleeves rolled up, and who briefly and plainly tell the best and most profitable way of doing things on the Farm and in the House, as learned from actual experience.

It is through strict adherence to this plan, in every department, that we are enabled to present as much useful information as the papers costing from four to eight times as much.

WILMER ATKINSON, Editor and Proprietor.

OUR BUSINESS METHOD.

The Farm Journal offers no premiums, gives no chromos, puffs no swindles, inserts no humbug advertisements, and does not devote one-half of its space to telling how good the other half is. It is published monthly and is furnished to subscribers at 50 cents a year, postage prepaid. Terms, cash in advance. At the expiration of the year the paper is stopped, unless renewed.

FAIR PLAY.

We believe, through careful inquiry, that all the advertisements in this paper are signed by trustworthy persons, and to prove our faith by works, we will make good to subscribers any loss sustained by trusting advertisers who prove to be deliberate swindlers. Rogues shall not ply their trade at the expense of our readers, who are our friends, through the medium of these columns. Let this be understood by everybody now and henceforth.

We are often asked for information upon the culture of tobacco. Well, we can't give any. We know nothing about it, anyhow, and if we did, we should not tell what we knew. We do not believe it is quite right to turn wheat, corn and hay fields into tobacco plantations. Let the soil be taught to bring forth that which administers to the sustenance and welfare of man, not that which is more or less an injury and a curse to him. That's our sentiment. Whenever we hear of a farmer going into the cultivation of tobacco, we are reminded of the one who sells out his farm and engages in keeping tavern—generally to his ultimate ruin. There may be profit in tobacco growing, but it is scarcely justifiable to the conscientious man and may burn a hole in his pocket.

CONCERNING TOBACCO.

The habit of using tobacco by male Americans seems to be on the increase, and that in spite of the generally admitted fact that such habit is a pernicious one, and it seems probable that before long more than one-half of our masculine adult population will be consumers of the weed, in some form. As a people we may deem ourselves fortunate if the women also do not in time succumb to the evil, and wear the yoke of the tobacco slave.

This state of affairs is not one to rejoice over, but it seems inevitable and must be so recognized. How to stem the tide of tobacco chewing and smoking is one of the unsolved problems of the day. Its solution probably rests with the mothers, and to them we must mainly look for an influence that shall arrest the evil in its present rapid progress.

Heretofore a majority of women have cried out against the tobacco habit, but they have not done so effectively. They have denounced it and abused the victims, ridiculed and contemned them, and they have done as much harm as good. The smoker has been called hard names, the chewer has been "gone on" at at a furious rate, as though he were really unfit to appear in respectable society. Such opposition has been more than useless; such tactics have served only to make matters worse. It is contrary to the nature of man to be reformed, or changed in his habits, by ridicule or denunciation, and the sooner this fact is submitted to by those who undertake to propagate reforms in the world the better.

Let it be confessed that good and excellent men smoke and chew; that those who smoke and chew possess a fair average of the human virtues; that they are just about on a level with those who are fortunately free from the grip of these habits. Of the smokers and non-smokers, chewers and non-chewers, whom one meets in business and in society, one class is a genteel, as cleanly and as manly as the other; as members of society one is as generous, as upright and as useful as the other.

But the confirmed tobacco users are beyond reform. Let the opponents of the evil cease wasting severe epithets on them. Let them take a less stilted view of the situation, be more persuasive and less condemnatory; let moderation take the place of exaggeration in dealing with the question.

Let the mothers come to the front and teach the boys the evils of tobacco using, its wastefulness in money and its injury to the physical system of its victims. In temperate phrase, and in a spirit of moderation, let them portray truthfully its bad effects, and the influence they will thus exert will be powerful for good, and perhaps in time succeed in arresting the progress of what all thoughtful persons are obliged to confess is becoming a great national evil.

Vineland, N. J. TIM.

Penn State: a "rat hole" in 1880, but worthy of "God speed. . ." in 1906

THE STATE COLLEGE.

A local paper of the county in which the State Agricultural College is located has its feelings lacerated by what the FARM JOURNAL said in the August number about the management of the College. We are sorry for that but we can't help it. The institution is a sore on the body politic and we declare it is high time that it be eradicated or reformed even though some editors should get angry at us. Let the friends of the college print a catalogue of the good it has ever done commensurate with its cost, and the FARM JOURNAL will not withhold credit if credit be due.

October 1880

The future prospects of the Penna. State College are declared by its friends to be of the most promising character. Yes, it always has been of the most promising character. There has never been any lack of promises from that quarter. It is fulfillment that is most needed! Let that rat hole be stopped up before another million of the people's money goes down.

November 1880

Wouldn't it be an improvement if some of the papers which are spending much time and labor in criticisms of the agricultural colleges and experiment stations, (some of which is justly deserved) were to devote a portion of their energies to candid statements of the credit which is due these same institutions for what they have contributed to the unexampled advancement of all farm knowledge? Try it once, brethren! Don't flatter them, nor pass by their delinquencies, but be just to the workers, and encourage the young people to take advantage of their facilities for practical farm education. As a rule we believe the agricultural colleges are fulfilling their mission fully as well as the older and better established classical colleges.

November 1891

ADVANCE IN AGRICULTURAL SCIENCE AND PRACTISE AT THE PENNSYLVANIA STATE COLLEGE

The policy of the Trustees of the Pennsylvania State College, to develop to its proper relative importance the agricultural side of that institution, is working out in gratifying results.

New buildings of the most substantial character, and especially designed for their several purposes, are being erected and equipped, and some of them—notably the dairy building, regarded by experts as the finest in the country—are in use.

Buildings and equipments, however, are but conveniences, and the real power which shall aid the farmer in his great task of feeding the world rests in the thoroughly equipped and trained students of science and practise, who constitute the Faculty of the School of Agriculture, and the corps of patient investigators in the Experiment Station; and the names of Armsby, Frear, Butz, Watson, Fries, McDowell, Hess, and others, will always stand well in the front of those who have given the impulses to Pennsylvania's advance and advancing agriculture.

To this goodly list has lately been added the name of Prof. H. E. Van Norman, recently of Purdue University, Illinois, with the title of Professor of Dairy Husbandry. Added to the enthusiasm of comparative youth, Prof. Van Norman has thorough training, large experience, attractive personality, and the rare quality of imparting inspiration to his students. His fine energy and extended knowledge are already making for the uplift of the great dairy interest of Pennsylvania, now ranking only second in the list of states in the annual value of her dairy products.

Of all the numberless subjects that have vital interests, both to the producing farmer and the great consuming public, perhaps none is of more importance than animal nutrition. Recognizing this, the National

NEW DAIRY BUILDING OF PENNSYLVANIA STATE EXPERIMENT STATION

Department of Agriculture some years ago cooperated with the Trustees of the Pennsylvania College in the erection of a new scientific apparatus, known as the Respiration Calorimeter, specially designed for deep research upon this subject, and Dr. Henry Prentiss Armsby, then Dean of the School of Agriculture, and Director of the Experiment Station, was placed in charge, in addition to his already heavy duties.

This is a highly organized and costly instrumentality, by means of which the most elaborate investigations are made, the ultimate purpose being to obtain from the living animal such knowledge of what he does with the food given him as may help in determining how to feed our live stock at less cost and yet produce more of the animal products which constitute so large and costly a portion of the food of the human race.

Realizing the paramount importance of this work, the Board of Trustees, at their last meeting in Harrisburg, carried into execution a part of their large and long-cherished plans for reorganization and development, above alluded to, by enlarging the scope of this particular line of research and investigation, and establishing it as a new department of the college, under the name Institute of Animal Nutrition.

Dr. Armsby was promoted to be its head, and was relieved of executive work so that, unhampered by other duties, he may apply his distinguished talents and ripened powers to these studies and investigations.

The work is of the utmost importance, its results touch every human interest, and it is a matter of general gratulation that a scientist of so distinguished rank as Dr. Armsby can dedicate himself to it as his life task, with the advantages of the superb organization and unique conditions at the Pennsylvania State College. God speed the good work.

May 1906

AGRICULTURAL EXPERIMENT STATIONS.

The Act of Congress, of March 2, 1887, commonly known as the Hatch Act, has resulted in the establishment of agricultural experiment stations in many states of the Union. These stations have already done a great deal of excellent work of a practical character, but are capable of vastly increasing their usefulness and their value to farmers. The stations should co-operate with farmers' organizations and individual farmers in the following ways:

Fertilizer analysis; manure analysis; soil analysis. Fertilizer analysis is now well under way in many states. Manure analysis is but just begun; we are just beginning to state in dollars and cents the value of home-made manures. Soil analysis, of supreme importance, has not yet been undertaken in any wide or general manner.

Water analysis; food analysis. This has to do with health. On a great many farms the water is not wholesome for drinking purposes, nor the food proper. We spare no pains to have a well-balanced feeding ration for cattle. Why not for children?

Plant examination and tests of new varieties. This work is now in progress.

Diseases of plants and animals. In this direction the stations are doing good work.

Extermination of insects and noxious weeds, and warfare against fungi. In this work the stations are making rapid progress.

Tests of new methods, new machinery and new implements. In this line good work has been done.

Lastly, above all, a closer relation with the farmers of the country, especially farmers' organizations, for the solution of the new problems that are forever coming up.

This closer and better intimacy between the stations and the farmers can be hastened and increased by farmers themselves. Outside of his club or grange the agricultural experiment station is the strongest and best ally of the intelligent American farmer.

February 1893

HARMLESS AND USEFUL.

Plain, hard-working, sleeves-rolled-up farmers, who keep their eyes open, may learn something from the fancy, booked-up farmer. With ample means at command, new methods can be tried, new machinery tested, new varieties of seed planted and improved stock bred. All these, the man who has to earn bread and butter for a family, and lift a mortgage from his acres cannot do, while it may be beneficial to him to have some other fellow try it, who can afford to run the risk of failure.

Let us all therefore, look on and learn what we can from the failures as well as from the successes of these experimental gentlemen, who come out of town for the purpose of showing how farming ought to be done. As a class they are not only harmless, but they are useful and ought to be encouraged.

January 1883

CONCERNING ENSILAGE.

We shall not proclaim ensilage a humbug because that may not be the right word to describe it. In France and Germany it has been adopted with a good measure of success. In this country many intelligent farmers, mostly of the fancy order, have become interested in it. Dr. Bailey, the father of the system in America, has displayed a wonderful amount of "push" and "brains" in bringing it before the people in the most attractive light. He figures the thing right out every time to a dot. He has made no mistake for figures won't lie. He can marshal a hundred or a thousand farmers, any day, who have tried ensilage with success. The weekly agricultural papers now give their readers several pages on the subject every issue, and the Farmers' clubs are discussing it. But it is only a nine day's wonder. Practical farmers won't adopt it, except one here and there, and in ten years from now the silos that are being built will be used for storing potatoes, turnips, beets or ice.

April 1881

FILLING THE SILO.

The Smalley Manufacturing Company, of Manitowoc, Wis., will furnish free to every subscriber of this paper, who will apply promptly, valuable Silo literature and complete information as to construction of Silos, Cultivation and Care of Ensilage, and one copy of "Silo and Silage," by Prof. Cook, of the Michigan Agricultural College.

Smalley Goods are so well and favorably known in every stock-raising or dairying section of this country, that it is hardly necessary to offer a single word in commendation, either of the firm or their products. We simply suggest to our readers that they write to them and let them tell their own "story" in their own way.

We illustrate a scene that has become familiar to farmers in every state of the Union—filling the silo. If you have not looked into the silo subject, hadn't you better do so before you get much older? Don't get left.

ROUND SILOS
AND HOW THEY ARE MADE

Most farmers have suitable stone for the foundation wall of a silo, and in building this there is nothing about it to require the services of others than those laborers usually found upon the farm. Cement and sand should be used in the upper portion of the wall, the balance laid up dry. The inside of this circular wall being the bottom of the silo, it should be made smooth with small stones and a free use of cement.

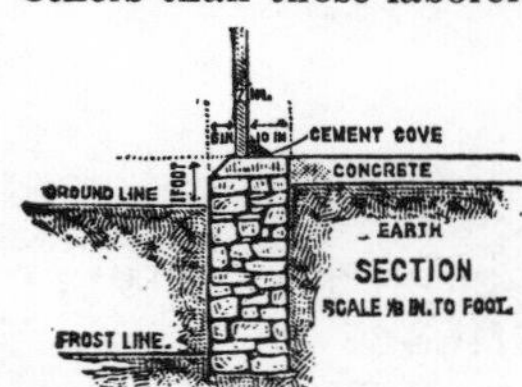

FOUNDATION OF SILO.

The first step in the erection of a round silo is to set up the front. Having determined where this should be, two crowbars or strong stakes should be driven in the ground against the edge of the foundation, letting the upper end of these project above the foundation, to prevent the front from slipping off from the edge. Care must be taken to have the front perpendicular. The nearer the silo can be located to the feeding stable, the greater the economy in handling the product. A slight elevation of the stone foundation above the surface of the ground near to it is wise.

BIRD'S-EYE VIEW OF BASE.

After the silo front is up and securely stayed, the staves are added, one by one, until the circle is complete.

A roofless silo is the right one for placing inside of a building, as is occasionally done. Many farms have a portion of a bay that might with profit be thus occupied. Experience has shown that the preference is for doing the filling of silos all at the top, by once setting the machinery. A roofless silo will allow the delivery of the carrier at any point around the circle.

SETTING UP THE FRONT.

Round silos are made of any size to suit the want or fancy of the user. More than any other, the size approximating one hundred tons capacity meets the average need of siloists. In one of this size built upon the door plan, *i. e.*, opening and closing doors for the removal of the ensilage, the style of construction generally is to have from one-third to one-half doors, and balance solid or not to be opened. This will therefore admit of about one-half of the ensilage being easily taken from the silo, while the larger portion must needs be lifted and pitched upward out of the nearest door or opening above. This *can* be done, but in these days of labor-saving devices, if the lifting and elevating of fifty tons out of a hundred can be saved, the readers of FARM JOURNAL will not fail to appreciate the economy. In the illustration herewith given we show a silo that has a continuous opening front.

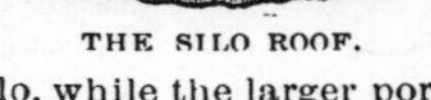
THE SILO ROOF.

SILO WITH CONTINUOUS OPENING FRONT.

In this style there are no doors. The front is one continuous opening, save the hoops and girders always there. By an ingenious arrangement of placing cross bars or staves horizontally across this opening, the silo is perfectly closed and sealed. The cross bars or staves are removed, one by one, from the top downward as the feeding progresses, keeping the opening on a level with the feeding surface in the silo.

July 1899

Silage got a frosty welcome in 1881, but silos were a "must" to see at the World's Fair in Chicago, 1893

CIRCULAR SILOS.

The two silos here shown were erected at the World's Fair for the benefit of the Live Stock Department, and to show the latest and most approved style of silo building. They are 30 feet in diameter and 30 feet high, and have a capacity of 300 tons each. In September, 1892, 360 tons of corn ensilage were put into them in 43 hours and 37 minutes, actual cutting time, by a Smalley Cutter and Carrier. Progressive dairymen should not fail to examine this silo exhibit when they visit the Fair.

FILLING THE SILO.

July 1891

SILOS AT THE WORLD'S FAIR.

August 1893

Editor Atkinson "sees the light" on RFD, then helps bring it about

FREE DELIVERY OF MAILS.

We are not in favor of free delivery of mails from rural post offices. The expense of such delivery would be enormous—almost beyond computation—and not justified by any advantage that would accrue to the people it is intended to benefit.

Moreover, there is no demand for such a system of free delivery among farmers and other rural people. The clamor now heard in behalf of the measure is fictitious. If there is a clangor made in certain directions in its favor, it is the artificial thunder of the stage, as if made by beating sheets of iron or tin pans; it is not real.

For one thing it will double the number of federal offices, and who wants to do that?

For another thing it will, if carried out, entail such an expense upon the Postal Department that we shall not see one-cent letter postage in this century.

Our most business-like and efficient Postmaster General desires a reduction in postal rates, and we believe he is ambitious to bring about such reduction during his term of office. He will have performed a vast service to the people should he succeed in the endeavor; but we warn him of certain failure unless he unload this foolish project, originated not by him, of free delivery of mails at rural post offices.

The FARM JOURNAL wants, and the people want, Mr. Wanamaker, one-cent postage. We don't want our country roads overrun with half-paid federal officials delivering two-cent letters at a cost of ten cents a letter.

December 1891

SHALL MAILS GO FREE TO FARMERS' HOMES?

ARGUMENTS IN FAVOR OF FREE DELIVERY.

BY MORTIMER WHITEHEAD.

Why?
What good?
Will it pay?
Yes, every time, to every question.

Tried, tested, proven a success. Arguments and the people, all in its favor. Let us see.

FIRST—WHY?—Because it is *right*. The FARM JOURNAL has for many years been telling the farmers that they should have seats at the first table, and farmers *are* coming to the front in more ways than one. They have joined the great army of progress and will never again take back seats.

Our fathers fought the battles of the Revolution to establish the principle and the *right* given us in the Constitution that "all citizens shall be equal before the law." A very large proportion of our citizens in villages and on farms are now very *unequal* before our postal laws. They pay the larger portion of the taxes, and whatever is paid for by the Government should be as freely given to the country as to the city.

When we pay our postage to have our mail carried, why should Uncle Sam carry the city man's letter right to his house or place of business, and then leave ours at a post-office perhaps several miles away from the person to whom we wrote. He only partly carries out the contract of carrying the mail for us, but fulfills it completely with our city cousins. Why should the machinery of Government be used so largely for the benefit of the favored few?

If the city man can't walk a few squares to *his* post-office to get his mail, why should we go miles through heat and cold, and spend hours in making the trip?

The city man is a business man? And so is the farmer, and becoming more so every day. If "time is money" to the city business man, it is money also to the farmer business man.

One-cent letter postage is advocated by some, and our post-office authorities say that the revenues of the P. O. Department will now almost admit of that step.

But rural free delivery is by far the more important step and should be taken *first*. It is the greatest good to the greatest number. What farmer would prefer to harness a horse and go a mile, perhaps three or four, to send a letter for one cent rather than have the letter taken by a carrier right from his door once a day and pay two cents postage as now?

Farmers and farmers' organizations are giving this new forward step their hearty support. Closely following it will surely come the postal telegraph and telephone, managed by Government for all the people, with telephone in each rural home to the postal telegraph station, and through it to the whole world. The not distant future will bring the postal savings bank, and *all* will bring the tide once more *to* the farm; will make it pay; make it brighter, more social, more intelligent, and therefore more patriotic on right lines, and be great factors in maintaining our Republic as given us by the fathers.

Urge this just measure *now* upon your Congressmen and United States Senators. Think about it; talk about it; work for it, and it will come. "Heaven helps those who try to help themselves."

(This question was brought before the National Grange at its late annual session by the Lecturer, who presented a comprehensive report, which was approved and ordered to be printed in pamphlet form for general distribution, and to be sent to each member of Congress and Senator. This pamphlet is free to all who will send stamps for postage to Box 222, Washington, D. C.—EDITOR.)

January 1891

FREE DELIVERY OF MAILS.

While there seems to be a demand for this measure in the country—a universal demand according to the view of some—there are those who fear it may, if carried, postpone other important reforms in the postal service.

What are those reforms?

One is one-cent letter postage, another is the establishment of a cheap parcel post, by which farmers and others living in remote places can have packages sent by mail at slight cost instead of having to pay extortionate rates to the express companies.

These great monopolies, the express companies, naturally favor any step that will weight our postal system so it cannot adopt a lower rate on merchandise. Another is the establishment of a cheap telegraph system by which the people everywhere can receive and forward messages at a few cents each.

It is fair to assume that it would bring joy to Jay Gould and his Western Union Telegraph Company to be able to stave off Government control of the telegraph in this way. It is not a bad rule for the people to consider what the monopolists want done, that they may the better decide what they ought themselves do.

This is what we did in this case. But the FARM JOURNAL is with its people in every well-considered movement for their benefit and convenience. If they want free delivery, if other and greater interests will not suffer thereby, if the times are ripe for it, then let it come. Sooner the better. See Mortimer Whitehead's argument on next page.

January 1891

POST-OFFICE ON WHEELS

"A very important reform is evident. The father, husband or son no longer has an excuse to go to post-office for mail, to be away from his family of evenings, but instead having received his morning paper or FARM JOURNAL in the morning, can spend the evening with his family where he ought to be."

"The experiment is giving good satisfaction through our entire neighborhood."

"I am now taking a a daily paper which I never did before, and all my neighbors are doing the same."

"While there are a few who oppose it, we say, 'Lord forgive them they know not what they do.'"

"When the post-office department gets its letter boxes along its routes as we understand they propose, every citizen will certainly be benefited."

The above shows the tenor of many other letters received, but most of them seem to have come from such as are well located, not far away from the line of the wagons on the morning delivery. They say, generally, that those who have not become reconciled to the innovation are those to whom free delivery has not yet been extended.

Original Post-office on Wheels, Standing in Front of the Residence of Edward Shriver, at Westminster, Md., who Designed the Wagon and Promoted the New System.

NO GOOD

A great many intelligent persons, besides dismissed fourth-class postmasters, have written in condemnation of the free mail delivery such as has been instituted in Carroll county without the knowledge or consent of a large majority of the people. They liked the old system and do not like the new and never can.

"Ninety-five per cent. of the people are against it. It does not even suit people that live on the road, and those that live three miles from a road have not received any mail since it went into effect. I live on the road myself but it does not suit me as it is too slow."

March 1900

John Wanamaker, Philadelphia's famous department store founder, was Farm Journal's first advertiser

BUTTERMILK.

The astronomer's business is looking up.

All men who open oysters do things by halves.

A coolness has sprung up between night and morning.

The beehive is the poorest thing in the world to fall back on.

A short-tailed dog is unable to express his feelings without great exertion.

After a young man has popped the question he generally has to question the pop.

A wife should be like roast lamb, tender and nicely dressed. No sauce required.

What is the difference between a fixed star and a meteor? One is a son, the other a darter

A man out West was offered a plate of macaroni soup, but declined it, declaring that they "couldn't play off any biled pipestems on him."

"Are you lost my little fellow?" asked a gentleman of a 4-year-old one day in Rochester. "No," he sobbed in reply, "b-but m-my mother is."

A correspondent asked if the brow of a hill ever became wrinkled. The editor replied: "The only information we can give on that point is that we have often seen it furrowed."

"Sleep on, my loved one, sleep!" This is the language of the first four months. After that, "Get up, Sally Ann, and get breakfast; I'm hungrier than a bear," seems to answer the purpose.

"Conductor, why didn't you wake me up, as I asked you? Here I am miles beyond my station." "I did try, sir, but all I could get you to say was, 'All right, Maria; get the children their breakfast, and I'll be down in a minute.'"

A farmer's wife, in speaking of the smartness, aptness and intelligence of her son, a lad six years old, to a lady acquaintance, said: "He can read fluently in any part of the Bible, repeat the whole catechism, and weed onions as well as his father.' "Yes mother," added the young hopeful, "and yesterday I licked Ned Rawson, throwed the cat into the well, and stole old Hinckley's gimlet."

My baby boy sat on the floor,
His big blue eyes were full of wonder,
For he had never thought before,
That baby by the mirror door,
What kept the two, so near, asunder.

He leaned toward that golden head,
The mirror border framed within,
Until two cheeks, like roses red,
Lay side by side, then softly said,
"I can't get out; can't you come in?"

The Great Store

The store covers 2¼ acres; a basement is under, and galleries are over, a part. The whole affords somewhere about 5 acres of room.

This particular business is 4 years old; it began in 1876 with clothing; in 1877 it became a general store with such goods as you see in the plan, with carpets, upholstery, furniture and kitchen-furnishing upstairs. Since that time gallery after gallery has been added: and there is not an inch of room to spare anywhere. To the surprise of many it has flourished while trade was languishing almost everywhere else.

To us there is no mystery about it; nothing surprising even; unless it be surprising that so conspicuous a business should ever be misunderstood. We do nothing more than simply to provide facilities for your getting what you want.

We don't mean to say that other facilities are not provided for distributing goods; but that's a different thing. We provide so that you get what you want, *exactly what you want!* If we send you the wrong thing, or if you think the charge is too much, you bundle it back to us.

In some goods we keep the richest things the world produces; in others we do not keep the richest. Most kinds we keep in as low grades as it is worth anybody's while to buy.

We tell of these things in the newspapers because there are thousands of you who don't know what we are doing; thousands of you who don't know the character of the stock that fills these 5 acres; thousands of you who, therefore, buy where you pay more money.

We are every merchant's fair and open competitor. We do not expect to gather millions of trade without meeting opposition and misrepresentation. Some will believe whatever is said against us. The only answer we make is a business answer. Send back whatever you don't want at the price.

We want your trade; you want our goods; or would want them if you knew.

When we get in communication with you, we shall have one means of winning your trade, viz., by pleasing you. When we have won it, we shall have one means of keeping it, viz., by dealing with you as we deal with everybody; giving you large return for your money, and supplying your wants so completely that you will look to us for what you want as naturally as you say "good morning" to your next friend.

During the summer we have been making more room. The administration, book-keeping and advertising offices have gone to 1317 Chestnut street to make room for Furniture and Upholstery. A workshop in the Market-street gallery has been turned into very excellent quarters for Custom-Tailoring. The removal of tailoring has left more room for Boys' Clothing. Another change has added one half more space to silks.

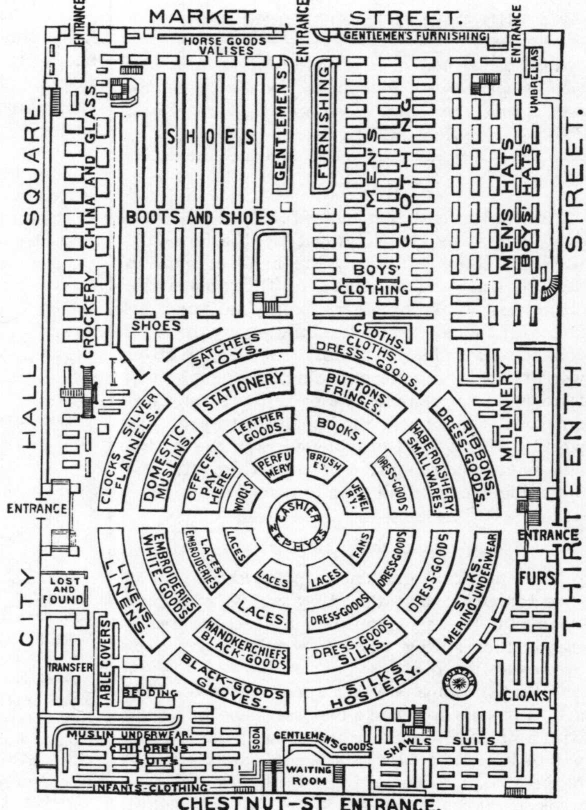

Ground-Plan of John Wanamaker's Store.

The galleries are now all connected together and are thereby not only enlarged, but made more available: they are about 1200 feet, nearly a quarter of a mile long. The electric lights, 64 in number, are in perfect order. Pneumatic tubes are being introduced to carry money to and fro between all parts of the house and the cashier at the centre so that "making change" often takes less than a minute (the journey both ways is made in 9 seconds).

Altogether we are ready for such a trade as we have never had before.

JOHN WANAMAKER.

Chestnut, Thirteenth and Market streets, and City Hall Square.

The nation mourns the assassination of President James A. Garfield

FARM JOURNAL.
(UNLIKE ANY OTHER PAPER.)
PHILADELPHIA, OCTOBER, 1881.

This paper has a larger circulation than any weekly agricultural journal in the United States, and larger than any other monthly, except one. Proof—Open Subscription Books.

IN MOURNING.

The Nation is in mourning for its dead President, who was struck down by the cruelest, wickedest blow aimed by the hand of man in modern times. The record of Gitteau's awful crime, the weeks of weary, weary suffering inflicted upon his victim, the long agony of those connected with him by family ties, and the bitter woe of a sympathetic and outraged people, will form and ever remain one of the saddest, most mournful chapters in the whole history of the world. May a kind Providence save the nation and mankind a repetition of such a dreadful and appalling event for all time to come!

SAVING TOMATO SEED.

Many practical gardeners do not know how to save tomato seed so that they will be white and clean and free from pulp, but purchase a new supply each spring when they might save their own as well as not.

Collect the most perfect specimens after they are fully ripe for seed purposes, slice in halves with a knife and remove the seed by hand into a pail or tub and set away in a cool shady place to ferment. In three or four days, or perhaps a week, if the weather be cool, the seed will readily separate from the pulp, and when poured into a larger tub of water and stirred with a stick the seed will settle to the bottom while whatever of pulp or skins it contains will float and can be poured off. In this manner they are washed in several different waters when they will be left as clean and bright as desired. They are then spread on a cloth in the sun and dried rapidly. The only danger of spoiling them is by leaving them too long in water in a warm place when they are liable to sprout.

Cucumber, melon, and other similar seeds, are saved in the same manner.

A few years ago the butterflies that were seen flitting about, during the summer, were mostly yellow ones, but now, if you will observe, many of them are white, with a dark spot on each wing. These are foreigners, and are the parents of those unmitigated nuisances, the cabbage worms. Now, if the sparrows would only eat the white butterflies, we could all have plenty of cole-slaw and sour-krout, and justice would be again triumphant.

Do not forget that James Vick declares that fall is the best time to set out a new asparagus bed. Get plants one or two years old. Let the rows be three feet apart and the plants three feet in the row. Use plenty of manure, of course. Plant five inches deep.

If an osage orange hedge is to be planted, now is the time to begin. Plow a trench where the hedge is to be eighteen inches wide and as deep as possible without turning up the subsoil. Let it remain over winter, setting out the plants in the spring.

The idea, so prevalent, that frost colors the leaves in the fall, is an erroneous one. The tints of the forest are the result of the perfect maturity of the leaves, and frost even though slight, destroys the tints of every leaf it touches.

Ah! soon on field and hill
The wind shall whistle chill,
And patriarch swallows call their flocks together,
To fly from frost and snow,
And seek for lands where blow
The fairer blossoms of a balmier weather.

(Gentle and harmless at ordinary times, but alert and savage when tramps and swindlers come in the front gate.)

Such is the skill of the modern counterfeiter that it requires much discernment to distinguish genuine from spurious coin, even with those accustomed to the use of money, but in the case of newspapers it is different. When an imitation article is thrown upon the public there are few so dull and inexperienced as to be unable to detect the deception, and to stamp it for what it is worth. Whether to issue false money, or to print a counterfeit newspaper, both practices are reprehensible and alike invoke the condemnation of fair-minded, honorable men.

When horse jockeys and beer guzzlers take control of an agricultural Society, its days of prosperity are numbered.

Holloway, the English pill manufacturer, has given upward of $3,750,000 for charitable purposes during the last six years. We suppose he is trying to repair the mischief his pills have done.

We see a prominent bee journal denounces a Mr. N. C. Mitchell, of Indianapolis, Ind., as a swindler, and an old one. Lizzie E. Cotton, of Maine, is another of alleged different sex, but of the same sort.

And now farmers are to be made rich by using ground unburnt limestone. Just as though the Silo was not sufficient, of itself! Green manuring, drainage, deep plowing, cooking stock food, sub-soiling, ensilage, muck beds, and ground limestone! What next?

In order to obtain enough milk to supply their customers, owing to the home demand for milk at the creameries, some city milkmen agree to allow farmers *to put enough water in their milk to pay freight*, and thus make it more profitable to ship milk to the city than to take pure milk to the creamery. How is that for honest enterprise?

A mare and colt belonging to J. Martin, of Kent county Md., were killed a few days since by getting entangled in a barbed wire fence. The colt's throat was cut from ear to ear and the mare was so mangled that she had to be killed. Now what was the use of J. M. building such a fence when he could have made one of plain wire cheaper, better and safer? That is what we should like to know!

Worm or beetle, drought or tempest, on a farmer's land may fall,
But for first-class ruination, trust a mortgage 'gainst them all.

TOPICS IN SEASON.

THE OUTLOOK.

There is just about one-half a crop of corn—not any more—in the United States. This is a tremendous fact.

Bad, very bad, harvests in England, owing to heavy rains.

Farmers that we know expect to get $2.00 a bushel next spring for potatoes.

Before harvest the FARM JOURNAL said, "Hold on to wheat; it will go up." And it did.

Tobacco growers are happy; an active demand for the weed and high prices make them so.

Dear pork next winter will make a strong English demand for American cheese—as a substitute.

Speculation in stock in the cities is quite wild and prices are up; but they are liable to tumble with a crash.

The cattle supply of Southwest Texas is nearly exhausted and the Northern markets must look elsewhere for beeves.

Prime timothy hay in this market is $1.40 to $1.50 per hundred; mixed, $1.25 to $1.35; straw 90 cts. to $1.00 Landreth quotes clover seed at $7 per bushel; timothy, flail threshed, $3.50.

Rot has carried off many sheep in England and on the continent, and sheep are in numbers far below the average, in those countries. So don't be surprised if there is a wool famine and consequently high prices in the near future.

Hemlock lumber is about one-third higher than it was three or four years ago. All kinds of lumber have advanced in price, and will probably continue to do so. Mill work for houses—doors, sash, frames, &c.—have risen greatly in price.

More than half the stock in Southern Illinois will have to be sold, or it will starve to death, on account of the failure of corn and the shortness of forage and hay. So B. F. J. tells the Country Gentleman, and thus it is in other parts of the West.

The apple crop of the country has been largely reduced in consequence of the fruit prematurely falling from the trees. We doubt if there will be one-half as many winter apples barrelled or binned as there was last year the country over. Big prices for these who have apples to sell!

While nearly all parts of the country have suffered by the drouth, New York and New England have not fared nearly so badly as the middle tier of states from Pennsylvania and Virginia west to Colorado. Farmers in the favored districts, having fair crops, and being sure of big prices, may set down 1881 as not a bad year for them.

THE FARM.

When the mountains are crowned with purple mist,
And the apples glow 'mid the orchard green,
When the grapes drop low on the clambering vine,
And the morning air is frosty and keen;

When the maples are blazing with scarlet flame,
The gorgeous flame of the quivering leaves,
Oh, then do we gather the golden corn
And bind it close in its ample sheaves.

We gather it in, our priceless hoard,
Ripened and crisped by the Summer's glow,
And up to heaven we lift our thanks
For this gift of grain ere the Winter snow.

This has been a hard summer on wheels, and loose tires prevail.

THE TRUCK GARDEN.

Onions are ready to be harvested when a large share of the tops lie down. After the bulbs are thoroughly dried they should be stored thinly in a cool, airy place.

Black raspberries throw up from the crown this season the new growth that bears next. After fruiting season is over cut out old bearing wood. The black raspberry is *not* a sucker plant, the stock being increased by burying the new growth in August and September with the tips above ground.

Fig. 1.

Fig. 2.

Thinning of the bunches of grapes is one of the most beneficial practices in vine-culture. As a general rule it is safe to cut off one-third of all the bunches formed. In regard to the shoots themselves it is a good rule to leave no more grow during the summer than we want to remain; but superfluous ones should be taken out before they have made much growth.

MANCHESTER.

"*Man may construct steamships and railroads, disembowel the earth for ores, measure the mountains of the moon, and make his voice heard across old ocean, but God alone can make a Strawberry.*"

Why shall we not all grow as many strawberries as the family can consume; and why shall we not also grow some to sell to our neighbors? It is a fruit always relished by the family, and the neighbors are usually quite ready to buy the surplus at a fair price. If the neighbors will not, the nearest town will.

What varieties shall we plant?

That depends on our locality, soil, and whether we want them for the home table or to sell. If for home use we will not plant Wilson's Albany because it is too sour; if for the market, and we are beginners, we will be sure to start off with this popular variety. If we set out plants of this sort we are sure of fruit, and plenty of it. Many other kinds fail; this rarely does.

CAPT. JACK.

Supposing still we are beginners, let us also plant Boyden No. 30, Charles Downing and Sharpless. We mention these three old sorts because they do well in nearly all locations and soils, while many other kinds succeed only under favoring conditions. We may possibly add Glendale and Capt. Jack to this list.

Have we a neighbor who has been engaged in strawberry culture? Perhaps he is clever enough to tell us what kinds do best in our section! Be it well understood that a variety may be bragged about in the newspapers and in the catalogues and yet prove absolutely worthless in our garden. We must make our own experiments and apply our own tests, if we would ascertain what are the best sorts for us to plant.

KENTUCKY.

Of the lately introduced sorts the Bidwell is worthy of mention, so also are Longfellow and Manchester. Mt. Vernon and Crescent have both acquired quite a reputation. The Cinderilla, Jucunda, Cumberland Triumph, Monarch of the West, Kentucky, Great American and Miner's Prolific are all worthy of trial.

Let us name some of the characteristics of the different varieties?

Sharpless very large, both berry and plant; Glendale, large, late, firm, prolific, not sweet; Jucunda, requires high culture for success; Seth Boyden No. 30, large, prolific, firm, succeeding almost everywhere; Longfellow, beautiful firm, sweet, late, in shape a long fellow; Cumberl'd Triumph, vigorous plant, prolific, rather soft for market; Crescent, very prolific, small size, rather early, fails in many places; Capt. Jack, firm, remains long in bearing, attractive but not sweet; Cinderilla, quality good, large, abundant bearer, bright g ossy red, quite saleable; Chas. Downing, rivals the Wilson in all respects; Kentucky, a beautiful late, sweet sort, does best on sandy soil; Bidwell, large, long, bright color, firm and of good quality; Manchester, solid, good size and quality, prolific and saleable color; Mt. Vernon, large, very handsome, prolific, but not very firm; Miner's Prolific, productive, large, well adapted to Prairie soil. So much for varieties.

BIDWELL.

Some kinds have perfect blossoms; others have not. Those that have not are not apt to do well in a beginner's hands. Fig. 1 is a pistillate, or imperfect blossom, and will not bear fruit unless a perfect flowered variety is planted near it. Fig. 2 represents a perfect blossom. We have before us letters complaining of the Crescent the past season that it produced no fruit. The reason is plain—it is a pistillate variety, and the blossoms were not fertilized. Old berry growers know all about this, but we are writing for amateurs, partly. Nearly all of the sorts we have named have perfect blossoms, and need no care in this respect.

CHARLES DOWNING.

How can we have a supply of berries next June if we failed to set out a bed last May? We may only do it on a small scale for the home table, but if any one thinks he will try and grow strawberries, it is worth while to start a small bed now, if simply for the purpose of giving the different varieties a trial. Potted plants, or such as have been dug up with a ball of earth attached, can be set out this month and may be depended on for a crop next June. Several advertisers in this paper will supply plants true to name at a cost of from $2.00 to $4.00 per hundred, with directions for transplanting and cultivation.

MT. VERNON, OR KIRKWOOD.

It will not pay to buy largely of potted plants now, because layered plants may be obtained much more cheaply for spring planting; we only state how this delicious fruit from one's own garden *may* be made to adorn our table next summer, if we neglected to plant out a bed last May.

Possibly you have a neighbor who can furnish you with plants, with earth attached to the roots; if so you are fortunate. An implement made like the post-hole digger shown on page 171, July number, only smaller, would be convenient for the purpose of taking up plants, earth and all, we should think, but a small spade will do.

Our friend Tillinghast, of La Plume, Pa., says that layered plants may be obtained now and potted by the purchaser. In two or three weeks they will have rooted and "will do as well as those that were potted before shipment." Hardly as well we should think, because later.

SETH BOYDEN, No. 30.

Except in a small way, as above suggested, spring is the best time for setting beds, for you then have a full crop in a year with slight expense for plants, as they do not need to be potted. It takes 14,000 plants for an acre 1x3 feet apart.

The time will come when hand-hoeing strawberry beds will be done away with. Why not set say four plants in a hill three or four inches apart, the hills in rows three feet apart each way? Cultivate by horse both ways, cutting off all runners. The hills will spread into immense stools from which three or four quarts of berries may be picked. We see this plan is recommended by J. H. Hale, a very extensive and intelligent grower of Connecticut. Old berry growers, on loamy soils where weeds and clover are much in the way and labor is costly, must come to this method. In light sandy soils, where weeds are easily kept down, the matted row system will be found the best, perhaps.

The bed that was set out last spring should be well worked and weeded during July. Cultivation should be continued until about October 1st, narrowing the cultivator as the rows widen. A noted Ohio grower sows turnips between the rows about August 1st, gaining a crop of roots, saving the labor of cultivation and keeping down weeds.

LONGFELLOW.

Some market growers take but one crop from a bed, plowing down the vines after the first fruiting and planting some other crop. Others mow the leaves, and then run a one-horse plow on both sides of each row, narrowing the rows to strips of plants six inches wide, thinning them out, cultivating between but letting new plants become established, for it is the new plants that are wanted. Manure freely in the rows with ashes and ground bone.

A one-horse harrow, with many small steel teeth kept sharp and bright, that can be narrowed or widened at pleasure, is recommended for use in a strawberry patch.

We are indebted to Mr. J. T. Lovett, of Little Silver, N. J., for several of the accompanying engravings. Mr. L. is a large grower and dealer in all kinds of small fruit plants.

Beginning with general uneasiness, giddiness, ringing in the ears, hurried breathing, headache, hot skin, high pulse, thirst, fatigue in the back and limbs. Then in a day or two commences the aching, gnawing pains in some of the larger joints which go on increasing until there is apparently not room for an additional pang. The affected joints swell, the fever gains ground, perspiration flows, appetite is lost, miseries multiply. The slightest movement of the body is attended with excruciating pain especially during the night, so that sleep, if any come, is made up of frightful dreams. You wish that the pain would move to another joint; this it is apt to do, but only to create redoubled torture. Such is Rheumatism—as I have found it. It is one tremendous and prolonged Ouch!

But we will drop that subject, hoping we may never need to recur to it again.

As hinted by the Editor last month I propose to make a change at Elmwood. I have been growing ordinary farm crops—hay, corn, wheat, oats —and I now am about to go into fruit growing and market gardening. I shall cultivate the large fruits to some extent, but berries and garden vegetables will, next year, claim most of my attention. I am satisfied there is more profit in this business than in plain farming for any one located near a good market, as I am.

I have been partly persuaded into the new departure by neighbor Webb, who says my land is admirably adapted to the growing of fruits and vegetables. He says there is "money in it," and I so conclude, for he has made money out of it. He is what is called in these parts a "Truck Farmer," gradually working into this line, until his fine farm is a huge garden. He has fully paid for his land out of his own earnings since he bought it, and now has a handsome income above expenses.

Neighbor Webb's success is no doubt due in part to his three hard-working boys—sturdy, honest, enterprising fellows—who would make anything "go" towards which their energies were directed.

Timothy, the youngest, is coming to Elmwood, and is to be my farm manager. He will be twenty-one next spring, and is to give me two year's service, for which I am to pay him a salary. I compensate him liberally, and he is to give me his entire time—except what he devotes to the girls on Sunday nights. We do not call him Timothy, but Tim; everybody calls him Tim, and a more popular young man cannot be found in the neighborhood. I shall be greatly mistaken if we do not make business hum for the next two years.

It will be my pleasure, the coming year, to write out for your readers a history of our operations, giving our methods of growing garden fruits and vegetables for market, with enough details to make it of practical use to all who would follow in our footsteps. It maybe that I can prevail upon Tim to keep a diary of proceedings—the times of seeding, planting, hoeing, marketing, the cost of labor, the value of crops, mistakes made, and so on, and if I succeed, the Farm Journal shall have the benefit of the same.

Ouch! There, the enemy has not quite left me yet.

OUT AMONG THE FARMERS.

A Hundred Acre farm in Berks County—Christopher Shearer and his Crops—From a carpenter's bench to a poor farm, and how gumption make a poor farm pay.

One of the features of the Farm Journal for the coming year will be a record of the visits the Editor makes to cultivators of the soil. We shall go among the plain farmers of our own State, the truckers and berry producers of New Jersey, the peach growers of Delaware, the vineyardists along the Hudson, the market gardeners of Long Island, the apple orchardists of New York, and among representative dairymen, stock breeders, poultry keepers, and sheep husbandmen wherever we may find them. We hope to extend our trips to the West and learn how they do things beyond the Alleghanies, telling what we see and hear to all the readers of the paper. We shall attempt no fine writing nor high-flown language; while our limited space will compel brevity even were we disposed to spin things out, which we are not.

In October last we visited Christopher Shearer and his 100-acre farm, five miles from Reading, in Pennsylvania. Christopher was once a carpenter, but tiring of that, bought the farm which he now owns, 27 years ago. The farm was poor then, but good tillage and much manure have made it rich. He values it now at $200 per acre, and much of the land in the neighborhood is worth $150 per acre.

"YOU MAY HAVE HEARD OF HER."

At first, Christopher, (we were told) devoted his energies to potatoes, and grew but little else for a time; but he soon began to set out fruit trees, and now has 50 acres of them. He has 3,500 peach trees, 1,500 apple, as many pear, 700 cherry, with twenty acres devoted to grapes, and two to strawberries.

Half of his apples are Baldwins, for these are the most profitable—more so, he says, than Smith's cider. There are many trees of Krouser, a native variety of Berks, which is a regular and tremendous bearer. Its quality is good, and its time about the same as Baldwin, which is a late Fall apple in this section. Of recent years the Krouser has developed a defect, in that it becomes "punky" about the core.

Of pears, nearly all are Bartlett. Mr. Shearer finds no other kind so profitable, and he has tried all of the best.

Of peaches he plants one kind only, which he calls "Variegated," in the absence of a better name. It is like Crawford's Late, but larger, smoother, and almost transparent. Up to this year we understood him to say that there was no failure in peaches for nine years. We went through his peach orchard and did not see a tree that was not full of health and vigor.

Yellows do not trouble Christopher. When a tree gets sick he roots it out quick as a wink, besides he selects peach pits from healthy trees, plants them, and thus secures freedom from the yellows.

We did not see a sickly fruit tree, either of apple, pear, peach, cherry, or plum on the farm. Every tree seemed to rejoice in kindly care. Every acre of orchard is kept cultivated in the fore part of the season, cultivation mostly ceasing about harvest. Speaking of growing pears, Christopher said to us, in reply to our question "Do you cultivate?" "Yes; if I did not cultivate, I would have no pears and no trees."

Other crops are grown among the trees. This season $3,500 worth of tobacco has been harvested from his fruit orchards. Clinton grapes fill up the vacant spaces in the apple orchard. A wine cellar, which holds five thousand gallons of wine, is nearly full, which finds ready sale at $1 per gallon. Part of this wine is made from grapes of Mr. Shearer's own production, but part from grapes bought from neighbors. It takes from 12 to 15 pounds of grapes to make one gallon of wine.

Two cider presses are kept running all Summer on the farm, Shearer's product this year, from his own apples, being about 3,600 gallons. The profits on that manufactured for neighbors, so great is the extent of the business done, are not less than $500 a year. The apple mills, driven by steam, will grind 200 bushels per hour, and the press will squeeze out the juice of the same in fifteen minutes.

Three acres of strawberries were grown the past season, yielding 10,000 quarts, and marketed at eight cents per quart in Reading. Crescent, Downing, Sharpless and Cumberland Triumph are deemed best, the first named excelling the others. The patch for fruit next spring, about two acres, is the best cared for, and in the finest condition of any we ever saw, and we have been among stawberries all our life. Six acres this year are devoted to artichokes. Drouth has made the crop a light one—not harvested at the time of our visit—but 400 bushels can be grown to the acre on ground that will yield 200 bushels of potatoes. The sole market is in New York, the price now being from $3 to $3.50 per barrel. They are grown precisely like potatoes.

There is but little live stock on the place—six horses and four or five cows—none other. No grain or hay is grown. Feed and manure are bought, the latter costing in Reading $2 for a four horse load. Five or six regular hands are employed, extra labor when wanted being quickly obtainable at from 80 cents to $1 per day, the laborers boarding themselves.

The one thing manifest in visiting the Shearer farm is the *thoroughness* with which everything is done. Of the thousands of trees and vines growing, not one but has intelligent, persistent oversight and care; of the various sources of profit not one that is lost sight of or neglected.

We find our space filled while our account is not closed. Next month we will present a portrait of Mr. Shearer—a plain, hard-fisted level-headed man—with a continuation of these notes.

DAIRY AND STOCK.

Dairymen will all come to the soiling system yet; no doubt about that. Pasturage is too costly. No interior fences and a ten pound cow on every acre—that is the high water mark. Please don't forget it.

The points and characteristics of the different breeds of swine are very carefully stated on this page. The man who wrote it knows what he is about.

It costs no more to make good butter than poor butter. Every pound of poor butter is made at a loss to the dairyman. There is profit in good butter.

If you want a good cow raise her yourself. The time is coming, and is now about here, when dairymen will cease to depend on bought scrubs, for the reason that they are unprofitable.

The man who give his cows water of a temperature a few degrees above freezing, in a place where they can drink it without shivering before they go back, and who keeps them where the manure will not freeze in the coldest weather, will make ten dollars on each cow during the winter more than he would if they were kept in a cold stable and driven to drink out of a brook or trough covered with ice. These matters of giving cows water of the right temperature, and as often as they will drink in cold weather, and of keeping them warmly sheltered, are of vastly more importance than most people suppose.

THE BREEDS OF SWINE.

Jersey Reds, Yorkshires, Chester Whites, Berkshires, Essex, Poland Chinas—Points and Characteristics.

The Jersey Red or "Duroc" swine have not been very generally disseminated, although they have many good qualities, especially for the grower of heavy weights. We believe they come as near being a grass breed of pigs as anything yet brought out, but must have time to develop and for that reason are not so well fitted for marketing at four to ten months as are some others. In color are dark sandy or light brick, have very coarse bone, deep hams and sides. Not as well sprung in the rib as some breeds, have heavy lop ears and coarse head. Weigh at maturity 600 to 1,000 pounds.

Small white Yorkshires are as near the opposite in every respect to Durocs as one can well imagine. In color invariably pure white, medium coat, very light in bone, remarkably short dished face and heavy jowls, broad, flat back, deep sides, short from loin to root of tail, and not remarkable for full round hams.

Their best card seems to be that they can be made very fat at a few months of age, weigh from 300 to 600 pounds at maturity.

Chester Whites have many admirers, and their claims have been strongly pushed. They are a white haired breed, with an occasional dark speck in the skin, great length of body, plenty of bone, good backs, deep hams and sides, with neat heads, somewhat dished, smallish well placed droop ears, grow to large size and can be fed off at a reasonable young age. Weigh from 500 to 800 pounds at maturity. They are as well suited, perhaps the best, for foundation stock to cross quick developing breeds on for light sale pork. Poland China or Magie, is a western breed in the fullest sense of the term. They are very rapid growers and great feeders, can be fed off at any time after six months, great length of body, deep hams and sides, with plenty of bone, rather long in the face, small wilt ear, in color nearly black, with occasional white on body, abou head and feet. Rather shy breeders and not as good nurses as some others, weigh at maturity 600 to 900 pounds.

POLAND CHINA.

Berkshires; more money has been invested in this breed in America than all other thoroughbred breeds combined, and perhaps there were good reasons for it. They are equally well adapted east or west, do not grow as large as some others, although they can be readily fed to weigh 500 to 700 pounds, and can be developed at any age. In color black or slate, with white on extremities, best of backs, deep sides and remarkably well developed hams, short dished face, small erect ears, and short straight legs, and stand up well on feet when fat, large breeders and best of nurses.

The Essex are the oldest established breed in England. They were brought to their present state of perfection by Lord Western and the late Fisher Hobbs. In color jet black, thin coat, broad back, round barrel with neat head and very light bones. Their mission seems to be to cross on the coarse native breeds for the production of quick maturing pigs, and for this purpose they are perhaps the best fitted of all the improved breeds.

ESSEX

LOOK AT THAT COW.

Probably most of our readers have heard of the famous cow, "Jersey Belle of Scituate," many have seen her picture, and some may have beheld the cow herself; yet there is no apology needed for presenting her portrait, which we do on the opposite page.

Jersey Belle became famous through her exploits at the milk pail, or rather, one might say, at the butter tub.

SMALL YORKSHIRE.

On February 25th, 1877, she calved, and on the 5th of March next following she made 3 pounds 6 ounces of butter; in the three days following she made 9 pounds 9 ounces; that week 21 pounds and 5 ounces and in 11 days 32 pounds; for five months she averaged 19 pounds per week.

One morning's milking in July made 1 pound and 10 ounces. Up to August 1st of that year she made 400 pounds; to September 472; to October 532, and to March 5th, 1878, she made 705 pounds.

She calved again May 10th, 1878, and in one week made 22 pounds and 13 ounces; her milking of September 29th and 30th, 1878, made 3 pounds 14½ ounces of butter.

Seven hundred and five pounds of butter—rich, golden butter in one year—would make any cow famous, especially as it is known that it takes more than six average cows to make that much.

The cows of the State of New York average 110 pounds of butter a year, of North Carolina 22, of Massachusetts,10of the Western States about 50. Jersey Belle weighed 950 pounds. Her color was rich yellow fawn, shading into a darker tint upon the head, diversified and mapped out with considerable white. She was ten years old last summer.

We use the past tense because the cow is not now living, having departed this life—kicked the bucket as it were—last July. She died of milk fever.

The record of Jersey Belle's butter yield is so well authenticated that it is not worth while for any one to dispute or doubt it.

The owner could have sold her the day before she died for $2,000, but he would not.

More purebreds . . . "Cobrollers" look funny now, but lard was an important product 100 years ago

THIS AND THAT ABOUT HOGS.

The hog used to be ugly and hardy. Now he is handsome, helpless and imbecile. Corn did it.

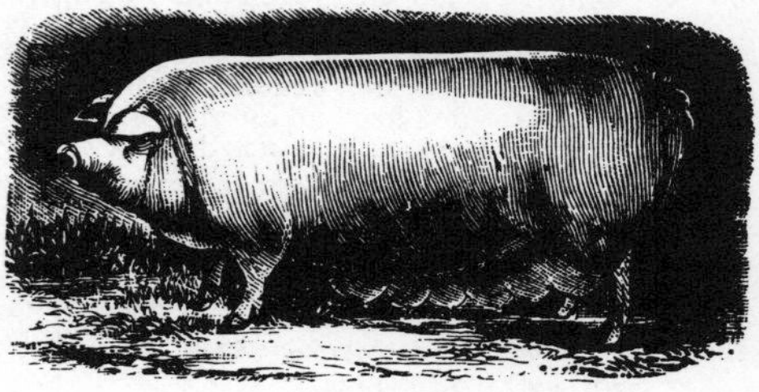

CHESTER WHITE.

It is safe to say that most of the diseases of swine are the results of inattention and neglect. Give the hogs clean pens, a large yard or lot in which to exercise and access to fresh earth, healthful food, pure water, and seldom, if ever, will they be troubled with disease.

For hogs that are kept closely penned an occasional dose of sulphur, charcoal or ashes is thought to be beneficial.

A store hog that is of a good breed and healthy should, according to experiments repeatedly tried, lay on a pound of additional weight for every five pounds and six-tenths of a pound of sound corn it eats. Thus one bushel of corn—a part meal and fed as slop, and a part in the ear or shelled—all the animal will eat, should make ten pounds additional weight, and ten bushels of corn will represent 100 pounds of pork.

BERKSHIRE.

Oblige the fat hog by knocking it on the head before sticking it so it won't want to run and squeal.

What this country needs is a little less hog and a little more mutton.

Three parts boiling water to one of cold is about right for scalding hogs.

A pig was never known to wash, but a great many people have seen pig iron.

There are lots of people who have been butchering hogs all their lives who do not know that a dressed hog, if frozen, will not produce good sausage. And yet such is the fact.

This issue of the FARM JOURNAL might be styled the "Pig Number," considering the looks of this page. Well, call it that.

The last one hundred pounds put on a fat hog costs the least.

Farmers who breed for market should never use pure breeds, but should cross the pure-bred boars on large, coarse, common sows.

It is the worst kind of waste to let pigs get poor at any stage of their existence. Don't keep hogs over winter except for breeding purposes. "Store hogs" should be done away with.

A potpourri of news and views from the editor's desk in 1882

Don't be *too* hard on oleo-margarine. It is bad stuff, which to sell as butter is a fraud, but the average price of good butter is as high as it has been for years. "Margey" may be a naughty girl, but she doesn't seem to injure the social standing of her sister to any great extent.

Akeley & Co., of 18 Devonshire St., Boston, Mass., want to advertise "Fine Old Brandies" in the Farm Journal and pay for it in goods. Well, no, we guess not. Try the Lydia Pinkham papers.

Smart Board of Health is that of New York City which declares that skimmed milk is unwholesome and which has had an ordinance passed prohibiting its sale. Where is the fool killer?

TOPICS IN SEASON.

THE FARM.

Blessed among men is he whose honest toil
Receives its guerdon from the fruitful land;
Who sees God's bounty in the teeming soil;
Who earns his bread with honest heart and hand!

Old rubber soles make excellent washers for carriages and are good to keep the shafts from rattling.

We are indebted for the several illustrations on this page to Landreth, Dreer, and Benson, Maule & Co., of this city.

Purdy recently speaks of "Clark's No. 1" potato as "the best I have eaten this season, and the handsomest I ever saw." An Indiana subscriber speaks very highly of Watson's Seedling.

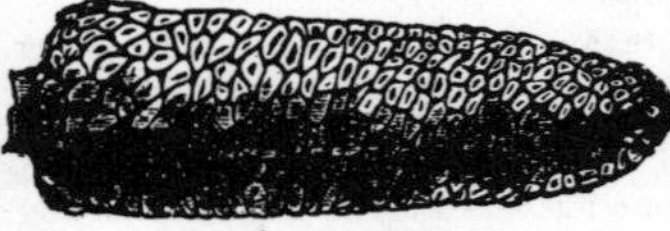

ADAM'S EXTRA EARLY.

Farmers should now bear in mind that a good township road mender will give them better roads with one-half the road taxes. Just whisper this information into the sound ear of the township supervisor.

Have you noticed the late decision of Land Commissioner that Catalpa and Ailantus are not timber trees and cannot be planted on timber claims? Yet he accepts cotton wood and box elder. See Dr. Warder's article in last Rural New Yorker. W. C. STEELE.
Little Silver, N. J.

A writer in the Country Gentleman gives his experience with Nash & Bro.'s Acme harrow. He says:—"On *once* going over the ground it accomplished the

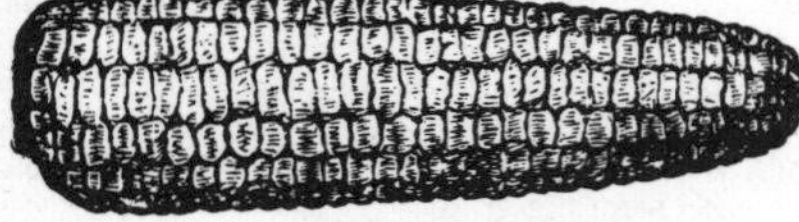

CROSBY'S EXTRA EARLY.

work of both roller and harrow, and more perfectly fitted the surface to receive the seed than both the others would have done. We would not now dispense with it for twice its cost."

We have before us an interesting letter from Seth Allen, of Rio, Col. Co., Wis., on the advantage of sowing salt on wheat in the spring. His experiments prove its great advantage. He uses about three-fourths of a barrel to the acre and harrows it in. Those who wish to try the experiment should address him for full particulars. S. A., is a practical and successful farmer.

Teams in prime condition, after a few days at the plow or harrow, are often badly galled by collars improperly made or carelessly fitted. To prevent or cure a galled neck or shoulder, give a thorough cleaning of the parts with cold water and salt every time the team is returned to the stable and wash the collar. This cooling application toughens the skin, and prevents fever and soreness.

One never knows how a new potato is going to turn out. Only careful and numerous trials, in different parts of the country, as a cropper, can determine its

TRIUMPH.

value. Tillinghast's "Belle" has taken the premium at our State Fair, in competition with fifty other varieties. It is large and handsome, and certainly appears to have unusual merit. It ought to have a general trial this season.

It is now pretty well decided that no matter what commercial fertilizers are composed of, there are but three substances or elements that should be valued in a fertilizer, because experience teaches that the application of these three substances, one, two, or the

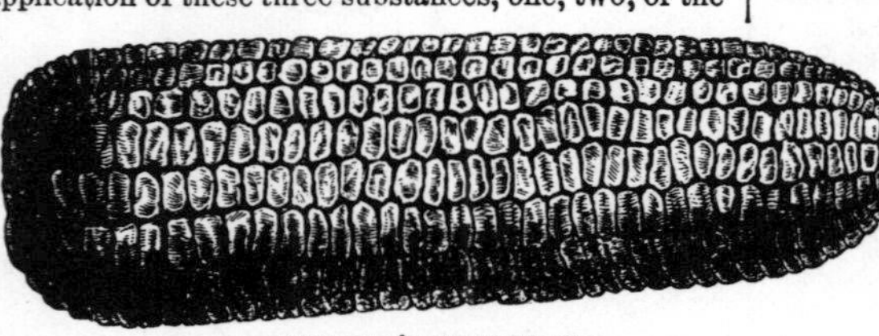

STOWELL'S EVERGREEN.

three combined, will supply all the lacking elements in any of our worn soils. While several other elements are found in soils and in crops, they are sufficiently abundant in every soil, and any outlay incurred in applying them would be a useless expenditure. These three substances or elements of plant food are phosphoric acid, potash, and ammonia.

EDITOR FARM JOURNAL:—How does Mr. Biggle know that "all the rich and costly fertilizing elements applied are still in the soil?" (See article in F. J. for Feb.) This is written in reference to the severe drought of last year. I have puzzled myself over this question a great deal, but am not at all clear that manure applied even in a dry season remains in an available form for future crops. I shall be glad to know that his statement is correct, but would like to know the reason for it. These elements may remain in the soil in other combinations it is true, or they may have disappeared in whole or in part; but the question is can manure be stored in the soil so as to be readily available for plant food? W. J. JENNINGS, *Green Farms, Ct.*

BAY VIEW CANTELOUPE.

That terrible pest of the farmer—Canada thistle—is slowly, but surely working its way south, and spreading over the country. It ought to be fought tooth and toe-nail by every farm owner and renter, wherever it appears. We have these notes concerning it from a practical man: To extirpate this nuisance, while it has not yet entire control of the soil, take each plant separately—dig about it as deep as you can, (which will not be very deep, before you will find other roots running off at right angles a little way, and then down a a long way) Cut the root off and throw on it a handful of salt, cover up, and rest secure from that quarter,

JENNY LIND CANTELOUPE.

PERFECTION DRUMHEAD SAVOY CABBAGE

but look out for its alternate. To distinguish it from the common thistle, which compared with the Canada becomes a moss-rose, pull or dig up the plant, if it has side or surface roots and tapers to a point it is common, but if Canada, it will have a root from one-eighth to a quarter of an inch in diameter from the crown downward almost indefinitely, but will break off at the first angle and be up in a few days. The neglect of a season may curse a life time.

The Osage Orange for a hedge should be planted 9 inches apart as early in the spring as the ground can be got in good condition. The soil should be as rich and as mellow as for corn, and receive the same cultivation the following summer. No pruning is needed the first season. The second spring most of the growth of the first year ought to be cut off and new plants should take the place of any that have died. Cultivate the second summer the same as the first, but not later than the last week of July, and do not prune. Early in the third spring, the upright shoots may be cut back to four or six inches of the previous year's growth, but the lower shoots may be left nearly their whole length, and the intermediate ones proportionately shortened, thus giving the hedge a pyramidal form. After the new growth has become firm it may be pruned once, and thereafter twice a year. As a rule the first trimming is given from the 15th to the 20th of June and the second from the 20th to the 30th of Aug.

THE TRUCK GARDEN.

We are bound to speak a word every year in favor of having plenty of sugar corn for the dinner table. "Plenty," means about once a day all through the season, and each time all the pot will hold. The first to plant is Adams' Extra Early, not sweet, but coming ahead of any other variety—sixty days from planting. It requires rich land and should be planted as soon as the ground is fit. Follow this with Crosby's Early and Triumph, both sweet, and both excellent. For the main crop take Stowell's Evergreen, northern grown seed, and make a planting every two weeks up to July 4th, beginning the middle of May.

When it comes to melons the old Mountain Sweet does to tie to. The Cuban Queen, introduced last year by Burpee is very large, and is said to be good. It ought to have a trial. Of canteloupes the "Jenny Lind," an old favorite, is perfectly delicious. The Bay View is large, luscious, and ought to be in every garden where

FIVE BELLE POTATOES ON A 9-INCH DINNER PLATE.

this fruit will thrive. It is a much larger melon than the Jenny Lind, though not so shown in the engraving. We may here add that many people can grow melons who think they cannot. An admixture of road sand with their soil will enable them to succeed.

Again we say plant Savoy cabbage for the home table. The "Perfection Drumhead Savoy," is a compact grower, large solid-heading sort, finely curled, short stalk, of excellent flavor, with the richness of the cauliflower. The Savoy is much sweeter and finer-tasted than sorts that are better grown for market.

Centerton, Burlington Co., N. J., is ripe for a canning factory. So we learn through a letter from a subscriber, Charles Stokes Jr., (whose address is Rancocas.) The location is an admirable one, the farmers are ready to supply the fruits, vegetables and poultry, and adjacent villages will furnish the helpers. Let somebody who understands the business wade in.—And now we are led to say that there ought to be ten canneries where there are now one. Let farmers in other sections ripen up to the point of wanting factories built and thus make a home market for their produce.

Conestoga wagons, early farm machines and a pitch for western land

PUBLISHER'S TABLE.

Should any errors be made in entering clubs received, and subscribers fail to get their papers, we hope to be early notified. An occasional mistake is unavoidable, but we gladly correct all errors when pointed out. Let all hands be patient, and we will serve them faithfully. We are bound that every subscriber shall get his paper the year round. You will find this is part of "our platform."

Philadelphia Club subscribers are charged 12 cents extra for postage. The postage to Oregon is less than across 7th street, and it is not our fault either.

Please keep business matters separate from what is meant for publication. Items of information for the Editor should be written on a separate slip of paper. Do not forget this, please.

Scarcely a month passes but it gives birth to some cheap agricultural paper, and about as many die as are born. This is a cold, cheerless world for such infants, unless they can give a mighty good reason for their existence.

We want your very best ideas for publication. Dress them up in a few words and let's have them. We want no thin, long-winded essays. Give us such facts, hints and wrinkles as will be *useful* to other readers of the paper.

Readers, what do you think of the notice, "Fair Play," on the first page? We mean exactly what we say. You may be sure we keep swindlers out of this paper, or if they accidently get in, we go for them with a sharp stick, and we UNCHAIN OUR DOG.

This paper is not the organ of the grangers or of anybody else. It is the people's paper, and they all take it—or expect to. Our Grange friends subscribe because it suits them, and read it because they can find nothing else as good for the money.

There are a great many interesting advertisements in this paper and the reader will observe that four pages are added to the regular number so that there will be as much reading matter as usual. It costs three hundred and fifty dollars for the four extra pages of this one issue.

Sometimes subscribers make inquiries of the Editor by mail which are not answered at once. There are various reasons for this. Sometimes he can't answer them; sometimes the answer would be out of season; sometimes we are so frightfully busy that we havn't time. We do the best we can and inquirers must be patient and excuse delinquencies. Better, also, enclose a postal card when asking for information.

Come on with that club.

ADVERTISEMENTS.

Advertisers like to know which paper benefits them most; therefore, our readers, in answering any advertisement in this paper, will please state that they saw it in the Farm Journal.

ODD MENTION.
(WHILE WE THINK OF IT.)

True "horsepower" from horses on a treadmill runs the grain thresher

The only machine that received an award on both Horse-power and Thresher and Cleaner, at the Centennial Exhibition: was awarded the two last Gold Medals given by the New York State Agricultural Society on Horse-powers and Threshers; and is the only Thresher selected from the vast number built in the United States, for illustration and description in "Appleton's Cyclopedia of Applied Mechanics," recently published, thus adopting it as the standard machine of this country. Buy the best. It is cheapest in the end. Catalogue sent free. Address, MINARD HARDER, Cobleskill, Schoharie Co., N. Y.

Farmers who have some nice seed wheat to spare, free from rye and cockle, ought to advertise it in the August and September numbers of the FARM JOURNAL. Four lines will be enough, and will cost only $2 per month.

=

I will send in, for June number, how I got rid of barn weavel without stacking out or burning the barn either. C. F. COX, *Oxford, Pa.*

Yes, but you did not. Here it is July, and the weavel business is not settled yet.

=

Owing to the rush of orders last spring Beatty was not as prompt in shipping organs as usual to our subscribers, and we had some complaints, among others one from J. K. Hancock, of Canterbury, N. H., who now writes to the F. J. as follows: "I have received the organ which I wrote you in regard to. It is better than I expected, far better. Beatty has done the generous thing by me."

=

Now, then, go at once and see if your insurance policy be good and tight. There may be a flaw in it somewhere, it may have run out, the company may be less sound than it ought to be, or the policy may be too small to save you from severe loss in case of a fire. The crops as well as buildings should be insured from fire and storm. The animals should be insured against thieves and disease. If you are burnt out, or blown down, or cut up by hail, or your stock die off, or are stolen, and you lose heavily, don't blame the FARM JOURNAL. For this is our warning.

=

We shall have our experimental farm—when we get one—embellished by a fine fruit-orchard, and will, no doubt, have a great deal of fruit to pick. Hence we must have some fruit ladders of the most approved kind, such, for instance, as the one shown in the engraving. The design was furnished originally by W. F. Bassett, of New Jersey, to the Gardeners' Monthly. Any reader of the Farm Journal is at liberty to make this kind of a ladder and use it when fruit gets ripe.

ADVERTISEMENTS.

Advertisers like to know which paper benefits them most; therefore, our readers, in answering any advertisement in this paper, will please state that they saw it in the Farm Journal.

THE POULTRY YARD.

EDITED BY DR. A. M. DICKIE.

Everyone's got "chicken fever," "But, good friends, go slow. Don't all of you rush into the raising of chickens by the thousands."

Possibly everybody does not know it, but eggs that are *right* when packed will bear long trips by express, if in neat light packages and properly marked, "Eggs For Hatching," and give fair results.

If you intend to use an incubator this spring for hatching chicks you should have it on hand now or should order it right away. It is prudent to become acquainted with these machines by running them a few days, before entrusting to their care one or two hundred high priced eggs.

You will contribute much to our happiness by sending us a rousing club for the F. J. Tell your friends that the poultry pages alone are worth much more than the subscription price. Let poultry keepers give us a lift on that 200,000 and we will reward them by making a better paper.

The "chicken fever" has never been more prevalent than it is now. But, good friends, go slow. Don't all of you rush into the raising of chickens by the thousands. It is not nearly so easy, nor so profitable in reality, as it is on paper. If you don't take our advice you will wish you had by the time you are two years older. Thousands of people, farmers, business men, villagers, mechanics are making money by keeping poultry on a limited scale. Those who have made a business of it and are successful can be counted on the fingers of one hand. These facts are significant. They do not prove that poultry keeping as a business is impracticable, or that success is not attainable, but they give point to our word of caution.

A VILLAGE POULTRY HOUSE.

What do you think of it? Is'nt it a beauty? Why should not FARM JOURNAL readers have tasty hen houses as well as fancy barns and dwelling houses. We have a large number of subscribers who are small farmers and villagers and who do not like to spoil the appearance of their lawns or yards with the mean sheds usually built for the chickens. Here is a model that is neat and convenient and can be so built as to ornament the finest lawn.

The whole structure is 10x20 feet on the ground with 8 feet posts. The enclosed part occupies a space 10x12 and the shed a space 8x10. The feed trough and water fountain are placed in the shed. In summer the nests are also placed here. If desirable the enclosed portion may be divided so as to have a laying and hatching room separate from the roosting apartment.

The house may be built on a smaller scale, 8x16 or 6x12 feet so as to accommodate 12, 24, or 36 fowls. It may be made to cost much or little according to the builder's purse.

The fence is made of No. 19 wire netting of 2 inch mesh, four feet high. The posts are 10 feet apart. The gate which is at the end of the house is made of lath.

The besetting sin of the village poultry keeper is overstocking. If you use only a bale of wire netting 50 yards long for a fence, don't keep more than a dozen hens, and don't keep them in this yard all the time if you can help it.

SUGGESTIVE FACTS AND FIGURES.

According to the census report of 1880 the number of barn yard fowls in the country at the time the census was taken was 102,272,135 and of other fowls, which we suppose includes turkeys, geese and ducks 23,235,187 or a total of 125,507,322 fowls of all sorts. We are expressly told that is "exclusive of the spring hatching," from which we infer that the figures are intended to represent only the number of fowls kept for breeding purposes or for laying and do not give what we might call the "new crop" or the chickens raised for market.

It is not unreasonable to suppose that the average product from each fowl would be five pounds of dressed poultry for market, worth 15 cents per pound. The market value of this product would be $109,130,491.

The number of eggs reported was 456,910,916 dozens. It is not stated whether this is the number laid or the number sold. But as it only allows 43 eggs to a fowl we suppose it is the number sold. Allowing 15 cents per dozen as a fair average price the season through and the country over, we have a market value of $68,536,637. Adding the meat and egg product we have a grand total of $177,677,128 as the value of the poultry product of the United States.

Our own opinion is that these figures might be doubled and more nearly represent the actual facts than they do now. However, taking them just as they stand, they show very forcibly the important contribution annually made to the wealth of the country by the poultry industry. It is one of our industries that is by no means overdone and that will bear indefinite expansion. We propose to do what we can in the F. J. to help along those who are engaged in it.

VILLAGE POULTRY HOUSE.

CHICAGO EGG MARKET.

Eggs are sold in the Produce Exchange at Chicago just after the call for cheese. They are classified as Extras, Firsts and Seconds. Extras comprise all fresh stock free from checks, clean, put up in barrels or cases; if in barrels, to be packed in sweet, clean, dry, cut straw, suitable for cold storage. Firsts comprise all stocks reasonably clean, put up in barrels or cases; if in barrels, to be packed in clean, dry, cut straw, as extras are packed, and not to exceed one dozen checks to the case or two dozen to the barrel. Frozen or leaky eggs are unmerchantable. Seconds comprise all eggs inferior to firsts, such as checks, dirty and cloudy. The description of limed and ice-house eggs is the same as those governing fresh eggs. A barrel of eggs is computed at 70 dozen; a case, 30 dozen. Eggs to pass as firsts must not lose to exceed 2½ dozen to the barrel or 1 dozen to the case.

ADVICE TO BEGINNERS.

The following sound and sensible advice we find in the circular of an incubator manufacturer. It is just good as if we had written it ourselves.

"I am often asked the question: Do you think I can make a success of poultry raising with your incubator and brooder? Now that is certainly a difficult question. Raising poultry is just like any other business, one will succeed where another will fail. In general terms I will say to all who desire to go into it as a business, if you don't know anything at all about the business, and don't intend to devote the necessary time to it to learn it thoroughly, you had better keep out of it. For my part, I do not want any one to go into it with their eyes shut, I had much rather lose a sale any time than deceive any one; whatever I tell you you can depend it is the best I know for your interest, as well as mine. I do not consider it to my interest to sell a machine, and then have the buyer make a failure of the business. On the contrary, the loss will be greater to me than to the buyer. If I had reason to think a person would make a failure of it, I would refuse to sell; in fact, I have in several instances advised intending purchasers out of the notion of buying, from the fact that they were so situated that I knew a failure would be the result. The real trouble is that so many have an altogether wrong idea about the care of the chicks, and that all that is necessary is to hatch them out, and then throw them a little feed occasionally. Well, a greater mistake could not well be made; any one who goes into it with that idea can either expect to change the idea very suddenly, or quit the business.

The real work comes in when the chicks are out of the shell; then is when the most care is required. It is no trouble for one who is used to the care of chicks, and knows just what they need, to succeed; but for a novice to go at it with the idea that he can do it as well as any one, is all a mistake. To all such I would say, either go in with the idea that you are going to give it the care and time to learn and a few failures will not discourage you, or else keep out of it altogether.

Poultry raising is a business that is especially suitable for women. There are thousands of farmer's wives and others, who, if they would try the artificial raising of poultry, could make it pay handsomely. These women all know more or less about the care of poultry and could make it a success from the start. Women generally understand the raising of poultry better than most men; one reason is that they attend to the numerous small details which are necessary, while but few men are willing to give the time that is required."

ROUP—ITS CAUSE AND CURE.

A disease more prevalent than any other in the winter season is roup. This is a disease of the lining membrane of the beak, extending, however, to the whole head and throat and finally affecting the whole constitution. It arises from exposure to cold winds and dampness, and from confinement in filthy and poorly ventilated houses. In its worst form it is contagious. Its first symptoms are hoarseness, sneezing and a slight running at the nostrils and frothy eyes. If not checked in this stage the discharge from the nostrils thickens and becomes very offensive, and at last the head swells, the eyes are closed, and the fowl dies. A. A. & L. H. Halladay, Bellows Falls, Vt., recommend as a preventive and a cure in the first stages the following: To one pint of water add two tablespoonfuls of carbolic acid and a piece of fine salt the size of a walnut. With an atomizer spray this all about in your houses after the fowls are on their roosts. Do this two or three times a week, or oftener, if your fowls get bad before you commence using it. They say, "With us it is a sure cure." We may add that the time to treat roup is in its first stage. After this the best thing to do, as a rule, is to kill the fowl and bury it, or burn it. A simple and generally effective treatment is to give each sick fowl a dessert-spoonful of castor oil at night for one or two nights and then feed on soft feed well seasoned with red pepper and charcoal.

It is needless to add that the producing cause must be avoided if any lasting benefit is to be secured by treatment.

FOOT NOTES.

A new campaign begins now. Map it out carefully, and don't count the chickens before they are hatched. Make provision for liberal care and attention to small details. Poultry keeping is mainly a matter of attention to details.

Do your fowls have access to gravel, coal ashes, shells or old broken mortar? They need such things

THE
FARM JOURNAL
DEVOTED TO THE FARM, ORCHARD, GARDEN, POULTRY AND HOUSEHOLD ECONOMY.

PHILADELPHIA. PUBLISHED BY WILMER ATKINSON, MAY, 1891. VOL. XV.—No. 5.

Price, Five Cents. *Practical not Fancy Farming.* 50 Cents a Year.

OUR BUSINESS METHOD.

The FARM JOURNAL gives no chromos, puffs no swindles, inserts no humbug advertisements, and does not devote one-half its space to telling how good the other half is. It is published monthly and is furnished to subscribers at 50 cents a year, postage prepaid. Terms cash in advance.

FAIR PLAY.

We believe, through careful inquiry, that all the advertisements in this paper are signed by trustworthy persons, and to prove our faith by works, we will make good to subscribers any loss sustained by trusting advertisers who prove to be deliberate swindlers. Rogues shall not ply their trade at the expense of our subscribers, who are our friends, through the medium of these columns. Let this be understood by everybody now and henceforth.

Note, (1) the above offer is to actual "subscribers," and only to them; (2) it holds good two months after the transaction causing the complaint, that is, we must have notice within this time; (3) we do not guarantee a pig's tail to curl in any particular direction; in other words, we guarantee against swindlers, but shall not attempt to adjust trifling disputes between subscribers and honorable business men who advertise. Bear these points in mind, hereafter.

CONTENTS OF THIS NUMBER.

It is a wise person who knows what to do next. The wise thing for the reader to do next is to see that the leaves of this paper are cut, and that the back is stitched with needle and thread.

A light supper is best.

Two dogs are at least one too many.

He that will have eggs must have cackling.

The girls should keep their lips for *him* alone.

The mysteries of the female mind are unfathomable.

The doctor that gives least medicine is the one to send for.

Just as like as not the chickens are drinking dirty water.

The ends of the fingers should never be dressed in mourning.

Don't shake hands with the devil when you say good-bye to him.

FARM JOURNAL is not a political paper; it is the people's own paper.

Small stones set on their edges make a good walk from house to barn.

It is a comparatively easy matter to test the vitality of all seeds before planting, and such a course will often be the means of saving much disappointment.

Fie, man! Why get discouraged! The honor lies in surmounting difficulties. You ought to be thankful that a chance is given you to show you are made of good stuff.

Buy what you want of FARM JOURNAL advertisers. They are honest. They have got to be honest. See "Fair Play" notice on this page. It is going to get a Million subscribers. Mind that.

Oliver Overtop is very particular about keeping his tools sharp. He says two men with sharp hoes will do the work of three men with dull ones. A dull harrow is lost time and wasted muscle. The farm with dull tools does not do well. Peter Tumbledown uses dull plows, and even his pocket-knife needs sharpening. It will hardly cut a plug of tobacco. His wife's bread knife is very dull.

THE FARM AND VILLAGE GARDEN.

BY ABNER HOLLINGSWORTH.

I am asked to state how pistillate and staminate strawberry flowers can be distinguished. In the convex heart of the female blossom is a yellow, velvety spot composed of the pistils, which are the female organs of reproduction. In the perfect flower, the stamens, as they are called, are seen growing around the margin or up through the yellow spot. On the tips of these are little sacks containing the pollen. These sacks open and the pollen falls over the pistils. This description is not scientific, perhaps, but may enable the unscientific reader to recognize the two kinds of bloom. Pistillate blossoms usually have a few stamens, but not sufficient to fertilize the pistils. An examination and comparison of a flower from a Sharpless plant and one from a Crescent will make my description plain.

Some time ago I spoke of the advisability of measuring the land with accuracy when about to apply chemical fertilizers. It is well also to gauge the fertilizer by some certain method so as not to put it on at random when applying it in the drill. My method both for field and garden practice is this: If planting a crop in drills three feet apart, for example, I calculate that 1 foot of drill occupies 1x3 feet of surface, or 3 square feet. As there are 43,560 square feet in an acre there will be one-third as many feet of drill, or 14,520. Now if I wish to apply 300 lbs. per acre I divide 14,520 by 300. This will give 48 and a fraction, which means that if I would apply 300 lbs. per acre I must use 1 lb. to each 48 feet (16 paces) of drill. To apply 400, 500, or any number of pounds per acre, I divide the 14,520 by that number, and learn how many feet of drill one pound will cover. If my readers have caught the principle of this method they can easily apply it to any width of drill or any quantity of fertilizer.

Frontier farming takes its toll. Biggle reports from a reader

HIGH FARMING AT ELMWOOD.

No. 136

BY JACOB BIGGLE.

I have here a tale of woe. It is from a woman, and the wife of an American farmer. If the Editor will print it, the act will be a good deed in a naughty world. There are a great many persons engaged in our calling both in the East and the West who are complaining of hard times and groaning under the burdens they carry, who had better read this letter two or three times over, for I think such perusal may cheer them up a little; at least it will convince them they are not so bad off as they might be and yet live.

Now, I do not know what it was that originated the poverty and misfortune of my correspondent, but I am sure she and her family are in a bad plight, and need some assistance from those who are better off; and I read in the public press that there are many others in that part of the country who are in similar straights.

Cannot some plan be devised for effectually rendering aid to these people in their dire distress? Whatever is done, should be done quickly, and I suggest that those of my readers who have a surplus of choice garden seeds, forward some to the writer of this letter for her own use and for her neighbor's. Harriet has sent some cash for the most pressing needs of Mrs. Hall. Perhaps the Editor of FARM JOURNAL will be willing to receive and forward such cash subscriptions as may be consigned to him for this benevolent purpose. *

Butka, Loup Co., Neb., February 29, 1891.

MR. JACOB BIGGLE. Dear sir:—

I have been one of your letter readers ever since you bought "Elmwood," and feel pretty well acquainted with both you and "Harriet." I have been much interested in "Elmwood." I think I can give you a history of "Low Farming on the Frontier."

We bought out a claim 35 miles from town and 10 miles from a post office, giving $50 for the claim of 160 acres. The land was raw prairie. We put up a little house of only one room. We moved in April 15, 1889. We spent our last dollar getting a sack of flour and a little meal to begin housekeeping with. We had come over 300 miles in a wagon, and brought most of what household stuff we have with us. Then began the struggle with poverty.

Mr. H. had to begin work away from home at once to be able to buy more food when what we had was done. With my help, the first week saw us with a well dug. We got water at 14 feet; finished up the well, curbing it up in June. Mr. H. got about 15 acres broken up that spring and planted in corn. I planted some of the sod in garden stuff. We also planted some potatoes and beans, which both yielded well for sod. Put in about 2 acres of buckwheat and did not get our seed back. Managed to live, and get a cow and hog, build a stable and milk-house the first year.

March 29, 1890, saw the fifth little one added to our family. The oldest is now four months past seven years old. Mr. H. took care of baby and me, and managed to get in the early garden and sowed crop. By that time I managed in the house alone, and he got the ground plowed and the corn planted. Everything was doing well, the corn looked splendid, so did the potatoes and garden up till the last of June. Then a hailstorm came, lasting fifteen minutes, which cut everything off to the ground.

Well, as we had no money, Mr. H. had to go off in search of work—there was none here. Dry weather set in and we raised nothing,—no corn, no potatoes, no beans, only a few turnips. Of course, as the hail cut the grain we had no harvesting to do.

Mr. H. came home in September, and Robbie, the oldest child, and I, helped him to put up hay. As we use hay for fuel, we had to put up lots. After putting up the hay and burning off guards, so we would be safe from fire, Mr. H. left us again in search of work to earn something to keep us through the winter. After he was gone but a short time, one of our only team was taken sick. He had to come home again, about Thanksgiving. For seven weeks the horse was not able to get up when he laid down, so it kept him at home attending it. Poverty was against us, as one thing needed was feed, and we could not feed him as he should have been fed. Just as we thought he was about almost well, he managed in some way to sprain one of his legs at the knee. He has not been able to get up alone since the accident. We have no feed but prairie hay, and he is very poor in flesh and gains no strength.

Well, my object in writing this letter is to ask you if you and your neighbors could not do something to assist us poor folks out here on the frontier. We have spent our last cent and have nothing to eat, and there are others who are very little better off than we are. We have done all we could to help ourselves, and unless God raises up friends to aid us, we will not be able to put out a crop this spring. We were *all* poor, and losing our crop put us so far behind. We must have feed for our teams (or they will not be able to do much work) and seed to plant. We need seed corn, wheat, oats, beans and garden seed and potatoes.

Those who live along the railroad have already received aid, but we away back have had nothing. There are quite a number who will have to receive help or cannot put in a crop. We decided last week that we must ask help of those who have been more blessed than ourselves. There has been so much of the western part of our state and Kansas that has suffered from drouth this year, and so many who are asking help in both states, I hope you can send a contribution to us. Seed can be shipped to Alfred Porter, Long Pine, Neb., whose post office address is Duff, Rock Co., Neb. Corn can be bought here at 50 cents, oats at 55 cents, wheat at 80 cents, beans at \$3.00 and potatoes at \$1.50 per bushel.

With kindest regards to you and Mrs. Biggle, I am, respectfully yours, MRS. A. J. HALL.

P.S.—March 7th. It has been cold, stormy weather ever since writing, and Mr. H. could not go to the post office. The horse was dead last Monday morning, so now we will have to get a horse. It's very discouraging. We could not spare money to take even the FARM JOURNAL this year, so I will not know how you are getting along at "Elmwood."

If you desire reference as to Mr. Porter's and my honesty and reliability, will refer you to Allen Mix, Duff, or A. A. Johnson, Butka. A. J. H.

* The Editor of FARM JOURNAL will, as suggested, receive and forward any sums of money that may be contributed for the purpose of alleviating the distress of Mrs. Hall and other Nebraska and Kansas subscribers who come within his knowledge as needing relief.

ALL ABOUT HORSE-BREEDING ON THE FARM.

ANSWER TO JACOB BIGGLE.—NUMBER SIX.

BY COL. F. D. CURTIS.

We should rear our own teams and then we can know of what they are made. When a man buys a horse he does not know how many hereditary spavins, ring-bones, curbs or blind eyes, or how much heaves he is purchasing at a big price per pound. When a farmer buys a horse he must pay for one which looks well, fifteen or twenty cents a pound: and he must get the money to pay this price out of farm products, which he sells for less than a cent a pound, and which never move unless he moves them; or he must pay for his horse out of beef, pig or sheep which he sells at less than half, and generally for one-third the price, live weight, which he pays for the horse.

The books do not balance good on this basis. We should know all about the blood and bones of the ancestors of our coming team, and then we should have it in our own hands so that we may know of what material the colts are made. Good blood is a good thing; but we can rear blemishes or weaknesses which will produce blemishes with good blood, as a foundation. Not so likely, I admit, as when the blood is contaminated; but mighty likely to show themselves when the colt is not properly fed. It takes much material to make much, and bone elements to make bone.

I am growing two teams of colts, and I shall have no fears of any unsoundness in any one of them. The parents on both sides were free from blemishes. The colts have been fed for development of horse points, which include feet. When not in the field they have always stood on the ground. Foods, which were lacking in elements to make much bone, sinew, hoofs, and nerves, have not been given to them. They have never been real fat; but they have been real vigorous. The joints have been fed, and so have the tendons. Their strength and maturity have kept pace with the development of body.

By this system of feeding the risks are reduced. Clover hay, bran and linseed meal are the foods for perfect growth in winter with the addition of oats when service is required.

The stable must be light or the eyes will be injured. The air must be pure or the lungs will be impaired. The hay must be bright, or the constant inhaling of dust will irritate the air passages. Good digestion is a virtue in a horse—a constant supply of salt will help in this. Feeding too much at a time, even of good food, is injurious. Tendency to colic comes from weak digestion. The home-grown horse need not thus be affected. If we buy we know not what these defects may be or how serious.

The useful horse is an educated one. The more intelligence the more comfort and value. The little colt can be taught the lessons which will make it a prize more easily than when older and its habits formed. It has a wonderful instinct for home, and it will naturally love the companionship of the family if those who associate with it are deserving, and the colt soon finds this out. Kindness is not lost on the colt.

The colt born in the autumn, costs less, as its dam may have done her summer's work, and the winter's vacation is turned to good account. There is time, also, for the owner to pet and associate with the little horse. In the spring it may go to pasture with soft food to eat and the best, for the change from milk, and for its tender gums caused by the shedding of its first teeth. It keeps right on growing, and is always gentle. It will come to you in the field as an old friend, and the winter's lessons and confidence may never be broken. Proper food and lots of sentiment will make with good blood a good horse. And such will always be profitable.

Charlton, N. Y.

PULLING TOGETHER.

Farmers should stand by each other and pull together—Other people combine for mutual help and protection, why not we?—Notes and news of Organization among farmers—The Grange—The Alliance—The League.

We believe that farmers should have seats at the First Table, and partake of the good things that abound, without crowding other worthy people away.

There is no use trying to force the millennium. The good time we all pray and work for will be slow in coming, at best, and we cannot hurry it up. Ill considered attempts to expedite its approach may result in a postponement of its arrival.

Hence movements of farmers to improve their condition, unless wisely planned and conservatively executed, are liable to set-backs, in which the good cause will seem to recede. Especially any selfish attempt to go forward at the expense of any other class, to acquire benefits which other people do not have, will certainly result in failure, as it ought to.

Therefore, let us be not rash; let us not ask nor expect too much; and let us be very sure that what we seek shall be for the good of the whole country, and not a part.

We must organize; we must discuss, educate; we must think and work; we must know what is good for us and what will not harm others; we must get together and stand together. Then all will be well in time.

It is folly for farmers' organizations to unite with other labor societies. Farmers must learn to manage their own team, before they hitch up with another team that has not learned to pull true. It is all right for labor to organize; if it does not it will be left in the mire. It is essential for farmers to organize in self-defence; but don't tie the two bodies together. Neither can run well so.

Farmers have elected lawyers to Congress and to the legislatures in times past, and now they are paying the penalty. It is a big job to undo the mischief done, and it will take years to accomplish it. One bad result is that it is now hard to find farmers who have had any experience in public office. Hereafter let us elect farmers to a fair share of the offices, especially the law-making offices, so that wise laws will be made that do not discriminate in favor of corporations. What folly to expect a Senate composed largely of corporation lawyers to pass equal and just laws for the benefit of the common people!

Here is a good plank from the "objects" of the League: "Encouraging all farmers to study political economy and the affairs of State, to qualify them to intelligently decide on political measures best calculated to improve their material interests, and also encourage all farmers to rely on farmers; to be true to themselves and their interests; to stand by each other in every good work."

The prayer book of the Episcopal church says: "In all times of our prosperity, good Lord, deliver us." Members of the Grange, Alliance, League and other farmers' organizations, remember those words in these days of your prosperity. Look out for wolves in sheep's clothing, beware of the professional politician, the chronic office-seeker, the summer-time friends. Trace their pedigree when they come around knocking for admission.

"The exchange of experience in the Grange, coupled with debate, advances progress and enlarges the mental caliber of men and women. 'Tis here we can fully develop our highest gifts, and if we have the qualifications for greatness or goodness it is brought to the surface and speedily utilized for the benefit of the world."

At a late term of court in one county in Kansas, the docket had 800 foreclosures of mortgage cases, sixty per cent. of those went to English and Scotch companies. How long will it take to close out at this rate? What is the doom of the small American farmer? No wonder farmers are pulling together, and we feel confident they *can* make things better.

There is likely to be a big crop of demagogues within the next two or three years. If you have any interest in such produce, sell it out now before the price goes down. They will be after the votes of the farmers on one pretense or another, sure. Look out!

Much of the fire insurance on farm buildings is placed in mutual (that is, co-operative) home companies. The New England Grange mutuals are very successful when pushed.

ONE MILLION SUBSCRIBERS.

FARM JOURNAL

Wants that many and will strive to get them.

Will You Help?

For the Largest Club Received on or before April 15th FARM JOURNAL will Pay Your Taxes for 1892 (under $100).

I have many times been told by subscribers and personal friends that FARM JOURNAL was good enough to have and ought to have ONE MILLION SUBSCRIBERS. Counting five readers to each copy printed it already has one million readers, but I want One Million subscribers and five million readers. To get so many I am sure will be

For Third Largest Club FARM JOURNAL will Pay Interest on Your Mortgage (under $40) for 1892.

A BIG JOB

But I do not mind that. It was a big job to build my circulation up from one subscriber to what it is now ; quite as hard, no doubt, as the one I now undertake.

I am assured that if my friends and supporters will stand by FARM JOURNAL the coming subscription season, that over one hundred thousand subscribers will be added to my list before the opening of Spring ; that is, if all old subscribers will renew and just talk up the paper a little among their friends and neighbors, each forwarding a small club, there is no doubt, whatever, that my readers will number a million and a half and perhaps two millions before the close of Winter. The question is, friends,

WILL YOU DO IT ?

$50 IN GOLD

Given for Second Largest Club.

A Good Fresh Cow for Fourth Largest Club.

1892-1893.

OLD FRIENDS in renewing, please send me a club which, in size, will indicate how well you appreciate the paper, and how much you desire that I may get my Million subscribers. The larger the club the better I shall like it.

NEW FRIENDS who now first learn of FARM JOURNAL (of whom there are multitudes, as 250,000 extra sample copies are being printed and distributed), I will thank you also to help along with the work.

CLUBS OF FOUR.

A club of 4 subscribers, for one year, at 25 cents each, will entitle you to a free copy one year. By getting 4 two-year subscribers, at 35 cents each, (only 10 cents more than for one-year subscribers) you will receive FARM JOURNAL Free for two years.

CLUBS OF TEN.

A club of 10 subscribers (and under 20) for one year, at 25 cents each, will entitle you to a free copy for one year, also a FARM JOURNAL binder, (holding FARM JOURNAL for two years). By getting 10 two-year subscribers, at 35 cents each (only 10 cents more than one-year subscribers), the clubber will get FARM JOURNAL free for two years, also a FARM JOURNAL binder.

A Good Silk Dress For Your Wife for the Fifth Largest Club.

A good Body Brussels Carpet, to fit your Parlor is one of the Alternative prizes for the Fifth Largest Club.

"Success stories" in FJ's Portrait Gallery —a warning about swindlers, too

FARM JOURNAL.

(UNLIKE ANY OTHER PAPER.)

PHILADELPHIA, JUNE, 1893.

NOT GOLD ENOUGH.

It is said that the entire annual production of gold is now consumed in the arts and dentistry, that there is no longer any new gold for money, and if not already, we soon shall be encroaching on the accumulated stocks of gold money for industrial purposes. Which makes it plain as the noonday sun that it will not do to discard silver as a money metal. Silver is the coin that the people must continue to jingle in their pockets, and their right to do so must never be denied them. Evil consequences must flow from any successful attempt of the nabobs of the old world or new to degrade and demonetize silver and make gold the only metal used for money.

THE CULTIVATOR AND ITS WORK.

It should have small teeth and plenty of them. It should have broad hoe attachments for skimming the surface and cutting weeds; these are usually called "sweeps." The width and depth of working should be easily and quickly regulated without the use of a wrench.

As a rule the cultivator should run close to the plant while it is young, and, if the soil is compact, it should go down deep. Later in the season it should run farther away and more shallow.

The frequency of cultivation must depend to a great extent on the weather. As soon as a crust forms after a rain it should be broken up by shallow culture. If the rain has been heavy and has compacted the soil it must be deeply stirred as soon as dry enough. It is an injury rather than a benefit to cultivate crops on wet, soggy soil. Weedy ground and frequent showers render frequent cultivation necessary.

Frequent shallow cultivation in dry weather makes a mulch that checks evaporation and holds the moisture in the soil for the use of crops.

IN THE HAY FIELD.

A modern mower cutting a five-foot swath can be drawn by a team of average weight. Haying time is too precious to be wasted by using a short bar machine.

No time is lost by stopping to sharpen a dull sickle.

Keep the sections of the sickle riveted tight and all the bolts screwed up, and save a general breakdown.

The man who is always sure it will rain before night lets his grass get overripe and cuts it just in time to catch the storm.

The wise man don't worry, but keeps his "weather eye" open, begins haying before all his grass is ripe enough, runs his mower only when the dew or rain has entirely dried off of it, cures it mostly in the windrow, and puts it in the mow before it has lost all of its grassy color and aroma.

Whatever nutriment there may be in grass,

W. B. LIPPINCOTT.

or any fodder plant, is all there when the seed is in the milk, or at latest in the dough state; and it is there in its most available form.

Much of the nutritious value of clover, and in fact of all grasses, is in the leaves and blossoms. By overdrying these drop off and are lost.

The spoiling of hay is due far more to the moisture that falls on it from without, in dew and rain, than to its own sap. This moisture dries off more quickly while the grass is standing than after it is cut. Hence the reason for cutting only when dry. Hence also the reason why it is safe to store while a little of the sap is in it, but unsafe to store when wet with dew or rain.

Peter Tumbledown's machine is broken and rusty and must go to the shop for repairs. But Peter won't think of this till he wants to mow.

Don't forget to take out the oil can and the water jug with you to the field—no other jug needed. A little and often is a good rule for using both.

That bright boy, as full of questions and ideas as he is of mischief, has in him the material for making a stirring, successful farmer. Answer his questions patiently, interest him in the farm work and business by taking him into your confidence and giving him something to do and to think about. As to the dull boy—your neighbor's boy—he can be a lawyer and politician.

Turn the horses into the meadow and let them roll and nip a few bites of grass while you make their night feed and bed ready.

Why not sow rye or clover among the corn, after cultivation is finished?

(Gentle and harmless at ordinary times, but alert and savage when tramps and swindlers come in at the front gate.)

A traveling man reports a great demand for glucose among the maple sugar makers of a certain state. Is this a slander, or have farmers concluded to destroy their own business by adulteration?

If any of our readers has been so successful (?) as to win a gold watch or any other valuable prize from anybody, we would advise them not to send a cent of money to pay for forwarding it. The firm that professes such generosity can afford to send their prizes free of cost.

A series of swindles has been committed recently in New England by sharpers who want to "put up a hay fork for an advertisement." A well-to-do farmer is selected in each community as the victim. He is told that the fork will not be charged to him, and that if he liked it, he is to recommend it and thus insure the sale of numbers in the vicinity. Soon after party No. 2 appears and demands pay for half-a-dozen or dozen similar forks. The indignant farmer of course protests. After a short controversy he is told that some mistake has evidently been made, and that if he will sign a document, which is presented, the order which party No. 2 claims to be collecting pay for will be countermanded. With the signature of the unwary farmer the schemer disappears only to put a bill for eight hay forks into the hands of local authorities for collection later on.

OUR PORTRAIT GALLERY.

New Jersey is known to strangers chiefly as a fruit and vegetable producing state. Those who frequent its noted seaside resorts see little else in passing through it by rail, but scrub oak, pine-lands and sand. It is, however, a fact that some of the best grain and grass land in the country is found within its borders. Upon this land the production of milk and butter is a rapidly growing industry, and here many noted herds of pure bred animals find a home.

The portrait we hang in our gallery this month is that of one of the state's successful farmers and dairymen, W. B. Lippincott, of Burlington County.

The kind of farmer he is may be inferred from the record of his gross sales for one year from a 139-acre farm, given below. While he does not state what the net profits were, it is safe to suppose that they were satisfactory. The statement is as follows:

Receipts from fruit and truck,	$2,527.69
Product of sixteen cows,	1,686.00
Young calves,	261.00
Hay,	550.86
Chickens, etc.,	177.62
Wheat (badly damaged by fly),	163.80
Total,	$5,366.97

Answering our inquiry as to his method of feeding and management to obtain such excellent results from his cows, he writes: "Their daily ration consists of four quarts of corn and cob meal ground together fine, with one quart of cotton seed meal, and one-half bushel brewery grains. They also receive cut corn stalks and clover hay fed dry. During inclement weather in the winter they are watered in the stable, on pleasant days are allowed a couple of hours in the yard for exercise. In summer they are turned to pasture. The night and morning ration consists of brewery grains and green corn fodder.

"I am satisfied my measure of success may be attributed to the breed of cattle, which is selected registered Jersey. The dairy business with common cows was tried for several years, their product not being satisfactory. Milk is shipped to Philadelphia."

Mr. Lippincott was born forty-three years ago, was reared and now resides on the farm owned by his family for nearly a century. His herd of forty Jersey females is his especial pride.

In 1873 he was married to Catherine B. Braddock. Both are interested in Grange work, Mr. Lippincott being a member of the executive committee of the State Grange.

TOPICS IN SEASON.

THE OUTLOOK.

Pineapple growing in Florida is increasing rapidly.

Peach prospects in Delaware and Maryland are excellent.

The grain and fruit outlook of California is full of promise.

The supply of the best quality of hogs for bacon does not equal the demand.

Abundant crops of fruit are in sight, but we must fight and spray or the insects and fungi will gather them in.

The grass crop of several states recognized as heavy producers is reported to be in a favorable condition.

It is estimated that the orange trees now planted in America will, in five years, yield thirty million boxes, while but eleven million boxes will be required for home consumption.

The wheat prospects at present writing are still unsettled. From all we can gather there has been a large increase in the acreage of spring wheat, quite enough to make up for any loss on account of damage done to winter wheat by unfavorable weather, etc.

THE FARM.

Now sweeter perfumes haunt the fields,
Now warmer shades are hiding
On leafy knolls, in mystic nooks,
Where lovers come with feint of books;
But read instead in downcast looks,
All sager lore deriding.

How they made old-fashioned pork products on the farm

BUTCHERING TIME

(Suggestions taken from the Bulletin of the North Carolina Experiment Station. They are good ones and this is why we copy them.)

AS THE FROSTS begin to whiten the landscape in the early morning, housekeepers in the country begin to plan for the approaching butchering time. Visions of the most substantial additions to the family larder lend enthusiasm as the event approaches, and especially so among the younger members of the household. The good wife and mother views it in a different light, as it will entail much exacting labor upon her and her assistants.

The blazing fire for heating stones; the squealing porkers and the sizzling noise of the heated stones as they are thrown into the water make the hearts of the lads jubilant. Nearby are the tables and clean tubs where the housewife and her assistants await to do their part. The first and most disagreeable task is the ridding of the fat from the intestines; this is best done before they cool; care, cleanliness and patient dexterity are essential in this work; the fat thus removed should be allowed to stand awhile in cold water, when it will make pure, sweet lard.

TO MAKE GOOD HAMS

To make good hams will require good hogs. By that is meant a medium weight hog, which has been properly corn fed, and watered with clean water. The choicest hams and bacon are made from hogs from twelve to eighteen months old, and weighing 125 to 200 pounds.

They are killed on the farms on a cold morning; well bled, well scalded and well *cleaned*. They should hang all day, be housed at night, not allowed to come in contact with each other, and cut and salted next morning.

Do not cut them up the day of killing.

Do not salt the meat before the animal heat has cooled out. More meat is spoiled by the salting and packing in bulk before it is thoroughly cooled than from any other cause.

Cut out the backbone and pull out the ribs. Trim the hams and shoulders close. Leave no surplus bumps or points and make the cuts as shapely as possible. The trimmings are worth more made into sausage and lard than if left to mar the appearance of the cured meat. The sides or middlings should also be carefully trimmed, and one or two four-inch strips cut lengthwise from the thin part, to be cured as breakfast bacon. This is important, as these cuts are much sought after, and bring two and a half cents more per pound than the whole sides, when properly cured.

When the meat has been properly trimmed then the curing begins; use about one pound of ground saltpeter to 400 pounds of meat. That is a heaping teaspoonful to the ham, more or less, according to size. This is rubbed in on the flesh sides and around the bones. Use fine salt and rub it in well, heaping it up on the flesh sides to some extent. Don't cut a gash for salt in the ham. If desired one pound of sugar may be added to each twenty pounds of salt.

The meat should then be packed up in piles on plank flooring of some kind, and raised off of the ground; a plank frame or large trough is better. The platform on which the meat is packed should be slanted so as to allow the melted salt to drip away. In about a week take down the pile, resalt and place the pieces in the pile and let them cure for four or five weeks longer according to size. When the meat is again taken up, brush off the salt and rub well with a tablespoonful of mixed ground pepper—red and black. If you prefer a body to hold this pepper, use a small quantity of good quality molasses well rubbed on; then the mixed peppers.

The joints are now ready to hang for smoking. With large wire needle or small knife, insert strong twine and hang in the upper part of the smokehouse, hock end down, and start a "smudge" or small fire made of green hickory, (preferred,) or red oak, beechwood or corn cobs. Smoke every day for about three weeks, or until the meat has taken on the rich brown color desired; and your hams are now ready for bagging; or if preferred, bagging may be done at time of first hanging.

To bag the hams, make bags of common unbleached sheeting; drop the hams into the bags, hock down, and sew or tie up tight at the top. Then saturate the sacked hams thoroughly in a thick solution of ashes and hot water; or as others prefer, into a lime bath, made up as for whitewashing. These dips serve to exclude all insect pests and to preserve the color and flavor of the meat enclosed.

It is better to hang the hams in the darkest part of the smokehouse.

Shoulders and breakfast strips treated like hams will pay well for the trouble.

SMITHFIELD HAMS

The hams made by a few individuals at Smithfield, Va., have a high reputation under their names, and sell in the best markets of the country at a fancy price—nearly double what ordinary hams sell for. But many hams are now sold under this name that are not produced at Smithfield.

The Smithfield people lay great stress upon proper feeding. In the fall the cultivated fields are thrown open to the hogs and they begin to fatten on the peas, corn-nubbins or pea-nuts left behind in getting in the crops.

From the field the hog is put into the pen and thenceforward fed upon corn and pure water. Absolute cleanliness is insisted upon. Swill-feed is thought to spoil the hams. The hogs when ready for slaughter must neither be too fat nor too lean. To secure the proper condition of flesh many raisers have several killings, thus selecting the animals as they mature. The desirable hog ranges in live weight between 125 and 200 pounds as extreme limits. The Smithfield method does not differ materially from that given above.

SUMMER SAUSAGE

To prepare sausage to be eaten cold next summer, use small, well-baked, earthen pots; take one handful of sausage after another, press firmly into the pot after it is nearly full. Then place in an oven hot enough to bake bread; bake a quarter of an hour for each pound of sausage; that is, if there are eight pounds, bake for two hours; and when done, place a weight on it until it is cold; remove the weight and fill with hot lard. Place upside down on a shelf in a dark, dry corner of the cellar until wanted; then put in the oven long enough to melt the lard; remove the sausage from the pot, and, when cold, slice for the table. Put no sage in sausage that is to be kept so long.

FAMOUS PENNSYLVANIA SCRAPPLE

made of all the scraps of pork not needed for sausage, lard, or for salting. Split the head between the jaws, remove the tongue, which is also used, cut off the end of the snout, remove the jaw-bone, eyes and nasal cavities. The ears may be used, if carefully cleaned, and the cartilage removed after boiling. Put the head meat and the skins, which have been removed from parts intended for lard and sausage, to boil in water to cover them; fifteen minutes after add the other meat, which may include the feet, nicely scraped, the trimmings of the hams and shoulders, the heart, a small part of the liver, and if desired the spleen, cracklings, and the kidneys with the white part all cut out, but these are not generally used. The meat must be boiled until it will separate from the bones, then taken out of the liquid and chopped fine. Strain the liquid to remove the small bones, and add to it enough water to make five parts liquid to three of meat. Set it to boiling, then stir in the meat, with an equal amount of corn-meal, made of new corn, well dried, before grinding, and ground fine. Stir while boiling and season with salt, black and red pepper and either sage, sweet marjoram, thyme or pennyroyal, whichever you prefer. Boil for about fifteen or twenty minutes. Put away in pans in a cold place, when it will keep two or three weeks if the weather is cold. Cut it in slices about an inch thick, lay in a very hot pan, fry only until brown on both sides.

"To the South Jersey boy the hog-killing season is one of as much rejoicing as the Fourth of July"

OUR EDITORIAL PLAN.

It is our constant endeavor to treat all subjects in season; to be concise and to the point; to be practical rather than theoretical; to exclude long-winded discussions and fine-spun theories of fancy farmers; in short, to give our readers CREAM, not skim-milk.

The Editor was born on a farm and reared at the plow handles, and our contributors are mostly practical men and women, who write with their sleeves rolled up, and who briefly and plainly tell the best and most profitable way of doing things on the Farm and in the House, as learned from actual experience.

It is through strict adherence to this plan, in every department, that we are enabled to present as much useful information as the papers costing from four to eight times as much.

WILMER ATKINSON, Editor and Proprietor.

Advertisers like to know which paper benefits them most; therefore, our readers, in answering any advertisement in this paper, will please state that they saw it in the Farm Journal.

FARM FENCE 18 to 24c. Per Rod.
Buchanan Fence Co., Box 256, Smithville, Ohio.

A MACHINE to weave fence of coiled hard steel spring wire at half price of factory fence. $25 buys wire for 100 Rod Fence. Catalogue Free. Address, CarterWire Fence Mach.Co. Box 10, Mt. Sterling, O.

IRON AND WIRE FENCE for Lawn, Farm and Cemetery.
ELLIS & HALFENBERGER, 159 Senate Ave. S. Indianapolis, Ind.

SAVE YOUR CASH
You need fence. The ready made kinds cost from 60 to 75c. a rod. We tell you how to make the best fence on earth for 20 to 35 Cents per Rod. Over 100 Styles, and from 50 to 70 rods per day. Send for our free Catalogue.
KITSELMAN BROTHERS, Box 35 Ridgeville, Indiana, U. S. A.

ORNAMENTAL FENCE!
25 different designs, they are all steel and cheaper than wood fence. Special prices to Churches and Cemeteries. Write us for catalogue.
KOKOMO FENCE MCH. CO., 409 NORTH ST. KOKOMO, IND., U. S. A.

ECONOMY IS THE KEY TO WEALTH.

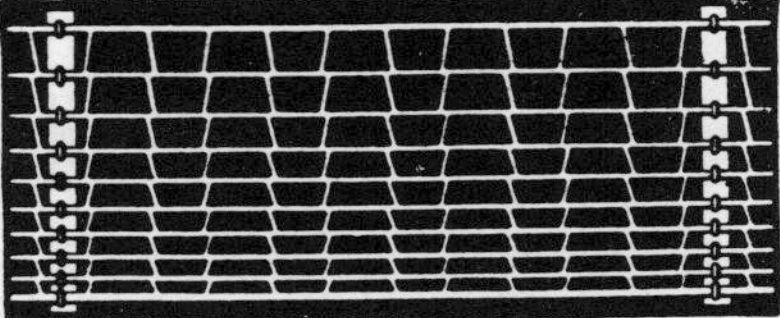

You can save money by buying your woven wire fence from us.
WE SELL DIRECT TO THE FARMER At Wholesale Prices.
We use only the best quality of steel wire, all galvanized; no small wires used; it's all interwoven; the stays can't slip. Write to-day for circulars and prices.
ADVANCE FENCE CO., 101 Old St., Peoria, Ill.

Do you want to go South? if so write to-day for our Journal free. It tells you about our great Chicora Colony and the finest of land for trucking, fruit and stock raising; the land of figs and tea. Land $5 per acre. Houses built and sold on $5 monthly payments. Cheap excursions weekly. D. L. RISLEY, 211 South Tenth St., Phila., Pa.

HOG KILLING DAYS IN SOUTH JERSEY

The animals for the killing are always in prime condition. When the day dawns for the killing there is an unusual stir about house and farm. The neighbors come early. All of the members of the family and the neighbors' families are present. Each man and boy, as well as each woman, is assigned to his or her part of the work. The killer does nothing except kill. Boys heat and carry water for the scalders and scrapers, whose work it is to remove the bristles and prepare the animal for the cutters, who take it when the carcass is cold, trim each part, and distribute them in the proper receptacles. If it is the ham or shoulder it is cared for by the master trimmer. As the feet and head go to the house for the women, who possess some secret whereby those parts of a porker are reduced to delicacies, the man who has this job is generally unmarried, and always a ladies' man. He and the killer are rivals if both are single.

A dinner in the house follows the day's work and to this, of course, every participant is invited. The dinner is oftentimes followed by a dance or some of the old-fashioned games of which copenhagen is a prime favorite.

To the South Jersey boy the hog-killing season is one of as much rejoicing as the Fourth of July. His interest lies in the fact that he is allowed to roast the pigs' tails in the ashes and also becomes the possessor of the bladder. These are inflated and used as foot balls, or are hung up until Christmas, and when taken down are exploded, the report fairly rivaling a gun shot.

Farmer's Handy Feed Cooker.

Reader's attention is called to this device, which is sold at $12.50 for 50-gallon capacity. By feeding poultry and animals cooked food during winter, at least one-third of the feed is saved; also having stock in a healthy condition, preventing hog cholera among your hogs, and insuring the hens laying freely during the winter months. On application to the Empire Manufacturing Co., Quincy, Ills., a catalogue giving full description may be obtained. They are made in all sizes.

THROW AWAY that horse-killing, out-of-date field roller and buy a machine that will make farming profitable. *The best field roller on earth* is made by the H.P.DEUSCHER CO.Hamilton,Ohio Write them for full partic'rs.

Farmer's Favorite
This is a thoroughly reliable, well made feed cooker, that is sold at a reasonable price. Best gray iron furnace, best galvanized steel boiler. In addition to cooking feed for stock and poultry it is unexcelled for heating water for scalding hogs, rendering lard, boiling sap, sugaring off, &c. Don't buy until you send for our free circulars and prices. It may save you money.
L. R. LEWIS, 17 Main St., Cortland, N. Y.

The Purchase of our FEED COOKER will pay the Farmer, Stock Raiser and Dairyman more profit on the investment than any article on the farm. Send for circular and prices of the best.
HENION & HUBBELL, 61-69 N. Jefferson St., Chicago, Ill.

AGENTS WANTED EVERYWHERE to sell the best Family Knitting Machine ever invented. Will knit a pair of stockings, with HEEL and TOE complete, in 20 minutes. It will also knit a great variety of fancy-work for which there is always a ready market. Send for circular and terms to the Twombly Knitting Machine Co., 409 Washington St., Boston, Mass.

JELLY. How made from cider. Sample by mail. J. A. WILSON, Chester Depot, Vt.

SEND a 2c. Stamp to the NORTH-WESTERN HIDE & FUR COMPANY, Minneapolis, Minn., and get a vast amouut of valuable information.

HIGHEST PRICES for RAW FURS. Send for list. Refer., 1st Nat'l Bank. LEMUEL BLACK, Hightstown, N. J.

SKUNK Highest Price paid for Skunk and other furs. Send stamp to M. J. JEWETT, Redwood, Jeff. Co., N. Y.

SKINS TANNED For Robes. SEND us your cattle and horse hides, calf, sheep and all kinds of fur skins to be tanned for Robes, Overcoats, Rugs, etc., to be returned to you. Left soft, smooth and moth proof. We guarantee satisfaction. Send for circular, tags, etc.
THE FOSTER ROBE & TANNING CO., Minneapolis, Minn.

Meat smoked in a few hours with KRAUSERS' LIQUID EXTRACT OF SMOKE. Made from hickory wood. Cheaper, cleaner, sweeter, and surer than the old way. Send for circular. E. KRAUSER & BRO., Milton, Pa.

COW HOPPLE FOR KICKING COWS either from habit or sore teats. By mail 50c. Also WART CURE
Guaranteed to remove warts from horses, cows' teats or man. Postpaid at 25 and 50 cents. Send for circulars. Agents wanted.
HENRY BASSETT. Salem, New Jersey.

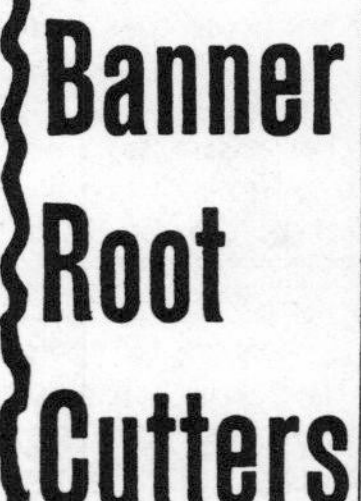

CUT BEETS, MANGELS, Turnips, Carrots, and all other roots and vegetables for stock feeding. CUT FINE. Choking Impossible. Run easy, have self feeder, separate dirt from cut feed. Five sizes, hand and power.
O. E. THOMPSON & SONS, Ypsilanti, Mich.
Largest Root Cutter makers in the world. *Catalogue free.*

THIS IS OUR VISITING CARD
The Appleton No. 9 Fodder Cutter
A Foretaste of "Appleton Quality."
Simply for the purpose of acquainting you with the superiority of "Appleton Quality" we have built the best exclusively hand fodder cutter on the market and will sell it at an extremely low price. It is as complete a machine for its purpose as any of our justly celebrated "New Hero" Ensilage and Fodder Cutters. Has 2 heavy 9-in. knives, 2 changes of cut, etc. Everybody will want one, and as the supply is limited, you should order at once to be sure of getting one. Should you want a larger power ensilage and fodder cutter or shredder, a husker, sheller, horse power, feed grinder, wood saw, wind mill, steel tanks, etc., we can supply you "Appleton Quality"—which is the best—there also. 160 page convincing catalogue mailed free.
APPLETON MFG. CO., 13 Fargo St., Batavia, Ill.

Technology is coming on fast

MORE TELEPHONES

The subject of rural telephone lines evidently interests Our Folks.

A Minnesota subscriber writes: "I am connected with a system which to us all has proven very cheap and durable. We use the Bell and Madison telephones, and the telephones are very important parts of a system. The line was built by us all, nine of us, and we got the privilege of putting the wire on the poles of another telephone company, and by means of a switch we are connected with this main line and act as sort of feeders for this company. It gives the neighbors a chance to use the company's line without going to the office in town.

"Telephones at $8, the wire at $4 per mile, and insulators and brackets at three cents for both, make a fine line and a cheap one."

A Virginia man writes: "Two years ago a small number of enterprising citizens in Rockingham county, in the Shenandoah Valley, formed themselves into a company for the purpose of building and operating a telephone system.

"We began with a nucleus of two lines and twenty-four members. It looked like a small beginning, and a great many of the wise-acres laughed at us. But on account of the vast resources of the country, and the peculiarly enterprising nature of the people, we hoped for success. We did not, however, expect such phenomenal success as since attended our efforts. In fact, after we once got things started we had to make no effort. The most serious question was how to accommodate so many. We overcame this difficulty, however, and to-day instead of the two lines and twenty-four members we have over one hundred lines and upwards of a thousand members. We also operate ten exchanges, and have run "commercial" lines to adjoining counties, towns and cities where there are located similar companies. By this means all our members have access to at least five thousand telephones. All the towns and cities in the valley are connected by wires, so that it would be possible for me to send a message from my telephone to Hagerstown or Baltimore. All this I get at the insignificant expense of $2 per annum, which goes to maintain the switchboard and pay the operator. I should not neglect to say we have a continuous day, night and Sunday service, and get the weather reports two hours after they are made out in Washington.

"Of course it would be impossible to accomplish such magnificent results unless you begin right. Your exchange must be located at the most business and central point, the lines must be properly constructed, and above all else the instruments must be of the best quality. There are but three or four standard instruments, and even among these there is a vast difference. Evidently a telephone constructed for a city exchange where there is but one on a line, will not work on a long country line where there are perhaps a dozen or more. If it is intended for this latter purpose it must be especially designed and constructed for it.

"In the cities the Series system is most satisfactory; on the long country lines it is a makeshift, at best. Here you want the multiple or bridging system. A first-class instrument with occasional repairing ought to be good at the end of ten years, and talk and ring distinctly one hundred miles. I have one that cost $16, that under favorable conditions will work nicely twice the distance."

An Indiana subscriber gives the cost of one mile of line as follows:

"Poles can be supplied by the farmers themselves, and they should be eighteen feet long, five feet in the ground and 150 feet apart.

"One mile of No. 14 galvanized telephone wire will cost you $3. Then you want twenty-four glass pony insulators and brackets. They will cost you $1.90, and binding wires for same thirty cents. Eighty feet No. 18 office wire thirty cents. Two No. 4 Kokomo transmitters will cost you $13 each, or $31.50 for line material, minus the post.

"You can get cheaper transmitters, but the one above mentioned is sure to give satisfaction.

"You can cut in as many telephones as you please on above line, but I only mention two for the sake of convenience."

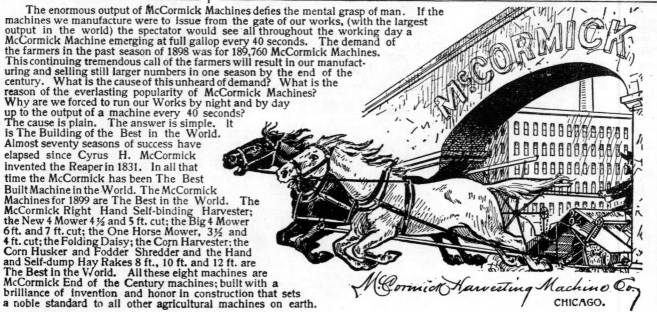

THERE IS THE BEST FEED COOKER ON THE MARKET

No Cooker offers a single real advantage which the "**Heesen**" lacks. It is the simplest, never out of order, and lasts for generations. It is quickest in heating, holds fire longest, is most economical of fuel, and burns anything. Wood or coal.

THE HEESEN FEED COOKER

is Guaranteed Full Measure. We don't stamp 50 gallon size "70 gallons." The "**Heesen**" will save one-third purchase money, and all cost of repairs. Seven sizes—15 to 70 gals. *Money back if not satisfactory.* Sold only direct from factory to farmer. Send for catalogue.

HEESEN BROS. & CO., 15 High Street, Tecumseh, Mich.

The enormous output of McCormick Machines defies the mental grasp of man. If the machines we manufacture were to issue from the gate of our works, (with the largest output in the world) the spectator would see all throughout the working day a McCormick Machine emerging at full gallop every 40 seconds. The demand of the farmers in the past season of 1898 was for 189,760 McCormick Machines. This continuing tremendous call of the farmers will result in our manufacturing and selling still larger numbers in one season by the end of the century. What is the cause of this unheard of demand? What is the reason of the everlasting popularity of McCormick Machines? Why are we forced to run our Works by night and by day up to the output of a machine every 40 seconds? The cause is plain. The answer is simple. It is The Building of the Best in the World. Almost seventy seasons of success have elapsed since Cyrus H. McCormick invented the Reaper in 1831. In all that time the McCormick has been The Best Built Machine in the World. The McCormick Machines for 1899 are The Best in the World. The McCormick Right Hand Self-binding Harvester; the New 4 Mower 4½ and 5 ft. cut; the Big 4 Mower 6 ft. and 7 ft. cut; the One Horse Mower, 3½ and 4 ft. cut; the Folding Daisy; the Corn Harvester; the Corn Husker and Fodder Shredder and the Hand and Self-dump Hay Rakes 8 ft., 10 ft. and 12 ft. are The Best in the World. All these eight machines are McCormick End of the Century machines; built with a brilliance of invention and honor in construction that sets a noble standard to all other agricultural machines on earth.

McCORMICK

McCormick Harvesting Machine Co.
CHICAGO.

Coupons Pouring In!

Everybody Buying at the New Cut Prices

Your Coupon Is in the Lower Left Hand Corner of This Page. Fill It Out NOW!

We believe the Economy Chief is the best and most satisfactory cream separator on the market today, regardless of price. We believe it to be the best in design, the closest skimming, the easiest running, the quickest cleaning; in short, the greatest separator value that money can buy. We have absolute confidence in the Economy Chief and we want every owner of cows to share this confidence with us. We want everyone interested in buying a cream separator to have an opportunity to find out for himself which is the best machine, which is THE SEPARATOR TO BUY.

Here Is the Challenge Offer That Is Bringing in the Orders by Every Mail

Deposit in your local bank the price of the Economy Chief Cream Separator you want to try, or

Send us a letter of reference from your banker stating that you are a reliable person; then

We will ship to you at once, freight prepaid, the separator you order, with the understanding that you are to set it up and try it on your farm for sixty days. Give it the hardest kind of a test; if possible try it alongside some other well known standard make, such as the Empire, United States or De Laval. Compare our machine in actual operation with any other. Note the amount of cream you get from each. Compare ease of running, time consumed in cleaning, and make any other comparisons you can think of. Never mind about the price; what you want from a cream separator is CREAM. If any other machine selling even as high as $85.00 or $90.00 will do better work, will skim closer, will give better satisfaction than our Economy Chief at $42.50, our advice to you is, buy the other machine and send ours back.

REDUCED PRICES FOR 1910

WE RECOMMEND THE BIG 600-POUND SIZE

No. 23T51 New 1910 Economy Chief. Capacity, 250 to 300 pounds, or 120 to 145 quarts per hour. Price reduced to	**$27.90**
No. 23T52 New 1910 Economy Chief. Capacity, 350 to 400 pounds, or 170 to 195 quarts per hour. Price reduced to	**33.80**
No. 23T54 New 1910 Economy Chief. Capacity, 600 pounds, or about 290 quarts per hour Price reduced to	**42.50**

When you have finished your sixty-day test, if you are perfectly satisfied that you have the best separator on the market, write us saying that you want to keep the machine, and we will send you a bill for your separator and the freight charges we paid on it.

If at the end of sixty days you are not satisfied that the Economy Chief is the world's best separator, you don't need to even tell us the reason for your dissatisfaction unless you wish to; just drop us a line saying you don't want the machine. We will then send you a return address card to tack on the box **and we will not only return all money sent us, but also pay you for your time and trouble in setting up the machine, repacking it and hauling back to the station. We don't want you to lose one penny in trying out the Economy Chief for sixty days.**

If you want to send cash with your order, as most of our customers do, you won't lose any of the benefit of the above CHALLENGE OFFER, for if at the end of sixty days you decide you don't want the machine, if you think after a sixty days' trial you can get along just as well without a separator, or if you have seen a separator in operation giving better results than the Economy Chief, just send it back at our expense, tell us how much we owe you for freight charges, hauling from and to the station, setting up and repacking, and we will promptly send you every cent of the purchase price, plus your bill.

THIS IS OUR CHALLENGE OFFER AND OUR WHOLE CREAM SEPARATOR PROPOSITION!

We think our Economy Chief Separator is the best machine in the world. We want to sell you an Economy Chief if you think the same as we do, not otherwise, and we make this challenge offer to give you a chance to find out all about the Economy Chief **at our expense** and to prove our confidence in our own machine.

IF THE MAKER OF ANY OTHER CREAM SEPARATOR IN THE WORLD BELIEVES IN HIS MACHINE AS WE BELIEVE IN OURS, LET HIM MAKE YOU THE SAME PROPOSITION WE DO.

That's all—Now fill out the Coupon!

FILL OUT THIS SPECIAL ORDER BLANK

☐ **CASH WITH ORDER.** If you are enclosing the full price, simply write the amount in this square.

☐ **CASH IN BANK.** You can deposit the purchase price of the separator with your local banker, to be held by him for a month while you are trying it. If you follow this plan make an **X** mark in this square and enclose your certificate of deposit signed by your banker.

☐ **BANK REFERENCE.** If you prefer not to send us the money, or to hold it in the bank subject to our order, make an **X** mark in this square and enclose a letter of reference signed by your banker, telling us you are a responsible property owner.

☐ **FREE DAIRY GUIDE.** Nearly everybody has a copy of our big General Catalog or our Cream Separator Catalog, but if you have not and want more information before ordering, make an **X** mark in this space.

Name ______________________

Postoffice ______________ **State** ______________

Shipping Point ______________ **State** ______________

R.F.D. No. ________ **P. O. Box No.** ________ **Street and No.** ________

Send me by freight on trial ____ **Economy Chief Cream Separator**

Size ______________ **Price** ______________

Farm Journal. (Please write plainly and carefully.)

SEARS, ROEBUCK AND CO., CHICAGO

THE FOUR-HORSE TEAM

BY JOHN M. STAHL

Saves Labor—Therefore Saves Money—Gets Work Done in Season—Does it Better—Is Up-to-date Business Farming, etc.

FARM labor is very scarce.

The complaint about the scarcity of good farm labor comes from all parts of the country, but especially from the upper Mississippi valley, where many of Our Folks live.

Farmers are paying for labor more than they feel they can afford to pay, yet can not get as much of it as they need.

Legislation has favored the manufacturer and railway man and banker and has not been just to the farmer.

That with some other things has made city labor more attractive and has drained the farm of its best labor.

But crops must be raised before we can remedy that.

To Our Folks everywhere, but especially to those in the upper Mississippi valley and wherever the land is smooth, we commend the four-horse team.

Many of Our Folks are already using the four-horse team.

With it one man can do nearly as much work in one day as he can in two days with two horses.

And with the four-horse team he can do better work oftener than poorer work as compared with the two-horse team.

With the heavy gang or sulky plow better plowing can be done in hard, dry ground than with the smaller plow.

The heavy plow will run steady and cut a uniform furrow and turn it well, where the light plow will wabble in spite of all the plowman can do.

The gang or sulky plow holds itself; the plowman must hold the lighter walking plow.

When one puts four strong horses to the disc harrow he can weight it down and ride on it.

He will get over more ground than if he has only two horses. He will also be able to do better work, for when it is well weighted down it goes to the bottom of the seed bed.

When one puts the four-horse team on the harrow he has a seed bed good all the way through and not on top only.

A cultivator that cultivates two rows is now manufactured and it is very popular where known.

Why not cultivate two rows at once instead of only half a row or only one row?

A good profit in farming will lie along the line of introducing the four-horse team idea wherever and whenever practicable.

It halves the expense for man labor.

Labor is money.

In many neighborhoods the two-horse team and even the three-horse team are already behind the times.

They are classed along with the negro, his mule, little plow and rope harness in the South.

Put four horses on to the self-binder and they can pull it along at a brisk rate without overtaxing themselves.

Four horses on the self-binder is business, if they are good, strong ones.

The farmer who wears the smile is going to be the man who is right up to date and possibly a little ahead.

He is the four-horse team man—the man who saves labor and all other expense whenever he can without any hurt to the quality of the work.

The farm is all right.

It is the best place in the world for the brainy, thinking, progressive man.

It will pay well for all the brains and thought he can give it.

He will have a windmill or gasoline engine to pump water, run the cream separator, saw wood, grind feed, churn, and so on; he will have the latest machinery that has been proved valuable; he will use the four-horse team.

Because economy is the road to wealth and such things economize labor.

But horses are still tops

HORSE COLIC—PREVENTION—CURE

BY JOHN M. STAHL

An Old-time Remedy That Seldom Fails—Causes of Colic—How to Prevent—Care in Feeding, etc.

The books learnedly distinguish several kinds of horse colic and give different remedies for each, but a remedy that will cure nearly every case of horse colic is turpentine.

When my father was a young man, before the days of railways, the goods used west of the Alleghanies were freighted from Philadelphia in great wagons, drawn by six-horse teams.

The men who drove these teams were great horsemen and had more real knowledge of horse ailments than some veterinarians have.

Their favorite remedy for colic was turpentine. An old driver told my father that in forty-eight years' experience he had never known it to fail. My father used it for fifty

On this page are advertisements of caster wheel, silos, mills, cutters, hay presses, drills and buggies.

ADVERTISEMENTS

When you write to an advertiser tell him that you saw his card in the Farm Journal. It is to your interest to do so, as Our Folks are treated honestly and served with the best. Read the Fair Play notice on first page.

NO NECK-WEIGHT. Get caster wheel for **binder** tongue. J. L. MARTIN, Clarence Ctr., N. Y.

For 40 Years

The above U. S. Registered Trade-Mark has been a safeguard to the farmer that he made no mistake in buying

Farmers' Favorite Grain Drills

For 1903 we offer to the Farmer many improvements and new devices of proven merit:

Steel Ribbon Grain Tubes,
New Balanced Angle-Steel Frame,
"Plowfur" Single Disc, Extension Chilled Hub,
"Perfection" Grass Seeder,
Improved Box and Roller Bearings.

Our **FREE** Grain Drill Literature tells all about it. Write for it to-day.

BICKFORD & HUFFMAN DIVISION
American Seeding Machine Company,
Dept. A. Springfield, Ohio.

OUR TOP BUGGY AT $24.95

Write for FREE VEHICLE CATALOG

exemplifies the wonderful vehicle values we offer in our **FREE VEHICLE CATALOG** which we send gratis to anyone on application. It illustrates and describes in detail the largest and most complete line of vehicles in the world (every kind made); tells all about the woodwork, trimming, ironing, painting and finish, gives hundreds of testimonials from people using our vehicles, and proves decisively that **ours are the best made, most stylish, strongest, finest finished and lowest priced vehicles manufactured.** Prominent among our specials are our

Extra Top Buggy	$24.95	Full Leath. Top Buggy	$55.00
RubberDrillTopBuggy	27.80	Extra Road Wagon	22.35
Leath.Quatr.top Buggy	27.90	Canopy Top Surrey	45.95
Leath.Quatr.top Buggy	32.95	Leath.Quatr.topSurrey	63.50
Leath.Quatr.top Buggy	39.50	Road Cart	9.25

Stanhopes, Phætons, Pony Rigs, Delivery Rigs and Farm Wagons at correspondingly low prices. **WE HAVE FACTORIES IN OHIO, MICHIGAN, MISSOURI AND INDIANA,** and ship direct from factory nearest customer's home, thus insuring prompt and safe delivery and low freight charges. **We guarantee our vehicles 2 years,** ship on easy terms, and extend every courtesy possible to accommodate our customers. No matter what others say, **send for our catalog before buying.** We lead in price, quality, style, guarantee and terms, and will save you money. **HARNESS AND HORSE GOODS** at lowest prices. Address **JOHN M. SMYTH COMPANY** 150 TO 170 WEST MADISON STREET **CHICAGO, ILLINOIS**

From Factory to Horse

MURRAY

Vehicles, Harness and Saddles are well known to all "Farm Journal" readers, as they have been advertised in this journal for the past 14 years, and thousands of "Farm Journal" readers are numbered among our valued patrons. Always offering a superior line of leading styles, our new line of "Murray" Vehicles for 1904 is even larger and more attractive than heretofore, and we know our 176-page catalogue, wherein we illustrate, describe and offer at tempting prices our complete line, will interest you.

Eighteen years of honest and straightforward business reputation is back of every "Murray" Vehicle, Harness and Saddle, and they cost no more than the unknown and questionable kind.

If you are pleased with our goods and business methods it is quite natural you will speak a good word for us to your neighbor, and it is on this simple principle of turning out only such work as in itself has brought us thousands of repeat orders and new customers, that has enabled us, from a modest beginning, to build up our business to its present mammoth proportions. We have at all times adhered strictly to this principle, and have never offered any "schemes" or "baits" to effect a sale of our product, but offer them solely on their well-established merits and low prices. In purchasing a "Murray" Vehicle, Harness or Saddle you are dealing with a known quantity and with a brand that has been time-tried and tested.

We place a guarantee of two years against breakage on all our goods, and a "Murray" guar antee means something, as it is backed up by our 18 years of continued success as leaders in our line.

Our line is exceptionally complete, and consists of Buggies, Stanhopes, Road Wagons, Driving Wagons, Bike Wagons, Phaetons, Surreys, Road Carts, Jump-seats, Traps, Spring Wagons, Delivery Wagons, Milk Wagons, Mail Wagons, Baker Wagons, Butcher Wagons, Laundry Wagons, Pony Vehicles, Farm Wagons, Farm Carts, Harness and Saddles, all of which we offer to you at lowest factory prices, with one small margin above actual cost of production.

A visit to our factory will convince you that we carry a larger stock of finished vehicles than any other factory in Cincinnati or the United States. Send for our new 176-page illustrated and descriptive catalogue No. 73; it is free for the asking. We are anxious to mail it to you.

WILBER H. MURRAY MFG. CO.

Nos. 323, 325, 327, 329 E. 5th St., CINCINNATI, OHIO.

Murray Surrey Seat Buggy. Price........................ **$44.90**

Murray Rubber Tire Driving Wagon. Price.................... **$44.00**

Murray Leather Quarter Top Buggy. Price.................. **$35.50**

Murray Canopy Top Surrey. Price.............................. **$59.75**

Murray Single Buggy Harness. Price...................................... **$4.68**

Murray Rubber Tire Buggy. Price.............................. **$59.50**

Murray Farm Wagon. Price.............................. **$26.95**

Murray Road Wagon. Price.................................. **$26.90**

Murray Jump-seat Buggy. Price.................................. **$49.50**

Murray Cut-under Surrey. Price.................................. **$72.00**

Murray Double Buggy Harness. Price......................... **$13.98**

Murray Top Delivery Wagon. Price.................................. **$54.75**

Murray Delivery Wagon. Price.................................. **$36.50**

April 1904

ODD MENTION

Old Year, dying, say farewell,
Soon will sound thy funeral knell;
New Year, come with hope sublime,
To the tune of gladsome chime.
Memory clings to joys gone by,
Sorrowing that the year must die;
But the future beckons fair,
Tells of pleasures we may share;
Hope leads onward, bright of view—
Farewell, old Year: welcome New.

No man can ever rise above that which he aims at.

Don't drive the hired man. Good men are often spoiled by hard masters.

The wonderful press of ours—have you seen it go? Two copies a second, just as you see the paper you hold in your hands. Drop in.

Lose no time in mulching the strawberry bed. Use strawy horse manure, and put it on three inches deep. Do as we say; don't flinch.

Washing made easy. No more stooping, rubbing or boiling

Avoid digging potatoes immediately after a rain. The keeping quality of potatoes is impaired by allowing them to lie in the sun long after digging. As soon as the earth on them is a little dry, gather them up and cart them to the cellar. Sprinkle air-slaked lime on the floor before the potatoes are emptied on it, and also sprinkle a little between each layer.

No live farmer will plow around a stump for four or five years wearing out his plow and his patience and wasting his land and labor. Blow them up or pull them out. If you want something to help pull, and to give you "a lift" write to H. L. Bennett, Westerville, O. He manufactures the Davis Stump Puller, illustrated herewith. We think it is a good thing.

“The auto is a fad . . . this is certain.” But the editor was a prophet on energy

FARMER’S PROBLEMS

I

IT is a common expression that the automobile “has come to stay,” but no one can be certain that this is true. This could have been truly said of the horse many thousands of years ago, and it can be said now for a surety that he “*is* here to stay.” Human beings, many of them at least, *love* horses; but it must be a strange kind of a person of whom it can be truthfully said, “He loves a gasoline engine.” There is, of course, a certain exhilaration in riding at a rapid rate, which many persons enjoy (even on forbidden·ground), and the machine that will get one along at twenty or thirty miles an hour has its admirers; but compel the machine to run at a moderate rate, say ten miles an hour, and few will care for it. In neither case can there be the feeling of affection between the rider and the machine, such as exists in man toward the horse.

II

The comparative *staying* power of the horse and the auto is involved in the question of the permanence of the *source* of power, the lands of the earth subject to tillage, and the oil wells and coal mines, discovered and discoverable. At this time the power used for driving the auto comes from oil or coal or water, nothing else has yet been discovered; and are we assured of a permanence in the supply of all these? A few hundred years, at furthest, may see the oil wells pumped dry and the coal mines exhausted; but the oats and corn, the wheat and hay, we are pretty certain of for ages to come. Those who say so airily that the “auto has come to stay,” rather imply by that expression that the “horse must go,” than which nothing could be further from the truth. The age that witnesses the departure of the horse will doubtless also observe the disappearance of man himself. They will go off together.

III

The auto is a fad just now, this is certain; as the bicycle was, with this difference: the bicycle fad extended to the entire population, while this later craze does not touch more than one in five hundred—except to annoy those whom it has not touched. The bicycle is here to stay, for certain utilitarian purposes, and no other; and the auto will have its uses, especially in the cities, from this on. But the present racing craze will die out; it will have to, for the people will not put up with it.

IV

THE PASSING OF THE HORSE

Every little while they tell us that the horse
has got to go;
First the trolley was invented ’cause the
horses went so slow,
And they told us that we’d better not keep
raisin’ colts no more.
When the street cars got to moting that the
horses pulled before
I thought it was all over for old Fan and
Doll and Kit—
S’posed the horse was up and done for—
But——he——ain’t——went——yit!

When the bike craze first got started people
told us right away,
As you probably remember, that the horse
had saw his day;
People put away their buggies and went
kitin’ round on wheels;
There were lots and lots of horses didn’t
even earn their meals.
I used to stand and watch ’em with their
bloomers as they’d flit,
And I thought the horse was goin’—
But——he——ain’t——went——yit!

Then they got the horseless carriage, and
they said the horse was done,
And the story’s been repeated twenty times
by Edison;
Every time he gets another of his batteries
to go

The first auto ad in Farm Journal, July 1908

“Get There”
at a price to suit
you direct for a
BLACK
MOTOR BUGGY
$375.00 $450.00
Built for country roads, hills and mud. Engine—10 H. P., 2 cylinders, air cooled, chain drive rear wheels, double break. Speed 2 to 25 m. per hr.—30 miles on 1 gal. of gasoline. Highest quality finish, workmanship and materials. Absolutely safe and reliable. Write for Book No. A-96.
BLACK MFG. CO., 124 E. Ohio St., Chicago, Ill.

ruthlessly taking possession of all the best roads to the detriment of the folks who made the roads and who are taxed to keep them in repair, and the word we get is that great indignation exists everywhere, and is rising to a higher pitch, month by month. The plaint, in some cases, is pitiful.

VI

One writer living in New York state says, “We never go to the city now excepting when it is actually necessary; and hardly anywhere else, for the most of the roads are narrow with very little room to turn out, so it would be a matter of life or death to meet one of those machines, of which there are several around here. There is no justice in one person indulging in a pleasure that endangers the life and property of another, and if the farmers have to find their future pleasure inside their own gates, there will be more boys and girls leaving for the city than have left yet. Let the automobilists build their own race courses. We have need of our roads for better uses.” G. C.

VII

Another writes: “I was going to town the other day and saw one of the auto enemies coming. I could not get out a handkerchief to signal, so I said, “Stop,” and the driver would not stop. I was thrown out, my horse ran away, my carriage was all smashed and the auto driver was not willing to pay any damage in the end.” The above letter is from a lady who is afraid to go to town again.

Another case from New Jersey: “We dare not go even to the village store for fear of meeting one of those autos. We must pay our taxes and help to keep the roads in a travelable condition, and dare not go out on them. Making the autos to stop would not help us, for our horses are afraid of them anywhere, under any circumstances.” This writer pleads for at least one day in the week, in which the autos are kept off the roads so he can drive out.

VIII

Herman Blenker, aged seventy, was dragged to death by a team of horses which he was driving, and which took fright at an automobile and ran away. He was unconscious when the horses were stopped and lived only about three minutes.

“There are five in our family,” writes another, “deprived of using the public roads because of the automobile nuisance. We dare not travel for fear of our lives. Many in this neighborhood are deprived of going to the neighboring town, of visiting relatives or even of going to church, on account of those frightful flying devils, dreadful enough to frighten even an old blind and deaf horse by the strong scent of gasoline.” From Kansas we have this: “We women dare not go to town for our purchases, so we have decided to send to the large stores in New York, Chicago and St. Louis, and have our goods freighted.” This writer thanks the FARM JOURNAL and says “Don’t forget to give those automobilists another blast.”

IX

We could fill the FARM JOURNAL full of complaints of this kind and many worse, detailing terrible accidents in which persons were injured for life, limbs broken and nerves shattered. It is true not all automobilists are so contemptuous of the rights of rural people, but that makes no difference as to the fact that the drivers of horses are liable at any time to meet the reckless driver, and suffer a runaway and smash-up in consequence. Even the well-meaning, usually careful driver not infrequently thinks he must “get there” by a certain time, and takes risks—with other people’s life and property—that he would not take with his own, especially if he is a distance from home where he is not known. The automobilist ought to keep off the public roads altogether, or behave himself.

October 1904

The question arises, Why not have roads made purposely for automobiles? These machines have their uses and should have a fair chance. And they would give far greater satisfaction to their owners if they could be speeded to their limit. Restrictive laws and ordinances are being passed everywhere, requiring them to go slow; on their own speedways they could travel easily fifty miles an hour and “get there” in advance of the locomotive. Would this not be better than to poke along on the horse’s road, and, besides, driving all the women on to the back roads, or keeping them at home altogether? Both vehicles would do better with a clear track, would they not?

MR. AUTO: “OUT OF MY WAY.” MR. HORSE: “WHO OWNS THIS HIGHWAY, ANYHOW?” MR. AUTO: “WELL, YOU DON’T.” MR. HORSE: “WELL, WHO WAS HERE FIRST, AND WHO HELPED TO BUILD IT—DID YOU?”

April 1904

When acetylene was the latest

How Lamps Eat the Life Out of Air.

HERE is a Lighting Test worth trying!

Take a common dinner plate.

Pour half a glass of water into it.

Then set an inch of candle upright in the water.

Then light the candle wick.

Now, turn an empty glass upside down on the plate, over the candle while it is still burning briskly as in picture No. 1.

—And note what happens!

The candle will die out a moment after the glass has been turned over it. Then the water will rush up *into* the glass, from off the level plate, and it

Fig. 1.

will *stay* in the upside-down glass which you can then turn over, plate upwards, without spilling. (See Figure 2.)

Now *why* does the candle die out so suddenly when the glass encloses it?

And *why* does the water rush *up* into the inverted glass after the candle has been lighted in it?

Because, the flame has instantly burnt out all the Oxygen of the Air which was originally in the glass.

That left a vacancy where the Oxygen used to be—a vacuum.

And that vacuum caused a *suction* which drew the water upward into the glass, like a pump, to take the place of the burnt-out Oxygen.

The candle flame died out so suddenly because no flame can *live* without Oxygen—just as no Animal nor Vegetable can *live* without Oxygen.

You see, the Air is about one-fifth Oxygen.

And, when you burn that vital fifth out of it with flame, or use it up in breathing, you take the very *Life* out of the Air. What then remains is chiefly poisonous Carbonic Acid.

You couldn't live *five* minutes in a room that had *all* the Oxygen burnt out of it.

Nor could you light a lamp, a match, nor a fire, in a room that had not considerable Oxygen left in it to support the flame.

If you want to *prove* this try the following experiment:

Take the same drinking glass as in previous Test and throw a lighted match into it.

That match will *burn* freely.

Then light another match, breathe outward *deeply into the glass* twice, with your face pressing against its edge closer than in picture. Then *quickly* drop the lighted match into it.

The flame will, *this* time, *die out instantly*.

What causes its sudden extinction?

Well, here is the cause: The Oxygen you breathe *inwardly*, with the Air, to your lungs, goes into your blood to purify it.

And, the Air you breathe *outwardly* from your lungs has therefore no Oxygen left in it to feed the flame of the match. It is full of Carbonic Acid—full of poisonous waste products, like the foul Air in a room from which the Oxygen has been exhausted through lamps or overbreathing.

You see Carbonic Acid is *death* to flame, just as it is *death* to Human Beings who re-breathe it too often without enough ventilation.

As we breathe 16 to 20 times a minute you will readily see what happens to our Lungs, Blood, and System, when we burn Kerosene Lamps, Gasoline-Gas, or City Gas, year in and year out, in our living and sleeping rooms.

These Lights burn a great deal of the *Life* out of Air—its Blood-purifying and Germ-destroying Oxygen.

And they leave behind an injurious excess of Carbonic Acid in the air we must breathe after it.

* * *

Now this excess of Carbonic Acid Gas, with want of Oxygen, in the foul Air of a room creates six injurious conditions:

1st,—It causes the Blood to partially stagnate.

2nd,—It causes the Muscles to feel Tired.

3rd,—It causes the Heart to act slowly.

4th,—It causes the Digestion to Delay.

5th,—It causes Headache, through clogging of Blood in the Brain.

6th,—It causes Catarrh of the Nose, Throat and Air passages.

These are well-known, easily proved, Facts. Ask your Doctor!

Of course, *you* may not have noticed these effects at the time the Lamps were burning, or if you did notice them you may not have *known* they were caused by want of Oxygen and excess of Carbonic Acid.

But, you may rely upon this—

In some degree these effects are produced *every time* you burn a Kerosene Lamp, or City Gas Jet, in the living or sleeping room, without wide open windows that create a draught to replace the burnt Oxygen.

And that Lighted Lamp, or City Gas Jet, for 365 nights in the year, eats up, little by little, a large share of the Energy and Life you get from Food and Sunlight.

That loss to your Health amounts to more than *you* probably *think* it does, year after year.

Put a lighted Kerosene Lamp in a closed up room and it will indicate your loss.

You'll find that lamp will burn itself out in time, though there be plenty of oil in the bowl and plenty of wick in the burner.

The flame will *die* out for *want of the very Oxygen it consumed.*

Now, *this* is where *Acetylene Light* comes into the story.

Acetylene Light uses up only *one-fourth* as much Oxygen as Kerosene Light, Gasoline Light, or City Gaslight does.

And, it leaves less than a *tenth* as much Poisonous Carbonic Acid in the Air that a Kerosene Lamp, a Gasoline Light, or a City Gaslight, of equal candle power leaves.

Moreover! Acetylene Gas is not poisonous enough to give you even a slight headache if you left a jet turned on full pressure and unlighted, for a *whole night* in your bedroom while you slept there.

Because, Acetylene is just pure, unadulterated *Light*, and nothing else *but* Light. Kerosene, Gasoline, and City Gas, are about *one*-tenth Light, and *nine*-tenths useless and poisonous other things.

Acetylene, because it *is* so pure and unadulterated, gives a beautiful *White* Light which is almost the same, in composition, as Sunlight.

It is so much like true, natural Sunlight that plants and flowers *grow* under its rays (24 hours continuously night and day) just as they grow under natural Sunlight during the day only.

That has been proven at Cornell University this very year—double growth under Acetylene Light.

And, the effect of Acetylene Light upon Human beings has been proven to be like the effect of Sunlight upon them, for the self-same reasons that it makes plants *grow* night and day under its wholesome rays.

That's *one* of the wonderful things explained in a little book, called "Sunlight on Tap," which I want to send you free, if you write me for it today.

Tremendous *improvements* have been made in Acetylene Lighting lately.

It is *cheaper* now than even *Kerosene* Light — a third cheaper.

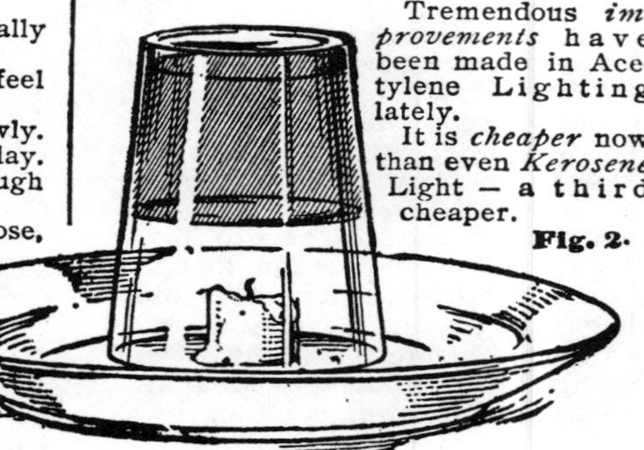

Fig. 2.

I'll prove *that* for you too,—if you're interested.

Two million United States People now use Acetylene Light.

They live chiefly in small Towns, and in the Country, where Acetylene is now found far more convenient, more economical, and infinitely *safer* than Kerosene or any other artificial Light.

No good Farmhouse, Country Residence, Village Home, or Village Store, would be without *modern* Acetylene Light if their Owners knew what *I* know now about it, since its recent *improvement* and reduction in cost.

And I want everyone who owns a home or store, in Village, Town, or Country, to write me for my free book called "Sunlight on Tap," which tells some mighty interesting facts about Reading Lights — and other Lights.

Just tell me how many rooms there are in your house. Then, I'll tell you about how much it would cost you to light them with brilliant Acetylene, instead of with murky, bad-smelling Kerosene, Gasoline, or City Gas.

Think of all the daily Lamp-Cleaning, Breakage, and *Risk* you could save by getting rid of Kerosene alone!

Just address me as — "Acetylene Jones," 161 Michigan Ave., Chicago, Ills., and write *today.*

November 1905

THEODORE ROOSEVELT AS A FARMER

All About the President's Country Home at Oyster Bay—How He Pitches Hay, Chops Wood and Improves His Farm

SOME folks do not know that President Roosevelt is something of a farmer as well as a nation-guider. On the northern shore of Long Island, N. Y.,–overlooking Oyster Bay, Center Island, and the blue, open sound beyond,—he owns about ninety-seven acres of high, rolling, fertile ground

FARMER SEAMAN'S HOUSE

It's on a rural free delivery route, three miles from the town of Oyster Bay. Yes, and it has a name,—as a good farmer's place should. Turning into the President's private driveway which opens on to the public road, I looked up and saw an unpretentious white board nailed to a tree at the entrance, with the wording, "Sagamore Hill," in modest small black letters.

There was no gate, no guardian fences, no fuss, no citified style. Just a plain farm driveway, winding up a wooded slope. I felt at home, instantly.

Presently the house came into view,—a rambling, comfortable-looking old-fashioned structure, with gables, porches and chimneys galore. I thought of open fires, blazing logs, and homey, country good cheer!—and felt still more at home.

Noah Seaman and his good wife acted as host and hostess, for the Roosevelt family were, at the time of my October visit, in Washington. Mr. Seaman has charge of the entire farm, and I found him to be a very pleasant man and an excellent farmer—just the kind we like to have among Our Folks. I spent a very instructive afternoon walking over the place, asking questions of everybody, taking photographs, and admiring the grand water view northward.

"How many acres under cultivation?" I asked.

"About forty-seven acres, counting pasture; the remainder is in woodland. The President is very fond of chopping. Nearly every day when he is here, he takes his axe, chops down a tree, and then cuts it up into firewood or fence material."

"I see that your soil here is a sandy-loam," I remarked. "What fertilizers do you use?"

"None,—except stable manure. We use all we can get of that. We keep, usually, about five horses, six cows, eight pigs and a flock of Barred Plymouth Rock chickens. Some turkeys, too. All the hay and straw needed for our stock are grown on the place."

I was much interested in the water and gas systems in use on this farm. Gas is made by an automatic machine, from gasoline stored in a covered underground place away from the house,—and thus the President's home, Noah Seaman's house, the barn, etc., are all well lighted throughout with gas. And in a snug little frost-proof building about a hundred feet from the house, I found a gasoline engine, pumping water from a tubular well 190 feet deep. I thought of the President's growing children, of his soft-eyed Jersey cows and his faithful horses, and wrote in my note book: "No darkness on *this* farm. No impure water; no typhoid; no tainted milk for the youngsters to drink. Of course not!—the President's big stick is after just such evils, and why shouldn't his ideas begin at home?"

The President is a real farmer

The water from the tubular well is pumped into a tank in the attic of the President's house; and the overflow goes to a large frost-proof outdoor tank, and from there to the barn and to Superintendent Seaman's house.

THEODORE ROOSEVELT'S COUNTRY HOME

When I saw the rustic entrance to the flower, fruit and vegetable gardens, I wished that Paul Plowshare could see it, too. He would have said, right off: "The owner of this rustic affair is the kind of a man we want in our Saturday Morning Fix-up-the-farm Club. Look at those graceful festoons of clematis paniculata, moonflower and crimson rambler; and notice those cozy seats at the sides beneath, and the straight, well-kept walk into the gardens beyond. Surely here are some good suggestions for our brother farm-adorners!"

The flower garden is very attractive, and in season contains some of the choicest varieties of bloom, including Mrs. Roosevelt's favorite roses and many other very beautiful flowers.

Adjoining the flower garden is the fruit and vegetable garden, and Superintendent Seaman, with his several assistants, keeps the farm tables well supplied with fresh products during summer and early fall. I saw a nice bed of strawberries; rows of grapes, raspberries, currants and gooseberries; peach, pear and apple trees; and all the evidences of a last-summer's carefully tended vegetable crop. Lima bean poles and asparagus plants are in such abundant supply that I'm inclined to suspect that some one in the President's family is especially fond of succotash and asparagus.

PATH TO THE PRESIDENT'S HOUSE

At the north end of the farm I was shown a recently-constructed rustic summer-house. It commands a magnificent view of bay and sound, and on a clear day the distant shore of Connecticut can be plainly seen. When Father Time has had a fair chance to drape some vines around this summer house, it will please even my critical friend Paul.

One July day last summer, Superintendent Seaman said to the President: "Mr. President, can you help us get in the hay?"

"Certainly. At what time?"

"After lunch."

"All right. I will be on hand."

But it began to look like rain, and so Noah Seaman called the President before the appointed time. He cheerfully responded and was quickly in the field, pitchfork in hand. He sprang into the work enthusiastically, pitching up great bunches of hay on to the wagon. "'Tis a great honor to stack hay with the President," said the man on the wagon.

But the President only laughed and pitched the harder. When the wagon was filled, the President followed it to the barn, and, going up into the mow, received the hay and stowed it away, trampling it down vigorously.

The Roosevelt estate has been in the possession of the family for many years. Theodore played there as a boy; he grew up to love it; and now, in the prime of his manhood, he joyously looks forward each year to a few months' sojourn amid the quiet peace and sturdy rural pleasures of Sagamore Hill farm. It isn't a pretentious place; quite the contrary. Around Philadelphia we have hundreds of country estates that are far more costly and elegant than the President's summer nest. But he is content. And the chips fly mightily and the axe rings true.—WALTER E. ANDREWS.

The Edison!

The latest style Edison Phonograph in our new outfit No. 10—this superb entertainer, Mr. Edison's latest, final improvement of phonograph—shipped

FREE

Yes, free. I don't ask a cent of your money—I don't want you to keep the phonograph—I just want to give it to you on a free loan—then you may return it at my own expense.

Read the Offer: I will ship you free this grand No. 10 outfit, Fireside Model, with one dozen Gold Moulded and Amberol records. You do not have to pay me a cent C. O. D. or sign any leases or mortgages. I want you to get this free outfit—the masterpiece of Mr. Edison's skill—in your home. I want you to see and hear Mr. Edison's final and greatest improvement in phonographs. I want to convince you of its wonderful superiority. Give a free concert; give a free minstrel show, music, dances, the old fashioned hymns, grand opera, comic opera—all this I want you to hear free of charge—all in your own home—on this free loan offer.

MY REASON—My reason for this free loan offer, this extra liberal offer on the finest talking machine ever made—see below.

MR. EDISON Says: *"I Want to see a Phonograph in Every American Home."*

The phonograph is the result of years of experiment; it is Mr. Edison's pet and hobby. He realizes fully its value as an entertainer and educator; for the phonograph brings the pleasure of the city right to the village and the farm home. **Now, the new Fireside Edison Phonograph** of our outfit No. 10, 1910 Model, is the latest and greatest improved talking machine made by this great inventor. Everybody should hear it; everybody must hear it. If you have only heard other talking machines before, you cannot imagine what beautiful music you can get from the outfit No. 10. This new machine is just out and has never been heard around the country. **We want to convince you;** we want to prove to you that this outfit is far, far superior to anything ever heard before. Don't miss this wonderfully liberal offer.

MY REASON **I don't want you to buy it**—I don't ask you to buy anything. But I do feel that if I can send you this great phonograph and convince you of its merits, of its absolute superiority, you will be glad to invite your neighbors and friends to your house to let them hear the free concert. Then, perhaps, one or more of your friends will be glad to buy one of these great outfits No. 10. You can tell your friends that they can get an Edison Phonograph outfit complete with records for only $2.00 a month—$2.00 a month—the easiest possible payment and, at the same time, a rock-bottom price. **Perhaps you, yourself, would want a phonograph,** and if you ever intend to get a phonograph, now is the chance to get the brand new and most wonderful phonograph ever made, and on a most wonderfully liberal offer. But if neither you nor your friends want the machine, that is O. K.; I simply want you to have it on a free loan, and perhaps somebody who heard the machine will buy one later. I am glad to send it on the free loan offer anyway. I will take it as a favor if you will send me your name and address so I can send you the catalog—then you can decide whether you want the free loan. There are no strings on this offer, absolutely none. It is a free loan, that is all. I ask not for one cent of your money; I only say if any of your people want to buy a phonograph, they may get one for $2.00 a month, if they want it.

Now, remember, nobody asks for a cent of your money. I want every responsible household in the country, every man who wants to see his home cheerful and his family entertained, every good father, every good husband, to write and get these free concerts for his home. Remember, the loan is absolutely free from us, and we do not even charge you anything C. O. D.

Write for FREE Edison Catalog

In this catalog you will find a complete list of music and vaudeville entertainments. You can pick out just the kind of records you want for the entertainment you want on this free loan in your own home. Get this catalog at once, then you can decide whether or not you want a free loan and when you want it. You can also decide just the music you want. Remember, I will appreciate it as a favor if you will give me the opportunity of sending you this latest style machine—the climax of Mr. Edison's skill—on this free loan offer. I will appreciate it especially if you will send me your name and address anyway right now, so I can fully and clearly explain our methods of shipping the Edison Phonograph on a free loan.

SIGN THE COUPON TODAY. Do it right now.

F. K. BABSON, Edison Phon. Distributor
Dept. 3011, Edison Bldg., Chicago, Ill.
Canadian Office: 355 Portage Avenue, Winnipeg, Can.

Just sign and mail the coupon at the left, and get this FREE catalog. Write today.

Write today for this interesting catalog, FREE.

FREDERICK BABSON, Edison Phonograph Distributor, Dept. 3011, Edison Bldg., CHICAGO, ILL.
Canadian Office: 355 Portage Ave., Winnipeg, Canada.
Without any obligations on me, please send your Great Edison Catalog, and also full explanations of your Free Loan Offer on the Edison Phonograph.

NAME ....

ADDRESS ....

No letter necessary; just sign and mail this free coupon right now today.

Seeds Of All These 12 Varieties, 6 cts.

Giant Raspberry-Blackberry.—Grows from seed and is a hybrid of the red raspberry and blackberry. Berry is dark red and grows in immense clusters sometimes $1\frac{1}{4}$ inches long. Flavor of both raspberry and blackberry, and ripens just after strawberries. Vine trails on ground like a dewberry. A few seeds will grow plants to start with.

Giant American Onion.—Introduced by us in 1908 and proved superior to any other light yellow skin mammoth variety with pure white flesh. Giant in size, grows fully from seed in a season; unusually mild in flavor; remains firm and solid all winter. We recommend it most highly. Very profitable.

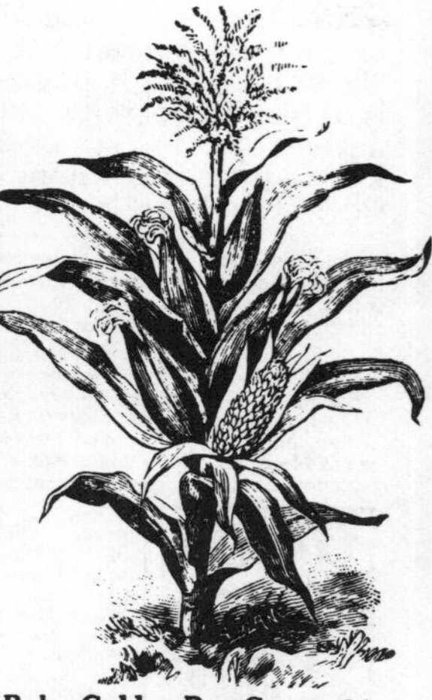

Baby Golden Pop-Corn.—Of rice type, the smallest in existence; very prolific; 5 to 10 ears to stalk; stalks not over 3 feet high, ears from $1\frac{3}{4}$ to $2\frac{1}{2}$ inches in length; kernels little smaller than rice, light, lustrous golden color and pops splendidly.

Sweet Peas.—Gorgeous mixture of 85 kinds. Seeds from healthy, vigorous, large producing, strong-stemmed plants. Flowers of gigantic size. All colors. Continue blooming all summer. This mixture can only be obtained from us.

Giant Japan Radish.—Grows to enormous size. Above is from photo of one 43 inches around and 21 inches high. Skin pure white, flesh solid and firm, more delicate flavor than our radishes; thrives in any soil; always crisp and tender. Good to eat at any stage of its growth.

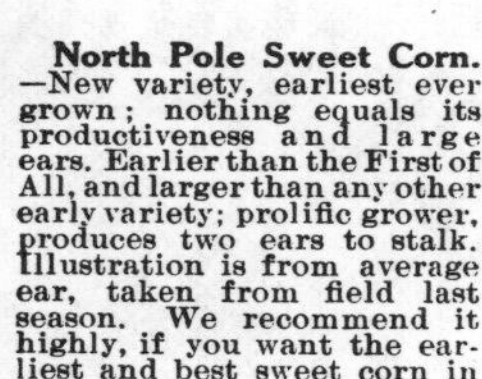

North Pole Sweet Corn.—New variety, earliest ever grown; nothing equals its productiveness and large ears. Earlier than the First of All, and larger than any other early variety; prolific grower, produces two ears to stalk. Illustration is from average ear, taken from field last season. We recommend it highly, if you want the earliest and best sweet corn in existence.

All-Summer Lettuce.—The very earliest, handsome, fine flavored, and the very best early Lettuce that grows. Can be grown in hotbeds or gardens at almost any season anywhere, and is good all summer and fall.

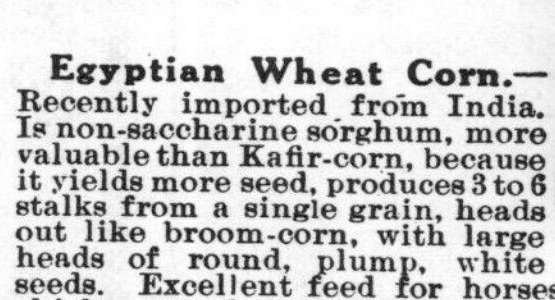

Egyptian Wheat Corn.—Recently imported from India. Is non-saccharine sorghum, more valuable than Kafir-corn, because it yields more seed, produces 3 to 6 stalks from a single grain, heads out like broom-corn, with large heads of round, plump, white seeds. Excellent feed for horses and cattle, unexcelled for chickens, makes excellent pan-cake flour and pops like pop-corn; has surprisingly good flavor; very tender and crisp. For a grain crop, not forage. We recommend it highly.

Chinese Lantern Plant.—Treat it like tomatoes and it fruits first season. Grows from seed. Produces numerous large unfolded husks that are shaped like Chinese lanterns, at first green, then yellow, and last bright scarlet. Delicious for pies, fruit cakes or puddings. Comes from Japan and will grow in any garden.

Peach Tomato.—Fruit resembles peach in size and shape; color deep rose, beautifully blended, with fuzz like peach; flesh rich and delicate in flavor, thin skin, tender, free from core; fine for eating from hand. Very handsome and great delight in garden.

Coffee Berry.—Very prolific and grows in any garden; very strong, and gives abundance of pods containing coffee berry; very nearly equals good Java coffee as a drink. Plant in May and cultivate same as beans. Much superior to other substitutes for coffee.

Large French Strawberry.—Grows from seed very easily and is far ahead of American varieties. Berries large, of luscious sweetness and very handsome. Seed sown early in hotbed, or in open ground in seed bed, soon as weather permits, and transplant when well started. Very interesting, pleasing and delightful for table use.

Remember all these seeds are for trial to prove to Farm Journal readers that our seeds will give the best of satisfaction. We are sure the above 12 sample lots growing in your garden will be your delight to show and surprise your neighbors, and we will mail all 12 Packets in a Coupon Envelope for **6 cts.**, postage and packing, and this **Coupon Envelope,** when emptied, will be accepted as a 10-cent payment on any seeds offered in our Catalogue.

Our Seed Catalogue for 1910 is a complete book, every page being filled with our offers of the choicest and best Seeds, Bulbs, Plants, Fruits, etc., some of which you can not obtain elsewhere. This New Seed Catalogue will be sent **free** with every sample lot. Do not fail to examine it before you buy your spring supply.

Address MILLS SEED CO., Box 599, Washington, Iowa.

Aunt Harriet before the days of "Dear Abby"

Heart Problems

BY AUNT HARRIET

[Aunt Harriet wishes to give advice, suggestions and sympathy to all Our Folks who are in doubt or in trouble, but her correspondents have become so numerous that it is impossible to answer all the letters in this column. To be sure of a reply, give full name and address and two-cent stamp, for only such answers as will benefit and interest the largest number of people will be given here. Address, Aunt Harriet, care of Farm Journal, Philadelphia, Pa.]

A WIDELY-READ newspaper recently published the following question: "Is the European plan of allowing parents to arrange a marriage likely to be more productive of permanent happiness than our way?"

From the American standpoint there seems, at first glance, something unpleasant in the idea of arranged marriages, but, after all, may we not make mistakes? The statistics of the divorce courts prove that there are many unhappy marriages, and to our shame we must confess that the number of divorces is larger in America than in other countries.

Marriage is ordained by God; the family is the foundation of the state and strength of the nation. It is not a thing to be entered into lightly, for health, morals, habits, disposition and means are important factors, and should be considered first. Love is necessary, but not enough; it does make burdens lighter; but love can not carry them alone, and only the young, the inexperienced and the ignorant think that it can.

European parents recognize all this, and are prepared to meet it. They know that a girl must have her dowry, and begin saving for it from the day of her birth. When the time comes for her to marry, they find out, and are expected to find out, all that is worth knowing about the man who is under consideration. They know his family, business and social connections; they have the means of finding out what sort of a life he leads, and they know to a sou just what he has to support her.

Contrast this with the American way, where our girls grow up in a haphazard way,—and what are her chances? If she belongs to the very poor, the illiterate class, she marries, or is looked down upon for not marrying. This class does not look ahead and does not consider "family," "social position," "congeniality," etc. So they marry and are happy or unhappy, as it may be. If they are happy and industrious, their position in life improves, and their children may belong to what we know as the middle class,. which we shall consider later.

The wealthy classes recognize their children's rights, and give them the chance to meet their own kind in society. The daughters of these people are sent to the schools and colleges where they make friends who will be of benefit to them. Dress, accomplishments and manner are all given attention, and with her "seasons" in society, the girl has her chance.

What is done for the average girl of the class between these two? In nine cases out of ten she must "fend" for herself. By this I do not mean that such girls are husband hunting, or that their mothers are to do it for them; but I do mean that the average girl must not only plan for all her little pleasures and outings, but in some cases has to fight for them, and it is usually through her intercourse with other young people that she gets her "chance." The tenth girl has sufficient initiative to go ahead, make friends and meet them. She is perhaps more attractive than the nine, has more attention and more opportunities. If she marries, the chances are that it is all arranged before the parents are spoken to, and they hand over the care of their child to a stranger who may be all that they can desire, or may not. As for the other girls, after their school years they settle down to a home life, helping mother, or they go out into the business world. There may be a happy home life. If there is, it may be so self-centered that there is never room for strangers. We have all known people to whom the idea of an outsider at table or in the living-room was a

On this page are advertisements of schools, department store, cultivators, patents, land, firearms and building materials.

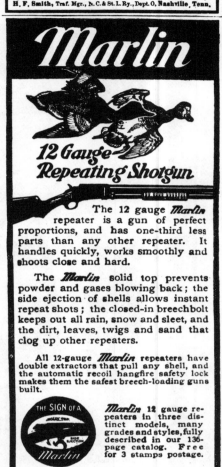

bugbear. We have all known families where father, mother or an aunt was queer and did not like company; the social life of the young in such homes is sacrificed to the selfishness of their elders, and while a young man who is well-dressed and well-groomed can go anywhere, a daughter's social status is that of her home, and the breadth of her life is measured by its walls; it is a narrow life if they do not expand.

A girl needs a good background as much as a picture needs a frame. Her people must not seem pushing, nor overdo matters by continually sounding her praises. Men do not enjoy being pursued; they should be the pursuers. But every girl, whether she is attractive or not, needs the background of a pleasant home life, where there is a certain regard for individual rights, a cordial greeting for neighbor and friend, interest in affairs of the day, opportunities for acquiring accomplishments, and the right and means to dress as well as circumstances allow.

Her friends, of both sexes, should be welcomed to the house, and she should have time and chance to attend any reputable gathering in her neighborhood. I have numberless letters from girls whose parents prohibit friends of the opposite sex. Sometimes the girls submit,—sometimes (oh, the pity of it!) they meet their friends outside; but I always wonder how such parents did their own courting, and if, in years to come, they will wonder why their daughters never married. After all, can we not learn something from the Old World on this subject? Whether happiness comes by way of marriage, or through the single life, we owe it to our children that each should have his chance. To have brought your children into the world is not enough, your debt to them is a large one; and if you expect love, respect and obedience from them, do your part to deserve it.

C. P.: Your letter came too late to be answered before this number, as we work two months ahead. By all means show the young woman that you are interested in her. It is supposed that you are acquainted with her? Then write and ask permission to call, taking with you a box of candy (Cupid's first aid to the bashful). When you leave, ask permission to call again, and ask her to go somewhere with you, for a walk or drive, or to church, or some entertainment. Once you get started, one thing will lead to another, and you will get on famously. Providing, of course, that you make yourself agreeable to her and her family.

"DOESN'T THE YOUNG MAN WHO CALLS ON YOU EVER TALK ABOUT MARRYING?" "YES, BUT NOT ABOUT MARRYING ME"

On this page are advertisements of rams, manure spreader, seed, taxidermy, roses, agents and buggies.

ADVERTISEMENTS

When you write to an advertiser tell him that you saw his card in the Farm Journal. It is to your interest to do so, as Our Folks are treated honestly and served with the best. Read the Fair Play notice on first page.

That suit is best that fits me

DURING the coming weeks there are very few women who will not endeavor to do a little "shopping," and a few words on the subject may not come amiss.

Of course Our Folks are looking for bargains, but remember nothing is cheap unless you need it. Avoid the "bargain counters" unless you are a good judge of materials. It costs just as much to make up poor material as good, and the difference in wear is of importance.

Remnants, suitable for children's clothes, or to combine with other goods, can always be found at reduced prices, and often, because of some great change in popular fancy, a piece of really good material is offered very low; but before you buy such be sure it is all wool, a becoming color, a firm and substantial weave, and a pattern of which you will not tire.

Standard goods are seldom reduced to any great extent, but this year, owing to the fancy for rough goods, the plainer weaves can be had at great bargains, but as a rule they hold their own.

The spirit of Christmas enters so largely into all shopping at this time of the year, that a few suggestions are offered. A great deal is said and written about the beauty of receiving or giving something at this time that you would not be likely to purchase for yourself, but the Fashion Editor fails to see the beauty of giving tidies to a woman who needs aprons and has no time to make them, or cologne to a girl who needs new handkerchiefs.

While by sending to this office for a catalogue, Our Folks can get any kind of a pattern they want, those illustrated in the FARM JOURNAL this month have been chosen with special reference to the holiday season.

What would please a young mother more than a tiny sack or flannel wrapper made according to patterns No. 20186 and No. 20184. The sack needs but three-quarters yard of flannel or any odd pieces of cashmere, albatross, nun's-veiling or like materials, in pink, blue, cream or grey. An embroidered edge is pretty, but an easier way is to briar stitch the hem with silk.

Wash flannels in neat stripes, either cotton or cotton and wool, are chosen for the wrapper, which must stand good service. Briar stitching is the only trimming required for this garment.

Wouldn't mother be pleased with an underskirt of black alpaca? Her daughters have long ago found out that for all the year round there is nothing so serviceable. It takes four to six yards to make a skirt with ruffle, and you pay from twenty-five to fifty cents per yard for it.

Housekeepers, girls, large or small, and children are remembered in the apron patterns Nos. 20404, 20456 and 20313. Why not try them?

Your eldest daughter will like a silk waist in her Christmas stocking, and you must be careful in buying it. Taffetas are always pretty, but it is not safe to pay less than seventy-five cents per yard for it. Pattern No. 20281 is the one to make it by, and she can trim it the way she likes best. Ribbon braces, collar and girdle, or three strips of insertion, or Vandyke points of lace, are all pretty ways to trim it.

A collarette, or a fancy collar of ribbon with bows at the back, a Scotch plaid necktie, all these are liked by young girls. The plaid necktie is tied in a bow at the back of the neck, over the dress collar, and is worn as a girdle, fastened with a clasp that comes especially for that purpose.

If you are giving a dress to some wee lassie, send for child's dress pattern, No. 20454, or if for an older girl, pattern No. 20457 to make it by. Both are sensible yet "dressy" styles. To avoid mistakes and delay be sure to read the directions for measuring carefully before sending for patterns.

A pretty hat of brown felt has a round crown and a slightly rolling brim, two ruffles of satin ribbon surround the crown, with a bunch of cocque feathers at each side. The ribbon is three and one-half inches wide, the under ruffle of green, the upper one brown. A yard and a half of each color is required, and the ribbon is doubled before being gathered, in effect it is more like a puff than a ruffle, and makes a very simple but effective trimming.

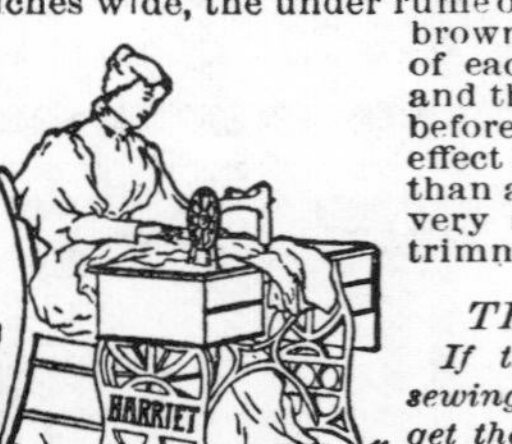

A "lesson" on dress and an opportunity to get your style from Farm Journal

Get Two Neighbors

to take the FARM JOURNAL two years at **30 cents each** and we will send you **free** any two (numbered) patterns shown on this page. Any 3 patterns for a club of 3. Send for sample copies FARM JOURNAL.

These patterns retail in fashion bazaars and stores from 20 to 40 cents each, but in order to make our paper more valuable than ever to our friends, we offer them to our lady readers for the low price of only **12 Cents Each, including postage.**

The patterns are all of the very latest styles worn in America, and are unequaled for style, accuracy of fit, simplicity in putting together and economy. For 25 years these patterns have been used the country over. Full descriptions and directions—number of yards of material required, number and names of the different pieces in the pattern, how to cut and fit and put the garment together—are sent with each pattern, *with a picture of the garment to go by*. These patterns are complete in every particular, there being a *separate* pattern for *every single piece* of the dress. Your order will be promptly filled.

For ladies, give BUST measure in inches. For SKIRT pattern, give WAIST measure in inches. For misses, boys, girls or children, give both BREAST measure in inches and AGE in years. See below for rules of measurement. Order patterns by their numbers.

Price of each pattern, 12 cents, including postage. Send a dime and a 2-cent stamp.

Send 2-cent stamp for large 4-page catalogue, showing many new fashion designs for December. Our Folks can have it free. **FARM JOURNAL, 1024 Race Street, Philadelphia, Pa.**

Ladies' Waist—20281. Cut in five sizes, from 32 to 40 inches bust measure.

Infants' Wrapper—20184. Cut in one size.

Ladies' Housekeeping Apron—20404. Cut in three sizes, small, medium and large.

Ladies' Five Gored Skirt—20306. Cut in five sizes, from 22 to 30 inches waist measure.

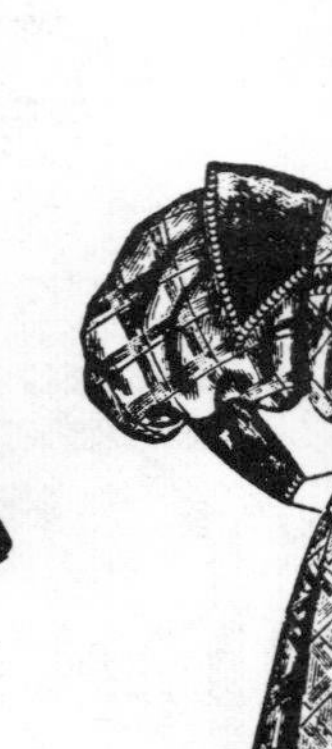

Misses' Costume With Seven Gored Skirt—20455. Cut in five sizes, from 12 to 16 years.

Infants' Sacque—20186. Cut in one size.

Child's Sacque Apron—20313. Cut in five sizes, from 4 to 8 years.

Little Girl's Apron—20456. Cut in five sizes, from 4 to 8 years.

Girls' Dress—20457. Cut in five sizes, from 8 to 12 years.

Ladies' Corset Cover—20014. Cut in five sizes, 32 to 40 in. bust measure.

Child's Dress—20454. Cut in five sizes, from 4 to 8 years.

That suit is best that fits me

THIS is decidedly an underwear number, quite timely, for the systematic woman likes to get her white sewing started during the lull which comes between the holidays and the spring rush. In these days of inflated prices it is well to make use of any little economies one may learn of, while anything that saves time and effort is doubly valuable. It is not worth while to make up any but good materials. This does not mean heavy fabrics, but good, firm weaves with durable trimmings. Longcloth is easier to sew than cambric or muslin ; cambric will outlast nainsook, while muslin (known as cotton cloth in some sections) is most durable for skirts. If you use embroidery, let the cloth upon which it is worked be of the same quality as the material it trims. Blind embroideries (*i. e.*, without holes) wear best, and the handloom products are the choicest. Avoid those made up of large holes, flimsily finished, and none of it is worth buying unless it has a firm edge. Machine-made torchons, from three cents per yard up, are preferred to poor embroidery. Buy pearl buttons always of the same pattern, you can then use left-overs. Brass buttons are good for the children's underclothes, as they do not break and will go through the wringer easily. This also applies to the flat lace buttons which are now used for fine blouses and children's dresses.

In buying materials for shirtwaists, select those with a smooth (not fuzzy) surface. They iron better and stay clean longer.

In selecting ginghams and other wash goods for yourself or the children, choose clear, clean-looking patterns. One color, combined with white, such as blue, black, brown, green or pink, washes and looks well to the last ; while a combination of colors looks pretty in the piece, but soon fades and washes to an indefinite shade.

For an inexpensive white dress, choose a striped or figured material, it will not need so much trimming. A pretty way to trim a striped gingham dress is to use bias bands of checked gingham, matching it in color, while the stripes and bars must be of the same width. A dotted lawn is prettily trimmed with bands of striped lawn to match, cut crosswise. Set in a waist, with lace insertion on either side, it is extremely pretty.

Waist No. 3127 is of chiffon cloth, in tucks, with the yoke and undersleeves laid over dotted net. Frills edge the upper sleeves and wrists, the yoke is finished with soutache braid, while the girdle is of messaline. The pattern provides for high or Dutch neck, long or short sleeves, and is suitable for any soft materials.

A princess slip is useful to wear under thin dresses, or the pattern No. 2565 may be used for the foundation of a dress, if some special style is desired. As a slip, silk, lawn or any lining materials may be used.

Kimono dressing sack, with French back, No. 2065, is comfortable, while neater than the all-'round kimono. Pretty flannels, challis, soft silks, lawn and dimity are all used.

There are three corset-covers to choose from. No. 2504 is quickly made from the deep embroidery which comes for that purpose, and needs only the beading at the waist and some ribbon to finish it.

Two styles of brassieres are given. No. 2390 was the first to appear, and is liked by those who do not object to the closing in the back. A brassiere is an excellent support to the bust, and is much liked by women inclined to stoutness. Strong wash fabrics must be used, with neat finishings and narrow edgings for trimming. The little tab in front is buttoned to the corset.

No. 3124 is cut on different lines, closing in front, and will be more popular with the older women than the first model.

Combination undergarments are growing in favor, and No. 2709 shows a neat design, suitable for stout figures. Longcloth, with torchon edging, was used in its development, but cambric, jaconet, nainsook, etc., may be used.

Simple and closely-fitting drawers are shown in No. 2508. The ruffles are of wide edging or cambric, lace-edged, hemstitched or feather-stitched.

Childs' petticoat and drawers are shown in No. 2453, the latter having seam only on outside of the leg. The petticoat may be made of flannel, cambric or longcloth, the drawers of the two latter.

Nightgown No. 2794 is very pretty with square yoke and embroidery sleeves. The pattern also provides for high neck and long sleeves and will do for muslin, cambric, longcloth, nainsook and outing flannel.

Only the thinnest fabrics should be used for nightgown No. 2389, made in one piece, to be slipped over the head. This is the easiest of all to make.

Infants' slip No. 1761 is in one piece, gathered at the neck and wrists. Made of soft nainsook, with tiny lace edgings, it does nicely for day wear. Made of outing flannel, it may have a tape run through the hem, and if cut long enough the gown can be drawn together with the tape in the hem, and the tape fastened to the bottom of the crib. This is a tried and true way to keep baby covered at night, and the long gowns will not be quickly outgrown.

Men's nightshirt No. 1631 is made of flannel, twilled or unbleached muslin, with the wash braid trimming in blue or red and white for finishing.

Transfer design No. 8052 shows a braiding design for waist, with front collar and cuffs, and to be used on linen, cotton, wool or silk materials. The dots are worked solid. We can furnish a design for a skirt panel to match, and the whole would be most effective done in white on a colored chambray or linen.

Design No. 8126 is the pattern for infant's dress so frequently asked for. The tiny roses to be done solidly in white, the leaves solid, or in outline stitch, filled in with seed stitches. The pattern is adaptable to either a long or short dress.

Farm Journal Patterns

are the best in the market, and they are guaranteed. Our Farm Journal Fair Play comes in with every order. Full directions, including quantity of material, accompany each pattern. In ordering, be sure to give *number* and *size* of the pattern wanted. For ladies' upper garments give bust measure taken over the fullest part of the bust; for skirts and under garments give waist and hip measurements. For misses' upper garments give age and bust measure; for skirts and under garments give age, waist and hip measurements. For children give age, breast measurement and length of back. Children of same age vary in size. For instance,—the average child of six years will measure 24 inches over the breast, but there are many young children of ten years who will measure only 24 inches. In such case you need a six-year-old pattern. Price, 10 cents. Address, FARM JOURNAL, Philadelphia.

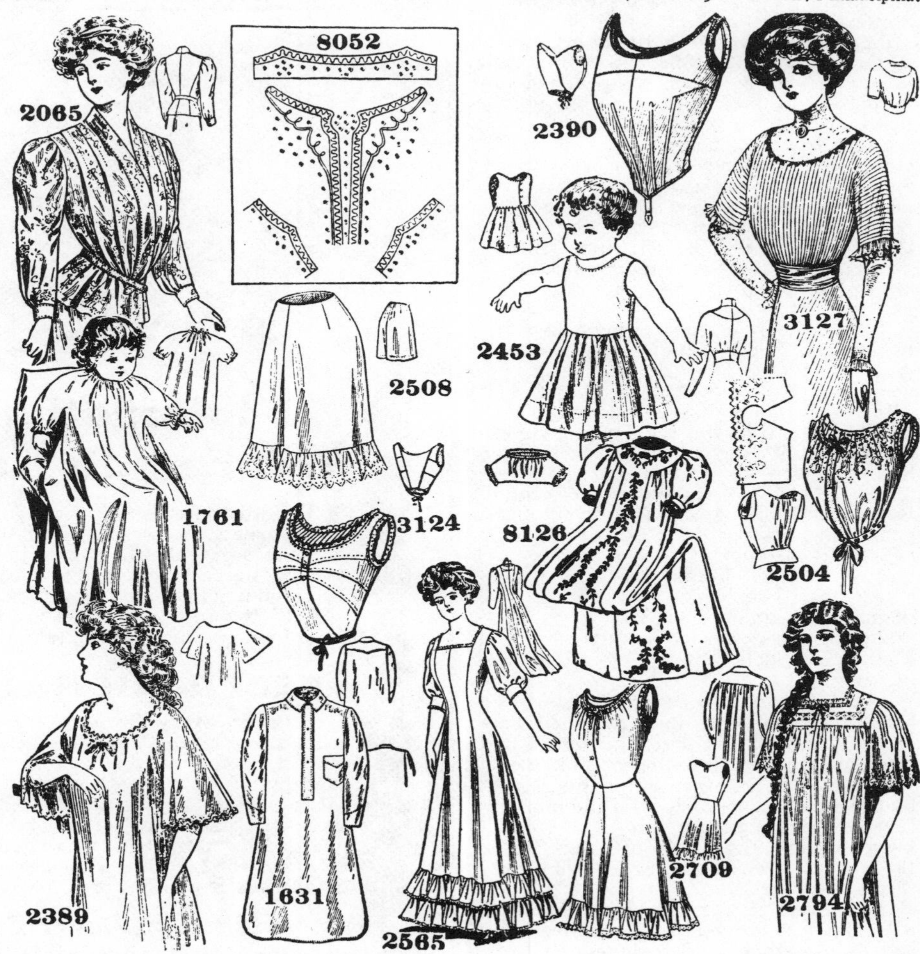

2065. Ladies' Kimono Dressing Sack. 7 sizes, 32, 34, 36, 38, 40, 42, 44 inches bust measure. **8052. Transfer Design for a Shirtwaist in Braiding and Eyelet Embroidery. 2390. Ladies' Bust-Supporting Corset-Cover.** 7 sizes, 34, 36, 38, 40, 42, 44, 46 inches bust measure. **3127. Ladies' Waist.** 5 sizes, 32, 34, 36, 38, 40 inches bust measure. **1761. Infants' One-Piece Slip.** One Size. **2508. Ladies' Open Drawers.** 8 sizes, 22, 24, 26, 28, 30, 32, 34, 36 inches waist measure. **2453. Child's Petticoat and Drawers.** 3 sizes, 1, 2, 3 years. **3124. Ladies' Bust-Supporting Corset-Cover.** 6 sizes, 36, 38, 40, 42, 44, 46 inches bust measure. **8126. Transfer Embroidery Design of Small Roses to be Embroidered Solidly. 2504. Ladies' One-Piece Corset-Cover.** 6 sizes, 32, 34, 36, 38, 40, 42 inches bust measure. **2389. Ladies' One-Piece Nightgown.** 4 sizes, 32, 36, 40, 44 inches bust measure. **1630. Men's Sack Nightshirt.** 7 sizes, 34, 36, 38, 40, 42, 44, 46 inches breast measure. **2565. Ladies' Princess Slip.** 7 sizes, 32, 34, 36, 38, 40, 42, 44 inches bust measure. **2709. Ladies' Combination Corset-Cover, Drawers and Short Petticoat.** 7 sizes, 32, 34, 36, 38, 40, 42, 44 inches bust measure. **2794. Ladies' Nightgown.** 4 sizes, 32, 36, 40, 44 inches bust measure.

How they built the "river-to-river road" in Iowa with 10,000 men

ROAD ACROSS IOWA

Three Hundred and Eighty Miles of Highway Made Good in an Hour

A GREAT piece of road building was completed in Iowa, says the Council Bluffs correspondent of the Pittsburgh Gazette-Times, when in the short space of one single hour a line of road 380 miles in length, and stretching entirely across the state of Iowa, was put in the most perfect condition of any road west of the Mississippi river.

And not the least interesting thing in connection with the tremendous piece of work, is the fact that not a man of the entire 10,000 engaged on the work received one cent of wages. Good will and patriotism are responsible for the splendid showing.

Last winter the Iowa roads became so fearfully bad that traffic was practically killed, and farmers were compelled simply to remain in their homes. Finally, the matter became a political question, and both parties got behind the movement. Governor Carroll called a good roads meeting at Des Moines, early last March, and out of this meeting was evolved the plan of a river to river road, stretching from Council Bluffs on the Missouri river to Davenport on the Mississippi, a distance of 380 miles straight across the state from east to west.

"Make the river to river road as nearly perfect as is possible to make just common dirt," was the sense of the good roads convention.

Instead of appointing new committees to handle the work, the regular Republican and Democratic committees in each county through which the road would pass were appealed to. The chairmen of the committees of each party were asked to get in the game and work for the road. Everybody agreed to do so, and soon a rivalry was created between Republicans and Democrats, each to see which party would have the most workmen on the job.

Saturday was selected as the day, and from nine o'clock to ten o'clock the hour of work.

In the weeks preceding the work all bridges and culverts along the road were repaired and put in first-class order, that no delay might come to the road builders.

The result of the organization was shown. Shortly before nine o'clock in the morning farmers began getting out in the road. Hundreds and thousands of plows, picks, shovels, scrapers, road drags, grading machines and other implements were brought along. Every farmer brought his team with him. Superintendents and overseers had been appointed in readiness.

And 10,000 determined men fell to. For an hour they continued working with might and main. At ten o'clock the job was finished, and the farmers went back to their fields, leaving Iowa the possessor of the finest piece of long-distance roadway in the West.

[A good example for other states.—EDITOR.]

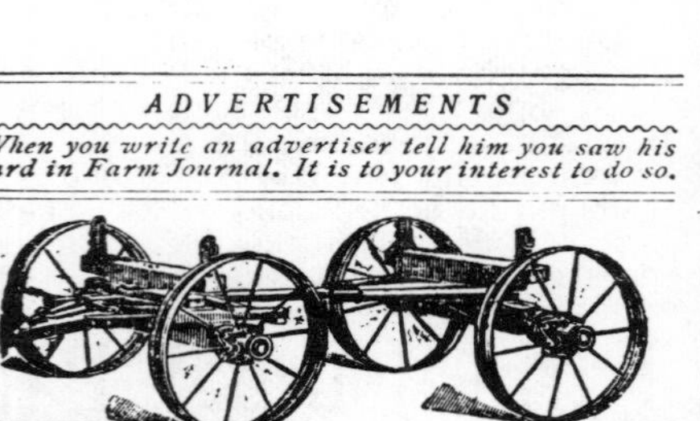

12

CUTTING UP A BEEF

The Various Parts as They Are Known in the Market

MANY housewives, both in town and country, who weekly or oftener patronize the butcher, have only hazy ideas with respect to the location and food and money value of the various cuts. They know in a general way that the sirloin and the rib-roasts are the choicest and most expensive parts of the beef, but only experienced cooks and housekeepers know that many of the coarser and less expensive parts of the carcass are as nutritious as the higher-priced parts. The cuts and their subdivisions are as follows:

Loin: The loin of beef is subdivided into porterhouse or short cuts, T-bone and sirloin. The porterhouse consists of the first five or six steaks from the small end next to the ribs. Next to this comes the T-bone steaks, regarded by many as the very choicest part of the loin. The last six or eight steaks next to the round are known as the sirloin. The tenderloin is the inside portion of lean meat near the rib end of the loin. Where the tenderloin is cut from the choice carcass, a fancy price is charged for it, as it seriously injures the value of the rest of the loin.

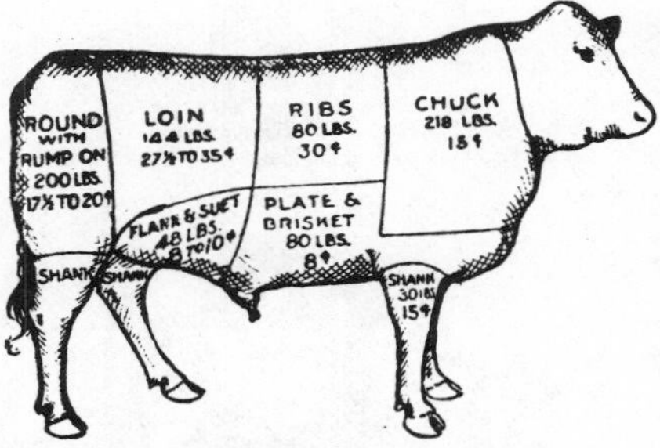

CHART SHOWING METHOD OF CUTTING UP A BEEF AND ALSO RETAIL PRICES OF CHOICE CARCASS

Round and rump: The rump is the fleshy portion over the thigh. After it is cut off, the round extends on down to the shank, having one bone near the center.

Flank: A section of lean meat overlies the flank which is stripped off and is known as the flank steak, and is much sought after. The balance of the flank is mostly used for sausage and hamburger, but may be boiled.

Ribs: This section consists of the first seven ribs and is mostly used for roasts. The cuts nearest the loin are considered the choicest and sell for the most money. Next to the chuck it is deeper and coarser.

Chuck: The lower eight or ten inches of that portion marked chuck is known to the trade as the "clod." This lies just above the brisket and extends up to the lower portion of the neck. This is cut mostly for pot-roasts and contains much lean meat. Most of the chuck is cut into steaks, the best portions being on the end nearest to the ribs. The portion next to the neck usually sells for pot-roast or boiling.

Plate: The plate is the lower portion of the carcass below the ribs, taking in the covering of the belly. It is mostly used for boiling but contains some good meat.

Brisket: This takes in the portion between the shank and the clod, or lower part of the chuck. It is a very fleshy piece with heavy bone, but makes fine pot-roast.

Shank: That portion of the shank from the knee or heel, to the cut above, is fleshy, though coarse, and is mostly used for boiling. The lower part is mostly bone and sinew and is for soup and boiling. In the forelegs this is called the shin.

Neck: This part usually sells with a part of the chuck and is fit mostly for boiling.

Sirloin ends: In some markets the ends of the sirloin and T-bone steaks, which run down into the flank, are cut off at the point where the flesh widens and are sold separately. These ends are coarser than the loin, but properly cooked are as good.

The illustration is made from a photograph of a prime steer that dressed 800 pounds. The weights given are actual but represent only the average for that class of steer. In cheaper steers the percentage of loin and ribs will be smaller and prices will also be lower. This class of steer will bring from eight to nine cents per pound wholesale in the carcass.

On this page are advertisements of patents, cooker, silos, dehorner, animal remedy and separators.

David Bradley Farm Implements

David Bradley Garden City Clipper Walking Plows. Wood and Steel Beam. A Style for Every Purpose. $3.68 Up.

David Bradley Light Draft Sulky Plows. Twenty-Six Sizes and Models. $22.95 Up.

David Bradley High Lift Foot Lift Gang Plows. $45.25 Up.

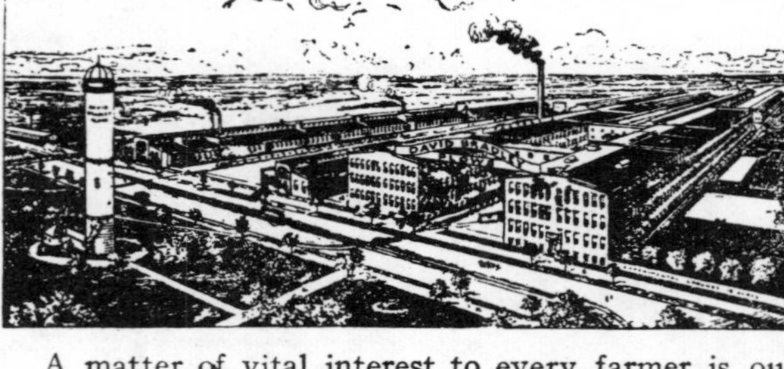

A matter of vital interest to every farmer is our recent purchase of the great David Bradley farm implement factory, the oldest and largest in the world selling direct to the farmer. The result is a sensational reduction in retail prices, brought about by the application of our famous factory to consumer selling methods. You pay actual cost of manufacture plus one single factory profit, eliminating at least three middlemen's profits.

Four generations of American farmers have testified to the absolute superiority of David Bradley goods. Plain old fashioned honesty stands behind every Bradley implement, an incontestable insurance policy against disappointment. **Bradley quality** has been supreme since 1832, and the sons and grandsons of the men who made it so maintain it today in our employ.

Send for our David Bradley Book of Farm Implements with full descriptions and prices of the complete Bradley line, sold under our guarantee of perfect satisfaction or money back.

We have the patterns for every Bradley implement ever made and can furnish promptly any Bradley repair or part, no matter when or where the original implement was purchased.

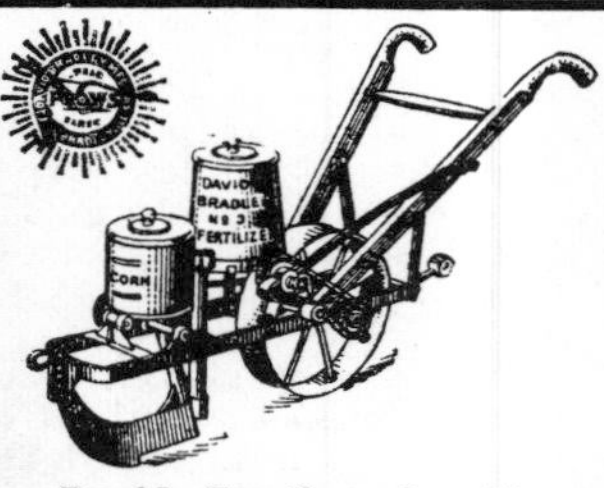

David Bradley One-Horse Corn Drills. Force Drop. Three Models. $6.98 Up.

David Bradley Listers. Three Styles, Walking and Riding. $16.95 Up.

David Bradley Force Drop Corn Planters. Flat Drop and Edge Drop. $22.85 Up.

David Bradley Ball Bearing Disc Plows. $29.85 to $52.65.

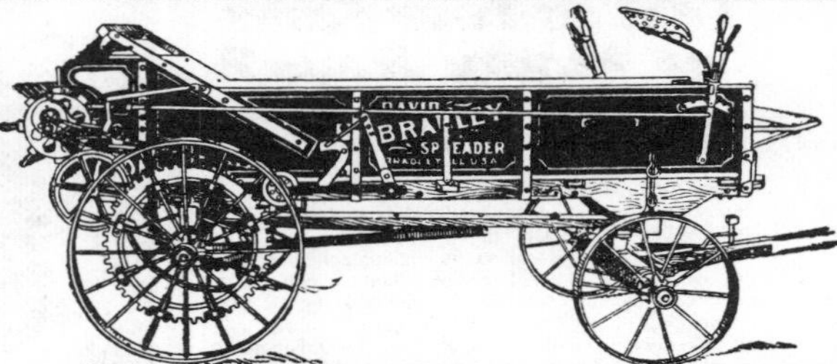

David Bradley Manure Spreader. The Strongest, Simplest and Best. Six Models. $42.50 Without Truck; $69.50 Complete, as Illustrated.

David Bradley Ideal Disc Harrows. Tongue or Tongueless. Solid or Cut Out Discs. $15.95 Up.

David Bradley Little Jap Disc Cultivator. Balance Frame. Pivot Axles. Seat Bar Dodger. A World Beater. $27.50.

David Bradley Double Cam All Steel Hay Press. Dealers Sold for $200.00 to $250.00. Our Prices, $135.75 Up.

David Bradley Cotton and Cornstalk Cutter. $18.95.

David Bradley Little Jap Riding Cultivators. Thirteen Styles of Shovel, Spring Tooth and Surface Gangs. Balance Frame. Pivot Axles. Seat Bar Dodger. $21.95 Up.

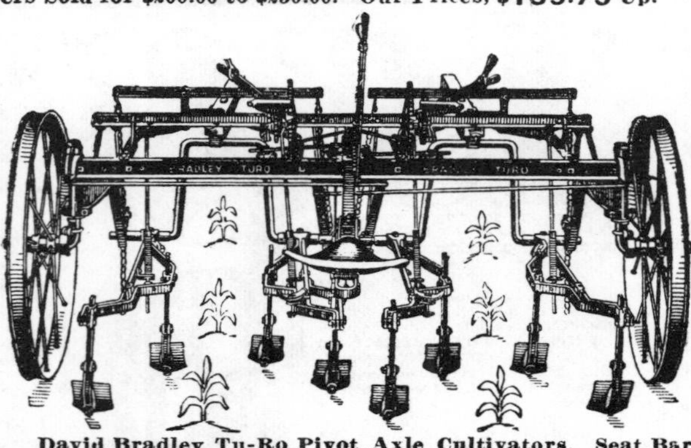

David Bradley Tu-Ro Pivot Axle Cultivators. Seat Bar Dodger. Expanding Lever. Cultivates Two Rows at Once. $41.00 Up.

David Bradley Walking Cultivators. $11.87 Up.

SEND TODAY FOR OUR DAVID BRADLEY BOOK OF FARM IMPLEMENTS

SEARS, ROEBUCK AND CO., CHICAGO

March 1911

Windmill Gets a "BLACK EYE!"

Daily Reports for the Three Windiest Months of the Year Indicate that Thousands of Windmills Throughout the United States Are Idle—

No Wind!

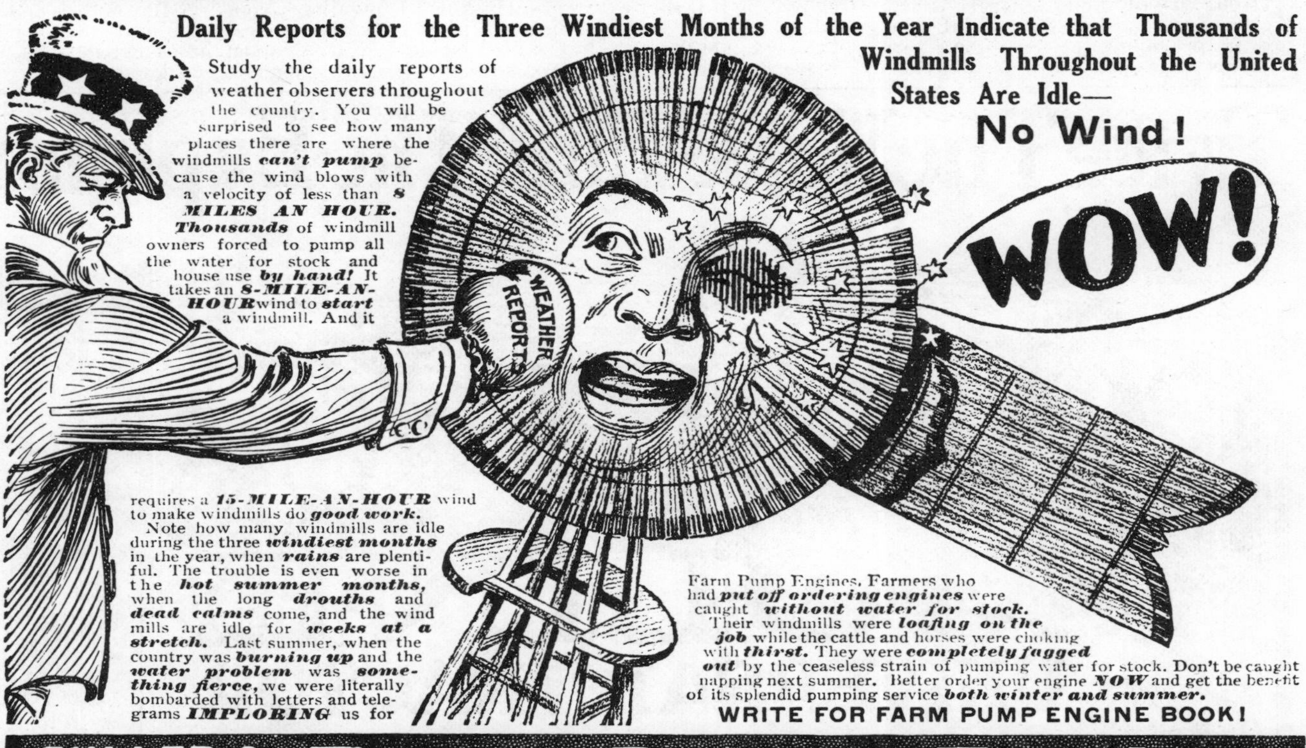

Study the daily reports of weather observers throughout the country. You will be surprised to see how many places there are where the windmills ***can't pump*** because the wind blows with a velocity of less than ***8 MILES AN HOUR. Thousands*** of windmill owners forced to pump all the water for stock and house use ***by hand!*** It takes an ***8-MILE-AN-HOUR*** wind to ***start*** a windmill. And it requires a ***15-MILE-AN-HOUR*** wind to make windmills do ***good work.***

Note how many windmills are idle during the three ***windiest months*** in the year, when ***rains*** are plentiful. The trouble is even worse in the ***hot summer months,*** when the long ***drouths*** and ***dead calms*** come, and the wind mills are idle for ***weeks at a stretch.*** Last summer, when the country was ***burning up*** and the ***water problem*** was ***something fierce,*** we were literally bombarded with letters and telegrams ***IMPLORING*** us for Farm Pump Engines. Farmers who had ***put off ordering engines*** were caught ***without water for stock.*** Their windmills were ***loafing on the job*** while the cattle and horses were choking with ***thirst.*** They were ***completely fagged out*** by the ceaseless strain of pumping water for stock. Don't be caught napping next summer. Better order your engine ***NOW*** and get the benefit of its splendid pumping service ***both winter and summer.***

WRITE FOR FARM PUMP ENGINE BOOK!

FULLER & JOHNSON Farm Pump Engine

Works 365 DAYS A YEAR!

COSTS LESS AND DOES MORE THAN BEST WINDMILL

Fits Any Pump and Makes It HUMP!

Patented in the United States, Canada and other foreign countries. Other patents applied for.

Pumps 400 to 1,000 Gallons Per Hour!

No Waiting for Wind!

Fits any force pump and makes it ***go the limit.***

Pumps 400 to 1,000 gallons per hour. Keeps it up ***day and night*** if required. Runs any of the domestic water pressure systems built for suburban or country homes. Supplies abundance of water, ***fresh from the well,*** for herds of stock.

Laughs at Zero Weather, Snow and Sleet

This service is ***doubly valuable in winter,*** when snow, sleet and storms put windmills out of commission.

No Need of Tank Heaters!

which not only keep water ***too hot or too cold,*** but cost as much to run as the gasoline used by this engine. By attaching a piece of pipe as an air head the engine will throw water sixty feet. Gives instantly available fire protection. Invaluable for watering gardens, irrigating, truck farming, sprinkling lawns and public parks, spraying trees, etc.

Runs Separators, Grinders, All Light Machines

The Farm Pump Engine is equipped with wide pulley for running the many machines that are ordinarily operated by ***hand-power*** or by ***foot-power.***

The engine is complete in itself. Nothing to buy but the gasoline. No "extras" of any sort—no pump-jacks, no belts, no walking beams, etc. No anchor posts to hold it down. No special platform needed. You simply fill the gasoline tank, oil up and ***start the engine!***

It's as high grade in every way as best automobile engines. Perfectly air-cooled, ***without cooling attachments!*** Self-oiling. Important working parts protected by metal case, easily reached for cleaning. Every engine ***tried out at the factory*** and shipped in perfect condition.

Thousands Sold! Write for Catalog

This little Portable Pumping Plant is the engine success of the century. Nothing else like it. The first gasoline ***engine*** to take the place of ***man-power*** in the everyday tasks of the farm. Little engine—Big Power. Over 100 practical uses. Think of such an engine for less than the cost of an unreliable, lazy, rickety, dangerous windmill!

Fuller & Johnson Mfg. Co., 4 Fisk St., Madison, Wis.

(Established 1840.)

Get a "Pumper" Going NOW! Don't Wait for Hot Weather!

Sooner or later you are going to have a Farm Pump Engine. Why not order your engine now and use it ***winter and summer?***

Farmers everywhere are doing away with windmills and installing Farm Pump Engines. They are getting perfect ***pumping service,*** and ***in addition*** using the little engine for countless odd jobs on the farm.

The engine runs indoors or out, rain or shine, zero weather or sleet. Weighs only 250 pounds—can be quickly and easily moved anywhere. Built and guaranteed by Fuller & Johnson, whose High-Power, Double-Efficiency Engines are internationally famous.

Send Coupon Today for FREE CATALOG

ENGINE BOOK COUPON

FULLER & JOHNSON MFG. CO.

4 Fisk Street, Madison, Wis.

Please send me your Engine Catalogs as indicated below.

Name ______________________

Address ______________________

☐ Farm Pump Engines ☐ Double-Efficiency Engines

April 1911

Will Machinery Prices Drop?

MANY of Our Folks want to know about buying machinery — should they buy now or will prices soon be coming down?

To our way of thinking, there is little chance of any immediate material reduction in prevailing prices of all farm implements. There may be individual cases where sale prices are slightly reduced, but we look for no general cuts.

The steel and iron already made up was bought by the manufacturers at prices about equaling those prevailing February 1, 1919. Labor costs are practically as high as they ever were. Unskilled labor is more plentiful in some parts than six months ago, but skilled labor is scarce. Transportation costs are still high, and apparently no decrease is in sight.

Thus, it is plain that all the elements that enter into the cost of making machinery, and that govern the price thereof, are likely to be high for some months to come. A few dollars one way or the other in the cost of a machine isn't so important as getting the work done when it needs doing.

After-Effects of Exposure Like This

RHEUMATIC twinges, sore muscles, stiff joints—must not be neglected. Ease them up right away with Sloan's Liniment.

Relieve other pains and aches, too, such as *lumbago, neuralgia, sciatica, strains, sprains, neuralgic headache,* with this most effective, prompt-acting remedy. Lay it on the affected spot and let it *penetrate* soothingly —*no rubbing* is required.

Don't fuss and muss around with smeary plasters or ointments. Sloan's Liniment is clean, won't clog pores or stain the skin.

Sloan's Liniment, as you know, comes in three sizes, 30c, 60c and $1.20. Most folks buy the biggest bottle, it's a generous size and they get more for proportionately less. Always keep it handy for emergency use,—it may be any minute.

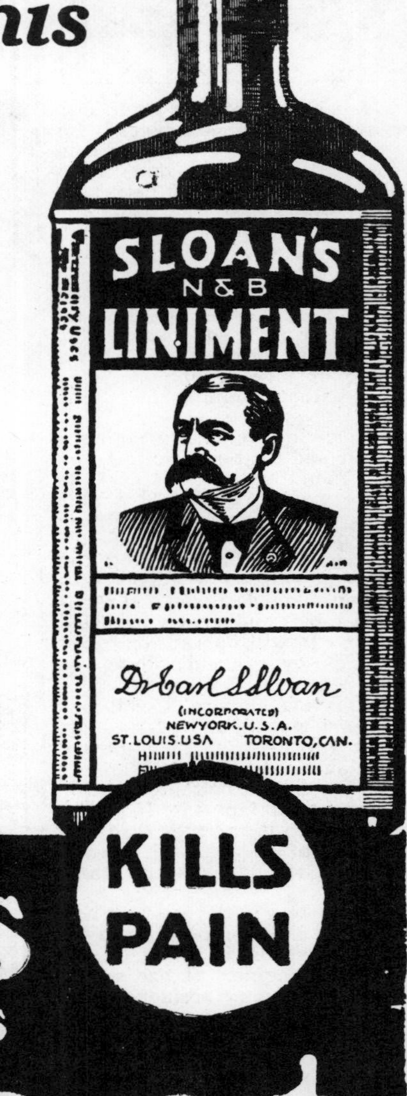

KILLS PAIN

Sloan's
The World's
Liniment

And now electricity and indoor plumbing . . .

FARM ELECTRIC LIGHTS

The Engine That Pumps Water Can at the Same Time Charge a Storage Battery. Thus Both Water and Electricity Can be on Tap in the Farmhouse so Equipped

THE outfit for supplying water and electric lights on a farm may be installed anywhere, the only requirements being that the place be clean and dry, and within no very great distance from points where the lights are wanted. To get the best and most economical service from the engine, it should be so installed that it can be used to drive other machinery in addition to the dynamo. If space will permit, it is easy to put up a small line shaft, and to drive from it the cream separator, churn, pump, washing-machine and other small machines. The engine will run all these and the dynamo at the same time, because to drive the dynamo for charging the battery takes less than one-third of the power.

The lights used may be taken directly from the dynamo or from the storage

battery, which stores up the electricity generated by the dynamo and holds it for use when wanted. Under ordinary conditions, most of the lighting is done direct from the dynamo, and it is not necessary then to charge the storage battery more than once or twice a week. When completely discharged, it will require about ten hours running to recharge it. When it is charged, however, it will be found to be extremely convenient, as it is not necessary then to run the engine for light. It will furnish lights for the average farm home for two or three evenings, when fully charged, without running the engine at all.

The accompanying half-tone shows a complete water-and-light outfit offered by a well-known manufacturer. It consists of a two-horse-power engine; dynamo; storage battery; switchboard; fifty Mazda (Tungsten) lamps; and the necessary shades, fixtures, etc., for installing the outfit. The engine has extra heavy fly-wheels and is specially designed and regulated to give a steady and unvarying speed to the dynamo. It will operate on kerosene, gasoline or low-grade distillates, as desired.

The dynamo is a 25 ampere, 32 volt machine, compound wound, and gives sufficient current for fifty 12-candle-power lights. It is automatic in operation and will maintain a constant voltage, regardless of the number of lamps in use. The low voltage at which it operates makes it entirely harmless to the operator, even if uninsulated parts should be accidentally touched.

The storage battery with the outfit has sixteen cells, and light or power can be taken from it whenever it is not convenient to run the engine. It has ample capacity for any ordinary residence and grounds, as it will carry nine 12-candle-power Tungsten lamps for seven and one-half hours of continuous service.

Such an outfit costs about $500—not including pump, air pressure tank, etc. All complete, the combined outfit shown would cost from $750 to $1,000, according to size of tank, pump, etc.

The cost of operating the electric plant will be found to be extremely low, considering the many benefits derived from it. If kerosene at ten cents a gallon is used as a fuel for the engine, fifty lights can be had for an hour at a cost of five cents. But if a farmer must pump water, the cost of the electricity is practically nothing, as the same running of the engine accomplishes both purposes.

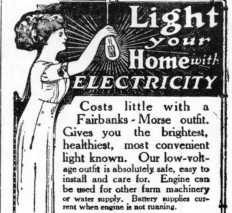

February 1913

October 1913

Farm Journal has its own "Experimental Farm" planned . . . half in fun, half seriously

Here is another little contrivance we shall have on our experimental farm when we get it started. We formerly had a cheaper concern—a simple stick of wood with a hole near one end to receive the plow point—when we used to farm at home, on which to slide the plow from one place to another, but we shall have to use wheels hereafter, such as are shown in the engraving. We are bound to have all the latest improvements, regardless of expense, and never let any other experimental farm get ahead of ours. No, indeed.

May 1882

We received two large, fine looking Kieffer pears from Wm. Parry a few weeks ago. They were ripe and we ate them. They were not very good and we are uncertain exactly how far they were from being bad. Sometimes we think they might have been worse and that if it were a question of no pears or Kieffer pears we should prefer the—latter. But we aver that for size, shape and beauty the specimens Mr. Parry sent us were superb.

When we get that experimental farm and our big dairy fully established we shall need a churn power, and here is the idea we shall work from. (Taken from the Rural New-Yorker, and none the worse for that.)

January 1884

Here is another illustration of a handy hook on which to hang almost anything. It may be used in the wood-house, the cellar, barn, stable or pig-pen. It is made of ordinary 3-16 annealed wire, and may be readily made at home. It should fit neatly over the board or cleat to which it is fastened. We intend to have a good supply of all these little conveniences on that Experimental Farm, when we get it.

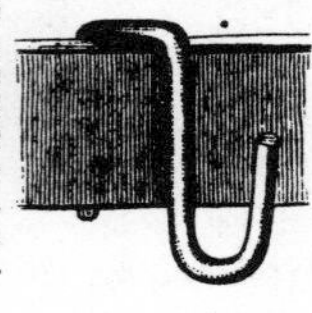

Now stand up so we can count you in that 200,000.

January 1885

If we do not have the best and handiest gates and doors about our prospective Experimental Farm it will be no fault of our friends. The cut shows the manner of making and operating a small door on pig and sheep pens or calf stables. It is pivoted on a bolt at the lower right hand corner. Gates for small stock may be made in fences on the same principle. Even large gates for horses and cattle may be operated by leaving off the top guard and letting the gate drop between posts at each side, which will hold it securely. B. U. Heister, Farm Ridge, Ill., kindly furnishes us the design.

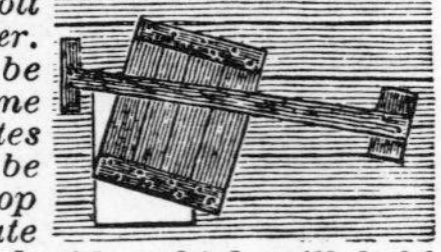

April 1889

Specialty farming is the order of the day. As we intend to keep up with the procession when we get that Experimental Farm of ours, we have planned to breed off the husks from our field corn to save labor of husking and exhaustion of the soil from growing useless fodder. We are confident this can be done. It is in line with the breeding of beef cows, butter cows, hornless cows, and the growing of seedless fruits, vegetable roots with little tops, etc. The variety, when we produce it, will be such a novelty that we hope by judicious advertising to sell several thousand dollars' worth for seed. Of course we shall grow corn for ensilage, but for that purpose we shall have a special variety. We have had an artist illustrate our Wonderful Mammoth Huskless and Stalkless Corn, as it will appear when perfected.

May 1891

When the editor gets that Experimental Farm, or perhaps sooner, we believe he wants to make a carry-all for fence-making like the one the good man of this house has made. Take an old rubber boot, cut the foot off at the ankle, tack the lid of an axle-grease box firmly to the bottom, fasten a strap to the top long enough to reach over the shoulder school-boy fashion. In this pouch he carries hammer, nails staples, and claw-hammer to pull old nails and staples, and wire stretcher, etc. On his shoulder he carries the post-hole digger and pounder; instead of hitching up the team.

Nebraska City, Neb. *Mrs. W. A. N.*

[The cut shows the editor as he will appear when he starts out on his tour of fence inspection, equipped as Mrs. N. suggests. It is to be presumed that he will take off his coat and roll up his sleeves when he reaches the fence!]—Associate Editor.

April 1891

I take the liberty of recommending to our Editor for use on his Experimental Farm in a dry season like this, the "only original," non-patented potato digger, a drawing of which I enclose. I do this on the following solid grounds: 1. It is self acting, is always in gear and will begin operations as soon as admitted to the field. 2. Its elevator has a double back-action, raising the tubers and earth with perfect ease and separating them perfectly. 3. The gearing is so ingeniously covered that it cannot be worn out or clogged by gravel, weeds or vines. 4. Its adjustment is automatic, and the point of the digger is self sharpening. It will follow crooked rows and dig deep or shallow in hard-pan or sandy loam, never missing a hill. 5. It will pick up the potatoes, carry them to market and get as much for small as for large ones. **John.**

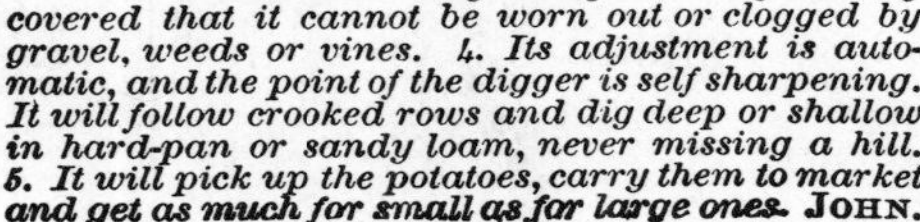

September 1893

Crocodiles are said to be quiet and inoffensive creatures when they are not hungry. (The same remark applies to man himself with equal force.) But the difficulty with the brute is that he is always hungry. Perhaps Secretary Wilson might find somewhere in our new possessions a breed with a less voracious appetite; if so, well and good. That sort of a snout looks as if it might prove to be a valuable subsoiler, or cultivator, but we are not yet quite ready to send in an order for one to be used on that Experimental Farm.

April 1900

To call the "men folks" from distant fields to their meals is often beyond the power of an old-fashioned horn,—especially if the wind be blowing the wrong way. The cut shows a good way to signal. The box is painted black, and can mean several things, according as it is fully elevated, or raised at other elevations. That Experimental Farm shall have one.

September 1900

When we get that Experimental Farm we shall have plenty of fruit-apples, pears, peaches, quinces and plums. No doubt about this. And then after growing as nice fruit as we can, we shall see that it is well assorted and sent to market in good shape. The wormy, knotty, poor fruit we shall keep at home for the stock. Already we have been looking

around for the right thing in fruit baskets, and have found it in the form shown above. This is the Seeley basket with cover at both ends. In filling the little end is up; after filling both ends are closed and the baskets can be stacked and packed close in wagon or car. They are very light and strong—a man heavy as Judge Biggle could dance on the lid of an empty. These baskets are to be made in the interest of growers, and we understand that a company is being formed for this purpose. Growers should have an eye on the project and address or see Mr. Seeley, 1027 Walnut st., Phila., Pa.

February 1897

One of Our Folks sends us a photograph of a wigwam wood-pile. He says, "The poles extend around a living tree and form a pretty tight protection for the wood stored inside. I have passed this wood-pile many times, and it always seems to be about the same size, which indicates a secret I have not been able to master in regard to our own. Ours gets smaller day by day until it is all gone." We do not exactly like the looks of this wood-pile, but if it holds its own, in the way described, we shall have to give it a trial on that Experimental Farm.

December 1904

A farmer said the other day, "When I was a boy my father gave me this advice, which I have always remembered and found to be good: 'Always have a string and a nail in your pocket when you go away from home, and when you go into the woods always take an ax with you.'" This seems to me worth passing along. E. L. V.

A fine ten-pound dairy cow, a ewe with two pairs of twins a year, a hen that will lay three eggs a week all winter, a horse that can go fast, look nice, keep fat and let a woman drive him, a collie that will guard the place day and night and not run the cows, a steer so fat that all the butchers want him—all are desirable on the farm, and worthy any man's ambition; but here's the bright farm boy, the prince, the lovely fellow who gets sleepy at night and is hard to call in the morning—this is the best stock on the farm far and away. And we shall have at least one on that Experimental Farm. Sure.

January 1904

HOME TOPICS, No. 50.

BY FAITH.

It is probably over twenty-five years since the first stir was made in this country for the so-called women's rights. I think the feeling was general that women were capable of taking a more active part in life than they had done previous to that time; a few were aspiring to the higher branches of education, and the question arose to what good and what else are they capable of? To the surprise of thinkers, both queries were speedily answered by a few who professed to speak for women generally, "she fits herself to take her rightful share in the government of the country; place the ballot in her hands." Of course a few upheld the idea, but it was repugnant to the large majority of women, though they naturally made no public demonstration against it, and its supporters were soon ridiculed as visionary and began to regard themselves as martyrs in the cause of woman's redemption from oppression.

Whether suffrage for women was right or not, it was certainly not desirable in those days, nor did its advocates take the right way to obtain it; there was entirely too long a stride from the stay-at-home, unbusiness-like women of those times who knew little and cared less about politics, to the excited crowds who filled the air about the polls with drunken profanity. But the reception which these reformers met, did not deter other women from trying in other ways to extend the sphere of woman's influence; females are the natural nurses in sickness; a few, under great difficulties and discouragements, obtained a medical education, and claimed the right to practice among their own sex and children; their capability once proved, that door of usefulness and influence was permanently open to women; the study of law was next attempted with the same results, and though a strong feeling exists in many churches against female pastors, there are a few who have filled even that position acceptably.

It is hardly necessary to name numerous trades and occupations now considered quite suitable for women, which fifteen or twenty years ago, were regarded as exclusively for men. A few moments thought will show that women have indeed become active workers in the world, and with their wider sphere of observation, and the intelligence possessed by the average American woman, they are necessarily thinkers as well, and far more capable of exercising the right of suffrage than many who now possess it. Of course there are many still, who are neither workers nor thinkers, but the changes of the past few years have caused many to think that placing the ballot in their hands, is only a question of time; already they take part in school elections in many of the states; and in Wyoming they are full voters.

The result, so far as I have been able to ascertain of the experiments is, that though women take no part in the primary or caucus meetings the men find it necessary to consider what kind of men they will vote for, it being well understood that the female vote will not be given to an immoral man, or to one whose character is in any way doubtful, no matter to what party he may belong. If this is to be the general result, we may be well satisfied to accept the right of suffrage when it is offered to us, little as we may desire it, simply for the good of the country.

July 1881

Here's an early declaration of women's rights, urging acceptance of suffrage "for the good of the country"

More in 1910

THE RIGHTS OF WOMEN

The women of England are greatly stirred up over the unjust laws under which they live, and are making a vigorous fight for a reform. Echoes of the contest are being heard on this side of the ocean, and many of our own women are on the war-path. These women want to be allowed to vote so they can take part in correcting the laws under which they live, and this, on the face of it, seems to be a fair proposition.

The laws of this country are less unjust to women than those of England, and yet some of them seem to be nearly of the same grotesque pattern.

For instance, if a wife who owns property fails to make a will and dies without issue, the widower is entitled to all the personal property and the use of all the real estate during his life. Thus it is in our own state and in some other states of the Union. Also the joint earnings of husband and wife belong under the law to the husband only; and when the husband dies the wife inherits not all of the personal property as in the case of the widower, but only one-third of the personal property and one-third of the income from the real estate.

Why, in the first place, the husband should get all, even money earned by the wife, and in the second, the wife receive only a third, is a question the women are asking, some in a loud voice and some in a subdued whisper, and it is up to the men who made the laws to give a proper answer. Such laws seem to have been based on the proposition that a widower needs the support which the inheritance can give, while the poor widow can largely shift for herself. It is enough to make an honest man blush to think that he ever had a hand in permitting such a partial law to remain on the statute books.

In many states a married woman has no right to her own children. The father is the sole legal guardian. He can take the child away from his mother. He can apprentice the child and send him out to work without asking the mother's consent; his services and wages belong to him; the mother is powerless to protect the child. She is a nonentity in the matter.

This is not right; it ought not to be and it will have to be remedied. If the child belongs to either one alone, it is the mother and not the father, for usually the mother is the child's best friend.

Some of the women are getting pretty cross about such unequality in the laws, and all manly men will not only sympathize with them, but will be ready to aid them in their struggle for justice.

February 1910

READS LIKE THE DECLARATION OF INDEPENDENCE

[Published by request of one of the signers]

THE following has been issued by the Woman Suffrage Association of Pennsylvania, and is well worthy of perusal and study by all Our Folks:

"The people of the United States live under a representative form of government. Under such a government it is necessary that those persons who are to be represented shall choose the persons who shall represent them. In the state of Pennsylvania the women citizens have no means of expressing such a choice. Therefore, it having become necessary that they should take steps to secure such means of expression, they have united to form a party which shall have for its sole purpose the securing of the ballot, through political action, for the women of Pennsylvania on the same terms upon which it is granted to the men of the state.

The founders of this Republic chose a form which was the most closely representative of any government then in existence, and in so doing took a long step toward the freedom of the human race. They found certain institutions in existence which were inconsistent with the principles of such a government, but which it was not then practical to dispense with, and which they left for future generations to abolish. The first of these institutions was that of human servitude as applied to a race. This was eliminated only after a long and terrible conflict, which ended in the establishment of the principle of freedom from physical servitude of the enslaved race, and the establishment of political freedom for the men of that race.

As our government derives its just powers from the consent of the governed, it is apparent that it must derive unjust powers from the lack of consent on the part of one-half of the people. This we have found to be the case in regard to the government of women who have no power to consent to the laws by which they are governed.

We, therefore, declare that in order to fully complete the plan of government formulated by the founders of this Republic, and sealed by their self-sacrifice and the devotion of their descendants, we will set ourselves to the task of removing this last obstacle in the way of a fully representative government, by securing the political freedom of women.

To this task we pledge ourselves, not in any spirit of self-seeking, but with that impulse of self-respect which has impelled all persons who have sought for freedom through all the periods of past history; that freedom of the individual which is only possible in a free state, where the government rests not upon the consent of a fraction of the people, however large, but upon that of the whole people."

This document was drawn up by Mrs. M. C. Klingelsmith, attorney for the Pennsylvania Woman Suffrage Association, and a subcommittee. The members of this Central Committee are:

Mrs. A. M. Orme, Chairman	Miss Julia Lewis
Mrs. M. C. Morgan	Miss Maie Atlee Bunn
Miss Lida S. Adams	Miss Annie Bunn
Mrs. Lawrence Lewis, Jr.	Mrs. F. D. Patterson
Miss Harriet Dulles	Mrs. Geo. A. Piersol
Mrs. M. C. Klingelsmith	Mrs. H. H. Donaldson
Miss Gertrude Atkinson	Mrs. Henry Justice
Miss Frances Bradford	Miss Helen McFogg
Mrs. L. M. B. Mitchell	Miss Sara D. Chambers

April 1912

Three meals a day—"nice for the husbands but death to the wives," wrote an early woman columnist. But feeding a threshing crew was "doing the impossible"

THREE MEALS A DAY.

BY MARY SIDNEY.

It is said that farmers' wives and daughters go insane oftener than other women; and if this be so I am of the opinion that it is the three meals a day they are tied to that is doing it.

What poor mortal could keep her head level if she is never able to get away from the thought, what shall we eat?

Nobody but a farmer's wife knows what a cavernous region there is under a farmer's vest; nobody knows so well as she how much stuff it takes to keep him from caving in. If there ever come a day, as is rarely the case on the farm, when the men are all away and there is no one left but herself and perhaps children, there will be simple fare that day. She will not put much work on her own stomach; but these days are of too rare occurrence to freshen and invigorate the mind to any great extent, and ten chances to one if they are not selected for canning or drying or preserving, and laying away stores for future needs.

The farmer's wife who does her own work, and they are more and more doing this as the business grows poorer, has really no time to call her own. Her position smacks of serfdom. The girl who is employed for general housework is a lady of leisure compared with her. She has an occasional day out, and frequent Sundays when the eating question does not concern her; not so with the weary wife; if she go to church she must hasten back to prepare the dinner for the men who are resting their bones and taking the world as becomes men. If she goes anywhere, she must leave plenty cooked for the family to eat in her absence, or rush back in time to have the next meal in season, or there will be mutiny among the hired men. I am sure the world must be easier and jollier for the wife of the untutored savage who eats when he is hungry, and swallows such things as he can get, than for the farmer's wife with cultivated taste, who wants to live like other folks, and has an eye to feeding her family in a civilized way. If the farm will not afford to hire help to wait on the men necessary to till the land, what is civilization but a burden to her? It has brought her lots of work and nonsense. It has invented little salts, little butters, little side dishes of every kind, with napkins, finger dippers, and untold troublesome culinary preparations that are enough to distract a poor lone-handed woman. If she wants to live her time out she should set her men down to one big dish with several spoons; as economical young men are said to treat the girls to ice cream by increasing the number of spoons, instead of plates, and as the German peasants pass round the mug of beer for the whole family, guests and all. It seems marvelous how it came to be so firmly established as a custom, that women shall do all the cooking and men only the eating. It was not so in the beginning, and one would think as he does the heavier end of the eating, he ought also to divide the burden of cooking. But it is no uncommon thing to find that women, even those who help in the field, and others who have to help support the family by washing and ironing and other laborious things, are obliged to break off to prepare the dinner and all the meals, while the men of the family are busy with their hands in their pockets looking on. Of course I am talking of farmers wives and other *working* women —not those appendages who "toil not, neither do they spin," and who would not nor could not cook a mess of hash if it were to keep the family from going to ruin. It seems to be the way of the world that those who will work, may work: while those who won't, tresspass upon others who do, to a ruinous extent.

I hear the girls singing a song not so elegant as suggestive—

"There is a married land far, far away,
Where husbands always eat three meals a day,
Oh, how those husbands eat,
Fish and fowl and bread and meat,
They say there is naught can beat
Three meals a day."

And three meals a day are nice, for the husbands, but death to the wives unless they get a lift once in a while that will give them a chance to soar away from the everlasting eating question, and think about other things. "Such as their neighbors bonnets and babies," the provoking Sidney head adds. I wonder if other women have the trouble that I have to get their husbands down into deep, solid thinking about things.

WESTERN CHIT-CHAT.

DOING THE IMPOSSIBLE.

We have been going to thresh for a month. Every time the cream man came I was afraid to let him have the cream for fear the threshers would come and we would run short of butter. Yesterday morning John woke me up at three o'clock and told me that the threshers would be here for supper. Then he asked me if I could go to town (five miles) and get some beef; he had no time, as he had to go round and hunt up hands. I left cousin Eva to tend to the bread, Jessie to bake the pies, Sarah to scour the spoons, and Harry to dig the potatoes, while Minnie and I drove to town. We were back at nine o'clock, and all the rest of the day was very full. The men did not get to work till half past three o'clock, and at four John came to the house and asked me to do two impossible things—one was to have supper at sundown, the other was to fix places for twenty men to eat supper at one time. The reason that it is impossible to have supper at sundown on a farm is that the milking and dish washing all come after dark, and everything is hurly burly, everybody screeching and yelling to each other about the cows and calves, and buckets and tins, and sheep and colts, and horses and slop buckets. I made a vow a long time ago that I would never get another threshing supper at sundown. Then as to seating twenty men—our table only holds fourteen men comfortably, and sixteen uncomfortably. When I seat sixteen men at it, they strike their elbows against each other and spill their coffee, drop the gravy bowls and spill the pies off the plate. We have another table in the kitchen that we made out of a discarded door; it is'nt just exactly tony, but it does pretty well for poor folks. It will seat six persons comfortably, three at each side, but when the table fell down one time John nailed some wide pieces across the ends, that cramp people's knees so that nobody likes to sit there. To eat at this table in the hot kitchen where we had had a blistering hot fire all day was *just* impossible. When five women are cooking in one kitchen at the same time there is no room for men folks. We had to take the table out doors and around to the porch and set it there and as soon as we put vicutals on it, one of us had to stand and mind the flies off. Then we had not dishes enough to feed twenty men all at once, and had to send the girls off to the neighbors to borrow tea-cups and goblets, and knives and deep dishes. We rang the bell at sundown and the men came running, and in a minute the tables were full, and such eating. "Twenty minutes for dinner" at a railroad restaurant is not to be compared with it, and the moment they were done they jumped from the table and ran—so as to get home and do up their chores—and I in the steaming precincts of the sweltering kitchen renewed my vow. And after this I *never* will have supper at sundown. Will I?

ROSE PARK.

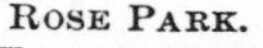

Feeding a threshing crew

Mrs. John B. Kelly, mother of Princess Grace of Monaco, as a Farm Journal cover girl

The Farm Journal

For Sleeves-Rolled-Up Farmers

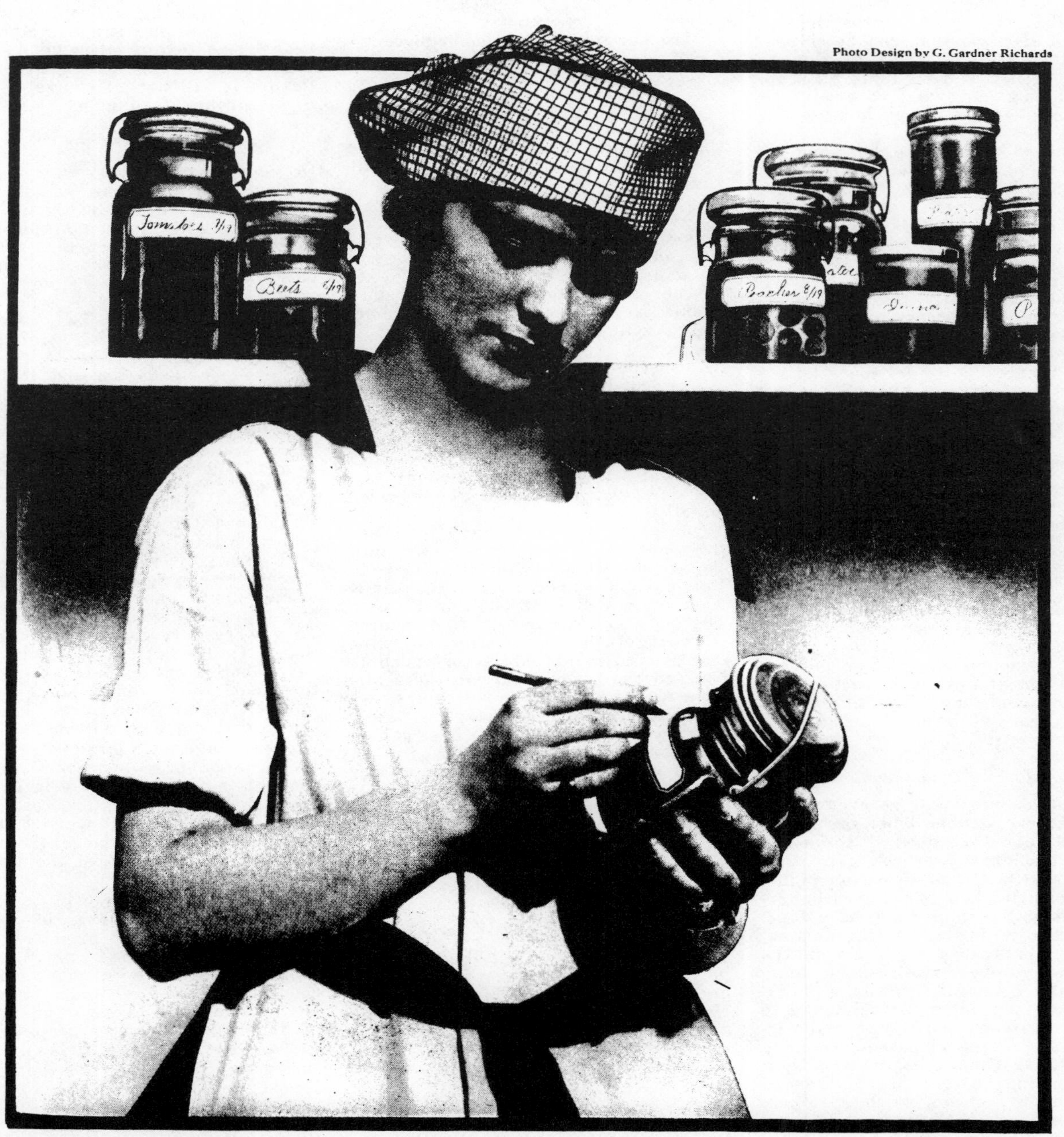

Photo Design by G. Gardner Richards

August, 1919 Peaches! *5 Cents*

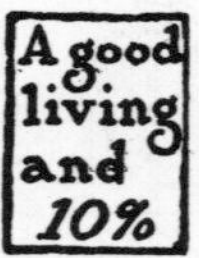

More Labor for 1919 or a Crash

A good living and 10%

THE critical problem this coming year is labor. Farmers can not make "A Good Living and 10%" unless the supply of farm labor is increased. Neither can they do their part in feeding the hungry nations of Europe.

Before Germany surrendered Mr. Hoover told us we must furnish Europe 22,000,000 tons of food this year. That is twice as much as we sent last year. Now the starving millions of the defeated nations, as well as those of Russia, are added to the list of those we must help to feed. We can not afford to be inhuman to our late foes—we hold ourselves higher than that; we shall help them to the extent of our ability.

Last year, with the largest part of our labor drafted, or enticed into war industries by wages higher than farmers could afford to pay, we grew a larger acreage of crops than ever before. We need to do still more this year. There is no possibility of overdoing the thing in the case of crops that can be shipped across the water. In fact, if the Government does not prevent hungry Europe from bidding our own food away from us, we shall ourselves go hungry next winter.

Europe will, of course, be doing the best she can next summer, but her labor has been slain in battle. Her work animals have been eaten, or worn out in war. Many of her fields have been torn up so badly that she can not raise a normal crop. Besides, she never was able to feed herself before the war. Hence it is absolutely imperative that our farmers have all the labor they can use next year.

We are shorter of labor on farms now than we were last year. The question now is, Where can we get more labor? It is yet too early to tell what effect the end of the war will have on the supply of farm labor. One big hope is that the closing up of war industries will free enough labor to meet the demand. Sending the boys home from camps will help, too. But we must remember that in former years we were in the habit of absorbing 1,000,000 immigrants a year into our growing industries. For four years past we have not had this immigration. We can not yet tell how many munitions workers will be absorbed by other industries, and how many will go back to the farm. Even if we could be assured of labor enough to go around, the problem of getting it back to the farm is no small one. The situation is really critical, but the prospects of meeting it are better than they were last year.

How To Save Labor

It is just as important as ever for us to use every possible labor-saving device this year. We need all the labor-saving machinery we can get. The farmer who last year drove an eight-horse team hitched to a big disk harrow, and at the same time led a four-horse team pulling a big drag harrow, will have to stay on the job. So will the farmer who drove a twelve-horse team hitched to a group of three gang plows.

We must depend on our neighbors to cooperate with us in planting and harvesting, and whenever possible combine to help those who are behind with their work, planning the work far enough ahead so as to know just how much extra help will be needed at all times. This will give those who are trying to find labor for us time to locate it.

Find How Much Labor Is Needed

Last year many of the states started in January to find out just how much help the farmers would need during the summer. Where this was done the problem of getting help was much simpler. Every state should follow this plan, not only this winter but every winter. This

"Just like running the family flivver," says this woman who is taking a man's place on the farm

work was carried on through the public school children, under the direction of their teachers, and with the assistance of county agents, school superintendents and various other interested parties.

Some Sources of Labor

The United States Employment Service is establishing offices all over the country to help move labor from one place to another as the need arises. County agents are in close touch with farmers and can find out how much labor is needed. In every state there is a farm help specialist.

These agencies can distribute to farms such labor as may easily be available. Every farmer who will need more help than he now has should tell his county agent his needs. The county agents in turn will call on the Employment Service for labor, if it can not be supplied directly.

Our soldier boys in Europe will be busy for some time. They must stay until settled governments are formed in Russia and Germany; for until that is done there will be trouble in Europe. The boys now in camps in this country will soon return home. Farmer boys now employed in munitions factories can go back to the farms. So can those who have been helping to build camps, nitrate factories, and the like.

Every effort will be made to send men with farm experience, who are thrown out of employment by stoppage of war industries, to the farms. It is impossible to tell now how much labor can be obtained from these sources; hence, we must leave no stone unturned to get labor from other sources, such as the Boys' Working Reserve and the Woman's Land Army.

Boys Were Good Workers

Farmers naturally do not like to employ inexperienced city boys on farms; they are liable to do as much damage as good. However, there are some things to be said in favor of this plan where experienced help can not be had.

Last year, under the guidance of the Boys' Working Reserve, many thousands of city boys patriotically volunteered to help on farms. Farmers accepted them because they had to. Those who employed these boys were agreeably surprised at their earnestness and willingness to learn. They were not of the type we see idling on the streets or smoking cigarettes.

Of those city high-school boys who had a brief course of training for farm work before going to the farms, even where the training did not last more than two weeks, ninety-five per cent made good; their employers reported favorably on them. This is very satisfactory. Those who had no training, especially those who were not high-school or college students, did not do so well; fifty per cent of them failed.

Most of these boys liked the work. Out of 170 city high-school boys who had two weeks' farm training in Indiana, twenty-seven liked farm work so well that they applied for admission into the State Agricultural College. Nearly all of these 170 boys made good on the farms to which they were sent.

A course of training in simple farm tasks has been prepared for use in high schools this winter, and every high school in the country is being urged to give this training. If this is done it will help to supply summer labor next year. This kind of labor will be better than most farmers expect it to be; although it will not, of course, be equal to well-trained farm help.

Women Saved the Day

In some parts of this country, notably in New York state, the Woman's Land Army saved the day last year. These women were mostly students and school-teachers; some were college teachers. They did plowing, harrowing, cultivating, fruit thinning and picking, mowing, pitching hay, shocking grain, fence making and milking. They were sent out in units ranging in size from four to seventy. Each unit had a chaperon-housekeeper, and they did their own cooking. They lived in vacant houses, barns and tents.

A former master of the New York State Grange employed some of these women. When asked how he liked them he said: "In common with other farmers here, when this camp was first established I thought it was a foolish scheme. But I couldn't get other help, so I gave the women a trial. I was agreeably surprised. Of course, the women didn't know much about farming, but they learned very quickly. They were very earnest and conscientious. On the hottest days, when ordinary laborers around here were lying in the shade, these women stuck to their jobs. After they had learned how to do things they made good hands."

The manager of a large farm near one of these camps, when asked what he thought about city women as farm laborers, replied: "You can judge what I think about it when I tell you that after my experience this year I shall ask to have one of the camps on my farm next year."

There are many women in every large city working like slaves in crowded tenements, who would consider it a god-send to get out on the farms where they could work in the open under healthful conditions. Women should not be denied an opportunity to take part in the work of feeding the hungry people of the world. They are eager to help.

Experience last year and the year before shows that where there is some one to look after the matter plenty of harvest labor can be had. Hundreds of towns shut up shop when harvest time came, and the people went out and helped harvest the crops. They will do it again next summer. All that is needed is to see that the proper appeal is made to city people. They are no less patriotic than farmers. They want to help.

3,633 Miles
Across the Wealth-Belt

Following is a record of the impressions of The Farm Journal's Automobile Party, after the five weeks' successful trip across Nebraska, Kansas, Missouri, Iowa, Illinois, Michigan, Indiana, Ohio, New York, Pennsylvania, New Jersey and Maryland

OUR first thought, now that we are home from our automobile trip, is to thank our good friends who gave us a friendly word as we passed along. All in all, we traveled 3,633 miles, were in twelve states, touched in 521 cities and towns, visited with many of Our Folks, called on 407 storekeepers, met 108 bankers, scores of Farm Journal Folks, and saw millions and millions of dollars in crops. In five weeks we drove across the world's wealth-belt, the prosperity section of America.

The foremost thing in our minds, as we traveled along day after day, was the question of roads. There is no larger problem today than crop transportation. Good roads are the basis of trade, just as crop production itself is the basis of all wealth. Where a road is passable only 300 days a year, there is not only great waste of time, but crops bring in less money and equally productive land invariably sells at lower prices.

We encountered every variety of road surface (or lack of surface) on the two main classes of roads—that is, the so-called trunk-line highways, between large cities, and the trading-center highways, between the smaller cities and towns. To make a first-class job for all time the main highways must be engineer-built, grades and right-angle turns largely eliminated, the roads must be built of concrete, wide enough for the traffic, preferably with a proper driving surface. It would pay to condemn land to straighten and shorten these through roads—the saving in distance would more than pay for the land itself.

These trunk lines are important, but we must not lose sight of the inter-town roads and the country roads; for if the latter are not put in good shape the towns would soon starve. In many cases we find that hard roads had added $100 an acre to the farm value, and it was also true that the better the roads the more prosperous the community. It was also true that no one ever willingly moved from a good roads district back to poor roads. The zealous advocates of good roads are those who have them.

All roads need not be concrete, but the main highways must, for nothing else will stand heavy hauling in fast motor trucks; and our prophecy is that it won't be long before trucks are almost as numerous in the country as automobiles are today. But all roads must be given care—scraped, dragged and drained, the chuck-holes eliminated and travel made safe.

We were obliged to make many detours. Some were clearly marked, others not. The most truthful sign said, "Road closed to Hope"—Hope being the name of a small town in New Jersey. But at that it was true,—the road *was* closed to hope, in most cases! More signboards are needed 'most everywhere. The trails, as through routes are called, are marked fairly well, but plainly worded signs would add to the comfort of strangers.

Crops

Everywhere, and generally speaking, crops looked good. Drought had done some injury in some places, too much rain had hurt in others, but prosperity for this year was manifest on every hand. There is noticeably less waste land than on our previous trips. The West is approaching the East in this respect. Diversification of crops is also more evident. Vegetable gardens are also increasing and so are orchards. More land is being put under cultivation through proper drainage. With continuing high prices for farm products,

an investment in reclaiming land is bound to yield large returns.

Buildings

Much more building, proportionately, is being done in farming communities than in towns or cities. Repairs are being made and much new construction is under way. Where labor is especially scarce, ready-made buildings are going up. The unsanitary, unsightly, ramshackle structures that never did help make profits, are being discarded and scientifically designed farm structures replacing them. The labor shortage has meant the building of modern tenant houses; for owners find they get dependable help only when they supply comfortable living quarters. Barns, granaries and bins are increasing in size, probably for the storage of grains and hay until prices are at the top.

The home grounds show marked improvement over past years. There are more flowers, more shrubbery and more care given to the lawns. It is a good sign and made us proud of Our Folks.

Furnishings

Inside the home the improvements are just as apparent as in the buildings themselves. Good plumbing goes into every new house and into most old ones that can be reconstructed. Electric lighting, adequate heating systems, hardwood floors, kitchen conveniences of all sorts, are also quite common and not to have the comforts of the city house is more and more the exception.

Farm Size

The labor shortage, the increasing price of land, etc., has cut down the size of farms. This, in turn, has intensified cultivation. Further development along this line will follow, as prices stay high and more machinery is used, and one man's labor can be made to accomplish more.

Machinery

Inasmuch as our only mechanical difficulty on the trip was the breaking of two valve springs, we had plenty of time to inquire about automobiles, tractors and farm machinery. There are thought to be 3,000,000 country-owned cars today, and we feel we saw most of them! Trucks, too, are becoming more common, as they ought to. The truck is a time-saver, and time is more valuable than ever, now that help is scarce and high priced. Tractors are coming slowly. The too-light machine is not making good, but the well-handled machine of adequate power is entirely satisfactory wherever used, especially as it is kept in operation more regularly and for an increasing variety of work. There are many more gasoline engines for belt work—the womenfolk seem to use them as readily as the men. The whole tendency is toward more machinery, thereby making human labor more efficient.

Live Stock

Pure-bred stock is coming strong. Breeders appreciate the value of pedigrees. Progressive bankers are helping this movement, which invariably increases a community's permanent wealth. There are naturally not so many horses where tractors are being used. Hogs continue to increase, and better hog houses are especially noticeable, despite vast room for improvement.

Conclusion

The country we saw is, generally, in splendid shape. Farms are better taken care of than ever, so is the machinery. Big crops seem assured and good prices, too. Never were we so proud of our subscribers and of publishing The Farm Journal, as after this journey across the wealth-belt.

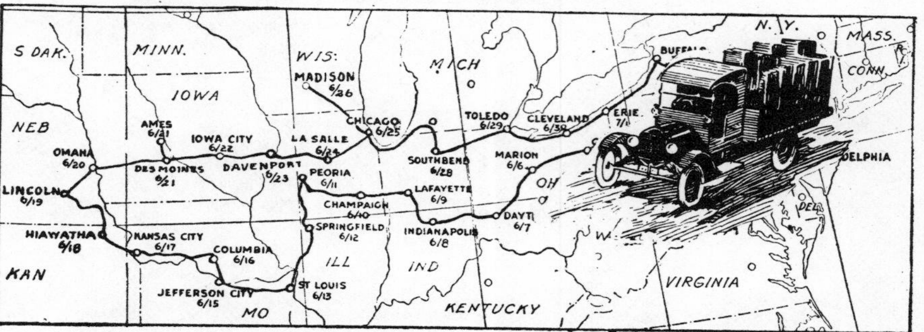

Farm Journal's 50th Anniversary issue reviews a half-century of progress in agriculture and rural life on the next 120 pages

The Farm Journal
50 th.
Anniversary
MARCH
1927
CONRAD F. LINKE

SOLID
fluid (TEXACO)
Your bearings cannot wait
till the oil warms up —

The oil must flow *instantly!*

Cold, thickened oil, slow to reach the bearings, can never save the first cutting, gripping wear of unlubricated metal on metal. Many a worn bearing and scored cylinder wall may be traced to a start on a winter's day—the costly effects of the first few minutes of cold idling. The right oil—zero flowing oil—is vital to your engine in winter.

No matter how cold the engine may be—Texaco Motor Oil never hesitates.

Texaco circulates instantly to every bearing. It splashes freely to every cylinder wall. The moment the engine turns — from that moment Texaco is vitally active in the protection of every moving surface.

The clear, golden color is proof enough. Texaco carries no paraffin wax, tars or other residues that congeal at low temperatures.

Such an oil adds miles to the life of your engine—miles of smoothness, quiet and power. Insist upon it. Look for the nearest Texaco sign.

THE TEXAS COMPANY, 17 BATTERY PLACE, NEW YORK CITY
TEXACO PETROLEUM PRODUCTS

TEXACO
MOTOR OIL

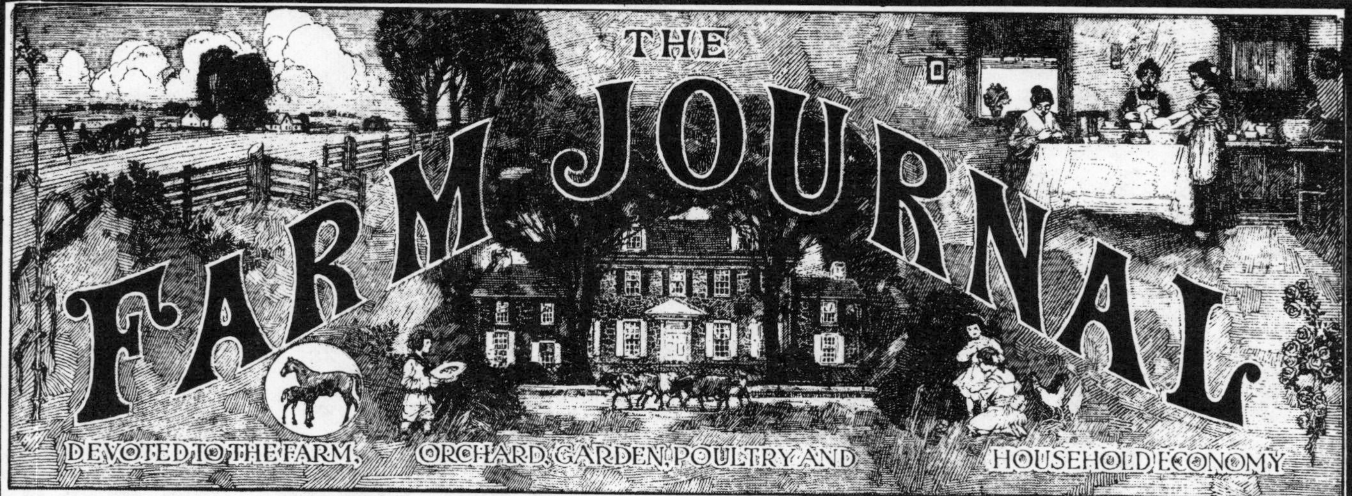
THE
FARM JOURNAL
DEVOTED TO THE FARM, ORCHARD, GARDEN, POULTRY AND HOUSEHOLD ECONOMY

March, 1927 Trade-mark Registered, 1905; Renewed, 1925. Copyright, 1927, by Wilmer Atkinson Company Vol. LI, No. 3

Practical Not Fancy Farming

"WE shall do our best to make The Farm Journal of *real* value to the cultivators of the soil and an entertaining visitor to rural firesides." So wrote Wilmer Atkinson in his introductory note to his readers in the first issue of The Farm Journal, March, 1877.

"We will let the paper speak for itself month by month as it appears," he continued, and this has been the policy of the paper ever since.

It is fair, however, on this Fiftieth Anniversary to look back, scan the present, and cast an eye to the future.

Wilmer Atkinson was a farmer boy, with a long line of farmer ancestors on both sides of the house, extending back to the time of William Penn. As a young man he had taught school, edited a local paper, published a daily in a nearby city, and in 1877 he conceived the idea of a farm paper that should be small in size, moderate in price, and of value to every member of the country home—men and women, boys and girls.

THE first edition of the little paper was 25,000 copies, representing mainly sample copies issued to secure circulation. The publisher at the very first adopted the plan of excluding all objectionable and harmful advertisements, such as lotteries, swindles, speculative, patent medicine and liquor. The article on page 8 tells something of how this policy turned out.

By 1882 the paper had passed its first 100,000 of circulation; by 1890 the 200,000 mark was passed and then the goal was set at 1,000,000. Thousands of Our Folks who read this will remember the long uphill pull until the million was reached in 1917.

Since then the circulation has grown steadily and healthfully, thanks to our friends, until, with this anniversary issue, we will print over 1,400,000 copies, giving The Farm Journal by far the greatest circulation among real farm folks of any farm paper in the world. If it is fair to count five readers to each copy, we have an audience of 7,000,000.

EARLY in its history The Farm Journal invented that deathless character, Peter Tumbledown, in whose name so many salutary lessons in industry, order, efficiency and thrift have been driven home and firmly clinched.

The Elmwood Farm letters of Judge Jacob Biggle and his wife Harriet can never fade from the memories of readers of the last 40 years.

Started at first to be only a local farm paper, The Farm Journal soon discovered that it was liked by farmers in far wider territory. It saw that many problems of farmers in Maine were identical with those in California, in Wisconsin and Texas and all other states. And so the magazine became itself national.

It would only cumber up this page to tell of the tons of paper that have been used in 50 years, the miles the sheets would extend, if placed end to end—many times around the world—the train-loads of mail stretching for miles in the postal cars. Nor perhaps is it worth while to tell, even without boasting, of the material things The Farm Journal has accomplished for its readers. You who read this are more interested in what The Farm Journal is doing and may yet accomplish.

AGRICULTURE has grown as The Farm Journal has kept pace with its development. The produce from the four million farms of 1877 amounted to $2,212,000,000; the produce from the nearly six and one-half million farms of *last year* will amount to about $17,000,000,000. The value of all farm property, land, buildings and equipment, when The Farm Journal started, was about $12,000,000,000. As the presses grind out this edition at the end of 50 years, this value has grown to about $60,000,000,000.

In the world of science, medicine, invention, mechanics, education, no 50 years in the history of the world has brought forth such profound changes in human thought and living. As Wilmer Atkinson and his one helper loaded type forms on a wheelbarrow to take them around to the nearby printing house, the horse cars were running, the telephone was still a toy, electric power and light undeveloped.

A trifling few farm homes had running water, all were heated by stoves or open fires, the roads were bad, every one went to the post-office for the mail.

With the stupendous growth and development in the comfort of farm living, The Farm Journal has kept pace. That we have been able to keep the plow in the furrow marked out by the founder of the business is a matter for self-satisfaction. It was his determination to make The Farm Journal a helpful, cheerful, stimulating monthly visitor for the rural homes of the country. It was not to be too large, for farmer folks were busy folks; it was to be well printed, for sometimes the farm light was poor; and what was said was to be boiled down—the "cream, not the skim-milk" of farm news. It aimed to "hit the nail on the head and not the thumb" and its determination was that all farmers should have "seats at the first table."

TO be 50 years old is one thing. To be 50 years young is quite another.

Wilmer Atkinson would have rejoiced to have joined in the happiness of this birthday. He passed away in 1920, at the age of 80, glad of what he had created; proud of its success and of the thousands and hundreds of thousands of friends that he had made. To only a few is it given to bring forth an idea, launch it on the stormy sea of life and see it mature as the heart desires. He had this rare satisfaction.

The Editor has a friend who maintains that those who have birthdays should do something for their friends on that day, and not expect gifts to themselves. Surely there is something in it. And so it is in this spirit that we have prepared this special issue, our Anniversary Number, filled to the brim with good wishes for our readers, and hopes for their continued health and happiness for the next 50 years and beyond that.

Arthur H. Jenkins
Editor.

THE FARM JOURNAL
Unlike Any Other Paper
Published Monthly by
WILMER ATKINSON COMPANY
Washington Square, Philadelphia, Pa.
CHARLES F. JENKINS, President
WILMER ATKINSON, Founder and Editor, 1877-1920
ARTHUR H. JENKINS, Editor

The Farm Journal is four years for $1.00; to new subscribers on trial, two years for 50 cents, one year for twenty-five cents; to subscribers in Philadelphia, Canada and foreign countries, two years for $1.00.

Entered as Second-class matter in accordance with the Postal Laws, at the Post-offices at Philadelphia, Pa.; Lima, Ohio; St. Louis, Mo.; Kansas City, Mo.; and La Crosse, Wis.

Table of contents of this issue will be found on page 117

50th Anniversary

WHATEVER YOU WANT IN A CAR WHATEVER YOU'RE WILLING TO PAY

CONSIDER OLDSMOBILE

Today *known factors* of merit, not price, determine the true value of an automobile.

Whatever you want in a car, check those known factors in Oldsmobile and you will find assurance of satisfaction . . . the satisfaction of spirited performance, of thrifty operation and long life, of comfort, convenience and distinguished beauty.

And whatever you're willing to pay, the more you go over Oldsmobile, point by point, and study every feature, the more you realize that here is, indeed, a car at a moderate price that gratifies your finer tastes as well as satisfies your every need.

Measure the car you want by these standards and good judgment and sound investment sense will tell you to consider Oldsmobile.

COACH $950 F. O. B. LANSING

The car illustrated is the De Luxe Coach

OLDSMOBILE SIX

Product of GENERAL MOTORS

The Farm Journal 50 Years Ago

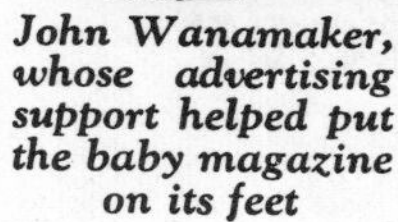

John Wanamaker, whose advertising support helped put the baby magazine on its feet

The first subscriber, Aunt Hannah Phillips

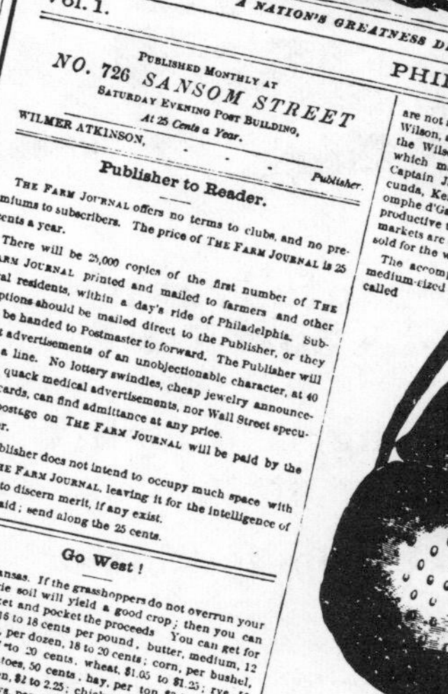

THE FARM JOURNAL

DEVOTED TO THE FARM, ORCHARD, GARDEN, AND RURAL ECONOMY.

Vol. 1. A NATION'S GREATNESS DEPENDS ON THE VIRTUE AND INTELLIGENCE OF ITS FARMERS. No. 1.

PUBLISHED MONTHLY AT NO. 726 SANSOM STREET, SATURDAY EVENING POST BUILDING, At 25 Cents a Year.

WILMER ATKINSON, Publisher.

PHILADELPHIA, MARCH, 1877.

Publisher to Reader.

THE FARM JOURNAL offers no terms to clubs and no premiums to subscribers. The price of THE FARM JOURNAL is 25 cents a year.

There will be 25,000 copies of the first number of THE FARM JOURNAL printed and mailed to farmers and other rural residents, within a day's ride of Philadelphia. ...

Go West!

Yes, go to Kansas. If the grasshoppers do not overrun your farm, the prairie soil will yield a good crop; ...

Strawberries—Essex Beauty.

BY WILLIAM PARRY.

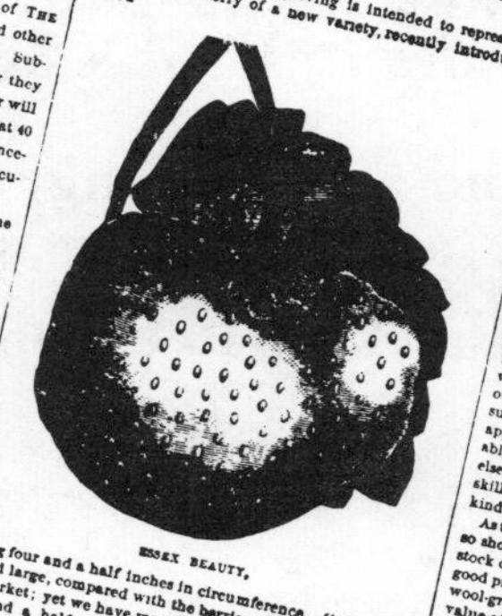

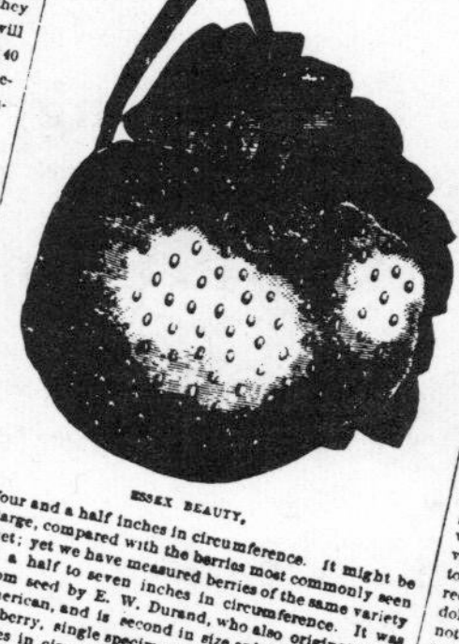

ESSEX BEAUTY.

Sheep on the Farm.

BY EASTBURN REEDER.

THE first Farm Journal was an eight-page paper, slightly larger than now, and the edition was 25,000. The March, 1927, Farm Journal has 116 pages. The edition exceeds 1,400,000.

You will note that the original subscription price was 25 cents a year. It is the same today. It has been lower, and also higher, at times, but at the end of 50 years it is the same as at the start.

The heading has been redrawn several times, as improvements suggested themselves. The last revision was by the famous artist, Franklin Booth. The fine old farmhouse that now appears in it, a picture of the home of General "Mad Anthony" Wayne, of Revolutionary fame, was first used in October, 1880.

The first colored cover was on the September, 1918, number, and the familiar old heading was moved to an inside page.

It is interesting to see that the office of publication, 726 Sansom Street, was in the "Saturday Evening Post Building." Three months later, the "Saturday Evening Post" was sold out by the sheriff. Needless to say, this was long before Cyrus Curtis bought the struggling weekly.

A great variety of reading matter of interest was printed in this first issue, including one feature, "Topics in Season," that still appears prominently in the magazine.

50th Anniversary

ESSEX *is* *a* SUPER-SIX

Yet Costs Little More Than Any Four

The Super-Six Principle now released to full capacity in Hudson is *also Amazingly Revealed* in ESSEX SUPER-SIX

50 miles an hour all day long, and ability to travel even faster if you want.

A smooth fast pick-up free from jerking or violence.

Long life to all wearing parts—accessibility, and the most advanced engineering for low maintenance and operating costs.

Riding and driving ease equaling anything you have ever experienced—surpassing anything ever achieved in a car of its cost.

No nerve shattering motor vibration, no chug-chug-chug-chug to mar the enjoyment of your trip. The smooth stream of Super-Six power whisks you along any road for any period of time or distance in carefree comfort.

No car of our experience has ever met with such enthusiastic reception. It has been the outstanding attraction at all automobile shows. The beauty, comfort and detail of each body type is commanding highest praise. And dealers everywhere are reporting sales that indicate the greatest Essex popularity of all time.

4-PASSENGER SPEEDSTER $750 · COACH $735 · COUPE $735 · SEDAN $785

All prices f. o. b. Detroit, plus war excise tax.

HUDSON MOTOR CAR COMPANY
DETROIT, MICHIGAN

Founder of The Farm Journal, and Editor from 1877 to 1917—forty years.

WALTER E. ANDREWS

FRANK G. MOORHEAD

Editor, 1920-21

CHARLES F. JENKINS

ARTHUR H. JENKINS

The nephew and associate of Wilmer Atkinson, Charles F. Jenkins, acted as Managing Editor from 1917 to 1920.

For several years previous to 1918, Walter E. Andrews, whose portrait appears above, carried the chief burden of editorial work, although he never bore the title of Editor. Mr. Andrews' connection with The Farm Journal extended from 1904 to 1918.

Since 1921, Arthur H. Jenkins, another nephew of Wilmer Atkinson, has directed the editorial policies of the magazine.

The Farm Journal was the first periodical in the world to guarantee the advertising appearing in its columns

50 Years of Fair Play

The Farm Journal's guarantee of advertising preceded by seventeen years the adoption of this policy by any other periodical

Truth in advertising and faith in advertising began with this notice

...., cash in advance. At ...
...ar the paper is stopped, unless renewed.

FAIR PLAY.

We believe, through careful inquiry, that all the advertisements in this paper are signed by trustworthy persons, and to prove our faith by works, we will make good to subscribers any loss sustained by trusting advertisers who prove to be deliberate swindlers. Rogues shall not ply their trade at the expense of our readers, who are our friends, through the medium of these columns. Let this be understood by everybody now and henceforth.

CONTENTS OF THIS NUMBER.

- New Head. High Farmi...

"Fair Play" notice in The Farm Journal for October, 1880—the first cash guarantee of advertising ever made by any periodical

"The Farm Journal says so; therefore it is so."

HOW many of us, growing up on fresh cow's milk, Mother's flapjacks and home-made country sausage, had this saying as firmly impressed on our minds as the daily family prayer? Probably few of the farm boys of 20, 30 and 40 years ago, whose fathers read The Farm Journal, can have forgotten that motto.

They say that truth shines through people's lives. It does. It shines through their business and business motives as well. It shone through the life and business—the lifetime business—of Wilmer Atkinson, who was not afraid to say "When my Farm Journal says so it is true."

The history of journalism reveals the necessity for a reform in advertising practise of 50 and 60 years ago. It was the heyday of misleading advertising.

Into this unhealthy atmosphere came Wilmer Atkinson and The Farm Journal. Born and raised on the farm, he did not forget how country neighbors had been cheated through advertisements. On the other hand, he had available the excellent example of the great editor, Orange Judd, whose "American Agriculturist," with its policy of excluding objectionable advertising, was well known to him. From the very start of The Farm Journal in 1877, therefore, Wilmer Atkinson barred all advertising of a questionable nature. He intended to see that folks of his own kind received a square deal.

But even this was not enough, and in 1880 he went still further, taking the final step of backing the advertising in The Farm Jounal by an absolute money-back guarantee.

The first "Fair Play" notice, printed in October, 1880, is reproduced above. It reads:

> "We believe, through careful inquiry, that all the advertisements in this paper are signed by trustworthy persons, and to prove our faith by works, we will make good to subscribers any loss sustained by trusting advertisers who prove to be deliberate swindlers. Rogues shall not ply their trade at the expense of our readers, who are our friends, through the medium of these columns. Let this be understood by everybody now and henceforth."

The part which Orange Judd played in this great reform deserves a little further mention.

The "American Agriculturist" was established in 1842. In 1856 it came under the control of Orange Judd, a born editor and a true friend of the rural classes. In 1859 he began each month to expose humbugs and frauds on a page devoted to that subject. The next step was taken in 1860, when he printed a notice to the effect that he would "exclude deceptive advertisements, also those persons who are reported not to perform what they promise." Later in the same year it was stated that advertisements would be admitted "only from parties who have a business character to sustain; suspicious persons known to treat their customers unjustly, are excluded."

But no notice that money would be refunded to subscribers who lost through dishonest advertisers was published in the paper, although until Orange Judd's connection with the "Agriculturist" was severed, sometime before 1884, his policy was carefully followed.

WHAT his "Fair Play" notice meant is well described by Wilmer Atkinson in his autobiography:

"The 'Fair Play' notice formed a conspicuous part in the paper's history, and helped contribute greatly to its success, eventually changing the attitude of all publishers in the United States toward their readers in respect to protecting them from fraudulent adventurers.

"No publisher in the United States had ever made such an offer. No matter, I meant it. I was shouldering great responsibilities. No matter, I had been doing it all my life. There might be risk in it. No matter, it was right."

The "Fair Play" notice is still nailed to The Farm Journal's masthead. In its present form it says:

> "We believe that all the advertisements in this paper are trustworthy. To prove our faith by works, we will make good to actual subscribers any loss sustained by trusting advertisers who prove to be deliberate swindlers. Just as we can not guarantee a pig's tail to curl in any particular direction, so we shall not attempt to adjust trifling disputes between subscribers and honorable business men, nor pay the debts of honest bankrupts. This offer holds good one month after the transaction causing the complaint."

Fifty years have passed, and the first readers of The Farm Journal who are still alive retain their faith in it. Fifty years from now, it is our hope that the coming generation will still say:

"The Farm Journal says so. Therefore it is true."

Wilmer Atkinson
about the time The Farm Journal was started

50th Anniversary

Distinguished Friends Write—

The Governor of Pennsylvania:

Dear Mr. Jenkins:

For many years, I have known The Farm Journal and the high position which it has held throughout the agricultural districts of this Commonwealth. Indeed, it was the farmers of Pennsylvania who first gave the stamp of their approval to the magazine in the days when it was started to serve them and with no thought of expanding to cover the entire Nation. It is gratifying to know that a publication which is resident in this State should have grown in influence until it has carried the lessons of better farming and of better farm living to every other State of the Union.

I am glad to send to you my congratulations on the occasion of the fiftieth birthday of your magazine and to express the hope that it may have yet another fifty years of useful effort in the cause of improving living conditions for the farmers not only of this Commonwealth but of the Nation as a whole.

Very cordially yours,

Jno S Fisher

The Secretary of Agriculture of Pennsylvania:

Dear Mr. Jenkins:

It must be a source of great satisfaction to you to know that there are today thousands of prosperous farmers in Pennsylvania and elsewhere whose earliest recollections include boyhood evenings in the farm home learning from the magazine which you now edit the lesson of better agricultural practises and improved standards of social life in their communities. The Farm Journal received its first support from the men and women who tilled the soil of this State and their judgment of the merits of your magazine has been confirmed by the intelligent farmers of the Nation.

You may well be proud of a record of fifty years of uninterrupted publication without change of name or of frequency of issue or of basic editorial policies. I congratulate you and your co-workers on this achievement and I trust that the future will bring to The Farm Journal a constantly growing success and a steadily increasing influence in the betterment of the farms and the farm folks of our State and Nation. Sincerely yours,

C. G. Jordan

The President of the Farmers' Union:

My dear Mr. Jenkins:

On the approach of the 50th Anniversary of the magazine which you are conducting, I want to congratulate you and your many readers on the completion of a half-century of real service to agriculture.

For years I have been a constant reader of your pages and they have been a source of inspiration to me. Your program of sane, constructive effort should be continued for another 50 years, and longer.

I am sure that in saying these things to you I am expressing not only my personal sentiments, but the sentiments which many thousands of members of the National Farmers' Union would wish me to send you on this occasion.

Yours sincerely,

C S Barrett

The President of the United States:

THE WHITE HOUSE
WASHINGTON

My dear Mr. Jenkins:

It gives me great pleasure to send my congratulations to the publishers, to you as editor, and to the many readers of The Farm Journal upon the celebration of its fiftieth anniversary.

It is unusual for a publication of this character to have enjoyed a continuous existence for half a century without change of name, ownership or basic policiés.

My best wishes go to you for an increased area of usefulness in your very important field.

Very truly yours,

Calvin Coolidge

Mr. Arthur H. Jenkins,
Editor, The Farm Journal,
Washington Square,
Philadelphia, Pa.

The President of the American Farm Bureau Federation:

My dear Mr. Jenkins:

For many years I have known and read The Farm Journal. And on this occasion, your fiftieth anniversary, it gives me a great deal of pleasure to extend to you, the editor of the Journal, the best wishes not only of myself but of the organization which I represent.

I am deeply conscious of the important role played by the farm press in the development of agriculture. The farm press was for many years the sole champion of better farm production and marketing practises and of a higher standard of rural living. The farm press is now seconded in its effort by farm organizations.

You should feel very proud to be the editor of a publication with the history and tradition of The Farm Journal and of its present record of continued growth.

Sincerely,

S H Thompson

The Master of the National Grange:

My dear Mr. Jenkins:

The Fiftieth Anniversary of The Farm Journal is an event of interest not only to its readers and to agriculture, but to the nation, for this publication has not only a long and most honorable record as relates to agricultural journalism, but it has likewise been a factor in our national welfare.

The last fifty years have been of far-reaching importance to agriculture; wonderful changes have taken place; it has been the greatest period of agricultural progress in the history of mankind. Through it all, there has been no one agency more consistent or persistent in its interest in farm problems, than has been the agricultural press, and in this field The Farm Journal has no superior.

For more than a quarter of a century the writer has been one of "Our Folks" and during the entire life of this publication, Grange members from the Atlantic to the Pacific have read the paper, have believed in many of its policies and have valued its counsel and advice.

May The Farm Journal celebrate its fiftieth anniversary with a feeling that it has rendered service and that before it are years of unequaled opportunity to serve agriculture and mankind!

Yours very truly,

L J Taber

50th Anniversary

The Next 50 Years of Agriculture

By William M. Jardine
Secretary of Agriculture

CENSUS figures show that American agriculture produced more in 1924 than in 1919, on fewer acres and with less labor. From 1919 to 1924 the country's area of harvested crops was cut down about 5 per cent. In the same period farm population declined nearly 400,000. Yet the output of nine principal crops plus the production from pasture was greater at the end than at the beginning of the half-decade.

I take this gain in efficiency to be an indication that our farmers are laying a foundation for future agricultural prosperity.

It is evident that our farmers as a whole have not been deprived of all hope for the future by the low returns, the heavy debts and the uncertain prospects of the last few years. On the contrary, they have been prompted to improve their uses of the land and to increase the effectiveness of their labor.

They are economizing land and labor as never before. As measured by production per man in agriculture, this country has led the world for a century or more. Its way of meeting the difficulties of the postwar readjustment process is to set a new record in individual production.

The Cost of Efficiency

This fact gives us a good starting point in guessing what the next 50 years may hold in store. Perhaps increasing efficiency in production is prolonging the disparity between the prices of farm commodities and industrial goods. It seems to be maintaining the *volume* of production at a higher level than consumption requirements justify.

That, however, is not an argument against efficiency, but simply a reminder that the problem of the group is not always the same as the problem of the individual. It is a warning that production, to be profitable, must be done not only at the lowest possible cost but with a shrewd eye to market needs. Ultimately, success in economizing land and labor, if coupled with skilful selling and wisdom in adjusting crop enterprises to the wants of consumers, is bound to bring prosperity.

Our increasing farm production on a reduced crop area and with a reduced farm personnel is partly due to the recent large-scale substitution of engine power for both human and animal labor on the farm. The mechanization of agriculture is going on today at a more rapid rate than ever before. It made big strides after the close of the Civil War.

More Crops for Human Consumption

Today, however, the mechanization process economizes land as well as labor, because it releases land that would otherwise be required to feed work stock. Power cultivation in the new cotton states and in the Corn Belt is cutting down feed requirements enormously, and in the wheat states the combined harvester-thresher, rapidly spreading even as far east as Ohio, is helping to solve the harvest labor problem.

What this mechanical revolution may mean to agriculture in the next 50 years can not be imagined. It is amazing enough to reflect on what is has already accomplished. Agriculture today appears to be increasing its production per person employed more rapidly than industry. With a tractor pulling gang plows, harrows and seeders, it is not uncommon for one man to prepare and seed from 80 to 100 acres a day. One man with a tractor-cultivator can take care of 250 acres of corn. In Texas last year there were many thousands of four-row cotton-cultivators in use. Ten years ago the combined harvester-tractor was unknown east of the Rockies. There are now more than 15,000 in the winter-wheat states alone. Tractors on farms have more than doubled since 1920, and now number over 500,000.

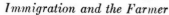

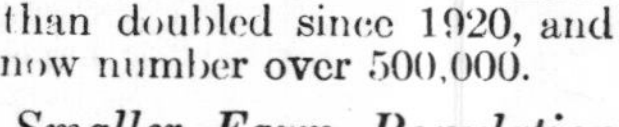

Photo Harris & Ewing

W. M. Jardine

Smaller Farm Population

Some of the things likely to result from this mechanical revolution are obvious. By reducing the amount of land necessary to maintain work stock, it will enable us to feed more people without increasing our farm-land area.

It will mean, to be sure, that we shall not require so many farmers for the job. The new machines now coming into use for plowing and harvesting will certainly cause a reduction in the necessary farm population. There will probably, however, be an increase in income per farmer. Farms, of course, will have to be larger. A hint of what may be coming can be seen on the Staked Plains of Texas, where, with modern cultivating appliances, five men can take care of 400 acres of cotton.

Supporting people on land formerly used to feed work animals simplifies our future food problem. It has been estimated that our population, by its natural increase alone and without any big addition from immigration, will amount to 150,000,000 shortly after 1950.

Immigration and the Farmer

If there is any large increase in immigration in the next quarter of a century, the 150,000,000 mark may be reached earlier. Our available farm-land area will not provide for 150,000,000 people and maintain our agricultural exports unless important changes take place in our present methods of crop production or in our standards of consumption, or in both.

In all probability, of course, there will be changes in both these directions. What we can expect in the release of land from the production of forage crops is shown by the drop in the number of horses and mules in the United States between 1919 and 1924. The decrease was about 2,500,000. It released no less than 10,000,000 acres of land for the production of food and fibers.

Among many uncertainties as to the next 50 years in American agriculture, one thing can be set down as fairly certain. There will be increased pressure of population on land resources.

All our good land that can be used for crops without drainage, clearing or irrigation is in use. Most of our fair land is in use, and a great deal of our poor land. In the comparatively near future it [*Continued on page 75*

50th Anniversary

50 Years of Farm Machinery

THE farmer who lived in 1877 in the comfortable farm home on the cover of The Farm Journal, as shown on page 5, undoubtedly considered himself fortunate in living in an age when machinery could do so much of his work. If we can trust the artist who drew the design, the farm possessed at least a one-horse plow and a watering pot!

But a farmer of the intelligent and progressive type who would like The Farm Journal doubtless possessed a full equipment of the tools of his day. Of plows and harrows he had the choice of a hundred designs. He probably had, in 1877, such implements as a disk harrow, a roller, a grain-drill, a corn-planter, cultivators, a mower, a reaper and perhaps a thresher. Doubtless he had horse-power of the tread-mill type, or perhaps the more efficient and powerful horizontal-geared horse-power. He raked his hay with a self-dumping rake, and got it into his mows with a hay-carrier and a double-harpoon fork. He could have had, for they were on the market, a hay-tedder, a hay-loader, a potato-planter, a digger, a corn-husker and a corn-sheller.

The 1927 cream-separator; this machine, with the Babcock test, "made" the dairy industry. Measuring a cow's value was a big problem before the Babcock test

In 1877 this plow was a standard type. Wood beams were still in use

A thoroughly modern 1927 plow—a two-bottom gang designed for use with any small tractor

The artist did not equip our 1877 farmer with a pumping windmill, but doubtless he had one.

He was looking ahead, too. He might explain to us that he expected soon to see inventors develop a binding device for his reaper. He had seen this tried out, using wire, but the farmers found the wire got into the stock feed, so that this idea had to be abandoned. The newspapers said a man named Appleby had perfected an attachment for binding with twine and making the twine tie itself into a knot, and that the machine would be on the market in a year or two. It would be a great thing if they could make it work.

Beginnings of Farm Power

And he had heard some talk of developing small steam engines that could run out to the fields and pull plows and harrows and reapers and all sorts of machinery after them.

Take dairy machines, too. He saw only a little while ago that an inventor was working on an outfit that would take milk just as it came from the cow and you could turn a crank and skim milk would flow out of one spout and cream out of another. He might even hazard a guess that some day some scientist would be milking cows by machinery. That sounded foolish, but inventors certainly were doing wonders.

Engines That Ran on Gas

And think what this steam idea might mean if they really got it into working order for the average farm! Gang plows of two and three bottoms were in use here and there, but they took a lot of horse-power. A steam engine could maybe pull the harrow right after it, so both operations could be done at once.

And he saw by the paper the other day that an inventor named Otto last year filed a patent for what he called an "internal combustion" motor that ran on gas. Some people said it was going to be better and cheaper and stronger and smaller than the steam engine and, if it proved to be really practical, it might do a lot of good for the farmer.

That is a fair picture of the progressive farmer of the day when this magazine of ours made its modest bow to the public in 1877. The basic principles of the most important of our present-day farm implements had been worked out. But many machines we regard as indispensable were not then sufficiently developed to make possible their wide-spread production and sale.

The farmer of 1877 never saw a silo. The basic idea goes back to Roman times and [*Continued on page 16*

Model threshing-outfit on the move 50 years ago

Newest type of milking-machine in a modern dairy

50 Years of Fashions

By Eudora Sellner

The "very latest" in March, 1877. It took time, material and ingenuity to make a dress when The Farm Journal was first printed.

MARCH, 1877! It was in this month that The Farm Journal made its first appearance, going into homes where ladies, gowned slight and tight above and voluminous below, rocked in their antimacassared rockers or stepped carefully and daintily amid their folds. A too-harsh movement might snap one of the many strings that held in place the wonderful array of ruffles, flounces, plaits, frills, ribbons and bows that went into the make-up of a feminine costume.

Those were indeed the days of costume! Life was not so complicated 50 years ago as it is today, but Dame Fashion was infinitely more so. Today our whole theme of style is built on "line." In those days it was "shape," and complicated indeed was the structure beneath to gain the outward ideal in "shape." We may speak of the "tailored" woman of today, but in those days, she was the "upholstered" woman.

As a costume in itself was elaborate, ornate and voluminous, so was the extent of the wardrobe. The well-dressed woman had to meet each event of the day with its particular costume. There was a housedress, a lounge dress, one for walking, one for carriage wear and one for evening, each of which consisted of yardage enough to supply a bride of today with her entire trousseau.

Our First Pattern Page

It appeared 30 years ago. Thirty years hence, observers of fashions will find the styles of today just as absurd as these seem to be

In the March, 1877, issue of "Godey's Lady's Book," one of the fashion periodicals of the day, attention is drawn to one of the difficulties of the extensive wardrobe in these words:

"It is an error which is very general and which shows great want of taste to spend large sums of money upon a few toilets to be worn only on grand occasions and to wear cheap or shabby clothes at all other times. Rather have more and keep them simple. Where the wardrobe is not very extensive, a colored dress is apt to be noticed as a particular dress much sooner than a black one." Also, Godey's book mentions that by use of the new fast dyes, frills or the entire dress can be changed so as not to be recognizable as the old one.

As today's garments seem to have shed all the "extras," those of 1877 seem to have accumulated upon themselves the maximum amount and variety of ornament. A polonaise is fastened slantwise with great ropes of braid and fringe; a scarf overskirt is looped up with lace and butterfly bows of pink and moss-green ribbon; a cuirass basque is trimmed with cords and ornaments and a band of chinchilla fur; a tunic of velvet falls over three deep falls of lace flounce held in place by bunches of pink roses twined with myrtle. Draperies of every shape, manner and form go to make up the costume of this period.

Needless to say, a gown that was evolved at such a price of labor, skill and materials was not an affair to be used for a few occasions and then cast aside, but must do duty for many years; and many such were handed down to the next generation.

Feminine sports of those days consisted of driving, boating and croquet, with sleighing, skating and tobogganing in winter. Surprise parties were a popular form of entertainment.

The Grecian Bend of the 80's

By 1883, skirt flounces had been picked up so they no longer swept the streets, but there was still a festoon of rufflings and flounces over a [*Continued on page 102*

It's a far cry from the puffs and frills of Miss 1883 to the bobbed-haired, short-skirted girl of 1927. Living conditions as well as clothes have changed; the "frilly" lady would find it hard to go through a modern day in the clothes of her period

50th Anniversary

50 Years of Livestock

By George M. Rommel

Red Rose, one of Cooper's imported Ayrshires, shown at the Centennial, 1876. Average for year, eleven quarts a day—pounds of fat meant nothing in those days

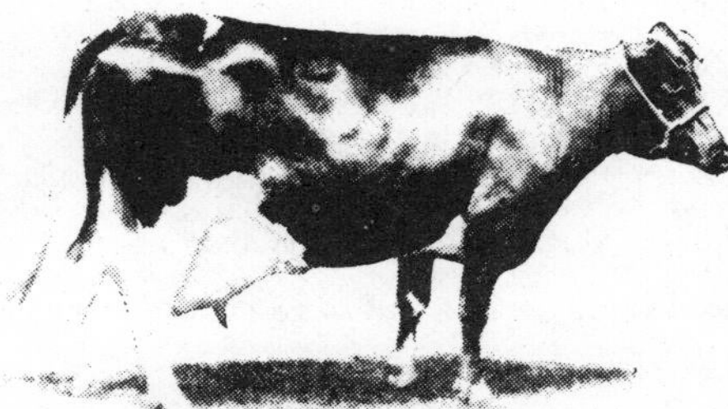

DeKol Plus Segis Dixie, 1926 world's champion cow—1,349 pounds of fat in a year. No striking difference in looks, but what a difference in production!

THE farm boys of the 70's lived in days of romance, excitement and hardship—days of the free range and the gun-toting cowboy, when a steer had five or six years of more or less happy hunting before he took the last long trail, when pigs were often driven 100 miles on their way to market, and Cincinnati was called Porkopolis.

Refrigerator cars were experiments. Hog-killing was a winter business for packers as well as for farmers. Farmers in the Corn Belt knew in a general way that ten bushels of corn would make 100 pounds of pork, but nobody used the words "corn-hog ratio."

So far as registered livestock was concerned, Thoroughbred horses and Shorthorn cattle had it pretty much their own way until 1870. The 70's and 80's witnessed a rush to bring to America the best of the established European breeds of livestock, as well as the rapid improvement of those which already had a foothold here.

Glorious scraps were staged whenever rival breed advocates met. Only pig-breeders were peaceful. They convened, in an assembly of great importance in American hog history, at Indianapolis in 1872, as the National Swine Breeders' Convention. That convention gave the Poland-China its name.

There was no "advanced registry" until the Holstein people started it in 1885. The fat production of cows was measured by churn tests up to that time. It was not until 1890 that the Babcock test, now so generally used, was invented.

Hog-cholera was almost continually rampant, and tuberculosis went unchecked in unventilated barns and stables. Cattle trailed up from the South left a wake of devastation behind them, for reasons unknown.

The Science of Feeding

Feeding was far from the science it is today. Corn was measured by the scoop and hay by the fork. Alfalfa, now the cherished dream of every dairy-farmer, was grown only in the western irrigated districts. Cottonseed was used by the gins as fuel or dumped into the river if there was a river handy to the plant.

Well—here we are at 1927—and 50 years older. We ought to be 50 years wiser, and we really do know more than we did in the 70's. Every breed of importance has its own association, but, instead of fighting each other like the Kilkenny Kats, they now show a tendency to work together. In spite of a hectic spot here and there, there is remarkable solidarity of thought and action among dairymen, and beef-cattle men have at last come together into an association for the promotion

Dan Bacillus and his boy Ike delivering milk in the 70's

of better beef and greater consumption of it. Organizations galore provide clearing-houses of information and animal-industry activity which increase the effectiveness of the work of the breed associations and the individual livestock producer. We have the greatest aggregation of livestock shows in the world, where the best steer, barrow or wether can be made grand champion [*Continued on page 54*

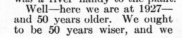

These two steers show the change in fat cattle types in 50 years. The white steer is the famous Clarence Kirklevington, champion yearling in 1882. This animal was also best Shorthorn steer of any age and best two-year-old steer of any breed at the Chicago Fat Stock Show in 1883; best steer, cow or heifer in the show; and best carcass, any age or breed at the same show in 1884. The Hereford was grand champion, 1926 International. Less than a year old when he won the purple. Upper right corner, a modern plant for bottling milk for city folks. The milk is brought to the plant by train and truck, bottled, then distributed in horse-drawn milk-wagons. Pasteurization, another modern process for safeguarding milk, is done at the bottling plant

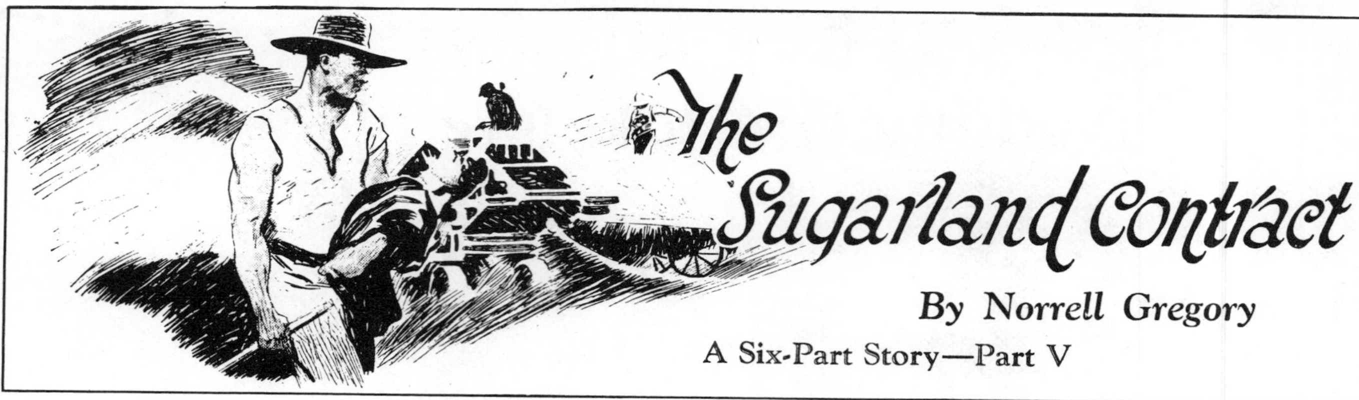

The Sugarland Contract

By Norrell Gregory

A Six-Part Story—Part V

PETRIE'S bound was so vigorous and so silent that it carried him within striking distance before Bly was aware of his approach. Petrie struck just as Bly turned, and Bly received a tremendous blow fair between the eyes. He went down, knocked entirely off his feet, so terrific was the impact, and he lay on the ground momentarily stunned. Petrie, thoroughly demented now, sprang over the fallen man and kicked him in the ribs again and again; lifted his heavy foot to trample Bly's defenseless face. But before his foot fell, a pair of frantic hands grasped his coat and yanked him violently backward. Petrie whirled with an oath and confronted a white-faced and defiant Anna. "What!" he cried, "you standin' up for *him?*"

"You'd better get away from here!" she said, tensely. "I've had enough of you. I won't stand for anything like this!"

"Anna!" he cried, all the rancor suddenly gone from his voice, "I didn't tamper with his engine. I'll swear it on a stack of Bibles. I *tell* you I didn't!" he repeated with increasing vehemence as she still stood defiant.

"You'd better go," she repeated. "If you didn't, who did? And why have you been making threats? And to kick a man that can't help himself!" At this point Bly stirred and struggled to a sitting position, still too dazed to comprehend the situation.

"Go on!" said Anna again. "I *never* want to see you around this place again as long as I live!"

"You don't, hey?" he said, grasping her arm in a grip that made her wince. "Don't go too fast, young lady!" He flung her from him with such suddenness that she almost fell. "You don't want to see me again, hey? You're likely to see a lot of me, you and that *thing* there!" He jabbed his thumb toward Bly, now struggling to get on his feet. Then, ignoring them both, he turned and went contemptuously to the car and drove away slowly, as Bly finally won his feet and set himself dazedly to resume the battle.

ANNA KELSO came to Bly and steadied him gently. "Are you hurt much?" she asked, a tremor in her voice.

Bly passed a shaky hand over his brow and laughed shamefacedly. "He handed it to me!" he said. "He certainly handed it to me good and proper." He felt his ribs tenderly and grunted painfully. "Funny it would hurt me so there," he muttered. "Thought he hit me in the face—anyway, I saw a million or two stars——"

"He kicked you!" she said quickly, "three or four times before I could——" she stopped suddenly.

Bly looked at her keenly. "Before you stopped him?" he finished. "Yes, you must have. Else he wouldn't have stopped so soon. He's not the kind that would." She did not reply. "You did stop him, didn't you?" he persisted.

"I had to!" she said, faintly.

He looked at her closely. "That was kind of you," he said.

"Kind!" she exclaimed, uncomfortable under his look. "No one could stand for that!" They had turned toward the house. At the porch step they paused and faced each other.

"Just the same," persisted Bly, "it was mighty kind of you. I'll sure remember you for that. Good night."

"Good night," she replied, and as he turned to enter the house, she made a motion as if to detain him, but desisted. And when Bly came out with Gandy, a few minutes later, she was no longer there. They found the rig apparently as he had left it. After a careful inspection of both machines they settled themselves in the engine cab. Bly was put to task to find a comfortable position for his battered ribs. He groaned a little as a twinge of pain shot through his body.

"What's the matter?" asked Gandy. "You act like you was all stove up."

"Stove up!" groaned Bly; "Gandy, I feel like every rib in my body was broken into toothpicks!"

"Thunder!" exclaimed Gandy, "what's happened?"

Bly told his story and Gandy sat motionless for some time after he had finished. "Bly," he said at length, "he'd a' tromped the life outa you if she hadn't stopped him. He's that kind."

"Don't I know it!" Bly spoke fretfully, like a peevish child. "I didn't dream he would come at me that way or I'd have been ready for him. I must have been mistaken about his trying to blow up the boiler."

"Right," said Gandy. "He had to go home and clean up before comin' over to Kelso's. He couldn't have had time to do it."

"No," Bly agreed after thinking a little, "I can see it now. It must have been LaFave. But it sure was lucky she stood up for me."

The animal snorted and gave a convulsive leap, and LaFave was catapulted from the saddle

GANDY looked at him and said nothing. Bly sat for some time, then he said:

"Gandy, I'm in a heck of a fix!"

"Are you?" said Gandy, innocently.

"Yes," said Bly, "I am."

"I can tell you a sure-shot cure for that kind of a fix," said Gandy, wisely.

"Let's hear it," requested Bly.

"Never knew it to fail," continued Gandy, grinning widely; "absolutely non-fail."

"Come through!" ordered Bly.

"Marry her!" said Gandy, shortly

Bly arose entirely too hastily for a set of badly battered ribs, and caught his breath sharply to stifle a yell. "You're crazy!" he said. "How would it look for me to propose anything like that to her? Like I was trying to buy a farm cheap, wouldn't it? That's the kind of stuff you could expect Petrie to pull off."

"You're crazy about her *right now,*" said Gandy. "Farm or no farm, you're crazy about her."

"Well, what if I am?" said Bly, unguardedly. "That's no sign she's crazy about me, is it, Gandy?" he said, dropping his voice. "You can see how it would look if I had the nerve to ask her such a thing, can't you?"

"Of course," replied Gandy, calmly, "if you look at it that way."

"There you are," said Bly. "I wouldn't think of such a thing, not for a million dollars. I'd sooner have my right arm cut off. Not that I don't think anything of her," he [Continued on page 88

They all say:
"Nothing can take the place of Fels-Naptha!"

"I always use boiling water"

"I always use lukewarm water"

"I always boil my white clothes"

No matter how you use Fels-Naptha . . . in boiling, cool or lukewarm water—in a washing machine or a washtub . . . you are bound to get *extra* washing help you would hardly expect from any other soap.

There's a very good reason, of course, for this *extra* help. Fels-Naptha gives you the *extra* cleansing value of two thorough, safe cleaners working together—*exceptionally good soap and plenty of dirt-loosening naptha.*

In the Golden Bar of Fels-Naptha you get the full benefit of this splendid teamwork between soap and naptha.

Fels-Naptha makes it so much easier to get your clothes white and thoroughly clean. It is so gentle to your clothes in the wash. And it leaves your clothes with that delightful clean-clothes smell.

When you consider, too, that Fels-Naptha is so economical and so handy to use, is it any wonder that millions of women say: "Nothing can take the place of Fels-Naptha"? Is it any wonder that thousands upon thousands of them come back to Fels-Naptha after trying all sorts of cleaners and soaps?

A great many farm women use Fels-Naptha for every cleaning purpose. For washing clothes—washing dishes—cleaning milk pails, cans and separator parts—removing spots from rugs and draperies—brightening painted woodwork—keeping their homes faultlessly clean and wholesome.

Don't you, too, want this *extra* help of Fels-Naptha? You can test it without cost, by writing Fels & Co., Philadelphia, for a free sample of the Golden Bar.

THE GOLDEN BAR WITH THE CLEAN NAPTHA ODOR © Fels & Co.

50th Anniversary

50 Years of Machinery

Continued from page 11

beyond, but the scientific structure of today is a development of this generation. In 1877 the whole theory was regarded with suspicion and doubt.

The reaper of that day was essentially the reaper of today, for the cutting machinery devised by Hussey in 1833 has not been materially altered since. Development has been entirely in better workmanship and materials, and in combinations with other devices to perform more than one job at once. And this has grown into the marvel of modern farm machinery—the combined harvester-thresher.

The mower was much the same in 1877 as today. If we believe the artist, "Safety First" had not been heard of!

The reaper used in 1877 and for some years thereafter. Binding with twine was just being perfected

Type of the first reaper and binder, about 1877, using the Appleby twine knotter

The manure-spreader and lime-spreader, twin necessities on the modern diversified farm, were still years ahead. Kemp's manure-spreader was patented in 1877, and advertised in The Farm Journal in 1881, but the first practical model was not on the market until 1887. The spreader of the modern type was patented by Oppenheim in 1900. The lime-spreader appeared in Illinois about the same time.

The splendid old firm of S. L. Allen & Company were already making their line of improved garden and field implements. Early in 1878 their first advertisement appeared in The Farm Journal, and "Planet Jr." tools have been advertised in our columns, in season, ever since.

Hand Work in the Dairy

Our farmer of 1877 kept dairy-cows. We know from the picture that he had at least two, for one of them is being milked in the barnyard by a stout female. And—alas for our artist!—on the wrong side.

Virtually all the dairy work was done by hand. The problem of winter feeding meant just so much extra care and trouble without a silo, and DeLaval had not yet put out commercially his continuous-flow cream-separator. This was conceived in our own first year of life, but it was not on the market until two years later. (Continued on page 28

Fifty years ago they were experimenting with seeding devices; this was an attachment to be added to the disk-harrow

The modern "culti-packer," drawn by an efficient small tractor. The rollers are so made that they not only pack, but also pulverize the soil

Better *and* Better Farming

THE Harvester Company congratulates The Farm Journal on the 50th Anniversary of its service to American agriculture. May the high aims and constructive policies that have guided it through a half-century show the way to a future of greater farm progress and prosperity.

LIKE The Farm Journal and like veteran farmers everywhere, the Harvester Company looks back on wonderful changes in agriculture. We have all traveled a long way together. Perfection can never be reached but each year the business of farming grows better and better.

The farm papers have preached the gospel of soil culture, seed selection, fertilization, scientific seed-bed preparation, diversification, swifter methods in putting in the crops and harvesting the yields. The inventors and builders of this Company have devoted themselves to providing the machines that make farming more profitable and easier. The farmers have combined *machines* and *knowledge* with good hard *work* and created the kind of agriculture for which America is famous.

Greater opportunities are ahead. Now the way to profit lies in big-capacity operations, maximum work with least labor, production of big crops at low cost all along the line. McCormick-Deering machines are helping millions of farmers in this direction and will continue to serve their best interests. They are sold by leading apostles of better farming in every community —the McCormick-Deering dealers.

A few machines among the 54 in the McCormick-Deering line are shown at the right

INTERNATIONAL HARVESTER COMPANY
606 So. Michigan Ave. of America (*Incorporated*) Chicago, Ill.

FARMALL, the new row-crop tractor planting 4 rows of corn

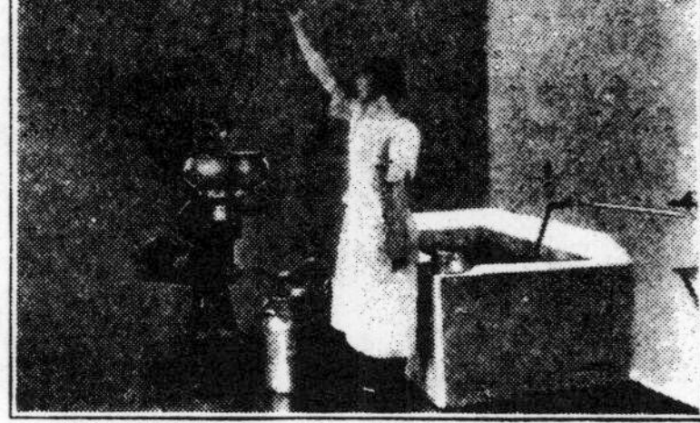

McCormick-Deering Harvester-Thresher and Tractor, saving 20 cents per bushel

McCormick-Deering ball-bearing Cream Separator

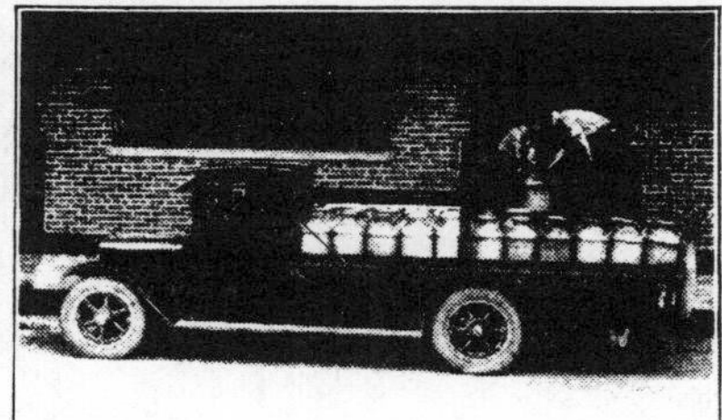

McCormick-Deering Corn Picker doing the work of six hand huskers

International Motor Trucks—Speed and Heavy-Duty—save time and money at farm hauling

McCormick Works, Chicago—world's largest farm equipment factory—one of the plants of the International Harvester Company.

McCORMICK-DEERING

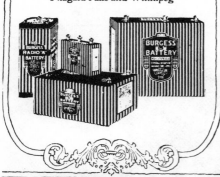

Ginseng and Riches

Ginseng requires shade

GINSENG grows wild, and formerly was quite plentiful throughout the northern and northwestern states, extending as far south as the mountainous sections of Kentucky, Tennessee and the Virginias. Ginseng is used only by the Chinese. They use it to some extent as a condiment with their food, in their religious ceremonies, and sometimes about the same as some people use a rabbit's foot or a horse-chestnut. But its main use is medicinal. Ginseng from the mountains of Manchuria and Chosen is considered the best. American comes next, and the Japanese last. The latter is not of much value. The annual export from this country for the last 50 years has averaged close to 175,000 pounds.

About 30 years ago, the wild root began to play out and an attempt was made to grow it in gardens, but for some years failed. After a time, would-be growers found that the seed would not come until the second spring after it was harvested and that during all that time it must be kept moist; also, that the plant must have at least partial shade. With this knowledge, fair success was attained. Location seems to have more effect on this plant than type of soil. It will thrive in any good garden soil, but it wants high and dry land. About the only drawback to its cultivation now is disease, and that can be avoided by using only naturally dry ground and planting in a high, airy location. Moderately rich soil is healthier than very rich soil.

Mature plant with seed-head

Ginseng is now grown with fair success in all northern and northwestern states as far as Oregon and Washington, provided gardens are laid out in airy locations. Warm, rich valleys are not adapted to its cultivation. Seeds or young plants should be planted in the fall. The roots should be set so the bud will be from one to two inches below the surface, and a mulch of one inch is desirable. This may be sawdust or well-rotted leaves. [*Continued on page 67*

Five-year-old roots

A garden of mature plants under artificial shade

NEW!

Low Model Melotte

It's Here!

NOW!—for the first time, the farmers of America have a chance—*if they act quick!*—to see and USE, on 30 days' trial, the New Low Model Belgian Melotte Cream Separator.

AT LAST!—a shipment of 2,000 of these new models has arrived—and if you write us at once, before this supply is quickly exhausted, you will have an opportunity to get a New Model Melotte for 30 days' trial. But don't delay!

The World's Leading Separator has taken a NEW Leap Forward! In ADDITION to the unsurpassed and unsurpassable Cream-separating efficiency and durability for which the Melotte has been world famous for 38 years, you NOW have, in the New Melotte, a greater convenience, a greater ease of operation and a more complete, all-around satisfaction that was ever known before. There is a new, swinging steel supply tank, waist high for your convenience. It is lined with white bath-tub enamel. Easy to handle. Easy to drain. Easy to wash. Sanitary! See the many OTHER refinements and improvements which have started the whole dairy industry of Europe talking!

Of course, the Melotte's wonderful Self-Balancing Bowl is NOT changed. A Bowl that NEVER gets out of balance—a Bowl that has NEVER had to be rebalanced—NEEDS NO CHANGE! YOU CANNOT IMPROVE PERFECTION!

Write for Special Low Introductory Price Offered NOW! Act Quick!

We KNOW that the New Melotte is going to be the talk of the dairy farmers of America—just as it now is in Europe—so, we are now making, for a short time only, a special low introductory price, to get this new model in the hands of American farmers right away. The price on later shipments may be considerably higher. Save money by acting NOW!

OUR CLAIM Which we Stand Ready to Prove

We claim that year in and year out, over a period of ten—twenty—thirty or more years, the Melotte will put the most cream in your cream can. The most cream because with its suspended, single-Bearing self-balancing bowl, the MELOTTE skims perfectly during its entire lifetime and never wastes any cream. The most cream with less expense, because the hand balanced separators wear themselves out of balance and waste cream before each rebalancing. There are no Melotte rebalancing bills, as it never, never gets out of balance.

Don't Pay for 4 Months

Write for the new Melotte literature today and find out how you may have the new model 77 Melotte on the same terms as the old Melotte. Don't pay for 4 months. Or, if you choose, pay only $7.50 down after 30 days' trial and then $7.50 per month.

Take this Melotte and set it up on your own farm. That's the right place to select a cream separator. Use it there just as if it were your own. Give it any test. After you have skimmed sixty times you will know it gets all the cream. You will know how handy it is. You will know how easy it turns. Your wife will know simple it is to wash. You will know the reason why we haven't been able to get any of these new Melottes until now.

Write for Full Details!

of this Great New Separator

Get the facts yourself. That's the first thing to do. Then you can decide. Don't be rushed into buying a separator from anybody until you have found out all about the new Melotte, until you haye tried it right on your own farm. Remember, you get a whole year to pay for it. When you have a new Melotte, you are through buying separators forever; for the new Melotte lasts a lifetime and stays in perfect balance every minute. Even if you won't need a separator for several months, let us tell you about the New Low Model 77 self-balancing bowl Melotte.

The Melotte Separator Department 25-03
2843 W. 19th St., Chicago, Ill.
2445 Prince St., Berkeley, Cal.
H. B. BABSON, U. S. Manager

The Melotte Separator, *H. B. BABSON, U. S. Manager*
2843 W. 19th St., Dept. 25-03, Chicago, Ill.
2445 Prince St., Berkeley, Calif.

Please send me at once full details about the new low model 77 Melotte Cream Separator and your "Don't Pay for 4 Months." Offer and Special Low Introductory Price to first buyers.

(Print Your Name and Address plainly)

Name ....

Post Office ....

R.F.D. .... State ....

How many cows do you milk? ....

Milking Machine Yes, we have a milker which is bound to interest you—Melotte quality—reasonably priced—terms. Check here if interested . . . . ☐

Topics in Season

50th Anniversary

SOAP for belt dressing is no good—it is slippery if it gets wet. Here is something that beats soap: Paint the belt with old crank-case oil and sprinkle on fine ashes (wood ashes preferred). The ashes are sprinkled on while the belt is running; the pulleys will then grind the ashes into the oil. This will make a real clinging belt and a dressing that will last much longer than soap. I use it in an emergency. *D.*

Opening a silo? Here's a tip: The way we used to get moldy ensilage out was either to throw it down the chute and carry it out of the barn, or throw it up out of a little door in the roof. One day

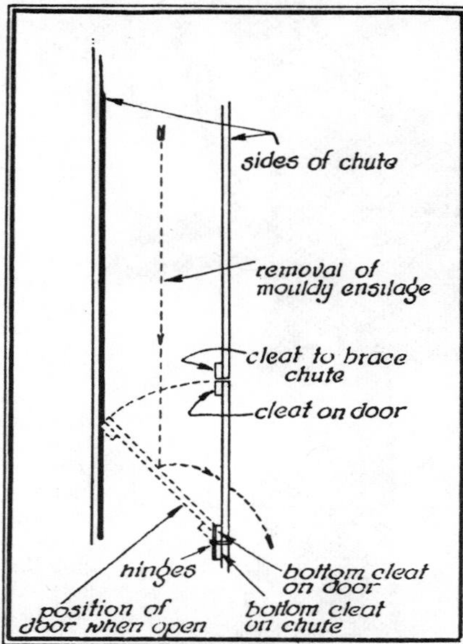

I thought of something better. I took a couple of hinges and four boards and framed a door in one side of the chute about six feet from the ground. Note the sketch. The hinges must be at the bottom of the door inside, and door must be about 18 inches longer than width of chute, so that the slope will cause the waste to slide out. After the moldy ensilage is thrown out, the door can be hooked shut again. *A. H.*

Don't cultivate alfalfa the first year after sowing—if you do, you'll do it only once, for the plants will be pulled out and there will be no alfalfa left. The best time of year to cultivate, nearly always, is early in spring or right after one of the cuttings. The best thing to use is an alfalfa-harrow—which is a type of spring-tooth harrow made especially for alfalfa.

One cause of rapid brake-lining wear, especially in these days of four-wheel brakes, is loose wheel bearings. Wheel bearings should be adjusted so there is no perceptible play in them. Furthermore, if the rear-axle shaft is sprung, or if because of loose bearings or for any other reason the wheels do not run true, the trouble should be corrected, for this wobbling motion tends to wear out brake-linings prematurely. *E. H.*

A soft cushion for the seats on tractors, disks or other hard-riding machines, can be made by doubling a small-size inner tube into a horseshoe shape and tying it in a grain sack. The tube can then be inflated to the amount desired. The valve-stem should protrude through the sack to allow easy inflation. This makes the softest and best cushion that I have ever tried. *L. H.*

Plow sweet clover under just as late in the spring as you dare wait before getting the ground ready for corn. That gives the biggest growth for green manure. Some folks like to let part of the sweet clover crop run over to give summer pasture for livestock, which is not a bad idea. Put an extra horse on the plow when turning under sweet clover. Roots are pretty tough. *G. R. H.*

Did your clover winter-kill? Try soybeans. Soybean hay is as good as clover hay for cows. If beans are broadcast for hay, use about six pecks per acre. You can count on one and one-half or two tons of hay per acre. Be sure to inoculate with nitrogen-gathering bacteria, unless the soil has grown soybeans successfully.

Seeding clover and grass in wheat in the latter part of March when the ground was honeycombed by freezing gave good results in comparison with other methods of seeding at the Ohio Experiment Station. A seed mixture of about six pounds of red clover, two of alsike, two of alfalfa and five of timothy per acre was satisfactory for hay on land where the lime need had been supplied. Red clover and alfalfa will not grow on acid soil without liming. A seed mixture need not cost more than one or two kinds of seed, and is more likely to produce a good crop of hay or a continuous pasture.

Whitewash for stables is made as follows: Make a thin paste of 50 pounds of hydrated lime in boiling water. Add one peck of common salt dissolved in hot water, three pounds of rice flour boiled to a thin paste and stir in while hot, one-half pound of Spanish whiting, and one pound of clear glue thoroughly dissolved in boiling water. This formula is more suitable for interior than for exterior use. Mix well in the order given, and let the mixture stand for several days before using. Apply as hot as possible with a brush or spray.

Whitewash makes the barns clean, light and cheerful

Quality First—then low price

But we never sacrifice quality to make a low price.

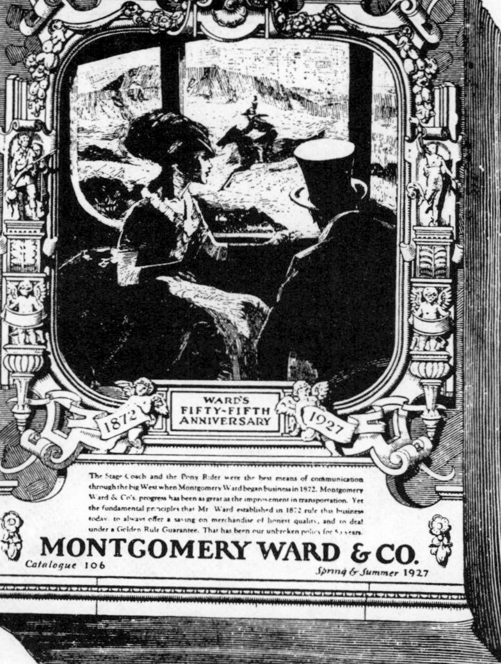

Your orders are shipped within 24 hours

Your orders will be shipped within 24 hours. That saves time. Besides, one of our seven big stores is near to you. Therefore, your letter reaches us quicker. Your goods go to you quicker.

88 Big Stores
are brought to you in the Pages of
Ward's Catalogue

A whole business street—88 Big Complete Stores—are combined in Ward's Spring and Summer Catalogue.

A vast furniture store, a shoe store, a men's store, a women's store—each filled with very large assortments of fresh new merchandise are shown complete in your Catalogue.

Almost your every need is supplied in one of these 88 Departments of Montgomery Ward & Co.

Do you "Shop" With Ward's Catalogue?

Do you look through each big store in your Catalogue? Do you look in your Catalogue as you would in the most modern complete store located near to you?

Do you *use* your Catalogue for everything you need to buy? Do you take advantage of its bargains *to save as much as you could save?* Do you always compare prices?

Here are lower-than-market prices for you. Low prices based upon sound business principles. A dozen of anything can be bought cheaper than one. Ward's buys by the thousand dozen for you and 8,000,000 other customers. We buy by the train load and *we buy for cash!*

$100,000,000 of Merchandise Bought for this Book—for Cash

Cash gets a lower price than credit. We pay cash for your goods. And *the saving is always passed along to you!*

So use your Catalogue. Use it every week for everything you need to buy. Take every advantage for saving this book offers you. You can save $50.00 in cash this season by sending all your orders to Ward's.

Quality—your satisfaction—comes first at Ward's. For 55 years Montgomery Ward & Co. has backed every purchase with an iron-clad guarantee that assures you of satisfactory quality always. At Ward's we never sacrifice quality, never cut serviceability to make a low price.

ESTABLISHED 1872

Montgomery Ward & Co.

The Oldest Mail Order House is Today the Most Progressive

Chicago Kansas City St. Paul Baltimore Portland, Ore. Oakland, Calif. Fort Worth

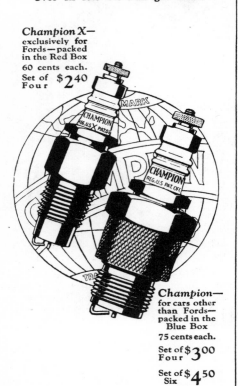

50th Anniversary

Success with Sweet Peas

By A. S. Kenerson

SWEET peas are undoubtedly one of the most popular annuals cultivated in our gardens. Although much of the improvement in sweet peas has been accomplished by our American growers and hybridizers, this flower is distinctly cosmopolitan. This graceful annual apparently is a native of Sicily, where it was first recorded in 1695. To England must be given credit for the early popularity of sweet peas, primarily through the efforts of Henry Eckford, but Holland, France, Algeria, Australia and South Africa have shared honors with England and the United States.

Elfrida Pearson, large shell-pink flowers

To produce the best results, sweet peas must be grown in a bright, open, sunny situation. If they are planted in shade, or even semi-shade, the vines make a weak, spindling growth, having sickly green foliage and producing few, imperfect flowers. It is advisable to select a new location each season to overcome diseases and insect pests. However, if the trenching method is followed and the soil is replenished each season, they can be grown in the same area for years.

It makes little difference whether the rows run east and west or north and south, but where double rows are planted there is a more even distribution of sunshine if the rows are planted north and south.

Soil and Its Preparation

Any good, friable, moderately rich, well-drained garden soil will produce excellent sweet peas. It is essential to consider drainage carefully, for the plants will not thrive in soggy or waterlogged soil. Under such conditions the seedlings are subject to damping-off, stem rot, root rot and various mildews.

No matter which system of planting is resorted to, fall preparation of the soil is preferable. If the trenching system is to be employed, a trench 15 to 24 inches deep and 16 inches wide should be excavated. It is well to loosen the subsoil and work coarse manure into it to facilitate drainage and to increase the feeding area for the deep roots. As the trench is filled, the poorer soil may be enriched with well-rotted manures, reserving the richer topsoil for the upper six inches of the trench. The trenches should be mounded up slightly to facilitate drainage and to allow for settling during the winter.

Four flowers to the stem

Fertilizers

Most garden soils are benefited by an application of hydrated lime to overcome acidity and to aid in making available fertilizing elements. Lime should, therefore, be incorporated with the soil at the rate of one pound for 20 feet of trench. A light dressing in the spring a week or ten days before planting will prove worth while. Sweet peas, being legumes, thrive best in an alkaline soil.

Bonemeal will supply nitrates and phosphates, which are essential to give color and substance to the plants and flowers. This is the best all around flower fertilizer, and it can be applied in liberal quantities without causing injury. Bonemeal is slowly available, so that the effect is noticeable throughout the season. When mixed with the soil, four to six ounces are added for each three feet of row. A top dressing with this fertilizer is advisable during the growing season. Additional fertilizers are not [*Continued on page 46*

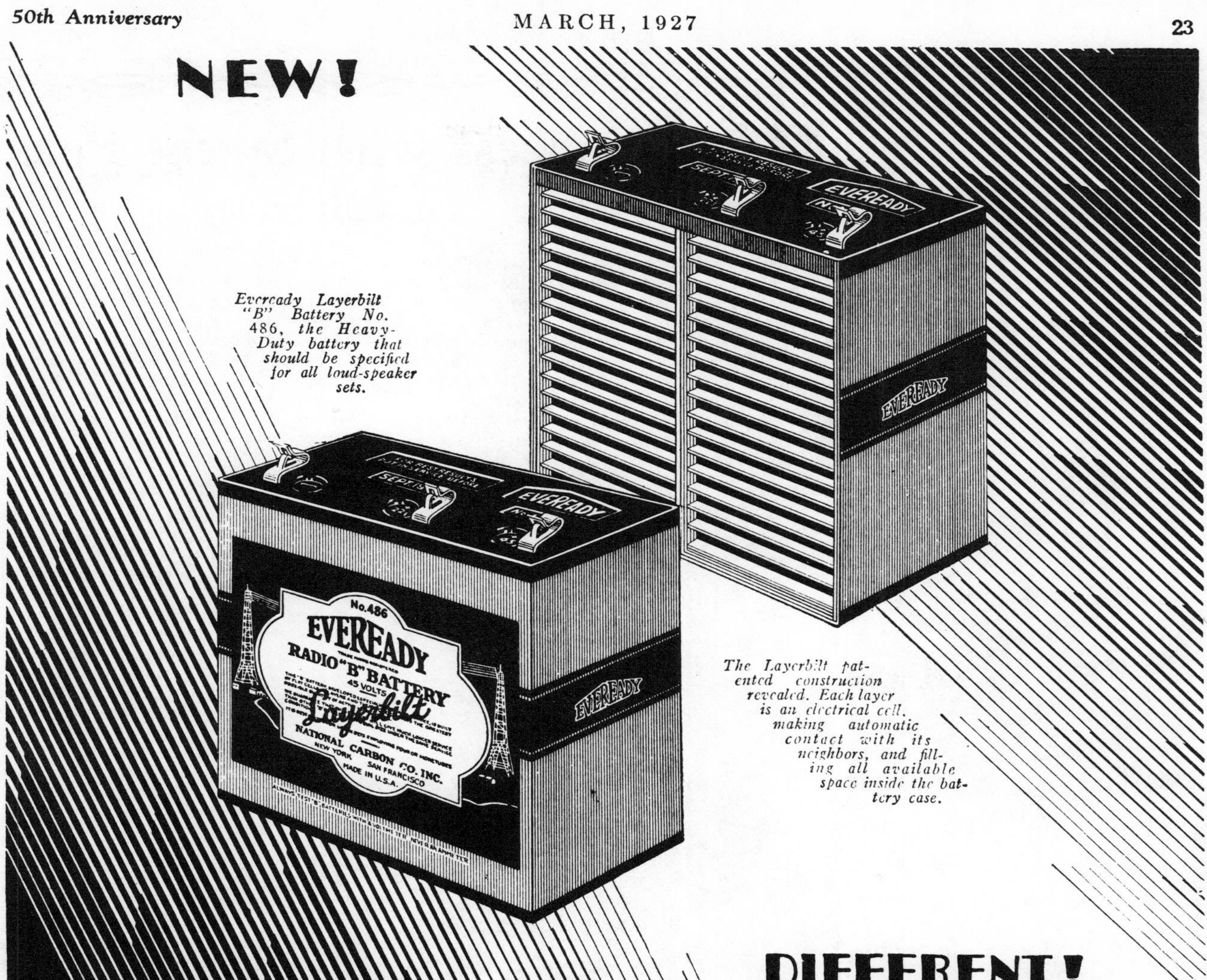
NEW!
Eveready Layerbilt "B" Battery No. 486, the Heavy-Duty battery that should be specified for all loud-speaker sets.
No. 486
EVEREADY
RADIO "B" BATTERY
45 VOLTS
Layerbilt
NATIONAL CARBON CO. INC.
NEW YORK SAN FRANCISCO
MADE IN U.S.A.
EVEREADY
The Layerbilt patented construction revealed. Each layer is an electrical cell, making automatic contact with its neighbors, and filling all available space inside the battery case.
DIFFERENT!

For greatest economy all loud speaker sets require the new Eveready Layerbilt "B" Batteries

IT WILL pay you, in convenience and reliability as well as in dollars and cents saved, to use this remarkable battery for farm radio.

The reason for the Eveready Layerbilt's surprising performance lies in its exclusive, patented construction. No other battery is like it. It is built in flat layers of current-producing elements, making practically a solid block. The layers make connection with each other automatically, and occupy all available space inside the battery case. Layer-building packs more active materials in a given area, and makes those materials produce more electricity.

Every farmer who has a loud-speaker set should use Heavy-Duty batteries, for they alone offer economy on modern receivers. When you buy new "B" batteries, be sure to get the Heavy-Duty size, and remember that the Eveready Layerbilt has proved to be the longest lasting, most economical of all Heavy-Duty batteries.

Our laboratories are continually testing batteries, and in all our tests we have yet to find a battery that is equal to the new improved and radically different Eveready Layerbilt "B" Battery No. 486. The development and perfecting of this remarkable battery is an outstanding battery-building achievement. It is the result of many years' experience plus the facilities and resources of pioneer manufacturers of all dry cell batteries.

NATIONAL CARBON COMPANY, Inc.
New York San Francisco
Unit of Union Carbide and Carbon Corporation

Tuesday night is Eveready Hour Night—
9 P. M., Eastern Standard Time

WEAF–*New York*	WGN–*Chicago*
WJAR–*Providence*	WOC–*Davenport*
WEEI–*Boston*	WCCO { *Minneapolis* / *St. Paul* }
WTAG–*Worcester*	
WFI–*Philadelphia*	KSD–*St. Louis*
WGR–*Buffalo*	WRC–*Washington*
WCAE–*Pittsburgh*	WGY–*Schenectady*
WSAI–*Cincinnati*	WHAS–*Louisville*
WTAM–*Cleveland*	WSB–*Atlanta*
WWJ–*Detroit*	WSM–*Nashville*

WMC–*Memphis*

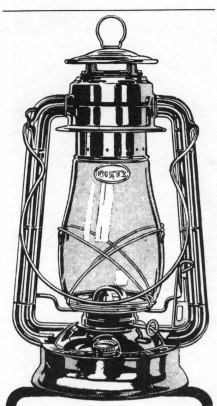

50th Anniversary

Alfalfa on Hillsides

By Ralph Kenney

MORE than 100,000 acres of good, profitable alfalfa-fields are grown on the hill slopes almost surrounding the blue-grass region of Kentucky. Here, alfalfa has been a profitable crop for the past 30 years. Hundreds of carloads of hay are shipped out of this territory every year. The experience of these farmers in Northern Kentucky disproves several erroneous ideas about alfalfa that have been current for a long time.

The territory mentioned includes all or parts of about 20 counties that fit around the central blue-grass area much like a ring with a large stone fits the finger. The most extensive area is on the north, between Cincinnati and Georgetown, extending from Lewis county on the east down along the Ohio River to Oldham county on the west. It runs south on both sides in a constantly narrowing band to Mercer and Washington counties on the west and Jessamine, Garrard and Lincoln on the east.

Alfalfa Loves Lime Soils and Dry Feet

The hills are continuous, with narrow ridges and deep draws, having generally 100 to 200 feet difference in elevation. The slopes are steep enough to give heart failure to a Corn Belt farmer who might be given a team and wagon and assigned the job of gathering hay. Land values range from $20 to $150 an acre, according to location and improvements. Fertility, as judged by corn yields, is much below that of the blue-grass area proper. This country is often referred to as the outer portion of the blue-grass. It grows grasses of all kinds to perfection. It is an excellent grazing country, and here, within the last 20 years, have developed the greatest milk-producing counties in the state. Likewise, the sheep industry of Kentucky is centered in the heart of this hill country.

The secret of alfalfa-growing lies in the lime-rich soils which, in this regard, are superior to the more level central blue-grass section. When the first alfalfa seed was sown in the late 80's and early 90's, it fell on sweet soil and made successful crops. As years passed, repeated trials showed landowners that the ridges were in most cases sour, hence little alfalfa is found on level land unless it has been limed in recent years.

This part of Kentucky is at present perhaps more comfortably situated from a financial viewpoint than any other group of counties of similar size in the state. Burley tobacco is grown to a limited extent, but experienced alfalfa-growers will tell you that alfalfa makes them more money than tobacco, and at the same time holds the soil from washing.

A Poor-Land Crop

The first ancient idea about alfalfa that went by the board was that one must choose the most fertile fields if he would be successful. These men choose their fields largely according to which will provide the cheapest seed-bed, paying little attention to fertility. They plan several years ahead and put the field in a cultivated crop the year preceding alfalfa in order to smooth over the gullies and clear the surface of rocks. Most of this land has been pretty well washed in the past 40 years, and the subsoil thus exposed grows as good a stand, that lives as long, as any alfalfa on more fertile soils elsewhere. Of course, they get larger yields with more fertile soil, but these men grow good alfalfa with what they possess now. It is not what they would like to grow, perhaps, in some cases, but it makes a fine quality of market hay and a stand lives ten or fifteen years. Three cuttings are obtained in average seasons, with a total yield of about two and one-half tons per acre.

Typical hillside slopes in Northern Kentucky, where 1,000,000 acres are ready to grow alfalfa as soon as the seed is sown

Their seed-bed practises have put away forever the old idea that uniform success in getting stands in this part of the United States is secured only on summer-prepared land sowed in August, for 99 per cent of all alfalfa in these hills is sown in the spring. The steep slopes prohibit working the land without a crop in the summer, a practise necessary to fall sowing, and which would result in sheet washing with enormous losses.

These Clay Soils Contain Lime

The choice of fields for alfalfa is of course confined to those known to be rich in lime. This is indicated by a covering of loose, thin limestone rocks. Generally these fields are located on the east, south or west slopes. As the thin rock layers broke up and the top-soil washed away, the rocks were left exposed and the thin alternating layers of clay have been worked up to become soil. [*Continued on page 90*

UNITED STATES TIRES ARE GOOD TIRES

Grade A Milk from Thoroughbred Rubber Trees
—the Basis for Quality Tires

IF you saw a pail of cow's milk alongside a pail of milk from a rubber tree, you probably couldn't tell which was which.

But appearance is not the only way in which these two milks are similar.

Take the matter of *quality*. The best milk comes from thoroughbred stock—be it cows or rubber trees.

Out in the Far East, the United States Rubber Company owns millions of thoroughbred rubber trees. The milk, or latex, from these trees is Certified Grade A.

In selecting the stock, caring for the young trees, preventing disease, gathering the latex, preparing it for shipment—every step is directed toward *quality*—and this quality means better tires.

Some of the pure virgin latex is shipped to the United States Tire factories just as it comes from the tree. Here it is used in making *Web Cord*—the special, patented cord construction used in building United States Tires. It is the secret of maximum strength and flexibility.

The rest of the latex is made into *Sprayed Rubber*—another United States Rubber Company achievement. It is really the "cream" of the latex—the purest, strongest, most uniform rubber known.

Because of its greater tensile strength, *Sprayed Rubber* is of vital importance in giving long-lasting service to United States Tires.

United States (US) Rubber Company
Trade Mark

Grafting buds from proven trees onto young trees is of great importance in obtaining quality rubber. In making the graft, the utmost precaution is taken that no dirt or bacteria touch the delicate grafting area. Not even the breath of the worker is allowed to come in contact with the wound.

As the result of the purer, stronger, more uniform rubber grown on the United States Rubber Company's plantations, you get more for your money in United States Tires.

A careful record is kept of every one of the 7,000,000 trees on the United States Rubber Company's plantations. The yield from each tapping, as shown by the measuring cup, is marked on the tree. In this way, it is possible to know exactly which are good producers. In the plantation laboratories, a strict check is kept on the quality of the latex as it is collected.

These natives are engaged in preparing the fertilizer which does so much to increase the yield and quality of the rubber trees on the United States Rubber Company's plantation in Sumatra—the largest producing plantation in the world.

Built by the FLAT BAND METHOD *from* SPRAYED RUBBER *and* WEB CORD

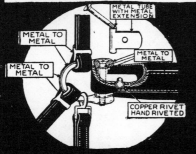

Various Grades of Cod-Liver Oil

50th Anniversary

A LARGE number of experiment stations are recommending cod-liver oil in one form or another for poultry. There is no argument as to its value for poultry. Not enough attention has been given to explaining the values of the various grades of cod-liver oil, however.

The truth is, cod-liver oil does vary in richness according to the condition and fitness of the cod, and the process of rendering the oil. Just as a flock of poultry must be in good condition in order to lay fertile eggs, so must a school of cod be fit and healthy in order to yield rich, potent oil. A cod netted during spawning season, for example, yields oil of low potency. The same fish, caught before or after spawning season, will yield oil of high potency—sometimes running 250 times richer than butterfat.

Rendering Process

The old-fashioned way of rendering—and it still prevails in some cases—is very insanitary as well as slow and cumbersome. The liver is taken from the cod and thrown into a large wooden vat. When practically filled, the vat is placed in a convenient spot, generally in the sunshine on the deck, and allowed to remain there for an indefinite period—maybe until the vessel makes port.

Gradually, the livers in the wooden vat become rotten and decayed, the oil in the tissues liberates itself and rises to the top. After a period of several weeks, the upper part of the vat contains a pool of reddish-brown oil, while the other remains of the livers have settled at the bottom. This old-fashioned way of rendering accounts for the disagreeable, sickening taste and odor which are very pronounced in some grades, and which oftentimes upset digestion.

One fleet of modern trawlers which trolls the Grand Banks of Newfoundland has developed a more sanitary process. Each trawler is equipped with a modern steam-heated boiler. The livers are thrown in right after the fish are caught and the oil is rendered fresh, a few hours after the cod is netted. This does away with the sickening taste and at the same time it results in a product that is exceptionally rich in vitamins, as well as being clean and sanitary.

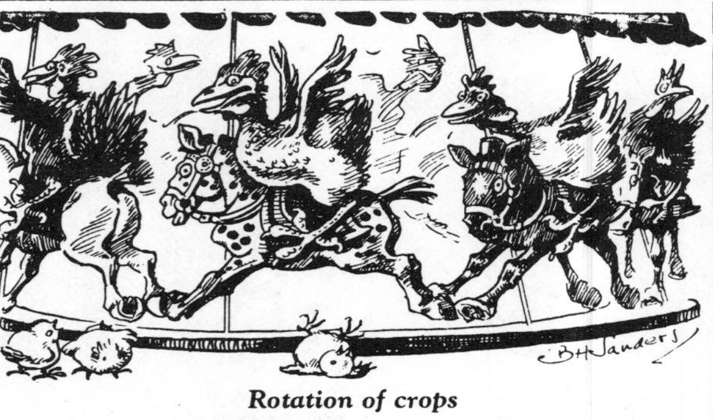

Rotation of crops

Penning Pays for Farm Flocks

I HAVE kept hens on free range and in pens, and I have found that free range has very little advantage over small pens, and is not nearly so valuable as a system of penning that gives the benefits of good range with the advantages of having the flock always under full control.

Last summer I saw what I consider about the best combination I ever investigated. The house was of the semi-open-front kind, 50 feet long, and had monitor roof with the row of glass seven feet from the front and ten feet from the rear, which was low. The house was divided into three pens inside, with corresponding pens outside in front. Large openings in the front for each pen were covered with poultry-netting and were provided with cloth-covered sash. Removable roosts, dropping-boards (with removable nests just under their front edge) filled the rear, while the front was given over to feeders and scratching material.

The house was located in the edge of a sweet-clover pasture. Every morning a gate from one pen was opened and the hens allowed free range over the pasture. They came in or were called in for the noon meal. In the evening the gate of another pen was opened, and that flock enjoyed free range. The next morning the last pen was allowed its freedom, and that evening the first flock had another chance. The flocks got the full benefit of free range, yet they could be kept separated fully, and the keeper could always keep track of them. *L. H. C.*

Johnny (as a locomotive passed): "It's a good thing they got a strong fence—he might get out o' there"

Rat killing: Here is method for eradication of rats that I have found effective: I found the rats had burrowed under the chicken-yard, with openings in a ditch in the rear. First I stopped up all holes by pounding stones into them, then with a crowbar I sounded the ground in the yard until I located their nests; then, placing a funnel in the hole made by the crowbar, I poured boiling lye-water into their nests. This practically eradicated them for more than two years. *J. S.*

Ultra-Violet Rays PASS THRU FLEX-O-GLASS

Pat. Pend:—Trade Mark Reg.

Weatherproof — Watertight — Unbreakable

1/8 Cost of Glass AND BETTER

POSITIVELY MAKES CHICKS GROW Fast and Strong

Build this Health-Producing Scratch Shed Easily and Cheaply

Give Chicks Actual Sunshine Indoors

Prevent Rickets, Diseases and Death!

Don't keep chicks behind glass. It shuts out the sun's Ultra-Violet rays, causing leg weakness (rickets), diseases and finally **death.** Leading State Experiment Stations have proved this in many tests. But these scientists found that chicks kept under FLEX-O-GLASS were safe from rickets, weak legs, stayed healthy, were full of pep and grew amazingly in this cozy sunlit room—because the chicks absorbed the energizing Ultra-Violet rays that FLEX-O-GLASS admitted. See proof in center column.

These tests were made for you. Put your chicks under health-producing FLEX-O-GLASS. Prevent weak chicks, diseases and death this easy way. Your chicks will mature or reach frying size much sooner than ever before. Thousands of poultrymen have replaced glass with FLEX-O-GLASS, which makes use of the sunshine—Nature's only health-producer—indoors too, where chicks are out of slush, snow and rain. Fast, strong chick growth will amaze you. Just build a FLEX-O-GLASS scratch shed easily and replace your poultry house windows with FLEX-O-GLASS. Use 15 yds. for 300 chicks. This cozy sunlit brooder-house will pay for itself many times the first season alone.

Proven Strongest and Best for Chicks

Ne'er Idle Poultry Farm of Indiana writes: "We used FLEX-O-GLASS on our brooder-houses this spring and were very well pleased. We placed it by the side of one window that was covered with—(another product). The difference in the color of the light was quickly noticeable. But one very convincing argument was that the chicks piled up in front of the FLEX-O-GLASS window, leaving the space in front of the other entirely empty. The FLEX-O-GLASS looks as well at the end of the season as it did at the first, while the other material is decidedly worn. I thought perhaps these observations of ours might be of interest to you."

Recommended by Leading Poultry Farms

"I have used your product the past 2 years, and find it O. K. Consequently I can recommend it to my Baby Chick customers."—Cornhusker Poultry Farm of Nebraska.

—o—

"FLEX-O-GLASS works wonders for little pigs." So writes A. P. Nave of Ohio.

Easy to Install

FLEX-O-GLASS is very easily installed. Comes in one piece 35½ inches wide any length desired. Just cut to size with ordinary shears, nail on and the job is done. Absolutely weather-resisting. Looks neat and attractive. Lasts for years. Millions of yards now in use.

Gather Eggs All Winter

Experts and users have found that a FLEX-O-GLASS scratch shed concentrates the sun's Ultra-Violet rays on hens which keeps them active and healthy, stimulates the egg glands and makes them lay in coldest weather. Under glass hens quit laying and chicks die because it shuts out these needed rays. Use 15 yards for 100 hens.

Enclose Porches

Just nail FLEX-O-GLASS over screen porches and stormdoors. Changes snow-trap into healthful sunroom or children's playhouse, cheaply.

Grow Plants Quicker and Stronger than Under Glass

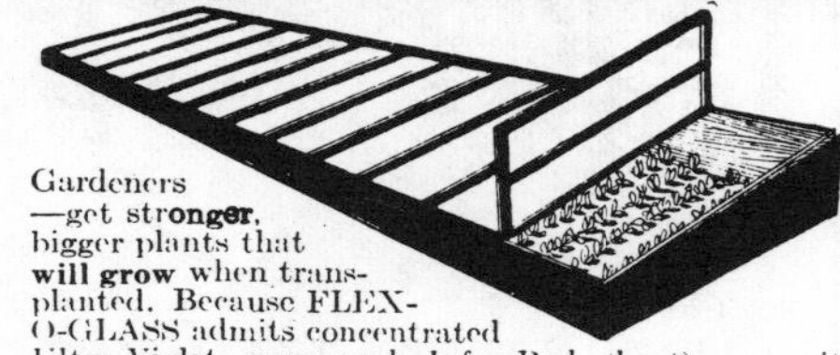

Gardeners—get **stronger**, bigger plants that **will grow** when transplanted. Because FLEX-O-GLASS admits concentrated Ultra-Violet rays and Infra-Red (heat) rays, it makes plants grow much stronger and faster than when under plain glass. (Glass stops these rays.) Have plants earlier. Get more money for them. FLEX-O-GLASS is installed much easier, holds heat better and costs far less than glass. Scatters light just as needed. Frames are lighter and easier to handle. 15 yards of FLEX-O-GLASS covers a hotbed of 135 sq. ft. Ideal for greenhouses.

Chas. Nerelius of W. Va. says—"I use FLEX-O-GLASS on hotbeds and it's better than glass. The plants do better under FLEX-O-GLASS."

Recommends It to Others

"I shall recommend FLEX-O-GLASS to others doing trucking. You sure have a winner." S. Krimmitz, Aliss, Wis.

"I use FLEX-O-GLASS on my hotbeds and brooder-houses with splendid success." Says Mr. Stewart of Ill.

Read This Scientific Proof

Tests by Leading U. S. Authorities

Specimens were furnished by Wis. State Exp. Sta. Published by U. S. Egg Society & Poultry Trib.

See the picture at left. The larger chicks received the Ultra-Violet rays in sunlight and the smaller chicks did not. All are the same age and were fed the same, at **Wisconsin State Experiment Station.** This seems almost beyond belief but it is true. Put your chicks under FLEX-O-GLASS and give them these wonderful sun's rays. Their fast growth will actually be amazing.

IOWA STATE COLLEGE states: "Believe your product (FLEX-O-GLASS) far superior to common glass for enclosing chicken houses for winter and brooder-houses."

OHIO STATE EXPERIMENT STATION, upon completing a 10 weeks' ricket test reports: "Enough of the effective Ultra-Violet rays were transmitted to offer protection against leg weakness."

KANS. STATE EXP. STATION says: "Up until 2 years ago no one understood the value of Ultra-Violet Rays. Some excellent results have been reported by practical poultrymen who have used glass substitutes, which will allow the passage of the health-giving portion of sunshine to a considerable greater extent than glass."

DR. MORSE, for 45 years Consulting Chemist of Connecticut says: "Congratulations are due you. Your statements I heartily corroborate, because the Ultra-Violet rays which penetrate Flex-O-Glass make hens healthful, chemically active and increase oxygenating power of the blood."

Alice W. of Worcester, Mass. says, "With these heavy snowfalls the baby chicks have had their outdoor yard indoors and are as lively as can be."

Mr. Latter of N. H. states, "Purchased 15 yards a year ago to replace glass windows and like it fine. Never would put glass in a hen-house again."

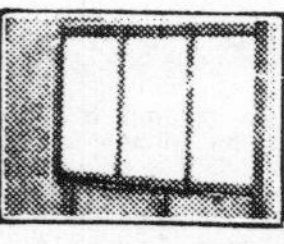

Replace Windows with the Genuine FLEX-O-GLASS

Chicks, pigs and plants eventually die and hens quit laying if deprived of Ultra-Violet rays. FLEX-O-GLASS admits these healthful sun rays. Glass stops them. THOUSANDS of people have replaced plain glass windows with FLEX-O-GLASS, the stimulating and beneficial Ultra-Violet ray filter; perfected by Mr. Warp years ago after careful research and experimenting, and recommended by best U. S. authorities and actual users everywhere.

Superior to Glass

"I put FLEX-O-GLASS on alongside of a glass window last summer. I found it superior to glass for light. I have had enough experience in the use of FLEX-O-GLASS to give advice to people I meet. I do not hesitate selling anything that has merit." T. S. Baird of N. Y.

FLEX-O-GLASS is Guaranteed Strong and Durable

FLEX-O-GLASS, an amazingly healthful product for admitting Ultra-Violet rays is unsurpassed. **Genuine FLEX-O-GLASS always has been** and **is today** made on a **strong, cloth base,** specially processed **to withstand all kinds of weather.** That's why it lasts so long, always lies flat and stays bright. FLEX-O-GLASS even **looks fresh** and **new** after **seasons** of exposure to wind, rain and snow. Don't confuse it with other materials. State Experiment Station **tested FLEX-O-GLASS thoroughly** before recommending its use—**Your Protection.** Reg. in the U. S. Pat. office, and used with **amazing** results everywhere, for **replacing** glass at **only ⅛ the cost.** Order Genuine FLEX-O-GLASS today at our risk—direct from the factory and save money.

Mrs. T. J. of Nebr. writes—"When Flex-O-Glass is installed beside another, it speaks for itself."

PRICES—All Postage Prepaid

Per yd. 35½ ins. wide: 1 yd. 50c; 5 yards at 40c [$2.00]; 10 yds. at 35c [$3.50]; 25 yds. at 32c [$8.00]; 100 yds. or more at 30c per yard [$30.00].

Special Trial Offer

15 Sq. Yards Postpaid for $5

The FLEX-O-GLASS MFG. CO. will send you 15 yards of FLEX-O-GLASS in a roll 35½ inches wide and 45 feet long, postage prepaid, for $5.00. This big trial roll covers a **scratch shed 9 x 15 ft.** (size for 300 chicks) or use for **brooder-house fronts, hotbeds, poultry, barn or hog-house windows, enclosing porches, storm doors, etc.** If after 15 days not satisfied FLEX-O-GLASS gives more warm healthful light than glass, or if it isn't stronger, better and more durable than other materials, just send it back and your money will be refunded by the FLEX-O-GLASS MFG. CO. without question. You take no risk. **You must be absolutely satisfied or your money back.** Order direct from factory and save money. Mail check or money order today. Use Guarantee Coupon below, which is backed by $1,000 deposited in the Pioneer Bank, Chicago. Send $9.50 for 30 yds. if you wish larger trial roll. Orders filled in 24 hours. FREE catalog on request contains valuable poultry information.

FLEX-O-GLASS MFG. CO., Dept. 37
1451 N. Cicero Ave., CHICAGO, ILL.

Find enclosed $.......... for which send me .... yards of Flex-O-Glass 35½ in. wide, by prepaid parcel post. It is understood that if I am not satisfied after using it for 15 days I may return it and you will refund my money without question.

Name ....

Town ....

R. F. D. .... State ....

FLEX-O-GLASS MANUFACTURING CO.

1451 N. CICERO AVE. Dept. 37 CHICAGO, ILL.

50 Years of Farm Machinery

Continued from page 16

The mechanical milker, now widely though not universally in use, was not to go on general sale for nearly 40 years.

Without the silo, there were naturally no shredders or blowers. Today's complete dairy equipment, with manure- and feed-conveyors, concrete floors and stalls, feed- and water-troughs, comfortable swinging stanchions, ventilating systems, and all splendid modern equipment for sanitation and health, were all things of the future for the man on page 5.

Grain-drills have not greatly changed. This is a model of 1880, built by Farquhar. Above, hand corn-planter

The arrival of the cheap internal-combustion motor, about a quarter of a century ago, brought with it many remarkable changes.

Gas engines, electric-light plants, commercial electric power, running water in home and barn, modern sanitary home equipment and electric labor-saving devices for the housewife—all of these are strictly present-day devices.

Power spraying-machinery was unknown in 1877. It was forced on fruit growers by the San Jose scale and the codling-moth

Nor have we any right to assume that the next 50 years will not show equal or greater progress. On the contrary, it is safe to predict that in 1977 the farm equipment of today will look as primitive and crude as does that of 1877 to us.

Combined planter and cultivator used 50 years ago

Power for pumping was generally from the windmill in 1877. This was a famous model of the "folding" or sectional type

We gratefully acknowledge the invaluable assistance of many of the large implement and machinery manufacturers in the preparation of the above brief review of the last 50 years. Many catalogs of early dates have been placed at our disposal, with important information; we regret being able to use so little of the interesting material made available to us.

Special thanks for illustrations and assistance are due J. I. Case Threshing Machine Company, A. B. Farquhar Company, International Harvester Company, Hayes Pump and Planter Co., Pine Tree Milking Machine Co., U. S. Wind Engine & Pump Co., John Deere Plow Co., Wiard Plow Co., De Laval Separator Co., Cutaway Harrow Co., The Russell & Co., and Mr. E. J. Baker, Jr., of the *Farm Implement News.*

In 1877 we got our power from this kind of treadmill, or from the horse-power of the horizontal type. Note the Arabian steeds that furnished the motive power

NASH

Leads the World in Motor Car Value

Quality and Value without an Equal

in the whole $1000 Field

By long odds the most distinguished motor car ever introduced into the $1000 field, this new Nash De Luxe Light Six is also the most remarkable performer.

Along with its notable beauty and classic body craftsmanship it has the vital superiority of a 7-bearing crankshaft motor—*the ultra-modern type.*

That gives you a superlative advantage over the standard 3 or 4 bearing motor in the way of matchless *quietness* and phenomenal *smoothness* thruout the full range of speed and power.

Colorfully finished in exquisite blue lacquer and enhanced with a wealth of refinements and appointments it stands out as a motor car value clearly above and beyond comparison.

The attractiveness of the interior is enriched with a walnut finished instrument board and window ledges and choice upholstery of genuine Chase Velmo Mohair Velvet.

Headlamps as well as cowl lamps are executed in the bullet design. The steering wheel is of real Circassian walnut. There are bumpers in front and bumperettes at the rear, and a motometer surmounts the winged radiator cap. 4-wheel brakes and 5 disc wheels are also included as standard equipment within the price. (4805)

Tree Planting on Rough Land

By Charles Goodwin

IN 1901 the writer was in possession of 18 acres of land on the shore of Skaneateles Lake, N. Y. All but about one acre of this land was rough and steep sidehills, or was cut up with a small stream that meandered through the place. This stream had formerly been used to operate a grist mill and cider mill, but had not been used for several years, and the whole place was in a run-down condition, well covered with burdocks, sumac bushes and poison-ivy.

In 1902, two hired men and I spent two or three days collecting and planting forest trees on the least rolling part of the place; about three acres were fairly level and this was bordered on each side by steep hillsides. I had planted a few trees the year before and have planted a few since, but most of the 300 or 400 trees on the flat land were planted at that time. We planted about 100 sugar-maples, about as many basswoods, and the balance were mainly elms and soft maples, with a few oaks and poplars. The trees were small.

Large Trees Now

From that planting we have soft maples from twelve to sixteen inches in diameter two feet above ground, sugar-maples from six to ten inches and basswoods from eight to twelve. The elms made a large growth, but we value them only for shade. I tapped 80 of the best maples the past two years and made all the sugar and sirup three families needed. I used a small bit for tapping (3/8-inch) and the holes close up the first season. The basswood trees are rapidly growing into valuable timber.

I was 49 years old when I planted the trees, and my friends told me I would never live to see much shade from them. The shade is so dense that not a thing grows under them. The real reason for my writing this little sketch is not so much the grove just described, but another grove planted to black locust on the steep sidehills and a few other rough places. The trees were three years old and grown in the nursery row. I transplanted them at the end of the first year so as to give them a better root system when we finally came to plant permanently. We had 900 and planted them about ten or twelve feet apart on one acre, and the balance of them were planted a few in a place as we found opportunity. Two men did the planting in two days.

Locust Fence Posts

I have already cut and used over 500 fence posts; I sold 200 more last spring and can cut 1,000 today. Perhaps some of my readers do not understand that locust is the best-lasting timber for fence posts that there is. It will even outlast red cedar. I know of posts that have been set for 80 years and today are sound. These trees make rapid growth and a few that we planted on the level land (a rich loam) made an annual gain of one inch in diameter. They should be planted fairly close together so they will run up straight.

Some trees of the original planting have been cut out. These posts, cut eight and one-half feet long, sell readily at from 50 to 75 cents each, according to size. This grove, which has cost almost nothing, has reached a value of a little better than $1,000, and it has taken 24 years to do it. Almost every farm has some place where all the fence posts needed for the farm could be grown and cost almost nothing. Don't plant these trees where you will ever want to till the ground later on, as the stumps will never rot.

A New Remedy for Tapeworm

By F. B. Hadley

MANY remedies have been recommended and tried to remove tapeworms from poultry, but none has been found satisfactory. For this reason, investigations were started at the Wisconsin Agricultural Experiment Station in an attempt to find some drug that would remove tapeworms and still not harm the bird. As a result of carefully controlled tests on a large number of birds, a drug known as kamala was discovered. Besides being nearly 100 per cent effective, kamala has a wide range of safety and can be given to the entire flock mixed with the feed, or administered individually, if desirable. When given in the doses prescribed, it has been found palatable and does not decrease egg-production, or cause any bad effects.

Kamala is a brownish-red, non-odorous and nearly tasteless powder obtained from the red glands secured from the capsules of a large evergreen shrub, which grows in tropical Asia, parts of Africa, the East Indies and in Australia. It can be purchased from any druggist. As kamala is often adulterated, only the best quality should be bought.

Mix Medicine with the Feed

The first thing to do when the entire flock is to be treated at one time is to group the birds according to weight and withhold feed for from 18 to 24 hours; next compute the amount of kamala that will be required to treat the flock according to the following dose table:

Birds weighing ½ to 1 lb.	¾ gram
Birds weighing 1 to 3 lbs.	1 gram
Birds weighing 3 lbs. and over	2 grams

The kamala should be thoroughly mixed with one-third as much cornmeal or dry bread crumbs as the flock will readily consume at one time. It is not necessary to follow the kamala with a purgative, as it acts in that capacity.

If post-mortem examination has revealed an extremely heavy infestation with tapeworms, it is likely that more than one treatment will be needed to remove all the parasites. In this event the treatment should be repeated, or a veterinarian should be consulted regarding the advisability of a second treatment, because some other complicating disease may be present.

It is always advisable with a small flock to treat each bird separately. This insures each bird's receiving the desired dose. Individual doses of kamala for birds of different weights should be based on the following dose table:

Birds weighing ½ to 1 lb.	½ gram
Birds weighing 1 to 2 lbs.	1 gram
Birds weighing 2 lbs. and over	1½ grams

For convenience in administering kamala to individual birds, the drug may be placed in one-half gram gelatin capsules, which are easily given by moistening with water and placing on the tongue.

Three hens each laid 300 eggs or better at the Vineland Egg-Laying Contest during the twelve months closing October 31, 1926, thus breaking all records for the eastern United States. The champion hen was a single-comb White Leghorn, owned by S. Baevsky, of Mays Landing; she laid 308 eggs. The second best hen in the contest, a White Orpington, laid 301 eggs. The third bird, a White Leghorn, laid exactly 300 eggs.

Water-Tank in Barn

50th Anniversary

Building a new barn? Why not put a water-tank inside?

ONE of the biggest improvements I ever made was by putting a tank for watering stock in the barn that I built a few years ago. Underground pipes which bring the water are below frost-line, so there is seldom any risk of having the water freeze. Relatively warm water is to be had during cold weather. The tank is set some distance away from the outside door and away from direct drafts. The hydrant comes up direct through the floor at one end, as shown. I'm really just as keen about the electric lights in the barn as I am about the tank—I couldn't get along without either. A light is placed directly over the tank so that the stock can drink their normal fill whether day or night, or winter or summer. If you use concrete, be sure to re-enforce the corners of the tank with bent steel rods or strips of woven-wire fencing. Your cement dealer will give you a booklet showing just how to do the work. Try it. *H.*

Bees in Spring

THE first examination in spring should take place just as soon after the bees begin work as weather will permit. At this time, see that each colony has a laying queen and plenty of honey to last until the bees can gather enough food from the field.

When there are bees of all ages in the colony, those less than two weeks old do the work inside the hive, and the older ones go afield in search of food for both young and old. In early spring all the bees are several months old, so some have to stay at home and carry on the house-hold duties, until there are young bees reared to take their places, which takes 21 days from the time the queen lays the eggs.

The average life of worker bees, after they begin going afield, is from eight to twelve weeks. So you can not expect those bees which have passed through the winter to live very long after they begin work in the spring. Therefore, you should do everything possible to help the colonies in rearing young bees just as early as possible, by seeing that the hives are tight and that the bees have free access to water and that they are supplied at all times with plenty of food.

Feeding Sirup

Whenever a colony is found short of honey, and you have no sealed combs to give them, you can make a sirup using equal parts of sugar and water, and fill empty combs with the sirup by using a wash-tub or any kind of tank that will allow the combs to lie flat on the bottom. Punch several holes in the bottom of a five- or ten-pound pail, pour the sirup into this pail and allow it to spray through the holes into the comb, holding pail several inches above comb. When one side is filled, reverse the comb and fill the other side, after which it is ready to be used the same as a sealed comb of honey. The sides of the tub keep the sirup from splashing on things and wasting. Of course, there are other good methods of feeding, but I like this way best.

Strength of Colonies

When a colony of bees comes out of winter quarters, it consists of from 30,000 to 40,000 old workers and a queen, with no brood or young bees. If we expect to get a honey crop from this colony, there must be from 75,000 to 100,000 workers at the beginning of the honey flow. You see the queen must be right on the job laying all the time from early spring until the main flow opens, if this is to be accomplished. Each colony in the apiary must be examined once every ten days, so as to be sure that all is going well. Whenever, for some reason or other, a colony is not doing as well as it should, we must right the wrong, even if we have to replace the queen with a young one. There are folks who specialize in raising queens for weak colonies.

If you can have a strong force of harvest hands (workers) plus a hive full of sealed brood at the opening of the flow, you are almost sure of a crop of honey, providing the flowers secrete nectar, and the bees are given plenty of storage room, in plenty of time. *Eugene Holloway.*

DEPENDABLE

People buy Dodge Brothers Motor Car because its dependability has won and earned their unqualified confidence.

This confidence has been solidified, moreover, by a policy of fair and reasonable prices; a dealer organization of the highest integrity; and a national service system that insures accurate work at fair, predetermined cost.

Special Sedan $945—De Luxe Sedan $1075
f. o. b. Detroit

DODGE BROTHERS, INC. DETROIT
DODGE BROTHERS (CANADA) LIMITED
TORONTO ONTARIO

DODGE BROTHERS
MOTOR CARS

Is Our Corn Soil Doomed?

Clear Streams and the Angleworm

By Arthur J. Mason

This is the second part of Arthur J. Mason's very important study of the permanence of soil in the Corn Belt.

Mr. Mason points out the vital differences between rainfall conditions in the Mississippi Valley and in a permanent country like England, and shows why the British earthworm is probably four times as efficient as his Illinois cousin.

He also makes this significant declaration: "Agricultural regions with dirty streams are, *must be,* temporary. Agricultural regions with clear streams are, *must be,* permanent."

Printing of Mr. Mason's paper will continue next month.

WE are the heirs of all the ages. In no other case is that so true as of the people of the United States. I think it was Lowell who said, "God winnowed a nation for seed"; and the occupation of this part of North America began.

For millions of years Providence had been storing and accumulating soil, timber, minerals, against that event. The property meanwhile was in the trusteeship of Indians, whose culture and institutions were exactly suited for the job of leaving Nature alone, and keeping others from interference. Nowhere on the earth's surface had Nature acted in such a large and generous fashion, in the storage of essential raw material, under favorable climatic conditions.

We came into this great property, and what a theater of action it has been for ardent, buoyant men to bring into existence this glorious, effective, happy thing we call the United States of America.

I, a foreigner, feel deep emotion as my mind's eye sweeps thousands of miles—from New York to the Pacific. [Mr. Mason was born in Australia—*Editor.*] Is this great heritage a permanent farm, or is it a *mine* undergoing exhaustion—not exhaustion of *fertility*, which is the plant-food *in* the soil, but the actual removal of what Professor Chamberlin terms the *body of the soil itself?*

I believe if you appeal to the fraternity of geologists and those whose duty it is to observe such things, the verdict will be fairly unanimous—*it is but a mine undergoing rapid exhaustion.*

Black Prairie Soil Turns Gray

My special interest, and doubtless yours, too, centers in this greatest of all continuous bodies of good land, the center of which we call the Corn Belt. Every discerning traveler recognizes it as the greatest feature of this country—a tract about 1,000 miles square, with Illinois near the heart. Mr. Bryce somewhere says: "The United States consists of the Mississippi Valley, and a fringe on either side."

I have lately acquired a farm; 160 acres of black corn land, not over 25 miles from this spot—smooth summit land, without a ravine or waste place, every inch cultivatable. For several years now I have affectionately watched this tract. There is no part 20 feet higher than any other. It has been under cultivation 50 years. Already the soil is gone from all the bumps—formerly the best part. My scrutiny led to the estimate, that almost half the soil has disappeared.

When I came to compare this belief with the view of two excellent old Germans, quite observant men, who had been on the farm from boyhood, their independent judgment had formed the same conclusion. The loss of soil is obvious, plain to any eyes that care to scan.

A fair estimate for the whole nearby countryside is that four to five inches of mold have gone. The soil and subsoil are very different in color—black the one, yellow the other. Let any man watch the plowed lands of this state; see the color change, in the depressions black, thence up the gentlest slope getting gray, then almost yellow on the tops of the bumps. *Once it was all black.*

Arthur J. Mason

How Rain Falls in Permanent Countries

To go back to my two pails of spilt water. [In The Farm Journal last month—*Editor.*] A whole school of agronomists points to Europe, an old country whose fertility is on the increase. Thus they allay the feeling of alarm at decreasing fertility in this country.

I would first point out that these men always quote Northern Europe, a land of small annual rainfall in inches, but frequent rains, a land having ideal conditions for the creation and retention of soil, *a land of clear streams.*

Let those same men quote the south of France. There the loss of soil is the despair of its people; it has involved enormous expenditures to arrest, in any degree, and is the subject of a large literature.

Now, what is the difference between these two parts of France? They have about the same annual rainfall, allowing for bolder topography in the South. Merely this, as our young soldiers who were in France can testify—in the North it rains about 200 days in a year, in the South the fall more largely accompanies thunder-storms. Perhaps there are half as many days on which it rains, and the total rainfall in both cases is 20 to 30 inches.

The whole question of rainfall is a strange and interesting one, full of surprises. London and the Sacramento Valley of California have a not very different annual rainfall. London the ever wet—Sacramento Valley the almost always dry. In one case, frequent little rains all the year, coming on 200 days. In the other, all the rain coming in three months, on 65 days, and for six months parched, baked dustiness everywhere.

Strangest of all, at Culebra, Isthmus of Panama, our Government found that it could not maintain a vegetable garden without irrigation; this in a place where it rains about 200 inches each year!

Where All Rivers Are "Brimming"

What is the situation in Little Green England, where our traditions were established and slowly indurated in the mass of minds?

Every Englishman passes through life clutching the handle of an umbrella. This becomes second nature; so he feels naked and defenseless without one, even during a California summer. Nevertheless, when the annual accounts are cast up, it is found that the total rainfall in London and the eastern counties is but two-thirds that of Illinois—specifically, 26 inches per year in London and 38 or 39 in Illinois—an average for the state, of course. Precipitation is but 36 inches in Chicago. The English rainfall more resembles our practise of sprinkling lawns—

[Continued on page 40

50th Anniversary

At peace with the world

PEACE and contentment, I say, are not a matter of how much money you have accumulated. They come with a clear conscience, good health, and the right companionship. No comrades mean more to me today than my trusty pipe and good old Prince Albert.

I start the day with a pipe in my mouth and a song in my heart. It has been like that for a good many years now. Before I settled upon Prince Albert as the one and only tobacco for me, I had "played around," as you young fellows say, with many brands.

I think it was the rich, rare fragrance of P. A. in the tidy red tin that spurred me to try a load of it in my pipe. I found the taste more than matched that wonderful aroma. It was cool. It was sweet. It was mild . . . mild, yet completely, delightfully satisfying.

Perhaps a leaf from my book of experience will set you on the road to peace and contentment. I tell you, in all seriousness, that you don't know . . . you simply can't know how much your pipe can mean to you until you have filled it with Prince Albert!

P. A. is sold everywhere in tidy red tins, pound and half-pound tin humidors, and pound crystal-glass humidors with sponge-moistener top. And always with every bit of bite and parch removed by the Prince Albert process.

PRINCE ALBERT

—no other tobacco is like it!

A Party for March 17

By Elsie Duncan Yale

THE cheeriness and wit of the Irish people naturally lead us to think of St. Patrick's day with good humor, and a party is quite in order.

Write the invitations on green correspondence-cards or note-paper decorated with shamrock seals, and use the following verse:

Come colleens and lads to a party so gay,
St. Patrick is calling, so come, come away,
We'll celebrate gladly by wearing the green,
So please be on hand at the festival scene.

Time Place

Abundant material can be secured for decorations. Crêpe paper in many charming designs appropriate to the day can be purchased for a small sum, and this can be fastened around the walls of the rooms as a border. Bright green festoons may extend diagonally from center of ceiling to corners, and showers of shamrocks may grace the doorways and windows.

BY way of a start for the festivities, the hostess may have in readiness slips of paper, upon each of which should be written the name of an Irish song, as "Mother Machree," "River Shannon," "Kathleen Mavourneen" and others. These slips are pinned on the backs of the guests, each of whom must guess the name of the song assigned him, as some one hums it. Naturally, in a few minutes the room will be a jolly babel of humming and laughter. As the songs are guessed the slips are removed from the back and pinned to the front of the coat or dress.

"Blarney" is a game highly appropriate for an Irish party. Choose a guest to sit in a chair facing the others, and let each in turn pay him or her a compliment, as a "bit of blarney." The complimented one is required to preserve gravity, with not even a smile, and each one who retains complete composure under the barrage of flattery is rewarded with an inexpensive prize, while the one whose compliment caused the smile must take the chair.

"Jaunting-Car Race." As jaunting-cars are associated with Ireland, two may be represented by children's express-wagons. A young man (preferably of light weight, for the sake of the wagon) is chosen to sit astride each wagon, and he must propel himself to a given goal with his feet. Of course, the winner is rewarded, and this time the gift may appropriately be an inexpensive little cup.

THE refreshment table is covered with the decorated crêpe paper. A toy horse and cart will do for centerpiece, the cart being loaded with "potatoes" made by rolling shaped bits of fondant in cinnamon. Roll the cart around the table so that the guests can help themselves to the candy potatoes.

As a variation from the usual party refreshments, the hostess may serve "Irish stew" from a large glass or china bowl. This "stew" is really fruit gelatin (colored green), on the surface of which are spoonfuls of whipped cream to represent "dumplings," which invariably accompany an Irish stew. Little cakes iced in green, salted nuts and coffee may complete the menu.

If more substantial refreshments are desired, serve bacon sandwiches and shamrock salad before serving the "stew."

Send self-addressed and stamped envelope for additional games for St. Patrick's day and for clever stunts for an April Fool Party. Address, Entertainment Editor, The Farm Journal, Washington Square, Philadelphia, Pa.

A cartload of "potatoes" for the centerpiece

A Country-Products Bazaar

A SPLENDID opportunity awaits farmers' wives who want a little income of their own. Every summer hundreds of farm women put up innumerable jars of good things in excess of what they will need for their families during the year to follow. City housewives delight in buying these home-canned products if they have the chance. It would be a simple matter for country housewives to arrange bazaars for the sale of surplus food.

The best way to proceed would be to organize a home economics club in your immediate community. Elect officers and have the secretary write to the secretary of the chamber of commerce of your nearest city, asking him to help you find a place where you can hold your bazaar. Chamber of commerce secretaries are the finest people in the world when it comes to extending favors or courtesies. They help folks to help themselves. It may be that your particular secretary can find space for you with very little (if any) expense to your club.

It will not be necessary for every member of the club to help at the bazaar. Members can take turns and you could plan to hold one sale in September and another the week before Thanksgiving. The secretary should then make arrangements to have the two affairs announced at meetings of various women's clubs and parent-teachers associations. Announcements could perhaps be placed on bulletin-boards, and notices printed in the local papers. Not only can you sell your canned vegetables, preserves, jellies and conserves, but fruit, eggs, poultry and other products could also be included. At the Thanksgiving sale, home-made pies, plum puddings, mince meat and cakes would sell.

Those who live in a summer-resort region might hold a midsummer bazaar, for the summer visitors would be interested customers. Or they could arrange to show their wares in a local store, keeping them on sale from the time they are ready.

Be most particular about your labels. Purchase large-sized gummed labels, print or write on them very plainly the names of your products, paste the labels on the jars and apply over each label a coat of clear shellac, which you can buy at any hardware store. You might also add your name and address to the labels, for this may mean future direct customers for your products.

When canning relishes such as chili sauce or chow-chow, you would do well to can them in pint or half-pint jars. Few housewives like large jars of such relishes. Jellies, jams and conserves put up in small glasses sell more readily than the larger containers. *Elsie S. Williams.*

50th Anniversary

What wonderful things you can do to salads *with* Jell-O

FRUIT salads? . . . So many, and so delightful! The colors of fruit made lovelier by Jell-O's clear, bright translucence. The flavor of fruit blended irresistibly with Jell-O's own luscious fruit flavor.

Vegetable salads? . . . More tempting than you ever imagined they could be! All the healthful things you ought to eat changed, by Jell-O's deliciousness, into things you long to eat.

And Jell-O supplies energizing, body-building nourishment that both adults and children need. *It requires very little digestive effort.* It is easy to prepare, and very economical.

For these reasons, serve Jell-O *often.* Dozens of different ways to serve it—scores! . . . We've a delightful recipe booklet for you, if you'll mail the coupon.

Your grocer sells Jell-O, of course. Five pure fruit flavors and chocolate.

SHOWER SALAD

Dissolve a package of Strawberry Jell-O in a pint of boiling water. When cold and beginning to thicken, stir in lightly one cup diced pineapple (cooked or canned), one cup diced mellow apple, and three Maraschino cherries cut in shreds. Then fold in one half cup of heavy cream beaten until very stiff. Turn into a fancy mold and at serving time unmold on a platter. Serve with or without dressing. A speck of salt added to the cream before whipping improves the flavor.

Individual Jell-O molds and a recipe booklet

A special offer!

For 30c (coin or stamps) and the front of one Jell-O package, we will send you six aluminum Jell-O molds, individual size, assorted shapes. With them we will send a Jell-O recipe booklet. Mail the coupon today!

The Jell-O Company, Inc., Le Roy, N. Y.

JELL-O

AMERICA'S MOST FAMOUS DESSERT

THE JELL-O COMPANY, INC.,
LE ROY, NEW YORK.

I am enclosing 30c (coin or stamps) and one Jell-O package front. Please send me six individual Jell-O molds, assorted shapes, and a Jell-O recipe booklet.

Name..........................

Street..........................

City.................. *State*..............

J.-F.J. 3-27

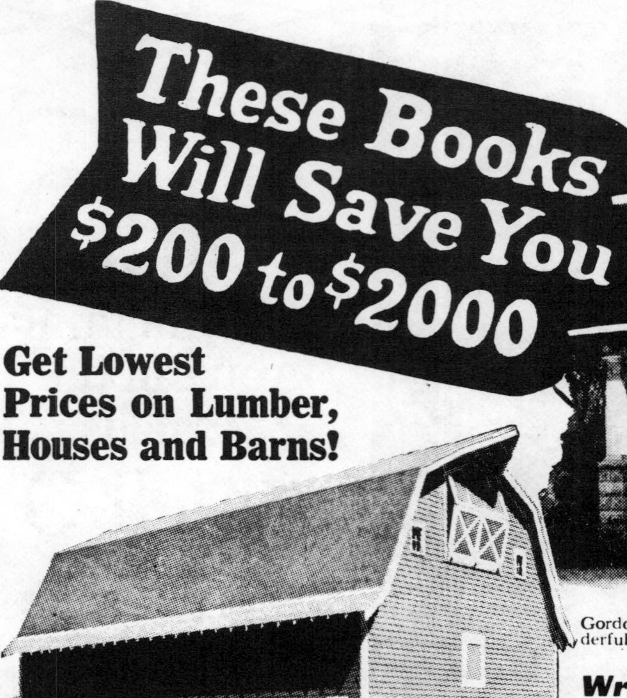

These Books Will Save You $200 to $2000

Get Lowest Prices on Lumber, Houses and Barns!

Gordon-Van Tine Home No. 508—Wonderful six-room farm home. Materials **$1716.00**

Gordon-Van Tine Gambrel Roof Barn No. 402—30 x 30. Materials **$802.00**

Write for These FREE BOOKS Today!

Book of 100 Home Plans
Shows photos, floor-plans, specifications of modern town and country homes, 4 to 9 rooms. Explains Plan-Cut system. Wholesale prices.

Book of Barns and Farm Buildings
Shows 654 sizes and kinds of barns, hog and poultry houses, granaries, feed and implement sheds. Barn plans to suit your needs.

Catalog of 5,000 Building Material Bargains
Everything for building, remodeling and repairing. Save even on a $25 order. Highest quality guaranteed.

Build Plan-Cut! The Finest Farm Homes at Amazing Savings!

Better Material—Better Construction—and at 30% Less Labor Cost!

This is what the Gordon-Van Tine Plan-Cut system gives you: A home especially planned by expert architects for farm needs; **highest quality material guaranteed;** a stronger, tighter, warmer home; a saving of 30% in labor cost in building, and 18% less lumber waste. All this you get at **wholesale prices** direct from our mill.

By the Plan-Cut method we saw, cut and notch the lumber at the mill for the home you select. All heavy rafters, joists, studs and framing lumber come accurately fitted to plan. No costly hand-sawing! Carpenters start nailing at once. Even unskilled workman can build successfully, because the Plan-Cut method compels accuracy! We supply complete plans free with material for your house.

Direct-From-Mill Wholesale Prices!

Homes Planned to Save Steps and Housework
Our farm homes are thoughtfully planned for farm conditions; separate dining rooms; roomy closets; wash-rooms; bath; handy kitchen cabinets; built-in bookcases; 1st floor bed-rooms; big basements and attics, etc.

One Guaranteed Price Covers All Materials
You know to a penny just what your house or barn will cost. We supply all materials as specified. Write for list.

5,000 Building Material Bargains

Lumber	Bathroom and Plumbing Supplies
Shingles	Roofing
Lath	Paints
Flooring	Glass
Windows	Furnaces
Doors	

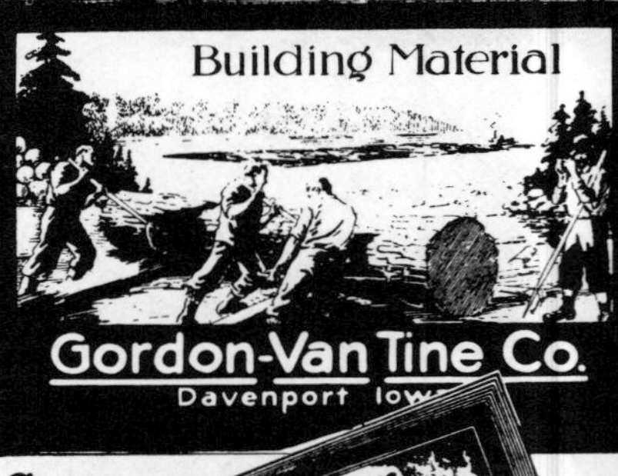

Hog House No. 482-B 24 x 30 $365
Well-built — plenty of sun and ventilation. Pens 6x8. Big passageway for easy feeding and cleaning.

Poultry House No. 489 22 x 24 $204
Built according to latest ideas of successful poultry-men. Lots of light, ventilation, warmth. Size shown accommodates 200 hens.

Garages $79 Up
Plan-Cut. Build yourself and save money. Ask for catalog.

Send Us Your Bills to Figure—Free Estimate

We sell lumber, millwork, hardware, and paints in any quantity. Whatever you are going to build, remodel or repair, send us your list. We will figure it free and give you lowest direct-from-mill prices, freight prepaid. Everything **highest quality** — you can't equal our material at usual sources. Write!

Gordon-Van Tine
(Established 1865)
PLAN·CUT Buildings

Gordon-Van Tine Co.
937 Gordon Street, Davenport, Iowa
Satisfaction Guaranteed or Money Back
Send me Free Books. I am interested in
☐ Houses. ☐ Farm Bldgs. ☐ Building Material.
Name..
Address..
....

50 Years of Home Building

By W. A. Foster

This house, called a "model residence," was shown in The Farm Journal, June, 1878. Frontage, 56 feet. Estimated cost at that time, $6,000. Just look at the "trimmin's"

"WHAT a funny house!" exclaimed John, on looking over The Farm Journal for May, 1878. "Did they ever build anything like this?" he asked.

John was 16 and he had just handed in a term paper on Gothic architecture in European history. No wonder the Gothic residence attracted his attention and aroused interest. He believed that Gothic architecture was confined to the famous cathedrals of France and England. The reading he had been required to do in preparing his paper had shown plans and pictures of Notre Dame, Rheims, Winchester, Lincoln and others, but not plans of farmhouses. It was plans such as this that Wilmer Atkinson had in mind when he said in his autobiography:

"In looking over the volume covering the first three years I note a lot of atrociously bad house plans that I seemed to be trying to palm off on my readers. I am sorry. If there be a man alive who copied any of them I ask his forgiveness."

FEW appreciate conditions through which our building has passed. The centennial year, 1876, marks an awakening of new interest in American architecture. From the lowly depths to which our architecture had sunk in the war period, this new interest was focused in the Philadelphia Centennial, and in the work of those master architects who so tenderly nursed an almost lost profession. The return of trained men from the Continent, the establishment of schools of architecture, the expansion of libraries, and the new interest in art, generally, all contributed a renewed enthusiasm to the architecture which followed.

Like a child, it floundered. Mistakes were common. With the eyes of the world dazzled by our opportunities, new peoples came—many crafts and trades. Our population became more cosmopolitan. Industry, a weakling, grew healthy and strong. These economic and social changes brought new problems. Health was the greatest, since cities grew rapidly about these industrial centers. Proper housing for the workers and their dependents was the first essential of health.

Another mile-stone was reached in the early nineties. The Columbian Exposition group doomed the lingering Romanesque style. Since 1900 the spirit in America has been restless and inventive. This restless spirit has given birth to new materials and constructions. Consequently, new materials will come into greater use in our realization of an American style in architecture.

America's most popular small house today, originally planned by J. F. Yewell. The plan (below) is simple

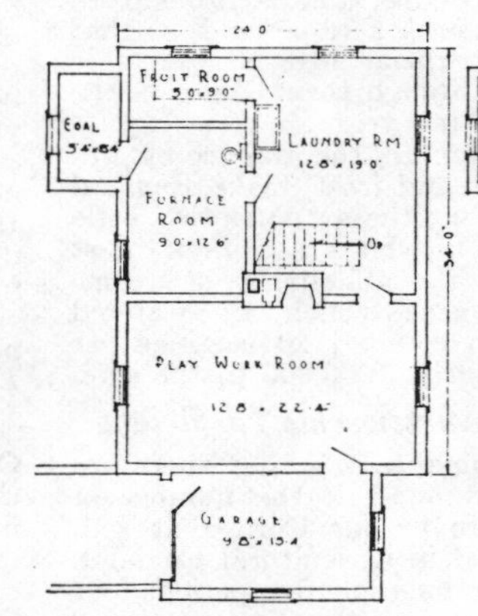

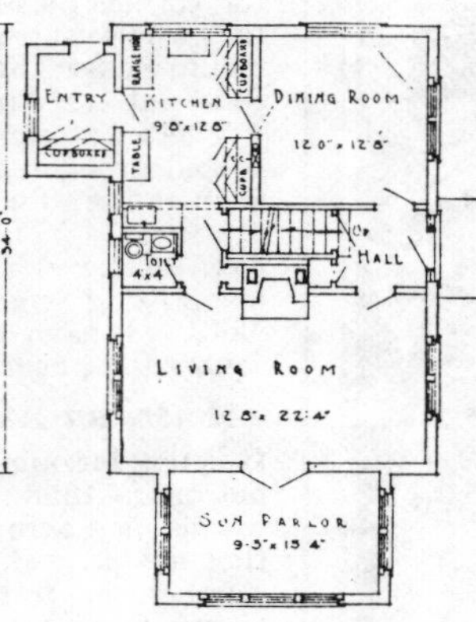

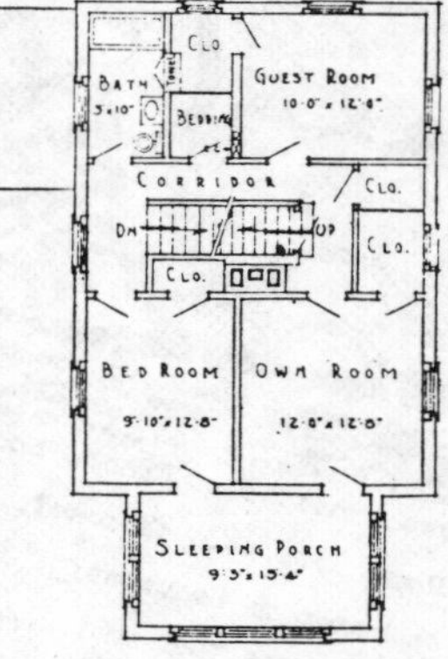

IN our American civilization, the farm or country house goes back to European precedent transplanted with a new environment.

The town house grew out of the country house. Limited space, economic needs and social limits brought about changes for health, convenience and comfort. The farmhouse of today has followed. It adopted the comforts and luxuries of the city home until today [*Continued on page 84*

This Gothic-roof house was shown in The Farm Journal, May, 1878. Estimated cost was $5,500

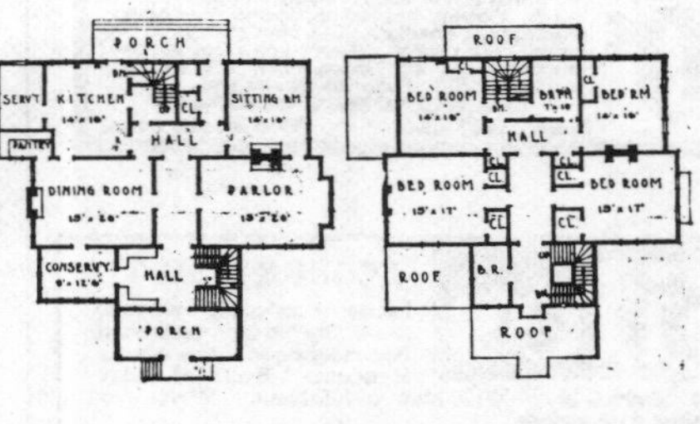

Floor plans of the Gothic-roof house shown at left. Cut off the conservatory, hall and porch from the front, and you have a fairly good floor-plan for modern home

50th Anniversary

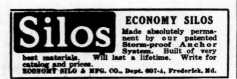

50th Anniversary

Is Our Corn Soil Doomed?

Continued from page 34

the best of reasons why our lawns are green, as English fields are green.

The streams of England are clear, stocked everywhere with the carnivorous game fish, preserving almost a uniform flow. Tennyson's brook joins a *brimming* river, if you remember—brimming, but not in flood—normally and constantly brimming and clear.

Such streams in agricultural regions can only exist where the rain comes often, but not much at a time. For then the water enters the ground, finding its way into the streams through springs—that is, underground. In this case no soil removal occurs. Soil removal—that is, erosion—only occurs when superabundant rain *flows over the surface*.

One might here announce the momentous principle: Agricultural regions with dirty streams are, *must be*, temporary. Agricultural regions with clear streams are, *must be*, permanent.

Darwin and the Angleworm

In 1837, Charles Darwin read a short paper "On the Formation of Mould." When he first announced that vegetable molds are created by the grinding and digestion of clays and soil material in the intestinal canals of the common angleworm, this announcement was greeted with some derision. Forty or more years later he followed this paper with a book of 300 pages on the same subject, in which he reiterated the early statements, now known to be true.

I quote from this book: "In many parts of England a weight of more than ten tons of dry earth annually passes through their bodies and is brought to the surface on each acre of land, so that the whole superficial bed of vegetable mould passes through their bodies in the course of every few years."

The moist climate, the absence of prolonged drought and frost, make England a paradise for these patriotic little creatures. You who are golfers must have observed the abundance of worms on putting greens, which are watered daily. I have counted 20 castings per square foot, nearly 1,000,000 to the acre.

American Angleworms Inefficient

It is not far amiss to say that there are not more than one-half the number of worms per acre in our Corn Belt soil, that are present in agricultural England. Further, due to long inactive periods, our worms do no more than half as much per annum as their Anglican brethren—a sad case of inefficiency, no doubt soon to be followed by demands for still shorter hours.

If my figures are sound, then the principal soil-creative agency is four times as effective in England as it is in the Illinois prairie.

Darwin found few worms in woods; a fair proportion in cultivated fields—most of all in pastures—some fifty-odd thousand per acre.

Here, perhaps, you will be cheered up a little if I announce that by the last census the angleworm population of Illinois numbers no less than 640,000 million worms—640 billion—6,000 for each man, woman and child in the United States. Is it Wall Street or some plutocrat that makes them so scarce when the boy wants to go fishing?

Further, these 640,000 million citizens of Illinois, in intelligent and long-sustained work toward the maintenance of the state, are more important than the 6,000,000 human beings in it, who only weigh one-tenth as much.

Now, about soil-removing forces: in the main they are twofold—surface erosion, and removal by wind in the form of dust. The former is manyfold more important.

Prairie Lands Were Treeless

A good deal has been said within ten years about soil erosion. Unhappily, indignation has been switched into a wrong channel. As usual, a scape-goat is found, and our wrath is poured out on the man who cuts down trees—"Woodman, spare that tree"—another dramatic, easily-roused sentiment, for we all love and enjoy trees.

Now the fact is, our good prairie lands *were treeless*. It is nearly always a sign of change from good to poor land to find woods appear—the black land is congenial to willows and cottonwoods; the oaks prefer slopes and brakes to creeks, where the gradient and accumulation of surface water-flow has naturally prevented the accumulation of mold. This is a fairly general rule.

Not forests, but *well-grassed sod surfaces* are the real creators and preservers of our vegetable mold. Such were our prairies when Abraham Lincoln was a boy; such they had been for thousands of years.

The sheltered mellow land, with its network of grass roots, mocked at erosion. It held the rainfall and led it underground; it furnished protection and an ideal home for our angleworm friend.

[The third part of Arthur J. Mason's paper will appear in an early issue—*Editor*.]

On page 86, February, Mr. Silver states that the combine does not save the straw but that some attachment will probably be devised by the manufacturers to do this. As a matter of fact, bunchers have been available on combines for many years and are commonly used in several sections. I am not sure that all makes of combine have such a buncher attachment, but believe they do. At any rate, many have it. It is my understanding that all combine manufacturers have some such attachment for at least some of their models. It is possible that some of the newest models may not yet have attachments, but one certainly will be available if it is needed, for it is easy to build. *Y.*

LUCKY MR. RABBIT
No wonder I am lucky,
For you can plainly see,
Where'er I go, I take along
My rabbit feet with me.

Charm dwells in the home where paint & varnish serve

Residence of Chester C. Bolton, South Euclid, Ohio, *Prentice Sanger, Architect*

"Save the surface and you save all" — Paint & Varnish
REG. U.S. PAT. OFF.

HOME is at its best when paint and varnish help the home-maker. They contribute beauty. They are infinitely adaptable to the decorator's needs. Keeping house becomes a lighter burden. Halls, stairs, corners have more light. Painted surfaces are more easily cleaned. Home is more healthy, more cheerful, more friendly — a better place to live in. To decoration, paint and varnish add protection. They save the structure of the house, outside and in, warding off rust and decay, wear and tear. The reasons for using paint and varnish are numerous and weighty, yet one short phrase holds them all — "save the surface and you save all". And this holds for all sorts of property.

SAVE THE SURFACE CAMPAIGN
18 East 41st Street, New York
A co-operative movement by Paint, Varnish and Allied Interests whose products and services conserve, protect and beautify practically every kind of property.

50th Anniversary

New Marglobe Tomato

By Grif McKay

MARGLOBE tomato is causing a lot of talk in eastern trucking sections. It is a new variety, produced by Dr. F. J. Pritchard, U. S. Bureau of Plant Industry, by crossing the Marvel and Globe varieties.

Earliana has been the mainstay of the eastern truckers, particularly in South Jersey, not because it suited the truckers so well, but because there was nothing better to be had. Marglobe is an improvement over Earliana, a lot of the Jersey truckers think.

Marglobe is red, smooth, and nearly round. It ripens well up to the stem, with a thick, solid interior of attractive color, and has a distinctly pleasing flavor. In season it is a week or ten days later than Earliana when grown under similar conditions, and only a few days later than Bonny Best, with a picking season that lasts longer.

The Marglobe tomato

The plant makes a vigorous vine growth and carries enough foliage to protect the fruit properly from scalding, and the foliage stays green for a longer period than most varieties under New Jersey conditions. It is wilt-resistant and a good yielder.

Small Potatoes, Few in a Hill

SOME farmers still use for seed the small potatoes left in the bin after the large ones have been eaten up during the winter. Small whole tubers are all right for seed purposes if they are free from disease and are from a vigorous stock. However, the trouble is that small tubers are in many cases small because they are from diseased plants. The diseases are carried over from year to year in the tubers. Thus, if disease is present in a farmer's potatoes, he is planting an increased percentage of diseased tubers if he uses the small ones only. Consequently, his potatoes will run out much more quickly.

The accompanying photograph shows what "spindle-tuber," one of the "running-out" or degeneration diseases of potatoes, does to the yield. The group of small tubers on the right is the entire yield from a plant of the Triumph variety. The plant was infected very severely with the "spindle-tuber" disease. None of the tubers is large enough for table use. They are all infected and will not reproduce themselves if planted. Plants from them will serve as centers of infection from which healthy plants in the patch will contract the disease.

The group of large tubers on the left is from a healthy Triumph plant. The yield is not exceptionally good for a plant of that variety, but every tuber is marketable. Plants from these tubers will be healthy, vigorous and productive of high yields. *R. W. S.*

P. C. benzene, standard remedy for killing peach-tree borers, has been tested for other fruit insects in California. Results show that it controls pear-root aphis, woolly apple-aphis, raspberry-cane borer, wireworms in dahlias, and garden centipedes. Tests in New Jersey have not been so favorable with some of these pests, so better go slow with the crystals of P. C. benzene if you live outside of California.

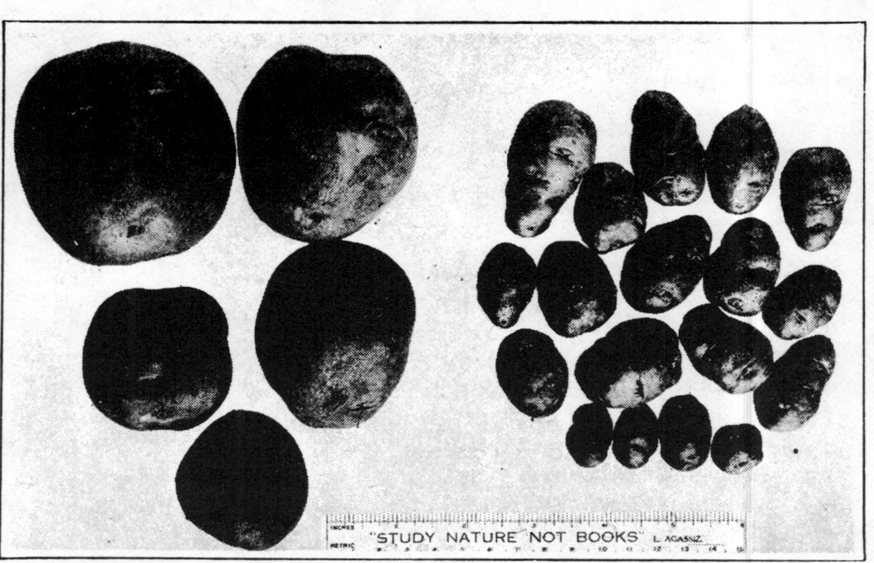

Left, yield from healthy Bliss Triumph. Right, plant had "spindle tuber"

The Improved STAR SIX SEDAN $925—*f. o. b. Lansing*

Again Improved

New improvements and refinements, plus well-known power supremacy, make the Star Car a greater value than ever before. See one at any Star Car dealer's and decide by comparison.

DURANT MOTORS, INC., 250 W. 57TH ST., NEW YORK CITY · *General Sales Department: Elizabeth, New Jersey*
PLANTS: Elizabeth, N. J. · Lansing, Mich. · Oakland, Cal. · Toronto, Ont.
Dealers and Service Stations throughout the United States, Canada and Mexico

Low-cost Transportation

Star Cars

STAR
DURANT MOTORS

IMPROVED STAR FOUR	
CHASSIS	$470
CONVERTIBLE ROADSTER	$550
TOURING	$550
COUPE	$650
COACH	$675
SEDAN	$765

HAYES-HUNT BODIES

IMPROVED STAR SIX	
CHASSIS	$650
TOURING	$725
COUPE	$795
COACH	$845
DE LUXE SPORT ROADSTER	$885
SEDAN	$925
LANDAU	$975
SPORT COUPE	$975

COMPOUND FLEETRUCK TON CHASSIS $950

Prices f. o. b. Lansing

The Dewberry Again

A LUSCIOUS, wine-colored dewberry, lost for 20 years to the public, has recently been revived from its long sleep and is now being recommended to gardeners and truck-growers for trial wherever dewberries are grown. This new-old dewberry, without a name up until a few years ago, is now known as the "Young" dewberry, named after B. M. Young, a nurseryman in Southern Louisiana who originated the hybrid in 1905. As early as 1896 Young had become acquainted with the qualities of the Loganberry on the Pacific Coast, and was desirous of growing that fruit on his own place. Repeated trials were unsuccessful. He then attempted to produce a berry similar to the Logan, that would be adapted to his conditions, by crossing the Phenomenal blackberry, a variety very similar to the Logan blackberry, with the Mayes dewberry of Eastern Texas. Numerous crossings of these brambles resulted in one outstanding plant which he noted "bore fruit that was large and of a Loganberry flavor." He considered it worthy of further attention, but because of business interests, it is related, the plant was discarded later.

The Young dewberry

The Lost Is Found

It was 16 years after the selection had apparently been lost to posterity, and during which time it was practically unknown, that a few plants came to the U. S. Department of Agriculture from J. F. Jones, a nurseryman at Lancaster, Pa., who requested the department to test them. The plants were set out in the horticultural field station at Bell, Md., and three years later came into fruiting. They attracted immediate attention because of the size and sweetness of the fruit, and other qualities superior to any dewberry previously grown there. George M. Darrow, of the Office of Horticulture, was impressed with the showing made in these first tests. In 1924 many plants were sent to experiment stations and other co-operators for testing under all conditions. These trials show that the Young dewberry is suited to the southern and southeastern states especially, but is also worthy of trial in other sections where dewberries are ordinarily grown. The variety has been found resistant to anthracnose disease wherever tested, and the foliage is entirely free from common leaf spot. The plants are more vigorous than other dewberries, and root at the tips more freely than does the Lucretia.

Some of the southern nurseries have the Young dewberries for sale. If unable to find plants, write the Garden Editor.

Dutchman's Breeches Is Poisonous

By Albert A. Hansen

IN the highlands of Southern Indiana and old Virginia, cattle have died in a mysterious manner since the days of the earliest pioneers from a strange malady that is characterized by trembling, frothing at the mouth and convulsions, and particularly by a staggering gait.

The trouble was attributed to plant poisoning, and suspicion pointed to a

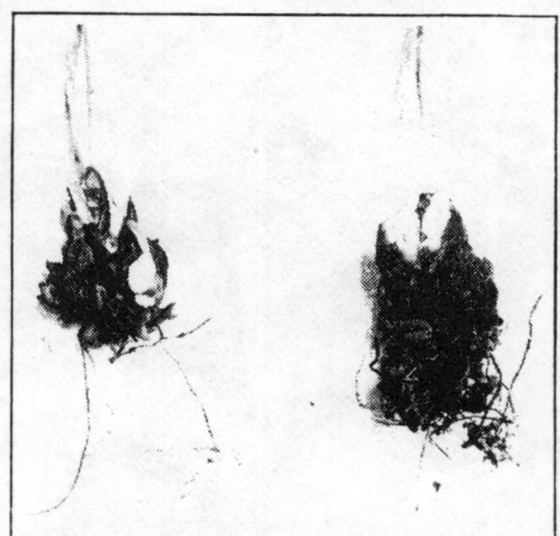

The poisonous bulbs

The lace-like foliage and spurred blossoms of Dutchman's breeches, or staggerweed, are distinctive

number of native species, but it was not until recently that the trouble-making plant was clearly exposed. It was found to be Dutchman's breeches, called staggerweed by the native highlanders of Virginia, a handsome woodland wildflower with poisonous foliage and bulbs. Most everybody knows this plant that comes up very early in the spring.

The bulbs are believed to be more poisonous than the foliage, but since the plant grows in the leaf mold on the forest floor, the underground parts are readily pulled out and eaten by grazing animals. When the animals are kept out of the woods until the grass has gotten well started, there is little or no danger of staggerweed poisoning.

Dutchman's breeches, or staggerweed, is found in wooded areas from Maine to Minnesota and southward to Missouri and North Carolina. Trouble may be expected wherever it grows in abundance.

Success with Sweet Peas

Continued from page 22

necessary, although some growers make use of weak solutions of liquid manure.

The foregoing information deals primarily with the trenching system, but the writer has grown equally good sweet peas without the elaborate, laborious trenches. During dry seasons, better sweet peas can be produced in trenches, and the flowering period will be prolonged. If, however, the soil is spaded and fertilized in the fall, and there is ample moisture during the growing season, an excellent crop can be produced. Trenching is fine for the man who has plenty of help, but for the average gardener it is questionable whether the reward is worth the extra effort.

Large blooms, lilac on cream background

Spring Plantings

For the greater portion of the country, spring plantings are preferable.

Early in spring the mound of soil over the trench or row should be leveled. At this time the second application of lime can be made, and bonemeal can be added when the soil receives its final fitting. The drills should be made three inches deep, spacing the seeds two inches apart in the drill If double rows are to be planted, they must be spaced at least six inches apart. After the seedlings are well established, they should be thinned to stand three or four inches in the row. At the above rate of planting, an ounce of seed would be ample for planting 40 feet of row.

In planting thinly, practically no allowance is made for seeds which fail to germinate or that are destroyed. It is far easier to thin out seedlings than it is to make a replanting. I would suggest, particularly for the amateur, doubling the rate given and sow one ounce for 20 feet. An average ten-cent packet will plant from three to five feet.

After the seeds have been scattered in the drill, they should be covered with one inch of soil. The balance can be worked in as the seedlings grow. As soon as the first plants appear, cultivation should start. It is very essential at this time that the surface of the soil be kept as dry as possible, to prevent damping-off disease.

Cultivate Frequently

During the growing season, the soil must be stirred frequently, especially after rains or irrigation, to conserve the soil moisture. Much labor can be saved if the plantings are mulched with finely cut hay, straw or grass clippings. These materials not only help to save moisture, but protect the soil from the hot sun. If the soil about the sweet pea roots can be kept cool and moist, the flowering period will be prolonged and the quality of the blooms will be superior.

When plants are well established and have been carefully thinned, they are ready for supports. In fact, as soon as the seedlings branch or produce tendrils, they should be supported. Brush is used quite generally for this purpose and it can not be improved upon for the training of sweet peas. If brush is not available, chicken-wire can be used.

Types and Varieties

There are two distinct types grown in the United States: the summer-flowering and the early or winter-flowering. The former is universally planted in the spring and, in the North, during the fall. The latter type is used for greenhouse plantings in the North, fall plantings in the extreme South, and spring plantings in the North where the seasons are very short. As a guide to new growers of sweet peas, I am listing below a few of the best varieties in the more-popular color classes:

Color	*Summer-Flowering*	*Early-Flowering*
White	Giant White	Snowstorm
Light pink	Daisybud	Peach Blossom
Dark pink	Hercules	Zvolanek's Rose
Lavender	R. F. Felton	Lavender King
Red	Royal Scot	Early King
Light blue	Mrs. Tom Jones	Blue Bird
Dark blue	Jack Cornwall	Blue Jacket
Bicolor	Sparkler	Columbia

Diseases, Insects and Other Difficulties

Briefly, sweet peas are susceptible to blight, anthracnose, root rot, mosaic stem rot, damping-off and mildew. The blight and anthracnose can be largely controlled by spraying at intervals of a week or ten days apart, using Bordeaux mixture. Mildew is usually controlled by dusting the foliage when moist with dew, using flowers of sulphur. For mosaic there apparently is no control.

Stem rot is really an advanced stage of damping-off which usually results from an excess of moisture in the soil or the presence of the organism from a previous infection. It can be controlled by keeping the surface of the soil dry when the plants are in the seedling stage. If an occasional plant is observed wilting, it should be removed at once, and the infected area be dusted with dry sand or sulphur to prevent the disease's spreading.

Root rot apparently is a soil-borne disease and can best be prevented by changing the soil in the trenches or by rotation so that sweet peas are not grown on the same area more often than every third year.

As for insects, only the aphis or lice on the tops and roots are likely to cause trouble. If the soft-bodied insect is observed on the under surface of the leaves, spray with 40 per cent nicotin sulphate in water, or dust with tobacco dust or nicotin dust, at intervals of a week. If the root system is infested, spray the soil on both sides of the rows with corrosive sublimate, using one ounce for eight gallons of water, which will treat 40 feet of row. Two or three applications, ten days apart, will rid the soil of lice, grubs and other insect pests.

Oil Sprays, Marigolds, New Peaches, etc.

AFRICAN marigolds, also called French marigolds, are well adapted to herbaceous borders. They are better in such locations than in beds. Plants grow

African marigold, an annual flower

about two feet high. Leaves and flowers have a strong scent. Range of color is from sulphur yellow to orange. Plant seeds in hotbed, or outdoors after freezing weather is past.

Yes, certainly, the paper plant-covers can be used as frost protectors as well as for heat protectors. Cheap, easy to put in place, and they enable the progressive one to get a few days' or a week's jump on the weather.

Oil sprays have in some cases come in for a lot of abuse because of poor results with home-made oil sprays. One of our contributors states that home-made preparations are likely to be "a curdled mess" that is likely to do no harm to insects and no good to the trees. Recent tests in Massachusetts show that two brands of commercial oil-spray material gave practically perfect control of European red mite, while home-made lubricating-oil emulsion gave poor control. The essential thing in home mixing is to get just the right concentration of oil in the spray, and this is not always so easy.

"For clubroot of cabbage, how much lime?" asks J. B. Just enough to make the soil a little above neutral. An acid soil turns blue litmus-paper red—just enough lime to overcome this color test.

Pull out Carman, Belle, Greensboro, Champion, Iron Mountain, and make way for some of the newer varieties of peaches produced by cross-breeding at the experiment station. That is the advice New Jersey peach-growers got at their last annual meeting.

Dry lime sulphur has not always been so effective as the liquid material for apples, but in Ohio tests lasting five years, the dry form was equally as effective as the liquid or bordeaux, and was safer to use.

Big savings have been made by New Hampshire folks who have for several years pooled their orders for fruit-trees. The state farm bureau is back of the pool. The saving lies in cheaper prices for larger orders. All nurserymen charge less per tree in hundred or thousand lots than they do in lots of ten or less.

Cyanid for Rats and Groundhogs

By F. L. Clark

THE farmers of Clayton county, Iowa, have been gassing groundhogs with calcium cyanid for two years, and now they are using it on rats with a great deal of satisfaction.

In Wagner township, 120 farmers last year used 850 pounds of calcium cyanid, putting it in about 6,000 groundhog burrows. They say that 92 per cent of the burrows treated were never opened, showing that over 5,000 groundhog homes had become family burying-grounds. This season the township was almost entirely free of groundhogs. Eight other townships in the county have been gassing groundhogs this summer, with most favorable results. The use of calcium cyanid has spread to the maintenance of country roads, also. The groundhog, it has been found, sometimes leaves the clover- and alfalfa-fields to make a cozy burrow around the ends of culverts, or pilings of bridges, or in the side of road grades. This may start serious erosion. The men who maintain the country roads this year have been carrying calcium cyanid, and whenever the burrow of a groundhog has been detected, a spoonful of the deadly chemical has been put in it. This gets rid of the groundhog.

Put in the Rats' Burrows

A number of the county farmers have been using the calcium cyanid to gas rats in their holes under the barns and granaries. R. G. Kinsley, near McGregor, Iowa, says he has practically freed his big dairy-barn of rats. The good work was accomplished almost in a single night. "We were having a perfect pest of rats in the barn," said Kinsley. "Cats and poisons didn't seem to make much difference. I decided to try calcium cyanid, as we had had such good results with it in getting rid of the groundhogs in our fields. We put a spoonful of it one night in every rat hole we could find under the barn. Next day, there wasn't a rat to be seen."

Kinsley says calcium cyanid is good to end the life of sick or aged or injured animals on the farm. He had an old horse which had become so decrepit that it was a merciful thing to kill it. "I hate shooting animals," he said, "so I took a nose-bag, put some wet bran in it and tied it over the horse's head. Then I dropped in a spoonful of the calcium cyanid. The horse was gassed so quickly that he fell over almost before I could get away from him. Death seemed to be painless."

Keeping in touch with the world

Electrical Hay-Hoisting

By E. R. and V. B. Meacham

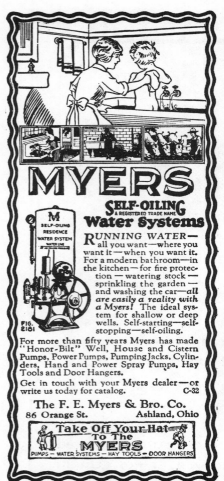

ELECTRICITY is doing away with a certain amount of the delicious dawdling with which we used to intersperse our periods of hard work. When I was ten—and afterward—I used to spend the long July days driving old Fan back and forth, back and forth, putting hay in the mow. But between loads, I could sprawl in the shade of the barn and look at the sky, and wonder if the catfish were biting down in Sugar River, and wiggle my toes and be glad I was barefoot, and hope Ma would make strawberry shortcake for supper.

Nowadays it is possible to use a simple device made up of power-driven winding drums controlled by suitable clutch and brake levers. This device is ready to start the instant the load comes to the barn, and hustles the hay into the mow without argument, confusion or loss of time. It is an electric hay hoist.

Hay hoisting is one of the incidental uses for a general-utility motor that comes in season this time of year. It takes the place of old Fan, or her successors, a brisker-stepping team. It also does away entirely with the need for that extra boy and releases him for weeding in the garden, because the electrical hoist can be operated by the man on the load. There is no delay while the team is taken off to be hitched on the draft rope, and no waiting for a slack rope to pull carrier back.

Just how much it is worth to the farmer to get this part of the haying job done with a saving of time and effort for both himself and his horses, he must decide for himself. The original cost of a hoist is from $70 to $120. This is no more than the farmer pays for other specialized machinery. There is little to wear out about a well-made hoist, and it should therefore last for many years, making the investment per season really very small. The application of the hoist to other uses, such as loading manure, or handling slings for unloading grain, would spread the investment over a wider range.

Hoisting hay at the Allen farm

Low-Cost Operation

The cost of running the hoist is low. On three carefully conducted tests made, one by Mr. Churchill of the Adirondack Power and Light Company, and two on the Wisconsin Farm Electric Experiment, the current necessary to lift a ton of hay into the mow ranged from 1/5 to 2/5 of a kilowatt-hour a ton. This means a cost of from two to four cents a ton where the electricity costs ten cents a kilowatt-hour.

On the Allen farm, a completely electrified farm near Lake Geneva, Wis., an electric hay hoist has been used for several years. Here the hay is unloaded from the rack at the end of the barn. The hoist is set up outside. Mr. Allen says of this hoist: "It makes a substantial saving in

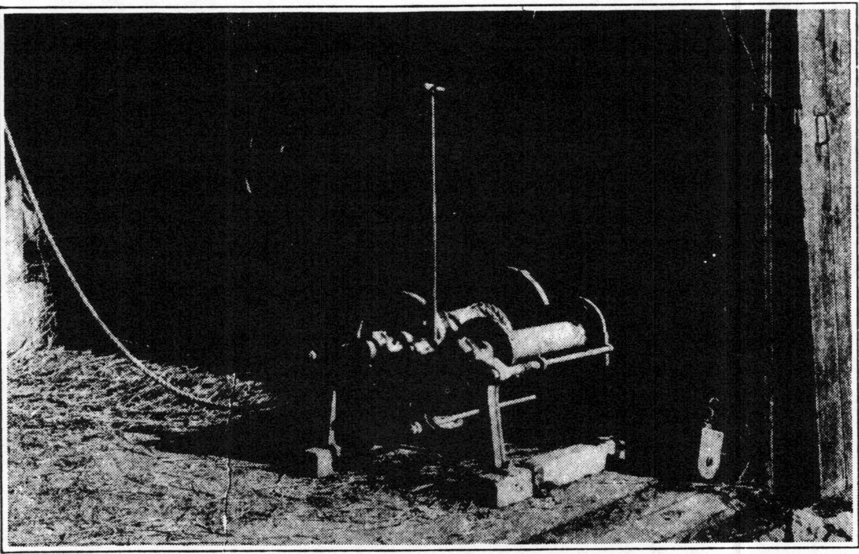

The hoist at the Stillmacher farm is conveniently situated just inside the barn on the driveway floor

the expense of hay rope, and in time. A team of horses is released for mowing, tedding and raking because we use it."

In 1924 George Stillmacher, at Ripon, Wis., used a double-drum hoist driven by a belt from a five-horse-power motor to lift his hay. His barn had the standard reversible carrier and a four-tine grapple-fork. When the loading was done by horses by twelve-year-old Jim, it took 13 minutes to unload the rack. At neighboring farms where the loading was timed, it averaged just over 16 minutes. After the hoist was put in operation, the load was put in the mow in nine minutes. This meant a saving of time of from 30 to 45 per cent. At three cents a kilowatt-hour, the rate Mr. Stillmacher paid, this saving could be made for a total cost of less than $1 for any farmer handling 60 tons of hay.

One Man Less in the Crew

The next summer a neighbor down the road, A. E. Smith, used a double-drum hoist with a five-horse-power motor for the same job. There was a saving of from four to twelve minutes on each unloading. And since the hoist was operated from the load, one less was required in the crew. One team was used to operate two wagons.

At Poynette, Wis., J. F. Forest runs a hay hoist with the power generated by his wind electric plant. At St. Johnsville, N. Y., George Nellis is running a double-drum hoist with a three-horse-power motor. If you ask him how he likes it, he will say enthusiastically:

"Fine. It works like a charm. I would hate to go back to driving horses back and forth on the hay-fork all day."

George uses the motor that runs his milking-machine for this job. The motor is hung from the ceiling of the cow-barn. By the addition of a short line-shaft, he was able to run a belt through the stairway opening to the hoist which sits on the driveway floor.

Getting On to the Ropes

The man who runs an electric hoist must have some of a sailor's knack with ropes, but after he gets on to it, the operation goes forward smoothly enough. When the men come in from the field with a load of hay, one of them jumps off the load, starts the motor, throws the rope from the control lever of the hoist to the man who stays on the load, and then gets into the mow. The man on the load pulls the rope which is attached to the clutch lever, releases the brake on the drum and pulls the fork down to the load.

After the fork is set in the hay, the man on the load pulls the control rope until the friction clutch is engaged, and holds it tight while the hoist lifts the forkful of hay from the load.

When the fork reaches the desired place in the mow, the operator slacks the control rope to stop the movement of the carriage, and jerks the trip rope to drop the hay in the usual manner. If the hoist is of the double-drum type, the operator can now put the reverse drum in operation and quickly return the fork. This relieves him of the hand-blistering work of hauling on the rope to return the carriage.

ℂ ℂ

Commercial fertilizers should be stored with care in order to prevent needless wastage and to keep in proper condition. We have found bags generally unsatisfactory. This is especially true with acid phosphate or with mixed fertilizers containing a high proportion of this material. Acid phosphate has a tendency to rot out the bags. With any moisture at all present, the material is also likely to become badly caked. Fertilizer can be dumped into dry wooden bins and held in good condition without danger of wastage.

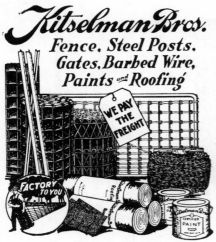

50th Anniversary

My Club Helped Me

By Leona Gale

Leona Gale, leader of the Ridge Road Canning Club, Washtenaw county, Mich., won second prize in the girls' group of last year's 4-H Leadership Contest. In this article she gives some of her experiences as local leader. The 4-H Leadership Contest, in which The Farm Journal offers $1,000 in prizes to the most outstanding boys' and girls' club leaders, continues this year. Prizes will be awarded as follows:

	Boys	Girls
1st prize	$250	$250
2d prize	100	100
3d prize	50	50

and ten prizes of $10 each for the ten next highest club leaders in each group.

THE credit for my success as a 4-H leader really belongs to my club girls who have co-operated so well in their work. Last year was the first time demonstration contests were held in our county, and our girls chose two members to be on the club team. Fair-time, with its usual run of warm weather, came the first week of September. Due to the fact that we wanted a very good exhibit of canned goods, we worked terribly hard trying to can "last-minute Blue Ribbon fruit," and also trying to decide which jars really looked the best.

After all that hurry and bustle we awaited the judge's decision. It came, at last, and you can just imagine how happy we were to find that we had won first place on all our club exhibits. Those same exhibits won third place at the state fair. All the girls were anxious to belong the next year, because the canning project proved to be a good financial venture. The girls won, on an average, $6 apiece in prizes at the county and state fairs. At the end of the season in 1925 our club was well known in this part of the county. When the farmers' club of Washtenaw county wanted judges at its exhibits, it chose some of our girls.

Our club extends over two counties, some girls living in Wayne and others in Washtenaw. Often some of our members have to drive about ten miles or more to attend the meetings. Do you blame me for being proud of them? Any girl interested enough to drive ten miles or more to a club meeting once every two weeks is, in my estimation, deserving of a lot of praise. We had a large club—for our county, anyway—and it was hard to find dates that were right for 20 girls—but we got along all right. We have the fine record of being a 100 per cent club for three years. By this I mean that every girl who started a project has finished it. Ever since this system was started our club has had one of these honor certificates.

Worth-While Work

I want to tell you the story of one girl who is particularly benefited through our club work. This girl has had many handicaps. While quite young, she was very sick with spinal menigitis. She lived—but was left impaired in health. She has not succeeded very well in school, although she works very hard. There are many boys and girls in our school who are unkind to her and make fun of these things that she can't help. This spring her father died, and she lived alone with her mother and her grandmother. As I thought of it, I couldn't see much happiness in store for her this summer and so I asked her to belong to our club. Later some of the other girls censured me quite strongly for inviting her, but I just waited—hoping that that girl would get a little pleasure out of the work this summer. At first I was rather disappointed, for she seemed so sad—but gradually we drew her into our circle until now you would hardly recognize her. She enters into our games and songs with as much zest as any of us. She has developed into an entirely different girl—happy, contented and interested, especially in club work.

Club Work Teaches Patience

Canning is our specialty, and our canning project is the one of which we are most proud.

All of our girls are quite young, but they surely do have a lot of patience. There is one girl in particular. She is only ten years old, and has been in club work for two years. The first year, even though competing with girls twice her age, she won third place on her exhibit. We thought that she was quite young to be in a canning club, and so this year she was only in the food-study work. But she expects to can a lot this coming year. In order to get into training for next year's project she tried a few canning experiments this year. I watched her can one pint of strawberries. Each berry had to be just the right size, shape and color, and each one had to be placed "just so." I didn't wonder, after seeing her can, that her finished jars looked better than most of those in our fair exhibits. However, she is rather young for the work.

This is Leona

I am hoping that our club will be able to live up to the high ideals set by the other clubs and leaders and those set by our own members in the past. I want our girls to get just as much out of the club as possible, and am surely going to work harder than ever this year to be a better club leader for our Ridge Road Club girls. I am going to try hard and do my very best in making our club more helpful and more instructive than ever.

The first issue of "Boys' and Girls' 4-H Club Leader" is out. Will be issued monthly by the Office of Cooperative Extension Work, U. S. D. A., Washington, D. C.

Sheet Steel Roofs Give Triple Protection Against Weather—Lightning—Fire

"SPARKS ON ROOF" and "lightning" are two of the greatest causes of farm fires, according to insurance statistics. Thousands of farms are protected against both these hazards by roofs of Sheet Steel.

Both the building and its contents are lightning-safe when covered with a properly grounded Sheet Steel roof. This fact is borne out by numerous tests and extensive field observation. So far as careful research has been able to discover, lightning has never fired a building protected by a grounded Sheet Steel roof.

A Sheet Steel roof is a fire guard that never sleeps. The smooth hard surface literally sheds fire. Sparks slide to the ground or harmlessly burn themselves out.

Sheet Steel roofs are durable, safe, economical. Ask your local sheet metal contractor or roofer for detailed information. Owners will tell you that for year-in year-out farm roof economy, Sheet Steel has no equal.

Roofing is just one of many uses in which Sheet Steel is giving farmers better service and increased economy. Grain stored in Sheet Steel bins can be held for market with entire safety. The grain cures perfectly in these fire-safe containers, and rats cannot gnaw through them. Sheet Steel watering troughs, brooders, feeders and ventilation systems provide improved sanitation for and better profits from live stock. Sheet Steel equipment in the home in many forms is of large value. These and many similar subjects are discussed in the interesting booklet, "THE SERVICE OF SHEET STEEL TO THE FARMER." A letter will bring you a copy. Address SHEET STEEL TRADE EXTENSION COMMITTEE, OLIVER BUILDING, PITTSBURGH, PA.

This trade-mark stenciled on galvanized Sheet Steel is definite insurance to the buyer that every sheet so branded is of prime quality—full weight for the gauge stamped on the sheet—never

less than 28 gauge—and that the galvanizing is of the full weight and quality established by the SHEET STEEL TRADE EXTENSION COMMITTEE specification.

SHEET STEEL

for Strength Safety Beauty and Economy

50 Years of Livestock

(Continued from page 13

without a declaration of war from the friends of the defeated contenders.

The modern dairy industry has come into being with the invention of the Babcock milk test, the perfection of the cream-separator and the application of pasteurization to milk. The fresh-milk business of the large cities has called into use huge thermos tanks on railroad cars, glass-lined tanks on motor-trucks, and uniformed milkmen. The practise of dipping milk from the can to the consumer's pail is only a memory. And a good thing it is.

All these inventions and changes have not altered the wedge-shaped body of the dairy-cow, though. Note similarity of type of the two animals—Red Rose, and the present Holstein champion on page 13. Red Rose was one of the Roadside herd of Ayrshires which took first prize at the Centennial in 1876. She had a record of eleven quarts of milk a day for a year. DeKol Plus Segis Dixie is the world's champion cow today—a Holstein. There were no cows with records of 1,000 pounds of fat 50 years ago. Today every major dairy breed has at least one 1,000-pounder.

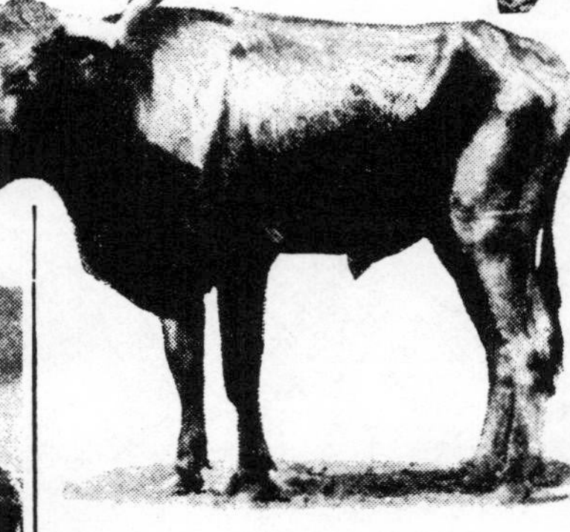

Above, inspector putting the purple federal stamp on meat. Government inspection was scarcely dreamed of in 1877. The beast with corkscrew horns (left) is the type of beef animal still common on the ranges 50 years ago. The breeding herd of Herefords (left) is a fair sample of range stuff today

Artificial refrigeration has made the modern meat-packing industry possible, and is of vast importance in the dairy industry, also. Nearly all the country's meat now comes from highly efficient packing-houses, where every step, from the time the animals reach the stockyards until the meat is loaded on the cars, is supervised by federal inspectors. Inspected meat is stamped with a purple stamp, reading "U. S. Inspected and Passed."

Control of Livestock Diseases

Through the agency of a superlatively effective organization of livestock sanitary experts, led by the United States Bureau of Animal Industry, we put pleuro-pneumonia completely out of business in this country over 30 years ago, and foot-and-mouth disease has never found permanent lodgment on American farms; we have had given to us without patent royalties a method of preventing hog-cholera that works.

Animal husbandry, within the last 50 years, has become a recognized branch of science at every important agricultural college, and, as a result of that development, beef animals are on the market at 1,000 to 1,200 pounds weight and two years or less in age. A calf that had yet to celebrate his first birthday walked out of the International show ring last fall wearing the purple ribbon of the grand champion. Ton litters and the "McLean county system" of hog sanitation are revolutionizing pork-production methods. Canny farmers market their pigs at six to nine months, weighing 225 pounds. The sheep-grower does not let his lambs go to market at greater weights than 80 pounds if he can help it. He has learned that early gains are cheaper, and early prices are higher.

With it all goes a knowledge of the science of animal nutrition which would have given the man of 1877 a headache to listen to. When the college professors first began lecturing about protein, carbohydrates and fat, they were criticized for talking over the heads of farmers. But the farmers raised their heads, talked back and called for more. So the professors gave them calcium and phosphorus, enzyms and vitamins, and the farmers never blinked. Now they ask many questions which the professors honestly admit they can not begin to answer.

An outstanding development in the last 50 years is the widespread recognition of the value of purebred sires. Nowhere is there greater evidence of this than in the quality of beef animals coming from the ranges. The Longhorn has given way to cattle carrying a large percentage of pure blood of the Hereford, Shorthorn and Angus breeds. Some of the range states have laws which forbid the use of sires, other than purebreds of the recognized beef breeds, on the ranges.

Just as outstanding in the dairy field is the cow-test association. The first organization of this kind was organized at Newaygo, Mich., in 1906. There are now considerably more than 700 associations. These associations, by showing the actual production of cows and their response to feed, have enabled us to draw the line clearly between profitable and unprofitable cows, regardless of pedigree. Hence, the place of the poor-producing purebred is insecure, and at the same time the good grade is coming into her own.

What of the future? We have come some in 50 years—no doubt about it. But one does not have to qualify as a prophet to say that the next 50 years will far surpass the past 50. We will certainly fit the livestock business more economically to the farming structure.

Chicago stockyards, 1871. Nothing here that looks like a modern packing-plant. Open country in the background

50th Anniversary

Those golden evening hours—

give them the brightness they deserve

Evening hours . . . precious hours . . . life's richest reward for a day's work well done . . . but robbed of their glory in thousands of farm homes by feeble, flickering kerosene lamps. Not until you have installed a Fairbanks-Morse Home Light Plant can you even begin to know how much more these hours can mean!

WHY have you waited? Is it because you are afraid a light plant will be just one more thing to attend to in an already crowded life? Then you have much to learn about this *protected* plant with its one-knob control that a boy or girl can operate *safely*.

Have you waited because you thought light plants were not all that they should be? Then remember that the present Fairbanks-Morse plant is the finished result of twenty years of experience. Yes, Fairbanks-Morse built *the first of all* home light plants and has been constantly improving it ever since!

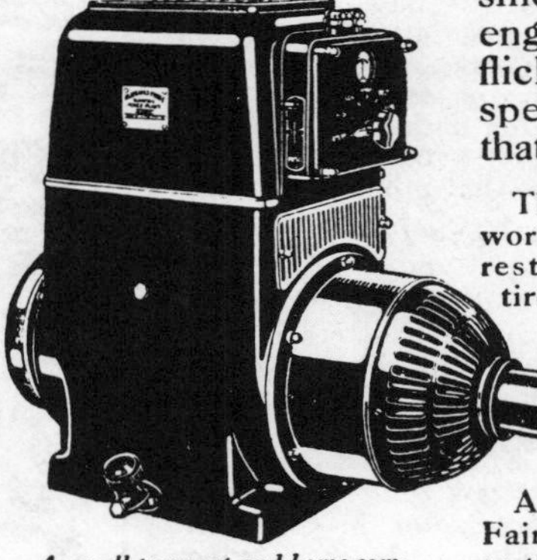

A small payment and home comfort is yours under the F-M Finance Plan

You have only to inspect the new Home Electric Power Plant to know that the ultimate in farm lighting has now been realized. See it in action. Listen to the smooth purr of its balanced engine. See the flood of unflickering light it gives. Inspect the advanced features that are possessed by it alone.

Then picture the wonders it will work in your home—the well earned rest that will come to mother's tired arms when electricity does much of the housework—the prideful smiles of the young folks when the old home grows brilliant under the magic of electricity.

All this is as close as your Fairbanks-Morse dealer—as close as the coupon below. Why have you waited?

PRICES quoted are cash f. o. b. factory; add freight to your town.

"Z" Engines	
2 hp. battery equipt	$ 48.50
2 hp. magneto equipt	58.50
3 hp. magneto equipt	101.00
6 hp. magneto equipt	153.00

Home Water Plants

Prices range from $84.75 and up, depending on type and size.

Feed Grinders	
Plate type, 4-inch	$ 11.00
Plate type, 8-inch	40.00
Plate type, 10-inch	55.00
All-Purpose Hammer Type	135.00

Fairbanks-Morse Products also include Hammer and Plate Type Feed Grinders, Fairbanks Scales, Washing Machines, Electric Motors, Pump Jacks, Power Heads, etc.

FAIRBANKS-MORSE
Home·Light·Plants

Manufacturers Branches and Service Stations Covering Every State in the Union Chicago, U. S. A.

Fairbanks-Morse Products F-M *"Every Line a Leader"*

FAIRBANKS, MORSE & CO., Dept. 3131
900 S. Wabash Ave., Chicago, U. S. A.

- ☐ Home Light Plants
- ☐ "Z" Engines
- ☐ Steel Eclipse Windmills
- ☐ Home Water Plants
- ☐ Feed Grinders
- ☐ Fairbanks Scales
- ☐ Washing Machines
- ☐ Electric Motors
- ☐ Pump Jacks
- ☐ Plate Type
- ☐ Hammer Type

Please send free book describing new Light Plant, also complete information concerning the items I have checked.

Name......

Address...... *R.F.D.*......

Town...... *State*......

Why you should have a Fairbanks-Morse

1 Compact. Completely enclosed. No separate tanks for fuel, oil or water.

2 Both electricity and engine power from *one* plant at *one* cost.

3 Easy to operate. Use with or without storage batteries. With battery simply press lever to start.

4 Selective control. Note single switch knob control in illustration for "start," "high charge," "low charge," "stop," "belt," and "line."

5 Advanced design. Rotating parts balanced as in finest automobiles. Has patented "Ricardo" cylinder head and unique cooling system of our own design. Pressure lubricated. And many other advanced features.

6 Economical. More power from same fuel. Operates on kerosene or gasoline.

7 Safe. Approved by Fire Underwriters.

8 No flicker of lights.

9 Completely equipped.

This new plant is built in two sizes, 750 and 1500 Watts.

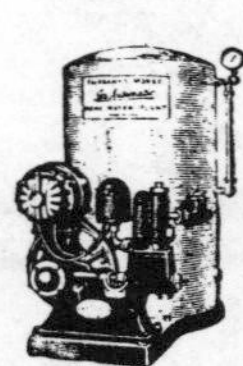

Automatic electric, engine or motor driven home water plants and pneumatic water systems, 120 to 5000 gallons per hour

"Z" Engines. A half million farmers regard these sturdy plants the biggest dollar-for-dollar value

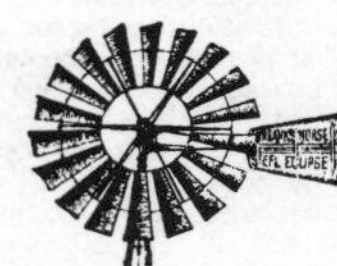

Steel Eclipse Windmills. Here is a windmill that will last a lifetime. Self-oiling, all-metal construction. All working parts carefully machined and completely enclosed. Built with the same care as a fine engine. Sizes 8 ft. and larger

Illustrated above is the Fairbanks-Morse Belt-Driven Home Electric Light and Power Plant, thousands of which have been in use for many years, giving general satisfaction to their many owners

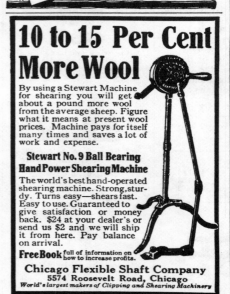

Watch the Gilts

By W. C. Smith

AN old sow will make a good bed and about nine times out of ten a gilt will not, which is the chief reason why we lost several pigs last April. Our old sows farrowed late in March and saved most of their pigs—97 per cent—partially because we watched a little closer than we did the gilts farrowing later, but principally because they burrowed down in the straw, carried litter where they wanted it and generally took care of themselves.

The gilts were bred purposely to farrow later, but one of those cold, dismal winds set in, that sometime chill the Wabash, Ohio and entire Mississippi valleys. Two gilts got back in a thicket and farrowed without bedding under some bushes and were not found for two days. These lost six pigs. Others just lay on top of the bedding in the houses and made no pretensions of protecting their litters. An older sow, farrowing under the same conditions, would have saved every pig. We have had them do that numbers of times.

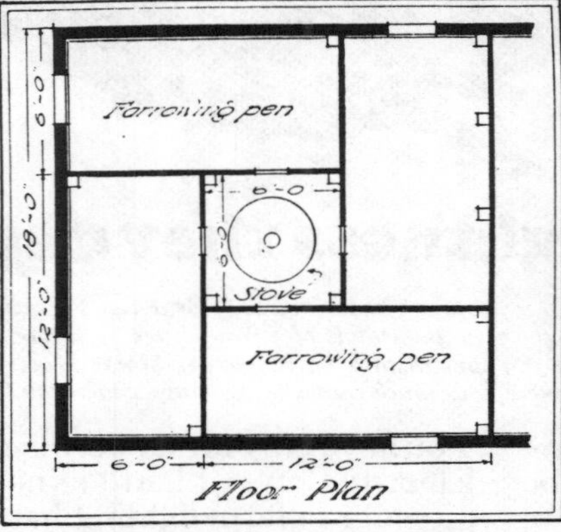

Arrangement of pens, stove in center

The Extra Pig Is Profit

Watch the gilts. The instinct of motherhood is not developed in them as it will be, and the first litters must be given plenty of attention unless weather conditions are ideal. One extra pig per gilt means a lot in the aggregate. Heavy rains during and after harvest last season spoiled so much straw that it is hard to get straw in some parts of the Corn Belt. Shredded corn-fodder, planer shavings, poor-quality hay and the grass used in packing chinaware and glassware can all be used as substitutes. We have already made arrangements to take all of the packing hay from the stores in our little town. Our old sows get by pretty well, but our gilts need all the attention we can give them. It pays.

If the weather is cold at farrowing time, you can heat the pens in the central house with a small brooder-heater. The arrangement shown in the sketch has been found ideal. Four pens are grouped about a space six feet square in the center. This can be adapted to practically any hog-house of the rectangular type.

Small doors, not large enough to allow the mother hog to enter, are cut through each side of the pen, so that small pigs can enter and take advantage of the heated hover. The type of brooder and stove used for baby chicks will be O. K.

When running the flue through the roof, cut a hole approximately twelve inches larger in diameter than the diameter of the flue itself, then cover the intervening space with a large sheet of tin through which has been cut a hole just large enough to take the flue itself.

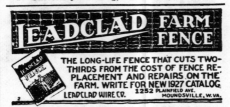

Rupture of Swine Is Hereditary

By R. F. Collins

FROM a total of 30 pigs, farrowed on farms in my locality not long ago, eleven were ruptured or became ruptured during the first few weeks of life. The owners were practical farmers who thought they knew all about hog-raising, and no cause for this trouble could be found until George E. Rollison, a local veterinarian, was called in. He investigated the cases and found that all the sows had been bred to the same sire. The sire was ruptured, and came from a litter where rupture was prevalent.

"Swine rupture is hereditary," Rollison explained, "and in most cases the tendency in little pigs to become ruptured can be traced to the parent stock. Boars with unnatural growths about the body, dropsical swellings or thin abdominal walls are always a menace and should never be used as breeders. It is just as important to see that breeding-stock is free from this condition as it is to inquire about type or pedigree. Failing to do this, the farmer loses money, and brings upon himself a lot of unnecessary bother and expense."

To Put a Ring in a Bull's Nose

First of all, when ringing a bull, see that he is securely tied. Use the dehorning chute, if you have one. If not, tie the bull's head to a strong post. To make the hole for the ring, get a punch made for this purpose. You can buy one from a dealer who sells dairy supplies. Some folks use a sharp-pointed pocket-knife blade for this purpose. After the hole is made, put in the ring. After the ring is screwed in its place, sandpaper it very carefully to remove rough edges near the screw or hinge that may injure the nose of the bull.

Breaking a Colt Isn't Hard

A good way to break colts, if you have plenty of time, is to begin by putting the halter on the colt and then turning it loose. After it becomes accustomed to the halter, then put on the bridle and turn loose. The next step is to put on full harness and allow the colt to walk around loose in barnlot for a while. No halter lead strap or hitch rein should be allowed to dangle to the ground from halter or bridle while on the colt's head.

The colt can soon be driven around singly with two lines, and before long it can be hitched with another horse—a gentle one—and both be driven around the lot. Soon the two can be hitched to a wagon and driven around together. Before you know it, the colt will be broken. *Willis Mehanna.*

Can You Answer "Yes" to These?

Are you feeding silage or roots, and legume hay, to your dairy-cows? Do you feed grain in proportion to milk production? Do you keep a record of each cow's feed, and milk produced? Do you use a purebred bull? Do your cows always have salt and plenty of fresh, clean water? Are your cows comfortable in winter as well as in summer? Do you keep your herd bull until you have had a chance to compare his daughters with their dams?

You would fire him quick!
IF you had a hired man who did this to your cream you would fire him quick. Yet your cream separator may be doing the same thing and you don't realize it. You can easily tell, without a cent of cost, whether your old separator is robbing you or not. Ask your De Laval Agent to bring out a new De Laval and try this simple test:
After separating with your old separator, wash its bowl and tinware in the skim-milk. Hold the skim-milk at normal room temperature and run it through a new De Laval. Have the cream thus recovered weighed and tested; then you can tell exactly if your old machine is wasting cream, and what a new De Laval will save.
Thousands have tried this plan and many have found a new De Laval would increase their cream money from $25 to $200 a year.
The new De Laval is the best separator made in 48 years of De Laval manufacture and leadership. It has the wonderful "floating bowl"—the greatest separator improvement in 25 years. It is guaranteed to skim cleaner. It also runs easier and lasts longer.
Send coupon for name of De Laval Agent and FREE catalog.
CREAM
7 SIZES Hand-Electric-Belt
$6.60 to $14.30 DOWN
Balance in 15 Easy Monthly Payments
SEE and TRY the New De Laval
TRADE in your old Separator
The De Laval Milker
If you milk five or more cows, a De Laval Milker will soon pay for itself. More than 35,000 in use giving wonderful satisfaction. Send for complete information.
See Your De Laval Agent
CLIP HERE
THE DE LAVAL SEPARATOR COMPANY, Dept. 1614
New York, 165 Broadway Chicago, 600 Jackson Boulevard
San Francisco, 61 Beale Street
Send catalog checked — Separator ☐ Milker ☐
Name
Town
State R.D.
No. Cows

EAR TAGS for all live stock. Breeders and Dairymen's Supplies. Quality high, prices low. Satisfaction guaranteed. Catalog free. C. H. DANA CO., 60 Main St., WEST LEBANON, N. H.

Annual Veterinary Inspection

By F. R. Cozzens

A GROUP of farmers in Dunbar community, Washington county, Ohio, are giving their dairy herds a yearly veterinary inspection at a cost of only 50 cents a cow. This fee covers a thorough examination of each animal, with suggestions and advice regarding any abnormal condition that may be found. The plan was put in force by an organized ring; and not only has it saved money for each member, but it has also enabled these farmers to check in the start many livestock diseases which would have proved fatal had they been neglected.

"Our nearest veterinarian lived twelve miles away, and it took a $10 bill to bring him out to our farms," Roy Malster, the organizer, told me recently. "For this reason the vet was called only as a last resort; the farmers treated various diseases with home remedies and often neglected minor ailments until they became serious. We lost many cows in this way, until the spring of 1923, when the county agent took a hand, and together we devised a plan to prevent it.

A Veterinary Co-Op

"A ring of ten farmers was organized for the purpose of getting veterinary service, and a committee was appointed to lay our plan before the doctor. Our combined herds numbered 30 cows, and the veterinarian agreed to examine these animals for the sum of $15, provided we furnish his transportation and lodging. His terms were accepted and a day was set for his visit.

"At the time mentioned, the doctor drove out to the central farm and inspected a herd. When he had finished, a man was waiting to take him to another farm, and this practise was continued until each member had been served. It required nearly two days to do all this, but during that time the veterinarian found six cases of garget, two cases of poisoning, one of rheumatism, treated an injured cow, and performed several minor operations. Some of the cases had been overlooked by the owners, and some would have proved fatal without proper treatment. It was estimated that our ring saved more than $100 by that visit alone.

"Since that time, we have followed the plan of having our herds examined each year, usually in the early summer. The main idea for these annual visits is to check disease before it infects a herd. By pulling together in a community ring we are making this possible at less than one-tenth the former cost."

Free-Choice Salt for Sheep

Allowing your sheep to lick salt freely is much better than mixing a limited amount with the ration. This we learn from experiments conducted at Ames, Iowa, ever since the winter of 1912-13. The sheep must, of course, be gradually broken in to helping themselves, or their salt appetite may bring them disaster.

The reason free-choice salt-feeding is better is that different feed rations contain different quantities of mineral, thereby varying a good deal the amount of salt required by the sheep or lamb. It is impossible, so far, to estimate the exact amount of salt required with each ration.

In this experiment, the feeding of beet molasses greatly decreased the salt consumption, while alfalfa stimulated the demand for salt.

Exercise for Bulls, Hog Prices, etc.

THE **dairy-bulls** at the New York State College of Agriculture, Ithaca, N. Y., number usually six to eight. They walk on an endless platform made of pieces of lumber hinged together, and with a slight slope. The wheels over which this runs are connected by belts through a countershaft to a pump. Thus, instead of turning a machine doing no useful work, the bulls pump all the water needed in the cow-barns, while taking their exercise. *F. B.*

Cottonseed and oat hulls: Frank Prucka, of Fort Crook, Nebr., fattens cattle on sweet-clover pasture, cottonseed-meal and oat hulls. He summer feeds only. The sweet clover puts on the first gain, and then for a few weeks 125 animals get 1,600 pounds a day of cottonseed-meal and 600 pounds a day of oat hulls. The hulls serve merely as a cheap compact roughage to balance the meal. Prucka has been feeding 20 years. *G. R. H.*

August Siebels, Harrison county, Iowa, used to run his hogs—from 500 to 600 head—all in a bunch. He changed that system to one of dividing up the bunch into three or four groups and handling these groups separately. The change resulted in fewer death losses and the hogs made much better gains on the same character and amounts of feed. August vaccinates all his hogs before they go on full feed. *B.*

The primer class in dairying, please learn this rule: The cost of grain is about half the total cost of feeding a cow.

To "dock" full-grown lambs or sheep, there is no better way than to tie a string around the tail, tightly, close to the body. Then place the tail on a block of wood, hold a hatchet or corn-knife or some sharp tool on the tail and with a hammer strike the poll of hatchet, or back of corn-knife, a good hard blow. Let the string stay on the stub for several hours to prevent bleeding. This method is easy and humane. This does not mean that lambs should be allowed to mature before docking. Dock and castrate lambs when a week or ten days old. *A. A. Colburn.*

Hogs harvest one out of 14 acres of Iowa corn. There is a great saving of labor in hogging down corn. Ever try it? The pigs do every bit as well as when fed by hand.

The best measure of a cow's efficiency is the feed cost of 100 pounds of milk. If you use this yardstick, you will not be misled by changing factors, such as selling price of milk.

A good living and 10%

High prices for hogs come, on the average, once about every four years. The relation of the price of hogs to the price of corn is an important price determiner. The average for the last 20 years shows that 100 pounds of pork would buy about eleven bushels of corn. In July, 1924, it would buy only seven and one-half bushels of corn. When corn is cheap compared to pork, as it is now, a large number of people go into raising hogs. If 100 pounds of pork buys only a little corn, people go out of the hog business. Cheap hogs follow cheap corn by a year or two.

50 Years of Poultry

By Michael K. Boyer

Courtesy of William F. Hillpot

Baby chicks shipped in boxes divided into compartments holding 25 chicks each, carry safely

ABOUT the time The Farm Journal was hatching from its shell, the poultry sharps of the day recognized 26 breeds of poultry. They were: Barred Plymouth Rocks, American Dominiques, Light and Dark Brahmas, Buff, Partridge, White and Black Cochins, Single-Comb Brown, White and Black Leghorns, White-Faced Black Spanish, Blue Andalusians, White, Silver-Gray and Colored Dorkings, Polish, Golden Spangled, Silver Spangled, Golden Penciled, Silver Penciled, White and Black Hamburgs, Mottled Houdans, Black Crevecours and Black LaFleche.

Today we have 24 distinct breeds in the American class alone, where 50 years ago we had only two. Besides, we have eight in the Asiatic class, fifteen in the Mediterranean, twelve in the English, two in the Oriental, two in the Continental, one in the Polish, six in the Hamburg and four in the French. In all, there are 64 recognized breeds, not including Games and Bantams, against 26 listed 50 years ago.

The incubator of 50 years ago was crude, but it did fairly good work

The Game fowls known 50 years ago were the Black-Breasted Red, the Brown Red, the Ginger Red, the Yellow Duck-Wing, the Silver Duck-Wing, the Pile, the White, Black and Gray—nine altogether. Today there are eleven breeds in the Game class.

Then the Game Bantams, too, were popular, and the sharps of that day disqualified cocks that weighed more than 24 ounces, and hens weighing more than 20 ounces. The judges of today set the weight of cocks not over 28, and hens not more than 26 ounces. Of Bantams other than Game, there were the Sebright, Black, White, Pekin or Cochin, and Japan. In all there were six breeds, including the Game, against 17 recognized today.

The List of Breeds Has Grown

Of ducks there were the Aylesbury, Rouen, Cayuga, East Indian or Labrador, Call, White Crested, White Muscovy and Pekin. Eight breeds in all, compared with 14 today.

Of geese there were the Toulouse, Emden, White China, Egyptian or Nile, and the African—five in all against seven today.

Of turkeys there were the Black, Buff, Slate, Narragansett and Bronze. Five breeds with seven today.

Fifty years ago judges were instructed, when disqualifying fowls, "to keep in view the Golden Rule." Probably much-needed advice at that time.

Wonderful advancement has been made in artificial incubation in the past 50 years. It was not until 1847 that the practical incubator was invented. It was a crude affair, however, and it was not until 1887 that a real, practical incubator was placed on the market. The authorities of 50 years ago were not very enthusiastic on the subject of artificial incubation, no doubt due to the fact that so little was known about it at that time. Failures were plentiful, and the late I. K. Felch, who lived to see the day when artificial incubation came into general use, at that early date sent out a word of warning: "No incubator is of any value, whatever, unless it contains within itself every principle, every phase and every condition that Nature furnishes for the incubation of the egg, and the successful hatching of the chick." As a rational deduction from this, he said, no one can invent a successful incubator unless he fully understands what those essential conditions are.

Early Incubators

The first machines, and their lamp attachments, were so crude that fires frequently occurred, and in a number of cases entire buildings were destroyed. But improvements came and danger from fire has now been reduced to a minimum.

In 1896 W. P. Hall, of New York, built and placed on the market the first mammoth machine, with a capacity of 5,700 eggs. Later on other makes [Continued on page 62

At left—Barred Plymouth Rock hen, 1927 model. Right—a specimen of 50 years ago. Some difference!

Records of production at the great egg-laying contests mount higher and higher each year. Imagine a scene in 1877 like this at the Vineland egg-laying contest

50th Anniversary

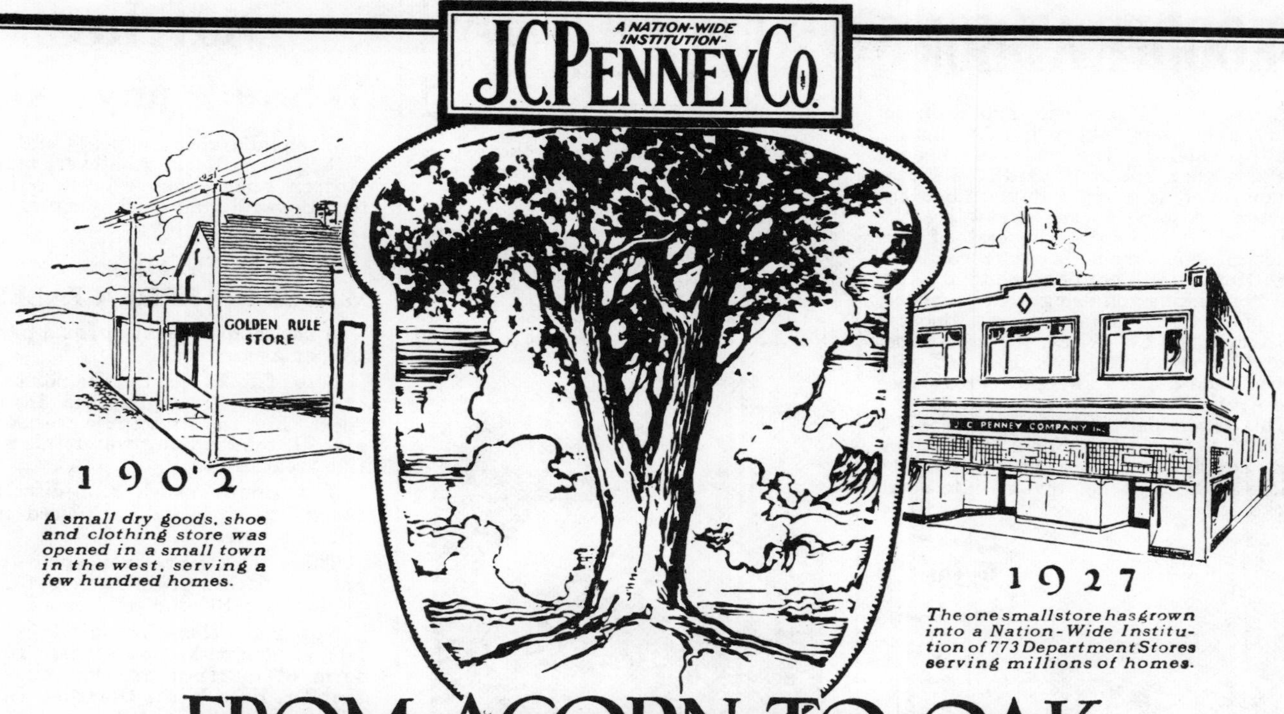

1902

A small dry goods, shoe and clothing store was opened in a small town in the west, serving a few hundred homes.

1927

The one small store has grown into a Nation-Wide Institution of 773 Department Stores serving millions of homes.

FROM ACORN TO OAK

After 25 years of growth now a nation-wide shopping service

773 STORES FROM COAST TO COAST

WE are celebrating with pride and thankfulness our Twenty-fifty or Silver Anniversary—with pride for the privilege of serving the American public—with thankfulness for the generous response that has come to our effort.

Since the Spring day in April, 1902, when Mr. Penney inaugurated, in a small and inconspicuous manner, a Retail Shopping Service which was destined to become one of Nation-wide Helpfulness, a quarter of a century has passed.

It has been a period of notable growth and expansion, of winning millions of friends, of serving them faithfully, of basing achievement upon the good will of mutual satisfaction.

During all these eventful years, we have been mindful of our responsibilities to the legion of patrons who have contributed and are today contributing, so continuously and so generously, in helping make our Service one not of profit alone but of the confidence that rests on good will.

Never for a moment have we knowingly wavered from the responsibility of this relationship. It has always been to us an inspiration to reach out for greater things, that we might be the better prepared to render a Service which should prove to be more and more beneficial to the increasing numbers who come to us.

Not only is that one little Golden Rule Store of 1902—now itself grown to far larger proportions—still serving the people in and about Kemmerer, Wyoming, but there has sprung from its applied principles and policies, others to a present total of 773 Department Stores, scattered over 46 States.

All these are children of what we now affectionately term, The Mother Store; all happily operate in the Service of the public under the name of the J. C. Penney Company.

The Founder of this Organization—Mr. James C. Penney—builded in his pioneering days more enduring and substantially than he knew.

His ideals and practices—square treatment alike to all always—and the extent to which he packed Value into every Dollar of purchase—these constitute the pattern according to which this enormous business has been shaped and which has caused it to grow until it has now become a Nation-wide Institution, serving more than 3,000,000 homes.

The dynamic selective and buying power of the Company created by its tremendous volume of cash sales, which, in 1926, amounted to $115,682,737.86, gives *a saving power to the public* which means much to the thrift and to the economic life of the people of every community where it operates a Store.

At this milepost in our history, we pause only long enough to express our thanks to the great American people for their continued confidence and appreciation of our efforts in their behalf and to offer the assurance that in the future as in the past we shall strive to serve not only well but better and better with each succeeding business day.

OUR ANNIVERSARY CELEBRATION BEGINS APRIL FIRST!

WRITE TODAY FOR "THE STORE NEWS"

beautifully illustrated by rotogravure, showing you how to save large sums on Dry Goods, Clothing, Furnishings, Shoes and kindred lines — standard quality goods! A post-card will bring it.

A NATION-WIDE INSTITUTION-

J.C.PENNEY CO. INC.

Executive Offices and Warehouse—330 W. 34th St., N.Y. City

RETAIL SALESMEN WANTED

experienced in our lines, to train for Co-partner Store Managers, providing for the continuous growth of our Company and especially the expansion planned for 1927. Write for particulars.

50 Years of Poultry

Continued from page 60

came into the field and today there are a score or more of large, successful machines, ranging in size from 1,200 to 40,000 eggs capacity. They are sectional in construction, are heated by hot-water pipes, using coal-burning stoves for that purpose. Some types use gas and others oil for fuel.

The first poultry-show was held in Boston, November 15, 1849, in a tent on Boston Common. But the first regular indoor exhibition was not held until five years later—in New York City, in Barnum's American Museum. The Hon. Daniel Webster was one of the leading exhibitors at the Boston show, entering "seven domesticated wild geese; also a pair of Java barnyard fowls, of good size and appearance." P. T. Barnum, the great showman, was president of the New York association, and he was ably assisted in the management of the exhibition by such notables as Horace Greeley, Orange Judd, George P. Burnham, A. B. Allen, D. D. T. Moore, Luther Tucker, etc. In fact, the entire management consisted of ministers, lawyers, doctors, editors and "honorables."

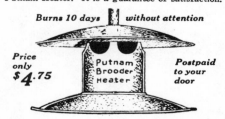

The modern brooder has taken one job away from the hen

Egg and poultry production is over four times what it was 50 years ago. Today the industry is a billion-dollar business and stands fifth in importance in the farm products of the United States. The center of production has slowly switched from the Atlantic to the Pacific. There are more people engaged in poultry work than in any other branch of livestock raising.

Changes in Diet

There have been great changes in methods of caring for poultry, such as in feeds and feeding, housing, preventing and handling diseases, etc. The error of the all-corn diet has been corrected.

Probably of still greater benefit than the home-mixed rations are the grains and ground-grain mixtures, put up and sold commercially as scratch feeds and mashes. Not only are these properly balanced, but they afford the keepers of small flocks an advantage they might not otherwise be able to obtain. Fowls do not tire so readily of feed that is properly mixed.

Great improvement has also been made in poultry-house construction. The old-time poultry-house was a mere makeshift, improperly ventilated, stuffy and uncomfortable. Fresh air in the hen-house used to be considered a menace to the health of the stock, and consequently the buildings were so tightly constructed that no air could enter.

We do not hear of the ravages of cholera, roup and kindred [*Continued on page 117*

The Baby Chick Says

By Alvin M. Peterson

Do not feed me as soon as I am out of the shell. I have a good deal of rich food in my body. Let me make use of this before you offer me something to eat. When I am 48 hours old I begin to get hungry. Then rolled oats tastes very good to me.

Do not put too many of us little fellows in the same box, basket or brooder. We are not nearly so likely to pile up and smother each other when there are less of us.

Give me plenty of warm sunshine. I like to be outdoors, the same as you, where I can enjoy the sunshine, run around all I like, play, and hunt worms and insects.

Do not feed me the same food day after day. How would you like oatmeal for breakfast, oatmeal for lunch and oatmeal for dinner—oatmeal the day in, and oatmeal the day out, week after week? I like rolled oats, but I also like other grain foods, milk, cheese, hard-boiled egg and other foods.

Give Me Shelter

I get cold very easily. I like a warm place to go to for a rest and a nap—especially do I like such a place on cold, windy days.

I do not like to be left out in the rain any more than you do. Be sure to give me a house or other shelter to which I can run when it starts to rain.

I like to be fed regularly, just as you like your meals at regular hours. Best of all, I like plenty of fresh, pure water. You can't imagine how often I get thirsty. If you will provide me with a handy drinking-fountain, I can get water whenever I feel thirsty.

I do not like dogs very well, unless they are very gentle. And I hate rats. Please do not let rats live near me.

Keep me in a safe place at night, one that is warm and comfortable, where I can sleep and rest in peace.

City man: "What kind of cattle are these hydraulic rams?"

The Cackle of the Hens

I know this is no lofty flight
Of poetry at all;
No doubt its subject's kind of slim,
And its object mighty small,
And you'll call me sentimental
And weak-minded, 'cause I sing
Of the pleasure that the hens give
By cackling in the spring.

STEALING chickens that roost in trees is an old trick. People here were having their poultry stolen right out of the trees. The thief would visit the farmer to inspect the fowls and see where they roosted, on the pretense of buying, and the next morning they would be gone. One woman who had padlocked her poultry-house, laughingly remarked: "My Thanksgiving turkey and a lot of my chickens roost in the trees, but if the thief can get them up there he is welcome to them." The next morning they were gone. Later on the thief was apprehended, and he admitted that he used a pole on the end of which he nailed a board. This he would push up under the breast of a fowl, the fowl would step on the board, and it was then lowered to the ground. *Mrs. J. W. Neiderheiser, Ore.*

Egg production is frequently brought on by the use of a wet mash fed in the hoppers in the same manner as the dry feed. A quart of fishmeal or meatmeal to every 100 birds should be mixed in the mash, says Oregon Agricultural College.

As a source of income, poultry has made the greatest relative increase on 4,666 Ohio farms, in 40 counties. This is evident from summaries of farm account-books compiled by the department of rural economics at the Ohio Experiment Station over a period of 15 years.

Turkey eggs for hatching should be kept in a room of even temperature, not above 50° F. Turn them every day.

Keep watch for the hen which eats no supper, and limps when she walks. Pick her up and examine for a torn side. Use a healing powder (not grease), and it will soon heal over. Then catch Mr. Tom and file his spurs until they are dulled. *Pennsylvania. Sara C. Reitz.*

A new farmers' bulletin, 1506-F, on "Standard Breeds and Varieties" has been issued by the United States Department of Agriculture, Washington, D. C. A copy will be sent free upon application to foregoing address.

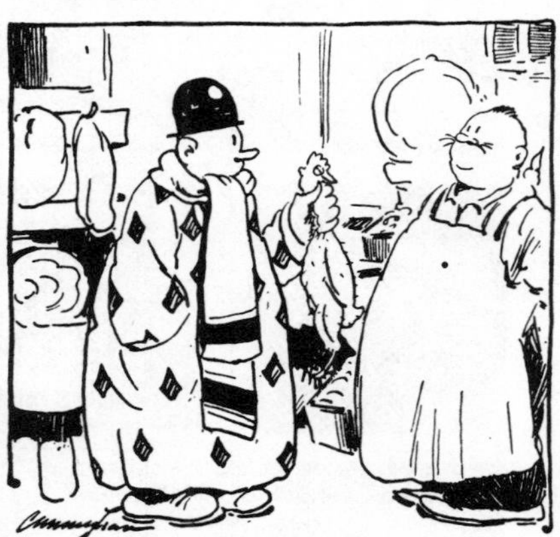

Customer, to butcher: "That chicken is so old it doesn't have a tooth in its head"

Stingless Bees

By Evangeline Weir

STINGLESS bees are found in the warm countries of both the Old and the New World. They live in colonies, working for the good of the community which has all things in common. This group consists of many species, and they differ somewhat in their methods of working and in the arrangement of their various nests. While hollow trees are the usual homes of the bees, they also build in wall cavities, and a few members are said to make nests in the ground.

The nest of this bee is made of wax, but differs from that of our stinging bee, for it is mixed with other substances, such as resin and earth, which change its color to brown or even black instead of the creamy white known to us.

The nest—at least in some species—consists of two parts: a nursery and a store-room. The nursery is a hollow, globe-shaped affair with thin walls of wax containing passageways, while the brood cells are arranged within this covering. Here the young are raised and receive such attention as is necessary.

Honey Stored in Pots

Outside the waxy, leaf-like walls, the round pots to hold pollen and honey are placed. These honey-pots resemble those of our humblebee in form, size and arrangement.

The doorways built by these bees are unique. Each species has a plan of its own for adorning the entrance to the nest. Some doors are simple—a small hole surrounded by a knob-like affair of wax which attracts little attention. Some are elaborate—shaped like a spout or a funnel, and extending some distance beyond the base. Others are masses of fluted wax built around the opening and spread some distance over the bark of the tree.

An Indian species makes a funnel-shaped door extending some distance beyond the tree to which it is attached, and smears the entrance with a sticky substance to keep out intruders. This is very wise, for ants and other small insects fond of sweets would creep in to sip from the honey-pots.

Guards at the Doors

In the wilderness of Brazil, we have one of the group that builds a spout of wax a foot or more long over the opening to its nest. The honey of this bee is said to be good, and the honey-pots quite large.

As these bees are stingless and unable to protect their homes in the usual way, they resort to other means. In a number, if not all, of our South American species, the doors are guarded during the day by a number of watchmen chosen for the purpose. Human beings find it quite unpleasant to force an entrance, for the bees—the whole community—will cover the head and face of an intruder, some biting and licking the flesh, others creeping into eyes, ears, nose and hair.

After the duties of the day, when the workers are all at home, a little wax screen covers the door for the night. Locked within the hollow of the tree, the little people go to sleep until the sun shines in the outer world, when they go forth to gather food, care for the queen and the children, and to guard the home. A well-regulated life, not unlike that of our own homes.

If the bees used for honey production in the United States were of the stingless variety, more folks would go into the bee business.

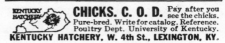

50th Anniversary

The Oxen of Old Lyme

By A. B. Champlain

A TEAM of oxen on our city streets would draw a crowd. Traffic would be blocked not only by the crowds that would assemble to view this unusual sight, but by the comparatively snail-like pace of the slow moving team. In these days of high-speed automobiles and electric conveyances, even the horse is becoming a rarity on city streets. Strange to relate, but nevertheless true, is a fact that oxen are still in use as draft-animals in certain parts of America.

The accompanying photos show oxen in action on the farms of Old Lyme, Conn., 100 miles from New York City. Oxen were ideal in their day for New England farming, but in localities where 25 years ago they were used extensively for farming and road work, and bred with care and pride for prize competition at fairs, they are now being replaced by more-modern appliances and methods of hauling, and are more valuable as beef for the market. Soon they will be seen no more, lumbering along the village streets with their loads of wood or hay. All through Connecticut the old-timers stick to oxen, especially in the woods, where other conveyances can not be used so well; but even here they are falling more into disuse as younger farmers appear.

Harvesting salt hay for oxen. The hay is gathered on scows from the marshes. Above, ox-cart

THE term oxen was originally used to designate cattle in general, but in the United States it refers to male cattle that have been altered when young to fit them for drafting purposes. They are steady at the yoke, quite intelligent, usually gentle and patient, sure of foot in the rugged, hilly country where they are used, and have great strength and pulling power.

Training is begun early; the little steers are hitched up two abreast by means of a yoke that is the replica in miniature of the one which they will wear when put to work. In this way they not only become familiar with the yoke, but are taught to obey the driving commands and signals of the teacher, and to work in unison with each other. They are usually taken into the team when about two years old. At first they are placed in the rear or middle of the team until they have become proficient to work alone or become leaders in turn. Each individual is always used in the same position in a team, after having been taught and broken in pairs as mentioned. Well-trained oxen soon learn to fall into their positions without more than a word of command.

THE yoke consists of a wooden main piece about five and one-half or six feet long, cut to fit over the tops of the necks of the oxen. Yokes are made of hickory, maple, birch and other woods, and the average weight is from 25 to 30 pounds. Placed about the neck of each ox is a bow that holds the yoke in position; it is inserted through the yoke on each side and pinned above. A large ring is fastened at the lower center of the yoke. Here the "neep," or tongue, of the wagon is fastened, or plow chain attached.

Oxen are more economical to keep than horses, and can do considerable work on forage such as they can find in the pasture, and on the salt hay from the tidal meadows. They are usually worked until five or six years of age, although sometimes until nine, or as long as their teeth hold out and they can eat, but at eight or nine they rapidly decline in value. The average life is from 15 to 20 years.

From two to six oxen is the number used for general hauling, such as wood, ice or hay, but I have seen as many as twelve pair or yoke on a single exhibition team. Sometimes one ox is used as a leader, with a single yoke.

Oxen hauling wood in winter

Oxen are shod with flat pieces of iron on each side of the divided hoof, especially for use during the winter-time on rough, slippery roads.

The animals are handled with an ox whip, which is a long, slender, pliable stick with a lash, usually made of sheep-skin, attached to the tip. Sticks of varying lengths are used, according to the

Nose baskets keep the oxen from eating while at work

number of yokes of oxen in the team. They are driven by motions with this whip, and light touches with the lash on the head or flanks, and by speech. The terms "gee," meaning right, and "haw," meaning left, are the principal words used in driving, and the oxen readily turn to the directions indicated; they also back or go ahead when the whip is lightly used and the proper terms called to them.

Devons, which are blood-red in color varying to dark bay, seem to be the favorite variety around Old Lyme; the Herefords run second.

Ginseng and Riches

Continued from page 18

Seeds should be planted about one inch deep and mulched same as the roots. Seeds are generally planted quite close together and then transplanted to about six by eight inches when the plants are two years old.

Beds may be worked up in the woods, but the growth there will not be over half what it will be under artificial shade. Hot, wet weather is the worst thing the grower has to contend with, and with that in mind artificial shade should be about six feet in the clear, as that makes the bed cooler than a low shade and it also makes it easier to weed and care for.

The crop may be harvested at five years, but is of much better quality if allowed to stand longer. I have had wild roots as old as 90 years, but that is rare. About seven or eight years gives the best results, considering both size and quality. A fair average weight for a five-year-old root, under artificial shade, is about one and one-half ounces, green; dry, about a half-ounce. Grown in the forest the weight would be less.

The roots are dug in the fall, washed and dried in the shade and are now worth from $8 to $12 a pound, according to quality. The growing of this crop requires close attention, and is no crop for the slipshod man to attempt. With proper care, it is not hard to grow and pays well. There is always a market, as fur dealers and others are always looking for it. Government bulletins will help the would-be grower some, and there is a paper published monthly that is devoted to ginseng culture and other similar crops.

The business is no get-rich scheme, and should not be entered into except where one has a proper locality and conditions to warrant success. *C. M. Goodspeed.*

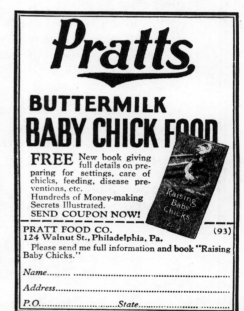

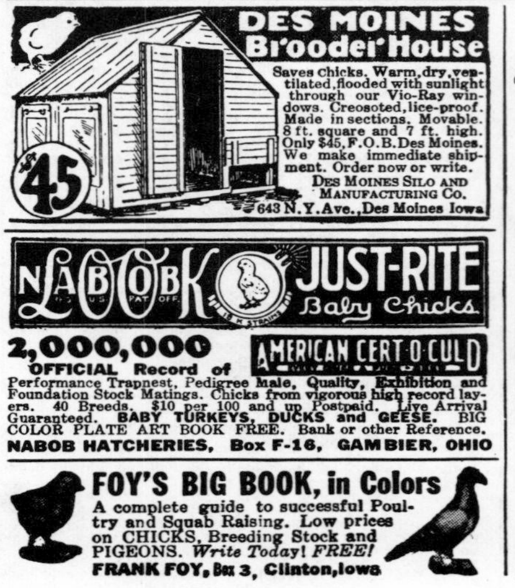

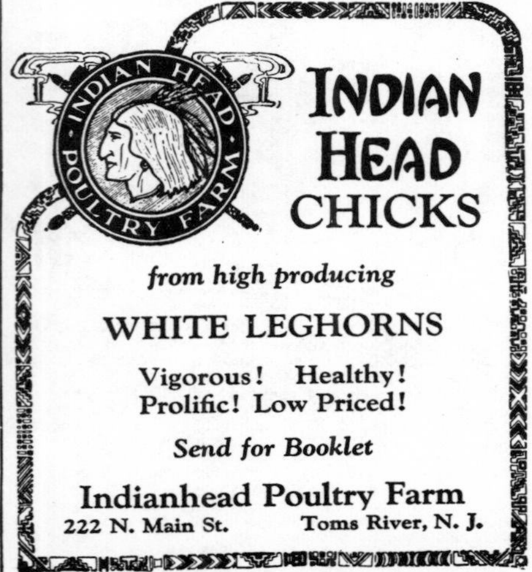

Marshall Breaks His Own Record

By C. J. Willard

THE world's record for large-scale corn-production has been broken by the man who made it. Ira Marshall of Dola, Hardin county, Ohio, grew 1,686.6 bushels of air-dry shelled corn on ten acres this year, breaking his last year's record of 1,600 bushels on that area. This achievement is the more remarkable because this year was not so favorable for corn in Ohio as last year, and Marshall made his new record on land which was in corn last year. Marshall is a stockman, who feeds most of his corn crop to beef cattle. He is a tenant farmer. The farm on which he has made these records belongs to a banker at the county-seat.

The record was carefully checked by W. E. Hanger and E. P. Reed, of Ohio State University. Six rows, selected at random and containing nearly a half-acre, were husked and weighed as a sample of the field. Then 50 pounds of ears were shelled to get the shelling percentage, which was 84. A sample of this shelled corn was sent to Columbus in an airtight can and the moisture determined, so that the field yield could be reduced to air-dry shelled corn.

Marshall's corn was of the Clarage variety, the same that he used last year. His son Glenn grew ten acres of Woodburn's yellow dent, and almost broke his father's previous record by producing 1,593.2 bushels on the ten acres. Altogether, the Marshalls had more than 25 acres of corn which averaged over 160 bushels per acre.

Muck Soil, Loam Subsoil

The soil on Marshall's farm is almost a typical onion muck, but the subsoil is a loam, and is tiled every five rods. Last year the land was in corn, and it had been in alfalfa for seven years before that. Six tons per acre of cattle manure have been used each of the last three winters. The land was plowed in April ten inches deep, and it was disked and cultipacked before seeding in May. Then 200 pounds of 20 per cent acid phosphate were sown broadcast and 100 pounds of high-grade complete fertilizer used in the row. The corn was harrowed once and cultivated three times. The most unusual of Marshall's methods is his way of planting corn. He planted four kernels per hill in hills 32 x 34 inches apart. This meant planting 23,000 kernels per acre, and his final stand was practically 20,000 stalks per acre.

Two "scoop-shovel" samples of the

corn harvested from the field, nubbins and all, averaged .52 pound per ear, green weight. Ears selected somewhat to get the run of the better ears, averaged .66 pound per ear. It is clear that Marshall has depended on a good stand of stalks bearing moderate-sized ears to make his remarkable yields.

Thick Planting

Will this method work elsewhere? It certainly does not mean that all that is necessary to produce 160 bushels of corn on an acre is to plant 20,000 stalks on it. But it is equally clear that to secure the highest yields on any land the stand must be thick enough to produce those yields. Rate-of-planting experiments from Ohio to Nebraska indicate that to secure the best yields from Corn Belt varieties of corn, the rate of planting should be adjusted so that one-half pound of ear corn to the stalk will produce the best yield the land will make in an average good season. None of these experiments has been conducted on land making more than 100 bushels per acre. Marshall has proved that the rule holds for higher yields as well. It is not desirable to grow more than four stalks in one hill, so that when large numbers of stalks an acre are required, it is necessary to put the hills closer together, as Marshall and several other Ohio growers of corn have done with a great deal of success.

Old Apple Trees Paid for Spraying

On Jim Kile's farm, in my locality, there are three apple trees of an unknown variety that produced a few scabby apples each year. No one gathered them, although the owner admitted they were excellent keepers, and made mighty fine eating when one large enough could be found. The trees were old, but since they shaded the poultry-lot, Kile made an effort to prolong their lives. In doing so he improved the fruit until the trees have paid him $80, with a prospect of profit for several years to come.

"The food elements in the soil about these trees had become exhausted," Kile explained to me. "A year ago in the spring I applied four loads of well-rotted manure, and arranged for ashes and mineral matter to be dumped there occasionally. I removed all the dead limbs from the trees, and then filled the larger cavities with cement.

"As the trees were badly infested with insects, I sprayed them before the buds opened, and after the bloom was shed. Still finding moths, I repeated the treatment, ten days later.

"The foliage was heavier than usual, but my big surprise came in July, when I noticed, among the leaves, some nice, smooth apples. At picking time, I gathered 31 bushels, which sold for $40.30. There were less than five bushels of cull fruit.

"I fertilized the trees again in the following winter, and last spring four sprays were applied. In the fall, I gathered 43 bushels of nice apples, valued at $55.90, making a total of $96.20. Cost of fertilizer, spraying materials, etc., for both years was less than $15, which left a profit of $81.20. This was brought about by adding plant-food to the soil and protecting the fruit from the pests and diseases which had formerly caused its poor condition. The work was done at odd times, without taking effort from regular farm routine." *C.*

THERE is much about poultry that must be acquired from experience. Go slow and learn the lesson well.

Party Clothes for Party Cakes

By Jane Hemmingway

Decorating tubes simplify the art of cake decoration

WE all know what a big part a birthday cake plays in a birthday celebration. Every one, from Grandmother down to the baby with his one candle, gets a thrill when it comes time to cut the cake. Then why not make the cake an important feature in other affairs?

A huge cake, properly decorated, makes a most attractive centerpiece for almost any kind of a party. What more appropriate centerpiece could you find for any sort of patriotic affair, Lincoln's or Washington's Birthday, Fourth of July, Memorial or Armistice Day, than a "monument" cake? Bake three or four cakes in pans of the same shape, but graduated in size. They may be different kinds of cake, too. Beginning with the largest, pile them up one on top of the other and ice all over with boiled icing. On the topmost cake place either a tiny plaster bust of one of our national heroes, or a small silk flag. Decorate with garlands and patriotic devices, done with icing pressed through a decorating or icing tube. Arrange piles of round cakes, iced all over to resemble cannon balls, around the base.

For a party given in the fall, make a big horn of plenty from a sheet of gilt or birch-bark paper. Place it on a bed of autumn leaves and fill with tiny cakes of all kinds iced in gay colors.

For a spring party, use a large round layer-cake as the foundation for the centerpiece. Cover with pale-green icing and across the top draw a bar of music, using the smallest-sized tube and melted chocolate. If possible, copy the first phrase from Mendelssohn's "Spring Song." Place small vases of spring flowers at the corners of the table. For place-cards perch a tiny bluebird on the edge of each glass, and for favors use Kewpie dolls, dressed as choir singers, holding postage-stamp-sized sheets of music in their hands.

A MOST realistic book can be made from an oblong cake if the edges are trimmed off a bit. Such a cake, iced in white with the title "CUPID'S DIARY" written on it in pink icing (with the icing tube), would make the table very pretty for an announcement luncheon. It could be further decorated with linked hearts, true love-knots, and other such symbols. There should be rose-colored ribbons extending from it to each place, ending in heart-shaped place-cards. Of course, every one scents a romance, and the hostess can then show the assembled guests her engagement ring.

A money shower for the engaged girl seems to be very popular these days: the girls give the guest of honor a sum of money with which to buy something she wants for her new home. A novel method of presenting the money would be to make a "Money Cake." Bake a very large round cake not more than two inches deep, and ice it all over with orange icing, colored a deep yellow with grated orange peel. Using the icing tube again, copy, as accurately as possible, the markings on a coin. Gilt tissue ribbons going from the cake to each cover make a most attractive scheme, and they could end in tiny place-cards on which bright Lincoln pennies are glued and the names written in gilt paint. Little savings banks from the five-and-ten-cent store can be used for favors. The money which has been collected should be changed into a new bill or gold coin, wrapped in waxed paper and hidden in the center of the cake. Invert a tumbler over the center of the cake, cut around the tumbler and serve this round piece to the guest of honor. Cut the rest of the cake into the usual slices.

AND now for the children. Four thin oblong cakes put together to form a box will make a perfect foundation for a fort for the boys. At each corner put a small round cake (baked in a muffin pan) for turrets, and ice all over with white icing. With melted chocolate and the decorating tube add the holes and windows. Stick a flag in each "turret" and stand a row of tin soldiers around it "in parade," one for each boy.

Another attractive cake is a round one having sloping sides and iced in green to represent a hill. On the very top place a little well made of a square box, and coming down the hill have a pair of dolls dressed to represent "Jack" and "Jill," carrying a small pail between them. At each cover place a small tin pail filled with candy.

What Cookery Means

THE art of cookery made the brute human. It was to improve, to vary what he ate, that he shaped his new life. And it is amazing with what promptness he learned further to vary his dinner by cooking it. As soon as we know anything about man, he was drying his food in the sun or baking it in the earth. As he began to cook, he adapted the details of his life so as to provide time and place for the cooking. To possess himself of a permanent oven instead of a chance hole in the ground, he built houses, he gathered with his fellow men in villages. The more elaborate his cooking became, the more civilized his life. Civilization came into being and grew, step by step, in the kitchen.

E. R. P.

The simplest decorations become ornate when the icing is pressed through tubes having variously shaped points. Paper linings for the muslin bags in which these tubes are inserted keep the bags from contact with the icing

Cake Secrets

Whenever you have questions to ask about cake-making, write us—we shall be delighted to give you any information we can.

If it's prizes you'd like to take on your cakes—or merely praises from those who eat them—you'll be delighted with this **Magic Three.** We call them that because by varying the fillings and frostings you can make practically any kind of butter cake you will ever want to serve, with just this White or Chocolate or Spice Cake for a foundation. Any one of them with ice cream or coffee makes a most delicious dessert.

Lemon Filling

1 cup sugar
6 tablesp. Swans Down
Grated rind 1 lemon
¼ cup lemon juice
¼ cup boiling water
2 egg yolks
1 teaspoon butter

Mix flour and sugar thoroughly. Add grated lemon rind, lemon juice, and beaten egg yolks. Add boiling water, set the mixture in double boiler, and cook until thickened, stirring constantly—then cook 10 minutes stirring occasionally. Add butter and cool thoroughly before putting on cake, by filling lower part of double boiler with ice water.

To make sure of having your boiled icing cooked to just the right consistency, add 1 cup granulated sugar to ½ cup boiling water and cook until it threads. Then remove from stove and pour in thin stream on beaten egg whites. Beat until creamy; place bowl in pan of boiling water and continue beating until the icing feels or sounds grainy on the edge of the bowl. Spread on cake immediately.

An oven thermometer is essential to proper baking. We can now supply you with a standard thermometer, postage prepaid, at $1.00 ($1.25 at Denver and west, $1.50 in Canada).

In writing, don't forget to give me your name and address, and remember we'd love to see you in our Swans Down kitchen.

Mary Jean Hart

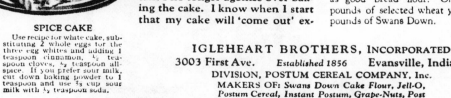

Domestic Science Dept.
Igleheart Brothers, Inc.
3003 First Ave.
Evansville, Indiana

Offices of The Farm Journal 1877–1927

The earliest office, a remodeled dwelling house at 726 Sansom Street, only a couple of blocks from our present building. After this the office was at 914 Arch Street, for a short time only

The third office, above, 114 North 7th Street, was occupied from 1879 to 1882

At the right is the fourth office of the magazine, 125 North 9th Street, used until 1895

1024 Race Street, the fifth office; three additions were built to this, and an abandoned church building in the rear was bought and remodeled, but eventually it, too, became too small

When The Farm Journal was started, in 1877, the number of employees was one. The first subscriber was Aunt Hannah Phillips, and one of the first advertisers was the late John Wanamaker, who was just about to open his great department store

Today machinery of the latest type does most of our work. The circulation is more than 1,400,000, and our advertising pages contain the announcements of most of the leading advertisers

The Washington Square front of our present building, occupied since September, 1912

The entrance hall in our present building, where Our Folks are always welcome

50th Anniversary

One of the huge 1927-type color presses, that prints the cover of The Farm Journal

Have Furnace Comfort Now!
Join the "Enjoy-It-Now" Club
It's an unprecedented opportunity. The most liberal home-heating offer ever made. It's so easy, now, to have Heatrola comfort during the raw, blustery months still ahead—healthful heat to ward off that end-of-winter illness. Ask your dealer about the Heatrola "Enjoy-It-Now" Club. Or, mail the coupon.

And only last winter.. Folks called them "*The hermits*"

YOU'VE seen it happen: A family who kept to themselves, who seldom entertained or were entertained, suddenly blossoms out. Their home becomes a popular gathering place. What made the difference? Chances are it was just this:

Before, they hesitated to invite people to their home, because—well, the house was never comfortable in winter, and then there was that hideous stove in the living room.

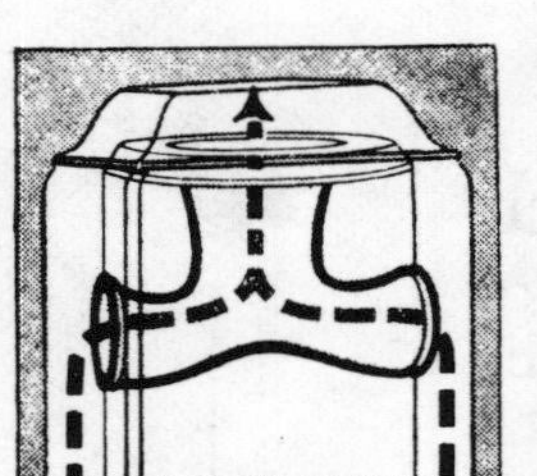

The INTENSI-FIRE *—exclusive with Heatrola*

The Intensi-Fire Air Duct is a patented device, built into the Heatrola, directly in the path of the flame. It tremendously increases Heatrola's heating capacity without using a single extra pound of fuel.

But since a handsome Estate Heatrola was installed—you should see the room! So charming, so modern. And so delightfully cozy. No wonder friends are always dropping in.

Comfort upstairs and down

When stoves "heated" the house, the few rooms that were warm enough were generally too warm. But with Heatrola there is cheerful comfort in every nook and corner, upstairs and down. And such healthful heat! No more of those persistent colds.

And Heatrola is so convenient and economical, too. It saves, on an average, 45 per cent in fuel over old-fashioned methods. A dust cloth keeps it looking like new.

Why risk end-of-winter illness?

A Heatrola installed in your home *now* may pay its entire cost in the doctor bills it saves. Your dealer will tell you how amazingly easy it is to have Heatrola's furnace comfort. Or, mail the coupon.

THE ESTATE STOVE CO.
Hamilton, Ohio
House founded in 1845
New York, 243 W. 34th Street
Minneapolis, 714 Washington Ave., N.
San Francisco, The Furniture Exch.
Portland, Oregon

There is only *One* Heatrola—*Estate* builds it

Estate HEATROLA
Heats the Whole House

Mail the coupon for details!

THE ESTATE STOVE CO.
Hamilton, Ohio
☐ Send me the details of your "Enjoy-It-Now" Club offer.
☐ I am planning to build. How can Heatrola save 15% on the cost of my new home?
(Check one you wish) 623

Name..........
Street or R. F. D...........
Post-office..........
State..........

NORMAN HALL

Experienced Cooks Prefer

Calumet, because they know by experience—by test—by actual results that

CALUMET

THE WORLD'S GREATEST

BAKING POWDER

gives them the best of good foods with the least effort and greatest economy. They take no chances. They don't experiment. They always use the leavener that millions of housewives agree is "best by test."

Double Acting

Calumet contains two leavening units. One unit begins to work when the dough is mixed—the other waits for the heat of the oven, then both units work together.

Makes Baking Easier

The certainty of Calumet—its infallible quality eliminates uneasiness and doubt during the entire process of baking. Try it. For best results, use the leavener that is employed by best cooks.

SALES 2½ TIMES THOSE OF ANY OTHER BRAND

The Next 50 Years of Agriculture

Continued from page 10

will be imperative, if we are to feed our increasing population without becoming dependent on foreign food supplies, for us to increase our yields per acre.

What is possible in this direction is indicated by the fact that average yields in leading European countries exceed ours by more than 40 per cent, and also by the fact that in some sections, particularly in the northeastern quarter of the United States, we have increased our yields per acre greatly.

It may seem a cheerful augury to the farmer that we are headed for a time when agriculture will have to hustle to keep pace with the country's needs. It is, provided farmers take full advantage of the opportunity they will have. But let us not suppose that they can achieve prosperity simply by letting their production drop down to or below the needs of our population. That looks like an easy way to boost prices. It is really inviting foreign competition in the home market. No nation can tolerate a food shortage.

Canadian grain, but for the tariff, would be moving already into the United States in large quantities. If our grain production drops much below our requirements in the future, consumers will have a strong motive to remove the tariff on wheat.

The same applies to all protected essential products. Our farmers are entitled to protection in the home market, but they will have a hard job to keep it if their production falls too much below the country's wants. A serious deficit of necessaries would force the country to draw on foreign sources of supply, no matter how much our own farmers were hurt.

I am talking, of course, about the comparatively distant future. Agriculturally, we are not on an import basis yet, by a long way. In recent years approximately 13 per cent of the net product of our agriculture has been marketed abroad. Fifty per cent of our cotton crop must find a foreign market annually. Last year nearly one-third of our wheat went abroad, and a fair proportion of our pork, tobacco and apple production.

The Downward Trend in Agricultural Export

It should not be forgotten, however, that the trend in our agricultural export trade was downward before the war and is downward again now, and seems likely to continue downward. Moreover, our imports of *competitive* agricultural products, such as sugar, wool, mohair, hides and skins, tobacco, dairy products, flaxseed and flaxseed-oil, make up an increasing annual total. Imports of these commodities last year, for example, amounted to more than $582,000,000. Sooner than we think, we may be heavily beholden to foreign countries for essential foods and fibers.

It will be necessary long before 50 years elapse to increase our crop yields. Transforming pasture into crop land and increasing the production per man engaged in agriculture will not solve our food problem. Larger production per acre will be required because the area of land that can be profitably worked is limited.

Changes in consumption habits may lessen the pressure to some extent. There is likely to be increased consumption of foods of vegetable origin and less consumption of foods of animal origin, except milk. Nevertheless, the pressure of population on land resources is bound to force intensity of cultivation beyond what is now profitable.

Farmers will therefore be impelled to make closer contacts with science. Improvement of plants by selection and breeding, for better performance under different conditions, is certain to make advances. There may be important discoveries in the laws of heredity, which will give greater control over plant growth and development.

Now and then some epochal discovery will effect spectacular results. But the main advance will probably come from the sum of many small improvements painstakingly developed by farmers. One can not speak with too much confidence as to prospects for the control of crop pests and diseases. Increasing knowledge of these things tends to be offset by increasing opportunities for them to spread. On the whole, however, it is fairly safe to predict considerable improvement in the use of the land.

Organization Is Necessary

There is another phase of agriculture that will develop greatly in the next half-century. I mean organization. Agriculture can not afford to remain unorganized in this age of large scale business operations.

Organization is necessary in agriculture, not merely for the purpose of regulating the movement of farm products into consumption, but to give farmers more control over the volume of their output. A million farmers acting independently in the production of a given crop are much more likely to throw markets out of balance by overproduction than is the case when the number of competing units is small. Organization enables farmers to accomplish the double object of adjusting production more accurately to anticipated market requirements, and feeding supplies gradually into the market so as to prevent needless price fluctuations.

The Coming Decision

The co-operative movement is now so firmly established in the United States that its future is certain. It affords the best approach to the solution of the surplus problem, through the two channels of merchandising and regulated production. It lodges effective bargaining-power in the hands of farmers, and makes possible great economies in distribution through the elimination of unnecessary waste, duplication of effort and overhead expense.

Perhaps the greatest danger faced by the co-operative movement is that it may not always be able to draw a distinction in practise between legitimate price stabilization and improper efforts at price control. But that mistake, whenever committed, will carry its own penalty. It is therefore not likely to be made very often. My own feeling is that organization in the next 50 years will do as much for agriculture as any other one thing.

Two paths open before American agriculture. One leads toward national self-sufficiency in essential foods and fibers and the other toward dependence on a foreign food supply. As to which path will be chosen, the country as a whole, of course, will have something to say. It can favor the right choice by giving agriculture all due protection and encouragement.

But the final word will remain with the farmer. If, knowing that he can have the domestic market as long as he continues to supply it adequately, he continues to increase his labor efficiency and his crop yields per acre, agriculture will regain and hold its place in the economic scheme on equal terms with other producing groups. It will be the surest guaranty of national progress and security

Field Peas Valuable in Washington

WASHINGTON Station not long ago put out a bulletin on field peas, reporting tests with the crop in rotations, and for hogging off in Washington. Here are the high points:

The yield of wheat following peas is less than wheat following good summer fallow, but greater than when it is preceded by corn or sunflowers.

A larger total yield of grain has been secured during equal periods of time in the rotations in which field peas have been used instead of summer fallow.

The average yield of field peas following wheat in four different rotations in which this crop succession occurs is 22.7 bushels, while the average yield of spring wheat following wheat in four rotations in which this crop succession occurs is 21.9 bushels.

The varieties, Bangalia, Canada and Alaska, seed of which is usually readily obtained, were among the high yielders.

Pigs fed limited rations on sweet clover or alfalfa pasture made more rapid daily gains later while hogging off peas. In two of the three years' experiments, the pigs fed limited rations were marketed with those fed full rations at the same weight, age and condition. The feed cost of the pigs fed limited rations on pasture was less than that of the full-fed pigs. The pigs made average daily gains of from .94 to 1.25 pounds each while hogging off peas. The pork produced per acre of peas varied from 141 pounds with a 16-bushel crop to 244 pounds with a 36-bushel crop.

Cheap Seed May Contain Noxious Weeds

Since the discovery that foreign clover and alfalfa seed from certain mild-climate regions is apt to give rise to plants subject to winter-killing in the American clover belt, there has been so keen a demand for native seed that the quality factor has in many cases been ignored. As a result, a great deal of home-grown clover and alfalfa seed is being used that is absolutely unfit for seeding purposes on account of the high weed-seed content.

Of the two evils, the low-grade native seed is by far the worse. When unadapted seed is used, the farmer loses only the crop, but when weedy seed is sowed it means not only a greatly decreased crop, but in addition a plague of weeds that may cause trouble and loss for years to come. If the weed seeds happen to include quack-grass or Canada thistle, it may mean a serious decrease in the value of the farm. A recent government statement declares that "in neighborhoods where good land is worth $150 an acre, a farm that is known to be infested with quack-grass often can not be sold for half that figure, while to many farmers quack-grass land is not considered a bargain at any price." Many real-estate dealers figure the average depreciation of land infested with quack-grass or Canada thistle is at least 25 per cent.

A little thought and care during the seed-buying season may avoid many hours of dreary toil in the hot sun next summer *A. A*

Love, joy, peace, long-suffering, gentleness, goodness, faith, meekness, temperance: against such there is no law. *Gal. 5:22, 23.*

Blue-Fox Raising

By C. E. Zimmerman

I WAS reared in a farming district in Ohio, and I am now raising blue foxes in Alaska. I believe it is practical for a farmer, as a side-line, to have a pen or two of blue foxes.

A breeding pair of blue foxes is rather expensive, and this is what prevents many farmers from going into the business. A good breeding pair will cost from $300 to $500. A pen 25 x 40 feet is big enough

Above, feeding puppies four months old. Below, puppies six moths old

for one pair, and the foxes do not require any more care than a half-dozen chickens. Table scraps from an ordinary family would feed a pair of foxes and their offspring. All foxes are very fond of milk. A pair will raise from four to twelve foxes a year.

Pelts Sell Well

The pelts of blue foxes sell for different prices, but generally at nine months old they average about $100. What other livestock on a farm would produce such wonderful returns in the same time? With proper facilities one man could easily take care of 50 pair.

Government statistics say about six ounces of food a day is necessary to nourish a fox properly. Fox raising is very interesting, and therefore might help to keep the farm boy at home. Of course, no one should go into this business without looking into it thoroughly, and knowing that it takes time and patience and hard work, and that there are many who fail in it.

It is a mistake to count on breeding-stock prices for all surplus animals. Count on pelt prices instead.

Pelting is not so hard. It can be done by any farmer, as it is no more difficult than with red fox or coon. Blue-fox pelts will become prime in any climate reaching zero weather in winter.

Farm Shop Work

SHEET or corrugated galvanized iron can be put right on over an old shingle roof. The old roofing provides additional thickness, and gives also a little dead-air space. Be sure to paint the metal as soon as it is laid. A trace of rust will cause damage. Coat the metal first with lead oxide and linseed-oil. Then give it a coat of red iron oxide. Litharge, used as a drier, will help to set the paint so it can not be scraped off.

❦

Get tillage machinery cleaned and sharpened early. Deep rust can be removed with sandpaper or emery-cloth and the cleaned surface polished with a brick. A plow will scour much quicker if you first

go over the share and moldboard. A small grinder will be a great help in polishing parts that can be removed. Another good idea is to put a small emery wheel on the end of the cable of an old sheep-shearing machine—then you can get at the parts that are hard to remove.

❦

To remove old wall-paper, soak with hot water. This can be done without damage, and easily, by filling an ordinary hand sprayer with hot water and going over the walls and ceilings several times; light applications, so the water won't run down. In a short time the old paper can be peeled from the walls with a putty knife. If there are several coats of paper on the wall, more soaking will be necessary. Cover the floor with old newspapers before starting a job of this sort.

❦

To loosen a rusted nut, saw down through the threaded bolt slightly more than halfway through the nut. Then squeeze the halves together, drop a little oil in, and turn the nut off. Later another nut can be used, the halves opened to their original width, and a metal wedge driven into the saw cut.

❦

Each time you put a saw or other tool away, wipe it with a soft rag which has been dipped in lard. This will effectively prevent rust.

❦

Small compartments, made by setting four-inch boards between the shop studding, will make excellent shelves and pigeon-holes for the many small articles which accumulate. A strip should be nailed across the front.

To put a quick edge on a pair of worn shears, try to cut a piece of glass, permitting the blades to slide back from the

edge as the hand closes down. A light, firm pressure will do the trick. Only two or three strokes will be necessary.

The flue sometimes burns out without warning. If this occurs at night in a wind, real damage may occur. Better than having a fire at night is to choose an opportune time and deliberately fire the flue. Place a wad of papers in the bottom, when it is raining or just after a rain (so the roof and other inflammable things will be soaked), then pour on some kerosene and light. This same plan has been used to clear furnaces of excessive soot.

Have you outfitted your farm shop? You do not want it so elaborate as the blacksmith shop in town, but if a definite space or place is set aside for repair work, then suitable, high-grade tools added as desired or needed, you will soon be able to save some money on repairs.

Sulphuric acid, or electrolyte, in storage batteries will quickly eat a hole in clothing. Ammonia will neutralize the solution without leaving a stain. By all means, keep a small bottle of ammonia in the shop to help in case of an accident of this kind. Just put ammonia on the spot as soon as the solution gets on.

To prevent soiling plaster or papered walls in the house when repainting the woodwork, get a flat piece of tin twelve inches square and make a slight bend through the middle. One-half should be bent up so when the other half is laid flat against the wall and pushed against the door or window casing, the tin can be held easily. This guard is moved along as the painting progresses and prevents getting any paint on the walls.

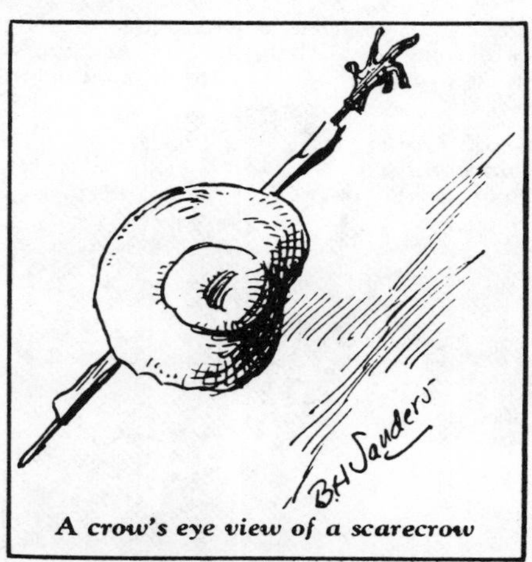

A crow's eye view of a scarecrow

50th Anniversary

Refinishing Your Car

By Berton Elliot

YOU can refinish your car yourself, and be assured of good results, if the following directions and suggestions, as well as directions on the can, are followed closely, and the work carefully done.

First, let it be said, there are two kinds of a job the car owner can do. One is done in about an hour, with a quart of auto enamel or new quick-drying finish, just daubed on without regard to proper methods of application—a "bright and shiny" job that looks good at 100 yards, but does not compare with a custom-shop job at close inspection, and has virtually no wearing qualities. The other is a workmanlike job that would pass anywhere for a paint-shop job. Beauty and permanence of finish will always be in proportion to the amount of care taken in the preparation of the surface and finishing.

Rubbing down the car with powdered pumice and water before applying varnish

The first step is to prepare a suitable place for doing the work. Two things are absolutely essential to good results—a warm room and entire freedom from dust. A satisfactory job simply can not be done in a cold temperature, as the finish will not flow out smoothly and level itself to an even surface when cold. The temperature should be at least 70°. One of the greatest obstacles to be overcome in enamel finishing is the settling of dust into the enamel coat before it has dried dust-free. This is not such an obstacle in the case of new quick-drying finishes, for they harden before dust has much chance to settle. They must be used indoors, though, else they dry too quickly. The place in which the work will be done should be thoroughly cleaned. Dust and cobwebs should be brushed from walls and ceilings. Sweep and sprinkle the floor with water so no dust will be raised.

Choose Clear, Dry Day

The best weather for doing the work is a clear, dry day. Damp, muggy weather causes slow drying, and the moisture is likely to interfere with good results. If there is any wind blowing, windows or doors should not be left open to let dust blow in.

The preparation of the car for refinishing is the first step. It should first be given a thorough washing. Removable parts, such as handles, curtain fasteners, etc., as well as spare tires, should be removed. Any tar or pitch should be removed with turpentine. Grease should be cleaned from hubs, axles, springs and joints with a stiff brush and turpentine. Corners where grease or dirt may have lodged should be scraped out with the point of a knife.

This cleaning up completed, we are ready to go ahead with the preparation of the surface, and application of the finish. Assuming the old finish is in reasonably good condition, not badly cracked and checked, proceed as follows:

Body and Fenders

Remove the hood (for future attention). Scrape off any loose paint. Sandpaper all rust or broken spots thoroughly with No. ½ sandpaper. Sand the entire surface lightly (preferably with finer sandpaper, about No. 00). Dust off loose particles of sand.

Touch up all bare spots with auto enamel of the desired color. For the new quick-drying finishes, there is a special primer that should be used to touch up bare spots. (A small camel's-hair pencil is desirable, although not necessary for this touch-up work.)

While these places are drying, under parts of the car can be done, as follows:

Scrape off loose paint, and sand rust spots. Apply one coat of black auto enamel. This is their only coat. An old brush should be used for this rough work, if one is on hand. Some folks don't care whether the under parts are painted—just keep them greased to prevent rusting.

Fittings, Small Parts and Top

Top-bows, windshield frame, etc., should be given a coat of black auto enamel, or quick-drying finish, this being their only coat.

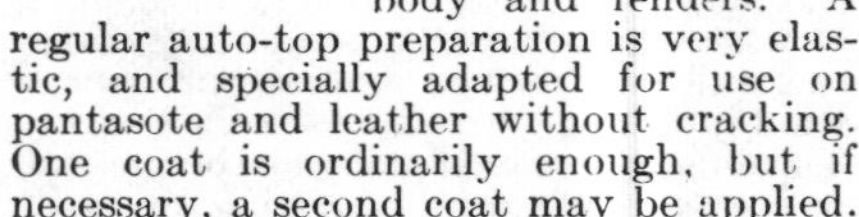

Three-inch fitch brush for body surface

Whether the car is an open or closed one, the top should be refinished with an auto-top dressing—unless the car is one of the closed types with a metal top, in which case it should be refinished the same as body and fenders. A regular auto-top preparation is very elastic, and specially adapted for use on pantasote and leather without cracking. One coat is ordinarily enough, but if necessary, a second coat may be applied.

The Wheels

Jack up the wheels, one at a time, so they will spin. Sand lightly, dust, and apply a coat of auto finish in the desired color.

Use small brush and black finish for door flange

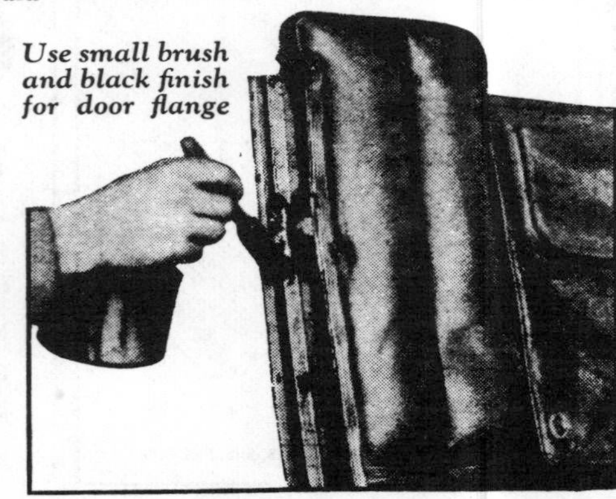

If one coat is not enough for a satisfactory job, sand again when dry, and apply another coat. Two coats of the new quick-drying finishes will be necessary for a first-class job—at least an hour between coats.

Enameling the Body

If there are any touch-up spots, sand them lightly, and dust. Stir the enamel thoroughly.

Start applying the enamel, doing one panel at a time, say one of the doors. Apply with up and down strokes. Then

Remove tires and clean wheels thoroughly before painting

go over the entire surface from left to right, which is called "laying off," and tends to spread the enamel out in a smooth, uniform coat, and cover any places that may be missed in flowing it on. Inspect the job quickly at this time for any "sags," or drips, especially at the hinges and corners. Then go over the entire surface with up and down strokes the entire length of the panel from the extreme bottom clear to the top. Laying off is not needed if a quick-drying finish is used. Let the finish flow from the brush; do no more stroking than is needed, and finish on the up stroke.

The Hood

The hood, having been removed previously, should be washed inside and outside with turpentine. It should then be sanded thoroughly and dusted off. The hood should then be stood on end and finished with the same method as on the body.

In case hood, fenders, radiator frame or lamps are finished in baking japan, and finish is still in good condition, it will be found preferable, after touching up the rusty places with black auto enamel, to go over the entire surface with a coat of clear auto-finishing varnish into which one-sixth the amount of black auto enamel has been added, instead of applying a coat of straight auto enamel.

Rims, Hubs, etc.

A coat of aluminum paint should be applied to the rims, and if desired, the hubs may be finished in black with auto enamel.

The car is now ready for use, as soon as dry, unless you want to apply a final finishing coat of clear varnish, a practise which is much to be recommended, as it increases the wearing capacity of the finish several fold. Do not apply varnish over the new quick-drying finishes.

Finishing Coat of Clear Varnish

If the car is to be given a coat of clear varnish, allow the enamel coat to dry for at least 48 hours. Then sand the entire surface lightly with fine sandpaper (No. 0000 or No. 00) preferably dipped in a mixture of half linseed-oil and half gasoline.

After sanding, all particles of sand should be thoroughly removed, which is most satisfactorily accomplished with what is termed a "tack-rag"—a piece of cheese-cloth dipped in varnish and wrung out as dry as [*Continued on page 89*

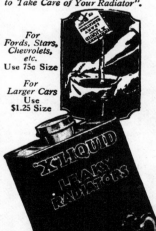

The Jolly Testator and His Will

By M. L. Hayward

IT is an old story, but a good one. A prominent lawyer at a legal banquet had been asked to propose a toast to "the lawyer's best friend," and immediately named "the jolly testator who makes his own will." The idea is, of course, that a lawyer might charge $25 for writing a will, but if the testator writes it himself it invariably leads to a law-suit—in which case the lawyers get the whole estate.

The underlying legal requirement in reference to a will is, generally speaking, that it be signed by the testator in the presence of witnesses, generally two; otherwise the will is void. Some state legislatures have stepped in, however, and provide that a holographic will is valid

Rich dog: "Lost a penny?"
Poor dog: "No, sir; I lost a scent"

without being witnessed; that is, a will "that is entirely written, dated, and signed by the hand of the testator himself."

It was, of course, not in the minds of the legislators when passing these laws, but they, too, have proved that they are also friends of the legal profession. This statement is borne out by the case of Clarence C. Beird, a decision of the Louisiana Supreme Court reported in 82 Southern Reporter, 881.

Question About Date

In this case, Clarence C. Beird died leaving the following instrument as his last will and testament, to wit:

"9/8/18.
"Should anything happen to me I want Mrs. C. A. Mains to have all my goods and money.
"C. C. Beird."

After signing this document, Clarence C. Beird "departed this life," and Mrs. C. A. Mains presented the document for probate to the Louisiana courts.

"It's not a valid will," the disinherited heirs argued.

"But the Louisiana law says that, 'in order to be valid, it must be entirely written, dated and signed by the hand of the testator. It is subject to no other form, and may be made anywhere, even out of the state,' and this document complies with all these requirements," Mrs. Mains contended.

"No, it's not 'entirely dated' by the deceased."

"Why not?"

"Because '9/8/18' is not an entire date," the heirs retorted, and the Supreme Court of Louisiana, in the case referred to decided that they were right.

"While it is true the custom prevails," said the Court, "and is in daily use of dating letters by the use of figures alone to represent the day, month and year, at the same time there is almost as much variance in the order in which the month and day are written as there is in the use of words and figures. Some write the month first and the day of the month next, while others write the day first and the month second, and in a case like the present, where both the figures intended to represent the day and the month are less than 13, under this well-recognized variance, it is impossible to tell whether the deceased intended to write September 8, or August 9."

Similar Law in California

The California legislature has passed a law in practically the same words, and in the California case reported in 156 Pacific Reporter, 464, the courts were called on to deal with a holographic will dated "10/1912," and the Supreme Court of California held that this did not comply with the law, as it was impossible to say whether "10" referred to the month of October or the tenth day of some other month.

"The general rule that the provisions of the law 'are to be liberally construed with a view to effect its object,' has never been stretched to excuse lack of substantial compliance with the statutory requirements that a holographic will must be dated by the testator," said the Court in handing down his opinion.

In another California case, however, the courts upheld a will dated "Nov. 22/97," and in another case the same courts upheld a will dated "4/12/17th," so that if Clarence C. Beird's will had been written in California and construed by the courts of that state, Mrs. C. A. Mains would have "all my goods and money."

A Job for a Good Lawyer

The obvious moral is that, notwithstanding the good intent of the state legislatures, it is still a safe rule to have a will drawn up by a practising lawyer. "in good and regular standing." Even then, the testator has no guarantee that there will be no legal battle over the disposition of his estate, which calls for a final story, equally old and good.

An honest-to-goodness but eccentric millionaire had employed a young lawyer to draw a will, leaving all the testator's property to his attractive and unmarried daughter.

"Now, you're sure that that will's perfectly valid, and that there's absolutely no danger of a flock of hungry lawyers devouring the estate in court?" the millionaire demanded.

"Absolutely sure," the young attorney assured him.

"And you'll guarantee that my girl'll get everything?"

"Certainly," was the positive reply.

"Well, I'll have to take your word for it," the millionaire demurred; "but, just to make me feel easier in my own mind, would you mind marrying the girl?"

ℭ ℭ

"Renting Farms in Virginia" is a new bulletin for Virginia folks. Tells what the prevailing custom is in the various Virginia counties. To get this bulletin free, write Virginia Experiment Station, Blacksburg, Va. Ask for Bulletin 249.

What a world!

50 Years of Home Building

Continued from page 39

it compares favorably with the city house in comfort, convenience and completeness. The appearance is not always good, but the outlook is hopeful.

The house already referred to, shown at bottom of page 39, is a good example of architecture 50 years ago. "This design in domestic Gothic style possesses considerable power, and is a decided change from the ordinary. As many admire this style, which is a new expression of taste, we present this design as a fair sample, though not an extreme in the style. It possesses a spreading

A "modern home" shown in The Farm Journal, April, 1901. A step nearer the simpler types of homes of today

effect, and if properly built, with harmonious surroundings, will be quite attractive. It possesses all the requirements of a refined family, finished in the Eastlake manner, now much admired, as it corresponds with the present styles of furniture. It will require a lot of at least 75 feet front and can be built at this time for $5,500."

That brief description appearing in The Farm Journal, May, 1878, enables us to understand the taste and need of people at that time. An examination of the plan shows a large hall, which is wasteful. The rooms are large and heated by grates. The stairs are steep and the winding treads are undesirable in modern home construction. The exterior gives us a real thrill or shock. The lack of permanence and the decorative effect bruise our feeling for mass and line.

Another house of the seventies is shown at top of page. The floor plan is triangular in shape—the house runs to a point at the back.

Most Popular Small House

America's most popular small house today, originally designed by J. F. Yewell, is shown, built of brick. It has a very pleasing exterior, showing the modern tendency in mass, proportion and line, yet simple and refined.

In plan this house is simple. The living-room is large and well-planned about the fireplace. Three nice bedrooms with cross circulation and convenient bath are placed on second floor. This house shows study and taste, making it desirable as a home for almost any section.

In conclusion, it is readily seen that the modern tendency is toward a refinement—a carefully studied plan and a better exterior. Planting has much to do with the final appearance. A careful choice of materials—greater permanence and lower fire risk—enters into most homes built today. Then there is a more pronounced need to build out both heat and cold, which results in saving on fuel. Close-fitted doors and windows, insulated walls and roof are contributions to this conservation.

It would be difficult to mark the changes in the short intervals of five years, but in a ten-year period the change is quite pronounced. The house, and the farmhouse in particular, has undergone great changes. To the present generation these changes have been for the better, although some few of the fleeting past still cling to the old-time parlor, the kerosene lamp and open grate.

Nuts To Crack

By Sam Loyd

The Mathematical Cop

IN the late nineties there was a policeman who patrolled New York's famous Park Row, and who was known to the newspapermen as "the mathematical cop." He was a wizard at figures, and challenged anybody to bring a problem in arithmetic that he couldn't solve. As an example of his quick wit and aptness at figuring, the following story was told about him:

"What time of the morning is it?" asked a roundsman who caught Clancy (that was his real name) arriving a few minutes late on his beat.

Clancy, realizing he was in a pickle, did some quick thinking. He pointed toward the City Hall clock, which the nearsighted roundsman couldn't see distinctly, and then startled his questioner with the following speech:

"Just add one-quarter of the time from midnight until now, to half the time from now until midnight, and you will have the correct time."

"Just so," assented the roundsman, who didn't grasp what Clancy was talking about, and he marched away to save his own confusion.

Now, if Clancy's statement was perfectly truthful, who can figure out what time it was when Clancy "put one over" on the roundsman?

He Warred Twice for Uncle Sam

In their given order write down words to fit the following definitions: Stamp-collecting; organ of speech; a land preserve; to gain as a just recompense; very small.

Now if the line is composed of the correct words, words to fit the following definitions can be struck out: Not long ago; equality; a white metal.

The letters that remain, in their regular order, will spell the name of a United States general who served in the Mexican and Civil Wars.

A Charade

Protect my first, wee, helpless elf,
It asks your tender care;
My second graced your grandma's head
At market, church or fair;
My whole, a retrospective glance,
Appears a summer's morn,
A fading dream of fairy joys,
Gone, never to return.
What is the word?

Concealed Geography

Find in each of the following sentences the name of a place in the state of Pennsylvania:

It is human nature to amble round an unpleasant subject.

Do not let your avocation divert your interest from your vocation.

If you wish to be a very decided success, start the drive now.

When in London or Athens it is well to adopt native manners.

She gave Caleb an onion for dessert and thus lost a boarder

ANSWERS TO FEBRUARY PUZZLES

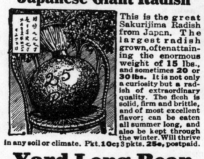

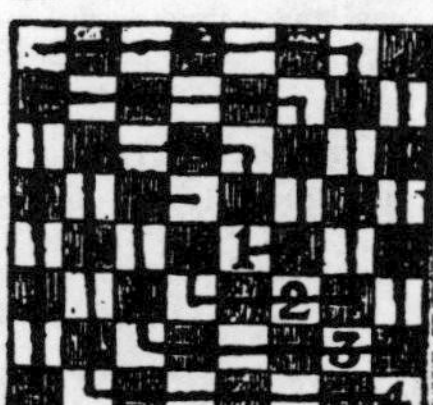

Mental Carpentry: In the accompanying diagram the four separate lines indicate the four similar pieces of which the checkerboard is composed.

Fractional fruit: Four cents would buy nine pears.

The morning star: Words set down: Lucid, roll, ferret, ire. Words struck out: Droll, retire. Remaining word: LUCIFER.

Rejected missives: Mary might have distributed the four valentines in 24 different ways, and of these, 15 would have given at least one of the boys back his own valentine; so the chances were nine for and 15 against such an event's happening as was described.

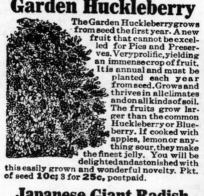

Making Every Edge Cut

By W. C. Smith

I HAPPENED to be over at neighbor Halstead's when a big car stopped and the driver inquired the price of fallen apples. The ground in Halstead's orchard was covered with fruit, principally because he had been too busy to spray and thin his fruit.

"Help yourself," said Halstead. "Don't know as I will have time to do anything with them. Couldn't sell them, anyway. Everybody has apples this year. Take what you want, just so you don't damage anything."

After the machine had left, well-laden with apples, I asked Halstead if there was not some way those apples could be marketed. It looked like a shame to lose those windfalls.

"It is a shame," he answered. "The trouble with apples in this country is that when I have apples every one has. You can hardly give them away."

"Don't give any away until I see you again," I said, and he laughed.

"Don't worry," he told me, "I never was lucky."

On my way home I stopped at Harrison Taylor's.

"Harrison," I said, "you have a lot of windfalls, I have some, Halstead has—every one with an orchard in the neighborhood has. Those apples are of some value if we could market them. What is your idea?"

Taylor has managed to pay for a good 80 largely by using his head for something besides a hat-rack.

"Cider, apple-butter, vinegar——"

"When do we start?" I interrupted.

Taylor grinned. "I never lost anything by trying," he said. "How about starting now?"

The Good Wives Helped

That is how Taylor and I and our good wives happened to turn a potential neighborhood loss into more than a $300 profit for ourselves and a gain to every one in the community. We got the proper permit, which is necessary in these near-Volstead days in our state, for making cider and vinegar. We ran a classified ad in the county-seat daily and found folks really hungry for old-fashioned apple-butter. We had three real orders for apple jelly—"the kind mother used to make"—and it was surprising to us to sell several baskets of sorted windfalls. We explained that those apples were just as good as any for immediate consumption. They had been sorted and graded. They did not bring so much as picked fruit, but they sold at the door and there was a profit.

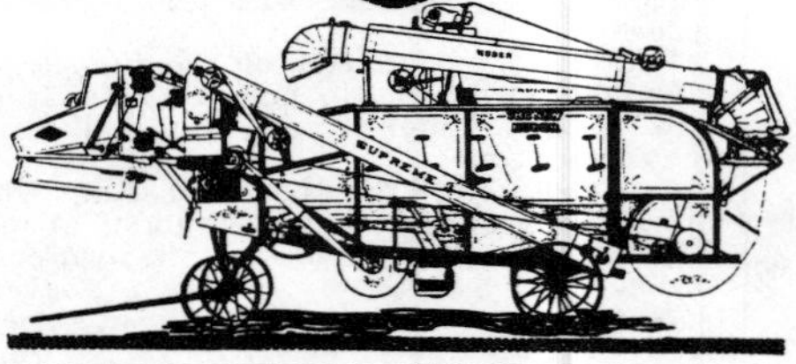

Details are tedious and unnecessary. This apple transaction is cited merely as an illustration, and is typical of many other examples of turning by-products into profit. It has been said that the big packing plants turn everything but the pig's squeal into a money return, and since my rather hectic experience with radio I am not sure they do not have some secret understanding with the broadcasters or others.

It is as necessary to eliminate waste on the farm as it is in Henry Ford's shops. We hear a lot about business farming, and a lot of good people confuse business with bookkeeping. Bookkeeping is necessary, but five years in the retail business taught me that no amount of bookkeeping would pay the bills. Goods must be turned. Turnover is slow, slow, slow on the farm, so everything that can be sold without depleting the stock must be turned. Furthermore, we often fail to get a fair price, with no one to blame for it but ourselves.

Berries were more plentiful in our neighborhood last season than they have ever been since we have lived in it. We started the season with strawberries at 20 cents a quart, $4 a crate of 24 boxes. Several others asked the same price and got it, but other neighbors dropped to 15 cents a box, and still others to 12½ cents, with crates going for $2 or $2.25. We talked the matter over, my wife and I, and decided to market only select berries—and most of ours were really select—and to get the price which we thought they were worth.

Not Much Surplus

"It will work no hardship on any one to pay what these berries are worth," my wife reasoned, "and we can always can or preserve any surplus."

The result was that we barely had enough berries for our own use. Folks wondered how we could sell at a higher price than our neighbors. They came and saw and bought. Most of our neighbors simply lost a good profit because they would not take it. No reason to kick there—except perhaps to kick themselves.

In our township, Mrs. Joe Neal marketed her by-products in cans and made more than $100 from a surplus in the home garden. That is business. My grandfather used to dwell on the necessity of "making every edge cut." That is simply another way of expressing the need of taking care of the by-products and getting the proper turnover. To be downright plain, we need to work the soil less and the public more—in the proper manner, of course.

Make This Drag

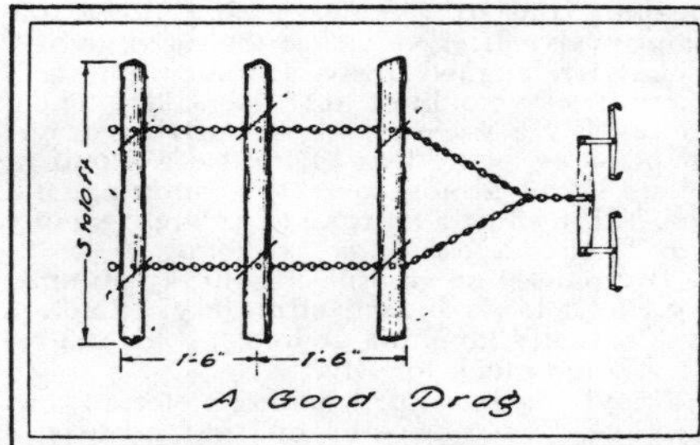

This drag works better than any I have ever seen. Take three round poles or scantlings, eight or ten feet long and four or five inches in diameter. Bore two 1¼-inch holes through each pole, about 14 or 16 inches from each end. Now string these poles on trace chains so that the poles will be about 18 inches from each other.

The three poles can be fastened to the chains by driving a spike through each and through a link of the chain. Now connect the free ends of the chains to a doubletree or large singletree with small singletrees, as shown in diagram. You now have your drag ready for service. On cloddy land each pole will give the clods a smash, and by that time the clods are well crushed and the ground is smooth and in good shape.

If a one-horse drag is wanted, simply cut your poles shorter and smaller—say about six feet long, and use a singletree instead of a doubletree. I have used the above drag to break down cotton and corn-stalks, and large weeds. It does fine work, too. *G. T.*

50th Anniversary

The Sugarland Contract

Continued from page 14

finished more quietly, "because I surely do."

"It's your puzzle," said Gandy; "I'm no good on such things."

"It's got me going," admitted Bly; "it's sure got me going."

AT dawn they started a fire and went back to the house for breakfast. "It'll be safe enough," said Gandy.

"Yes," agreed Bly. "They won't try that trick twice; besides, they couldn't get up steam enough to hurt anything before we get back."

They found Kelso choring about the barn when they arrived. He received the news they had to impart with a set countenance. Bly did not mention his trouble with Petrie.

"It must have been LaFave," said Kelso; "he would do such a thing. He's as ornery as they make 'em. Just got out of the pen last year; he'll be back before another."

Breakfast was late, and Chris grumbled. "Where did Anna run off to?" he asked. "Looks like she'd know enough to stay around and help you in a time like this."

"She had to go, Chris," Mrs. Kelso replied.

"Had to!" snorted her husband. "She always has to go. Where did she go?"

"She had a telephone call from over where her aunt lived," explained Mrs. Kelso, patiently. "She'll be back sometime today."

Bly wondered at the manner with which she referred to Anna's aunt.

"Isn't your wife a sister to my stepmother?" he asked.

"No," replied Kelso. "I've been married twice. My first wife was a half-sister to her. Anna's father was a half-brother. They've both been dead several years. Sort of mixed-up relationship."

"I see," said Bly, and went off to the rig, thinking.

THEY were threshing wheat shortly after sun-up. An ugly, gray morning it was, close and oppressive. So thick was the atmosphere that they could scarcely see the smoke from Petrie's rig, less than a half-mile away.

"We'll git it today," predicted Gandy; "see if we don't."

"It won't hurt us any more than it will Petrie," said Bly. "Sol, you keep them donkeys moving today. We'll need lots of water. And stay away from Petrie's rig." He eyed the water-hauler suspiciously.

Sol was in an unusually jovial humor. He saluted smartly and said, "All right, cap'n!"

Gandy watched him drive off. "Believe that old scalawag has been drinkin'," he said. "Don't you?"

"There's something wrong with him," agreed Bly. "He's altogether too lively."

"Have to watch him," said Gandy. "Wish we'd fired him long ago and got a reliable hauler."

Although Bly agreed with him, he said nothing. As the sun climbed higher the heat increased. The atmosphere took on a peculiarly yellow tint; an ugly color. Sol had not got back with the first tank at nine o'clock and barely an inch showed in the water glass when Gandy came around for a drink and to wash the dust from his eyes and nose.

"Hain't Sol got back yet?" he asked, staring at the water gauge.

Bly shook his head. "Can't run much longer," he said. "Head of steam she's carrying and the rate she's putting it out, we'll crack a crown sheet if the level gets much lower."

Gandy leaped down from the engine. "Where does he get the water?" he asked.

"Below the bridge, just above Petrie's rig. Only place he can get down to the river on this side."

"I'll go see what's wrong," said Gandy, swinging astride a saddle-horse that was tied to the fence nearby. He leaned forward and yelled into the drowsy animal's ear. The horse reared and shot off on the path down to the river.

A half-hour passed, and Gandy did not come. Bly shook his head, surveying the tree-fringed river. A single cloud had pushed a sharp nose above the trees. No water showed in the glass at all, and the engine was steaming with very little fire. Bly knew that if the water got too low in the boiler, and the fuse plug did not blow out, he would either crack a crown sheet or else what water remained in the boiler would be suddenly converted into steam and burst the boiler. The steam gauge stood at 175. The safety valve seemed unable to take care of the excess steam, so rapidly was it being formed.

He got out the jacks and was jacking up the front end, to keep the crown sheet covered, when he sighted a horseman coming up the river at a smart trot. It appeared to be the horse that Gandy had ridden away, but as the animal approached Bly saw that it was not Gandy, but Pip LaFave, who bestrode him.

MARCH

NEST STY HIVE COTE COOP KENNEL HUTCH

An old home week

LAFAVE rode up on the belt side and stopped a few feet in front of the engine, between the engine and the separator. Bly noticed that the cloud that he had noticed but a few minutes before was leaping into the sky at an astonishing rate, turning the day into dusk.

"Hello," said LaFave cordially, stopping the horse three or four rods ahead of the fly-wheel and resting his weight on his thigh thrown across the saddle. "Here's a horse I found runnin' loose down by our rig. Thought mebby he belonged up here."

"He does," said Bly, shortly, eying him.

"Gittin' short of water, ain't you?" said LaFave, grinning insolently.

"We'll make out," Bly told him, and tried a shot at random. "Don't mind running low on water half as much as some skunk opening the drafts and wiring down the safety valve after we've left the rig at night."

LaFave laughed freely. "That would be a dirty trick, wouldn't it?" he said. Then, giving Bly a wicked look out of the corners of his eyes, he added: "Didn't see a pair of pliers layin' around here this morning, did you? I'm short a pair, and I thought mebby you might have run across them."

Bly paused stock still, absolutely stunned by the fellow's brazen effrontery. LaFave was actually laughing at him, up his sleeve. It was too much for Bly.

"Say!" he exclaimed, taking a step toward LaFave, "you just step off that horse and I'll do my best to repay you for that little job! Step off or I'll take you off."

LAFAVE laughed sneeringly; the horse stepped closer to the belt, almost touching it.

"Looks to me," said LaFave, "like your services are needed worse down the river. Last time I saw that long-legged partner of yours he was goin' down the river tangled up with a team of drownin' mules in about 90 feet of water."

Instinctively Bly knew that he was not lying; the picture sickened him. Then blind rage gripped him. He knew that LaFave was in some way responsible for whatever had happened to Gandy and Sol. He took a menacing step toward LaFave just as the approaching cloud obscured the sun, bringing with it an erratic blast of wind. Bly did not know exactly what he meant to do, but whatever he had in mind was never acted upon.

That gust of wind caught the pitchers unaware and tossed bundles this way and that. One of these stray bundles struck the lower section of the belt, speeding toward the engine, and stuck there for an instant. The bundle was snatched instantly toward the engine, caroming off just back of LaFave's horse, striking the animal on the hindquarters. The animal snorted, gave a convulsive leap, and LaFave was catapulted from the saddle, alighting squarely on the belt at almost the exact spot the bundle had occupied but a split second before.

BLY was not a yard from the fly-wheel when this happened. He shut his eyes in horror at the sight, and opened them just as LaFave's form shot between the belt and the fly-wheel. LaFave's body struck the ground just as the storm struck with insensate fury—like the blast from some gigantic cannon. Wheat shocks flew like feathers and thunder crashed like siege-guns. The force of the wind flattened Bly against the boiler. As he struggled into the cab to shut off the engine the gale was creating a gigantic pipe out of the smoke-stack. Bly closed the throttle, slammed down the drafts and leaped for the horse, now humped with its back to the driving gale, and went scudding riverward, blown before the storm like an autum leaf.

Concluded in April

Refinishing Your Car

Continued from page 81

possible, then shaken until it commences to become sticky or "tacky." Then rub the entire surface with pumice stone and water, using a sponge dipped first into the water then into the pumice stone, rubbing lightly and using lots of water. Wash thoroughly with clear water and dry thoroughly.

Apply one coat of clear auto varnish, following the same procedure as in applying the auto enamel previously described—flowing on the varnish with up and down strokes, laying it off with cross strokes and straightening it out with strokes from the extreme bottom to the top. Varnish should preferably be strained before using.

If Car Is Badly Checked

In case the finish is badly checked and cracked, such surfaces should first be given a coat of auto-enamel primer, sanded and dusted. (For the quick-drying finishes, use a special metal primer or undercoating.) Proceed with auto-enamel coat, and clear varnish coat, if desired, as previously described.

The inside of car can also be brightened up by giving all wooden surfaces a coat of spar varnish. The surface should be sanded lightly before applying the varnish. If in very bad condition, two coats of varnish may be necessary.

A Word About Brushes

A word or two should be said about brushes. Good brushes and the right kind of brushes are necessary for good results. It is practically impossible to avoid showing brush marks with a worn-out or stiff, hard brush.

Two brushes should be used—a two-and-one-half- or three-inch varnish-brush for the body, and all large surfaces, and a one-inch varnish-brush for all small surfaces. It is also desirable to have a small camel's-hair pencil for small touch-up spots and fine work.

New brushes should be brushed out a few times on an old board to work out any loose hairs before starting. When through with the job the brushes should be cleaned thoroughly with turpentine, and washed with soap and water, then put away in a dust-tight bag.

It is essential that a clean brush—one that has no old paint in it—be used for the quick-drying finishes. If there's any doubt, get a new brush.

The dog: "You've heard of a crocus? Well, that's the kind of a crow I think you are"

Alfalfa on Hillsides

Continued from page 24

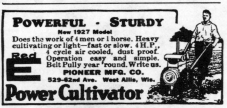

Most of these clay layers on such slopes are in reality marls, some of which have as high as 20 per cent or 30 per cent lime materials. The old idea was that the large supply of lime had leached out of the rocks, but now it is recognized that the marls are a good source of supply. The rocks have to a large extent been removed and used to fill gullies, left in piles, or sold to the road-builders.

For the most part, the crop preceding alfalfa is corn or tobacco, and in many

Left, alfalfa sowed alone. Center, sowed on rye, and rye removed

instances the land has lain bare through the winter. The ground is prepared for oats, the oats seeded, and alfalfa broadcast afterward, using from ten to as high as 25 pounds per acre. The tendency is toward less seed. Sometimes it is covered with a brush drag or other light working of the ground, but often there is no covering. Failures are rare.

Soil Already Inoculated

Few men inoculate alfalfa in these hills, yet there seems to be an abundance of bacteria in the soil. They have learned that alfalfa is much more likely to make a stand than red clover on the same land, and their methods of seeding make it cheaper to seed alfalfa.

Since erosion is a constant danger, the more careful growers sow some other grass or clover in low places where gullies are apt to start. For this purpose, alsike clover, orchard grass, Kentucky bluegrass and timothy are most often used.

This brings to light another erroneous old notion these men have discarded. The fear that blue-grass will run out the alfalfa is constantly present among inexperienced alfalfa-growers in other sections. These hillside growers, on the other hand, welcome the grass. They know of no cheaper way of establishing a blue-grass pasture than to have it grow up in the alfalfa.

More than 1,000,000 acres of lime-rich fields are in cultivation in these 20 counties. All are potential alfalfa-fields. There is also a large area of ridge land in cultivation. In recent years the ease of handling hay on more level land, together with a desire to grow it near the barn, has started the use of pulverized limestone. Thousands of tons of such lime are being applied annually, followed by alfalfa.

Not less than 30,000 acres were sowed last spring. Campbell, Grant and Pendleton counties already have over 10,000 acres of alfalfa each, and are sowing more.

Last spring we moved a grain-binder for 27 miles over a rough country road. To do this without jarring all the nuts off the machine, we took two old 30 x 3½ automobile tires and put them on the truck wheels of the binder. They went on a little hard, but once on didn't come off. *J. D.*

Got a Spring? Try Raising Trout

By F. L. Clark

IN the Gay's Mills neighborhood, Crawford county, Wis., lives Robert Collins. On his farm there is a spring which has been turned into a small trout hatchery. Collins has found this a most profitable side-line to Duroc-Jersey hogs and White Leghorn chickens. The spring-water, as it flows in the creek and into tanks, is used for the farm stock, and there is also running spring-water in the house. So the trout are just so much extra.

"Trout Fries"

In one week last summer the Collinses sold as high as $100 worth of trout. The fish are marketed in two ways. They are shipped dressed and packed in small wooden boxes. Besides, Mrs. Collins, who is a good cook and a master hand at preparing trout for the table, has a little business of her own, serving "trout fries."

A couple of picnic tables have been put out under the pines on the front lawn of the home. Here every once in a while through the summer, parties come and enjoy fried-trout dinners.

By securing a license number from the state, a farmer can obtain the right to hatch trout artificially and to sell and ship those he raises just as he sells chickens, hogs and other products of the farm.

A Stream Back of the House

Back of the farm home at Pinehurst, as their farm is called, a large spring pours out cold and clear in a deep, shaded ravine. By building a series of three small dams in the creek just below the spring, four ponds ten or fifteen feet in diameter have been made. A spring-house is built directly over the spring. The two ponds just below are open, but a quantity of planted moss grows in them and floats on the surface, providing shade and a hiding place for the wary little creatures. Over a portion of the fourth pond is the little frame hatchery provided with tanks.

Collins, in starting the trout business, hired an expert to come to the farm to teach him how to strip the females and milk the males for artificial hatching and how to care for the spawn after they are hatched. The inch- and inch-and-a-half-long fish are kept in tanks in the hatchery. The year-old ones are kept in one of the open ponds, the two-year-olds in the other. In the spring-house are the big ones, weighing up to three and three and a half pounds. These are seined out with a small hand seine for shipment and for the trout fries. In preparing them for market they are fed hamburger, milk curd and noodles cooked with meat three times a week. The yearlings and two-year-olds are fed liver.

ℭ ℭ

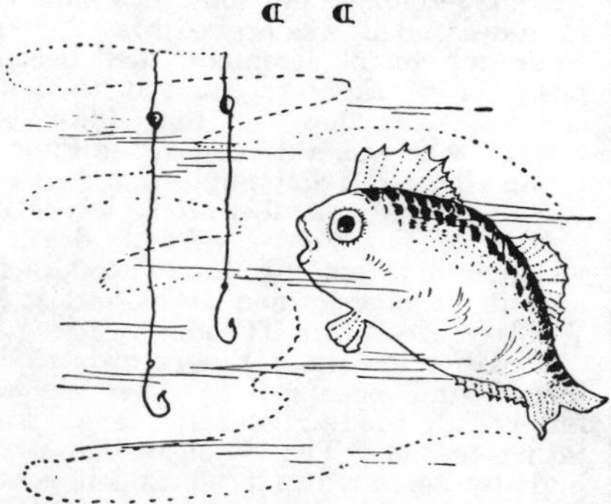

Hungry fish: "Say, I want the third course! Ate up the first two courses an hour ago!"

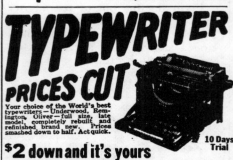

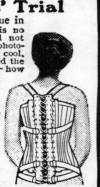

New House Around Old One

By J. L. Graff

YOU have heard that old saw about the man who built a new house out of his old one and let the old one stand until the new one was finished. John Madsen, Cook county, Ill., comes close to matching the story. His new house, shown in the photo, was built around and over the old one, and the family lived in the old one all the time. You can not see a sign of the old house, built 60 years ago, for it was torn out piece by piece as the new one was finished.

Plenty of porches on the new house.

Another Handed-Down Farm

I am sending a picture of the house on the Woolsey homestead, on the north side of the stone road leading from Pennington to Washington Crossing, N. J.—the place where Washington crossed the Delaware River with his army during the Revolutionary War.

George Woolsey came from Jamaica, L. I., in the year 1700 and settled on this farm. George Woolsey, his grandfather, came to this country in 1635, and his son, known as Captain George, was the father of one of the original settlers whose will was proved March 11, 1762; and the will of Jeremiah, his son, to whom the farm descended, was proved May 2, 1801. Ephraim, son of Jeremiah, then became possessor of the farm, and it then descended from him to the eldest son George, who was a deacon in the Presbyterian Church at Pennington, and served three years as a member of the legislative council of New Jersey. At his death it was heired to his only son, Theodore F., and it is now owned by Charles M. Woolsey, the son of Theodore.

Thus for 226 years this farm has been owned and occupied by the Woolsey family, descending in all cases from father to son. The Woolsey house was built by Jeremiah in 1765, and it is still in a good state of preservation. We are now the sixth generation in this house and the eighth that has lived on this farm. *Chas. M. Woolsey*

Raises Fishworms for Market

By Y. P. Bhosale

FEW people would think that earthworms, valuable as they are to our soil, could be grown as a cash crop. But those who think not must change their minds. William Paggi, who owns a fishworm farm near Lake Austin, Tex., has proved that they net a good income. William raises earthworms, sells them for $1.50 a quart, and is still unable to meet the demands.

At first, William produced earthworms in the flower-beds around his house in spare time, but he found the business so profitable that he intends to produce them on a large scale and devote his entire time to their production. In 1924, when he first started to raise earthworms, his net profit was $150.

William has a local market and ships to nearby places as well, both retail and wholesale. Whenever a customer calls to buy some worms, William goes out in the garden and digs fresh worms for him.

Worms are fed milk, leaves and water from cooked rice. They also get food around the roots of chrysanthemums and balsams where they live. When worms are dug, the whole plant is dug out. The overhead expense lies chiefly in the amount of rice water that is necessary to soak the plant-beds every day.

Whenever an order comes in, the big worms are sold first. The small ones are kept for sale when larger, and for restocking. Sometimes it is necessary for William to restock his beds, and he transplants worms from somewhere else.

Wet weather is an enemy of this business, but when drought comes, or there are few late-summer showers, he is able to sell all that he can possibly raise. He gets a large number of orders from distant places. He ships worms in cartons that contain moist dirt covered with leaves. These leaves supply food to the worms and help to keep them alive.

Sayings of Uncle Levi Zink

They say we'll have cobless corn in the near future. Fine! my old pipe will fetch a fancy price as a curio! Myrtie Hack gets her good looks from her father—who is Briarville's leading druggist

How Strong Is an Egg?

ONE of the best attractions at the New York State Fair at Syracuse last fall was a device which showed, without the aid of a lecturer, that thick-shelled eggs are best, and that they can be produced by breeding and feeding. The photo of this device was kindly sent to The Farm Journal by Bristow Adams, Cornell University, Ithaca, N. Y.

Crowds that viewed the exhibit at the fair openly avowed that "it isn't a real egg," and so general became this comment that the exhibitors (the Poultry Department at Cornell) had to print an extra sign: "This is a real egg, laid by a hen; it is not hard-boiled."

Out of the many people who stood in front of the device, some, at least, got the educational message that strong, thick-shelled eggs will ship best and evaporate least, and that egg-shell strength can be modified by the poultryman if he will feed shell-forming foods (grit, bonemeal, oyster-shell, cod-liver oil) and if he will breed from birds that habitually lay eggs which will stand a 16-pound weight.

As if 16 pounds were not enough, some of the eggs put to the test by this device did not break when a weight of 23 pounds was applied. Perhaps they might not have succumbed to an even heavier weight, but the scales used would not register more than 23 pounds. In several trials, strong-shelled eggs withstood a pressure of 50 pounds. Thin-shelled eggs, on the other hand, broke at from two to three pounds pressure, and this means loss to the poultryman in handling and shipping the eggs.

Scales Told the Weight

The device to show the strength of egg-shells is a simple one, as indicated in the illustration. The hammer is not an essential; any weight would do. But it had the value of being a familiar object, known to be heavy. It gave no sudden impact, but when it pressed on the egg, the scales told the weight of that pressure, going up and down throughout the day. The wheels under the table on which the test was made had no relation to the test itself. They are merely a set of gears to reduce the speed from the electric motor which furnished the power for raising the head of the hammer, with its handle as a lever.

It was a good exhibit because it moved, and because it exemplified the motto that "Knowledge begins with wonder."

So much for the device. As to the economic waste from soft-shelled eggs, government reports show that over 13,000,000 dozen eggs, most of them laid in the spring, spoil in cold storage simply because their shells have been thin, or have been cracked slightly, while en route between the hen and the cold-storage room.

Once an egg is cracked, even so slightly that the eye can not see it, germs and molds find ready entrance and spoil its contents. Nature has provided the egg with a delicate protective, gelatinous coating, which, as long as it is intact, tends to keep out air and germs. Once this coating is pierced, the keeping quality of the egg is lessened immediately.

In eggs of first quality, the shell must be strong and sound (free from cracks or checks). Strength and soundness are necessary to insure good shipping and good keeping quality. The shell of the egg is about one-sixtieth of an inch thick, in normal, strong-shelled eggs.

An egg-shell is chiefly composed of carbonate of lime, phosphate of lime and a little animal matter.

It is estimated that a hen laying 100 eggs in a year produces in that time 24 ounces of carbonate of lime, which it secures from such materials as shells, dust, stones and pieces of bone it picks up while on range. When hens are confined, oyster-shell, gypsum, grit, etc., must be given to supply the deficiency.

It should be the rule never to ship thin-shelled or cracked eggs to market. Thin-shelled eggs, by the time they reach market, are usually in the class of cracked eggs or "checks." They should never be permitted to enter the regular channels of trade, but should be used at home instead.

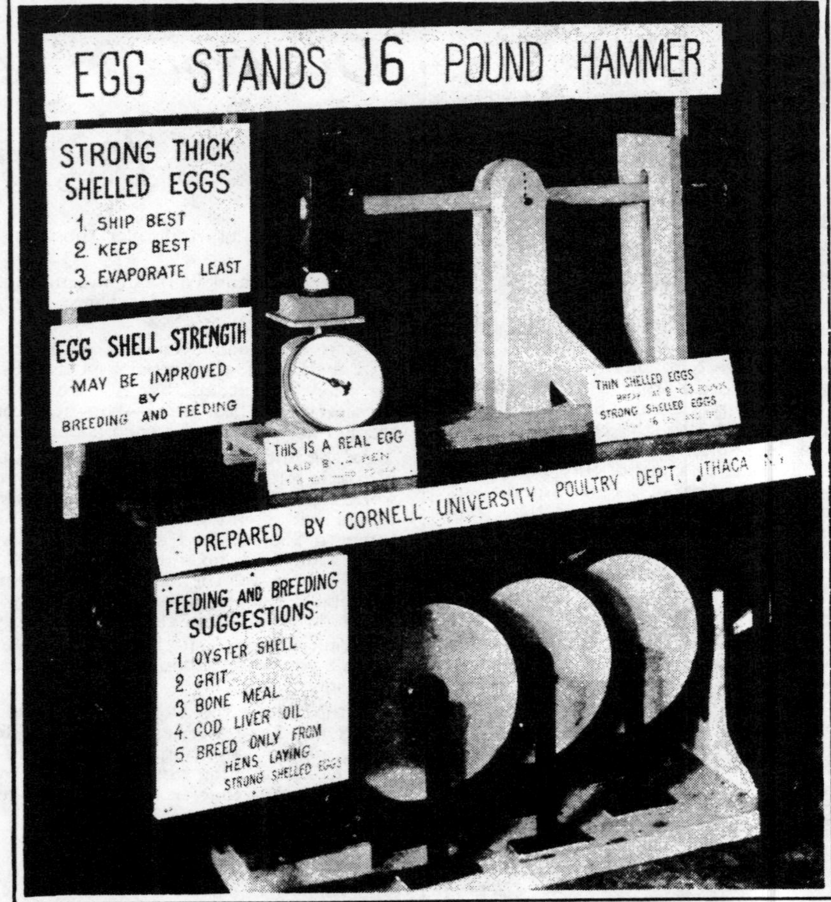

The exhibit at New York State Fair showed, without a lecturer, that thick-shelled eggs are best, and that they can be produced by breeding and feeding

Roup and colds in poultry are common ailments during the winter-time on many farms. Much of this trouble can often be avoided. When roosts are on a slant the birds always try to get on the top two or three roosts. The lower roosts will often be entirely vacant. This tends to crowd the birds together so that they become very warm during the night. In the morning as the birds get down on the floor their bodies cool off very rapidly. Colds and roup are much more common in houses where the birds are crowded together on the roost. Level roosts will help in avoiding this trouble. The roosts should be four feet above the floor for the heavy breeds, and four and one-half feet from the floor for the light breeds.

Just Look!

Hundreds of Dollars Profit from Small Investment

—GIVES CHICKS VIOLET RAYS

BELANT FARM
Independence, Mo.

VIO-RAY CO.

We like your products fine. Used Vio-Ray in one of our semi-monitor houses, 24 x 75, where we have been having trouble for several years because of dampness. After taking out the glass and using your Vio-Ray have had no trouble.

Don't know why any one would fill the front of a chicken house with glass now that Vio-Ray is out and is cheaper and better.

Belant Farm,
F. F. Bellew.

Save your Baby Chicks
Speed Plant Growth
Make Hens Lay.

YOUR BABY CHICKS MUST HAVE VIOLET RAYS (VITAMIN D)—OR THEY PERISH

VIO-RAY GLASS

ASSURES CHICK SUCCESS

PREVENTS DEATHS—LEG WEAKNESS

These are actual money making facts! Each day thousands more are proving how easy these profits are made, simply aiding nature by supplying actual SUNSHINE (violet rays or vitamin D energy), which is scientifically transmitted through VIO-RAY GLASS (plain glass stops violet rays). VIO-RAY GLASS is cheap and easy to put up. You will hardly lose a single chick. You prevent sickness, leg weakness (rickets) and deaths. Chicks grow faster, stronger and weigh more. (College tests prove 37% increased weight.) Think! what that alone means. Earlier and higher markets with more weight. Hens lay more eggs. Keeps them safe and warm. Provides extra scratching space. You do not risk a cent to try VIO-RAY GLASS. Our guaranteed trial offer is made to convince and show you this easy way to profits and success. If for any reason you may doubt these wonderful results we will gladly send further proof and free samples upon request.

CHICKS THRIVE—GROW FASTER—HENS LAY

Surely you will believe your own eyes and are willing to take a few moments to simply tack VIO-RAY GLASS over a scratch shed, put it in windows or even tear off a few front boards and put VIO-RAY up. We don't ask you to merely take our word or even the thousands of users. VIO-RAY GLASS will quickly prove its own merits and we make you a liberal guaranteed test offer. Should VIO-RAY for any reason fail to prove these beneficial results you are not out one cent. Just try VIO-RAY once. You will stop your losses, increase your profits and come back for more—bringing your friends, too, for there is only one genuine VIO-RAY GLASS—made only by us.

HERE'S WHAT COUNTS

We have hundreds of these letters. VIO-RAY will do the same for you, just give it a chance. We quote: "Saved over 100 chicks." "Saved all but 19 out of 386." "Vio-Ray doubled my egg yield." "Hens laid all winter." "Chicks healthier in every way." "Unbeatable for hotbeds." "Never saw greener or prettier flowers." "Sure made money for me." "Send us 3,100 yards at once." "Only lost 8 chicks this year."

VIO-RAY GLASS A MONEY MAKER

Genuine VIO-RAY GLASS is the only glass substitute made on both screen and cloth base by scientific process. VIO-RAY is tough, durable, unbreakable, translucent and weatherproof. Comes in rolls, any length, 36 inches wide. Easily cut with shears and tacked over opening or frames. There are many uses—let us show you.

FREE

SAMPLES

CATALOG and Full Information Sent Free Upon Request

If you want samples and more information about VIO-RAY GLASS and its many uses, we will gladly furnish same free, without obligation. Just send your name and address. We will also send new catalog showing latest poultry raising improvements and inventions and the new steel poultry house we want a name for.

WIN THIS 500 CHICK BROODER—FREE

Here is your chance to get one of our famous "HEART OF AMERICA" houses free. We want a name for our newly invented sectional steel house. Get our new catalog and see it. It's a dandy. Then send your suggestions. The adopted name receives this house free.

GET THIS FREE CATALOG "PLAIN WAYS TO PROFITS"

See the 1927 improvements and inventions. New brooder and poultry houses, steel, wood, round and square. All sizes, built so you can add new sections at any time. As many windows as you want—fit any section. No other catalog like it. Brim full of money making ideas. Your copy is ready—ask for it today before you forget.

VIO-RAY COMPANY

903 Interstate Building - - - KANSAS CITY, MO.

IDEAL FOR HOTBEDS

VEGETABLES 6 WEEKS EARLIER

VIO-RAY GLASS is the ideal covering for hotbeds. Cheaper and better than glass for VIO-RAY keeps cold out, holds heat in and freely passes violet rays. Spreads soft sunshine to all corners—no dark edges and lost growth. Will not glare or burn plants—grows greener, hardier plants and produces vegetables 4 to 6 weeks earlier for higher markets. Frames are light and easy to handle. Both large and small growers now use VIO-RAY GLASS. J. B. OBERMEYER, a grower of Sayner, Wisc., says: "Vio-Ray was worth over $500 to me." IT PAYS! And you can try VIO-RAY at our risk—order as many rolls as you wish. Our guarantee holds good.

OVER $100 PROFIT FROM SMALL BED

Nashville, Ark.

Vio-Ray Co.:

By using Vio-Ray on my hotbed of tomato plants I sold over $100 worth of plants from a 6 x 9 bed. Plants grew right through severe weather. Any one doubting Vio-Ray write me.

J. B. Ramage.

SEE OUR NEW HOTBED FRAMES

Get our catalog, see our newly designed sash and frames. Light, rigid and cheaper than you can make.

SPECIAL OFFER

We will prove these wonderful results. You need not risk a penny. We have arranged special test rolls. Order as many as you want under our full money back guarantee. VIO-RAY GLASS is made on both screen and cloth base. State which you prefer—most people use both. Send $5 for each roll and we will send prepaid.

Special test roll cloth base contains 144 sq. ft. (16 running yards). Special test roll screen base 36 sq. ft. (12 running feet). Or you can order any lengths at these special prices. Fill in coupon below—check what you want. This offer fully guaranteed. You risk nothing. Try VIO-RAY NOW.

VIO-RAY

VIO-RAY Co.
General Offices
903 Interstate Bldg. Kansas City, Missouri

I am enclosing $______ please send me______ special offers (36 sq. ft.) VIO-RAY screen glass—Or ______ special offers (144 sq. ft.) VIO-RAY glass fabric or ______________. If no money is enclosed send me free samples and catalog______.

NAME______________________________

ADDRESS___________________________

TOWN_____________________STATE______

Cook for Tomorrow, Too

By
Florence Taft Eaton

HEADWORK must help housekeepers if they are to keep pace with the times. Nowhere is this principle more successfully applied than in cookery. Therefore, if you keep the following day in mind when cooking for the present day's meals, you will cook not only what you need for the dish you are concocting for Tuesday's dinner, but will also have Wednesday (or Thursday) in mind.

There are certain every-day cooked staples that I always make in quantity and plan to keep on hand (in ice-box or pantry), and I find this habit a great time-saver.

Potatoes, for instance—I always boil more than needed for the meal impending. Next day they are ready to cream, fry or hash. For breakfast, I can dice, sauter in bacon fat (adding left-over corn the last five minutes), and season with salt, pepper and minced parsley. Or dice, sauter, and just before taking up, push aside in the middle, break in an egg or two, and scramble potato and egg together lightly after the egg has begun to set; or, the potatoes are all ready for vegetable or meat hash. Or, escallop the potatoes, mixing them, diced, with cream sauce, pouring them into a buttered glass baking-dish, topping with grated cheese, and browning lightly. For salad, dice, mix with diced celery and any cold vegetables on hand, and mayonnaise or other dressing. Shredded cabbage is a nice addition.

Mashed Potatoes

I always make a double quantity. Smoothed into a buttered baking-dish, topped with grated cheese or melted butter, you have a delicious

potato dish with no trouble. Or, you can brown it in the frying-pan like an omelette. Also, we often mix left-over mashed potato with shredded fish and brown it in the frying-pan, providing a nice, quickly made main dish for breakfast or luncheon.

Sauces

Make twice as much cream sauce as you need for the dish at hand, and the next day's creamed dish can be prepared in a minute. Or, plan to use the sauce left over as foundation for cream soup for next day, adding enough hot milk or water in which vegetables have been cooked to make it the right consistency, and a little puréed left-over cooked vegetable for flavor. If milk is used, season highly.

Make enough sauce of fresh tomatoes for two or three days; in winter make a quart can of tomato into sauce at once. The surplus is ready to add to cream soup for mock bisque, to add liberally to chopped meat which is to be warmed up and put on toast for lunch or supper, or to surround Hamburg steak. There are dozens of delicious dishes of which tomato sauce is a part.

Home-made mayonnaise or boiled salad dressing can be made in liberal quantities, as both keep well.

Hamburg Steak

I always plan to have from one-fourth to one-half pound of cooked Hamburg steak left over. Next day I run that "left-over" through the meat chopper, add a very liberal amount of highly seasoned tomato sauce and put on toast for a main lunch or supper dish; or I make "beef patties," using the same mixture as a filling for baking-powder-biscuit patties (a slightly richer baking-powder-biscuit dough cut in rounds and baked in two half-inch layers, the bottom one brushed with melted butter). Pour more of the sauce and beef around, garnish with parsley, serve very hot. If you have luncheons to put up, use the minced left-over Hamburg, just moistened with tomato sauce, for a sandwich filling—a sandwich always especially liked by the masculine members of my family.

Canned tomato soup is a nice substitute for home-made tomato sauce—but remember that this is one of my recommended double-quantity concoctions.

Uses for Bread Dough

Coffee cake is often made on "bread day." To two or three cupfuls of dough add one egg, one-fourth cupful sugar, butter size of an egg (melted), a little nutmeg. Work with the hand until perfectly blended and smooth, pour into a greased tube pan, let rise until very light, brush top very lightly with melted butter, sprinkle with sugar and cinnamon, and bake. Add a few seedless raisins to the dough for variety.

Cinnamon bun (left) is delicious with or without apple sauce or canned fruit. Coffee cake (above) is at its best when baked in a tubular pan

Make cinnamon buns, too. Roll a piece of bread dough thin, brush with melted butter, sprinkle with sugar, a little cinnamon and a few currants or seedless raisins, roll, cut off inch-thick rounds, stand them on end in a pan, dot with butter and sprinkle with sugar, let rise, and bake.

Tuna Fish

Buy the large cans (the economical plan), flake half the fish, mix with diced cold boiled potatoes and a liberal amount of cream sauce, put in a shallow buttered glass baking-dish, grate cheese over—or cover with crumbs and butter—and brown in a quick oven; this is delicious. Next day flake the remainder of fish, add to more diced potato and a little diced celery if on hand, combine with home-made mayonnaise or boiled salad-dressing, and serve the delicious resulting salad on lettuce or shredded cabbage. Always wash a whole (big) head of lettuce or several small ones, roll in a piece of cheese-cloth, put in a cool place and have it ready for two or three salads. It is no more work to wash and roll a lot than a little. Also, in winter, keep cabbage on hand for cole-slaw or combination salads; this is full of vitamins, very healthful and should be served often.

Pastry

Of course, all housekeepers make enough pastry for two or three pie-bakings, don't we? It improves by staying in the ice-box two or three days. With pie-crust all ready and a double quantity of squash (cooked for yesterday's vegetable), squash pie is an easy proposition. Also, the pastry is ready for a suddenly-decided-upon meat pie.

Enough has been said to show the great advantages to busy housewives of this planned surplus, the utilization of which is as interesting as a cross-word puzzle. The result is less work and shorter hours in the kitchen, and more time saved for other duties, pleasures and for rest.

50th Anniversary

Four of a series of eleven illustrations showing the building of foundations and walls

Placing the concrete. A board should be placed along the trench to keep the soil from caving.

Forms for the wall are built over the foundation. Bolts to fasten the sill are placed in their proper position in the form.

A convenient method of pouring concrete in the wall-forms. Note the movable boards to prevent wastage of concrete.

Wall-forms completely filled. During hot or cold weather, protection should be given the concrete while hardening.

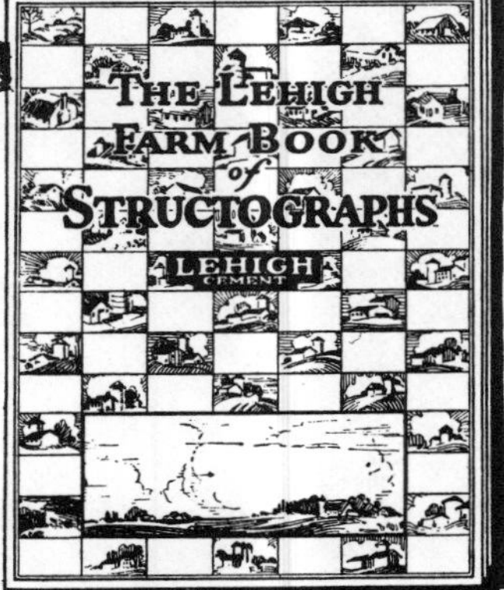

Structographs!

featured in this New Lehigh Farm Book

Concrete farm work now made easier

THE new Lehigh Farm Book of Structographs is unlike any previous book on the subject of concrete farm improvements. To a large extent pictures have taken the place of words—pictures which anyone can understand and follow.

There are 280 illustrations and working plans covering 18 distinct concrete jobs. The illustrations for 9 of these improvements are grouped in separate series—each series becoming a progressive picture-story of the building of some one job from start to finish.

You can imagine, as you look at these pictures, that you are watching the actual construction. Enough non-technical description is given to make each operation doubly clear. In addition, practical and easily-understood directions for mixing and making concrete.

In the column at the right you may find the improvements you have wanted to make.

FREE!

STRUCTOGRAPHS on the following subjects are included in this new book—each a complete picture story of how to build correctly and economically.

- Foundations and walls
- Dairy barn floors
- Hog houses, storage cellars
- Concrete walls and steps, and cellar entrance
- Fence posts, manure pits
- Septic tanks, water troughs

These additional subjects are pictured and described.

- Concrete block garage
- Feeding floors for hogs
- Barnyards, milk houses
- Wells and cisterns
- Barn approaches
- Tobacco curing-houses

LEHIGH PORTLAND CEMENT COMPANY

New York, N. Y.; Chicago, Ill.; Allentown, Pa.; Birmingham, Ala.; Spokane, Wash.

Other offices in principal cities throughout the United States

WHATEVER YOU BUILD—"LEHIGH" MEANS DEPENDABILITY

20 MILLS FROM COAST TO COAST

Lehigh Portland Cement Company,
Box 15-C, Allentown, Pa.

Please send me, without cost or obligation, a copy of *The Lehigh Farm Book of Structographs.*

Name..........................

Street..........................

City..................*State*......

Concrete Septic Tanks

By John R. Haswell

WE have learned, in building over 1,000 tanks on Pennsylvania farms, many short cuts which make the construction work easier, but the original design of this one-chamber tank which we are building remains the same. This tank has given satisfactory results in actual use over a period of years. We now have over 75 wooden forms for casting concrete septic tanks, distributed in practically all the counties. Five-sixths of the state is covered, and occasionally a form is borrowed from an adjoining county where none is available locally.

The forms are all, with two exceptions, three feet wide, six feet long and four and one-half feet deep. This size serves well for the average farm family. The long, narrow, rectangular shape with a flat bottom is easy to build, holds the sediment in the tank, and the effluent is readily purified in subsurface filtration lines made of common farm drain-tile twelve inches long. This tile must be laid very shallow —from ten to eighteen inches deep —and has roofing-felt or old oilcloth over the slightly spaced joints.

Water-tight joints in tile line from house to tank; open-joint tile line for effluent. Put building-paper over the open tile joints. Outlet baffle board in place in this photo, other board removed. You are looking at this from the inlet side. Outlet line curves around the slope

Photo. Lehigh Portland Cement Co.

The wooden form has been removed and both baffle boards are in place. Sewage from house enters through tile at left. Tile at right is outlet

Above, wooden form used for casting concrete. Paint the form with engine-oil before pouring concrete around it

Left, form in place in the ground and concrete is being rammed between boards and earth. No outside form needed

Quite a few farmers, in their hurry to get the work done, neglect to put the plugs in the inlet and outlet Y sewer-pipe branches. We find these better than other forms of pipe fittings, and for most farm conditions give the best service. The finished plugs should set before being used. Where cast-iron pipe is used, from the house to the tank, a double hub should be leaded to the cast-iron Y branch. These are only half as long as the terra cotta, and the double hub or collar will be required to extend through the concrete to make a joint as shown in photos where terra-cotta pipe is used.

A handy little concrete-mixer which will revolve as it is being emptied is a great labor-saver. The whole job can be done by three men in three hours. A few old barn doors laid on the ground will keep the stone clean, and the concrete will be better. Use a small water-bucket in dipping from barrel. Better too little than too much water in the concrete mixture.

Fill the bells of inlet and outlet tiles with cement mortar. Leave a vent in outlet tile, as shown by trowel. Put disk of tin in to hold mortar till it hardens

All of our forms are bolted together with square-headed bolts, with the heads on the inside so that they can be withdrawn after a day or two, when ready to remove the form. The form is put together, as soon as the 4 x 7-foot hole is ready, and the boards are given a coat of old engine-oil. This should be well-soaked-in at the corners and along the baffle cleats.

The form is easiest held in place, where there is ample grade for the sewer, by blocking under the cross-arms. In most locations it is simply sufficient to dig four feet one inch below the sewer grade, put in the form and block up the cross-arms until the inlet hole is opposite the sewer line. On flat layouts it is often advisable to set very carefully-leveled stakes on which to rest the cross-arms of the form.

This year we [Continued on page 113

50th Anniversary

Tired Muscles for Happiness

By A. E. Dee

Getting his ultra-violet-ray treatment

WHEN I was asked sometime ago how I would vote on the control of child labor by Congress, I replied that my vote would be "No."

I have an adopted son, 14 years old, who had been laboring all summer—and "laboring" is the proper term, for he worked for a man, part of whose land is drained swampland devoted to the production of market truck. The boy sought the job of his own volition. He knew that he must work, for we have no income from our little farm except from fruit, and there is not too much of that. He went "job-hunting" the Saturday before school closed and returned in a few hours, saying he had a job for the summer at 20 cents an hour.

He worked every day except holidays, Saturday afternoons and a few very rainy days. His work varied and included pulling weeds, dropping or planting celery, pulling, washing or bunching vegetables, hoeing, making hay and threshing grain, but much of it was in the level stretches of brown velvety muck which absorbs the heat of the sun until it shimmers in waves.

Cruel, you think? But he gained nine pounds in weight and about an inch in height. He averaged nine and a half hours' sleep every night and went "swimmin'" on an average of twice a week. He ate and digested quantities of wholesome food, his eyes are bright, his breath sweet, his skin clear and brown, and he was happy. The same results you would hope to obtain by sending your boy to an expensive summer camp.

Sometimes "my boy" returned from work so tired that I have allowed him to lounge at the supper table and helped him to care for his blistered feet, but he has also returned home from games of baseball and tag "consid'able skun up" and also dead tired. That's different? Oh, no it isn't. The muscles don't know why they exert a certain amount of energy; they just appropriate new energy and new tissue-food from the blood, relax and assimilate and are ready for the next task, whether hay-pitching or ball-batting. But the mind knows!

He shares this treatment with his pets

THE exertion of games is pleasurable, after sitting in a schoolroom two or three hours with mind and body confined to school work. The muscles cry out for use. The boy wants "fun." The school games provide for both. But no such conditions exist during an unused idle vacation. The boy, left to himself, kills time or gets into mischief. Home work with a wise and companionable father or elder brother, with sufficient firmness, patience and tact to keep the boy at work a certain number of hours, should care for the situation, but many boys are not so fortunate as that. Girls, too, can be provided with home work, but for both boys and girls it should be organized, regular, and part of it at least be muscle-tiring, which is another term for building; and it should have a fixed financial rating the same as if performed away from home.

There are homes where the question of filling hungry stomachs and covering growing limbs is so urgent as to crowd out other considerations. The undersized, undernourished, nervous children of such homes are the product, not of work, but of conditions. They would be much better off laboring at some outdoor work with clean air for the lungs and clean sunshine to open up the pores and induce perspiration. In some homes the rooms are often hot and crowded, the children are allowed to drop off to sleep unwashed, only partly undressed, and awake cross and unrefreshed. This leaves an impress upon all but the strongest. Most of such children live in or near towns or cities, for people must live where work is found. The home struggled for and planned for by the newly married pair, perhaps paid for at last, seemed large enough at the start and will be again, when the brood has flown; but now, while they are growing, the struggle and inconvenience seem at times unendurable, and parents are often driven by it into the mistake of reproaching the child, an attitude so obviously unjust as to embitter and harden him. Society requires that his person be covered, his stomach demands a satisfying fulness at all times. What is to be done about it?

MUCH more dangerous is the problem of the children whose father's earning capacities make it possible to meet living expenses. The children's money is not needed. The Y. W. and Y. M. C. A., the boy scouts and girl scouts conduct all sorts of healthful outdoor activities for such girls and boys. Mother and Father breathe sighs of relief, buy the required outfits, hand over the money and are thankful for the beautiful simplicity of it all. Then there is the expensive camp which meets the approval of those who are on a higher round of the financial ladder. There are so many kinds of families, such diversities of climate, occupation and race, that only Nature finds a sure solution. Treat them all alike and the fittest survive, but civilization, modern education and intelligence demand that even the unfit shall be cared for and, if possible, made fit.

The last-mentioned families live under what we consider the most desirable of conditions. Twenty years ago, I should probably have thought the same, and even now, had I the means, I might be weak enough to ease up on my boy. For I do not believe it is enough to keep him pleasantly occupied, exercised, fed and lodged under good conditions. But exercise and occupation for the youngster alone, simply as exercise, occupation and amusement, leave out something of vital importance as a character- and muscle-builder. The desirable thing is regular, organized, sustained, muscle-tiring labor for a certain length of time at regular intervals, with a definite objective, preferably the benefit of the child and its family, and for a definite wage. If John wants a new knife, let him earn it, thus determining the relation of labor to capital. Point out to him that while earning he was also bestowing the benefit of labor on some one else, the money being only the medium, and earning power the real capital.

The attitude of both public and family is so illogical and so harmful, as regarding child labor, that to hand child-labor control over to any body [Continued on page 109

50th Anniversary

The Greater National Catalogue First in Style always . . .

Now offers the greatest savings for the home

You need look no further than this National Catalogue to see and to know—and *to have*—the *Best* and *Most Beautiful* styles for Spring.

Every important source of Fashion, all that New York has to offer in beauty, in exclusive design, has been utilized in making this most important collection of Fashions for Spring.

Thirty-eight years' experience in the Style World of New York has given the National a mastery, a supremacy in Fashion that stamps every offering in this book with the Seal of Style authority.

Best Style in Things to Wear Best Taste in Everything for the Home

This Greater National Catalogue is filled with unusual bargains in the most interesting things for Your Home—Furniture and Rugs that are outstanding because possessing more beauty in design—actually in better taste. Curtains and draperies that are truly artistic, that not only serve their purpose but add charm to the home. This Greater National Catalogue is therefore a Home Book of great importance to You. It couples utility with good taste, and brings you your greatest opportunity for Saving.

38 Years' Experience in Creating Bargains

With all its reputation for Style and Quality, the National has always been famous for low prices, for the Saving it always offers.

Whether it be a Cross Country Tire—made of new live rubber and finest fabrics—or a pair of shoes, or a kitchen cabinet, Your Saving is always assured. For 38 years the National has given the biggest possible dollar's worth for every dollar.

And back of every purchase is our guarantee. The National has always said to every customer: "Your money back if you are not satisfied."

Write today for your free copy of The Greater National Catalogue.

This Greater National Catalogue also Saves You Money on —

Auto Tires	Jewelry
Storage Batteries	Kitchen Cabinets
Furniture	Paints
House Furnishings	Vacuum Cleaners
Electric Appliances	Draperies
Rugs	Curtains
Wall Paper	China and Glass Ware
Stoves	

The NATIONAL CLOAK & SUIT Co.

NATIONAL CARALEY COMPANY, Inc.

289 West 24th Street, New York City — 645 Hardesty Avenue, Kansas City, Mo.

Send for Your Free Copy

TO NATIONAL CLOAK & SUIT COMPANY
289 West 24th Street, New York City — *645 Hardesty Ave. Kansas City, Mo.*

(If you live east of the Mississippi River mail this coupon to our New York house—if you live west of the Mississippi River mail to our Kansas City house.)

Kindly send me the free copy of the Spring and Summer "National" Money-Saving Catalogue.

Name..................................

Address..................................

P. O...........................*State*.........

National Arts Wall Paper is outstanding in beauty of design and artistic patterns. If interested in Wall Paper, please make a check here.........

50 Years of Fashions

Continued from page 12

bustle, out of which rose the hour-glass waist-line (with tight bodice above) known to us as the "Grecian bend."

It was during the 80's that tennis became fashionable, and daring indeed was the girl who gathered up her flounces and tied them into a cascade that floated behind her as she frisked gently about on the tennis court, her ankles exposed to all beholders.

In 1890, ruffles and frills had disappeared, and all padding except in the back, leaving a rather straight and severe figure. The excessively feminine had disappeared for a brief respite, giving place to a more practical type, for this was the period in which women began to think of "doing things." The sleeve, however, is an item of interest, for it began to have an inverted look, with gathers at the top which grew rapidly into the famous "leg-of-mutton."

Leg-of-Mutton Sleeves and Gibson Girls

Women in 1897 were struggling with the problem of how to put themselves and their sleeves into a jacket. There was not only the sleeve to get crushed, but stiff epaulet shoulder-trimmings as well. This was the famous starched "shirt-waist" period; they were worn for day, dinner and dress, with a stiffly lined and much-gored skirt measuring about six yards around the bottom. These are the fashions shown in the early Gibson drawings.

Bicycles were the rage, and rash females discarded their skirts for voluminous bloomers; and though they were accused of trying to ape the men, there was a wide margin between trousers and the shapeless "tailored" bloomer.

By the time sleeves had a chance to diminish, flounces increased, and by 1901 we again have the distinctly feminine type known as the "Gibson girl." She wore a stylish picture hat above the new pompadour hair-dress. Her waist was well-bloused in front, and ruffled skirts swept the sidewalks.

High-Waisted and Princess Styles

The cycle moved on and simplicity again held sway, bringing semi-fulness in 1908, and by 1910 a drastic change, with long, narrow skirts and high waist-lines, and straight princess styles for those who had well-molded figures. For several years we thought we were enjoying the acme of simplicity in dress.

From Sheath to Full Skirts

To break the monotony, skirts took upon themselves loops and draperies, full above and so narrow beneath that the inevitable happened—a slit was necessary to make walking possible. The sheath skirt was so impractical and dangerous a garment that it is not surprising that it could not stay long in mode. To relieve her outraged feelings, Dame Fashion took a turn. In one season she jumped to the opposite extreme of skirts of voluminous fulness. It was 1915 when this radical change took place, and it was almost too sudden to grasp. Some of us said we would never wear them, but we did. It was so much more comfortable and sensible.

The Debutante Slouch, Flappers and the Charleston Girl

The next important change, and one hard to get used to at first, was the dropped waist-line. It fell steadily down until belts and sashes fell well below the hips, and we had the tall, slim figure of 1921, with the debutante slouch. By this time there had also evolved a figure not to be ignored. Young America stepped forth with bobbed hair, soft collegiate slouch hat, flat shoes, striped wool socks, sweater or tweed suit, knee length—thus we have her, the flapper of 1922. She liked the short skirts and would not give them up—we have them yet!

Compare the two extreme types pictured, 1877 and 1927. Can your mind fathom the whys and wherefores of changing fashions?

Fashions Change, Styles Never

The story of the evolution of costume is as full of interest and romance as is the evolution of the human race down through the ages. Geography, history, art, all have their tale to tell of their bearing on the evolution and revolution of costume. Always has woman adorned herself for her man; the vagaries of the changing mode go hand in hand with the changing whims of femininity. The cycle of adaptation, change and revision goes on without seeming rhyme or reason, delving into past modes, evolving something new never dreamed of before, here today, gone tomorrow; and what tomorrow will bring, who can tell?

But it is fashion that changes—style never! Style is the distinction that belongs to the well-dressed woman of every age, who takes that which fashion dictates and, considering good taste, becomingness and appropriateness to time and place, gives to her clothes the touch of individuality that makes them an expression of her own personality and not one of the thousands whose garments are "cut from the piece." So future generations will look upon our present era, for we have just passed through such a period. But more and more we find indications that the "despotism of mass fashion" has had its day, and we are ready to experiment with new ideals, with individuality and style the keynote of fashion.

ℭ ℭ

Tea leaves should not be thrown away. Place a pint of used leaves in a pail, pour over them one quart of boiling water, and leave for one hour. Strain and bottle the brown liquid. If used with a piece of soft flannel on mirrors, glasses or windows, it makes them shine like crystal. It is also a good cleanser for varnished wood and doors and furniture; also for linoleum. A little of the liquid put on flannel will clean linoleum better than water, and if the linoleum is polished afterward with a soft duster, you will get a polish like that given by beeswax.

Mother: "Hilda, did you empty the pan under the ice-box?"
Hilda: "Yes, Mother, and I put some fresh water in it"

New Styles for the Spring Seamstress

5759. *Girls' Dress.* 4 sizes: 8, 10, 12, 14 years.

5753. *Ladies' Dress.* 7 sizes: 34, 36, 38, 40, 42, 44, 46 inches bust measure.

5715. *Ladies' Dress.* 6 sizes: 34, 36, 38, 40, 42, 44 inches bust measure.

5742. *Ladies' Dress with Slender Hips.* 9 sizes: 38, 40, 42, 44, 46, 48, 50, 52, 54 inches bust measure.

5732. *Child's Dress.* 5 sizes: 1, 2, 3, 4, 5 years.

5712. *Ladies' Dress.* 6 sizes: 34, 36, 38, 40, 42, 44 inches bust measure.

5690. *Ladies' Dress.* 6 sizes: 34, 36, 38, 40, 42, 44 inches bust measure.

5709. *Child's Dress.* 3 sizes: 2, 4, 6 years.

5697. *Ladies' Combination.* 4 sizes: Small, 34-36; medium, 38-40; large, 42-44; extra large, 46-48 inches bust measure.

5738. *Girls' Dress.* 4 sizes: 6, 8, 10, 12 years.

5743. *Ladies' Apron.* One size: Medium.

Prices of patterns obtainable from The Farm Journal will be found in first column on this page

Farm Journal Dress Patterns

12 cents each

Patterns are postpaid; send coin. Send 15 cents in coin for our up-to-date 1927 Spring and Summer Catalog, containing 500 designs of ladies', misses' and children's patterns, and 30 embroidery stitches. Be sure to give *number* and *size* of pattern wanted. *Please do not send stamps.* Send all orders to The Farm Journal, Philadelphia, Pa. *Adv.*

Patterns for the Little Folks

5762. *Child's Dress.* 4 sizes: 4, 6, 8, 10 years.
5729. *Child's Play Suit.* 4 sizes: 2, 4, 6, 8 years.
5737. *Girls' Dress.* 4 sizes: 6, 8, 10, 12 years.
5726. *Boys' Suit.* 4 sizes: 2, 3, 4, 5 years.
5527. *Child's Dress.* 5 sizes: 1, 2, 3, 4, 5 years.
5728. *Underwaist.* 5 sizes: 2, 3, 4, 5, 6 years.

Prices of patterns obtainable from The Farm Journal will be found in first column on page 104

Portable Breakfast Table Is Handy

A small pine table was fitted with trunk casters so that it would roll easily and with just a touch of the hand. At breakfast and at suppertime I set the table in the kitchen, with the lunch cloth, necessary china and silver. The food is placed on the table, then the table (dishes, food and all) is pushed to any spot where we may wish to eat. In hot weather it goes to the shady porch, where we find that the fresh air revives jaded appetites. On cold winter mornings the table is rolled close to the kitchen range so that we can enjoy its warmth. For Sunday night suppers, the table goes into the living-room, where we gather around the table before a cheery wood fire.

This rolling table saves much time and many movements, because it can be completely set in the kitchen, within arm's reach of the worker as she prepares the meal. It is better than a tea-wagon because it can be used as a table and we can draw our chairs up to it. Then, too, it enables us to eat wherever we want without inconvenience, and I am saved the trouble of setting the large table in the dining-room three times a day. As our family is small, this scheme works admirably for us; it might not be so practical for a larger family. However, a large family would find uses for such a table, especially for Sunday night suppers. *Q.*

Bags Made from Dish-Cloths

WHEN persuaded to "come out of the kitchen," dish-cloths form interesting foundations for very pretty bags. The work is quickly and easily done, being nothing more than a darning-stitch worked in plain wool or the glossier yarns.

The geometrical patterns used for cross-stitch are used, but instead of working each stitch, the yarn is carried over as

far as required by the design. For example, the two rows at the top of the trees on the bag shown cover the foundation for one stitch. The next two rows cover three stitches, the next two rows cover five, etc.

The trees are worked in rose color with lines of black and gray above and below, and blocks of rose above. The main parts of the borders at bottom of bag are worked in rose, the lines in black and gray.

The bag measures 10 x 8¾ inches finished, but could be made larger. Strips for handles are cut 2 x 18 inches and worked in the colors used for the bag. The strips are overcast over thick, soft cotton cord and attached to the inner sides of the bag, which is then lined with sateen, brier-stitched to the upper edge. We do not provide patterns for these bags.

Mother Pencil: "It's so rainy out, Peter; be sure to wear your rubbers"

Seasonable Recipes

MACARONI and spaghetti should always be cooked in double quantity. After cooking, rinse in cold water, add more salt, take out what you wish for that day's meal, and save the rest, plain. Use that reserved to top a meat pie (meat mixed with some sauce on hand), or to combine with sliced hard-boiled eggs and a liberal amount of cream sauce; top with grated cheese and brown in the oven for a delicious main dish for lunch or supper. Bits of red sweet pepper and minced parsley are a tasty addition.

Savory rice is prepared thus: Simmer 2 tablespoonfuls of rice in 1 pint of milk until nearly cooked, then add 1 ounce of finely-grated cheese, ½ ounce of butter and a pinch of salt. Mix all together and put into a buttered pie-dish, sprinkle ½ ounce of finely-grated cheese on top and bake in a moderate oven for half an hour.

Potato snow is toothsome. To make, beat with 4 cupfuls of freshly-boiled hot potatoes ¾ cupful of boiling milk, 1 heaping tablespoonful of butter, salt and white pepper to taste. Beat first with a fork, then the egg-beater, adding more hot milk if very stiff. The mixture should be perfectly smooth, very light and almost as thin as cake batter. Pile in a baking-dish and sprinkle thickly with grated cheese, then set in the oven until the cheese has melted and crisped.

For potato puffers, mash enough freshly-boiled hot potatoes to make a pint. Beat with these 1 cupful of hot milk, 1 heaping tablespoonful of butter, salt and pepper to taste. When a little cool, beat in 1 egg and 2 tablespoonfuls of flour with which has been sifted 1 teaspoonful of baking-powder. Fill iron gem pans (which have been well-greased and heated) three-fourths full with the potato mixture and bake in a hot oven until well browned.

Jam fritters make use of stale bread. To make, spread 12 slices of bread on one side with jam, put another slice on top of each. Cut into neat shapes and if stale, soak in a little hot milk. Sift 1 cupful of flour into a bowl with a pinch of salt. Break 1 egg into the middle of the flour, add ½ cupful of milk gradually and beat the batter well. Dip the pieces of bread in this batter and fry in plenty of smoking-hot fat, to a golden brown. Drain and dust with sugar. Serve with hot milk or sweet sauce.

For maple-walnut pudding use 4 tablespoonfuls of corn-starch (level), 2 cupfuls of milk, ½ teaspoonful of vanilla, ½ cupful of maple (or brown) sugar, ½ cupful of nut-meats cut into pieces. Scald milk in double boiler. Mix sugar and corn-starch. Add hot milk slowly to the mixture and return to double boiler. Stir until mixture thickens. Add flavoring and nut-meats, pour into a mold and serve with cream and sugar.

Nut brown bread requires 1 cupful of Graham flour, 4 teaspoonfuls of baking-powder, 2 tablespoonfuls maple sugar, 1 cupful of sweet milk, 1 cupful of white flour, 1 teaspoonful of salt, 1 cupful of chopped nuts or raisins. Place in a well-greased pan and bake one hour in a moderate oven.

BEFORE washing windows fill all places where the putty has loosened with a mixture of plaster of Paris and water applied with a case-knife.

High-School Party—Reducing

By Aunt Harriet

PLEASE suggest invitations and inexpensive menu for a Senior-Junior high-school party. Our colors are

Red and Purple.

Attractive and inexpensive refreshments would include sandwiches made with chicken filling, for which I am sending a recipe. With these you could either serve a salad or make part of your sandwiches with the chicken filling and part with lettuce and mayonnaise and omit the salad.

A fruit salad would be inexpensive, especially if the lettuce is finely shredded and you use canned fruit. Arrange on plates. Place a sandwich on each plate, also, then pass additional sandwiches. Ice-cream, dainty little cakes (home-made), coffee and cream peppermints would complete the menu.

The form of invitation given below is decidedly informal, but will arouse the curiosity and interest of your guests. Use white correspondence cards.

(In red ink)	(In purple ink)
The Time:	Friday, March 25, 8 to 11 p.m.
The Place:	63 North Main Street.
The Event:	Party for the Class of 1927.
The Invitation:	Comes from the Class of 1928.

The members of which hope to see you there!

PLEASE suggest the quantity of food to eat in order to reduce ten pounds and make reduction permanent. My weight is normal, but all but three of the 24 members of our club are underweight, and the girls tease and call me *"Fatty."*

I can not furnish this information, and would not furnish it if I could. In order to resist disease and take our places in the world, we need healthy bodies and sound minds. While the undernourished may seem to flourish for a while, the breaking point comes sooner or later. Unfortunately, the burden of ill health can not be borne by the individual alone; it has to be shared by the family, the friends and the community.

In a recent issue of "Baking Technology" (a trade magazine), Dr. Thurman B. Rice speaks of the present fad for reducing under the title of "Fatness and Fitness." Dr. Rice says:

"It may surprise some people to know that all age groups in both sexes are showing a marked decline in tuberculosis death rate, save one. The group to which young women and adolescent girls belong shows a slightly increasing rate as compared with the rates of a few years back.

"Several reasons for this condition are set forth. One of the commonest is that scanty dress is responsible. . . . . . . It is more likely that the reason lies for a large part, at least, in the scanty diet of girls who are willing to go to any extreme to remain thin or become thin. The ideal type of girl from the standpoint of fashion is far too thin to satisfy the requirements of the hygienists. Many women and not a few men are injuring themselves to attain fashionable silhouettes.

"We do not defend the soft, flabby flesh of the person who eats too much and works too little. That kind of fat is a nuisance and a burden, which shortens life and hinders efficiency. But fat that is the result of proper eating and good health, and which is able to stick on during normal muscular exercise, should be regarded as an asset—money in the bank which can be drawn on in time of need.

"Any prediction concerning the trend of fashion is a risky undertaking for mere man, but we will guess that a return to fuller figures will take place in the rather near future. It will certainly be in the interest of health, as has been the general trend of fashion for the last half-century."

AUNT HARRIET wishes to give advice, suggestions and sympathy to all Our Folks who are in doubt or in trouble, but only such answers as will benefit the largest number of people will be given here. For prompt reply, send a stamped, self-addressed envelope to Aunt Harriet, this office.

Tired Muscles for Happiness

Continued from page 100

or organization that has not abundant time for exhaustive study of the requirements of the situation, would be useless and harmful. And as for Congress, has it not many matters of importance pressing it at all times? Then why add this duty and responsibility to those of an already overworked body?

Do you not think that, if the control of the child's labor activities is handed over to any one besides the parent, who, no matter what that parent's mistakes and failings, may be likely to come nearer to the right thing for the child and the family than some person or body of persons who never has known, never will know anything about that child as an individual or its family as a home unit? Do you not think it should be given to some body of persons who have no other matters to consider and who are entirely free from political influence or interference? Would it not, perhaps, be even better to reach it in some other way, in the way that so many other matters and situations have been bettered and alleviated—through educating the parents concerning the relation of child labor to the welfare of the child, the family and the country? An incalculable amount of good has been done through the schools, the home-and-school leagues and the mothers' meetings, along many lines. Why not educate the mothers of the children who are now in school?

DON'T give your boys and girls large amounts of money, send them to expensive colleges or schools, allow them to pass their vacations in care-free, money-spending play, then sternly tell the boy "Go to work," and start the girl on a matrimonial campaign and disown her if she marries an idle bounder. When, pray, did you teach your boy to work? Why should your daughter not marry an idle bounder, since you have made her life all play? The other sort has not had time to play with her, and she finds that a man who attends to business and takes life sanely is too slow.

I know that child labor is in many localities misapplied and exploited, that it is employed and carried on under conditions detrimental to the child; and that, of course, should be remedied as speedily and thoroughly as possible. But the question is more far-reaching and important even than that one phase of it. Persons chosen for the work of controlling, adjusting or regulating child labor should be peculiarly fitted for the work by nature, intelligence and choice, such persons to have no other public duties and be as free from and independent of political influence as the justices of the Supreme Court. They should be as carefully chosen as are those justices.

"Here's the chicken's heart, Martha —it's just your size."
"No, thank you, Aunt Harriet; I like chicken, but I unlike its machinery"

50th Anniversary

Make a Picture Kite

KITE season will soon be here again. Who will fly his dragon the highest? You may have envied the boy who had a fancy kite his uncle had brought him from a toy shop in the city, but you can have one just as nice. A boy with a little bit of ingenuity can make as pretty a kite as can be purchased anywhere. Many of you have made kites of some kind—if nothing but a rag kite. Why not make one with a nice picture on it? A picture kite is beautiful to see when 20, 30 or more feet from the ground. The picture, whether it be a huge butterfly, a dragon or a wild bird, stands out prominently, and everybody, old and young, who sees it will express admiration.

The photograph shows how the frame of such a kite is made. The picture can then be put on—sewed, pasted or attached in the way easiest for you. Be sure that it is firmly attached, so that the wind won't take it from the frame of the kite.

All kinds of designs can be used. The ones girls and boys seem to like best, however, are pictures of dragons, birds or persons. One boy I knew painted the red, white and blue insignia of American aviators on his kite. When the kite was flown, it looked just like one wing of an airplane.

Look at the two pictures printed below. The little fellow holding the two kites made them himself.

Kites are more than toys, too. They create imagination. Ben Franklin discovered that lightning was electricity by flying a kite. The first wire on which was built the cable bridge at Niagara was carried across the water by means of a kite. And the principle of kite flying started the dream which led to the discovery of the principles which have been embodied in the airplane.

Uncle Sam ready to go up. Above, some bird!

The Prize Pony

WHEN I was a boy living near an Indian village, the Indian boys used to stage pony races. At one of these races I recall a pony which none of the redskin lads could straddle.

The Indian boys all laughed. I laughed, too. Then the owner of the pony saw me and laughed louder than ever as he said, "White boy ride um pony?"

I shook my head, and all the Indians laughed at me. Then the owner spoke again.

"White boy ride pony, white boy take um home along with him."

I knew I couldn't ride the pony, but also knew that if I didn't try, the Indians would laugh at me every time they saw me, and I couldn't stand that. As I started to pull off my jacket, I thought about a lump of sugar in one of the pockets. I took it and held it in the palm of my hand as I threw my coat under a tree. I walked up to the pony and rubbed his head, at the same time letting him smell the sugar. He sniffed at my hand, then began to lick it, so I slipped the sugar into his mouth while I stroked his head.

Then I put my hand on his back and stuck my bare toes against his leg, and climbed on. I expected him to pitch me off as fast as he did the Indian boys, but he only turned his head around and bit my foot. Then I grabbed his ears in both my hands, dug my bare heels into his sides and shouted, "Giddap! giddap, Ginger!"

With that he reared up and turned around on his hind feet, dropped down on his front feet and started away on a gentle trot. The Indians set up a loud laugh, not at me this time, but at the pony's disgusted owner.

The only explanation I could ever think of why the pony started off with me was that he had been raised by a white boy who had given him sugar, and he remembered. *G. R.*

Lonesome Master Donkey

He's lonesome, I can tell it,
And wants a home and friend;
And I am lonesome, also,
For I've no pet to tend.

My puppy died last August,
My parrot flew away,
My chicken that I loved so
much,
We ate him Saturday.

So if you could arrange it
That he could live with me,
I'm sure he would be happy
And so would I—you see!

A. M. Cahill.

Our Native Deer

DOES any wild animal present a more picturesque appearance than the deer? Above is shown a white-tail buck and doe, native on the slopes of our western mountains. There are more than 50 species of deer in all parts of the world. In Europe the male of the red deer sometimes grows to a size four feet high and seven feet long. The American deer, however, is considerably smaller.

"The deer is the most timid creature I know," writes Kenyon Wilcox, Wideawake from Connecticut, near whose home deer can still be found. "The slightest sound will sometimes send it bounding off over fences and through the brush. When the mother doe runs, she waves her tail as a signal to the little ones that danger is near, and they dart after her through the brush. The bucks are sometimes ugly, especially at the mating season, and will occasionally put up a stiff fight. The game laws here protect deer so that they are growing very plentiful in numbers."

ℭ ℭ

Perseverance did a lot for Kenneth Hinshaw, of Goldendale, Wash. In 1925 he won second place in the Moses 4-H Leadership Contest. He did not allow second place to discourage him, however, and when the winner for 1926 was announced at the International in Chicago, Kenneth was awarded the cup for the coming year. Stick to it, boys and girls! That's one thing 4-H club work teaches us.

ℭ ℭ

"Our clan has learned how to use the heliograph in signaling. It's hilly here and the heliograph always works in sunshiny weather." *Blair Lindsey*, 👁, *W. Va.*

Know how a heliograph works, boys?

ℭ ℭ

The Wideawakes

A Brotherhood of Farm Boys

Brotherhood Chieftain, *Charles P. Shoffner*
Brotherhood Steward, *Werner P. Meyer*

Motto: Plow a Straight Furrow

Every farm boy should become a member. To join, copy the pledge, write name and address, send to us, and your name will be enrolled and the button and folder will be sent you free. There are no dues, no fines, no assessments. Wideawakes now number 54,023; 834 clans have been formed. Membership Certificate printed in two colors, with gold seal attached, 10 cents.

PLEDGE: *I desire to become a member of The Wideawakes, and promise to play fair, to lend a helping hand, to believe in farming, and to have a brotherly love for farm boys everywhere.*

The Meeting Place

An Advertisement of the American Telephone and Telegraph Company

It is not so long ago since people met in town hall, store or at the village post-office, to talk over matters of importance to the community. Then came the telephone to enable men to discuss matters with one another without leaving their homes. With the growing use of the telephone, new difficulties arose and improvements had to be sought. Many of the improvements concerned the physical telephone plant. Many of them had to do with the means of using the apparatus to speed the connection and enable people to talk more easily. This need for improvement is continuous and, more than ever, is a problem today. Speed and accuracy in completing seventy million calls daily depends upon the efficiency of Bell System employees and equipment as well as upon the co-operation of persons calling and those called and numerous private operators.

It is not enough that the average connection is made in a fraction of a minute or that the number of errors has been reduced to a very small percentage.

The American Telephone and Telegraph Company and its associated Bell Telephone Laboratories have practically for their sole task the making of the telephone more serviceable and more satisfactory—as a means of conversing with anyone, anywhere, any time.

Money In This For You, Too!

Benjamin Sargent, of Illinois

No matter what your age or previous experience, there's Farm Journal subscription money for you near home. Actual records by thousands like Mr. Sargent and George Norvell prove it.

Spare minutes now bringing you nothing can and will bring you *cash*. All equipment furnished free; also valuable assistance in getting started. Dignified work leading to permanent business.

Special opportunity also open to girls and women. Any one can succeed; information costs nothing.

George Norvell, of Kansas

Especially Profitable Season Now Starting—Send This Coupon Now

The Farm Journal, Department FM-3, Washington Square, Philadelphia, Pa.

Gentlemen: Send me free equipment and information about this wonderful Farm Journal business.

Name__________ Box, Street or R. F. D.__________

Post-Office __________ State__________

Bird Day of The Liberty Bell Bird Club

Don't forget that April 8, the second Friday in April, will be Bird Day of The Liberty Bell Bird Club. On this date suitable exercises should be held in all schools and clubs. In time, this day will be universally-celebrated.

The Great Horned Owl

This owl is a great consumer of rats, mice and sometimes, unfortunately, small birds. An owl authority who watched a pair of the owls learned that they ate 1,596 mice, 134 rats, 54 shrews and 39 birds in one season.

Juncoes at Wyncote, Pa.

Here we have three juncoes enjoying their dinner at a feeding-shelf. Did you have one this winter?

The Liberty Bell Bird Club

Motto: *Protect Our Feathered Friends*

Pledge: *I desire to become a member of The Liberty Bell Bird Club, and promise to study and protect all song and insectivorous birds, and do what I can for the club. 907,587 good folks have signed this.*

Copy the pledge, sign your name and address, enclose ten cents, send it to us, and your name will be enrolled and the club button and 20-page guide sent you. The Liberty Bell Bird Club, The Farm Journal, Philadelphia, Pa.

Concrete Septic Tanks

Continued from page 99

decided it was safer to pour the side walls first and finish off the top edge before placing the bottom.

It is best not to let any water get into the tank while the form is in place, for it may swell the wood to such an extent as to make removal difficult. The form can be removed in a day or two if there has been no freezing. The lines to the house

Completed tank, one piece of cover on, baffle boards wedged down a few inches from top. The X means "This side up"

and purifying tile should then be connected. All curves are made in the outlet line after it leaves the tank. This is usually 100 feet of farm tile laid in one string with only a few inches fall. Some of our layouts look like a big snake laid on a hillside. The curves are cemented to prevent seepage at the steep places, and the straight parts, laid across the slope, total 100 feet.

Cover slabs are most easily made at the

Cover is made in four pieces, each four feet long, 21 inches wide, reenforced near under side. Should cure two weeks before being used

same time as the tank. Some paper on a level floor will keep them from sticking. Pieces of 2 x 4-inch material are used for a form, and if a little wider strip is placed on a slant for the edge of one of the middle slabs, it will help in lifting them off. It is best to mark this No. 1.

Before covering the tank, it is a good idea to fill it with clean water. This will help cure the concrete and show if there are any leaks.

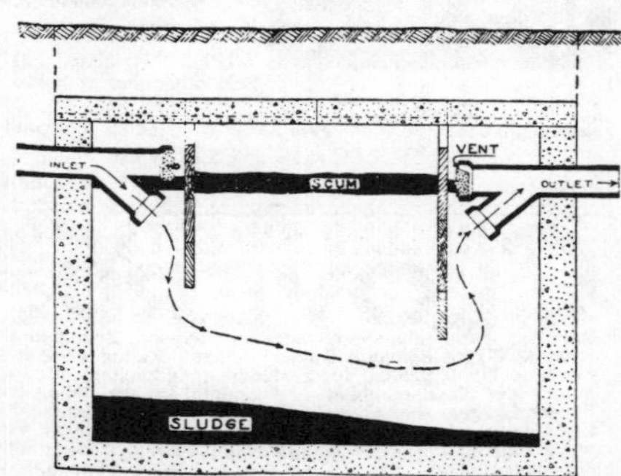

Cross-section of completed tank, showing how sewage is turned into liquid effluent. Top of tank is a foot beneath ground

What Do You Want To Know?

The Editors of The Farm Journal, assisted by a large corps of research investigators and practical workers and advisers, are at the command of each and every one of Our Folks. They are prepared to answer inquiries and give advice on questions referring to any branch or phase of farm work, farm life, farm home, farm activities or general farm conditions (including legal, veterinary and medical matters), this constituting what we call

National Service

Questions are answered in The Farm Journal if of interest to the general reader. Others are answered in personal letters, provided the inquiry is accompanied by a two-cent stamp.

Questions of General Interest

Answered by Experts

Waterproofing Stucco

I COVERED part of my house with cement (stucco), but find it is not waterproof. I read of a process of waterproofing with water-glass, without any rule or proportion to apply. If you can tell me how, it would do me a great service. *E. H.*

The water-glass method is a brush treatment applied to the surface: two coats are usually enough. Water-glass is commonly known as sodium silicate, and is purchased in the liquid form from any drug store. This treatment is more expensive than the soap-and-alum treatment, which consists of alternate applications of alum and soap by brush treatment; use eight ounces of alum per gallon of water and one and one-half pounds of hard soap per gallon of water. The surface to be treated should be perfectly clean and dry, and the temperature should not be cold—not less than 50° F. The soap solution should be applied first, boiling hot, with a whitewash brush, rubbing so that the surface is entirely covered, but not enough to produce a suds. This must dry 24 hours, or until thoroughly dry. The alum is then applied, and allowed to dry. This is followed with another wash of soap and alum separately, as before. This is one of the most effective treatments which you can use, and is known as the Sylvester wash.

You can also use paraffin dissolved in gasoline or naptha, applied with a brush. The gasoline or naptha evaporates, leaving the pores filled with paraffin. At least two coats should be used.

Moss on Tree Trunks

Is there any way I can get rid of moss and lichens on the trunks of trees? *W. E. J.*

Spraying with Bordeaux mixture 6:6:50 in fall will prevent the growth of moss. The application must be thorough, so that the liquid will penetrate to the bark of the tree. The moss and lichens will not drop off immediately after spraying, but will gradually disappear.

Veterinary Questions

Answered by Dr. H. H. Havner

Sow Weak in Hind Parts

We have a sow about due to farrow and she has gotten weak in her hind parts. She is on pasture and has been fed a stock conditioner, but that did not seem to help her. Can you aid us in any way? *B. O.*

The only help for this sow is a ration high in mineral, vitamin and protein content. Try this mixture: Corn, 50 pounds; ground whole oats, 30 pounds; wheat middlings, 20 pounds; tankage, 6 pounds; oilmeal, 3 pounds; alfalfa-meal, 3 pounds. All of these ingredients are important, but particularly the addition of tankage, oilmeal and alfalfa-meal. By all means do not omit any of the last three feeds. Doses of cod-liver oil may prove helpful. Give one or two tablespoonfuls on the feed twice a day.

Hoof Won't Hold Shoe

I have a horse that has a bad hoof—won't hold a shoe. The hoof is rotten. What would you advise? *D. J. McC.*

Make a strong trough out of two-inch lumber and slip it into the front of a single stall. The box or trough ought to be at least six inches deep and three feet across. Put water in trough to a depth of five inches, and add one and one-half ounces of any standard stock-dip for every gallon of water. This will make a suitable antiseptic foot-bath. Soak the feet for six-hour periods three times a week until improvement is noted.

Radio Questions

Answered by Henry M. Neely

Home-Built or Manufactured Set?

I have made up my mind to buy a radio set, but I am puzzled about whether to get a manufactured set offered by a dealer in our nearest town or to let a young expert there build me a set. This expert is a young fellow who seems to know his business, and he tells me he has some parts in what he calls a "kit" that make a better set than the factory one. Will you please advise me?
Montana. *L. D. F.*

Now, that seems like a perfectly simple question to answer. All I have to do is to advise you to buy either one or the other and let it go at that. And, as a matter of fact, the chances are that you would be satisfied either way—for a time, at least.

It is true that there are one or two complete "kits" on the market which, when properly—don't overlook that word *properly* —assembled, make a mighty fine outfit. This is because such kits combine two or three patented principles, but if the manufacturers tried to turn them out as completed sets, they would find themselves facing patent prosecution. So they get around that by selling a lot of parts and, if you put them together into a set, they claim they have nothing to do with that. This principle, however has been declared illegal by the courts and such kits are gradually being driven from the market. Consequently, if you had such a set, and trouble developed in it later, you probably would find it impossible to get replacement parts. Furthermore, the average service man finds it extremely difficult to service these kit combinations.

On the whole, I have no hesitation in advising you to stick to the set turned out complete by the reputable manufacturer. You know where you stand with such a set today, and you can depend on service as long as you want it. You would not think of buying a car or a cream-separator or a tractor on which you couldn't get replacements or service when needed, and the same principles should apply to any other piece of mechanism—including the radio set, which is the most delicate piece of mechanism to be found in the home.

Health Questions

Answered by Dr. F. O. Hendrickson

A. S., Mich.: Appendicitis usually manifests itself by a generalized pain in the abdomen. The pain gradually localizes itself in the right side of the abdomen on a level with the top of the hip bone. Nausea and constipation usually are present. As the symptoms progress, fever comes on. If you think you have trouble with your appendix, above all, do not take a cathartic or any kind of a laxative. Keep the bowels quiet and you will get along better.

L. O., Wis.: Prominent ankles and elbows probably are familial characteristics, and I do not believe they can be corrected. We know of no method whereby flesh can be added to one part of the body and removed from another.

Reproduction of the first Odd Mention heading, October, 1878

It always pays to use one's brains. A half-dozen young folks went skating and when they reached the pond, were not quite sure whether it was thick enough to bear them. One young man rushed on and said, "It bears me up," so all the rest skated to him, with the consequence that the added weight broke the ice and they all got a ducking.

The new rubber-block pavement tried in London is said to be a success. Each block has a rubber cap vulcanized to a brick base, and measures $10\frac{3}{8}$ by $5\frac{5}{8}$ inches. The foundation of the road is twelve inches of concrete. The rubber bricks are laid upon a sand bed and then joined by a patent process.

Chas. L. Hill, president of the National Dairy Association, advises farmers to laugh at least once each day as a present aid in the solution of their surplus problems.

Has your wife a big pile of dry wood and chips in the woodshed?

F. J., March, 1901.

Just think how dead a paper would be without live advertisements. The Farm Journal is not dead, is it?

F. J., March, 1880.

Who has the good luck to possess copies of The Farm Journal, for AUGUST, 1877, and AUGUST, 1878? New York Public Library needs them to complete its 50-year file of this magazine. $10 each will be paid for the first copies of these two issues, in good condition, to reach this office. Send to us, not to the library.

The Man Who Drew Our Cover

This is Conrad J. Linke, a Philadelphia artist who studied at the Pennsylvania School of Industrial Art, the Spring Garden Institute, the Chicago Art Institute and the Pennsylvania Academy of Fine Arts. Mr. Linke specializes in portraits, murals and figure work in oil. He has drawn many covers for The Farm Journal, and his work is always of interest. We are sure you will enjoy the beautiful cover on our anniversary number.

It is said that the normal useful life of a lemon tree is 30 years.

If there are some bare patches on the lawn, now is the time to sow some blue-grass and white-clover seed on them. A little fine hen manure and wood-ashes may be added to help the growth.

F. J., March, 1895.

These horses are investigating the stalled auto and are evidently thinking, "Perhaps he will call on us yet"

50 Years of Poultry

Continued from page 62

diseases today that were so prevalent 50 years ago. Poultrymen have learned the art of prevention. They not only know how to prevent epidemics, but they have been drilled in the proper care of stock, know how to treat slight ailments, and thus prevent serious results.

We have also wonderfully improved in the art of culling and mating, and are now able to pick out the laying hen. We know how to increase egg production, and how to have stronger generations.

During the past 50 years our knowledge of egg production has grown to such an extent that the 300-egg hen has become a fact. Not general as yet, but gradually increasing each year. The invention and use of the trapnest has been of untold service in raising the standard of good laying—from 120 eggs, considered high 50 years ago, to 200, which is accomplished on many farms today. A study of the records at the various state egg contests shows remarkable improvement in this particular with all breeds.

Another wonderful improvement is noted with our fanciers, who are not only giving us new and good breeds, but are improving the old ones so that we have a combination of beauty and utility in all breeds. The "fancy fowl" of 50 years ago was not, as a rule, a good layer.

Contents—March, 1927

What type of beef meets the popular demand?

WHY are shrewd livestock producers turning toward lighter beef cattle?

Because they know that the average consumer determines the kind of cattle the market wants, and the average consumer today wants well-finished beef from light cattle.

Swift & Company, being obliged to supply the retailer with the type of beef the consumer wants, has felt the force of this light-beef demand very definitely. The reasons are these:

The trend toward kitchenette apartments and economy has increased the demand for small cuts of beef. The housewife has found that beef from light animals can be more easily cut into roasts and steaks of the size that best suits her needs, and the lighter beef cuts have less waste. The elimination of the old-fashioned coal or wood kitchen stove in the cities, the reduction in the size of families, the trend toward smaller living quarters, and the growth of the delicatessen business in cities, have also added to the unpopularity of heavy beef.

Hence, cattle weighing between 950 and 1150 pounds and yearling or baby beef between 650 and 950 pounds alive are most frequently in best demand.

Heavy beef is now used mostly by fine hotels and restaurants. A light corn crop may mean too small a supply of them but it takes only a small percentage of these big cattle to saturate the market.

How were these facts strikingly illustrated by conditions in 1924-'25-'26? The story is told in detail in the new Swift Year Book, along with many other vital facts, statistics and timely information of value to every farmer and livestock raiser.

Swift & Company will be glad to send you a copy of the Year Book on request—just fill out the coupon and mail.

Swift & Company, Public Relations Dept.
4102 Packers Ave., U. S. Yards, Chicago, Ill.

Please send me free of charge, Swift & Company's 1927 Year Book.

Name..........

Address..........

Swift & Company

Founded 1868

Owned by more than 47,000 shareholders

*The pattern shown above is the "*KURDISTAN*" Gold Seal Art-Rug No. 500*

Beautiful, Easily Cleaned Rugs
—*for every room in your home*

WHATEVER room in your home needs new floor covering, there is a wide assortment of money saving *Gold Seal* Art-Rugs from which to choose. Rich Oriental patterns for living and dining room, floral effects in delicate colors for bedrooms and neat geometric designs for kitchen and pantry. Each one expresses the latest ideas in artistic floor-covering!

Lighten your housework

In addition to being attractive *Gold Seal* Art-Rugs are so practical, so labor-saving! The smooth, water-proof surface can be kept spotless with just an occasional light and easy mopping. How different from the hard, tiresome sweeping and beating that old-fashioned floor-coverings require!

Another point—*Gold Seal* Rugs lie flat without any kind of fastening—never ruffle or curl up.

Real bargain prices

For over fifteen years *Gold Seal* Rugs have been unequalled in quality, durability and value. Right now prices are lower than they ever have been! A genuine *Gold Seal* Art-Rug offers floor-covering value no housewife can afford to overlook. Sizes range from small mats to 9 x 15 foot rugs.

Remember, there is only one genuine Congoleum. For your own protection, insist that the Gold Seal appears on the rugs you buy. No floor-covering without this Gold Seal is genuine Congoleum.

CONGOLEUM-NAIRN INC.
Philadelphia New York Boston Kansas City Chicago Atlanta San Francisco Cleveland Dallas Minneapolis Pittsburgh New Orleans Rio de Janeiro
In Canada—Congoleum Canada Limited, Montreal

CONGOLEUM
GOLD SEAL
GUARANTEE
SATISFACTION GUARANTEED
OR YOUR MONEY BACK
REMOVE SEAL WITH
WET CLOTH

CONGOLEUM
REG. U.S. PAT. OFF.
GOLD SEAL
ART-RUGS

Insist that this Gold Seal appears on the rugs you buy!

"WOODLAND"—*a restful foliage effect and a pretty border of primroses in delicate colorings. It's Gold Seal Art-Rug No. 581*

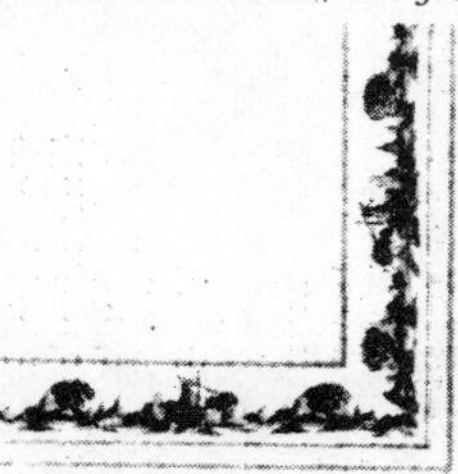

"HOLLAND"—*delightful blue and white Dutch tiles with a quaint windmill border. It's Gold Seal Art-Rug No. 594*

"OMAR"—*a striking border of black with graceful motifs framing a field of cool soft gray. It's Gold Seal Art-Rug No. 596*

"SIAM"—*turquoise blue in a clouded effect delightfully sets off the quaint Oriental scenes. It's Gold Seal Art-Rug No. 589*

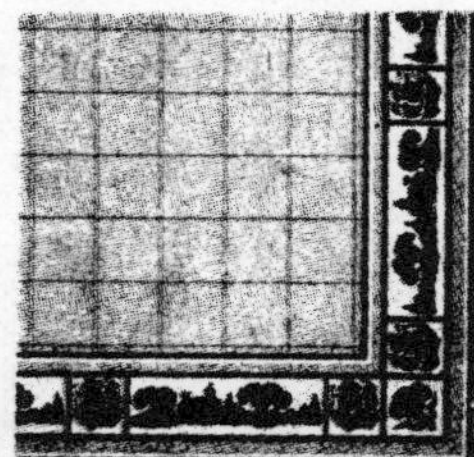

"PLYMOUTH"—*an interesting border showing wooded landscapes and pilgrim ships. It's Gold Seal Art-Rug No. 580*

"CAPRI"—*a copy of an antique Kermanshah rug on an Oriental blue background. It's Gold Seal Art-Rug No. 534*

. . .and now the 30s

The Madhouse *Called* Washington

What the Capital thinks of the New Deal—the agricultural rejuvenation—and 15 per cent salary cuts

By Frederic William Wile

NEVER except in wartime has the National Capital been the scene of so many dizzy and kaleidoscopic events. President Roosevelt's inaugural pledge of "action — and action now," has certainly been kept, and the end is not yet, for the keynote of the whole Roosevelt economic recovery scheme is that nothing is necessarily final.

Repeatedly the President has referred to his program in terms of experimentation. Lapsing into baseball lingo, Mr. Roosevelt says he doesn't expect to "make a hit every time he goes to bat." His attitude toward the farm program is characteristic. When the plan was launched, it will be remembered, he specifically explained that it embarks upon new paths, and that if it fails, he'll be the first to say so and try something else.

WASHINGTON'S chief emotions about the New Deal revolve around the President's courage and what appears here to be an amazing stranglehold on popular confidence. Politicians recall nothing to equal it. Through the Capital stream men and women from all sections and of every party affiliation. They bear a universal message: that the whole country is "with Roosevelt"; that, irrespective of politics, the people are "for him," and will go blindly anywhere he leads.

The "folks back home" don't pretend to fathom all the intricate economics of the Roosevelt policies. They can't follow the mental processes of the presidential Brain Trust as it leaps mysteriously from proposition to proposition. But as reported to Washington, the country seems satisfied to know that action has supplanted inaction, and content to feel it is "on its way."

Whether this is a correct picture of public sentiment Washington is not sure, and would very much like to know. On the surface, with telegrams and assurances of 100 per cent support rolling in, and Washington swarming with codemakers, all seems going well. But Washington knows that many industrial leaders lack confidence in the principles of NIRA, and are "going along" simply because they want prosperity to return, and do not want to be in the position of appearing to oppose the administration.

INDUSTRIAL recovery under NIRA is dominating all thought and activities at Washington, which has known few such human dynamos as bluff, gruff General Hugh Johnson. Some find him dictatorial and hard-boiled, but nobody denies his intelligence, determination and go-getting capacity.

EVERY whiff of evidence available in Washington indicates that farmers and farm leaders are feeling better than they have in years. Dollar wheat, 60-cent corn and 11-cent cotton have had their traditional effect in injecting new hope and a considerable amount of enthusiasm into American agriculture, though the cash benefits are just beginning to reach the farmer's pocket.

Washington is surprised and pleased at the smoothness with which the "processing taxes" on wheat, cotton and certain types of tobacco have "gone over." It is expected that there will be difficulties over the tax on the floor stocks of retail stores, particularly as to cotton goods. But as this is only temporary, and not a continuing tax, the Treasury Department is expected to work it out successfully.

THE apparent success of the midsummer cotton drive was also gratifying to Washington. In the course of a mere 10-day campaign, a force of something like 20,000 local agents of the Government and farm leaders dived into the sea of 2,000,000 cotton growers, and came up with agreements to reduce acreage by approximately 10,000,000 acres. Cotton is now being plowed up all over Dixie in accordance with this undertaking, and the first bonus check amounting to $500 was paid to a Texas cotton-grower on July 28.

The Agricultural Adjustment Administration under Mr. Peek is jubilant, and justly so.

THE Federal economy program produced two tempests-in-teapots which threatened to become major agricultural hurricanes. One arose from the insistence by Director of the Budget Douglas that the Market News Service be eliminated. There was such an uproar that the service had to be speedily restored, though in curtailed form.

The economy bugaboo also called for a 25 per cent cut in agricultural extension forces. The natural rebellion of the extension job-holders, fostered by the farm organizations, proved sufficient to compel continuance of extension activities on more or less normal lines.

ECONOMY is indeed a word of execration in Washington. The 15 per cent pay cut and wholesale dismissals in every branch of the civil service have produced anguish, and in many cases downright suffering. There are repeated assurances that as many old government workers as possible will be absorbed in the innumerable new bureaus and agencies set up to carry out the recovery program. But the woods are full of Democratic job-seekers, and it remains to be seen just what will happen. At the moment the Jacksonian theory that "to the victors belong the spoils" seems to have the upper hand.

ANOTHER matter over which Washington is inclined to be critical is the extra-official activities of the President's private and official households. The Capital has what is perhaps too high an idea of official dignity, and lampoons the magazine jobs of Mrs. Roosevelt and Mrs. Dall, the $1,000-a-week broadcasting of Colonel Howe, the President's secretary, the newspaper syndicate column of Professor Moley, and all that sort of thing.

Perhaps Washington is a little envious of the liberal incomes that are thus earned, without any 15 per cent cut by Act of Congress.

If Washington is a mad-house just now, this is the violent ward. The magnificent Department of Commerce building where the NIRA hangs out. On the right the splendid new group of the Labor, Post-Office and Interstate Commerce Commission buildings

New Equipment *for the* Farm

THE small rotary tiller, designed to prepare seedbed at one operation, now has some big brothers and cousins. C. W. Kelsey tells us that the manufacturers are now making one with two-speed transmission for truck farms and nurseries; a larger model cutting 28 inches wide and 12 inches deep; a straddle row attachment that can be used on all the small models for all widths of cultivation up to 24 inches; and also rotary tillage tractor attachments to be pulled by your farm tractor. Have you seen one of the rotary tillers work?

MORE to say about wind electric plants. One of the manufacturers announces a wind-driven generator that sells around $75. This outfit, unlike a larger, heavier, higher-priced outfit, can be mounted on top of a pole or iron pipe. The price does not include tower or batteries. Regular automobile batteries are used to store the electricity. Some of the first users of this set used automobile light bulbs; but there is now a six-volt bulb on the market that fits standard sockets. This plant will light the home and run the radio—that's what the plant is designed for. This plant is not to be compared with the $700 outfits, but worth considering if you want a plant for little money.

CAN you think of any bigger contribution the implement folks have made to farm progress than the manure spreader? If so, name it. As big a blessing as the first spreaders were, they seem crude and clumsy when compared with the newest ones on the market. Sounds like a sales talk, but let's see the new features:

Box of galvanized, rust resisting iron or copper-bearing steel, non-warping. Mounted low for easy loading. Wider at rear than front to prevent wedging as the load moves back. Large capacity, 70 to 80 bushels, which is no more than two horses can pull, because the axles are equipped with roller bearings. Roller bearings on the beaters, too.

Grease gun lubrication, same as on your auto. Five apron speeds, for thick or thin or in-between rates of spreading. And you don't have to stop to "unwrap" the beaters because they are so designed the manure won't wrap around them.

Levers near the driver's seat enable him to change the rate of spreading as he goes along. Thus the poor spots of soil can have a heavier poultice than better land.

Steel wheels and steel frame construction; in short, all metal. Lime spreader attachments readily put on when wanted.

STAINLESS steel has entered the dairy. The separator makers are using it for disks. One of the manufacturers now offers a separator with stainless steel disks that have no numbers on them. You don't have to arrange the disks in definite order when you wash the separator —just wash them and put them back as you pick them up. That's something the separator user will like.

IF time is an item in your painting job, use a power spray outfit. You can do the job in about one-sixth the time. Low-priced outfits, consisting principally of the spray gun and hose, can be attached to the motor of your car, truck or tractor. Neighboring farms might purchase one jointly. Better still, form a paint spray ring and doll up the buildings on all the members' farms. Whitewash and disinfect poultry houses, hoghouses, and dairy barns, too.

Prices *and* Failures

Two grain crop disasters in a row, and possibly a third making—Will prices advance enough to compensate farmers?

By Bernard W. Snow

AS AN example of fast action and prompt decision the crop disaster of 1934 establishes a record in American agriculture. As I write, early in August, we are already taking stock of our food supplies to determine our ability to "carry-on" until another crop gathering season shall come around.

Not in our history, and perhaps never before in world history, has there ever been such volume of crop destruction concentrated into a space of four months. Not even the famine years in China, in India and in Russia will show such crop losses, measured in volume.

Of course our situation does not approach the famine conditions experienced in other countries. We have enough food here. In the famine countries the margin between sufficiency and want is always narrow. With us our productive capacity is so great that the range between plethora and want is too wide to permit thought of real physical suffering.

The fact remains that we are facing a year of the smallest grain production per capita that we have known since our agricultural resources were drawn from a domain continent-wide.

A Billion Bushels Short

LET us put this into figures as far as figures are now available. Our principal crops are usable either as direct or as secondary food products. A considerable part of what we class as animal feeds must therefore be included in a comparison of human food supplies. For this year I am quoting my own August 1 estimates, and the comparison is with the average for the five years 1928–32.

Grain Crops in Millions of Bushels

	1934	1927–31
Corn	1,720	2,516
Winter Wheat	385	632
Spring Wheat	74	254
Oats	498	1,187
Barley	115	157
Rye	17	41
	2,809	4,787

In grain crops alone here is a shrinkage of nearly two billion bushels, the production this year representing only 58 per cent of the average of recent years. If our margin between production and minimum of need were as narrow as it is year after year in lands where gaunt famine is always just around the corner, we would already need ration cards.

But grain alone does not measure our situation. The meat supply per capita is shrinking rapidly. The deliberate destruction of some six or seven million pigs and sows, coupled with forced slaughter of possibly two or three million heads of cattle to save them from starvation, means the elimination of a large volume of meat products from our daily food.

Thus a year of crop disaster, plus an economic experiment intended to raise general prices by creation of an artificial scarcity through destruction of available food supply, gives promise of sharply and perhaps permanently lowering our American standard of living.

Two Droughts at Once

THIS year we are seeing two distinctly separate types of drought operating at the same time, and to a very considerable extent over the same area. The first a periodic drought which has been under way for several years, gradually removing the sub-surface water supply and forcing plant growth to rely increasingly upon current seasonal rainfall. This period has been under way, in some districts of the central northwest, for as much as five years, with steadily shrinking crop possibilities. The weather records locate the area involved as the Great Plains district, the semi-arid area between the 100th and the 105th meridian and reaching from the pan-handle of Texas well into the Canadian province of Saskatchewan.

This type of drought damage can be readily forecast, almost a year in advance, merely by a study of records showing actual moisture supply during certain months prior to the time for crop planting. That portion of our arable land lying within the limits specified is suited only to wheat as a standard direct cash crop, and in the winter wheat area from and including Nebraska southward, the rainfall of July, August and September, before the seed is planted in October, bears a closer relation to final crop yield the next June than does the rainfall of any other three months of the crop season.

Drought Visible Last December

IN other words, the stored-up moisture accumulated in the ground during these months by reason of the fact that the old crop is matured and removed in June, is a principal determining factor in the new crop yield nine months later. A severe mid-summer drought of one year largely determines the wheat yield of the next year in this portion of our wheat area.

The warning of impending wheat crop disaster in both spring and winter wheat which I voiced in *The Farm Journal* last December, when I declared that the proposed wheat acreage reduction program was "flirting with famine," was based upon knowledge that the sub-surface moisture supply in the wheat area of the semi-arid belt had been further reduced through lack of summer rainfall.

The fact that a second drought of an altogether different type has appeared over a much wider area accounts for crop losses far greater than I anticipated last winter. In the humid area east of the Missouri River sub-surface moisture is of only secondary importance, because the current seasonal rainfall during the warm or growing crop months is ordinarily sufficient, with a large margin of safety, to supply crops with all the water they need.

Rainfall records are not complete enough to warrant conclusions as to probable moisture supply in advance, and so predictions of seasonal drought are of small value. This year seasonal rainfall was deficient over the greater part of the central valleys from May to July.

Short feed grain crops mean short meat and milk crops; feeding the pastures will pay better than ever for the next year

Helen Westley and Shirley Temple in "Dimples." Below: Norma Shearer and Leslie Howard in "Romeo and Juliet"

Rating the Autumn Pix

What our chief Rate-Master thinks of the new, the nearly-new, and the coming films

By CHARLES F. STEVENS

Must See

Romeo and Juliet Don't be scared of Shakespeare. The movie crowd has taken this immortal love story and made an extraordinarily fine film of it. The magic of the lines plus the ability of the films to give reality to scenes, far better than the stage can ever do, gives us one of the best pictures ever made, I think. *Norma Shearer* as Juliet, *Leslie Howard* as Romeo, and a

well-nigh perfect cast. On your MUST list.

Dodsworth Notable film version of Sinclair Lewis' novel and play, both almost classics. As in the play, *Walter Huston* is again the supreme virtue. No better actor in the country. Playing with such perfection, you forget *Huston* and see only Dodsworth—the American business man with all his fine characteristics and crude faults. Splendid supporting cast headed by the able *Mary Astor*. Sincere and absorbing.

Nine Days a Queen A British film that ranks right up there with the one we all admired, "The Private Life of Henry VIII." The tragedy of the young girl who was Queen of England for nine days—Lady Jane Gray—and then walked to the headsman's block. A true, unadorned story out of history, by a large and well-chosen cast. *Nova Pilbeam* as Jane, and *Desmond Tester* as Edward VI, may well claim to be the cinema world's leading child actors, along with our own Shirley. Prepare for some tears.

Sing, Baby, Sing One of the funniest, fastest comedies in many a weary moon. You've heard the story—temperamental Hollywood actor comes to New York, gets tipsy, implores unknown girl to be his Juliet and let him be Romeo; in the next day's cold gray light dashes madly for Hollywood with the gal in hot pursuit. *Adolphe Menjou* hitting on all cylinders, and a grand cast of merry-makers. Tops in its class.

Goodish

Craig's Wife *Rosalind Russell,* as the single-minded, selfish and essentially bad woman who sacrificed her husband and everything else to one end—she wanted her house to be hers alone. Tense. Women will prefer.

Dimples *Shirley Temple,* — and no more need be said. Here little *Shirley,* captivating as ever, is a waif who wanders into the stage troupe and heart of a theatrical producer eighty years ago. Eventually she plays Little Eva in "Uncle Tom's Cabin." *Frank Morgan* and comical *Stepin Fetchit* also good. *Temple* fans all go.

Ramona The latest in color films, and pretty good photographically. Helen Hunt Jackson's familiar love story, with its Indian and American Spanish setting. Done once before in silent films, if memory serves me right. And also the source of the popular song of ten years ago. I prefer the play to the song. With *Loretta Young, Don Ameche, Pauline Frederick.* Nice love story.

Fairish

Missing Girls The audience at the start of this one won't know what really happens to missing girls in the Great Metropolis, and at the end they still won't know. The film forgets to tell. Aside from that, a fast tale of rackets and politics, with *Roger Pryor, Muriel Evans.*

Thank You Jeeves Another by P. G. Wodehouse, whose English butler, Jeeves, has pleased so many Americans. In this one, all's well as long as Jeeves and his master, the Hon. Bertie, are on the screen together, and all off when they aren't. *Arthur Treacher* as Jeeves, and *David Niven* as Bertie, are good. As a whole, only so-so.

The Texas Rangers *Jack Oakie, Fred MacMurray, Jean Parker* in a curious mixture of Wild West "horse opera" plus "cops and robbers." Aims to be an epic film of the Texas Rangers, without much success. Amusing and exciting enough to please small boys and big boys. Thass all.

Valiant Is the Word for Carrie *Gladys George,* brilliant actress of "Personal Appearance" on the "legitimate" stage, in her first talking flicker. Here she's in the pix herself, playing the part of a "bad woman" who had her hard heart softened when she found and cared for two little orphans. A good cast, with *Dudley Digges, Arline Judge.* Class A tear-jerker.

Time for a modern magazine

Wilmer Atkinson's old desk was still around in early 1939. FARM JOURNAL acquired *The Farmer's Wife*, and I came to work just in time to help prepare the May issue, the first of the combined magazines. Because from boyhood I had admired FARM JOURNAL, it was a proud moment to join the staff with the fancy title of "editor-in-chief," and to be allowed to sit behind that big, old-fashioned desk. For most of the next 25 years it was to be my work bench.

Although the time had come for a more modern magazine, I was reluctant to abandon all the homely, forthright policies Uncle Wilmer had established. To retain some of the familiar flavor, we continued for years to run the Peter Tumbledown cartoon, the "Now is the time to—" column, and a few other prized features. But the old idea of farming as simply "a way of life" rather than a real business was fast fading out, just as tractors were displacing horses. More and more, the pages had to be filled with new kinds of material. We quit printing fiction. Until Pearl Harbor left no choice, we opposed getting the United States into the war that was raging in Europe.

Remembering that FARM JOURNAL'S columns had helped to establish rural mail delivery and parcel post, we had our say on numerous national questions. Of many New Deal actions we were critical, although we favored the Rural Electrification Administration and soil and water conservation.

Looking back from here, I am sure that we were usually looking forward. Confident that the war would be won, and knowing that the problems of peace would be tremendous, as early as 1942 we began to advocate a world program "to help others to help themselves." That was before the Marshall Plan.

But we never spent too much space on global problems. When Warfarin, the first really effective rat killer, became available, we hammered away in little paragraphs month after month, until our readers, and I am sure my co-editors, may have tired of the topic. But we knew how destructive farm rats could be, and thought that killing rats might be almost as important as reporting the new weedicides and other profit-making aids to farmers. On one topic we never let up. That was the importance of research to find new facts about soils, crops, animals, and all that concerns farmers.

Along in the late 1940s I got to wondering what an inch of rainfall would be worth on a midwest cornfield about August 10, if it had not rained for ten days. That question led to another. Suppose that, besides irrigating his corn field, a farmer were to do everything else that science and experience had indicated would build up his yields! In 1947, with the help of an Illinois fertilizer and seed dealer, Joe Schrock, we found seven farmers who were willing to try. We called this the "300-Bushel Corn Adventure." It was not to be a contest, but an experience. We didn't know that a 300-bushel yield might be possible, but we set the target high. We hoped if anyone ever reached it, we would know how he did it.

Each winter we invited the year's participants, along with hybrid corn company representatives and others interested, to a dinner in Chicago. Higher and higher yields had been reported. One evening Jimmy Holbert, then Funk's top researcher, rose and made a statement. "We have been trying," he said, "to provide farmers with hybrids that would average 75 bushels an acre, or might help them to make 100. *Our sights are too low.* We must develop hybrids that can turn more sunshine, more water, more fertilizer into corn on the cobs."

Jimmy Holbert and his competitors tried. In 1955 Lamar Ratliffe, a 4-H Club boy in Mississippi, came up with 304 bushels, but no one was sure about what factor did it. Three times since then the 300-bushel mark has been exceeded, once in Louisiana, once in Michigan, and in 1975 Herman Warsaw in Illinois brought the record up to 338 bushels.

I like to think that FARM JOURNAL'S "300-Bushel Corn Adventure" had more than a little to do with opening the route toward this tremendous achievement. We supported USDA'S Regional Research Laboratories. From one of them came the cheap process for making penicillin and other antibiotics; from another, the potato flakes now in every grocery store and dozens of other items that have widened the farm market and have served the public. We urged that the whole worldwide vegetable kingdom should be fully explored and the contents of every kind of plant be analyzed for possible uses. Plants can be fully renewed every year, while mineral resources once gone can not be replaced.

I can not recall those busy, fascinating years without a welling-up of gratitude to many associates. The temptation to talk about the people who really made the magazine is strong; I resist it because so many would have to be named. But I do have to speak of Arthur H. Jenkins, who had been editor for some twenty years. Arthur adjusted at once to our new relationship and was unfailingly helpful and inspiring; he deserves long remembrance. The best day's work in my nearly 25 years at FARM JOURNAL was done one evening. Carroll P. Streeter had come in with the 1939 merger to head up *The Farmer's Wife* section. Some years later, over a dinner table, I told him I wanted him to become managing editor of the whole magazine. He was a bit hesitant, but finally agreed. He was the right man—constantly in touch with changing farm interests, and especially gifted at finding brilliant field editors and other associates. It was not long before he took practically full charge, and later, when editor, he performed magnificently at fitting the magazine to farm needs.

With all due respect to co-workers on the multitude of other types of publications, I have long believed that agricultural journalism is the highest and happiest kind of all. Farm writers have to peek through no keyholes, raid no files, destroy no reputations, ask no impertinent questions in order to quote silly answers, nor report rumors as probable facts. Their work is always constructive, always helpful. They believe in the right to choose, the essence of American liberty. And day after day, they meet the finest people on earth.

What a glorious privilege!

—Wheeler McMillen
Editor-in-chief, 1939 to 1955

Ada the Ayrshire— Every farmer knew her antics and recognized his own contrary cows

ALL OF US
are in the War

FARMER

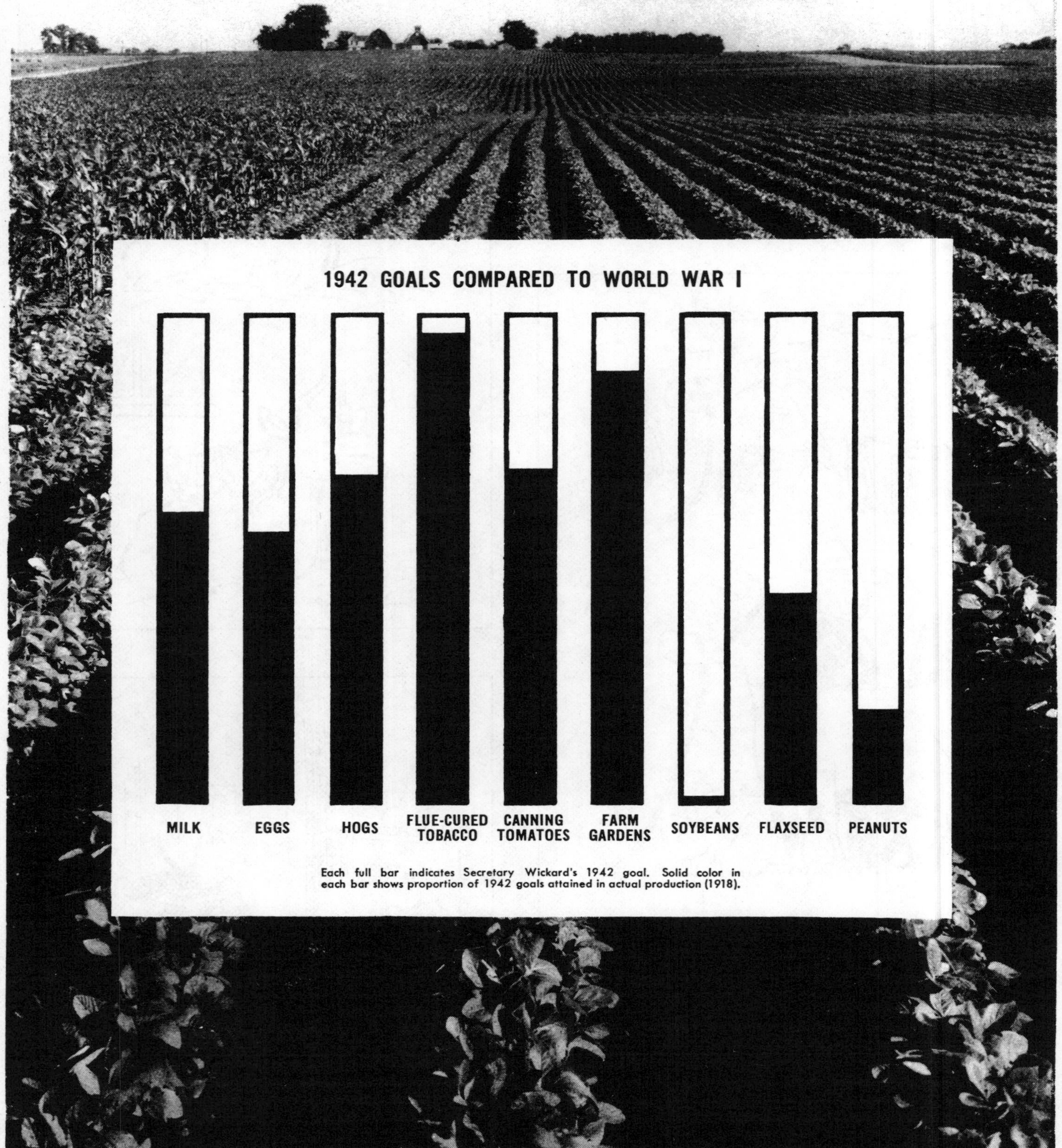

Each full bar indicates Secretary Wickard's 1942 goal. Solid color in each bar shows proportion of 1942 goals attained in actual production (1918).

Lambs at Arminto, Wyoming, awaiting shipment to Iowa feed lots. Never have there been so many sheep and lambs on feed as there were January 1, 1942 (6,775,000 head).

Can a tractor feed steers? Henry Marshall, West Lafayette, Indiana, cuts down labor by using his general-purpose tractor in hauling feed and manure, moving feed bunks, etc.

YESTERDAY, agriculture looked out upon surpluses; today, it looks out upon deficiencies; tomorrow, perhaps, on acute shortages. Thus total war changes the economic landscape. Napoleon said the same thing another way: "An army marches on its stomach."

Our problem is now production. With scantier facilities, the farmer will try to produce this year the greatest output in history. Secretary Wickard used exactly the right adjective when he said: "The burden and responsibility upon American farmers are *staggering*."

Some of the increases asked for in 1942 are: 7% more milk than last year; 13% more eggs; 10% more chickens; 14% more hogs; 30% more gardens; 8% more corn and cotton; 13% more dry beans; 73% more dry peas; 32% more canning peas; 18% more canning tomatoes; 54% more soybeans; 31% more flaxseed; 57% more cover-crop seed; 6% more rice; 58% more turpentine; and two and one-half times as many peanuts.

Acreage restrictions are removed from sugar cane and sugar beets. Wheat is about the only major crop on which no increase is asked. There will be no marketing quotas on corn this year. The chart on facing page, set squarely into a photo of an Indiana soybean field, compares some of the 1942 goals with the magnificent job agriculture did in 1918 during World War No. 1.

Fortunately, our war effort hits into an upswing production cycle on some farm products which, by their very nature, are difficult to increase quickly. Never have we had so many meat animals on farms as there were January 1. Cattle and sheep numbers set new all-time high records. The 1941 pig crop was the second highest on record, and all signs point to a 1942 spring pig crop that will beat any we ever had.

Production of milk in 1941 left all previous figures behind,

Evaporated milk being loaded for export. We milked 372,000 cows to supply Great Britain with cheese, evaporated milk and dried skimmilk in the last eight months of 1941.

With two rotary hoes behind his rubber-tired tractor, Paul Meyer goes over the cornfield in a hurry on John Stuart's 480-acre grain and livestock farm in Lake county, Illinois.

Power is a good hired man. Harrowing 300 acres is an average day's job with this Diesel tractor, used by Reichelt and Beal, Holyoke, Colorado. Fuel? One gallon to 5½ acres.

This California rig grinds dairy and poultry farm manures. Minerals are added to make complete organic fertilizers for Salinas Valley truck growers. Hammer mill does the grinding.

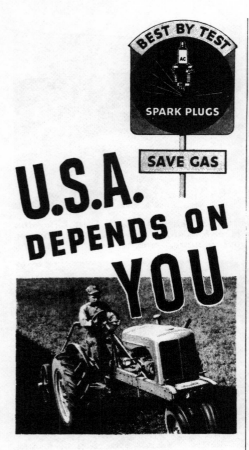

not because of a record-breaking number of dairy cows, but because of more milk per cow. The poultry and egg crop last year topped all previous records. Total cash income to farmers last year from all farm marketings touched eleven billion dollars for the first time since 1929.

What became of last year's milk production is a story in itself. An unprecedented demand for cheese for our own use and for export to lend-lease countries caused 125 plants to make cheese for the first time. Total output broke all records (916,590,000 pounds).

There were booms, too, in evaporated and dried milk. Total for 1941 (3.165.-906,000 pounds) exceeded the goal set last March by Secretary Wickard following passage of the Lend-Lease Act. British lend-lease shipments took 443.556.493 pounds from April 29 to December 31. 1941. As 1942 began, the output of evaporated milk was 93% higher than a year earlier.

Production of dried skim-milk for human food is 13% ahead of what it was a year ago. The government is buying this for distribution under lend-lease, relief and school lunch programs. Production of dried whole milk is 38% ahead of a year ago.

For another story of all-out production, interview the Little Red Hen. A year ago Secretary Wickard asked for an 8% increase in young chickens on farms. When Uncle Sam counted chickens seven months later (January, 1942), he had an army of layers 12% greater than a year earlier, and they were laying 17% more eggs. The number of potential layers now on farms is ample to meet the 1942 egg production goal. In January this year, hatcheries turned out 47,000,000 chicks. It was their biggest January on record. On February 1, advance orders for baby chicks were 35% larger than a year earlier.

One pound of dried eggs (center) equals 48 fresh ones roundabout. John Bull gathered the eggs from 13,600,000 Yankee hens from May 1 to December 31, 1941. Dried eggs are shipped to Britain in moisture-proof barrels.

To take care of the increased output of eggs, the Little Red Hen has built 54 egg-drying plants since a year ago (there are now 70). Drying reduces a 30-dozen case of eggs weighing 45 pounds (without the case) to ten pounds of powder. The dried product takes less ocean shipping space, and there is less danger of breakage and spoilage. Dried eggs (shipped in barrels with double liners of paraffin paper) keep well as long as they are kept dry.

To win their major objective of greater production, farmers this year will have to fight on several fronts. One of the toughest sectors is labor. Agriculture has already lost a million workers through the draft, enlistments and defense jobs. Employment agencies are able to supply few farm helpers, and fewer still who are competent.

Something is being done about it. The government plans to build 18 mobile labor camps for farm workers on the East Coast. In New York the state legislature has passed a measure that will give 30-day leaves to school children over 14 who want to help on farms during planting and harvesting. Sugar beet growers in the western states want the child labor provision of the 1927 sugar act suspended so children can work in sugar beet fields.

One of the leading farm implement companies announces a plan to have dealers train women and girls to operate milking machines and other farm implements. Boy Scouts in Iowa are being trained by both farmers and implement dealers to take the place of farm hands. In many localities F. F. A. groups are helping to train town boys for farm work. Add to all these the willingness of farmers to pool labor with their neighbors, to work longer hours without any thought of extra pay for overtime, and then compare everything with the attitude that has been displayed by some industrial labor leaders.

Agriculture still awaits more favorable consideration of farm help from the draft boards. During World War No. 1 President Wilson openly sponsored putting farmers and their helper sons into deferred classifications, and draft boards generally went along. Some draft boards, unacquainted with farm needs, are sending to camp farm boys badly needed on the farm but unwilling to claim exemption for fear of being called unpatriotic. If draft boards can not correct this, then why not assign these men to work in the fields, just as other soldiers and sailors are detailed to build planes, superintend construction of guns, munitions, etc.?

Another tough sector is farm power and equipment. Agriculture is mecha-

Sugar beet growing yields to mechanization. This giant rig loads beets faster and prevents sugar losses (anywhere from $10 to $20 an acre) caused by delay in getting sugar beets to the factory.

nized to a much larger extent than during World War No. 1. In 1915, the peak year of horse population, there were only 25,000 tractors on farms. Now there are close to 1,600,000; every fourth farm has a tractor. In some states there are two to every three farms. The number of trucks has climbed from a few thousand to more than a million during the same period: automobiles, from a half million to over four millions.

Unable to get tractors, farmers can not fall back on horses because there are only half as many as in 1915. It takes three or four years to bring a colt to working age. Most farm implements have been redesigned for tractor use, and would not give satisfactory results with horses, even if horses were available.

With tractors, implements and other equipment hard to get because of low manufacturing quotas, this problem is being attacked from a different direction —that is, greater usage and longer life from equipment now on farms. Farmers will pool their equipment, operate their own rigs longer hours, load their tractors to full capacity, and hire custom rigs to help out in rush periods.

Farm machinery clinics have suddenly become almost as much of a country institution as the old-time literary society. California has held 200 clinics this year. California farmers claim they have 50,000

Co-op livestock shipping associations show up in a new light now. P. O. Wilson, secretary of National Livestock Marketing Association, discusses 1942 plans with market analyst H. M. Conway.

welding outfits. There are 200 high schools in California with welding outfits used by vo-ag boys for farm machinery repair. In Kansas, high school boys studying agriculture have repaired and rebuilt many farm implements, made surveys of old machinery parts suited for repair, and held farm machinery clinics.

Production costs are definitely a part of the farmer's problem, too. It is traditional (and frequently true) that the prices of things farmers buy go up faster than what they sell. Feed costs are up already. Bran is $12 a ton higher than a year ago; cottonseed meal, $12; soybean meal, $17; tankage, $28; meat scraps, $29; fishmeal, $24; distillers' dried grains, $10; alfalfa meal, $8.

To a considerable extent farmers are able to cut feed costs by growing more grain and legume hay; but when under pressure for greater production per animal, it is hard to get along without some purchased feed. Feeding ratios the country over are generally favorable to producers of hogs, beef and poultry products,

Imports cut off, American farmers turn to seed growing. G. C. Passmore, Prattville, Ala., combined 45 pounds of White Dutch clover seed per acre from his pasture, and put it in used feed bags.

but not to dairymen. Wages for farm help are up about 10%.

Cost of living has gone up 10% in the past year. Food prices are 21% higher than a year ago; clothing, 15%. The cost of food for the farm table, however, can be the last thing for farmers to worry much about. As specialists in food production, they can grow most of the food they need—fruit, vegetables, meat, eggs, etc.

In the Tennessee grow-your-own-food campaign, one farmer in seven was able to produce 75% or more of the food for his family without any radical change in his farming program. A farm that produces most of its food makes a major contribution to the war effort for these reasons: The family health is benefited; cost of living is reduced; commercial supplies are made available for city people, for armed forces and for our allies; transportation and packing plants are relieved.

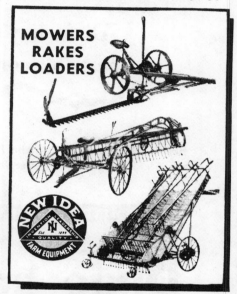

Farm Journal • December, 1948

Corn Beats 200 Bushels

Farm Journal • October, 1946

300 Bushels or Bust

Farm Journal • May, 1950

300 bushel corn—no pipe dream

Farm Journal • January, 1953

Dixie boy claims best '52 corn yield

HEADLINES from some of the *Farm Journal* articles reporting farmers' efforts to grow 300-bushel corn, after our October 1946 issue startled everybody with the idea. It's been a 9-year campaign that taught us a lot.

Dixie boy does it—304 bu.!

BACK-PORCH FIGURING. 4-H Club Agent J. W. Archer (rt.), Lamar, his dad (left) show weight slips to *Farm Journal's* Ralph Wennblom.

Lamar Ratliff, 16-year-old 4-H'er in Prentiss County, Mississippi, tops *Farm Journal's* 300-bushel goal

BY RALPH D. WENNBLOM

NINE years ago last month, *Farm Journal* startled corn growers with what sounded like a crazy idea.

"Will anybody ever raise 300 bushels of corn an acre?" asked George D. Scarseth, well-known soils scientist, in an article entitled "300 Bushels or Bust" in the October 1946 issue. "*I think it's possible,*" wrote Scarseth.

Some people snorted, others just laughed. Best official yield on record at that time was 190 bushels.

But *Farm Journal's* Wheeler McMillen believed in the idea. He and Joe Schrock of Schrock Fertilizer Service, Congerville, Ill., found five farmers who were adventurous enough to shoot for 300 bushels in 1947.

All five "busted." Top yield was only 115 bushels. In December, the farmers met in Chicago with the country's best corn scientists to figure out what had gone wrong—and to lay plans for doing better. This was the first of a series of Golden Acre Dinners, sponsored by *Farm Journal.*

The idea really caught fire in 1948 when more than 250 farmers entered the "Adventure." Top yield was 224 bushels—considered phenomenal. But 100 guests at the Golden Acre Dinner agreed: "We'll make 300—someday!"

From that year on, top yields kept bobbing above the 200-bushel mark—207, 233, 214, 218, 243.

Then, early this month, just nine years after *Farm Journal* first popped the "300-bushel question," 16-year-old Lamar Ratliff and his dad, Paul, grew the answer—304.38 bushels of No. 2 shelled corn on a solid acre!

I saw the field that made corn history. The Ratliffs call it their "club patch." It's barely 1½ acres in a small

Photos: George Ambrester

25,850 STALKS did the trick. Here, Lamar shows the 6″ to 8″ between plants. His rows were 30″ apart.

hollow that's surrounded by steep hills.

Farm Journal's 1946 article was prophetic. It had said that the best place to try for 300 bushels would probably be "a very well-drained, light, sandy soil. It should be in a valley or a muggy corner where there is little air drainage, and where there'll be the most growth-promoting carbon dioxide."

That description fits the Ratliff field to a T!

Just what else do you need to grow 300-bushel corn? We still really don't know, but here's what Lamar had:

● **25,850 stalks.** "How did you estimate that?" I asked. "We counted 'em," said Paul Ratliff, the father.

They planted a hybrid, Funk's G-711, in rows running north and south. "I'd guess there were two ears on 75% of the stalks, and three ears on 5%," said Paul, adding: "*We never found a barren stalk in that acre.*"

● **Plant food.** They spread 25 loads of manure—about 15 tons—last fall; cleaned out the neighbors' henhouses to get enough. Before planting, they put on 1,000 pounds of 14-14-14 and 200 pounds of nitrate of soda (16% nitrogen), side-dressed with 300 pounds of 33-0-0 when the corn was knee-high.

● **He had moisture.** Records from the U.S. Weather Bureau at Tupelo, Miss., only 18 miles away, show 43.58 inches of rainfall during the corn's growing season: 12.52 in March, 7.06 in April, 10.80 in May, 3.50 in June, 6.56 in July, and 3.14 in August.

Total rain from September 1, 1954, to September 1, 1955 was 66.79 inches.

● **He had Dolly,** a nimble eight-year-old mule to do the cultivating. "That little mule minds. She won't step on a corn plant if she can help it."

● **He had luck.** Five mule shoes—one for each year that they've tried for the record—hang from a sweet gum tree alongside the patch.

● **And a dad** who loves to grow corn, and a mother whose shirt-factory wages helped pay the fertilizer bills.

Lamar didn't have much time to talk about corn when I was there, so his dad told me how they grew the crop.

"The field has been in corn every year since '26 when it was cleared, I guess, except for '44 when we grew cotton," says Ratliff.

"Well, last October we disked down those stalks—the corn made 218½ bushels last year—and spread the manure. Then I broke it with a middlebuster plow that had a subsoiling chisel welded underneath. I put her down as deep as the mules could pull it—about 12 inches, I guess.

"Two or three weeks later, I went in and busted it back again. Kept doing that all winter. Whenever the soil dried out, I turned it. Plowed it eight times during the winter.

"Then in March, we put the 14-14-14 and the soda in the furrow and busted once more. This put the fertilizer about 15 inches below where the seed would be.

"On March 23, we drilled a whole bushel of seed on that acre—thinned it to a plant every 6″ to 8″ after we cultivated. Then we side-dressed and laid it by.

"*That's all we did. We just let it go to suit itself, and it went!*"

Mrs. Ratliff piped up. "It didn't grow by itself. Paul was down there watching it, night and day."

County Agent W. T. Smith and his assistant, J. W. Archer, measured off the acre—132 feet wide, and 330 feet long—supervised the harvesting, and certified these yield figures:

Weight of the ear corn: 19,776 pounds. Three 20-pound samples of ear corn shelled out 84.5%. Based on this, the 19,776 pounds of ear corn contained 16,710.72 pounds of shelled corn.

A sample, sent to Mississippi State College, tested 13.93% moisture. The standard for No. 2 corn is 15½% moisture, 56 pounds to the bushel. A bushel of 14% moisture corn actually weighs only 54.9 pounds. So, to correct the yield to 15½% moisture, they divided 16,710.72 by 54.9. This figures out to 304.38 bushels.

Any way you look at it, that acre is quite a piece of ground. Since 1950, it has produced 1,264.6 bushels of corn—an average of 210.8 per year. **End**

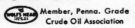

Photos by the author

It was Mrs. Warsaw, shown driving the tractor, who hauled the corn to town and brought back the elevator scale ticket. It told an incredible story of a 338-bu. yield that came from a measured 1.00018 acre in an 80-acre field that had been in corn for 14 straight years! It was no contest yield.

New corn yield record 338 bu.

By BOB COFFMAN
Farm Journal Field Staff

■ Herman Warsaw couldn't believe it, but there it was on the elevator scale ticket: 20,500 lbs. net weight, at 21.96% moisture. Converted to No. 2 corn, it came out to 338.02 bu. And he had harvested it from a measured acre on his McLean County, Ill., farm.

Warsaw had been thinking about 300-bu. corn for 20 years, but he was still speechless when he found out he had actually produced that much—and more to boot.

His first thought, he admits, was "Nobody's gonna believe it. Do we have to tell anyone?" But you can't hide a yield like that under a bushel. This was not a contest yield. "He just did it on his own," a friend and eye witness to the harvest, Don Swanlund, told us.

Warsaw had his eye on one 80-acre field all summer. In continuous corn for 14 years, it had yielded 267 bu. two years ago. Finally, curiosity got the best of him, and he made some pre-harvest checks with a slide rule calculator developed by University of Illinois ag engineers. Gulp! More than 300 bu., the calculator predicted after accounting for harvest plant population, ear size, number of rows and kernels per row.

That did it. Warsaw quietly went out and staked and flagged an area 2,334′ long by 18′8″ wide in the 80-acre field. (It comes out to 43,568 square feet, eight square feet more than an acre—1.00018 acres to be exact.)

With no thought of ever breaking the 306.6-bu. mark set by Michigan grower Orville Montri two years ago, Warsaw invited seed company representatives to come out while he cut the patch. No big deal. But it certainly was a big deal for the combine! Black diesel smoke

Herman Warsaw holds some 338-bu. ears. They weigh an average .7 lbs. each and came from a harvest stand of 33,000 plants per acre. Kernel depth exceeded ½″, bigger than average.

started rolling; he shifted the six-row rig into low gear and let the machine creep forward.

The acre had a measured harvest stand of 33,000 plants. Random ear samples showed an average weight of .7 lbs. with 18 or 20 rows of kernels prevalent and 50 kernels per row. Kernel depth exceeded ½″, a factor not considered in the pre-harvest guesstimates. The local elevator recorded the net weight and moisture and converted it to No. 2 basis.

For the record, the hybrid that produced the incredible crop was FS 854, purchased from his local co-op, a branch of FS Services, Inc., an affiliate of the Illinois Farm Bureau.

He planted in 28″ rows on April 22, at 34,300 kernels per acre. Rainfall from May 1 until harvest totaled a few drops over 24″.

The crop was fertilized with 400 lbs. per acre of nitrogen, 228 lbs. of phosphate and 286 lbs. of potash. Then, for good measure, he added 20 tons per acre of hog manure. "Not so much for its nutrient value as for its contribution to organic matter," Warsaw explains.

When *Farm Journal* visited with Warsaw, he had not finished harvesting the entire 80-acre field where the record was carved from, but he conservatively estimates that his entire 380 acres of corn in 1975 will beat a 200-bu. average.

That is not at all unusual in his area of central Illinois. His neighbors have teased the 200-bu. mark, too, in field after field this year.

"I must be crazy," he thought to himself last spring when he buttoned up against an April 22 snow squall to go out and plant corn. But as an official U.S. local crop reporter for more than 40 years, he knew the merits of early planting—snow or no snow.

Later, he observed that the crop got an unusual amount of sunlight during the growing season. Even after a rain, the sun came out brightly and tagged on a few extra growing degrees. He points to the uniform size and quality of the ears as the payoff for plentiful sunlight.

The crop that started in snow flurries almost ended in a hurricane. The backlash of hurricane Eloise in late September put some of Warsaw's corn down, and he hustled to harvest his prize field earlier than he had planned. As improbable as it seems, he thinks they left some corn on the ground in the record field.

What does it cost to grow 300-bu. corn? "I honestly haven't figured that out," he told us. He knows he has about $125 in fertilizer, chemicals and seed. He'll know to the penny when he gets the time. Warsaw has been a cooperator with the Farm Business Farm Management record service since 1948.

"There has to be some profit in there," he grins. Let's see, 338 multiplied by $2.50 per bushel comes to $845 gross per acre.

Warsaw has a rare sense of stewardship for his soil. Frankly, he gets more excited telling about his conservation tillage program than he does big corn yields.

"We haven't used a moldboard plow for six years," boasts Warsaw, pointing to the five-bottom hulk of steel gathering feed room dust in a side shed.

Then he shifts your attention to an aging chisel plow he has used since the late Sixties for all his tillage. Near the door of his machine shed you notice his new corn planter has a tool bar of fluted colters up front.

"We prefer the combination of deep tillage in the fall, coupled with no-tillage in the spring." It wasn't until he switched to deep chisel plowing that he was able to break the 200 yield barrier.

About the time he was able to produce 200 bu. of corn per acre, a 16-year-old lad in Mississippi—Lamar Ratliff—was turning the corn-growing world on its ear by picking an unheard of 304.38-bu. yield in 1955. "That became the target for all of us to aim at," Warsaw remembers. "I wondered then just what the soil's potential was on my own farm. I guess a lot of guys did."

But 300 bu. seemed as far away as the moon 20 years ago. Now we know both can be reached. Warsaw got serious about 300-bu. corn when his field hit 267 in 1973—the same year Ratliff's record finally toppled.

"I set the goal for myself to hit 300 bu. by 1978. That meant doing everything we thought was necessary, then waiting for the weather and everything to fall into place."

Well, you know what 1974 was like—wet spring, summer drouth, early frost and light brittle corn. But 1975 has rewarded him handsomely, and presented a challenging goal that the next generation of farmers will try to surpass.

After I visited Herman Warsaw, I was convinced his achievement was legitimate. I also came away satisfied that the honor had gone to a quiet, dedicated farmer and not to some sort of hard charger blowing on the horn and trying to elbow into the national limelight. ◁

Farm women... partners in the family business

The millions of farm women who have been reading FARM JOURNAL during these 100 years were fortunate that the magazine was founded by a man "grounded in the faith," as he himself put it, for women's equality. For all through those years, building on Wilmer Atkinson's editorial policy of the first forty years, FARM JOURNAL editors have recognized the abilities of women not only in the home, but also in the farm business—and in the world.

The first editor was brought up in a Quaker home, and he writes in his autobiography: "I did not have to go through a period of tardy conversion . . . as so many other men did, but had graduated, a full-fledged friend and advocate of the woman's cause. . . ." The "cause" was the ballot. He was a friend and admirer of Lucretia Mott, the little Quaker woman to whom he gives full credit for starting the woman's movement in America.

In 1915 he headed the Pennsylvania Men's League for Woman Suffrage, lent his presses and set apart office space in the FARM JOURNAL Building. The Men's League joined the women in a march from the front steps of its present headquarters. Such activity led to the amendment a few years later to the Federal Constitution, franchising all women in the country.

Atkinson deplored the common law decree that when a woman married "she ceased to be a distinct person; husband and wife were one, and that one was the husband." It is not surprising that this man edited his new magazine for the farmer *and* his family. In eight months, he wrote, "I had the Household Department going in fine shape . . . I early saw that one of the fields to cultivate comprised the firesides of America. . .Practical farmers and farmers' wives," he wrote, "tell each other through the FARM JOURNAL how to do things the easiest and best way on the farm and in the home. . . ." In 1902 he described "the real reasons" for FARM JOURNAL's success: "It is a home builder and home preserver . . . its keynote is happy, prosperous, and contented rural homes before fat hogs . . . hogs do not come first. . . ."

Over the years, much of the magazine's copy for the home was help for the day-to-day routine—recipes for good food, plans for more efficient kitchens, patterns for home sewing, decorating suggestions, new products. But attention also was given to the psychology of bringing up children, of a happy marriage partnership, of bookkeeping and handling of finances, of community concerns—church, school, entertainment. Many farm women helped, as they still do, with chores and with field work in emergencies and were at home with articles on livestock and crops as well as homemaking. So are women editors:

On the current staff a woman writes on farm finance, and a woman is editor of the dairy section. FARM JOURNAL has been—and is—edited for farm men and women as partners in a family business.

While men were at the helm, women writers appeared in the very first issues. The first woman hired by Wilmer Atkinson used a fictitious name, so unusual was it for women to venture into the workaday world. In 1939, *The Farmer's Wife*, published in St. Paul, Minn., was merged with FARM JOURNAL, bringing its home economics professionals, a Test Kitchen and an editor, Carroll P. Streeter, whose philosophy that FARM JOURNAL readers were "human beings who happen to live on the farm" strongly influenced the JOURNAL's content. In 1945, a woman editor was brought in to head the magazine within a magazine and expand the staff.

Magazine content was supplemented beginning in 1959 with books staff-produced on subjects of interest to farm men and women. In 1970, a separate book division was established and, by this Centennial year, had distributed 10 million books on subjects both of everyday help and of inspiration. Family-oriented copy has become even more dually directed—to both men and women.

On the next dozen pages are several sample articles; the first epitomizes the progress of the farm woman in the first three or four generations of FARM JOURNAL readers: "The Farm Woman Wins Her Place." The second article was one of the most widely read and discussed in the magazine's history: "How Does a Young Wife Manage?" grew out of the frustrations of young women coping with "so much to do . . . so little time." FARM JOURNAL readers—1,500 of them who had lived through this typical small-children, limited-income, heavy workload period—volunteered advice and reassurance. In the third article, farm women themselves distilled the pros and cons of their lives on the land: "We Have the Best of Two Worlds."

—Gertrude Dieken
Editor, Farmer's Wife, 1945-1970
Creative Director, Book Division, 1970 to the present

Photo: Nebraska State Historical Society

To be a farmer's wife 75 years ago meant hardship, if home were a sod house on the prairie. This homemaker's loneliness was broken by a visitor who rode twenty miles.

THE FARM WOMAN

One spring day, less than a hundred years ago, Martha Wilson stopped her stirring spoon in midair to make sure she heard right. No mistake: wheels scraped against a wagon turning around the bend into the house yard.

Her hand went only halfway up to straighten her hair as she flew out the sod house door—that sound meant mail to this Nebraska prairie wife. Bert Young, nearest neighbor, was back from Nebraska City, 50 miles away, with the first news from East of the Missouri since before Christmas.

The rest of the day, in between twisting slough grass to feed the fire and minding the baby, Martha read, and read again, the letters from Her People. "We had a little party last night for Papa's birthday," her sister Ellen wrote from Philadelphia. "Just a few nearby neighbors, thirty in all."

Martha held her hands over her ears to shut out the everlasting moan of the prairie wind. When Thomas came in after dark from sowing, he could see that his wife had wept buckets.

After the usual supper of cornbread, molasses and salt pork, Thomas pinched off the wick to make the candle burn bright, and settled himself with a thick brown book. It had come in the mail, from his Uncle William, back East.

This was an important book—the first report of the

Photo: Cornell University

Home demonstration workers brought new ideas, a new outlook. Here a Cornell group cranks up for a bread-making meeting in 1915.

Today farm women work together in organized groups. This picture shows Associated Women of the Farm Bureau at Chicago meeting recently. Presiding is Mrs. Raymond Sayre, a farm woman who has been around the world, plans a trip to Africa. →

WINS HER PLACE

BY GERTRUDE DIEKEN

first Commissioner of Agriculture to the President, Abraham Lincoln—and 100,000 extra copies had been distributed. It was a big book, but that was good. A man didn't get much to read out here.

Thomas leafed around in it here and there, but on page 462 his mind fastened on the title *Health of Farmers' Families*. Martha wondered briefly what held a man's attention in that dull-looking fine print.

Thomas read that there was some concern over the large numbers of farm people in lunatic asylums: "The statistics of the insane in Massachusetts show that the largest number of cases were farmers' wives." And, on turning the page, Thomas read: "This is the key . . . their subjects of thought are too few; *their life is a ruinous routine. . .*"

"Let the farmer never forget that his wife is his best friend . . . and equal partner," he read. The United States Department of Agriculture reminded Thomas that Martha was not a machine—that "few things will bring a more certain and happy reward to a farmer than for him to remember his wife is a social being." (He glanced with new eyes at Martha, sitting in the candlelight perimeter with her beloved letters.) And he read further that "a bunch of flowers or a shilling ribbon" would be "a good investment."

The author even reported reproachfully that he had been in a farm house where the wife sewed industriously by the dim light of a candle, when the same farmer owned "600 acres of fine grazing lands, every inch paid for." At that point, Thomas blew out Martha's homemade tallow and went thoughtfully to bed.

MARTHA WILSON'S GRANDDAUGHTER, Alice Haley, recently came across that brittle, brown-edged "First Report" of the United States Department of Agriculture, the inside cover inscribed in faded ink: "Thos. Wilson, Esq." She found it in a long-untouched trunk in the attic of her spacious, two-story brick farmhouse that stood on the selfsame site as the sod house in the Sixties. The quaint language amused Alice until she realized, suddenly, that this "neglected drudge" was her own grandmother!

Alice was thoughtful as she tripped down her carpeted stairs. In the kitchen she switched on the exhaust

"I AM NOT AFRAID OF TOMORROW, FOR I HAVE SEEN YESTERDAY AND I LOVE TODAY."

fan, set the oven timer, started a refrigerated casserole to bake, and began folding clothes that had been automatically washed and dried. All in less time than it took Grandma Wilson to stoke up her "hayburner."

"Drudge," the United States Department of Agriculture had called the farm woman in 1862. Alice's eyes traveled around her streamlined kitchen. "We-l-l, there is still lots of work on the farm, but I could hardly be called a drudge," she mused.

She began listening with one ear to the hog prices broadcast from Chicago; the telephone rang, and her mind registered the metal slam of the mailbox at the end of the gravel drive. *Isolated? Lonely?* With something doing every night last week? With two cars in the garage and a plane in the hangar? With a trip to town every day or so? Hardly.

Ignorant? With magazines, radio, television, newspapers, Home Extension club? No.

Inferior? Timid? Poorly-dressed? Culture-hungry?

I'M A LUCKY WOMAN, Martha Wilson's granddaughter exclaimed right out loud, on her way to answer the phone.

She is, of course. And there are thousands of farm women as fortunate. Most farm families now can make a good enough living to have a good life. Not all. There are still, in 1952, far too many farm homes without even such an elementary thing as running water. Some still lack electricity, and hundreds of thousands more got it only within the last ten years. Many are still without furnaces, bathtubs, and the other creature comforts that most people consider ordinary essentials of living.

But *any* farm woman's lot today would be beyond the wildest dreams of the lonely young mother who made a home in that remote one-room sod house.

Not only the smooth, shiny machines would surprise her. The pioneer woman who went West bravely armed with her mother's well-meant admonitions, a walnut bureau, a few iron kettles, and often unusable recipes (no white flour in Nebraska City), also would disbelieve that housework could become a science and a profession. That "ruinous routine" has taken on real dignity.

"Domestic economy" it was called when the first Midwest colleges started offering a few courses. That was about the time of the first *Farm Journal* (75 years ago) and the first Farmers' Institutes. In 1950, 1¾ million students were enrolled in high-school home economics and 60,000 in college were studying cooking, sewing, buying, child rearing, home decoration. In the nation's capital, a whole corps of women were researching on homemaking problems in a government bureau—Human Nutrition and Home Economics.

But—and here Martha Wilson would well-I-never—*farm women have been the ones really to take advantage* of home economics study. They have the biggest adult education program in the world. And they haven't forgotten to interpret the "culture" in agriculture their own way—they study music, art, books, as well as homemaking skills.

If farm families live well today, chances are it's not *just* because they make more money or because factories make more things. It's because Mamma set her mind—and spirit—to work as well as her hands! The Home Demonstration Agent had a lot to do with it, too.

Now, many years later, city women are clamoring for the same sort of homemaking education. It is spreading to foreign lands. Because farm women know what Home Demonstration work has done for them, they are helping get it to their less privileged sisters in Europe, in Asia, and to bring foreign home economists here for training. Better homes, they reason, will produce sturdier, stabler people—the first essential to peace.

TO BE SURE, BUILDING this "ruinous routine" into a profession of homemaking was slow—and often grievous—business. Those early women deserve bronze plaques and statues if anyone ever did.

Take Martha Van Renssalaer, who began poking around in the curriculum at Cornell University in 1900 (she founded home economics at Cornell, and the home economics building bears her name). She asked about bacteriology, because it seemed to be the closest she could get to something housekeepy.

"Bacteriology? Whatever for?"

In patient terms, she told the bacteriologists: To teach women the importance of keeping the dishcloth clean.

"Oh, just tell them it's nicer that way," said the men! Women wouldn't understand science anyway.

But pioneers in "domestic *(Continued)*

economy" were determined that women could reason. It was a fight: When Vermont first allowed women to enter the University (1871), it was a "bold and rash step . . . at considerable risk."

Letters like this, written by a farm woman to Liberty Hyde Bailey (Cornell's Dean of Agriculture), spurred the early women on: "I cannot tell you what it means to me to know that somebody cares. My life is made up of men, men, mud, mud. Send me the bulletins and remember me in your prayers."

Such gratitude inspired early Home Demonstration Agents to "set yeast" in dreary, cold hotel rooms at night and to tote the dough, cozy in a valise with a hot water bottle, to the farm women's meeting next morning. With the buffalo robe over the valise, not over teacher!

Not all farm women jumped at the chance to improve. (There are still several million who have no part in Home Demonstration work, many who have never heard of it.) They sometimes looked witheringly at the school-trained homemaking "expert" who was teaching them how to can beans. Humph! No older than their own daughters!

So these experts had to step carefully. A former Texas state leader of Home Demonstration work told me herself that she once turned down a home agent candidate who drove a red Ford. Red was too flashy for farm women!

A little group of women gathered around an early Arizona home agent with challenge in their eyes: "They said you can get a whole hen in a quart jar. We want to see you do it."

For the most part, however, strong affections sprang up between the home agent and "her women." She was their friend. In North Carolina, women in one county asked Jane McKimmon, the state leader, to replace their agent. Their reason: "The one we have is well educated and can do things, but she doesn't *love* us, Mis' McKimmon!"

BUT FARM WOMEN learned to fight for "the program." (Some first had to fight their husbands, who didn't believe in such folderol.) As late as 1919 courthouses were considered by most women as places where it was not quite respectable to be. Farm women went anyway, to ask county supervisors about money for Home Demonstration work.

Farm women learned the power of sheer numbers. When the Texas legislature tried during the depression to cut almost by half the funds for all educational institutions (including their Home Demonstration program), no less than 1,800 farm women descended on the capital. Times were hard and taxes hard to pay (the farm woman who was State President had to borrow a hat for the trip). But they didn't intend to see Home Demonstration work crippled. Instead of a 41% cut, the legislature reconsidered, ended with only a 25% cut.

Meanwhile, farm women have fought alongside their men to better farm income and the farmer's status. When the National Grange was organized as a farm fraternal group, soon after the Civil War, women and children over 14 were equal members in their own right. A truly enlightened stand for those times!

Memberships in the Farmers Union and in the American Farm Bureau Federation have likewise always been family affairs. In 1934, however, Farm Bureau women organized their own special arm of the federation to focus their attention on schools, health, laws and the like. Farm women serve on the AFBF's Resolutions Committee, which makes the organization's national policy.

And it is no accident that the liveliest and soundest of the co-operatives are those in which women are the most active. Such co-ops have the least trouble getting—and keeping—members!

In all these ways the farm woman has gained, above all, new respect for herself as a homemaker *and as a person.* The Home Demonstration Agent might explain what made the "tunnels" in bread, but she was doing more—she was shaping farm women into leaders. Part of their payment for learning how to make better bread was standing on their own two feet and showing the same thing to other women in their own neighborhoods. Right now there are more than ½ million such leaders.

Each year the President of the United States proclaims a special Home Demonstration Week to call the nation's attention to this group of women, whose current slogan is "Today's Home Builds Tomorrow's World."

The farm home *especially* has something to give to tomorrow's world. It produces people of high courage, who have faith in tomorrow. Nature tempers them with favors and failures. They meet the changes of Nature and seasons, start young and work hard, know how to share toil as a family instead of going it alone. They believe in God because He is all around them. They can win, or they can sacrifice for the group—it's all part of farm life.

The farm home sends out into the world young people who can face it serenely, but vigorously. People who don't panic easily and who have the independence and strength of free men (with more common sense than any single group in our population). We *need* them on our farms, in business, in schools, in government, in world affairs.

FARM WOMEN KNOW this. They haven't merely *favored*, they have *fought for*, better schools, better churches, better income, better living, advantages for their children. They are not afraid to fight for a better world.

That courageous but lonely prairie woman of less than a century ago would be surprised (but wouldn't she be happy?) to find herself today a part of a globe-encircling sisterhood of 5½ million rural women—the Associated Country Women of the World. Her granddaughter sailed to the international convention in Copenhagen in 1950—with 150 other American farm women. There she went to the same opera as the King and Queen of Denmark and attended meetings in Christiansborg Castle. A far cry from Martha Wilson's mind-reeling solitude.

Woven in among the bushels and tons and acres and dollars is every farm woman's unspoken contribution to the American farmer's success:

"I am the keeper of the farm home. I provide the physical—and mental—food for our children's growth, smooth out their faults and problems, keep everybody healthy, happy, strong and encouraged. I manage evenly an uneven load of work.

"I am the purchasing agent—I buy for the house and family, often for the farm; I keep books and pay the bills. More than is usually realized, I hold the balance of power in deciding what we need and what we shall postpone or do without—this decides how we live.

"I am the steward of neighborliness, beauty, truth, and spirit that produce strong character for the world's work.

"The American farmer—*and I, his wife*—have done these things."

BY LAURA LANE

How does a young wife manage?

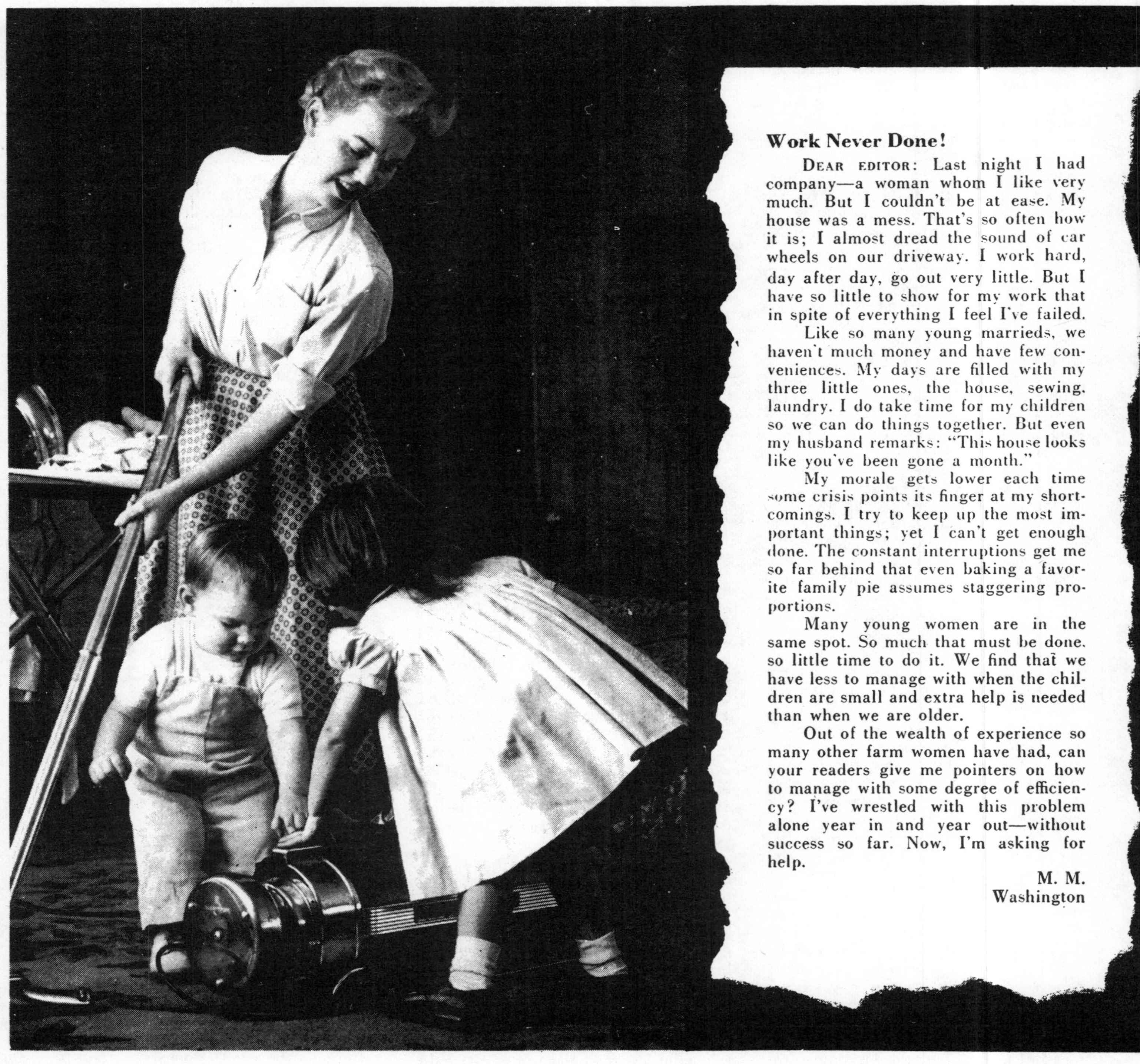

Work Never Done!

DEAR EDITOR: Last night I had company—a woman whom I like very much. But I couldn't be at ease. My house was a mess. That's so often how it is; I almost dread the sound of car wheels on our driveway. I work hard, day after day, go out very little. But I have so little to show for my work that in spite of everything I feel I've failed.

Like so many young marrieds, we haven't much money and have few conveniences. My days are filled with my three little ones, the house, sewing, laundry. I do take time for my children so we can do things together. But even my husband remarks: "This house looks like you've been gone a month."

My morale gets lower each time some crisis points its finger at my shortcomings. I try to keep up the most important things; yet I can't get enough done. The constant interruptions get me so far behind that even baking a favorite family pie assumes staggering proportions.

Many young women are in the same spot. So much that must be done, so little time to do it. We find that we have less to manage with when the children are small and extra help is needed than when we are older.

Out of the wealth of experience so many other farm women have had, can your readers give me pointers on how to manage with some degree of efficiency? I've wrestled with this problem alone year in and year out—without success so far. Now, I'm asking for help.

M. M.
Washington

Here—in a single letter written as if it were from one homemaker—we have woven together the best ideas from 1,500 women. They tell Mrs. M. M. (see her letter at left) how they cope with dishes, diapers and farm chores

● Dear Mrs. M. M.: Reading your letter was like looking in a mirror. I have days that are variegated, mutilated, animated and frustrated. I, too, am an "almost" type of housekeeper—almost through with the cleaning, almost finished ironing—almost dead.

"My house was a mess. That's so often how it is . . . ."

Until I overhauled my viewpoint, I regarded housework as menial, monotonous, degrading. My eye was on the circumstance and not on the goal—to be a good wife and mother and have pride in this career I chose.

In a young mother's years of *doing* it's easy to get the false notion that hard work in itself is a virtue. (You may know women who make drudges of themselves with too much dig-dig, rub-a-dub and moppy-plop.) But in spite of good management, life's unexpecteds can knock those perfectionist housekeepers off their well-dusted pedestals.

Ask yourself first: "Whom am I trying to help and please in this job?" My husband, myself and our children, in that order, I finally discovered. Not my perfectionist mother-in-law, my own indulgent mother, nor visitors—whether drop-in callers or lingering guests. Most over-worked homemakers set their standards too high. So my advice is: Don't strive for perfection.

Yes, it's frustrating to be caught between a critical husband and several young master-mess-makers. When my own husband made the crack, "Looks like I'd better bring my shovel over from the barn and dig out," I answered: "Thank you, dear, for offering to help. Where shall we start?" That worked.

The two times my husband washed diapers made such an impression on him that he went out and bought a washer, money or no! We women like to be reassured over and over that our work is appreciated. So we value our spouse's moral support as much as his actual help.

When the house isn't up to snitch, the children and I try to give Dad a specially warm welcome so he notices us and not the clutter. (Too much chaos makes him homesick for his mother's neat-as-a-pin housekeeping.) But I think a husband needs a cheerful wife more than a perfectly kept house, for men resent their wives always being tired.

"My husband remarks: 'This house looks like you've been gone a week.'"

I've read that resentment is the most tiring of all emotions. You can use up all your energy for a whole day in a few moments of rage. On the other hand, when your mind is at peace, your body can perform many tasks without fatigue. You're more likely to organize, not agonize.

A flexible plan, not an impossible one, is the best answer I've found to cope with "so-much-to-do, so-little-time." Let's face it, you can't really schedulize because your farm setting and your role of mother guarantee interruptions. The idea is to break those endless tasks into bite-size pieces, then work like sixty. Being productive, even for a short time, will give you a glow of competence. After accomplish-nothing days, tell yourself: "There's always tomorrow."

I list my jobs to be done in my reminder book under the headings: *Gotta, Oughta* and *Hope To.* If you don't assign jobs a priority in some way, you'll be tired before you're halfway through your list. One other bit of psychology I use on myself: I'm sure to include some jobs that give me special satisfaction. When I need a lift, I go outdoors. (Usually I feed the sheep, stopping long enough to burn papers and empty garbage.)

"...give me pointers on how to manage with some degree of efficiency."

Don't put off the *Gottas* and *Oughtas*—putting off makes jobs harder since you suffer through them mentally and they still aren't done. Dread of a task is more tiring than the actual work itself. So things I dislike doing, I do as early in the day as possible. Makes the whole day go better.

Have you ever counted up the number of decisions you make in a single day? They're enough to tire you—especially if you make them alone. But making up your mind about what to do and when to do it comes easier with experience. Deciding what's right or best in rearing the children often ties me in knots. When you can't avoid mistakes, learn to live with them peaceably.

It's monotony, not routine, that women dislike. And routine without frustration is a giant step toward efficiency. Here's an example: I can automatically take out of the refrigerator whatever I need for fixing breakfast, so I open the door only one time.

I timed myself for several days once to see how long it took to do the dishes. Actually I found it was such a short time that my fuss about them was hardly worthwhile. And meantime, I speeded up the process. See if you can figure out the things you do the hard or wrong way and how you can improve. (Just now I'm struggling to dress our youngest quickly in a way that will foster more self-help on his part and less irritation on mine.)

"I have so little to show for my work."

But routine and habit are blessings since they free your mind to think. Fortunately, ideas aren't confined to an 8-hour day. Doing dishes is my time for contemplation. While your hands grade eggs, you can look ahead to how you're going to redecorate the living room. The next time you iron, first read something that really interests you. Then as you iron, ponder on what you've read. ◁

We have the best of

Have you ever thought how or whether your life would change if you lived in town? Most conveniences are possible on the farm now, and you can take advantage of much the city has to offer as well. Are there any real differences left between farm and town women?

City woman's world, or the farm wife's? Town-reared Pat Tullis leaves no doubt about her choice—their Ohio farm with its new ranch-style home.

THE FARMER'S WIFE editors have put that question to hundreds of farm and ranch women all across the country. Over coffee cups and in letters women have agreed: You can't pick us out of a crowd; even so, our lives are different. Indeed, it's in the differences that a farm woman finds her special gripes—and her deepest joys.

Farm wives are business partners with their husbands (usually not true of

BANK ACCOUNT IS THE SAME for the farm business and family, so "we talk things over and decide together," farm women say. The Orville Swensons, Minnesota, make big- and medium-sized decisions over a cup of coffee.

TWO WORLDS

city wives). So a farm woman must know the business. "I love being able to share fully my husband's problems and successes," a Kansas homemaker said. "And I'm glad his work is close to home. On the farm we are our own boss. Together we work hard and together we enjoy the fruits of our labor." (This includes the children, of course.)

Being your own boss may take more self-discipline and better management than holding a town job. "Sure, it's nice to take off when we want to," one woman said. "But I envy a city woman at 5 p.m. when her husband's on his way home—while mine still has half a day's work to do at the barn."

Lack of time off is bemoaned by many. As a New England woman put it, "Every morning, every night—there the cows are, and there we are."

As a partner, a farm wife helps decide how to spend the money, since a new grain dryer and a new dishwasher are paid for out of the same pocketbook. "We talk things over and decide together what we'd better buy first," said most of the women we visited. Few complained because they had to postpone wants, though many sighed over the big amount of capital today's farming requires. As a Nebraskan explains, "The business comes first—if it didn't do well, we'd never get anything for the house or farm; but when John gets his new tractor, I'm likely to get my new vacuum."

Living out in the country has its pros and cons. Privacy is one plus: "When I need a green cathedral, I merely go for a walk by myself," an Ohio wife writes. "Here is a tree formed in perfect symmetry. It's clothed in lacy buds and ethereal mist on a spring morning. There, on a fall evening, a copperplated sun rests against the sky, on a shelf of bare treetops. I return to my family, feeling like Emily Dickinson that 'Instead of getting to Heaven, at last—I'm going, all along.'"

While Mom usually likes living on and from the land, she would as soon keep that good earth out of the house! "Mud, mud, mud! Town women wouldn't dream how impossible it is to keep a farm house clean." . . . "We get our towels and sheets dirtier; give our floors more wear and scrubbing." . . . "Why doesn't someone invent a dust-filtering system for those of us who still live on dirt roads?" An Iowa homemaker had this remedy: "I keep flowers around the house to distract the eye from dirt."

But there are lots of compensations for mud. "I love the emotions packed into our outdoor life—even the excitement of getting hay into the barn when a storm threatens," said a Wisconsin farm woman. "There's the fun of showing the children a nest of robin's eggs in the old crabapple tree; the pleasure of taking a work break in the garden; the satisfaction of another heat lamp in the brooder house when a May night turns chilly. Such happenings make heart-to-heart conversation with my husband."

Living in "the best of two worlds" may be a mixed blessing: "Before good transportation, our place was isolated; now we're only 20 minutes from town, and oh, the miles we rack up each month—nearly a thousand!" From Nebraska: "Soon as I start in on some big project, Verlon will yell, 'Say, will you quick run in to town for a tractor part?'" But no matter how mobile you are, "Living out can mean being shut in, when winter snow or spring mud fills your long lane."

A farm woman's work is "different" in ways both pleasant and irritating. A Connecticut homemaker dovetails farmwife duties with the farm bookkeeping and barn chores. She's also a 4-H leader, an active member of her Homemakers group, and chauffeur-on-demand for her large family. She uses spare time to help a shut-in neighbor!

"Each day unfolds such a variety of tasks, interruptions and surprises that planning a strict time schedule is as impossible as budgeting our unpredictable income. I like the challenge—I'll tell you for sure that this life is never boring!" (Indiana)

On the other side of the coin . . . "I wish I had 10 hands and the constitution of a horse," said one wife. An Okla-

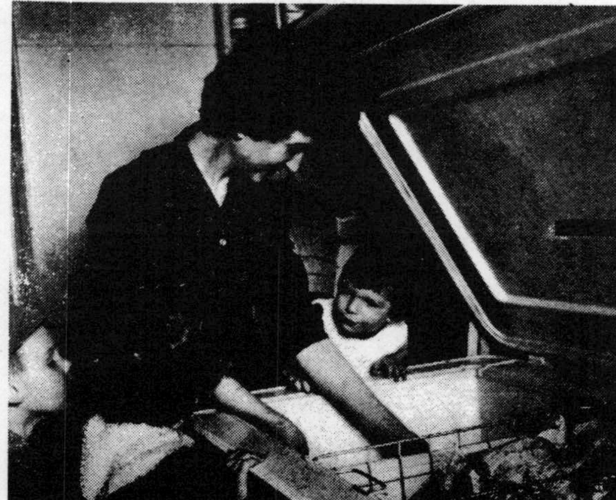

AN EXTRA PERSON—OR TWO OR THREE—for dinner is an everyday happenstance on the farm. A freezer saves the day, especially if (like Peggy Forrest's in Ohio) it's well stocked with ready-to-heat dishes.

BY JEAN ANN NIMROD

Family Living Department

Photos: Betty Gregory LaRoche, Editorial Assistant

homan: "During busy seasons, seems as if I just can't get out of the kitchen. Getting three big meals every day—some served in shifts, plus some carried to the field—taxes my imagination, fills my time and strains my disposition."

Farm women are especially thankful for today's conveniences, such as a freezer full of farm-grown pork, beef, chicken and vegetables. They praise time-saving appliances—from fryers to dryers. Said an Ohio woman: "A farm wife's efficiency means efficiency in two businesses—homemaking and farming. My husband likes my help and companionship. Modernizing our kitchen and laundry has given me time to be outside with him."

Entertaining on the farm is likely to be more frequent and more casual—and on a bigger scale—than elsewhere. "People are neighborly—always dropping in to visit or to help," one farm wife commented. "Last year we fed 230 'extras'—not counting those who ate with us often."

But occasionally a farm woman would like to hide her welcome mat: "Six visitors today—each staying for a long chat—have made me feel crowded. Town friends don't realize that seasonal work can't always allow much sociability."

Farm houses are different from other houses, too. Farm women want a special area for "all that paperwork and bookkeeping"; a large, well-planned utility room and back entryway with roomy closets for chore clothes, plus a shower to "save the bathroom."

Although farm houses contain "miles" of floors to mop, many farm homemakers set as much store by wall-to-wall carpeting as their city sisters do—but for different reasons: "A good carpet saves so much wear and tear on good floors" . . . "A vacuum twice a week saves twice-a-day mopping."

The average farm home is likely to have a large kitchen, with maybe a daybed "where George can catnap in his work clothes."

Picture windows are the pride of many: "There's some point to having one out here—you'd never have a view like this in the city."

"A farm is *the* place to raise children"—just about everybody volunteered. From California: "Though ours lack next-door playmates, they have special closeness with brothers and sisters. They're with their dad a lot, too, and that's important."

From Ohio: "Do I have to invent situations where my children can learn thrift and industry and perseverance? Well, hardly. A plot of corn or a 4-H heifer shows the world the care it's getting."

A Colorado homemaker reflected, "Many of our young will have to adjust to urban life, but their farm background will serve them well. There's a crying need for country-style initiative, creativeness, dependability, and willingness to work."

Farm children learn to feel valuable. "They can see that the work of a farmer is necessary for the well-being of his fellow men. Moreover, in a rural community there is always great demand for leadership and talent." (Ohio)

Some grievances against city people and city attitudes came out. "Too many people put farmers in a separate category—after all, we're no more separate than bankers or bakers." . . . "Urbanites think of the country as it was years ago. We're as modern as most." . . . "I deplore the way TV portrays the farmer as a creature of outlandish clothes and corny speech."

While the truth is . . . "You can't tell a farmer from anyone else these days, either by speech or dress, as long as he isn't talking about farming. You might pick a farmer out of a group by noting his white forehead above tanned cheeks, if his wife hasn't made him go hatless at times to even up his sunburn!"

Some readers are emphatic that farmers need to do a better job of public relations. Illinois: "It's important for us not to whine. Better to make ourselves heard constructively—in politics, for instance. Farmers as a whole aren't any more aware of urban problems than vice versa. Let's get together with our town friends in their organizations. Town and country should be one community."

Glories of farm life outweighed the gripes, by and large. A Missouri wife expressed well what we heard from many: "As a person, I have the same hopes, dreams, joys and frustrations as any woman anywhere. As a farmer's wife I'm happy about some differences, and I put up with those that irk me. Our work is harder, our responsibilities greater; but our rewards and joys are more wonderful. I wouldn't trade places with anyone." **END**

KNOW-HOW AND COMPANIONSHIP—farm dads are around to provide both. Safety-minded Robert Grieser, Ohio, teaches his boys to use tractor.

A popular recipe—one of thousands printed in Farm Journal and 19 cookbooks over the years

Homemade bread...

fresh from the oven

Make 4 crusty loaves—all alike or deliciously different—from a single recipe

Two golden-crusted loaves of bread cooling on a rack and two more baking—no wonder the kitchen's so inviting. Maybe your oven will hold four loaves, but whether you bake in pairs or fours, you'll have bread to eat right away and some to freeze.

If you bake two loaves together, you let the dough for those baked last rise twice, the old-fashioned way. They should be ready to bake when the first two come from the oven. Their texture may be slightly different, the flavor more yeasty.

Homemade White Bread

Crusty loaves with rich wheat flavor

3 pkgs. granular or compressed yeast
½ c. warm water
½ c. sugar
4 tsp. salt
⅓ c. melted shortening
5 c. water
16 to 18 c. sifted flour

- Sprinkle granular yeast over warm (110°) water, or crumble compressed yeast into lukewarm (85°) water.
- Combine sugar, salt, shortening and water in 5 qt. bowl. Stir in 8 c. flour. Add yeast and enough of remaining flour (8 to 10 c.) to make stiff dough that cleans the bowl when you stir.
- Knead on lightly floured surface until smooth and satiny (5 to 8 minutes). Place in greased bowl; turn to bring greased side up. Cover; let rise in warm place (80° to 85°) until doubled, about 1½ hours. Punch down dough.
- Divide in half. Set aside one half to rise again. Divide other portion in half; shape each half into smooth ball; let rest 10 minutes. Shape into two loaves; place in greased 9x5x3" pans. Grease top lightly; cover and let rise until doubled, about 1 hour. Bake in hot oven (400°) 40 to 45 minutes. Immediately turn out of pans on rack.
- When portion of dough set for second rising is doubled, punch down and repeat above process. Makes 4 loaves

To bake four different kinds of bread, make 1 loaf of white, 1 loaf whole-wheat, 1 two-tone loaf and 2 two-tone swirls. For directions, see photo below and these variations:

Variations

Whole-Wheat Bread: Substitute whole-wheat flour for half the white flour (do not sift whole-wheat flour).

Two White and Two Whole-Wheat loaves: After adding yeast to batter, divide batter equally into 2 large bowls. To one bowl add enough more white flour (about 4 c.) to make a stiff dough. To other bowl, add 4 c. whole-wheat flour. If dough is too sticky to handle, add more white flour. Knead each kind of dough separately.

Raisin Coffee Bread: Make 3 loaves, and knead ½ c. raisins into fourth loaf just before shaping. Place in greased 8" square pan to rise. Before baking brush top with melted butter and sprinkle with cinnamon sugar.

Potato Bread: Reduce amount of water to 3 c. Add 2 c. instant mashed potatoes to water mixture before adding flour and yeast.

Milk Bread: Substitute 5 c. scalded milk for 5 c. water. Add sugar, salt and shortening. Cool to lukewarm before adding yeast to batter. **End**

← TWO-TONE LOAF—make from half white and half whole-wheat doughs. Coffee Swirls (dough for Two-Tone Loaf makes 2 swirls) start as ropes of risen white and whole-wheat doughs—roll under hands, dip in melted butter and cinnamon-sugar mixture, coil alternately in two greased 8" round pans, let rise until doubled and bake in hot oven (400°) 35 to 40 minutes.

PHOTO: PETER DANT STUDIOS

BY RUTH BEHNKE
ASSOCIATE FOOD EDITOR

January 1960

Adventure toward abundance

Every generation believes that it lives in the most momentous period of history; that change is occuring at a record-breaking rate.

So it will remain for historians to confirm our biased impression: The fourth quarter-century of FARM JOURNAL's existence has been one of unprecedented vitality and transition for American agriculture.

The collapse of farm prices during the 1920s followed by the drouth and Great Depression of the '30s had stagnated American agriculture. It took the 10 years of World War II and the Korean War to restore not only the economy but farmers' confidence. Also, the great storehouse of science and technology, accumulated since the turn of the Century but delayed by depression and war, was now ready for use. Dr. Firman H. Bear, the famous Rutgers University agronomist, gave voice to this confidence when he declared in an article for our 75th Anniversary: "The U.S. Can Feed a Billion People."

As if to indicate how, a headline the following March asked "Can Land Take Corn Every Year?" To Ralph Wennblom, our crops editor at the time, the idea wasn't as tentative as that title made it sound. Dr. Bear and other agronomists had been telling him that farmers no longer had to grow legumes in the rotation to supply corn with the nitrogen it needed. They could now buy it cheaper in a bag. And that meant they could grow their most productive crop year after year, as we confirmed two years later: "They're Growing Continuous Corn."

By 1954, the lingering benefits of war demand were gone, crops prices had fallen to government support levels, where they were to remain for almost 20 years. So the only routes open for the crops farmer to improve his income were to increase his yields or cut his costs.

In the mid 1950s came another of those tentative questions: "Are 40" Rows on the Way Out?" The article declared that row width had been set at 40" because that was the width of a mule. Later articles suggested that commercial fertilizer was capable of feeding thicker stands; that closer row spacing would shade the middles sooner and preserve soil moisture. By 1964 the question was all but settled: "Will Narrow Rows be 20" or 30"?" Improved practices such as these almost doubled average corn yields in that 25-year span. Development of hybrids had the same effect on grain sorghum production.

The mid-1950s saw the rise of another trend: minimum tillage. A March 1954 article reported: "Corn Planter Follows the Plow," meaning that it wasn't really necessary to make all those trips with disk and harrow to work up a fine seedbed. By 1961, FARM JOURNAL was demanding: "Why Plow and Cultivate? "

The rapid adoption of chemical weed killers during the 1960s confirmed the realization that the reason for most tillage was to kill weeds.

Soon farmers began crowding their crops another way: by growing "Two Crops in One Season" (June 1954). As FARM JOURNAL began its Centennial year, farmers were "Interseeding Soybeans in Standing Wheat."

How to save labor became the most urgent question with livestock producers, especially after jobs became so abundant in the 1960s. The most promising answer: Finding ways for animals to feed and clean up after themselves.

Dairymen, tired of carrying feed to and milk away from their cows, welcomed the idea of herringbone milking parlors, introduced from New Zealand in 1959, and "free stalls" in 1960, which leave stabled animals protected from being stepped on but free to move to the milking parlor and to self-feeders.

More pounds of meat or milk from less feed became the focus of breeding efforts with all three types of livestock. FARM JOURNAL proclaimed the need for production-testing of beef in March 1953 with the question: "Have Purebreds Jumped the Track? " Under the leadership of Livestock Editor John Rohlf, it kept up the campaign all through the 50s and 60s with such articles as "The Dwarf Riddle" in 1956 and "More Red Meat, Less Fat" in 1968. Dairy cows were considered primarily "roughage burners" until 1961, when New York scientists reported that "You May Have a 20,000-lb. Cow and Not Know It." By 1965, FARM JOURNAL was telling how to "Full Feed Grain to Cows."

The magazine campaigned for a variety of causes. When vesicular exanthema tied up the hog business in 1952, Claude Gifford, now head of information for the USDA, found that the disease was spread through the feeding of raw garbage. So in 1953 he was saying "Let's Make 'em Cook Garbage," and kept publishing the state-by-state boxscore until virtually every state had passed a garbage-cooking law and the disease had been wiped out. When hoof-and-mouth disease broke out in Mexico in 1948 and in Canada in 1952, FARM JOURNAL sent editors to report "I Saw the Cattle Shot." The editors were so impressed by the destructiveness of this disease, FARM JOURNAL demanded "Let's Get That Disease Lab," and campaigned for it until the special foot-and-mouth lab was constructed on Plum Island off eastern Long Island.

The campaigns extended to social and political questions. "Want One of These Blotting Your Farm?" the magazine asked, showing pictures of car graveyards, trailer camps and string-towns as it urged adoption of rural zoning. And when the Kennedy Administration proposed a system of rigid acreage allotments for wheat, FARM JOURNAL took a strong stand against the proposal and helped defeat it. Editor Carroll Streeter's Opinion page on the subject was one of the most influential he ever wrote.

Production advances which the magazine promoted helped prepare the United States for the sudden heavy export demand beginning in 1972. In spite of the millions of "reserve" acres brought back into production, commodity prices climbed and became so volatile that farmers needed to recapture their marketing skills. In response, the magazine more than doubled the space devoted to Farmcast and articles offering market advice.

As the nation begins its third century and FARM JOURNAL its second, it is clear from the booming export demand that farmers will be needing help with both production and marketing for the foreseeable future.

—Lane Palmer
Editor, 1968 to present

Photo: Robert Nunn

THESE SOILS LOOK ALIKE, but they're a lot different. Soil at right is Joe Svercl's, and is chock-full of the soil organisms that rot down residues. It's from a field that's been in corn since '44, and has averaged 125 bu. for 6 years in a row. At left, Joe Svercl Jr., with soil from field of neighbor who grows corn in a rotation. Note the un-rotted stalks.

They're

BY RAY ANDERSON

JOE SVERCL is no crops and soils scientist. He's a butter-maker by trade.

When he started farming in Steele County, Minn., he didn't know that "you can't grow high-yielding corn year after year on the same ground," the prevailing opinion at the time.

So he grew it.

He also wasn't aware that "you have to rotate with legumes to build up and maintain soil tilth."

So he didn't rotate.

He did know that corn is a profitable crop in southern Minnesota. And he knew from his butter-making that micro-organisms—"culture," as butter-makers call it, and "bacteria," as most of us know it—can be tremendously helpful little busy-bodies.

In 1954, Svercl harvested 14,375 bushels of corn from 115 acres. That's 125 bushels to the acre.

***And 125 bushels per acre** is the average yield that he has cribbed from those 115 acres for six years in a row.*

Svercl grows his corn on two fields—one, 75 acres, that's been in corn for

TROUBLE HERE. Corn every year for 37 years, but no fertilizer of any kind. Yield: 32 bu., and dropping every year, at the Iowa State College Farm. But look...

Photos: K. Robert Kern

. . . WHAT HAPPENED when scientists fertilized part of the plot with 500 lbs. of 33-0-0 and 300 lbs. of 0-20-20. Soil snapped back — grew 75-bushel corn.

growing continuous corn

He uses bagged fertilizer and lots of manure

11 consecutive years; and another, 40 acres, that has grown corn 10 years.

Continuous corn, with no rotation at all, is not a brand-new idea. *Farm Journal* has told about several farmers who do it (see article below), and thousands of others now include corn in their rotations more often than they used to. Why they can do it, and still get high yields, is still a subject for speculation among both scientists and farmers.

I've known Joe Svercl nearly two years, and have been back to his farm several times.

Svercl is convinced that soil bacteria—the billions of "bugs" too small to be seen by the naked eye—are the key to his success. They feed on nitrogen, and in Svercl's fields, they get nitrogen from *both* commercial fertilizer and manure.

Most of the continuous corn growers that I know use no manure, and plow down most of their commercial fertilizer *in the fall*.

Svercl, on the other hand, spreads about 12 loads of manure per acre, and plows down commercial nitrogen *in the spring*. Here's his system:

He disks down the stalks in the fall, figures that they add as much as 4 to 4½ tons of dry matter per acre. During the late winter and early spring he spreads manure, some from his own feedlots, some from a dairy near by. (He gets it for hauling it away.)

After the frost goes out in the spring, he broadcasts 300 pounds of 33-0-0 on top of the manure and stalks, *then disks again*.

"I want to get the manure, the stalks, and the ammonium nitrate all mixed up, so there won't be any layers of manure and stalks when I turn them under," he explains.

Adds Svercl: "That heavy shot of nitrogen is for the 'bugs' to feed on, so they'll be able to rot the stalks and manure into organic matter and humus."

He plows eight to ten inches deep with an ordinary moldboard plow, then harrows, packs, and plants four kernels every 38 inches, in rows 40 inches apart—16,000 stalks per acre.

He uses a starter fertilizer. If the spring is cold and wet, he puts as much as 160 pounds of 5-20-20 in the row. If the weather is more favorable, he uses less—maybe only 100 pounds. He cultivates shallow with sweep shovels; twice as a rule, never more than three times.

In 1954, Svercl put on $15.50 worth of commercial fertilizer per acre—$12.15 for nitrogen, $3.35 for starter—and spent $2.35 for lime. Actually, he limes once every three years, three tons per acre; figures that his successive corn crops use up about a ton a year.

Is Svercl ruining his land? I was curious about that. So was M. C. Bray, who farms across from Svercl, and rotates corn with small grains and soybeans. We wondered whether Svercl's soil has more and busier "bugs" than Bray's soil.

So Joe Svercl Jr. and I did some spading. We bagged soil samples from both of the Svercl fields. We also bagged samples from Bray's field of second-year corn, which averaged 80 bushels per acre in 1954. Then I lit out for

(Continued)

These farmers rely on commercial fertilizer

DO YOU have to spread manure, and lots of it, to grow continuous corn? You do not!

Manure does supply organic matter, and some scientists suspect that it also contains helpful hormones or antibiotics that make it a superior plant food, but that hasn't been proved.

Yontz Bonnett of McLean County, Ill., doesn't use manure, yet he's averaged 111 bushels of corn per acre from 80 acres for seven consecutive years. That includes 1954, when drought and excessive heat during tasseling and silking cut his yield to 50 bushels.

The first six years, Bonnett plowed down 600 pounds of sulfate of ammonia, 250 pounds of rock phosphate, 200 pounds of muriate of potash, and two tons of blast furnace slag (contains phosphorus and lime) per acre, *in the fall*, on top of the chopped-up corn stalks. At planting time, he put 200 pounds of 3-18-9 in the row.

In the fall of 1953, Bonnett cut his sulfate of ammonia to 500 pounds, and his muriate of potash to 100 pounds. Last spring, he changed his starter fertilizer to 150 pounds of 5-40-0, and spray-applied one pound of aldrin per acre to control soil insects.

Last fall, after 1954's short crop, Bonnett cut his sulfate of ammonia to 300 pounds, figuring that the 1955 crop will benefit from the left-over nitrogen that the 1954 crop didn't use.

In White County, Ind., C. V. Conder grows continuous corn without manure. He has 32 acres that's been in corn for eight consecutive years.

Conder limes every five years, three tons to the acre. His fertilizer treatments vary, but average about 1,000 pounds of 10-10-10 each fall, plus 100 pounds of 8-32-0 starter at planting time.

Conder, like many other growers of continuous corn, has had his troubles. Some years, parts of the field have yielded as much as 50 bushels less per acre than others, because of soil insect damage. He's had serious compaction, too, but now feels that micro-organisms have "reactivated" his soil to the point where tilth is improving.

"Profits depend," says Conder, "on the attention that you give to details like stand, weeds, insects, erosion, and tilth."

In Woodford County, Ill., Lester Pfister grows hybrid seed corn continu-

(Continued)

Svercl corn: *125 bu. per acre for 6 years in a row*

(Continued)

the University of Minnesota.

At the University, W. P. Martin, head of the Soils Department, and biologist E. L. Schmidt, explained that incubating a soil sample, and measuring the amount of carbon dioxide given off, would tell them just how active the microbes in a soil are. Here's what they found out:

The soil in the 75-acre field that grew Svercl's eleventh continuous crop of corn is really hot stuff! During 18 days of incubation, the sample "breathed out" 2½ times as much carbon dioxide as the sample from neighbor Bray's field of second-year corn.

What about organic matter? Bray's tested 4.2%, which is better than average. But the 11-year soil tested 5.2%.

As a clincher, the scientists tested to see which soil would make the most nitrogen available to a growing crop. Again, the Svercl 11-year soil won out. During 18 days, it produced nitrate nitrogen—the form plants can use—at the rate of 10 pounds per acre. The Bray soil produced only 2 pounds.

"*We are impressed by the consistent and marked superiority of Svercl's 11-year soil,*" say Scientists Martin and Schmidt. "It has high reserves of organic matter nitrogen, and also contains the large number of soil microbes needed to transform that nitrogen into the nitrate form."

The Minnesota scientists also took their own samples, repeated the tests, and got similar results.

What about the soil in the 40-acre field that grew Svercl's *tenth* continuous crop of corn? Well, there wasn't much difference between it and Bray's soil.

Both "breathed off" about the same amount of carbon dioxide, transformed equal amounts of nitrate nitrogen, and tested about the same in organic matter. Both lacked the soil bacteria that Svercl's 11-year soil contained.

This would seem to indicate that ten straight crops of corn have not harmed the soil. And Svercl believes that it's improving each year.

The Bray fields are farmed like most of the other naturally-fertile soils in the area. No particular rotation; usually corn, corn, small grain, and soybeans. Bray used 150 pounds of 4-24-12 starter on his corn in 1954.

Both farms are fairly level. The topsoil is 16 to 28 inches deep, underlain with clay loam and gravel. Natural drainage is excellent.

Joe Svercl isn't a typical farmer. But sure as shooting, he's cribbing a whale of a lot more corn per acre than most of us. **End**

Continuous corn: *"The key is enough nitrogen"*

(Continued)

ously, with irrigation and gets good yields without using manure.

In the fall. Pfister spreads a layer of cobs on top of the stalks. then broadcasts heavy applications of nitrogen, phosphate. and potash. He fall-plows deep—down to 18 inches—with a special plow.

George M. Scarseth, Tippecanoe County. Ind.. has a thin. light soil that's underlain with a tight clay pan. Scarseth has experimented for four years with mulch planting of continuous corn. He uses the IHC Till Planter which works up the ground and plants the corn in slits. without any plowing, disking. or harrowing.

Scarseth has had problems. too. He's down to six acres of continuous corn this year. after starting with 35 acres in 1951. He is interested in growing corn every year. but he's also trying to reduce labor. measure the value of weeds as soil-builders. and determine the effects of cultivation on soil tilth. Scarseth is a part-time farmer—a scientist with a yen for trying the unusual.

Is corn a soil-builder? "You can improve your soil with corn as quickly as with anything else." say S. W. Melsted. R. H. Bray. and E. H. Tyner. soil scientists at the University of Illinois.

"The 'key thought' in growing high-yielding continuous corn," adds Bray. "is to supply enough nitrogen."

Could *you* grow corn continuously? Probably. providing you have:

1. *The soil.* Many scientists maintain that you have to have a fairly level, well-drained. deep. heavy soil. that's high in organic matter and has good tilth to start with.

Others claim that any *good* soil can be made to grow corn every year.

2. *Moisture.* A good crop of corn pumps the soil dry. most years. and there's little or no carry-over of moisture. Of course. irrigation will solve the moisture problem.

3. *Plant foods,* including enough nitrogen to feed *both* the corn and the soil organisms that digest or rot the left-over stalks from each crop. Otherwise. plant foods won't be released, and tilth won't be maintained.

4. *Skill.* The hazards multiply, and it takes precise management to keep down insects. diseases, compaction.

I'm convinced, after talking with growers and scientists, that continuous corn is no longer a stunt for a few adventurous farmers to try. With proper management. it's a sound, profitable practice—one that large numbers of farmers will adopt in the years ahead. **End**

NARROW ROWS YIELD MORE. Irrigated grain sorghum consistently racks up 10% to 15% more yield in 20-inch rows. Pairs of 14-inch rows on 40-inch beds yield almost as well—let you cultivate with regular 40-inch equipment.

Photo: Texas Experiment Station

Are 40" rows on the way out?

Photo: C. B. Spencer

COTTON IN 23" ROWS. This 12-acre field made 1,030 lbs. of lint per acre—25% more than adjacent 40-inch-row cotton on the Paymaster Farm, Hale Co., Tex.

Photo: Frederick Walker

CULTIVATES SIX 22-INCH ROWS. Ray Cryder, Grundy Co., Ill., spaces 12-inch sweeps on a 138-inch tool bar. So his tractor would fit between the rows, he fabricated spacers that extend each rear wheel eight more inches. "My soybeans yield 3½ bu. more in narrow rows," says Cryder. ▷

Photo Paymaster Farm

"NO 40-INCH SOYBEAN ROWS FOR US," says Harold D. Loden, Paymaster Farm, Hale Co., Tex. "We get two to five more bushels per acre in 23-inch rows—plant 300 acres that way with six unit-planters on a 4-row tool bar."

BY CHARLES E. BALL *of Farm Journal's Southern Field Staff*

SOUTHWESTERN farmers are taking a hard second look at the 40-inch "walking plow" row.

In fact, some have already chucked it in favor of rows only 20 to 30 inches wide. Results: 10% to 20% more grain sorghum and up to five bushels more soybeans per acre. A few adventurous farmers are even trying cotton in 20-inch rows with surprising success.

The narrow-row idea doesn't work everywhere. For some crops in certain areas, the conventional 40-inch row appears to have definite advantages.

But the swing to narrow rows is already under way in the Midwest. Implement manufacturers have sensed the trend—you can see it in their tool-bar equipment that's easily adjusted to almost any width of row.

Plant breeders are ready to change their thinking. One told me recently that "we've known that some crops prefer narrower rows, but we've settled on varieties that do best in 40-inch rows because we thought they were what farmers wanted and needed."

Farmers already growing irrigated grain sorghum in narrow rows think highly of the idea. "*It's sure to spread,*" says R. G. Peeler, president of the Deaf Smith County (Tex.) Grain Sorghum Producers Assn. "Our 27-inch rows averaged 8,000 pounds per acre last year—a good 15% to 20% more than our 40-inch rows."

At least three experiment stations in Texas confirm Peeler's results:

1. At the Lower Rio Grande Valley Experiment Station, irrigated sorghum in 40-inch rows averaged 4,100 lbs. of grain per acre. Alongside, the same varieties in 20-inch rows yielded 16% more with no fertilizer; 23% more with 60 lbs. of nitrogen per acre; and a hefty 35% more with 120 lbs. of nitrogen per acre. These results show how narrow rows make better use of fertilizer.

2. At the Lubbock Experiment Station, irrigated sorghum consistently yields 10% to 15% more in narrow rows.

3. At the USDA Southwestern Great Plains Field Station, in the Panhandle, the three-year average yields were: 5,879 lbs. in 40-inch rows; 6,434 lbs. in 30-inch rows; 6,849

lbs. in 20-inch rows; and 6,969 lbs. in 12-inch rows.

"We've tried various seeding rates," says agronomist K. B. Porter, "and have concluded that six to eight pounds per acre—80,000 to 100,000 plants per acre—is about right regardless of row spacing. *It's the better plant distribution*—not the increased number of plants per acre—*that makes the narrow rows yield more.*"

Narrow rows also make better use of irrigation water. In Porter's tests, each acre-inch of water made 273 lbs. of grain sorghum in 40-inch rows; 297 lbs. in 30-inch rows; and 317 lbs. in 20-inch rows. In 12-inch rows, it dropped back to 314 lbs.

But narrowing the rows doesn't usually increase sorghum yields if moisture is a limiting factor. For example, in Kansas Experiment Station dryland tests at Garden City, highest yields—a 40.8-bu. average—during the last four years have come from plants spaced six inches apart in 40-inch rows. That compares with 35.9 bu. from a plant every six inches in 20-inch rows.

It's difficult to cultivate sorghum in 12- or 20-inch rows. But Porter says that you can get the advantages of narrow rows by planting two 14-inch rows on top of 40-inch beds. That leaves 26 inches between pairs—enough space for the tractor's wheels while cultivating. And it gives you a furrow for irrigating. This is exactly what a lot of High Plains farmers do.

For example, Edmund Schlab and his brothers, Charles and Raymond, Parmer County, Tex., space eight unit-planters on a four-row tool bar to plant four pairs of 14-inch rows with 26 inches between pairs. On the lister beams, ahead of the planter openers, they use a 14-inch solid sweep with the inside corners cut off two inches to let trash go through.

Other farmers plant pairs of 14-inch rows on 42-inch centers with their wheat drills—plug up holes to get the combination.

To keep down weeds, the Schlabs first rotary hoe the sorghum two or three times. Then, with a rear-mounted cultivator, they run one 6- or 8-inch sweep between the 14-inch rows and regular sweeps in the 26-inch middles.

Soybean growers on the High Plains are swinging to narrow rows, too. "Every one of our 300 acres is planted in 23-inch rows," says Harold D. Loden of Paymaster Farm, Hale County, Tex. "Not only do we get a two-to-five-bushel increase in yield, but we have less lodging, and we leave fewer beans in the field."

"Because beans in narrow rows shade the ground earlier," he adds, "we don't have to cultivate as much—only one time after using the rotary hoe, and this is to give us a water furrow."

In the Midsouth, advantages of narrow rows aren't as clear-cut for soybeans. "Most of our southern varieties have been bred for growing in 40-inch rows," says E. E. Hartwig, in charge of USDA soybean research in the South.

"As a result, we don't get the increases in yields from narrow rows that Midwesterners do," he continues. "They're growing a different type bean, which usually doesn't lap in the middle like ours do."

So Hartwig is sticking with his previous recommendation of 42 to 45 lbs. of seed per acre, which will give 10 to 12 plants per foot (Lee variety) in 36- to 40-inch rows.

In Arkansas—now the nation's fourth-ranking state in soybean production—only a few growers have switched to narrow rows. "But they are interested and narrow rows have some advantage for some growers," says C. E. Caviness, University of Arkansas soybean researcher.

For example, "where there's a hardpan and the beans don't grow tall, 24- to 30-inch rows will make three to five bushels more than 40-inch rows," says Caviness. "But in the Delta, where soils are fertile and beans grow waist-high, the 38- and 40-inch rows are as good as any."

A few cotton farmers are trying narrow rows, too. R. A. Pickens of Desha County, Ark. has "played with it" for four years. Last year, a poor stand cut the yield on 45 acres of 20-inch rows to only 690 lbs. of lint per acre compared with 751 lbs. for the rest of his farm. "But the three previous years, our narrow-row cotton made from 60% to 95% more lint than our 40-inch rows," says Pickens.

To get 20-inch rows, Pickens simply doubles back and plants in between 40-inch rows. Then he broadcasts a pre-emergence weed killer and "forgets the cotton until harvest." That's right—no cultivating!

"No doubt about it," he declares, "we can make more cotton this way. But since we can't harvest it mechanically, I'm doubtful that it will ever become a general practice."

But the harvesting bottleneck may be only temporary. "If narrow rows will increase yields enough, we'll develop machines to harvest it," agreed agricultural engineers at the recent Cotton Production-Mechanization Conference in Memphis.

At the Lubbock (Tex.) Experiment Station, cotton planted in two 14-inch rows on 40-inch beds—the same pattern used for sorghum—yielded from 15% to 25% more than regular 40-inch rows.

Cotton, especially tall cotton, is one crop that makes good use of row space. In fact, in some areas, skip-row cotton outyields regular 40-inch plantings (FARM JOURNAL, February 1960).

In the Corn Belt, farmers are successfully growing soybeans in 24- to 28-inch rows. In 352 University of Illinois tests, soybeans racked up a 15% yield bonus in 24-inch rows.

A few Midwesterners are trying corn in narrow rows. Yields go up about 10%, but lodging is still a problem that corn breeders will have to solve.

What the outcome of all this interest in narrow rows will be, no one can say yet. But we'll likely see new varieties, chemicals and equipment in the next few years that will permit even more farmers to try narrow rows. **End**

LAY MIS-CUTS and random length lumber flat, spike 'em together and tie corners with one-inch iron rods.

Built like a TOWN ELEVATOR

FOR THE FIRST 5′, Wilbur Garrels used 2x6s; finished with 2x4s. Bin partitions are mortised into walls.

Photos: A. M. Wettach

ELEVATOR IS 10′ x 50′ x 27′. Garrels, Henry Co., Iowa, estimates it cost 24¢ per bushel of capacity.

This month, *Farm Journal* starts a new department, "Machinery Parade." You'll see it every month from now on.

In it, we aim to show as many of the new machines as possible—just as soon as they can be announced. One of our editors will make it his chief business to watch the machinery front. You, in turn, can know what's doing in the farm machinery world, if you watch *Farm Journal*.

MACHINERY

Pick corn with

Photos: Bob Fowler

This combine can pick about 1½ acres an hour in 125-bushel corn. Hopper Machine Co. makes and installs the picker head for $1,980 in areas near Bakersfield, Calif.

YOU'LL be hearing a lot more this fall about harvesting corn with a grain combine.

Machinery designers are improving on the corn-combining ideas of state college engineers and farmers that *Farm Journal* told you about last year. ("Harvest More Corn," September 1953.)

Several companies—including John Deere and International Harvester—already have experimental machines in the field (see photos right). But they're not yet on the market, and probably won't be for a few years. Company officials say that they want to run all kinds of field tests before they decide whether to build any for sale.

Another company—Allis-Chalmers—started work on the idea more than a dozen years ago, shelved it during World War II, now is working on it again.

Meanwhile, farmers in all parts of the country—especially in the South and West—are reporting successful corn harvests with their present combines. California manufacturers are building picker attachments to fit all makes (see photo, left, and *Farm Journal*, January 1954, page 23).

In the irrigated West, growers can turn off the water and dry corn down to 12% to 15% moisture in the field. Combines do best when corn is exceptionally dry—dryer than it usually gets in the Midwest.

To see whether grain combines can do a passable job in the Corn Belt, engineers are trying different types of cylinders and concaves. They're also going over their combines, piece by piece, to see whether any parts need "beefing up" to handle tough, high-moisture cobs and stalks.

At the University of Nebraska, agricultural engineers are working on a combine that snaps off the ear and tosses out the stalks *before* shelling.

If this corn-combining idea pans out, you may some day get by with one machine where you now need two. You'll probably need a dryer, but you can store in bins instead of cribs.

New machinery

Just touch the hydraulic lever to raise this drill. Spiral spring agitator (inset) puts a band of plant food alongside drilled seed, lifts out for easy cleaning. 9- and 11-foot models, $335-$380 f.o.b. LaCrosse, Wis. Allis-Chalmers Mfg. Co.

Green-chop harvester. Fan blades on the cutter rotor blow chopped forage up through the wagon spout. Rotor has 4 knives, takes a 54-inch swath. You can raise or lower complete unit with tractor hitch. $565, f.o.b. Racine, Wis. J. I. Case Co.

PARADE *your combine?*

Self-propelled combine with an appetite for corn. Engineers moved this John Deere experimental machine down the rows at a 2¾ mile-an-hour clip in 12½% moisture corn. It lost no more corn than a picker-sheller in this field, but left a few kernels on the cob in corn with 20% moisture.

These machines snap off the ear before it hits the cylinder; both have been working in 110- to 120-bushel corn in California. International Harvester Company engineers are also experimenting with combines that take in the whole stalk.

you'll be seeing this fall

New hydraulic hitch for rear-mounted equipment on Massey-Harris 33 and 44 tractors. With a "Hitchall" kit, you can pull new three- and four-bottom plows with present tractors. Although the Massey-Harris and Harry Ferguson companies have merged, dealers will continue to operate separately.

Lay plastic pipe or electric cable from the tractor seat—up to 18 inches deep. First, you make an "exploring" run to find any rocks, then put in pipe, and close gap with rear tractor wheel. Sub-soiler $51, pipe attachment, $24, f.o.b. Detroit, Mich. Ferguson Div., Massey-Harris-Ferguson, Inc.

Hybrid

BY OVID BAY

HYBRID sorghums really have that extra zip that we've been hearing about.

And while there isn't enough seed to go around this year, growers expect to raise hybrid seed on 20,000 to 25,000 acres this summer. Barring a widespread crop failure, *you'll be able to plant about half your sorghum ground to one of the new hybrids next year.*

In case you have any doubts about these new feed-makers, take a look at these results, racked up in 1955 tests:

▶ Experimental hybrids averaged 27% more grain than ordinary sorghums in Iowa State College tests. At Ames, on good soil, *hybrids averaged 90 bushels an acre alongside corn that made only 61 bushels.*

▶ In Monroe County, Mo., Fred Forsyth's hybrid sorghum averaged 147 bushels an acre. Ordinary combine kafir alongside made 102 bushels.

▶ Hybrids developed by the DeKalb Agricultural Association, Inc., outyielded ordinary sorghums at several locations in 1955:

At Chambers, Neb., Redbine 60 averaged 87 bushels, but Hybrid 4 came through with an even 100.

At Rocky Ford, Colo., irrigated Caprock yielded 98 bushels. Hybrid 3, also irrigated, hit 119 bushels.

At Dayton, Iowa, the score read: 83 bushels for Hybrid 2; 54 bushels for Combine 7078.

And in Texas tests, Hybrid 3 made 87 bushels as compared with 68 for Plainsman at Slaton; Hybrid 4 averaged 64 bushels while Redbine 66 made 49 bushels at Renner; and at Corpus Christi, they grew 19-bushel Martin alongside Hybrid 2 which made 34.

Even better hybrids are on the way. "Most of the hybrids we now have will be replaced by much better ones in a few years," says Orrin J. Webster, USDA agronomist at the University of Nebraska.

The scientists are crossing U.S. varieties with a yellow-seeded sorghum from Africa—hope to get a hybrid with as much Vitamin A as corn. *Pound for pound, present hybrids almost equal corn in feed value.*

Some experimental hybrids show surprising resistance to chinch bugs. Still others mature earlier and store better. High moisture at harvest time is a real problem in humid areas.

Most scientists even foresee the day when we'll have dozens of hybrid sorghums, all tailor-made for specific areas, the same as hybrid corn varieties.

Meanwhile, the push is on to get seed for planting next year. "We expect to grow enough hybrid seed in '56 to plant two million acres in '57," says J. Roy Quinby, superintendent of the Chillicothe, Tex. Experiment Station. "We'll have four new hybrids growing in 200 county plots this summer, so farmers can see what they look like."

The female parents of the four Texas hybrids are white-seeded combine kafirs. The male parents are red-seeded. When crossed, they produce red seed which, when planted, yields about 40% more grain than ordinary sorghums. (*Farm Journal*, September 1953.)

The Nebraska Experiment Station expects to grow hybrid seed on about 250 acres this year. Nebraska scientists are also working on hybrid *forage* sorghums. Some yield well, but the forage appears to lack quality.

DeKalb has been distributing 10-pound samples of their new hybrids for planting this year. Their agronomist, R. F. Holland, who headquarters at Lubbock, Tex., predicts *"a plentiful supply of seed for planting next year."*

Growing hybrid seed is quite a feat, and a real tribute to the ingenuity of the sorghum breeders.

Back in 1943, they discovered a peculiar plant of sorghum on a farm near Cookeville, Tenn. It looked exactly like all the other plants, but it didn't produce a single grain of pollen.

This no-pollen trait—scientists call it the "male sterile factor"—gave them the key to hybrid sorghums.

When the scientists set out to make a hybrid, they first select the strains, then breed this no-pollen trait into the female parent. This female parent produces no pollen of its own, but it does accept pollen from a male, pollen-producing plant growing nearby. (See photo, page 105.) Result is a mating that produces hybrid seed.

But the male pollen has to do more than simply fertilize the female parent. It also has to snuff out the no-pollen trait. Otherwise, when you planted the seed, none of the plants would produce pollen, and no seed would be set.

Getting this "pollen restorer" into the male parent is tricky, but the scientists have figured out how to do it.

Because hybrid seed looks just like ordinary sorghum seed, fly-by-night peddlers are reportedly selling so-called hybrids in some areas. Our advice: Don't be a sucker. What little certified hybrid seed there is hasn't found its way into the hands of fast-talkers. **End**

sorghums yield ⅓ more.

Photos: De Kalb Agricultural Ass'n., Inc.

EXTRA SIZE WHERE IT COUNTS. New hybrid isn't much taller than ordinary sorghum at left, but the longer, fuller heads make from 30% to 50% more grain. There isn't enough seed to go around this year, but you may be able to get a 10-pound sample to try out. In '57, seed of the new hybrids is expected to be plentiful.

HYBRID IN THE MAKING. White rows in center pollinate red female rows alongside. The female plants shed no pollen—they're male sterile. So the seed they produce is a hybrid.

NEW YELLOW SORGHUMS, crossed with white and red varieties, may give us hybrids with as much Vitamin A as corn.

The tractor tires make the seedbed. Be sure to space the tractor wheels so that the corn planter runs in their tracks. Otherwise, you'll get poor stands. This field at Funk Research Acres, McLean Co., Ill., was plowed and planted on May 15.

Corn

BY RALPH D. WENNBLOM

Photos: Funk Brothers Seed Co.

Look at the grassy weeds! This part of the field was plowed, disked, and harrowed before the corn was planted, then harrowed again after planting—the way most of us put in a crop of corn. Was it worth it? Well, let's compare it with . . .

. . . corn planted immediately after plowing, without disking or harrowing. Why so few weeds? Soil between rows is so loose and lumpy that the weeds sprout slowly. The corn comes up fast, and one cultivation covers weeds in the row.

Crops and Soils

planter follows the plow

Twice over the field—once with the plow, once with the planter—puts in a corn crop; saves disking, harrowing, a cultivation or two

MOST of us over-do it when it comes to working up our corn ground.

We plow, then disk it once, maybe twice, and if there's time, we may even give the field a harrowing or two. Nothing like "doing the job right," and the field does look nice.

What we forget is this: a kernel of corn actually needs only a few square inches of seedbed—just enough *firm* soil to get the plant started and keep it going for a few weeks. After that, the plant gets its food and moisture from the *rootbed*.

No one needs to tell you that a loose, spongy rootbed beats a tightly-packed one all hollow, when it comes to growing good crops. And running over a field with implements can't help packing the soil.

Farmers who've tried it are sold on the idea of planting right behind the plow. "I planted half of my '53 corn on the furrow," says Bill Rhodes, Kalamazoo County, Mich. "If there was any difference in yield, it was in favor of the corn on the furrow. It seemed to take the dry weather better."

Another Kalamazoo County farmer, Dick Seelye, got 85-bushel corn on a field that was plowed, planted, and cultivated just once.

Andrew Shugars, Allegan County, who was one of the first to try furrow planting (*Farm Journal*, May 1952), reports that the method has paid off five years in a row.

These Michigan farmers agree that it doesn't pay to wait too long after plowing to plant. Depending on the weather, plant within a day or two, so that the soil doesn't dry out and harden on you.

At Ohio State University, they've compared furrow-planted corn with corn planted in the usual manner since 1940. During the last 14 years, the yields from furrow-planting have averaged 56.8 bushels per acre—*about a bushel more* than corn planted on land that was plowed and disked twice before planting.

The idea might work with other crops, too. Why not try it on a few rows of soybeans, potatoes, sorghums?

Photo: Cameron Hervey

The pay-off. Row at left, on land worked up in the usual manner, made 92 bushels. Row on right, planted on freshly turned furrows, yielded the same. "We got just as much corn, with less work," says R. J. Laible.

AFTER small grain is off, hustle right in.

PLANT a second feed crop, like sorghum or Sudan.

OR soybeans. Use a short-season variety.

OR a 90-day hybrid. Make silage if frost catches it.

TWO CROPS

in one season

Team up moisture, speed, and fertilizer with a short-season variety, and harvest a second crop

YOU may want to try growing two crops on the same land this year if you're pressed for feed or hemmed in by acreage allotments.

Farmers who make double-cropping a regular practice admit that it's risky, they tell *Farm Journal* that "you won't get much if you have a dry summer."

But if you double up on fertilizer—put on enough to feed both crops—and get average rains, including a "sprouting" shower soon after planting, your second crop will usually yield from ½ to ¾ of normal.

Hustle off the small grain. Farmers in the southern half of the Corn Belt grow good corn or soybeans after they've harvested their winter wheat or barley.

But there are numerous other combinations. For instance, you can chop oats in the heading-out stage for silage (to gain time), then plant grain sorghum, soybeans, or corn.

If silage is what you're after, use either a "silage hybrid" or forage sorghum. Sweet sudan grass will make either pasture or silage.

Another possibility: soybeans for hay. Plant thick, and cut after the pods form. Soybean hay is generally considered to be worth only 80% to 90% as much as alfalfa, mostly because cattle won't eat the coarser stems.

Cattle don't like straight *soybean silage* as well as corn silage, but in Florida tests, 2.9 tons of soybean silage equalled one ton of No. 1 alfalfa hay.

A mixture of soybeans and sweet Sudan grass makes good silage, say Illinois farmers. They seed 15 to 20 pounds of Sudan with 1½ bushels of soybeans per acre. Other farmers prefer to plant soybeans with forage sorghum for silage.

Speed is the secret to successful double-cropping. "By using a crop dryer, we're able to combine wheat about five days sooner," says John McCarty, Gibson County, Ind.

Ohio State University tests back up McCarty. Last year, they shoved the wheat harvest up six days by using a dryer; also got ¾ bushel more per acre. What's more, the early-harvested wheat graded higher, reports Engineer W. H. Johnson.

Continues McCarty: "To make the wheat straw rot faster, we put on liquid nitrogen—100 pounds of actual nitrogen per acre for corn, 25 pounds for soybeans.

"When early-planted corn yields 70 bushels, our late-planted, 90- to 100-day hybrid usually makes about 50 bushels per acre. Late-planted soybeans make 15 or 20 bushels," says McCarty.

Paul Primus, Gibson County, Ind., says that "we've pulled the combine out of a field one evening, and the planter out the next."

If Primus can get his *winter barley* off and the corn in by June 25, he plants corn. Otherwise, he puts in soybeans. Last year, a 12-acre field of corn on the heels of winter barley made enough silage to feed 100 cattle for three months.

Buckwheat matures in about 60 days, fits in well as a second crop for Carl Burcholz, DuBois County, Ind.

An alfalfa-corn combination works well for Lloyd Gearig, Fulton County, Ohio. He gets a couple of tons of first-crop alfalfa hay. Then, *if there's moisture*, he turns under the alfalfa and socks in a 90-day hybrid.

This same idea is being tried by Ersel Walley, Allen County, Ind. He fertilized his clover crop heavily with 10-10-10 this spring, plans to put the first crop in the silo, then plant silage corn.

Or you can put in soybeans. Despite the drought last year, Owen Rhoades, Macoupin County, Ill., got 1½ tons of hay and 13 bushels of soybeans from each acre. In '51, better moisture-wise, his soybeans made 25.

Although not a sure-fire proposition, double-cropping may be a risk worth taking this year. So the land won't suffer, put on *extra plant food*, and give the field *more than its share* of manure next year.

—Dick Braun

June 1954

By BOB COFFMAN
Farm Journal Field Staff

Farmers tell of success...and failure...with INTERSEEDING

■ Interseeding soybeans into standing wheat drew mixed reviews last year—some cheers and some jeers. The same is true for farmers who tried a reverse twist and flew wheat into corn, soybeans or sorghum.

Where the idea worked, they got two crops for less effort and expense than they would have gotten with conventional double-cropping. Where it didn't work, all farmers got from the experience was the feeling they'd been had!

Phil Ellis, Vermillion County, Ind., can hardly believe what happened to him. He seeded 12 acres by air May 30. He clipped the top leaves on his Amsoy 71 beans when he combined wheat.

"Beans looked good early, but they lodged so badly that by harvesttime it didn't look as if they'd amount to much. They were flat on the ground when we tried to combine them, so we just gave up."

He continues his story, "After we got the corn out I decided to have another go at it. The hired man brought out one truck. We thought that would hold the whole crop. We filled that truck in nothing flat."

Now, the punch line: "Those beans made 54 bu. per acre! Heck, I couldn't lose!"

But some did lose. Ellis's neighbor Max Bishop plowed up his 30 acres of interseeded soybeans and will go back to normal double-cropping methods in 1976. "Our trouble started when our wheat lodged badly before harvest. We had to cut so low to get the wheat that we did irreparable damage to the beans. On Sept. 1, our beans were only a foot tall, and might have made 15 bu., but we gave up on them," Bishop told us.

He'll go back to plowing wheat stubble and then planting soybeans; he figures there's a better chance to make 25 bu. per acre that way.

Harry Woodyard, Edgar County, Ill., shared Bishop's disappointment, getting only 9 bu. per acre off 40 acres.

He was beat from the beginning, when only 30% took root. Then weeds moved in—foxtail, cocklebur, ragweed and smartweed.

Everything that could go wrong did, he feels. He'll go back to double-cropping after wheat.

Other detractors didn't mince words with us when we asked about their failures. One told us his crop was a "flop." When asked what advice he'd pass along to other farmers, he responded, "Don't do it."

Another said, "Don't believe everything you read."

Down South, Charles Berry's first try at interseeding produced a gratifying yield of 45-bu. soybeans after 40-bu. wheat.

He timed his seeding on May 15 to take advantage of heavier-than-normal rainfall forecasts for the second half of the month. The gamble paid off. Eleven days after planting, he got 1.2" of rain that saved this stand.

It also helped that he dropped the seed onto level ground, in a heavy-textured soil.

Not everyone hired an airplane to interseed. We know of several who used tailgate seeders on the backs of pickup trucks with favorable results. Others actually planted the beans in the ground while the wheat was ankle high in April.

One of those was Robert Buker, Tippecanoe County, Ind. He pulled a corn planter through young wheat on April 15, seeding ¾ bu. per acre in 15" rows. The planter was equipped with disk openers, tilling ½" deep.

Those soybeans eventually yielded 24.4 bu., while a comparison of soybeans broadcast on top of the ground in standing wheat on April 15 resulted in only an 8% stand and an 8.2-bu. final yield.

One of Buker's neighbors, Paul Shepherd, seeded 1½ bu. of soybeans per acre pulling a tailgate seeder behind his pickup on May 14. His wheat made 74 bu., but the beans that followed got awfully weedy. Shepherd, in fact, gave up on harvesting them. But after he got his corn picked, he went back to the beans and much to his surprise, harvested 22 bu. per acre with no problems from the frost-killed weeds.

Farm Journal has quizzed nearly four dozen farmers who tried interseeding on approximately 5,000 acres in 1975. Here are some of their conclusions:

- Results still seem to outweigh the risks in most cases. For the $15 to $20 most put into seed and aerial application, even low soybean yields beat nothing.
- Weather clearly is the key. Ideally, soybeans should be flown on at 2 to 2½ bu. per acre, into dampened ground, with a nice shower within two or three days after seeding.
- Clipping the top few leaves of young soybeans when you cut wheat doesn't do much harm. But later varieties seem to grow back better than earlier ones. ◁

Less than a third of the acreage got a chemical weed killer 10 years ago. Now . . .

It's the way to grow cotton

Photo: Delta Photos

By JOE DAN BOYD
Farm Journal Field Staff

■ Cotton growers treated more than 9 out of every 10 acres with a chemical weed killer in 1972. In fact, an estimated 93% of the total acreage—almost 12½ million acres—got at least one herbicide of some kind last season.

"I honestly don't know where to find a single acre of Arkansas' 1.4 million in cotton that didn't get a pre-emergence treatment and at least one post spray in 1972," says Extension Cotton Specialist William Woodall.

In the 14 major cotton states, growers used pre-plant or pre-emergence chemicals on 10,132,000 acres, and applied post-emergence sprays on 6,952,000.

Assuming that only two-thirds of the post-emergence sprays were put on acres that had already received pre-emergence treatment, 12,449,000 acres got at least one herbicide of some kind.

The graph at right shows the progress of cotton weed chemicals over the last 10 years that FARM JOURNAL has been making a survey in co-operation with Extension Cotton and Weed Specialists.

Certain troublesome weeds gained ground in the last decade too, but so far new weed killers and new techniques are holding most in check.

"Nutsedge came on strong in the early '60s," says James M. Brown, manager of production technology for the National Cotton Council. "Teaweed was a real headache by the mid-60s, and spurred anoda was giving Mid-South growers fits by the late '60s."

"Annual morning glory is the big trouble now in Arizona," says Stanley Heathman, the state's Extension Weed Specialist. "Our most effective approach is post-emergence chemicals like Telvar, Karmex and Caparol, but we badly need a pre-plant chemical to handle it."

"We have our share of annual morning glory, too," says New Mexico Extension Agronomist William Jackson. "Growers usually fight it with an overlay of Caparol—behind a pre-plant herbicide that is also effective against spurred anoda."

"Bindweed and nutgrass made a comeback in 1972 in El Paso and Pecos areas of Texas," reports Fred Elliott, Extension Cotton Specialist. "Farmers dusted off flame cultivators for both."

"We're seeing more of a troublemaker called bristley starbur that's related to cocklebur," says Charles Swann, Extension agronomist in Georgia. "So far, pre-emergence Cotoran and Karmex or early post sprays are doing a reasonably good job against it."

Last season pre-plant Treflan and Planavin went on some soils that are usually considered un-

Photo by the author

Stop early weeds before they start. Boom and tanks on the tractor apply a pre-plant spray of Treflan for Howard and Anderson Reed, Dooly County, Ga. Disk and a smoothing board behind incorporate the spray (above). In Tallahatchie County, Miss., Bouldin Marley sprays 14" bands of Karmex behind the planter (left), then follows with two post-emergence sprays of Cotoran-MSMA, cultivates three times and lays by with a spray of Lorox.

likely candidates for incorporation tools, reports Fred Elliott.

"Some of the Texas Houston clays are tough to incorporate with chemicals," he explains. "But, enterprising growers turned the trick by using Rotovators ahead of 'flex type' planters that disturb the incorporated zone very little."

Pre-plant tank mix combinations of Treflan and Caparol will continue to gain in popularity, believes Heathman of Arizona.

"Growers can band the mixture and cover lightly with a layer of soil thrown by lister points mounted just behind spray nozzles," Heathman explains. "Later, growers 'mulch down' rows with harrows, rotary tillers or Rolling Cultivators without disturbing the band. Narrow planters knife seed just below the bands of chemical, and irrigation provides the moisture."

In winter vegetable areas of California and Arizona, growers prefer Dacthal as a pre-plant cotton herbicide because of its short residual life.

"They incorporate a Dacthal band across the bed just before planting, then irrigate to activate the chemical and germinate the seed," explains Marvin Hoover, California's Extension Cotton Specialist. "This is light incorporation very near the surface, often done *(Continued)*

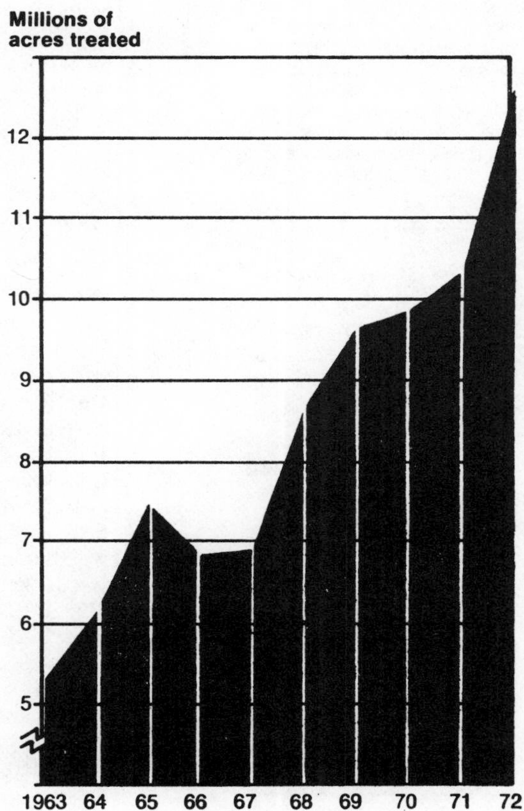

The way to grow cotton *(Continued)*

with a powered rotary tiller and bed shaper combination rig."

In the pre-emergence or planting-time arsenal, Cotoran has already made lots of headway, particularly on farms plagued with teaweed.

"In northeast Arkansas, pre-emergence sprays of Cotoran, Telvar or Karmex are almost as universal as a pre-plant of Treflan or Planavin," says grower Chauncey Denton.

"Cotoran at the 'cracking' stage may get a try by a good many Missouri growers in 1973," speculates Extension agronomist Joe Scott. "They hope to improve cotton stands and knock out more of the early germinating, hard-to-kill weeds."

In Madison County, Ala., Albert McDonald broadcast Cotoran on practically every acre—even the 2x1 skip-row fields.

"Broadcasting means I have to cultivate two or three fewer times later in the season," he says. "What's more, it usually means I don't have to use a layby spray, except on heavy bottom land."

Where he did use layby in '72, McDonald went with Lorox and Karmex.

In Tallahatchie County, Miss., Bouldin Marley kept cotton clean with a 14" band of Karmex at planting, followed by two post applications of Cotoran-MSMA; three mechanical cultivations; and, Lorox at layby.

"Johnson grass was a problem on soils that had been in soybeans the year before," he admits. "Spot sprays of DSMA from a riding crew helped clean that up."

The biggest growth area in cotton weed control in recent years has been in directed post-emergence and layby sprays.

"In North Carolina, use of post-emergence directed sprays doubled here in 1972," says Glenn Toomey, Extension agronomist, North Carolina State University.

In South Carolina, C. N. Nolan, Extension agronomist reports: Cold weather early in the season helped weeds get the jump on cotton in '72. But, growers responded with increased post treatments, including directed sprays of MSMA or DSMA mixed with Caparol, Cotoran and Herban; followed by Karmex or Herban at layby.

"Where larger weeds were still around at layby, many growers went to Lorox," he adds. "By harvest, most of the cotton was clean."

Even more exciting days lie ahead for cotton weed control. Here are some of the possibilities:

- "A new chemical named Probe plus MSMA in a directed post-emergence treatment was one of the most promising new treatments in 1972, both on farms and at experiment stations," says Louisiana State University agronomist Thomas Burch. "Teamed with MSMA, the new chemical, under development by Velsicol, got just about any growing weed up to 3" tall."
- At the Northeast Louisiana Station, a 3M experimental compound called MBR 8251 gave outstanding control of nutsedge in 1972 tests.
- Another experimental herbicide named Sancap by its developers, CIBA-Geigy, offers real hope for broadleaf control on light sandy soils where many current sprays aren't now recommended. In Oklahoma, for example, where up to half the cotton is grown on sandy land, this could be a real boon.
- Still another new chemical, named Zorial, looks good against a raft of broadleaf weeds in cotton. Under development by Sandoz-Wander, Inc., it will be tested further in 1973.
- And finally, the Zapper, an experimental microwave weed control rig has been announced by Phytox, Inc. Based on research at Texas A&M, the Zapper focuses electromagnetic energy into the soil to kill weed seeds and emerged weeds.

Cotton treated with weed killers in 1972
(estimated)

	1972 Pre-Emergence Acreage	1972 Post-Emergence Acreage
Ala.	570,000	300,000
Ariz.	153,000	170,000
Ark.	1,426,000	1,411,000
Calif.	568,000	131,000
Ga.	438,000	285,000
La.	650,000	640,000
Miss.	1,720,000	1,700,000
Mo.	402,000	320,000
N. Mex.	75,000	75,000
N.C.	220,000	170,000
Okla.	325,000	75,000
S.C.	360,000	325,000
Tenn.	475,000	350,000
Tex.	2,750,000	1,000,000
TOTAL	**10,132,000**	**6,952,000**

Photo: Washington State University

SHORTIE WHEATS lodge less and yield more. One semi-dwarf variety may be released this fall. "It's 12″ to 18″ shorter than Omar, yet averages a third more yield," says USDA scientist Orville A. Vogel.

NEW DWARF WHEAT ...ready this fall?

THERE'S a good chance that one of the semi-dwarf wheat varieties developed at Washington State University will be released by the Washington, Oregon and Idaho experiment stations this fall.

The variety, labeled CI 13448, still must meet final test requirements and pass a commercial milling trial. But if CI 13448 is released, there will be a considerable amount of foundation seed ready for seeding this fall.

"We're growing about 60 acres of foundation seed in several eastern Washington locations," says USDA scientist Orville A. Vogel. "This should yield 4,000 to 5,000 bushels of foundation seed for registered growers to increase to 250,000 by 1962 when it would go to certified seed growers."

Vogel first started work on the variety in 1947 when he began crossing a low-grade, dwarf wheat from Japan, called Norin 10, with the Brevor and Burt varieties.

What can you expect of CI 13448?

"It has the same smut resistance as Burt," says Vogel. That means it's resistant to all known races of common smut and everything but a new race of dwarf smut found only in the Flathead Lake region of western Montana. In the higher rainfall areas of eastern Washington, the new variety produces plants about one foot shorter than Brevor and 18 inches shorter than Omar.

With present farming practices in the higher rainfall areas, Vogel expects the semi-dwarf variety to yield 10% to 25% more than Omar. But if you fertilize heavily, he believes it will average at least 33% more than Omar.

Last year CI 13448 yielded up to *96 bushels per acre without lodging, compared with 55 bushels for Omar.*

WSU has started soil management experiments which scientist Fred Koehler hopes will provide much of the information farmers need to have in order to consistently grow top yields of the semi-dwarf wheats.

WSU plant breeders have speeded their work on semi-dwarf varieties with growth chambers furnished by the Washington State Wheat Commission. "With this chamber, we now can tell in five days how tall a wheat will grow," says Vogel. "It used to take five to seven months." —*Glenn Lorang*

Ralph D. Wennblom and George W. Wormley, Crops and Soils Editors

Spraying Soil with Asphalt Film May Speed Up Crops

You know how vegetable growers cover the soil with black plastic.

Now comes this idea: A liquid derived from an asphalt-type material which you spray onto the seedbed. It covers the soil with a black film only one-thousandth of an inch thick that seals in moisture for days—even weeks.

But more important, the black film absorbs more heat from the sun which in turn warms up the soil as much as 10° at the two-inch depth. If the weather is cool and sunshiny after planting, the seeds come up five to ten days sooner.

The film-forming chemical, called EAP-2000, comes as a liquid that you can apply in 6- to 8-inch bands with a conventional sprayer. Discovered by the Esso Research and Engineering Co., Linden, N.J., it is not yet on the market. Results in on-the-farm tests, although promising, have been erratic.

For one thing, the soil has to be smooth in order to get an even layer of film. In some tests, the sprayed-on mulch speeded up emergence, but the crops didn't mature any sooner.

Even so, the company believes their sprayed-on mulch may do an even better job than sheets of plastic and at far less cost. The material doesn't seem to harm the soil. "It disappears with the first cultivation," says Esso engineer Jim Davidson, who is running tests at the University of Arizona.

The scientists have also used the sprayed-on mulch to get new range seedings "over the hump."

In one Colorado trial, blue grama grass, mulched with EAP-2000, came up in five days compared with a month for the un-mulched. Four months later, the mulched seedlings were vigorous—a solid stand—while the un-mulched plants were spotty and stunted.

Meanwhile, Arizona farmers are trying the sprayed-on mulch on melons, cotton, corn, sugar beets, grain sorghum and cucumbers. We'll let you know how their tests pan out. **END**

Photo: Donald R. Tindall

NEW HANGING HERRINGBONE is latest one on the market. All pipework is suspended from ceiling, leaving clear area underneath for washing, milking, cleaning.

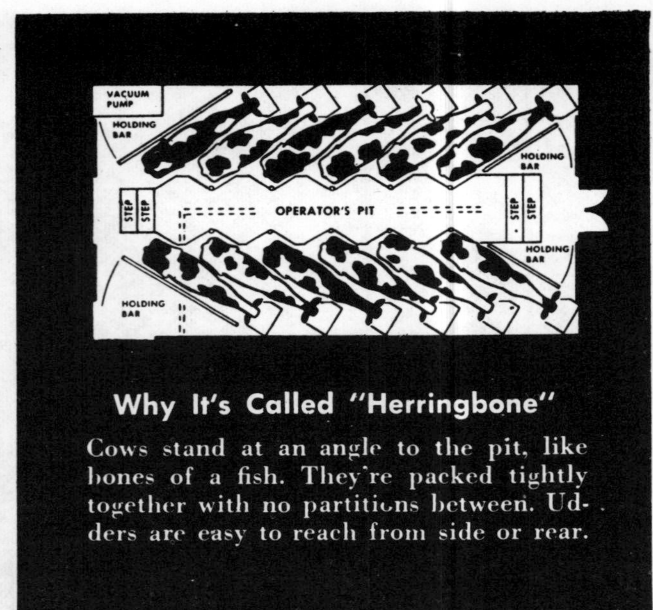

Why It's Called "Herringbone"

Cows stand at an angle to the pit, like bones of a fish. They're packed tightly together with no partitions between. Udders are easy to reach from side or rear.

Herringbone milking ...it's moving fast

You can fit this new idea into any kind of set-up from stanchion barns to loose housing

By RAY DANKENBRING and BILL HARDY

LOUIS MAXFIELD had his shirt off as he flipped milker units from the business end of five big Holsteins across to five on the other side of him.

"Better start the fan in here to get a little breeze" his mother told him, as she showed us through the door.

Louis was in the pit of a herringbone parlor. It was a hot summer afternoon, and he was really too busy for visitors. On top of that —the cow tester was there meaning that each cow's milk had to be weighed and sampled.

"But you should have seen us before we had this parlor," said Mrs. Maxfield. "We were milking in stanchions, and it took at least two—three if they had time—to do the milking and carry the milk to the bulk tank."

That's just one reason why the Maxfields were among the first in their area to try a radical new idea—herringbone milking. They ordered one shortly after reading that the idea had been brought from New Zealand and was working out well on the Illinois farm of Clarence Aavang (FARM JOURNAL, June '57). Now, the Maxfields in the hills of Vermont are only one of hundreds of dairy families with herringbones.

One brand alone—Chore-Boy—already claims 70 parlors operating in Ohio, 50 in Michigan and about the same number in Indiana, to mention *just three states.* Kaiser Aluminum has distributed 1,500 plans, based on that original Illinois parlor. Clay Equipment Company has parlors operating in 31 states. And still newer ones are popping onto the market, like the new "hanging-herringbone" developed by Southern States Cooperative. *They all add up to a first class boom!*

What's the magic of herringbones? While we slowed up Louis Maxfield some with our questions, and the cow tester stopped him to get a sample from each cow, he milked 50

Photo: Hanson Carroll

HERRINGBONE IN OLD BARN? Carroll Stanley and son feed grain and milk batch of eight cows at once in "half a herringbone" across end of barn; put 'em back in tie-stalls for hay and silage.

high producers in less than two hours.

"Some folks say you can average a cow per minute," we baited Louis.

"We're interested in production—not just milking speed," was his comeback. The herd average of *15,190 lbs. milk and 585 lbs. fat per cow on 54 cows*, proved his point! "But it's still faster than two of us in stanchions."

You don't have to switch *to loose housing to make a herringbone practical.* The Maxfields keep their cows in stanchions.

Carroll Stanley, another Vermonter, had a pretty good barn with 62 tie-stalls in it. Milking was too big a chore for both Carroll and his 17-year-old son. "I had reached the point where I had to reduce the herd, or really get set up for milking," Stanley told us.

He read about herringbones in FARM JOURNAL. Later, he and Mrs. Stanley drove to Indiana to look at one. They liked it, but hesitated to spend money for a *separate new building.*

Finally Stanley and his son ripped a 12-foot-wide strip across one end of the 38-foot-wide barn and put in a pit and *just one line* of eight herringbone stalls.

Now they simply run eight cows into the herringbone, milk while the cows eat grain, then run 'em back to their stalls.

"The whole job of modernizing our complete dairy set-up cost $8,000," says Stanley. $3,000 went for the "parlor." The rest went for a pond, piping water to the barn and installing cup, a $2,600 bulk tank and a gutter cleaner.

While Stanley talked to us, it took less than two hours to milk 86 high-producing Jerseys.

As we talked to more herringbone-users we picked up a sprinkling of commendations and answers to the problems they've encountered.

Dave Syme, manager of Hilly Land Farm at Scotland, Conn., has a Clay parlor and says: "Cows behave fine. They don't bull around in the stalls. The closeness of cows to each other has a quieting effect."

Another told us: *"A cow that will kick your head off in the stanchion won't even bother you in the herringbone!"*

What about manure splatter? While most dairymen said they had no "splash" dangers in working directly behind the cows, manufacturer Joseph Clay suggests a six-inch high curb.

John Hansen of Snohomish County, Wash. put a ¾ x 2-inch mesh grate on each side of his 12-cow herringbone *and gutters underneath* which he hoses into a sump outside.

A. J. Christiansen of Massachusetts not only put in grates, and a bevelled splash board to protect him—he put a gutter cleaner underneath.

Feeding systems can be a problem. But some dairymen, like Christiansen don't feed in the parlor at all. "We feed in the stanchions, and the cows have more eating time," he says.

Some say that when feed sticks in the down chutes it's a problem to crawl over the backs of the cows and jar it loose. But the Maxfields say: "We use pelleted feeds, and never have to worry about it clogging."

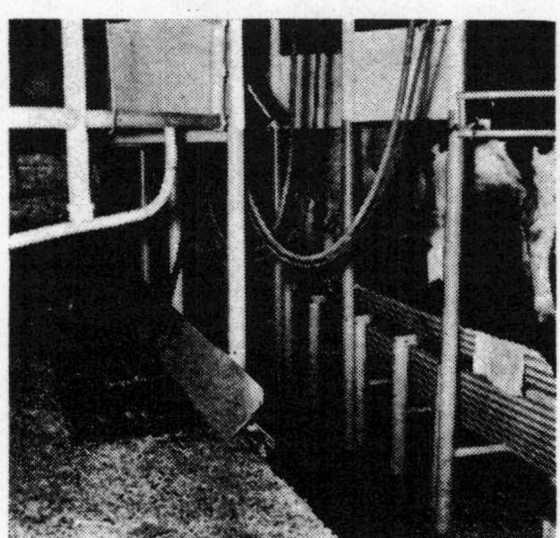

Photo: Bill Hardy

"SPLASHBOARD and grates are the best things we've found to keep a herringbone clean," says A. J. Christiansen. Gutter cleaner underneath handles manure.

What size herd do herringbones fit? "We first thought the herringbone was for herds of 80 or over," says Clay. "But in 30 users, we found that nine out of ten milking less than 50 cows."

Don Golay, president of the Farmer Feeder Company that makes Chore-Boy equipment, says Clarence, George and Dave Heimerdinger of Clinton, Mich., were operating separate herds until they put in a herringbone. Then they combined their 50 cows; expect to go to 100.

W. N. Stoneman, president of the co-op that is selling the hanging-herringbone, says herringbones fit almost any size herd *by the number of stalls you put in.*

"The important thing is that you're saving steps and time by bringing all those udders close together and at a handy height," he says.

And that's the real advantage of *all herringbones.* **End**

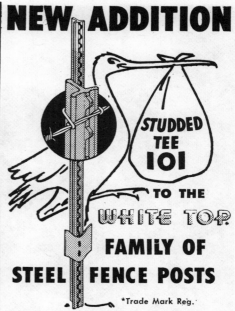

1

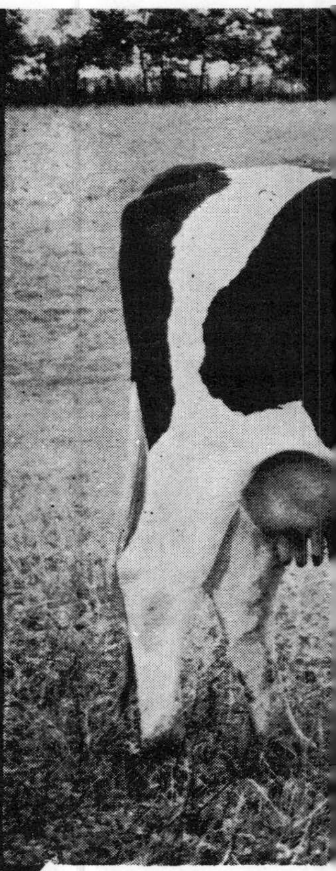

You may have a 20,000 lb. cow...

3

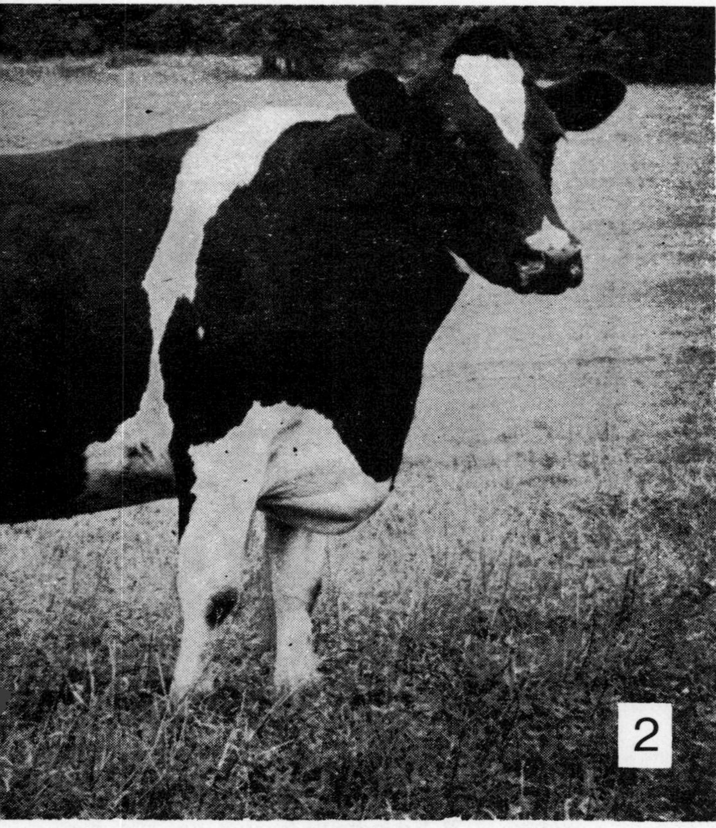

2

and don't know it

One of these four cows made 20,000 lbs. of milk; one made 15,000; one 14,750; one 11,250. *Answer, page 58*

BY BILL HARDY
Farm Journal's Eastern Field Editor

Nearly all of these 101 Eastern dairymen found "sleepers" in their herds. Here's one of the most surprising dairy stories we've printed.—The Editors

JOHN ROAT of Broome County, N.Y. has been feeding his cows "by the book" for some time and feeling pretty well satisfied with the results. And why shouldn't he—with a herd average of 12,234 lbs. of milk for 40 milk cows?

But last fall, research workers from the Grange League Federation Cooperative Exchange (GLF) in Ithaca, N.Y. asked Roat if he'd be willing to put a few cows on a high-grain test to see what happened.

What happened was a real eye-opener to Roat and to 101 other New York and New Jersey dairymen who took part in these GLF feeding trials. Some of the results promise to knock the props out from under several of our firmly-held beliefs about feeding.

For instance, one of the four Roat animals shown in the pictures at the left is Millie. Before the test, Roat had been feeding Millie about like he had the other cows in the herd—17 lbs. of grain a day, 18 lbs. of hay and 35 lbs. of silage. And Millie was producing about like the other cows—12,000 lbs. seemed her limit.

But when the GLF folks upped Millie's grain to 36.8 lbs. a day, *her milk production zoomed to 20,000 lbs.!* Without question, she had the breeding potential to make a lot more milk—*but not on the kind and amount* of feed she had been getting!

Here's how the four cows shown at left performed:

COW	GRAIN FED BEFORE	GRAIN FED ON TEST	PREVIOUS MILK PRODUCTION	TEST MILK PRODUCTION
Pug	18 lbs.	36.8 lbs.	12,000 lbs.	14,750 lbs.
Paula	18	37.0	11,000	11,250
Millie	17	36.8	12,000	20,000
Petal	20	36.8	14,000	15,000

Note that while Millie went up 8,000 lbs., Paula, who got slightly more grain, gave only 250 lbs. more milk.

Robert Mead, Courtland County, N.Y., has 44 milk cows and a herd average of 14,000 lbs.—a high-producing herd. Here's how his five cows on test made out:

COW	GRAIN FED BEFORE	GRAIN FED ON TEST	PREVIOUS MILK PRODUCTION	TEST MILK PRODUCTION
36662	20 lbs.	41 lbs.	15,000 lbs.	22,250 lbs.
36683	20	41	19,500	25,000
94059	20	41	15,000	18,000
32948	20	41	17,000	17,500
318382	20	41	14,500	17,000

Mead's results ought to make any dairyman sit up and take notice. Two of his *(Continued)*

4

Laughs from the COUNTRY PRESS

If Communism's as great as the Russians claim it is, you'd think they would take down that Iron Curtain and put in a picture window.—*News*, Longview, Wash.

Getting old is merely reaching the point where you feel your corns more than your oats.—*Journal*, Belton, Tex.

A miser might be pretty tough to live with, but he makes a nice ancestor. —*Times*, Inman, S.C.

Many an old settler settled out West because he didn't settle up back East.—*Journal*, Kingman, Kan.

Successful door-to-door salesman to housewife: "I'd like to show you a little item your neighbors said you couldn't afford."—*Spokesman-Review*, Spokane, Wash.

Three meals a day, a good house, two cars, a boat, a power mower and a contented wife—why shouldn't I be in debt?—*Plainsman*, Huron, S.D.

At the table, it's not the minutes that increase the weight, but the seconds.—*News*, Jackson, Miss.

People are a little like tea bags—they don't know their own strength until they get into hot water.—*Advocate*, Cumberland, Wis.

Now is the time to:

Paint.
Fix gates.
Pay taxes.
Tell jokes.
Clean closets.
Dance the polka.
Go duck hunting.
Read Psalm 118:6.
Watch your weight.
Buy shotgun shells.
Burn the mortgage.
Enjoy autumn colors.
Fill up on apple pie.
Invest in a chain saw.
Plant more lily bulbs.
Repair storm windows.
Have your eyes examined.
Green-wrap some tomatoes.
Have a family portrait taken.
Have flapjacks for breakfast.
Admire Mom's chrysanthemums.
Start planning a winter vacation.
Keep an eye on the cattle market.
Give Aunt Minnie slips from your best geraniums.
Take Shorty with you when you visit the stockyards.

20,000-lb. Cow

cows took to high grain feeding so well that they gave him more than 100 lbs. of milk a day! All but one responded generously. *Leaving out cow No. 32948, the other four averaged 4,563 lbs. of extra milk for the 21 extra pounds of grain each received.* His highest producer gave the second-highest response.

How many made enough more milk to pay for the extra grain?

Here's how Ernie Charron, manager of applied research for GLF went about getting the answer: In his first test, he selected cows in 48 farm herds, paired them up as nearly as possible by age, weight, freshening date, feeding rate and general condition. For the first 14 days, he had the farmers keep all the cows on the same grain that they had been getting (which averaged 12% above the recommended textbook feeding standards.)

Then for one cow in each pair, the farmers started increasing the grain by 2 lbs. per day until the cows were getting 2 lbs. per 100 lbs. of body weight—or 35% above standards.

Of the 442 cows getting extra grain, 95% responded with extra milk. But *only 40% of them made enough more to pay* for the extra grain.

In a second test with different cows, the grain was increased until the cows were getting all they'd eat or all that the owner was willing to feed (the average was 57% above the standard). This time, 24% of the cows responded with increases of 4,000 lbs. or more (roughly the break-even point).

Charron's results bear out exactly the advice that Michigan State University's C. F. Huffman gave in FARM JOURNAL just a year ago (See "Dairy with Nothing but Corn," FARM JOURNAL, October 1960, and for the latest Michigan results, see page 54.)

"You can under-feed a cow and not know it," Huffman said then. "Some heavy producers should be on a full feed of grain for the highest profits, while other cows simply don't have the inherited capacity for using that much."

What's so new about feeding according to production? Haven't we been doing that in DHIA for years?

"Only within limits," says Michigan's Huffman. "Dairymen on DHIA have seldom gone above 16 to 18 lbs. of grain per cow per day. Many have been afraid to go higher for fear of hurting the animal's health or because they didn't think they could afford to feed the extra grain."

J. T. Reid, Cornell University dairy nutritionist, points out that our present-day dairy feeding standards are based largely on the old Haecker experiments conducted at the University of Minnesota in the early 1900s. "The mean yield of fat-corrected milk in those experiments was only 24.4 lbs.," he says. "And only one cow produced over 40 lbs. Present-day breeding and management have given us better cows—but we haven't been feeding to take full advantage of their milk-producing abilities."

The results chop down a bunch of widely-held ideas. For instance:

- High-grain rations don't "just add fat on the back of the cow." Both tests *exploded* this belief. Seventeen cows that weighed an average of 1,086 and produced an average of 34.5 lbs. of milk per day at the beginning, *gained* an average of 23 lbs. during the test. But the 19 cows that weighed an average of 1,407 lbs. each and produced an average of 77.8 lbs. of milk *lost* an average of 85 lbs. each during the test. In other words, some big, high-producing cows will lose weight right while they're eating as much as 60 lbs. of grain a day!
- Cows respond with extra milk when fed extra grain *anytime* during lactation. But because they produce so much of their total output during the first 120 days, it's especially important to feed extra grain then.
- High-grain feeding did not hurt the cows, according to veterinarians who checked them before and after.
- High-grain feeding did not increase mastitis. It was actually less of a problem with the high-grain group than with the others.
- High-grain feeding had *no effect on the butterfat content* between control and test cows.
- Big cows produced the most and showed the greatest response to extra grain. Cows averaging 1,086 lbs. in body weight at the beginning gave $26.98 worth of milk above feed costs. Cows averaging 1,407 lbs. ended up with $124.96 worth above feed costs. (These figures are based on grain at $66 a ton, hay at $25 a ton, silage at $8 a ton and milk at $4.63 per hundred.)

How can you single out the cows in your herd that will respond to high-grain feeding?

"All cows have to be challenged—and the limiting factor in this challenge is appetite," Charron says. "Some cows quit at 25 lbs. of grain, others will eat up to 60 lbs. or more."

"So long as a cow will eat more grain and pay for it, keep feeding her!" Charron urges. "For some cows, the profit level is 20 lbs. a day—for others, 50."

Maybe you have some 20,000-lb. cows in *your* herd. Why not find out? **END**

Answers to Quiz on Page 33

COW NO.	NAME	PRODUCTION
1	Pug	14,750
2	Paula	11,250
3	Millie	20,000
4	Petal	15,000

Photo: Ovid Bay

Photo: Dick Braun

KEEP 'EM OUT OF THE MUD with slats: Louis Kirshner, Benton County, Mo., built 6'x12' slatted "patios" in front of his individual "A" houses. Total cost, including water and electricity for heat lamps: $117 per pen. A portable slat-floor house (above, right) solves manure problems for Cedric Pursifull of Huntington County, Ind. He skids the 16'x24' structure with his tractor, uses it for finishing. It will house 50 head, or six farrowing stalls.

SLATTED HOG FLOORS are sweeping the Corn Belt

A MIDWEST FIELD STAFF REPORT

Edited by Dick Seim

IT'S THE best thing we've done in 20 years!"

That's the Regier brothers, John and Arnold, Cottonwood County, Minn., talking about the slatted floor they put in their hog finishing building.

Their enthusiasm is typical of the thousands of Corn Belt farmers who are rushing to install slats as an answer to their biggest hog-raising problem—handling the manure.

Even though the idea is too new for you to find much in the way of "hard" research facts, farmers aren't waiting. It looks too good, with its possibilities of saving labor, eliminating bedding and carrying more hogs on given floor space.

And they're getting encouragement from such college people as "Mac" Whiteker, Iowa State University hog specialist, who advises:

"I'd give serious consideration to slotted floors if you plan to build an enclosed, insulated, ventilated hog house."

FARM JOURNAL's Midwest field editors talked with dozens of hog producers from Nebraska to Ohio who are raising hogs on slats.

A few admit trouble learning to use slats, but the big majority say "why didn't someone tell us about them before?"

Here are their reasons:

A Time Saver

"We've had to clean our pit only twice since February," say the Regiers. "Slats have really made the job easy."

Their "new" finishing house is actually an old horse barn that they converted for $800. They tore out the stalls, dug a 68' long pit right down the center. It's 6'4" wide, 4' deep at one end and slopes to 5½' at the other. They slatted the area over the pit with elm 2 x 4's. They keep the water level in the concrete-lined pit high enough to cover the accumulation, clean out with an ordinary 5" grain auger.

A producer with a different approach, but the same interest in saving labor, Warren Waitt, Hamilton County, Ind., uses six 18' x 36' "package" houses, each designed to hold 100 pigs. Cost apiece, complete, about $3,500.

Waitt says, "You can't beat these houses for cutting labor. I haven't spent 30 minutes cleaning time in the six of them since last February."

He provided 15 square feet of lagoon per pig adjacent to each house.

Bob Brenton, Dallas County, Iowa, experimented by installing slats in seven pens of a finishing building. He raised the slats 16 inches from the floor, walled up the space underneath, and filled it with water.

He says, "Those seven pens saved us 15 minutes of labor a day. At the end of two months, one man cleaned the whole area under the pens in 35 minutes with a hose."

In a 113-day comparison at the University of Illinois, A. H. Jensen found

(Continued)

Slatted hog floors are sweeping the Corn Belt

it took an average of only 1¼ *minutes per day* to clean a floor completely topped with slats—17 minutes per day to clean a concrete slab floor.

No Bedding Either

When you put slats in, you cross bedding out. But how much does that save you?

Jim Frieden, Kosciusko County, Ind., figures he saves $1.50 per day on 100 hogs during the bedding season.

Tom Chrystal, Greene County, Iowa, says he figures you have $40 per ton in bedding by the time you have it on the manure spreader. He estimates that it costs at least $10 per ton to grind cobs—and he points out that straw can be a high-priced item. Of course, some growers use little or no bedding on solid concrete.

More Hogs

While the cost of slat floors often may be double or more the cost of a slab—some say two to four times—the cost per pig can be held to near the same level by allowing less space per pig on slats.

Says Lloyd Broderius, Renville County, Minn., "I nearly doubled the capacity of a 34′ x 60′ barn by putting in a complete slatted floor."

He says the building accommodates about 330 market-weight hogs now. That's roughly 6 square feet per hog.

Normally, you'd have pigs of different ages going through the house. The firm that manufactured the slatted floor in Broderius' barn makes these recommendations:

Pigs from 50 to 100 lbs., 3 square feet. From 100 lbs. or 125 lbs. to 150 lbs., 6 square feet. For pigs 150 lbs. and over, 9 square feet.

Another Minnesota farmer, Charles Steffl, Redwood County, crowded 50 pigs in a 12′ x 24′ portable house with a slatted floor 12 inches above the ground.

He says, "Going fine so far."

Steffl built his house for $550 in materials, plus his labor. He's a tenant, so finds advantages in being able to push up capacity on slats, and yet keep construction costs low.

While most growers and researchers agree that you can get by with less area per pig on slatted floors—there's no one formula generally accepted. Again, detailed research hasn't caught up with farmer adoption of the idea.

Early results from A. H. Jensen's trials at the University of Illinois may provide some guidance.

Says the scientist, "We got satisfactory results with 4 square feet of space per pig up to 120 lbs. For pigs up to 190 lbs., there was no difference between 6¼ and 8 square feet."

Jensen thinks that hog performance may prove to be similar on solid or slatted floors if hogs are allowed equal space. "But from a cleanliness standpoint, slatted floors are ahead."

Arranging capacity so manure gets trampled through—that's one of the secrets to success with slats, stresses Dick Hollandbeck, Purdue University.

A researcher for Central Soya, Leo Curtin, advises keeping the number of pigs per pen down to 20 or 25. What size pens? Last year he allowed 7½ square feet per hog—dropped that to 6½ square feet this year.

A Few Problems, too

Although most of the producers FARM JOURNAL editors visited are sold on slats, none claims they're foolproof.

Several reported trouble with tail-biting. "We had a lot of it until our vets suggested feeding an iron compound," says Waitt. Producers with only part of their pens slatted sometimes have difficulty training hogs to use the dunging area. Some have had ventilation problems

Iowa State University emphasizes that you should use slats or slatted floors only in insulated, draft-free buildings with good mechanical ventilation in winter. Specialists say it may be necessary to control both temperatures and humidity in cold weather to be sure slats clean well.

There's no general agreement yet on what one type of slat—wood, steel or concrete—works best. Costs vary, but generally, hog producers pay 55¢ to 60¢ per square foot for wood slats, around 65¢ for concrete bars, and about $1.30 for steel "T" bars.

One thing sure, however—even without all the answers we're going to see more slat floors used by all kinds of hog raisers, big and little. **END**

Now is the time to:

Pay bills.
Chop wood.
Mulch roses.
Wean calves.
Hull walnuts.
Buy snow tires.
Watch football.
Go deer hunting.
Thin the woodlot.
Order baby chicks.
Clean up the garden.
Start a Christmas list.
Check water warmers.
Plan a winter vacation.
Put up a basketball hoop.
Read the 23rd Psalm, again.
Buy Mom a big box of candy.
Get extra turkey legs so each member of the younger set can have a Thanksgiving drumstick.

Let's make 'em cook Raw Garbage

BY CLAUDE W. GIFFORD

IF YOU raise livestock of any kind, or grow feed—or pay taxes—it means something to you to stop commercial feeding of raw garbage in your state.

This practice—which breeds livestock diseases and is a spring-board for epidemics—already has cost farmers millions of dollars. And it endangers human health as well.

One of these raw-garbage feeding establishments is probably as close to you as your nearest town. To get the kind of protection you need, it's high time that your state passed a garbage cooking law. Now—at this next session.

But why such a fuss over raw garbage anyhow?

Look at some of the diseases it carries: Hog cholera . . . Trichinosis . . . VE disease . . . even Foot-and-Mouth.

We should be in no mood to trifle any longer in view of what we've been through: *The last two outbreaks of foot-and-mouth in this country started in raw-garbage-fed hogs.* Before stopping the outbreaks, 975 farmers had their herds killed and buried. It cost us more than $100 million to stamp it out.

Garbage feeding establishments are also hotbeds of hog cholera. "We can never eliminate hog cholera in this country as long as we feed raw garbage," says Dr. B. T. Simms, Chief of the USDA's Bureau of Animal Industry.

Look at the increased chances of spreading trichinosis, one of our most feared human diseases. The rate of trichinae infection in these hogs is 1,800% higher than in grain-fed hogs, and the trichinae worms are usually present in much greater numbers.

This summer we saw the final blow from a disease, born and bred in raw garbage feeding. It was VE disease in hogs—which raced to 87 townships and counties in 29 states within a few weeks. If you think that cost you nothing, just add this up:

Instead of hogs hitting their expected peak price of $25 in August, they started dropping as VE mounted in July. During August prices slid $2.50; a dollar in one day—the day VE hit the Chicago yards.

This wasn't a general meat-price drop: fat steers went up $2 in August; lambs hit their top for the year.

Much of the reason for the decline in hog prices was that VE scared packers away from the Midwest markets which set hog prices.

People in the know maintain that VE has cut from $1 to $2 a hundred off every hog that has gone to market since.

In addition, all farmers have shared other losses: such as the $2 million in indemnities, which shows up in taxes; and the expense of cleaning and disinfecting several stockyards, more than 6,000 stock cars, and countless trucks—which shows up in yardage fees and hauling charges.

And this is going to go on as long as commercial raw garbage is fed to hogs—VE can't be eliminated without cooking garbage.

Perhaps the greatest threat is this: VE looks so much like foot-and-mouth that every case must be checked, by an involved method, to see that it isn't. This increases the possibility that foot-and-mouth might get a head start on us under the guise of VE. Thus, it is a threat to every livestock man—dairyman, cattleman and sheepman, as well as hog raiser.

The answer is plain. It's time to get garbage cooking regulations in every state. We'll show how in a moment.

There'll be plenty of opposition from the garbage feeders. There always has been. They say that cooking is too much bother; it costs too much; the heat destroys the vitamins in the garbage; and that hogs won't eat it or do well on it.

Is this really true? Garbage feeders in Canada cook their garbage. The hogs do well—and there's no cholera or VE in Canada!

Garbage feeders in Virginia have been cooking their garbage since September. One feeder with more than 1,000 hogs on garbage tells *Farm Journal* this:

"The hogs seem to eat the cooked garbage just as well, and gain as well. And I find that it costs me only between 50 cents and $1 a ton to cook it.

"My death losses, which have run from 10 to 20 hogs a month for years, dropped off to two hogs a month. I also find that whereas I formerly had to buy 80 to 110-pound pigs—big enough to stand the shock of going on a full diet of raw garbage—I can now start 40-pound pigs on cooked garbage.

"I believe other garbage feeders in this area are finding the same thing. It's more work, but I don't see how I can afford to go back to the old way."

We can end raw garbage feeding, and its dangers, once and for all, with state and Federal co-operation.

The essentials of a satisfactory state law are simple:

1. License all commercial garbage feeders—then you can yank their licenses if they don't cook.

2. Inspect them to see that they do cook, and that they keep things reasonably sanitary. A license fee can help pay the inspection cost.

3. Allow hogs to move off garbage feeding establishments only with a health certificate.

4. Refuse to pay indemnities for disease to any establishment that feeds commercial raw garbage.

If each state did this, the garbage feeders would fall into line overnight.

In addition the Federal government should:

▶ Enforce the cooking regulations for garbage moving across state lines.

▶ Quarantine on a state-wide basis, and refuse to allow live hogs or raw pork to move out of a state that doesn't require the cooking of garbage (except when those hogs move directly to an approved plant for immediate slaughter and processing).

▶ Refuse to help pay indemnities for disease control in states that have no garbage cooking law.

If this were done, the states would fall over themselves to get their regulations pronto. It's not enough that a few states pass a law, such as Nebraska has done in a special session. If a few states hang back, we stay in the same pickle.

Why hasn't all this been done long ago? There's only one reason. Farmers haven't demanded it; and the garbage feeders have fought it. Government responds to the loudest squawks, sometimes without too much regard to where they come from.

We look pretty silly letting unsanitary, unsafe conditions in a $50 million garbage feeding business threaten the welfare of the farm families who raise more than 99½% of the nation's livestock—a $21 billion business.

Your state legislature is meeting soon. Send this article to your governor at the State House, or to your State Representative. Tell him that you want action, then stay with it. See that your livestock and farm organizations do the same! Then you'll get something done.

January 1953

BY JOHN A. ROHLF

how they made FED BEEF NO.1

☐You can tell the story of the beef-feeding boom in many different ways.

You can tell it in terms of hard facts and show that fed-beef tonnage has more than doubled in the past 10 years; that there's more *fed-beef* on the market today than *all* beef put together as recently as 1958; or that Texans, long No. 1 in *feeder* cattle, have quadrupled their *feedlot* production in this period.

You can tell it in terms of people, such as Jack Carrothers, whose photo is on the cover of this issue of TOP OP. Carrothers, who came to Texas from the Greeley, Colo., area in the early 60s, is typical of the "new breed" of feedlot managers and operators. They have been largely responsible for propelling beef-feeding into the No. 1 spot in all of agriculture.

You can tell it in terms of a new business phenomenon—one that may some day emerge in other segments of agriculture. Some economists suggest that beef feeding is becoming a "conglomerate," with increasing integration—both vertical and horizontal. They point to the sophisticated new production technologies, the highly-efficient business procedures, new breakthroughs in processing, distribution and merchandising that have shot fed-beef to the top.

You could write a book on any of these three approaches, and it would make inspirational reading. For fed-beef production is one of the most exciting growth stories in our entire dynamic national economy.

The formula has been the basic: Start with a product that consumers like, make it better and then produce it in volume and at a cost that creates a ready demand.

Beef feeders have done all this and more. They've combined agriculture's two biggest "raw materials"—cattle and feed grains—and "manufactured" them into the favorite food of the world: fed beef. And they produce it in such quantity, that every American now eats an average of five ounces of beef per day.

Describe the typical American cattle feeder, we were asked recently by a European visitor. Our first instinct was to tell him of the big commercial lots of the High Plains and Southwest and the businessmen-who-happen-to-be-feeders who manage them. Then we thought of the 200,000 farmer-feeders, most of them in the Corn Belt, who have likewise been increasing their output and still produce more than 50% of the total fed-beef supply. Both groups are "typical" of the industry.

Top Operator

But the Mr. Magic of the business is the commercial feeder, such as Jack Carrothers or Joe Easley of Texas, Ladd Hitch of Oklahoma, the Monforts of Colorado, the Entz of Arizona, V. V. Williams of California.

Their beef-making factories run up to 75,000-head capacity. Whirring computers calculate rations, figure their costs. Chattering teletypes bring market information from around the country. Buyers jet from one feeder source to another in search of replacements. Others scour feed sources for the best buys. Corps of health specialists and nutritionists are on call.

Many commercial lots custom feed—that is, finish cattle for other owners. California's Williams, who started running what he called a "cattle hotel, American plan" 40 years ago, may feed cattle for 50 or more customers over a year. Some are cowmen, others farmers, dealers, packers or investors. In a typical custom contract, the cattle owner pays feed costs plus a daily yardage charge and veterinary fees.

Most of the big feeding operations are corporations, with the stock held primarily by large farmers and cattlemen. A few recently have "gone public" and others, looking toward further expansion, plan like moves.

If this all sounds like big business, it is. The 1800 feedlots with more than 1000-head capacity averaged a "cash flow" of nearly $2 million each last year. And the 200,000 farmer-feeders, who raise most of their own feed as well as selling other farm products, averaged about $20,000 each from just fed-beef marketings.

Now that it has climbed to the No. 1 spot, how financially solid is the fed-beef business?

A recent survey of commercial banks — the primary source of feed-lot operating capital—produced a consensus of a "good" to "excellent" rating. One reason: Availability of futures markets for both feed and cattle so feeders can hedge against price fluctuations. Astute managers, with precise information on costs, lock in their profits, even before animals go on feed, by trading in futures contracts.

Beef economists agree that feeding will continue to grow, with the bulk of the increase coming from commercial lots. And that the primary expansion will be in the new beef-feeding "belt" stretching from the Texas Panhandle to the Western Corn Belt.

That, briefly, is fed-beef, the Cinderella story of agriculture. And a story with a happy dynamic future ahead. ◁

PHOTO BUD FICHTE

WHICH IS BETTER FOR WHEAT GROWERS?

Here is probably the most interesting and controversial farm question of the year. The outcome will be of far-reaching importance—not only for wheat growers, but for other farmers as well. Even if you can't vote, you'll have a stake in it.

The question will be settled sometime before mid-June when the nation's wheat growers vote in a referendum on whether to adopt a wheat certificate program offered to them last fall by the Agricultural Act of 1962. It will take a two-thirds majority of "yes" votes to pass this program. If

says JAMES G. PATTON

President, National Farmer's Union

MOST great decisions men must make are extremely difficult. Seldom are vital decisions easy to resolve.

In this year's national wheat referendum, the nation's farm families who grow wheat are being asked to make the most important decision in agriculture since the passage of the Agricultural Adjustment Act of 1933.

Yet, paradoxically, wheat farmers will find this year's great decision an easy one to make. This is true, not merely because the ballot is a simple one—requiring only a "yes or no" or "for or against" choice. Rather the decision is easy because the alternatives are purely economic—the decision can be (and will be) made on the basis of dollars and cents by each individual farmer.

I'm convinced that all but a few farm families already know this and their decision will be a resounding approval of the wheat certificate program for 1964.

After nearly 35 years of association with farm people, it is difficult to imagine that they will view this referendum as a political battle, or an ideological struggle, or a test of their loyalty to any farm organization. Today's modern farmer with his great capital investment and his fierce pride in being a farmer, is, first of all, a shrewd businessman. Price times bushels add up to income and it's income that gives farmers the security which genuine farm independence requires.

I think it is significant to note that all the major farm organizations—with one exception—all the commodity groups directly interested in *(Continued)* more than one-third vote "no", this particular wheat program will be rejected, and the matter will be back in the lap of the Congress.

This is no ordinary wheat referendum with the usual simple choice between (1) supports at 75% to 90% of parity with acreage controls for all growers, and (2) supports at 50% of parity for those who abide by the same acreage allotments—and no supports for those who don't. In this referendum, a "yes" vote will bring a completely new wheat program for the years ahead. A "no" vote will tell Congress that this isn't the wheat program that farmers want for the future.

How would the wheat certificate program work? What are the prospects if it's voted in or out? How will the outcome influence farmers other than wheat growers? These vital questions are tackled head-on by Mr. Patton and Mr. Shuman. Their statements appear just as they wrote them.

FARM JOURNAL is pleased to present both sides of the question as a service.

says CHARLES B. SHUMAN

President, American Farm Bureau Federation

Drawings: Sam Dion

WHEAT producers have been voting for government programs in a more or less routine fashion. But they have not had to face up to the issue of really restrictive controls until this referendum.

In most years, the national allotment could not be reduced below 55 million acres. There was a 15-acre exemption for small farmers. Diverted acres could be shifted to other grains or forage crops. The support price could not be lowered below 75% of parity (currently $1.84 per bushel).

All of this has now been changed. The present Administration's wheat-control certificate scheme on which wheat producers will vote in this year's referendum includes *the tightest, most binding controls ever seriously considered for a farm commodity.*

In addition to providing much stricter acreage allotments than growers have experienced in recent years and a new type of marketing quota, the Administration's plan provides for diverted-acre controls and cross compliance. It also gives the Secretary of Agriculture vast powers to regulate all handlers, processors and distributors of wheat from the farm to the ultimate consumer.

The referendum is not just another vote on wheat marketing quotas. This referendum will determine whether farmers want to go all the way down the road of government supply-management of their business over to a government bureaucracy, all of *(Continued)*

YES—Patton

(Continued)

wheat—and all the big grain marketing cooperatives are in solid agreement that the 1964 wheat program should be approved in this year's referendum.

In fact, all these organizations have agreed to pool their resources and their manpower to conduct a nationwide program of information and action to secure a "yes" vote in the referendum. The federation of these groups is called the National Wheat Referendum Committee.

Briefly, let's examine the factors that will weigh in the farmer's mind as he makes his decision to vote "yes":

1. First of all, there is the matter of income. How will farm families fare under the new wheat certificate program? The program is so designed that their total wheat income will be as great as the 1961-62 level. Nationally, this means a total of $2.3 to $2.4 billion.

If an individual wheat farmer had a 1963 wheat base of 100 acres and a normal yield of 20 bushels per acre, his projected wheat income for 1964 would be $3,531. This is how it figures out:

- His acres will be reduced 10%—so his allotment will be 90 acres.
- On the basis of yield, his quota will be 1800 bushels.
- Of this, 1530 bushels will be certificate wheat at $2 per bushel or $3060.
- His noncertificate wheat of 270 bushels he can sell for at least $1.30 or $351.
- For his 10% cut in acres, he will receive diversion payments of $120—or for a final total wheat income of $3,531.

To realize the same gross wheat income at $1 a bushel, the wheat farmer would have to increase his acreage from 90 to 171 acres—and in addition would have to stand the cost of planting and harvesting these additional acres.

2. In addition, there is a built-in crop insurance feature in the program. In case of crop failure and the farmer doesn't even produce enough to meet his certificate quota, he will not be penalized. Furthermore, a farmer does not have to market his certificate wheat immediately—he can hold it until the end of the marketing year. If enough farmers did this, the market price of cash wheat would be stabilized at a higher level than $1.30 or $1.40 a bushel.

3. This program also carries the advance payment feature for diversion payments, providing many farmers with much-needed ready cash at the beginning of the year.

4. If a feed grain program is passed by Congress this year, then wheat farmers could use allotted feed grain acres for wheat—thus giving farmers flexibility of operation and new independence in judgment.

Now, let's take a look at what happens if one-third of the wheat farmers vote "no" and the program is rejected.

In the first place, for all practical purposes, there will be NO program and for all practical purposes, NO price supports.

It is conservatively estimated that if there is no wheat program for 1964, something like 65 million acres will be put in production as the wheat farmer frantically tries to dodge disaster. As a result, around 1.5 billion bushels of wheat could be produced, further aggravating the surplus situation.

In the desperate effort to pay bills, every wheat farmer who depends on wheat for a cash crop would be dumping his crop on the market.

It is frightening to imagine what would happen.

No one has ever denied—even those who oppose the program—that wheat prices would be depressed to $1 a bushel or less.

On the foreign market, the picture would be equally dismal and bleak. This nation would have no choice but to dump cheap wheat on the world market—thus wrecking world prices and immediately causing justified resentment and retaliatory countermeasures from friendly countries that would endanger our entire foreign farm trade business which amounts to nearly $6 billion annually.

NO—Shuman

(Continued)

agriculture will be vulnerable. The wheat certificate plan is a complicated one and many growers are confused as to what they are being asked to vote on. The Administration forces are capitalizing on this confusion by presenting the program in its most palatable form for the first year of operation. *This can only mean that the plan would have to be tightened in future years.*

What are the facts? In the long run, wheat farmers' income would be hurt by adoption of the certificate plan. Despite the proponents' claims of short-term advantages, these facts must be faced:

■ Under the provisions allocating wheat production to certificate and noncertificate classifications, *every grower would be forced to take a feed price for part of his crop.*

Under the certificate plan, producers of high-quality wheat for which there is a demand for milling would receive the same share of the certificate market as the producers of low-quality wheat for which there is little demand. Marketing certificates—entitling producers to the higher of the two support prices—would be distributed on the basis of base production history, without regard to milling and baking quality, or the use actually made of the wheat. All producers would have to sell part of their production in the noncertificate market.

■ The portion to be sold at the substantially lower noncertificate price may be small in the first year, but who can tell what it will be in the second, third and later years of the plan? Legislative history indicates that the portion of production for exports that receives certificates is to be reduced in the future.

■ Attractive payments are promised for diversion of wheat acreage in 1964 and 1965, *but the Administration has stated it will be possible to cut the cost of the program after 1965 because diversion payments will be eliminated!*

■ Allotments can now be cut to the acreage necessary to produce one billion bushels of wheat after allowances for small farms. At 1962 yields of almost 25 bushels per acre, this means the national allotment could be cut to around 40 million acres. Secretary Freeman has indicated that the allotment will not be cut more than 10% to 15% below 55 million acres the first year, but much greater cuts could be made in the future.

■ Farmers growing less than 15 acres of wheat will be subject to controls regardless of whether they wish to participate.

■ The certificate plan could result in the dumping of huge quantities of noncertificate wheat on the feed market with depressing effects on feed grain prices.

■ The wheat certificate plan would hamper U.S. efforts to sell wheat, and other commodities, in foreign markets. The two-price feature of the plan could lead to retaliatory restrictions on U.S. exports. The plan is utterly inconsistent with our efforts to get the European Common Market to adopt farm policies that will not exclude our products.

■ Proponents of the wheat certificate plan are using "scare" tactics to secure a "yes" vote in the referendum.

For example, Secretary Freeman says that the choice for wheat growers is between $2 wheat with a "yes" vote and $1 per bushel wheat with a "no" vote.

With support prices at $2 for certificate wheat and $1.30 for noncertificate wheat, the average obviously would be less than $2 per bushel under the certificate plan.

If the plan is defeated, the law provides that acreage allotments would remain in effect and the Secretary would be required to make price support loans to cooperators at 50% of parity (currently $1.24). The price could not be beaten down to $1 per bushel unless the Secretary should deliberately dump accumulated surpluses. The law, which can and should be strengthened, already contains restrictions against such action. *Defeat of the certificate plan will not lead to overproduction or chaos in the world wheat market.*

As part of his "scare" program, Secretary Freeman has warned farmers that the Department will seek no new legislation in the event the certificate plan is rejected. Apparently the Secretary assumes that Congress has abdicated all of its Constitutional authority and responsibility for development of commodity programs in favor of dictatorship by the USDA. *I am sure this has not happened.* **END**

FARM JOURNAL'S OPINION

A Rigged "Choice"

BY ALL odds, the most important farm policy question of the year is the wheat plan so ably debated in this issue by Mr. Patton and Mr. Shuman. It affects not only wheat farmers but everyone raising feed grains or feeding livestock. In the long range it affects almost every other farmer, too, for what happens to wheat farmers today could happen to other farmers next.

Wheat farmers have had quite a measure of control already, but nothing like they are asked to accept now. If they vote this plan in they would be required to take an immediate 10% cut in acreage. (The Secretary of Agriculture would determine acreage, as guided by law but with a considerable measure of his own judgment.)

Wheat farmers would get marketing certificates, in bushels, for their higher-priced wheat—a quota they could no longer beat with fertilizer, new varieties and better farming. They could no longer plant diverted land to something they could sell. (The Secretary could allow it to be grazed.) If those with 15 acres or less in wheat signed up, they would get the same controls as the bigger man, for a change. In '64, at least, all wheat farmers would get the same price supports, and all would get certificates for the same percentage of their crop, regardless of the kind of wheat they raise or its suitability for the food trade. (The Secretary determines this.) The present pattern of wheat growing in the U.S. would be frozen—as is.

In exchange for these compulsory controls the government would offer $2 a bushel for 80% of farmers' wheat. (The Secretary sets the price anywhere between 65% and 90% of parity. Also the Secretary sets the percentage of the crop qualifying for certificates.)

For the other 20% of the crop the Secretary would also set a price he deemed in line with the world price and the feed price, now around $1.30 a bushel. Also a payment would be made for diverted acres in 1964 and probably in 1965—again at a level set by the Secretary. The law allows no such payments after 1965.

In the above you'll note that "the Secretary" would make seven major decisions about how much wheat you could grow and what you'd get for it. Nor is this a complete list. Reading the whole law we find *78 instances* where "the Secretary" must make some judgment about wheat for farmers or handlers! Wheat is admittedly in trouble but do you want to give *any* one man, no matter how well intentioned, this much power over the conduct of your business?

Actually this referendum is as rigged as those in the past have been. The reward for voting "Yes" has been put high (for the first year), and the penalty for voting "No" has been made unreasonably stiff. It's another case of strong-arm tactics, which farmers can rightfully resent.

Mr. Freeman himself has been proclaiming that "it's a choice between $1 and $2 wheat," and President Kennedy darkly warns that the wheat country would return to "depression conditions." We happen to think that both threats are considerably exaggerated, in an obvious effort to scare farmers into a "Yes" vote. But whether so or not, why must it be tight government control or a threat of ruin?

If the referendum loses we doubt mightily that Congress would let the wheat country go to pot—not when half of U. S. farmers raise wheat and several times that many town and city people depend on how wheat farmers do! This needn't be the last chance the country will have to do something about wheat. Last year, you recall, the Administration "had to have" a compulsory feed-grains plan. When it didn't get it it settled for continuing the program we had. Now it finds a voluntary set-up will do the trick after all! Why not continue the '63 wheat program for a year while we devise something better, whether it's a better two-price plan or something else? Congress could vote a continuation within a week.

The question farmers have to decide is whether to take a bad deal with an attractive price or vote it down and ask for something reasonable to live with.

Carroll P. Streeter Editor

THE BARN'S HAUNTED

By GEORGE W. WORMLEY
Machinery Editor

MACHINERY PREVIEW FOR 76

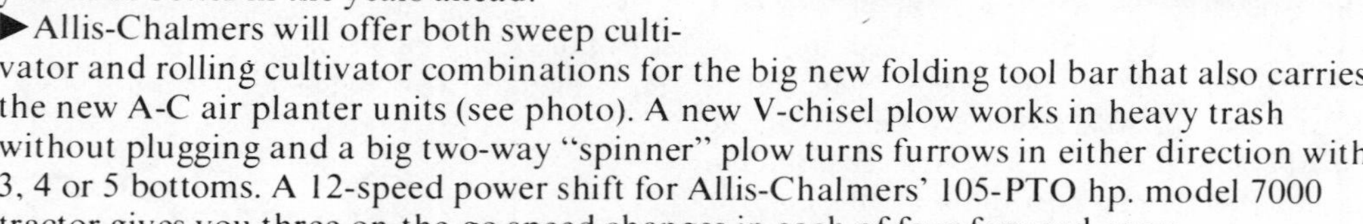

■ As the U.S. begins its Bicentennial year, you—as an American farmer—are recognized around the world as the greatest food and fiber producer of all time. And you'll likely be called on to step up output even more in the years ahead, probably without extra manpower, without abundant supplies of low-cost fuel and without a big jump in the unit price of the things you produce. The machines shown on the following pages are designed to help you do just that—and still produce at a reasonable profit, while cutting down on the long hours and tiring backwork that have been a part of farming over most of this country's first 200 years. Besides the machines pictured, here are others to help you farm better in the years ahead:

▶Allis-Chalmers will offer both sweep cultivator and rolling cultivator combinations for the big new folding tool bar that also carries the new A-C air planter units (see photo). A new V-chisel plow works in heavy trash without plugging and a big two-way "spinner" plow turns furrows in either direction with 3, 4 or 5 bottoms. A 12-speed power shift for Allis-Chalmers' 105-PTO hp. model 7000 tractor gives you three on-the-go speed changes in each of four forward gears.

▶J I Case Company will have a new chisel plow that's easy to convert from a mounted to a pull-type hookup, a heavy offset disk that comes in sizes from 10′ to 20′ wide, a 12-row cultivator with a hydraulic lift tool bar, an "1845" hydrostatic four-wheel-drive skid loader with a 45-hp. gasoline or diesel engine, and two new loaders—one for David Brown tractors and the other for the big Case 1270 and 1370 tractors.

▶Deere is introducing loaders and blades for their new line of utility tractors announced earlier this past fall and will also have hydraulically controlled scrapers and land levelers for use with bigger tractors. New Deere seed monitors give you a running seed count on planters up to 12 rows wide; a pitmanless-drive "450" mower will cut with a 7′ or 9′ cutter bar and a "350" offset disk will come in widths from 16′ to more than 20′.

▶Ford's new line of three- and four-cylinder tractors, ranging from 30 PTO hp. to more than 80 PTO hp., features more efficient engines, increased hydraulic flow and lift, changes in styling, improved access for servicing and alternators which step up electric generating capacity. Diesel engine improvements include changes in the cylinder head, intake manifold, air cleaner and fuel pump.

▶International Harvester is offering 33″ of vertical clearance in "Hi-Clear" plows which you can get with either automatic reset beams or with a new "Toggle Trip" reset feature. A new nine-furrow model will be added to the big "800" Flex Plow series, which goes on up to 12-furrows in size. Other new IH machines include a folding Packer Mulcher and a chisel plow with a "Conser/Till" attachment that disks stalks ahead of the chisels.

▶Massey-Ferguson is introducing an economy model MF 230 tractor that develops 34 PTO hp. with either a gasoline or diesel engine and is offering a gasoline engine MF 235 that develops 40 PTO hp., compared with 42 hp. for the diesel version introduced earlier. MF also plans two new rectangular balers, and is offering medium-duty Quick Attach loaders and new offset disks 10½′ to 18′ wide.

▶White Farm Equipment's newest Field Boss tractors are ready for 1976 farm use. The 2-85, a diesel, develops 85 PTO hp., while the 2-70 cranks out 70 PTO hp. with either a gasoline or diesel engine. A Field Boss 2-60 will develop 60 PTO hp. and a 2-50 model will turn out 50 PTO hp. White also has a new folding Plant/Aire planter for up to 12 narrow or 8 wide rows.

January 1976

1 High-capacity hay baler for farmers who put up a lot of hay is "all new from the ground up," says Sperry New Holland. Named the "320," it rides on high-flotation tires and is supported by a tongue that connects directly to the axle. Pickup, with dual-speed drive, is 75" wide; feeder adjusts for light or heavy windrows.

2 Works up a strip 25' wide. Wings on a new Brillion Pulvi-Mulcher fold up hydraulically to an overall width of only 13'10" for transport. Spring teeth between front and rear gangs of rollers are also positioned hydraulically. The big machine weighs over 5 tons.; wide tires on dual wheels add flotation in soft fields.

3 Heavy duty forage harvester chops with an 8-knife cutting cylinder. Blunt knives on the new CB800 forage harvester resist bending and chipping, stay sharp longer, say Gehl engineers. An optional hydraulic sharpener grinds cylinder knives right in the field. Electric shift and in-cab spout deflector controls are also optional.

4 Cuts up to a 14' swath with an auger header, up to 20' with a draper header for grain. Hesston 6200 "regular duty" windrower also can be outfitted with 10' or 12' auger heads or with a 16' grain header—all with hydraulic lift. A 57-hp. water-cooled engine powers variable-speed drive. Cab with blower is optional.

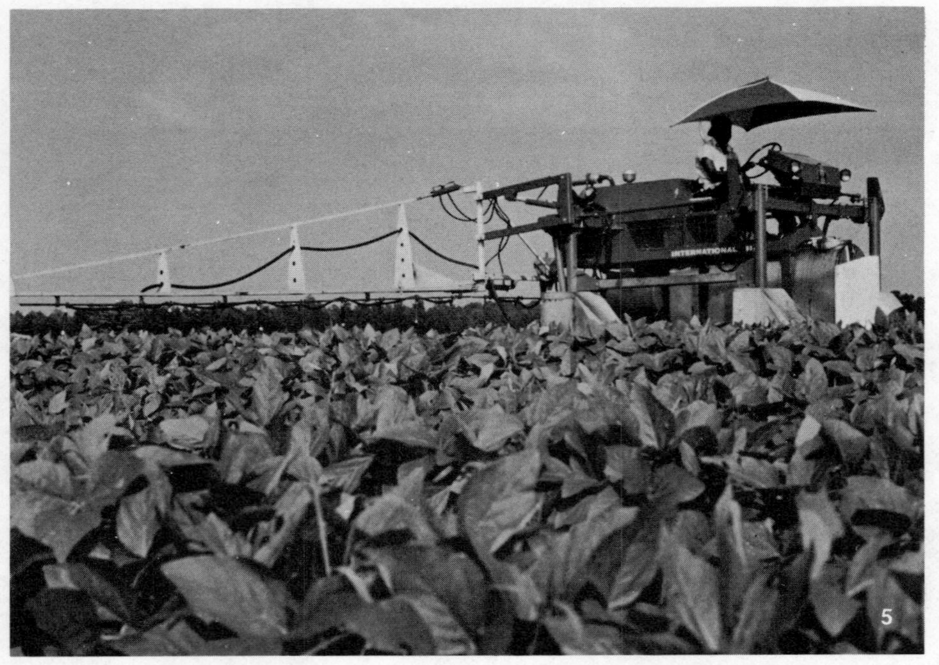

Machinery Preview 76

5 Sprays 12 wide rows or a 40' strip. A 58-hp. water-cooled engine and hydrostatic drive power the new International 800 Hi-Clear sprayer. Four wheels and a narrow 275-gal. tank, which rides between the rows, add stability on slopes. The boom mounts on front or rear, and wheel tread adjusts to fit row spacings.

6 Leaves a mulch on top. Adjustable gangs of cone-shaped disks on the front of the John Deere 1710 Mulch Tiller work up crop residues. Chisel plow shanks behind disks can be equipped with sweeps or twisted shovels that mix soil with the mulch. Tandem wheels keep the frame level; four widths: 11', 13', 15' and 17'.

7 No ridges when you disk with the new Case Double Offset Tandem (DOT) disk-harrow. Front and rear gangs "overlap" to leave a level surface. Big dual wheels help support the main frame of the DOT, while the wings, which lift hydraulically, have outrigger wheels for extra flotation. Three disking widths: 25', 28' and 31'.

8 Plows up to 10 furrows. A vertical clearance of 30'' under a heavy 6'' X 8'' box-beam backbone lets the big White 449 plow turn tall cover and slice through heavy trash without plugging. The frame adjusts for 16'' or 18'' furrows, and you can add or subtract bottoms. A smaller 549 model ranges from 5 up to 8 bottoms.

9 Four-cylinder turbocharged diesel engine in the Ford 7600 tractor develops an estimated 84-PTO hp. A two-speed 540/1000 rpm PTO is standard and so are an 8-speed transmission and Load Monitor draft control. A 16-speed Dual Power transmission on Ford tractors with over 100 hp., is optional on the 7600.

10 Air planters on a tool bar fold for transport. A two-way hydraulic ram for each wing controls new Allis-Chalmers 5'' X 7'' folding tool bar. Two wing widths and two center section widths give you a choice of four sizes ranging up to eight wide 40'' rows. Flexible hoses connect the air supply to all of the air planter units.

11 Disks a strip up to 33½' wide, folds to 12½' for transport. Six different sizes of the Massey-Ferguson 820 Flex-Wing tandem disk-harrow range from 19' to 33½'; disk blades come in three sizes: 20'', 22'' and 24''. The wings lift hydraulically, and a self-leveling hitch is standard. The disks cut with 310 to 380 lbs. per foot of width.

Machinery Preview 76

12

13

12 Grinds hay and grain. Slanted throat drops down to open a 20'' bale table, which leads to the live-action feed-roll on new Farmhand 110-bu. grinder-mixer. The mill, 20'' wide and 21'' in diameter, is fed by a drop feeder with a variable speed range from 0 to 275 rpm.

13 Builds up to 1½-ton stacks of hay or stover. A pickup 6' wide whisks windrows into the Owatonna 540 stacker while blower spout and compression roof build a uniform stack. To unload, stacker bed tilts up while a hydraulic cylinder operates a push-off that leaves the stack intact.

14 Mows, conditions, windrows a 9'3'' swath of hay, straw or stalks. The New Idea Cut/Ditioner features a new spring assist suspension, high flotation tires and a full-width ground roll for a uniform cutting height. Rotating flails won't plug or skip in down, tangled hay.

15 A new look and a new model are part of the Versatile ''Series 2'' four-wheel-drive tractors for 1976. The new tractors will be powered by a six-cylinder Cummins diesel engine that cranks out 220 hp. All the Series 2 Versatiles will have hinged hoods for easier servicing.

14

15

By **DICK SEIM**
Farm Journal Field Staff

TOMORROW'S FARMER...here today

Photos: Perry Struse Jr.

"First, you must learn to manage yourself; then you can learn to manage others," says Bob Haworth, who farrows and finishes more than 2,000 hogs yearly and farms 900 acres. He employs a college graduate and also part-time help. You'll find Bob in his office most evenings. His wife, Gladys, keeps the books that take up to 40 hours a week.

Maybe you're one of them. See if you agree with these insights into the kind who will succeed in the next 25 years.

■ How mechanized will farmers be in the year 2000? How nuclearized? How solarized? You'll have to look somewhere else for that kind of "farm of tomorrow" stuff. Or make up your own—plastic domes and robot tractors and the rest of it.

Because it doesn't matter. Men and women run today's farms, and they'll run the farms of tomorrow. The farm operator's ability to structure a business, attract capital, select enterprises and manage labor will determine whether he succeeds.

That statement pegs tight to the opinions of grain-livestock producers who run growing businesses today. Four such men counseled us on this subject. We think they demonstrate qualities and skills that will be increasingly essential in 5, 10, 25 years. We'll briefly sketch their operations. Then we'll expand on their views of what it will take to survive and succeed in tomorrow's agriculture:

Harlan Murley, 39, Buchanan County, Iowa. This year he'll crop 950 acres, split between corn and soybeans, with a small acreage of seed oats. The straw beds hogs. He'll finish 1,500—half that he farrows and half feeder pigs.

He employs one full-time man, production manager David Pech, 23. Murley's wife, Karen, helps outside when needed, shares in management and bookkeeping.

Murley recently incorporated his operation and allowed Pech to buy in. Corporate shares provide a way to bring deserving, compatible employees into the business.

He expects to farm at least 1,200 acres by 1977 and wants to expand in hogs, too. He'll add a man—prefers an animal science graduate who likes hogs.

Bob Haworth, 35, Poweshiek County, Iowa. He farms 900 acres, heavy on corn,

Flexibility. "You must be open to change," Murley says. Stoner comments, "You need the ability to adjust, to anticipate."

Raikes adds, "It's a quality that grows in importance each year. You must try new things—look at something in a different way. It applies to labor utilization and management, and selection of enterprises."

Labor management ability. This ranks high with all four. If you have it, or can develop it, you can grow past your personal physical limits. And all see the farm of the future as a multiple-man unit.

but raises 300 acres of seed soybeans. His corn, plus the share he buys from his landlords, goes into the more than 2,000 hogs he farrows and finishes each year. He has bred a lean, growthy line, and sells many of his gilts for breeding.

Haworth recently lost a young assistant to a home farming opportunity. He hired a new graduate through the Iowa State University (ISU) agriculture placement office. He also employs part-time help.

Incorporation may be in the picture for Haworth, too. He perseveres on the business side, spending most evenings in his office. His wife, Gladys, puts in 30 to 40 hours a week on the firm's books, preparing a complete cash flow, month by month.

Tracy Stoner, 35, Webster County, Iowa, farms just over 1,000 acres and rents some additional grassland for pasturing cattle. He and three full-time men also handle a 250-sow continuous farrowing operation and feed 750 to 1,000 cattle per year.

His production manager, Ed McWeeny, 31, an ISU graduate, has full responsibility for hogs. In addition, McWeeny serves as second-in-command.

Stoner says his immediate goal is to convert everything raised on his land (including cornstalks) into animal protein—beef and pork.

Ron Raikes, 33, a PhD economist on the ISU staff. And . . . a member of the board of directors and vice president of the Raikes family farm corporation in Saunders County, Neb.

He actively consults with his father, Ralph, firm president, on farm matters—OKs major purchases and investments. He spent the 1975 crop season in on-farm management of the 1,600-acre plant—1,350 acres of row crops, four to five employees.With this experience, and his professional economics background, he brings a valuable perspective to the subject.

As you've noted, all four represent farm operations of close to 1,000 acres or more. That doesn't mean smaller farms don't pay now, or won't in the future. But in the view of these men, the farther ahead you look, the more likely it is that a smaller farm will pay only for the man who holds it comparatively debt-free.

You've gotten some feel for the men who've advised us on this topic. What personal qualities do they deem most important for the farmer of the future? They show general agreement on four "big ones:"

"It's important to me that we work together," says Karen Murley. That includes sharing office work and phone time with husband Harlan. "I'm willing to work wherever I'm needed. Farming allows this close relationship more than many occupations," she says. Murley is shooting for 1,200 crop acres by next year. More hogs, too, even though he markets 1,500 a year now. He incorporated and allowed his manager to buy in. "I consider people a resource to build around," he says.

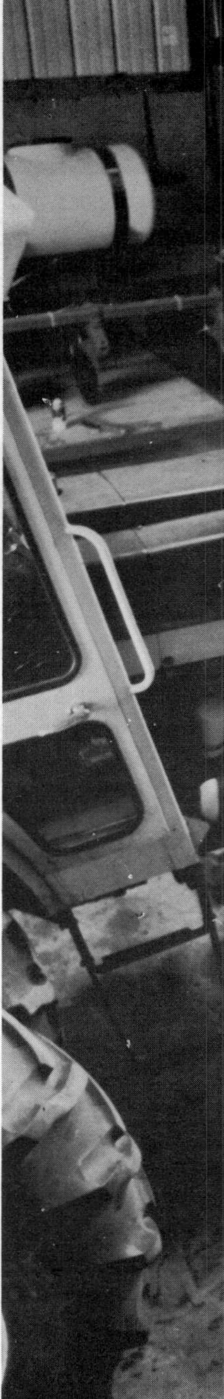

"There are real advantages to multiple-man operations," Haworth points out. "You can go for size that gives you economic and marketing advantages. And you have the backup management you need. Particularly in livestock operations, a one-man operation is vulnerable—too complex for neighbors to handle if you're knocked out."

Murley agrees: "We'll see more two- and three-man operations. This allows each man time for some opening in the routine to take a vacation. And, of course, it gives you backup management. I don't know how closely banks look at this factor now, but it seems likely to be a factor in their thinking in the future."

Raikes observes, "As you succeed and grow, you soon find yourself more an administrator than a worker. I found that out last summer—could hardly afford time on a tractor. So you're right into labor or personnel management. And it's not long before you need a man who can be your assistant. You need to keep such men challenged, motivated and rewarded."

The others also express concern on this point. Murley says, "We want to provide more than a job for a good man, we also want to make available a good future for him." He's at work on a plan involving incentive pay (based on net accrual) and opportunities to acquire stock in the farm corporation.

The ability to obtain and handle credit; finances. "We may have to yield on pride of ownership," Stoner says. His point: Own less of the operation outright; use capital for operation, getting it "outside" if necessary. Raikes agrees. All the men see difficulties ahead in obtaining financing for large operations from conventional bank sources.

And when you've got the money . . . We've explained how the Haworths spend much of their time. The Murleys develop cash flows even though their banks don't always require them. Murley personally relies on net worth changes. The point is they know where they're at—think no one will find credit or survive even 10 years ahead without firm, sure command of his financial picture.

Marketing ability. "It's the difference between break-even and profit," Murley asserts. Stoner shakes his head, "I need to get better." None of the four are completely satisfied with his marketing ability—but all are conscious of the need, and working at it.

Other qualities they rate highly: a personality that can stand pressure, the discipline to seek self-improvement and education, the ability (one you can develop) to recognize what services and consultants can help you and when to use them. Does the next one surprise you? Mechanical aptitude. Also, ability to see the other man's side—vital in labor management, consumer relations and obtaining credit.

Now, an additional note on size and why these men want to grow. Murley explains, "My oldest son is 16. I need an open-end, continued expansion, if I'm going to have a place for him in three to five years. I could drag along, hold a spot for him—but his chances are better if I keep the operation growing."

All three on-farm operators in the group share this situation, and would agree with Stoner on this added point: "To keep the men you need, and to keep their opportunities and rewards growing, also requires that you expand— in output, if not always in acreage.

It all ties together, doesn't it? And demands tough, smart, determined men and women. But farming wasn't easy 200 years ago, either. Here's hoping you or your children will be in the business in the year 2000. In fact, we're betting our business on it. ◁